# Folk Groups
## and
## Folklore
## Genres

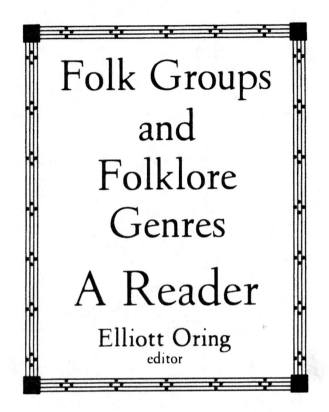

# Folk Groups
# and
# Folklore
# Genres

# A Reader

## Elliott Oring
### editor

UTAH STATE UNIVERSITY PRESS

LOGAN UTAH

Manufactured in the United States of America.

00      99      98                          05      06      07

Library of Congress Cataloging-in-Publication Data

Folk groups and folklore genres.
        Bibliography: p.
        Includes index.

        1. Folklore       2. Folklore--United States.     3. Folklore--United
States--Social life and customs.      I. Oring, Elliott, 1945-
GR66.F64          1989      389      88-27810
ISBN 0-87421-140-9 (pbk.)

*For Ernestine Friedl,*
*teacher and friend*

# Contents

# Preface

*Folk Groups and Folklore Genres: A Reader* is designed to accompany *Folk Groups and Folklore Genres: An Introduction*. The thirty-four essays included here are organized according to the chapter headings of that introductory volume. This common organization is meant to simplify the articulation of the essays in the two books.

Although the volumes are designed to be used together, they also can be used separately. The essays in this reader have been chosen to reflect a broad range of ideas, issues, and perspectives in contemporary folklore studies. They are more than replications or illustrations of the discussion in the introduction. They extend the discussion in diverse directions, alert the reader to new problems, and introduce alternative perspectives. For example, the three essays that appear in the "Occupational Folklore" section of this volume broach the functional theory of magic, introduce performance perspectives, and highlight the romantic and commercial forces that condition public display. These, however, are not the ideas and issues central to the chapter "Occupational Folklore" in the introductory volume.

Many of the essays in this volume focus on American folklore and this emphasis is deliberate. Analyses and interpretations of cultural phenomena with which students have some familiarity are the most likely to provoke critical response, since students can draw upon their own experience for counterexamples. Furthermore, it is familiar, commonplace experience that is the genuine measure of our theoretical achievement. If the theories of folklorists and anthropologists yield no compelling insights into our own everyday behaviors, they are unlikely to provide a framework for understanding the practices of others.

I do not mean to suggest that the study of other cultures holds little value or that it must necessarily await our own self-knowledge. The study of the self and the study of others are one and the same process. We come to see ourselves only through our reflections and refractions in others. The study of folklore can never be commensurate with the study of a single society. Indeed, essays concerning folk traditions in other cultures have been included in this volume to register the imperative to look beyond our own social and cultural boundaries. Whether we are making any headway in understanding the human condition, however, will first be registered through insights into our own behavior and belief.

Each essay in this volume is preceded by a brief headnote. Neither summaries, analyses, nor critiques, the headnotes frame key questions or issues to orient the reader and promote recall. References cited in the headnotes direct the reader to related discussion and are keyed to the "References Cited" section in the back of the book.

# Preface

Reprinted articles appear as they were originally published, though some minor changes were made to enhance readability. The general style of citation has not been changed, although internal citations and footnotes have been converted to notes at the end of each article. Several of the selections were originally published in the 1960s and 1970s, and dated references and gender-specific language remain unchanged.

There are many to be thanked for the publication of this volume. First and foremost are the authors for their fine essays. Others, whose names do not appear in the table of contents, also contributed. Mahadev Apte, Larry Danielson, William Ivey, Michael Owen Jones, Dianne Smith, and Donald Ward all read portions of the manuscript and made valuable suggestions. Although not all of them could be heeded, they helped clarify what needed to be done. Linda Speth and Nikki Naiser of Utah State University Press once again proved efficient yet creative publishers. Judit Katona-Apte, Foley Benson, Benjamin Fass, Robert and Mary Georges, Bruce and Gen Giuliano, Adolph Hofmann, Jane Jones, Norman Klein, Taffe Semenza, Barre Toelken, and Judith Terzi all contributed in their own ways, as did Irving Levinson, whose primary motive, however, was to finally see his name in print.

# I
# On the Concepts of Folklore

## Folkloristics:  A Conception of Theory
### Thomas A. Burns

*An assortment of theoretical perspectives inform the study of folklore. Although some theories are clearly more avant-garde than others, no single theory can rightfully claim the field of folklore for itself. Few folklorists have restricted themselves to only a single theoretical approach in their work. Moreover, there is no theory employed by folklorists that is uniquely folkloristic. Folklore theory has derived from, or is at least intimately tied to, theoretical developments in a number of other fields such as anthropology, sociology, linguistics, literary criticism, psychology, and history.*

*This state of affairs can make the mastery of theory in folklore something of a problem for the introductory student. The following essay outlines the perspectives that have been and are being employed in the analysis of expressive lore. Because the author refrains from describing the development of these perspectives historically, or fleshing out these perspectives with descriptions of the personalities involved or relevant bibliography, the essay provides only an abstract conception of theory. This essay is basically a map. Like a map, it is helpful to study it in advance, but its usefulness can only be fully realized in its application to a territory. Therefore, students are likely to benefit from rereading this article toward the end of their course of study to see whether they can locate the theoretical perspectives employed in the other essays in this volume. For a single-volume history of folklore theory in Europe see Cocchiara (1971). For the history of British folkloristics see Dorson (1968a, 1968b), and for the United States, Zumwalt (1988). A useful bibliography of folklore histories, surveys, methodologies, and biographies can be found in Bronner (1986).*

An academic discipline is generally defined by the nature of the materials it studies and the types of questions it explores with respect to these materials. The materials of folkloristics are generally recognized to be traditional ideas, actions, or consequences. Whether traditional materials are defined in terms of mentation, behavior, or product is largely a matter of the theoretical interest of the particular researcher. The domain of traditional ideas, behaviors, and/or consequences is further delimited by most folklorists in one of two ways. The first group of folklorists does not consider all traditional things, but only those held to be expressive (artistic, non-instrumental). This group consists of the traditional arts folklorists within which there may be further narrowing to include only the arts that depend heavily on a verbal component (the traditional verbal arts). Generally the traditional arts folklorists define "traditional" in terms of some process or basis of artistic expression (oral transmission, face-to-face communication) and not in terms of a particular culture level. Consequently, they are free to explore this art among all cultural levels and groups. The second group of folklorists (folklife scholars) delimits the domain of traditional ideas, behavior, and/or consequences in terms of culture level and not in terms of whether these traditional ideas, etc., are necessarily expressive in nature. Folklife scholars study traditional or folk culture where traditional tends to mean some combination of the following traits: rural, pre-industrial, non-mainstream, non-elite, preservationistic (past oriented, old time), regional, or ethnic.

While a definition of the materials of folkloristics involves a recognition of alternative viewpoints, it is easier to discern the nature of these materials and the criteria that inform their selection by different groups of scholars than to grasp the types of questions they explore—the theoretical dimension. Two aspects of the theoretical situation in folkloristics make this aspect of the discipline particularly difficult to grasp at the present time. There has been an enormous expansion in the past fifteen years in the scope of theoretical viewpoints that have come to be regarded as legitimate perspectives in the American study of folklore. Besides the emergence of new interests within the foundation disciplines of anthropology and English literature, major perspectives of the disciplines of linguistics, sociology, psychology, history, and communications have been incorporated into the study of folklore. The inclusion and subsequent impact of these new viewpoints is reflected in the expanded course offerings in the major folklore departments in the country. The increased breadth of theory regarded as pertinent in the discipline is one factor contributing to the difficulty of a person gaining an adequate command of the theoretical dimension of modern American folkloristics.

Compounding this problem is another factor. As yet there has emerged no theory or perspective that has been able to unify the many disparate viewpoints, past and present, that constitute the theoretical pursuits of scholars in the discipline. The communications approach is the only perspective that even has the capacity to propose itself as able to generate a unified theory of folklore. Still, the tools of communications analysis are only emerging, and their exploratory use is largely restricted to the domain of the micro-analysis of the folkloric act. The communications approach is simply not well enough developed to offer folklorists interested in more "macro" questions of symbolic function or symbolic change a viable alternative to their current theoretical orientations. In the absence of anything more than the remote promise of a unifying perspective, the reality of the theoretical situation in folkloristics is that we have many relatively separate perspectives being pursued by scholars, with the interrelations among these perspectives represented only by the eclectic and often idiosyncratic contributions of a few scholars. In light of both the increased breadth and lack of unity among the different theoretical perspectives in modern folkloristics, it is not surprising that among students and scholars alike, there exists a considerable difficulty in grasping the theoretical state of the discipline.

Short of a truly unifying theory for folklore, what is needed now in folkloristics is a comprehensive book length exposition and evaluation of the many perspectives that have formed and currently form the basis for research in the discipline. In light of the situation described above, it is not surprising that no comprehensive work of this sort has been forthcoming from any one individual. With so many inputs it is virtually impossible for any one scholar to feel competent to undertake the project.[1] The possibility of an edited volume of solicited expository and evaluative essays seems a reasonable alternative. The time for such a work is certainly ripe. The sketch of expressive culture theory presented in this paper is one that I have found necessary to produce for beginning graduate students in folklore in the absence of a comprehensive theoretical work and in light of my own reservations about recent alternative formulations.[2] These recent formulations are useful as bibliographic surveys of the major work in the various domains of research pursued by folklorists. They do not make it their task to spell out the basic argument that underlies and motivates these works. The present article supplements these earlier surveys of theory by reversing the emphasis and making the statement of the argument of each position focal while minimizing the bibliographic aspect.

The theory sketched in this paper does not encompass the theory of the discipline as a whole but rather of that portion of the discipline concerned with expressive culture, the theory informing the work of the traditional arts folklorists. General social, economic, political, and technological theory that is of concern to the folklife scholar studying instrumental as well as expressive aspects of folk culture is not included here. The intention of the sketch is to summarize the nature of the interest explored and the salient features of the position of each of the perspectives on expressive culture. Names have been purposely eliminated so as to highlight the ideas. Evaluative and historical remarks have been kept to a minimum with an effort to portray each perspective as equally viable and open to current exploration. Each section is followed by a very few references to more detailed expositions of the position. The sketch is designed as a point of departure and brief synthesis of the central notions that are being or have been explored by traditional arts folklorists. Elaborations, subtleties, and complications of the argument for each position have not been pursued.

The organization of the conceptualization originates with the realization that theoretical interests and perspectives transcend the boundaries of area, genre, and academic discipline. The only way to productively organize theory is by criteria inherent to it. Disciplinary divisions of theory which are currently popular are inadequate because the same theoretical concerns are shared by many disciplines. For example, literary, linguistic, and communications approaches to folklore all pursue the matters of structure and style, while anthropology, sociology, and psychology all investigate the issue of function. To formulate categories of expressive culture theory in terms of disciplines invites either redundancy or the arbitrary exclusion of theoretical pursuits from certain disciplines so that stereotypes emerge. In the following theory sketch (which by no means resolves all the difficulties of redundancy or researcher bias), the concerns of any one discipline with expressive materials may emerge at several different points.

---

### Chart 1: A Conceptualization of Expressive Culture Theory

## I. DIACHRONIC PERSPECTIVES

### A. EVOLUTIONARY THEORY
1. *Cultural Evolutionists*
2. *Myth-Ritualists*
3. *Comparative Philologists, Mythologists*

### B. DEVOLUTIONARY THEORY
1. *Elitists*

### C. DIFFUSION THEORY
1. *Single Point Diffusion Theories*
   a. The Indianists
   b. The Egyptianists
   c. The Finnish Historic-Geographic School
2. *Tempered Diffusion Theory*

### D. HISTORICAL USAGE

## II. SYNCHRONIC PERSPECTIVES

### A. FUNCTIONAL THEORY
1. *Behavioristic (Stimulus-Response) Functionalism*
2. *Psychoanalytic Functionalism*
3. *Cohesion*
4. *Functionalism of Analytic Psychology (Jungian Psychology)*
5. *Diachronic Study of Function*

### B. STRUCTURAL THEORY
1. *Structuralism*
2. *Structure of Performance*
3. *Development of Expressive Competence*

---

## I. Diachronic Perspectives (The Study of Expressive Materials Over Time)

Diachronic perspectives are frequently combined with geographic perspectives (the study of expressive materials over space) resulting in the investigation of folklore over time and space.

### A. Evolutionary Theory

Evolutionary theory rests on the assumption that the history of culture has been one of advancement or progress from simpler, less adequate, less accurate intellectual conceptualization and institutional structure to more complex, more adequate, more accurate conceptions and conditions.

### 1. *Cultural Evolutionists*

Expressive behaviors reflect and are the product of men at different stages of mental and/or cultural development. Three stages of development are generally recognized from savage to barbaric to civilized. Each culture stage is characterized by an integrated array of institutions, each of which is said to display certain traits. Progress is seen in terms of a culture's advancement from one stage to the next through a relatively fixed sequence. Only through contact with a much more advanced culture can a less developed culture by-pass or skip a stage or condition in the "natural" sequence of development. The folk (peasants) tend to be seen as the residual barbarians of the civilized stage.

Cultures do not require contact with one another for their development in similar directions. Rather there is held to be a basic psychic unity of all men which results in fundamentally similar responses to the common experiences all men confront in satisfying their requirements. Progress is a function of the quality of the thinking that underlies the responses of men as members of their cultures. As man's thinking becomes more adequate, man's social behavior changes and becomes more satisfactory in the fulfillment of his needs. As social behavior becomes more adequate, culture is said to evolve.

Particular expressive behaviors are said to arise at particular stages in man's cultural development and to reflect man's mental competence and thought processes (not necessarily his mental capacity) at those stages. As such these products are "at home" in the stages where they originate. However, expressive and other behaviors of earlier stages can survive into later cultural stages as residuals, having lost their original and "primary" function and meaning and having taken on secondary function and significance. Cultural residuals are called "survivals." The notion that some cultural forms survive in the context of cultural evolution is referred to as the doctrine of survivals. Evolutionists tend to equate modern primitive cultures with the savage stage of culture and look to primitive cultures for the nature of the savage mental and cultural condition. More advanced cultures reveal their previously less advanced heritage through survivals.

5

Expressive behavior plays a central part in evolutionary theory because it is expressive phenomena that are said to most decisively reveal the nature of man's thought process at different stages of culture and because expressive behaviors are likely to be those that survive to later stages, thereby revealing the participation of all cultures in a common pattern of cultural development.[3]

While earlier evolutionists tended to equate supernaturalistic conceptualizations and analogic thought modes with the savage or primitive on the one hand and naturalistic conceptualizations and logical or rational thought modes with civilized man on the other, later evolutionists have discussed cultural advancement in terms of the ever-widening domain of experience that becomes subject to naturalistic-rational modes of explanation and the ever-narrowing domain of experience that remains subject to supernaturalistic-analogical-magical modes of explanation.[4]

Modern parapsychology is itself questioning the contention that the conceptualizations underlying magical behavior are necessarily supernaturalistic. The implication of most parapsychological research is that much of what Western man has regarded as magical behavior may be based on naturalistic conceptions of communication and influence that simply utilize communication modes that Western man has either suppressed or ignored in his pursuit of the nature of his world in terms of the five "accredited" senses and the rational mode of thought.[5]

## 2. *Myth-Ritualists*

Myth-ritualists are a specialized group within the cultural evolutionists. Their focus is on the evolution of the expressive arts themselves. From their viewpoint, culture and art begin in the ritual acts of primitive men, especially sacrifice. As culture evolves, ritual becomes progressively verbalized, giving rise to myth. When the verbal description of the rite achieves autonomy, myth achieves independence as an expressive form. Rite is the primary form and myth is its immediate derivative. From myth and rite the secular verbal and performing arts subsequently evolve. As the sacred character of myth and ritual is lost or forgotten, myth becomes tale or song, and rite becomes drama, dance, music, or game. All the secular arts are said to have sacred formal precursors, and ritual is the original sacred expressive form. Ultimately all expressive forms and particular products can be traced back to ritual and to particular rites. The myth-ritualist concerns himself with reconstructing the ritual basis of particular expressive products by identifying the elements of the original ritual that survive in these products.[6]

## 3. *Comparative Philologists, Mythologists*

Using the tools of the historical and comparative linguist, usually in conjunction with an Indo-European theory of the basis of the language and culture of the Western world, the philologist attempts to reconstruct the nature of the parent or sub-parent Indo-European language and culture. Since many of the early written documents are religious in nature, the reconstruction of the parent belief system, particularly its mythology, has been the focus of much of the cultural reconstruction effort. The comparative mythologist assumes that this parent mythology survives in the residual tales and customs of the Western peasantry and attempts to organize this folk data in conjunction with previous records and the insights provided by comparative language studies to reconstruct the parent mythology and ritual. Reconstruction arguments setting forth the nature of the interdependencies of narrative records tend to rely heavily upon the etymology of terms, especially proper names. Not all comparative mythologists who pursue mythologic reconstructions make significant use of the tools of the historical linguist and not all comparative philologists concerned with mythological reconstruction are tied to the Indo-European theory of Western cultural development. Some employ the techniques of comparative language study within general cultural evolutionary theory.[7]

Current investigations of the Indo-European origins focus upon the reflection of Indo-European social structure offered by the comparative study of mythologies rather than upon the use of comparative linguistics to assist in the reconstruction of the parent mythology itself.[8]

## B. DEVOLUTIONARY THEORY

Most devolutionists are really devolutionists only in the sense that expressive products are seen to deteriorate while culture in general advances. Indeed this is the notion implicit in the "survivals" or "residuals" conception of the evolutionists. There is a sense then in which evolutionary theory contains within it a devolutionary conception of expressive culture. There are, however, some devolutionary theories of expressive culture that are linked to devolutionary conceptions of culture as a whole. Devolutionary culture theory is in tune with the Christian conception of the perfect (civilized) state of the world before man's fall from grace. The fall of man is, in the devolutionary sense, the fall from the civilized state—with some groups "falling" or "degenerating" further than others. Of course the Christian world, struggling after salvation through the "true" religion, is logically the group that gives witness to having fallen the least and is logically the most culturally advanced (civilized).[9]

### 1. *Elitists*

From this viewpoint, the elite arts evolve with developing culture while the folk arts trail behind as the residue of imperfect imitations of elite products by the artistically unsophisticated folk (peasant, common man). Traditional expressive arts are "naturally" rudified elite arts. Art is seen as flowing from the elite to the popular to the folk and as degenerating continuously.[10]

Most modern research into the relationship of the folk, popular, and elite domains of expressive culture recognizes that there is a complex interplay of dependencies among these different levels and that adaptation at any level is a function of the artistic tradition at that level. From this modern point of view the assessments of rudification and degeneration by elitists appear largely as judgements of the consequences of adaptation from a point of view outside the tradition in which the adaptation occurs. Most modern research approaches the question of the interrelationships of folk, popular, and elite arts in terms of intra-cultural diffusion theory rather than devolutionary theory.[11]

## C. DIFFUSION THEORY

Diffusion theory asserts that expressive culture products, like other culture traits, originate some place and spread elsewhere through a process of transmission. Diffusion theory assumes a theory of cultural transmission, however unsophisticated, in terms of cultural interaction and in accord with broad principles of social psychology and learning theory. The diffusionist is interested in tracing the spread of expressive products from their point of origin through time and space to their present distribution. Usually his efforts involve working in reverse from present distributions to reconstruct the process of diffusion and to propose the nature of the original creation.[12]

### 1. *Single Point Diffusion Theories*

Single point diffusion theories assume that cultural forms or products arise at one point in time in some one place. When found elsewhere, these forms and products are to be accounted for in terms of their diffusion from the one place of original creation.

#### a. The Indianists

Particularly with respect to narrative literature, this group holds India to be the fountainhead of virtually all Western narrative art. The basis for the proposal rests on the fact that the oldest known versions of many of the traditional narratives of the Western world are found in ancient Indian written records. The Indianists tend to assume that transmission of literature over any significant distance is a function of written rather than oral means. They are inclined to adopt an elitist position with respect to the oral versions of narratives performed by the folk. Assuming the primacy of writing in literary transmission and of ancient Indian culture in the Western world, Indianists sought to demonstrate that when found elsewhere, narrative literature could be traced back to sources in India. The legitimacy of the Indianist contention, however qualified, probably rests upon the Indo-European basis of Indian literature and culture.[13]

#### b. The Egyptianists

The Egyptianists were more expansive than the Indianists in two senses. First, they considered the full scope of Egyptian culture, not just the domain of literary creation as was the case for the Indianists. Second, while the Indianists were mainly concerned with India as a source of Western literature, the Egyptianists proposed Egypt as the source of advanced cultural phenomena world wide. Although the Egyptianists include in their theory the expressive domain of myth, ritual, and the arts, this cultural dimension is not the singular focus of their attention.[14]

scant or among any group where historical records consist of largely ideal statements without the balance provided by materials revealing the real anxieties, frustrations, and desires the group experiences in the pursuit of its ideals and goals.[18]

## II. SYNCHRONIC PERSPECTIVES (THE STUDY OF EXPRESSIVE BEHAVIOR MORE OR LESS AT ONE POINT IN TIME AND SPACE)

### A. FUNCTIONAL THEORY

From this viewpoint, expressive behaviors and products are significant because of the services they render with respect to individual and social needs. Functionalists primarily concern themselves with the relationship between general cultural behavior and the behavioral and symbolic content found in expressive forms. The first step in any functional proposition is the realization that expressive materials reflect in their content the normative and/or anti-normative behavior of the groups for which they are relevant.[19]

### 1. *Behavioristic (Stimulus-Response) Functionalism*

Expressive behavior from this viewpoint is regarded as a stimulus realized through either the individual's observation or participation and is said to evoke a response in the individual which reinforces or instills the values and attitudes displayed and/or approved in the expression. Also involved here is the notion that expressive behavior constitutes a safe arena within which the individual can practice or test himself for cultural competence with respect to particular skills or roles. Notions of expressive culture as providing charter, validation, sanction, or justification for values, ideas, and institutions are all essentially behavioristic-functional propositions.[20]

Behavioristic theory is most adequate for explaining the function of expressive behaviors where ideal behavior is displayed and approved. It is less adequate in explaining expressive behavior where anti-normative behavior is displayed and denied, and it is least adequate in accounting for the function of expressive behavior where anti-normative behavior is displayed without denial. While behavioristic psychology includes within it the notion of behavior motivated by drives and the reduction of drives through the location of and participation in appropriate behaviors, the derivation of the symbolic response for this purpose is vague in behavioristic theory. Although behaviorism has in its broad theory the capability to regard expressive behavior as response to these drives, the domination of behaviorism by learning theory leads to the identification of the behavioristic viewpoint with the notion of expressive behavior as stimulus.[21]

Ego psychologists from the psychoanalytic domain tend to stress the stimulus function of expressive behavior in their conception of the consequences of involvement in expressive behavior. Although ego psychologists derive their viewpoint from within psychoanalytic theory, they examine expressive involvement primarily in terms of what it reflects about and how it works to stimulate ego growth in the individual.[22]

Thomas A. Burns

## 2. *Psychoanalytic Functionalism*

Expressive behavior is regarded by the psychoanalyst as a response to psychological needs, a response which is realized through either participation in or vicarious identification with aspects of the content of expressive products. Anxiety or impulses not allowed gratification through direct behavioral outlets due to the restrictions of society are said to be released through more indirect or symbolically representative expressive behaviors. The expressive arena constitutes the carefully controlled, bounded domain for the expression in disguised (symbolic) form of these feelings, desires, fears, and impulses that receive inadequate direct expression because of the inhibiting nature of social rules. The consequences of symbolic expression of these feelings in the expressive arena is to reduce the level of these feelings, though not as much reduction occurs as would be the case for participation in directly gratifying behavior. The final result of the reduction of the levels of these feelings is that the individual or group is said to be put in a better situation to endure and so to cope with the strictures of society in its everyday normative format. From this perspective, expressive behavior serves as a safety valve, as a coping mechanism.

The psychoanalytic viewpoint allows for the possibility that expressive behavior assists the individual and the group in coping not only by releasing repressed anxieties and inhibited impulses or desires, but also by denying these very same impulses or desires. It is therefore possible, from the psychoanalytic perspective, for expressive behavior to operate in behalf of repression on the one hand and as a vehicle to release repressed feelings on the other. The psychoanalyst attempts to resolve this paradox by saying that at the conscious level expressive behavior frequently services the forces of repression or denial, while at the unconscious level, anxieties and impulses are released in symbolic or disguised forms.

While the above psychoanalytic theory of expressive behavior is commonly utilized in the assessment of the meaning and function of folklore by many different researchers, the psychoanalytic school itself has come to be identified with the symbolic interpretations of applied psychoanalysts. This group follows Freud's early suggestion that expressive behaviors enjoyed by groups were likely to be heavily laden with symbols. The meaning of these symbols was taken to be essentially universal and was known to the psychoanalyst from his study of their appearance and meaning in the dreams of patients undergoing psychoanalysis. The assumption of the universal meaning of symbols, along with the assumption that these symbols formed the basis for collective expressions, freed the applied psychoanalyst from the need to justify his interpretations of folkloric materials. It was no longer necessary for the analyst to specifically identify the shared experience and affects of the group that underlay the relevance and meaning of these collective expressions. The assessments of the symbolic meaning of folklore that have resulted from psychoanalytic scholars have been severely criticized by folklorists and anthropologists for their failure to take into account differences in the perception and understanding of collective expressions by different cultures and different individuals within cultures.[23]

### 3. *Cohesion (a secondary consequence of the behavioristic or psychoanalytic function)*

Cohesion is a secondary function of participation in expressive behavior by a group. It is held that the feeling of groupness is increased by mutual involvement of the group's members in expressive behaviors that either release anxiety and aggression or promote values and ideals. Through the sharing of anxieties and/or values in expressive behavior, the group affirms its sense of groupness—its identity. Likewise, in venting its antipathy for outgroups through the expression of stereotypes of outgroup members in folkloric behavior, the ingroup defines its identity in terms of what it is not.[24] Of course while the ingroup may gain in cohesiveness by rejecting the outgroup through stereotypes, these same stereotypes and the expressions that embody them are the source of antagonism and disunity in the relations between the ingroup and the outgroup. Cohesion gained at one level of social inclusiveness through traditional expressions may be countered by divisiveness resulting from these same expressions at a more inclusive level of groupness.

In line with the cohesion proposition is the research with symbolic behavior that suggests expressive behavior serves, through its symbolic representations, the significant interactional, social structural and cognitive conflicts of society. Expressive behavior addresses these conflicts or points of stress and either vents in symbolic form the feelings that underlie them or gives the periodic appearance of having resolved them by the effective manipulation of symbols. The consequence of engaging in these expressions is held to be maintenance of group integrity.[25]

### 4. *Functionalism of Analytic Psychology (Jungian Psychology)*

This group attributes to expressive behavior a more creative role than does the psychoanalytic group, of which it is an offshoot. Jungians posit a collective dimension to the unconscious of the psyche of all men. This collective unconscious is never directly known, but is held to be the reservoir of the pervasive experience of mankind stored as an array of innate predispositions or archetypes. Archetypes are usually seen as being filled by culture-specific images which nevertheless reveal their archetypal underpinnings by their basic similarity across widely divergent cultures. Images of archetypes are symbolic since these images are indirect representations or manifestations of the archetypes of the collective unconscious in the personal unconscious and conscious mind of man. Jungians regard most expressive behavior as they regard archetypal dreams; as drawing upon the collective experience of man, residually stored in the collective unconscious, to recommend through symbolic manifestations the appropriate course for the resolution of individual and social problems. It is this creative, prognostic function of expressive materials that Jungians tend to emphasize. In pointing the direction for potential growth, the function of expressive materials is to assist the individual in the realization of the individuation process; the realization of the balanced or "complete" adult and society formulated in the collective image of such adults. Expressive materials are seen as revealing the progress of cultures and individuals in developing toward the ideal state of self-awareness: a balance between (1) the fully differentiated faculties of feeling, thinking, intuiting, and sensing, (2) the well adjusted personal unconscious, and (3) the creative contact with the collective unconscious. Jungians examine expressive materials to determine their archetypal basis, the nature of the creative recommendation they make in symbolic terms, and the condition they reflect in the growth of cultures and individuals toward a state of self-realization.[26]

## 5. *Diachronic Study of Function*

While most functional studies tend to be synchronic, the function of expressive material can also be studied over time. The role of expressive behaviors in the culture change and culture contact situations is a major avenue of investigation. In such situations expressive systems of different groups are usually in conflict and competition. Indeed, where physical confrontation is disallowed, as among ingroup factions, the competition among groups may be primarily expressed and even resolved in terms of the opposed systems of expressive behavior.[27]

## B. STRUCTURAL THEORY

There are two different approaches to the structural examination of expressive behavior. The first is concerned with how expressive behavior, as a product of man's mind, reveals the structure of man's perceptual and thought processes. The second is concerned with determining the nature of the systematic knowledge (competence) that underlies the ability of the individual as a member of his culture to generate expressive behavior. This systematic knowledge is held to be reflected in the systematic nature of expressive behavior itself.

## 1. *Structuralism*

The French school of structuralists contend that the nature of man's mental operations is binary. They further hold that because mental operations are binary, man perceives and organizes his world in terms of binary categories. Culture as ideation depends on the processes of perception and cognition, so cultural conceptualizations must be binary in nature (e.g. nature-culture, life-death). Unfortunately nature and experience do not always accord with the oppositional categories of culture and as such there is tension between the "real" world and the conceptual system. Moreover, there are some oppositions that are emotionally laden for man (e.g. life-death) and whose conflicts require at least the illusion of successful resolution (e.g. in favor of life in death). Expressive behaviors arise to service points in the binary conceptual scheme where tension exists as a result of significant conflicts between conceptualization and reality and as a result of man's emotional desire to resolve some categorical oppositions in particular directions. Expressive behavior symbolically addresses these cognitive conflicts and assists in their resolution by creating the illusion of their successful mediation. The appearance of successful mediation or resolution is achieved through successive transformations of the symbols representing the conceptions in conflict. Ultimately, expressive culture works to maintain the cultural cognitive system by periodically reducing cognitive tension created by the conflict between reality and the binary basis of cultural conceptualization. The structuralist examines expressive materials to determine what conceptual conflicts are being addressed and mediated through what symbolic representations and by means of what symbolic transformations.[28]

## 2. *Structure of Performance (folkloric behavior as communication)*

Performance-structuralists are concerned with the process whereby a traditional artistic message is realized in a performance context. They assume that all behavior is rule ordered and that what a performer and audience learn are the rules for generating different types of artistic communications that are appropriate in different types of social situations. That is to say, a participant in a folkloric act is held to draw upon his knowledge of how to behave in order to generate behavior that constitutes appropriate participation in the shaping of the artistic result. His knowledge is thought to be systematic, and the adequacy of his systematic knowledge is said to represent his competence to perform. The performance-structuralist is interested in characterizing the nature of the system of competence that underlies each participant's behavior and the systematic way in which the competences of the various participants in a folkloric act interrelate to produce an overall result that is judged to be, to varying degrees, appropriate and aesthetically satisfying. Since there is no way as yet to determine directly the structure of competence, competence being an ideational matter, the performance-structuralist must try to determine the nature of this competence by examining its behavioral consequences. Close observation and analysis of the process and product of performance are the means the performance-structuralist utilizes in trying to construct a model of the systematic shape of folkloric competence. The structure of performance competence is assumed to be similar to the structure of receptive competence upon which the understanding and aesthetic judgement of a performance rest. Indeed, developmentally one would expect that the competence to receive and understand the artistic performances of others is continually ahead of the competence to translate that receptive understanding into the competence to manifest such artistic performance oneself.

How the folkloric act should or can be structurally conceived is far from resolved in performance structure theory. Until recently three domains were identified as important because of the significance of the variables in these areas for determining appropriate performance behavior. The separation of the domains was recognized as being artificial but analytically useful. The three domains were those of text, vehicle, and context. Each of these domains was held to be structured, and any folkloric performance was regarded as a function of competence in dealing with structure in all three domains. Text structure referred to the domain within which the content of the folkloric act was determined. Study of textual structure involved the identification of the units of content, the dependencies of these units at different levels of inclusiveness in a generative hierarchy, and the rules for combining these units of content to create complete, acceptable, generic texts. Vehicular structure referred to the process whereby content was manifested. Vehicles for content manifestation included all codes passing in all channels of communication that are utilized in expressing content. Vehicles included language, music, graphic representation, all forms of movement, and material or artifactual products. Study of vehicular structure focused on the rules for the use of each code and the rules for integrating the use of the various codes in performance. Contextual structure referred to the social rules of artistic behavior. A folkloric act occurred in a social situation, and social situations delimited and restricted the range of acceptable folkloric texts and the appropriate manner of their manifestation. Competence to perform or participate in a folkloric act referred, then, to the participant's ability to formulate texts and to manifest them in vehicles in such a way that they were appropriate and acceptable in particular social situations.

Later structural conceptions of performance have called attention to the artificiality of the text vehicle, and context division of the variables of performance. In addition it has been observed that this division gives undue emphasis to the realms of content and vehicle structure while lumping together a number of quite distinct and equally important variables under the umbrella term, "context." From the point of view of more recent performance research, there are not rules of text, vehicle, and context that somehow act conjointly, but rules for acceptable expressive interaction. Regarded in this way, the distinction between the performer as expressive message transmitter and the audience as message receiver is seen as spurious. All participants in an expressive act are performers. Together, by their interaction, these performer-participants negotiate an expressive act. Expressive competence is seen as the ability to participate in such negotiations. Successful expressive acts are ones resulting from a willingness on the part of the social interactants to participate in a creative negotiation, and the ability of each participant to execute adequately the behavior required of him during the negotiation. Different types of participation require different abilities, different competencies. Individuals differ in the range of participatory roles they are competent to fill in particular types of expressive acts.

A performance-structuralist analyzes a folkloric act as a negotiation among the participants. He does not analyze "a" text because there is no "one" text of the performance. The notion of a single performance text is superorganic; it is not realized in anyone actually interacting in a folkloric event. Rather a performance consists of a set of texts, one for each participant since each participant receives somewhat different information and each selects differentially among what he receives. Each participant is continually receiving a text of the act as it builds and each is continually contributing by what he does to both his own text and the texts of other participants. There is a text of "the performance" only in the sense that the texts of the individual participants are systematically related. A recording of a performance, however detailed, is a record, not the text of either the performance or a participant. Such recordings are useful only as means to try to reconstruct the system of texts of the interactants.

Since the variables of time, place, occasion, and the social aspects of age, sex, rank, etc., are all cued by features of the information received by each participant, the variables of context are really aspects inclusive in the text of each participant. Vehicles, or the codes passing in the various communication channels, are the carriers of this more inclusive notion of text. It follows from this viewpoint that a performance consists of the set of systematically related texts of the participants, texts that are realized in terms of vehicles.

Ultimately the performance-structuralist tries to reconstruct the system of texts of the participants in an expressive act. Studying many such sets of texts of the same kind of folkloric act, the analyst tries to understand the way in which these texts reflect a rule regulated negotiation. Once he has formulated the rules for participation in a type of folkloric act, the performance-structuralist is in a position to understand in a rigorous way the "native" basis for aesthetic evaluation of folkloric acts of that type. Ultimately the performance-structuralist pursues the aesthetic system that underlies participation in, and evaluation of, different types of traditional expressive acts among different social groups.[29]

### 3. *Development of Expressive Competence (the diachronic study of competence)*

Developmental studies of competence investigate the growth of the conceptual-generative system that underlies performance. The evolution of a sophisticated performance competence is recognized as being incremental with less adequate competence characterized by less sophisticated incorporation of the rules of performance. Understanding the sophisticated, elaborated system of performance can greatly benefit from studies of that system in the simplified versions that characterize the competence of beginners. Developmental studies of competence contribute to an understanding of how traditional artistic behaviors are learned and transmitted. Developmental studies explore the relationship between the expressive competence of the individual at different stages and the individual's general development of (1) vehicular skills, (2) perceptual abilities, (3) conceptual or cognitive abilities, and (4) social interactional abilities. The structural developmentalist is concerned with the growth of expressive competence in each genre of performance and in the relationship between the growth schedules among genres.

While the focus may be structural, studies of developing expressive competence may also deal with the parallel issue of developing affect as reflected in the changing content focus of expressive behaviors at different stages. The notion here is that just as the formal competence of the individual grows in systematic ways, so his emotional concerns change and develop in a fairly regular pattern. The development of expressive competence reflects in content and form, developing affect and perceptual-cognitive abilities respectively. Investigations of developing performance competence usually focus on the period of development from early childhood through adolescence.[30]

Thomas A. Burns

## Conclusion

In the absence of a unified theory of expressive behavior and of a comprehensive, current work on folklore theory, it is hoped that the above sketch of the theory pursued by traditional arts folklorists will prove useful to the beginning student in suggesting the range of ideas currently explored in this division of the discipline. As a discipline, folklore is currently defined by this range of theoretical concerns, plus the more general social and historical theory of the folklife scholar. Folklorists, whatever their special material interest or chosen theoretical pursuit, are first and foremost persons knowledgeable about the full range of both traditional behaviors and the various potential approaches to their study. They differ from persons trained in other disciplines studying expressive material in that they have a greater awareness of the range of both theoretical alternatives and traditional materials, and because of this knowledge, are in a position to be more sensitive to the implications of each theory and type of material for alternative perspectives and materials.

---

[1] A work in progress by Dan Ben-Amos tentatively entitled *Folklore: History, Forms, and Methods* constitutes the only modern, comprehensive, intellectual history of the discipline to be undertaken by a single scholar.

[2] Richard M. Dorson, "Current Theories of Folklore," in his *Folklore and Folklife: An Introduction* (Chicago, 1972), 7–47; Jan Harold Brunvand, "The Subject in Context," in *Folklore: A Study and Research Guide* (New York, 1976), 7–33.

[3] Edward Burnett Tylor, *The Origin of Culture* [vol. I of *Primitive Culture*](New York, 1958 [orig. 1871]), esp. chapters 1, 2, 3, 4, 8, 9, and 10; David Bidney, *Theoretical Anthropology* (New York, 1967 [orig. 1953]), 183–214, 286–290; Richard M. Dorson, *The British Folklorists* (Chicago, 1968), 187–265; Marvin Harris, *The Rise of Anthropological Theory* (New York, 1968), 142–216; Robert H. Lowie, *The History of Ethnological Theory* (New York, 1937), 68–127.

[4] Leslie A. White, *The Evolution of Culture* (New York, 1959), 3–32, 261–278.

[5] Arthur Koestler, *The Roots of Coincidence* (London, 1972); Allan Angoff and Betty Shapin, eds., *Parapsychology and the Sciences* (New York, 1974); Lyall Watson, *Supernature: The Natural History of the Supernatural* (London, 1973).

[6] Stanley Edgar Hyman, "The Ritual View of Myth and the Mythic," in *Myth: A Symposium* (Bloomington, Indiana, 1965 [orig. 1955]), 136–153; Lord Raglan, "Myth and Ritual," in *Myth: A Symposium* (Bloomington, Indiana, 1965 [orig. 1955]), 122–135. For an anthropological position that gives as much credence to the mythic source of ritual as the ritual source of myth, see: Clyde Kluckhohn, "Myths and Rituals: A General Theory," *Harvard Theological Review* 35 (1942): 45–79.

[7] Stith Thompson, *The Folktale* (New York, 1946), 367–375; Richard M. Dorson, *The British Folklorists* (Chicago, 1968), 160–186; Jacob Grimm, "Preface to the Second Edition," in his *Teutonic Mythology* (New York, 1966 [orig. 1843]), III, v–lv; Wilhelm Grimm, *Grimm's Household Tales*, trans. Margaret Hunt (London, 1884 [orig. 1856]), II, 575 ff.

[8] C. Scott Littleton, "The Comparative Indo-European Mythology of Dumezil," *Journal of the Folklore Institute* (1964): 147–166.

[9] Alan Dundes, "The Devolutionary Premise in Folklore Theory," *Journal of the Folklore Institute* 6 (1969): 5–19; Clyde Kluckhohn, "Some Reflections on the Method and Theory of Kulturkreislehre," *American Anthropologist*, 38 (1936): 157–196.

[10] Emma E. Kiefer, *Albert Wesselski and Recent Folktale Theories* (Bloomington, Indiana, 1947); D. K. Wilgus, *Anglo-American Folksong Scholarship Since 1898* (New Brunswick, New Jersey, 1959), 35–42.

[11] See section following entitled "Tempered Diffusion Theory."

[12] Harris, 373–392.

[13]Thompson, 375–379.

[14]Lowie, 156–176.

[15]Thompson, 391–405, 428–448; Richard M. Dorson, ed., *Studies in Japanese Folklore* (Bloomington, Indiana, 1963).

[16]Franz Boas, "The Growth of Indian Mythologies," *Journal of American Folklore* 9 (1986): 1–11; Frank Hamilton Cushing, "The Cock and the Mouse," in *The Study of Folklore*, ed. Alan Dundes (Englewood Cliffs, N.J., 1965), 269–276; Harris, 250–300; Fred Kniffen, "Folk Housing: Key to Diffusion," *Annals of American Geographers*, 55 (1965): 549–577; Henry Glassie, "The Types of the Southern Mountain Cabin," in *The Study of American Folklore*, by Jan Harold Brunvand (New York, 1968), 338–370.

[17]Jan Vansina, "Recording the Oral History of the Bakuba: I, Methods," *Journal of African History* 1 (1960):43–51; Jan Vansina, *Oral Tradition: A Study in Historical Methodology* (Chicago, 1965); C. Gabel and N. R. Bennett, eds., *Reconstructing African Culture History* (Boston, 1967); Richard M. Dorson, "The Debate over the Trustworthiness of Traditional History," in his *Folklore: Selected Essays* (Bloomington, Indiana, 1972 [orig. 1968]), 199–224.

[18]Richard M. Dorson, *American Folklore and the Historian* (Chicago, 1971), essays four through eight; Richard M. Dorson, "History of the Elite and History of the Folk," in his *Folklore: Selected Essays*, 225–259; Merle Simmons, *The Mexican Corrido as a Source for Interpretive Study of Modern Mexico (1870–1950)* (Bloomington, Indiana, 1957); Bill Ivey, "The 1913 Disaster: A Michigan Local Legend," *Folklore Forum* 3 (1970): 100–114.

[19]Franz Boas, *Tsimshian Mythology*, 31st Annual Report of the Bureau of American Ethnology (Washington, D.C., 1910), 393–477; Ruth Benedict, "Introduction to Zuni Mythology," in her *Zuni Mythology* (New York, 1935), I, xi–xliii.

[20]Bronislaw Malinowski, "Myth in Primitive Psychology," in *Magic, Science and Religion* (New York, 1954 [orig. 1926]), 93–148; John M. Roberts and Michael L. Forman, "Riddles: Expressive Models of Interrogation," *Ethnology* 10 (1971): 509–533; Elliott M. Avedon and Brian Sutton-Smith, "The Function of Games," in their *The Study of Games* (New York, 1971), 429–439.

[21]The behavioristic investigation of the function of humor is one area where the drive reduction dimension of the behavioristic theory has received considerable attention. For a review of this research see: Thomas A. Burns with Inger H. Burns, "Humor and the Joke" in their *Doing the Wash: An Expressive Culture and Personality Study of a Joke and Its Tellers* (Philadelphia, 1975), 18–36.

[22]Jacob A. Arlow, "Ego Psychology and the Study of Mythology," *Journal of the American Psychoanalytic Association* 9 (1961): 371–393; Eric Erikson, *Childhood and Society*, 2nd ed. (New York, 1963), 209–234.

[23]Sigmund Freud, *Jokes and Their Relation to the Unconscious* (New York, 1963 [orig. 1905]), chapters 1, 3, and 6; Thomas A. Burns with Inger H. Burns, chapters 1, 3–6; Ernest Jones, "The Symbolic Significance of Salt in Folklore and Superstition," in his *Essays in Applied Psychoanalysis* (New York, 1964 [orig, 1912]), II, 22–109.

[24]Wm. Hugh Jansen, "The Esoteric-Exoteric Factor in Folklore," *Fabula* 2 (1959): 205–211; Roger D. Abrahams, "The Negro Stereotype: Negro Folklore and the Riots," *Journal of American Folklore* 83 (1970): 229–258.

[25]Victor Turner, *The Drums of Affliction* (Oxford, 1968), 1–24, 198–268; Clyde Kluckhohn, *Navaho Witchcraft* (Boston, 1967 [orig., 1944]), 5–9, 76–128; Scarlett Epstein, "A Sociological Analysis of Witch Beliefs in a Mysore Village," *The Eastern Anthropologist* 12 (1959): 234–251.

[26]Carl G. Jung, "The Psychology of the Child Archetype," in *Essays on a Science of Mythology* (Princeton, New Jersey, 1969 [orig. 1941]), 70–100; Carl G. Jung, "On the Psychology of the Trickster-Figure," in *Four Archetypes* (Princeton, New Jersey, 1970 [orig. 1954]), 135–152; Carlos C. Drake, "Jung and His Critics," *Journal of American Folklore* 80 (1967): 321–333.

[27]Anthony F. C. Wallace, "Revitalization Movements," *American Anthropologist* 58 (1956): 264–281; L. P. Mair, "Independent Religious Movements in Three Continents," *Comparative Studies in Society and History I* (1959): 113–136; Edmund Leach, "Myth as a Justification for Faction and Social Change," in *Political Systems of Highland Burma* (London, 1964), 164–278; Clifford Geertz, "Ritual and Social Change: A Javanese Example," *American Anthropologist* 59 (1957): 32–54.

[28]Claude Lévi-Strauss, "The Structural Study of Myth," *Journal of American Folklore* 78 (1955): 428–444; Edmund Leach, Claude Lévi-Strauss (New York, 1970); Claude Lévi-Strauss, "The Story of Asdiwal," in *The Structural Study of Myth and Totemism*, ed. Edmund Leach (London, 1967), 1–47; Elli Köngäs Maranda and Pierre Maranda, *Structural Models in Folklore and Transformational Essays* (The Hague, 1971).

19

# Thomas A. Burns

[29] Alan Dundes, "Texture, Text, and Context," *Southern Folklore Quarterly* 28 (1964): 251–265; Roger D. Abrahams, "Introductory Remarks to a Rhetorical Theory of Folklore," *Journal of American Folklore,* 81 (1968): 143–158: Roger D. Abrahams, "The Complex Relations of Simple Forms," *Genre* 2 (1969): 104–128; Dan Ben-Amos, "Toward a Componential Model for Folklore Communication," *Proceedings of the Eighth International Congress of Anthropological and Ethnological Sciences, 1968, Tokyo and Kyoto* (Tokyo, 1970), II, 309–311; Dell Hymes, "Models of the Interaction of Language and Social Setting," *Journal of Social Issues,* 33 (1967): 8–28; Richard Bauman, "Verbal Art as Performance," *American Anthropologist* 77 (1975): 290–311; Vladimir Propp, *Morphology of the Folktale,* 2nd. ed., (Austin, Texas, 1968); Benjamin N. Colby, "A Partial Grammar of Eskimo Folktales," *American Anthropologist* 75 (1973): 645–662; Henry Glassie, *Folk Housing in Middle Virginia: A Structural Analysis of Historic Artifacts* (Knoxville, Tennessee, 1975); Albert Lord, *The Singer of Tales* (Cambridge, Massachusetts, 1960); Robert A. Rothstein, "The Poetics of Proverbs," in Charles E. Gribble, ed., *Studies Presented to Professor Roman Jakobson by his Students* (Cambridge, Massachusetts, 1968), 265–274; Barbara Kirshenblatt-Gimblett, "A Parable in Context: A Social Interactional Analysis of Storytelling Performance," in Dan Ben-Amos and Kenneth S. Goldstein, eds., *Folklore: Performance and Communication* (The Hague, 1975), 105–130; Thomas A. Burns, "Riddling: Occasion to Act," *Journal of American Folklore* 89 (1976): 139–165.

[30] Brian Sutton-Smith, "The Expressive Profile," *Journal of American Folklore* 84 (1971): 80–92; Howard Gardner, *The Arts and Human Development* (New York, 1973); Rosalind Eckhardt, "From Handclap to Line Play," in *Black Girls at Play: Folkloric Perspectives on Child Development* (Austin, Texas, 1975), 57–99; Evelyn Pitcher and Ernst Prelinger, *Children Tell Stories* (New York, 1963); Martha Wolfenstein, *Children's Humor* (Glencoe, Illinois, 1954).

# Herder, Folklore and Romantic Nationalism
## William A. Wilson

*The collection and study of what has come to be called "folklore" began in Europe at the close of the eighteenth century. The enterprise was an outgrowth of the twin movements of romanticism and nationalism—ideologies that transformed the artistic, political, and social life and thought of all Europe. Perhaps the central figure in both articulating and crystallizing romantic-nationalistic consciousness was Johann Gottfried von Herder. In the following essay, William A. Wilson outlines the development of Herder's philosophy to demonstrate the central importance of folklore in the romantic-nationalistic program.*

*Folklore both creates and is created by a romantic-nationalistic consciousness. Interest in the documentation, analysis, and display of folk traditions has characterized virtually all emergent nations in the last two centuries. Nazism was also a romantic-nationalistic ideology—an ideology that recruited folklore to the service of the Third Reich (Kamenetsky 1972, 1977; Mieder 1982). Dorson (1966) has surveyed the role of folklore in a variety of new nations, and Wilson (1976) explored the case in Finland in some depth. The deep nationalistic motivations underlying both scholarly and popular interest in folklore suggests the importance of reflecting upon the ideological bases of our own research.*

> Methinks I see the time coming when we shall return in earnest to our language, to the merits, to the principles and goals of our fathers and learn therefore to value our own gold.
>
> —Johann Gottfried Herder

English-American folklore studies began as the leisure-time activity of scholar-gentlemen intrigued by the quaint body of customs, manners, and oral traditions called *popular antiquities*—rebaptized *folklore* in 1846. With the advent of evolutionary anthropology in the second half of the nineteenth century and with its emphasis on folklore items as survivals among the peasants of ancient practices and beliefs, folklore became the object of serious study by scholars like Tylor, Lang, and Gomme. Since then both English and American folklorists have devoted much of their time to the study of survivals and to the historical reconstruction of the past or of past forms of present lore.

Reproduced by permission of the publisher, from *Journal of Popular Culture* 6, no. 4 (1973):818–35. Not for further reproduction.

William A. Wilson

On the continent serious folklore studies began earlier and followed a different path. There they were from the beginning intimately associated with emergent romantic nationalistic movements in which zealous scholar-patriots searched the folklore record of the past not just to see how people had lived in by-gone days—the principal interest of the antiquarians—but primarily to discover "historical" models on which to reshape the present and build the future. In this paper I shall attempt to show how this marriage of folklore research and nationalistic endeavors occurred and to describe some of its results.

Nationalism is a term not easily defined. Hans Kohn calls it an idea,"a state of mind, in which the supreme loyalty of the individual is felt to be due to the nation-state."[1] In words of about the same effect, Carlton J. H. Hayes calls it "a fusion of patriotism with a consciousness of nationality."[2] A nationality he defines as "a group of people who speak either the same language or closely related dialects, who cherish common historical tradition, and who constitute or think they constitute a distinct cultural society."[3] In other words, the nation-state to which the patriot owes his allegiance is defined according to ethnographic principles. Both as an inspiration for the idea of nationalism and as a means of winning the minds of men to that idea, folklore has served well.

In Western Europe and America the rise of nationalism in the late eighteenth century was, at least in the beginning, in line with the liberal and humanitarian philosophies of the Enlightenment. It was precipitated in no small degree by Rousseau's doctrine of popular sovereignty and "by his regard for the common people as the true depository of civilization"[4]—ideas which found their most powerful manifestations in the French and American Revolutions. Adherents of the new nationalistic philosophy looked forward to the day when the entire human community would share in those rights recently won in America and France. To them, as Kohn points out,

> the nationalism of the French Revolution . . . was the triumphant expression of
> a rational faith in common humanity and liberal progress. The famous slogan
> of 'liberty, equality, fraternity' and the Declaration of the Rights of Man and of
> the Citizen were thought valid not only for the French people, but for all
> peoples.[5]

In Central and East Europe, however, a different kind of movement—romantic nationalism—developed. In these areas, where the people were generally socially and politically less developed than in the West, national boundaries seldom coincided with those of existing states. Hence nationalism here became a movement not so much to protect the individual against the injustices of an authoritarian state, but rather an attempt to redraw political boundaries to fit the contours of ethnic bodies. To be sure, the adherents of this nationalism took over Rousseau's concept of popular sovereignty, but to it they wedded the idea that each nationality is a distinct organic entity different from all other nations and that the individual can fulfill himself only to the degree that he is true to that national whole of which he is merely a part. Thus individual will became secondary to national will, and service to the nation-state became the highest endeavor of man. In contradistinction to liberal nationalism, romantic nationalism emphasized passion and instinct instead of reason, national differences instead of common aspirations, and, above all, the building of nations on the traditions and myths of the past—that is, on folklore—instead of on the political realities of the present.

The man most responsible for the creation of this romantic nationalism was the German scholar Johann Gottfried Herder (1744-1803).[6] In its beginning stages, romantic nationalism was little more than the wistful dream of scholars and poets who endeavored through constant education and propaganda to kindle the spark of national consciousness in the hearts of their lethargic countrymen. As Kohn points out, they "became the voice and the conscience of their people, interpreting its history or mission and shaping its character and personality." And "always they developed a philosophy of history and society, in the center of which stood their own nation and the principle which was to sum up its idea and faith."[7] Such a man was Herder, whose philosophy of history not only inspired the German nationalistic movement but, for better or for worse, seems to have served as the foundation for most such movements since his time. By showing the German people why their building a national culture on native foundations was not only desirable but absolutely necessary, Herder formulated a set of principles of nationalism that have generally been held applicable to all nations struggling for independent existence.

Some of the principal tenets of his philosophy Herder took from other sources. In 1768 he received a copy of Michael Denis's *Die Gedichte Ossians, eines alten celtischen Dicters*. The book, a translation of Macpherson's *Poems of Ossian,* contained elaborate notes which had originally been written by Melchiorre Cesarotti for the Italian translation of Macpherson and which had been taken over by Denis, translated, and added to his own work. In these notes Cesarotti had relied heavily on the *Scienza Nuova* of Giambattista Vico—particularly on Vico's ideas about poetry and history. From Vico—via these notes—Herder received two ideas that were to become cornerstones of his own philosophy.[8]

The first of these was the idea of different historic ages, each of which evolves naturally out of the preceding age—in other words, the concept of continuity in history. "All things," said Herder, "rest upon one another and have grown out of one another." And again: the fatherland "has descended from our fathers; it arouses the remembrance of all the meretorious who went before us, and of all the worthy whose fathers we shall be."[9] This idea was soon to have tremendous national significance.

The second concept which Herder took from Vico was that each historical epoch forms an independent cultural entity whose various parts are integrally related to form an organic whole. Applying this concept of culture patterns to the historical stages of individual nations, Herder was soon to argue that since each nation was organically different from every other nation, each nation ought to be master of its own destiny. "Every nation," he said, "contains the center of its happiness within itself."[10]

From the writings of Charles de Montesquieu, Herder received further support for his concept of independent culture types. From them he also received a new idea—that these culture types are to a large degree determined by the physical environment in which nations are located. "Nature," said Herder, paraphrasing Montesquieu,

> has sketched with the mountain ranges she formed and with the rivers she made flow from them the rough but definite outline of the entire history of man. . . . One height created a nation of hunters, thus supporting and necessitating a savage state; another, more spread out and mild, provided a field for shepherd peoples and supplied them with tame animals; another made agriculture easy and essential; and still another began with navigation and fishing and led finally to trade. . . . In many regions the customs and ways of life have continued for millennia; in others they have changed, . . . but always in harmony with the terrain from which the change came. . . . Oceans, mountain chains, and rivers are the most natural boundaries not only of lands, but also of peoples, customs, languages, and empires; and even in the greatest revolutions of human affairs they have been the guiding lines and limits of world history.[11]

Herder contended, then, that from the varying circumstances of nations' physical environments had emerged national differences and that these, enhanced over the years by historical developments, had gradually evolved into distinct national units, the organic structures of which he considered to be reflected in what he called national characters, or national souls. "Those peculiar national characters," he said,

> which are so deeply implanted in the oldest peoples, unmistakably manifest themselves in all their activities on earth. As a spring derives its component parts, its operative powers, and its flavor from the soil through which it flows, so the ancient characters of nations arose from family traits, from the climate, from the way of life and education [for Herder education and tradition were synonymous], from the early transactions and deeds peculiar to them. The customs of the fathers took deep root and became the internal prototypes of the race.[12]

Since no two nations had shared common environments and common histories, then no two nations could share common characters.

Herder next argued that since each nationality was, in effect, created by nature and history, man's duty was not, as the advocates of the Enlightenment maintained, to work for the creation of a common community of nations governed by universal, rational law, but rather to develop each nation along those lines laid down by nature and history. In bold defiance of the Enlightenment, he declared: "Every [nationality] carries within itself the standard of its own perfection, which can in no way be compared with that of others." He insisted that "we do justice to no nation by forcing upon it a foreign pattern of learning." And over and over again he proclaimed that "the most natural state is *one* people with *one* national character." Therefore, nothing seemed to him so unnatural as "the wild mixture of various breeds and nations under one sceptre."[13]

In advocating this position Herder was again influenced by Montesquieu. In the *De l'esprit des lois* (1748), Montesquieu had argued that the laws of a nation are merely the necessary relations arising from the nature of that nation's social character and geographical environment. Since these factors vary from place to place, there are no universal laws—only national laws. The laws of a nation best suit itself and only by chance can be applied to other nations.

Herder took over this relativistic position and made it a central part of his philosophy. "O, that another Montesquieu," he said, "would enable us to enter into the spirit of the laws and governments on this round world of ours."[14] Throughout his works Herder himself tried to become this other Montesquieu—though the real Montesquieu may not have agreed with the image—and repeatedly reminded his readers that every nationality must develop in accord with its own innate abilities, in line with its own culture pattern. As Alexander Gillies points out, he attempted

> to show and assess the value of what had of necessity to emerge, and to point out the universal moral, for peoples as for individuals, namely that each must fulfill nature's intention, indeed cooperate with her, by achieving what it is possible to achieve in given circumstances.[15]

For a nation to do otherwise—to attempt to develop on a cultural foundation other than its own—meant breaking the continuity of past development and disrupting the nation's organic unity. The consequences would be the stultification of native cultural forms and ultimately the death of the nation itself. "The stability of a nation," said Herder,

> which does not forsake itself, but builds and continues to build upon itself, gives a definite direction to all the endeavors of its members. But other peoples, because they have not found themselves, must seek their salvation in foreign nations, serving them, thinking their thoughts; they forget even the times of their glory, of their own proven feats, always desiring, never succeeding, always lingering on the threshold.[16]

I should emphasize that, as the above quotation indicates, when Herder spoke of self-fulfillment he spoke of peoples, not of people, and of nations, not of individuals. Inherent within his philosophy was the idea that the individual could receive his fullest development only as an integral part of his particular nation. "Since man originates from and within one race," he said, "his development, education, and way of thinking are genetic." Thus "every human perfection is national," and the individual achieves his own salvation only through the salvation of his nation.[17]

Like Vico, Herder sought to explain the nature of a thing by studying its origin. But also like Vico—and like Aristotle—he put the nature of a thing in its end, in its final cause. Aristotle said man was made for life in the city-state. Vico said he was made for civilization. Herder said he was made for humanity (Humanität). "Humanity," said Herder, "is the character of our race. . . . We do not bring it with us ready-made into the world. But in the world it must be the goal of our strivings, the sum of our exercises, our guiding value."[18]

Herder defined humanity in a number of ways,[19] but in each case, as Gillies says, it was clearly "something of which man alone is capable, and which he must learn to develop for himself in this life."[20] The important point for our purposes is that Herder believed that humanity was something man could achieve only as a member of a nation[21] and that nations could arrive at humanity only if they remained true to their national characters, or souls. Each nation, then, by developing its own language, art, literature, religion, customs, and laws—all of which were expressions of the national soul—would be working not only for its own strength and unity, but for the well-being of civilization as a whole. Each nation had a special "mission" to perform in the progress of man toward humanity—the cultivation of its own national characteristics. "All nations," said Herder, "each in its place, should weave [their part of] the great veil of Minerva."[22]

But as Herder looked around he was greatly distressed to see that his own land was not fulfilling its mission—was not developing along nationalistic lines. At the close of the sixteenth century, German intellectual life, which had once held such great promise, had begun to decline. By the beginning of the eighteenth century, after suffering through the disruptions caused by the Reformation, the Counter Reformation, and the Thirty Years War, "Germany was a masterpiece of partition, entanglement, and confusion."[23] The country was divided into 1800 different territories with an equal number of rulers. There was no unity in commerce and industry, and the air was rife with religious feuds.

Worse still, the people had abandoned their own native cultural forms for foreign models—particularly those of the French. The German nobility, to Herder's despair, had widely imitated the brilliant court life of Versailles with the unfortunate consequence that French ideas and customs had filtered down to the middle classes and had widened the gap between them and the common people. French was the language of refinement and culture, and the German of the common people was considered vulgar. Those who had to use it padded it with so many foreignisms that it was scarcely recognizable to the lower classes. In literature, matters were equally bad. German writers not only used French as their principal medium of expression; they also based the form and content of their works on French and classical models and extolled the cosmopolitan ideals of the Enlightenment.

All this spelled disaster to Herder. He insisted that Germany must return to her own foundations—and do so immediately—or Germany was doomed. "The remains of all living folk (or national) thought," he warned, "are rolling with an accelerated final plunge into the abyss of oblivion. The light of the so-called culture [Enlightenment] is eating around itself like a cancer. For half a century we have been ashamed of everything that has to do with the fatherland."[24] He begged his countrymen not to abandon their native traditions in favor of those of other nationalities, but rather to cherish their own ways of life inherited from their fathers and to build upon them. And to those who found delight in aping foreign models, he declared: "Now seek in Germany the character of the nation, the manner of thinking peculiar to it, the genuine mood of its language."[25]

The point at which Germany had begun to lose the true spirit of its nationality and to ignore its historical antecedents had been, thought Herder, the end of the Middle Ages. At this time native traditions had been interrupted by foreign influences introduced by the Renaissance. To regain its lost national soul, then, Germans would have to return to the Middle Ages—to the point where the break had taken place—and resume their cultural development from there. A healthy, durable culture, Herder repeated again and again, must be built on a native foundation. He did not suggest, I must add, that the Golden Age lay in the past. For him, with his concept of humanity, the Golden Age was in the future. It was just that Germany had unfortunately gotten off the only cultural track that would lead it to humanity, and for its own salvation, had to be put back on. As Robert Ergang points out, Herder wished to lead his people to the national past, the spring of the national sentiment, "so that they might refresh themselves by clear draughts and then go onward to a great future."[26]

But how were the Germans to bridge the chasm between the present and the past? How were they to rediscover their lost soul? For Herder there was only one way—through folk poetry.

To understand Herder's concept of folk poetry we must turn once again to Vico. For Vico mythos equaled history. The first poets, he claimed, were actually historians who spoke in metaphorical language. Later ages distorted and misunderstood their meaning, but originally the poems of Greek mythology were descriptions of actual events. Thus for Vico, and for Herder, who accepted Vico's point of view, poetry could be used to explain history—to get otherwise unobtainable data about past epochs. Applying Vico's thesis to the Bible, Herder concluded that the creation story in Genesis was a folksong dealing with the institution of the Sabbath, that the Song of Solomon was a collection of folksongs of Solomonic antiquity, and that Revelations was, as Robert T. Clark puts it, merely "the historical reaction of the aged Apostle John to the destruction of Jerusalem by the Romans—which John might conceivably have seen—and an application of images from the prophecies and from this terrible event to the Second Coming."[27] Thus from these Biblical folk poems it was possible to learn a great deal about past events. In the same way, argued Herder, Germans could learn the events of their own history by studying the folk poems which still survived among the peasants.

Still more important, Vico claimed that folk poetry reflected the sociocultural pattern of the society in which it originated. Homer, he said, was nothing more than a projection of Greece—a disguised name for the people. He

> composed the Iliad in his youth, that is, when Greece was young and consequently seething with sublime passions, such as pride, wrath, and lust for vengeance, passions which do not tolerate dissimulation but which love magnanimity; and hence this Greece admired Achilles, the hero of violence. But he wrote the Odyssey in his old age, that is, when the spirits of Greece had been somewhat cooled by reflection, which is the mother of prudence, so that it admired Ulysses, the hero of wisdom.[28]

Thus "Homer was an idea or a heroic character of Grecian men insofar as they told their histories in song,"[29] or, in the idiom of Herder, Homer was the summation of the national soul expressed in the poems of the folk.

This idea—that the national soul, or the cultural pattern, of a people expresses itself best in that people's folk poetry—is found everywhere in Herder. "Poetry," he said,"is the expression of the weaknesses and perfections of a nationality, a mirror of its sentiments, the expression of the highest to which it aspired." Folk poems he called "the archives of a nationality," "the imprints of the soul" of a nation, "the living voice of the nationalities." From them "one can learn the mode of thought of a nationality and its language of feeling."[30] What better place, then, could a man go to discover the soul of a nation than to its folk poetry?

But who were these "folk" poets whose poems were the key to national character? They were, said Herder, those who were organically one with their culture—those most in tune with the national soul. Through the free use of their imaginations and through reliance upon their emotions—instead of their reason—they allowed the creative force of the folk character to work through them and thus became the producers of truly national poetry—poetry which bore the stamp of both the physical and cultural environment in which it had been created. Herder wrote:

> To ... chain and to interrogate the Proteus which is usually called national character and which manifests itself no less in writings than in usages and actions, this is a noble and fine philosophy. It is practiced with greatest certainty in the works of poetry, i.e., of imagination and feeling, because in these the entire soul of a nation reveals itself most freely.[31]

Folk poets, then, were national poets—the agents through whom the true character of a nation made itself manifest.

These folk poets, I must emphasize, did not have to be anonymous, nor did they have to speak from hoary antiquity. For Herder the only requirement was that the folk poet reflect the culture in which he lived. "The most indispensable explanation of a poet," he insisted, "especially is the explanation of the customs of his age and nation."[32] Homer and Shakespeare he considered two of history's greatest folk poets because they had so adequately expressed their own nations in their poetry. Of Homer he wrote, in words strongly reminiscent of Vico, "I consider him the most successful poetic mind of his century, of his nation.... But I do not look for the source of his happy genius outside of his nature and of the age that shaped him."[33] Again he emphasized that the great folk poets of Greece—Homer, Aeschylus and Sophocles—had succeeded because they "wrote with a Greek pen, on Greek faith, for Greece."[34]

Herder would have been only too glad to turn to contemporary German folk poets to seek guidance for his country, but unfortunately there were none. With the exception of perhaps Klopstock, they had all bartered their German birthright for a mess of French pottage. For this reason it was essential to turn to the peasants, to those Germans who had remained the most unspoiled by foreign influence and who had kept on their lips those songs created by folk poets in the days when German culture had rested on its own foundation. Of these old poets, Herder said, they "are our fathers, their language the source of our language, and their unrefined songs the mirror of the ancient German soul."[35] In their works, then, lay the road to salvation.

As the above quotation indicates, folk poetry had still another value for Herder: it had retained the national language in its most perfect form. National language was extremely important because, according to Herder's organic view of culture, only through it could one think naturally and respond to and express the national soul. "Every language," he wrote, "has its definite national character, and therefore nature obliges us to learn only our native tongue, which is the most appropriate to our character, and which is most commensurate with our way of thought."[36] Therefore, he argued that

> a nation . . . has nothing more valuable than the language of its fathers. In it lives its entire spiritual treasury of tradition, history, religion, and principles of life, all its heart and soul. To deprive such a nation of its language, or to demean it, is to deprive it of its sole immortal possession transmitted from parents to children.[37]

But, unfortunately, the language of the fathers had been demeaned. Latin and French instruction in the schools and the general use of French by members of polite society had, as has been pointed out, so loaded it down with cumbersome foreignisms that it was hardly recognizable. Only in folk poetry had it retained the pristine beauty found in the literature of the Middle Ages. Hence only to this earlier literature or to folk poetry could the poet wishing to remain true to the idiom of the fathers go for inspiration.

Much of the stimulation for Herder's work with folk poetry came from his reading of Bishop Thomas Percy's *Reliques of Ancient English Poetry* and James Macpherson's fraudulent *Poems of Ossian,* both of which were published in England in 1765. These works—particularly the Ossianic poems—convinced Herder that the earliest Celts, Germans, and Norsemen (at first no distinction was made between these races) had possessed cultural values equal to those of the Greeks.[38] English literature had become great—and consequently also the English nation—because it had developed continuously out of these ancient cultural values. For example, Shakespeare had, believed Herder, based many of his works on ancient popular ballads, stories, and myths.[39] On the other hand, German literature—and so too the German nation—had languished because German poets, unlike the English, had ceased to remain true to their native traditions. Herder said:

> From ancient times we have absolutely no living poetry on which our newer poetic art might grow as a branch upon the national stem. Other nations have progressed with the centuries and have developed on their own foundations,...
> . from the beliefs and tastes of the people, from the remains of the past. In this way their literature and language have become national. The voice of the people has been used and cherished, and they have in these matters acquired a much larger public than we have. We poor Germans have been destined from

the beginning never to be ourselves, always the lawgivers and servants of foreign nations, the directors of their fate and their bartered, bleeding, impoverished slaves.[40]

It was in emulation of the success of the English, then, that Herder began his campaign to revive his nation's past and to make it the basis for a new German way of life. The first and most important step in this campaign was to collect and publish the surviving folk poetry—"to make available," as Gillies says, "the lost treasures of the past as a foundation for future writers to build upon; to bring about in contemporary Germany a set of literary conditions similar to those of Elizabethan England, out of which new Shakespeares and Spensers might grow."[41] With the taking of this step, European folklore scholarship was officially begun.

Herder made one of his first pleas to collect folklore in 1773 in an essay called *Auszug aus einem Briefwechsel über Ossian und die Lieder alter Völker.*[42] The essay awakened an immediate interest in folklore and inspired G. A. Brüger to write his *Herzensguss über Volkpoesie,* published in 1776. Then in 1777 in his essay *Von Ähnlichkeit der mittleren englischen und deutschen Dichtkunst* Herder wrote a moving call to arms:

> Great empire! Empire of ten peoples, Germany! You have no Shakespeare. Have you also no songs of your forebears of which you can boast? Swiss, Swabians, Franks, Bavarians, Westphalians, Saxons, Wends, Prussians—have all of you together nothing? The voice of your fathers has faded and lies silent in the dust. Nation of heroic customs, of noble virtues and language, you have no impressions of your soul from the past?

> Without doubt they once existed and perchance still do, but they lie under the mire, unrecognized and despised. . . . Lend a hand then, my brothers, and show our nation what it is and is not, how it thought and felt or how it thinks and feels.[43]

In typical form, Herder set an excellent example for his countrymen by answering his own call. As a young man he had begun collecting folk poems and had continued the practice over the years. In 1778 and 1779 he published part of these poems in his now famous *Volkslieder* (after his death retitled by his editors *Stimmen der Völker in Liedern*). This work, along with his continued admonitions to save the nation's old literature, finally overcame the opposition of those who looked with scorn on songs of the "common" people, and folklore collecting began in earnest.

Two of the first to respond to Herder's call were Friedrich David Gräter and Christian Gottfried Böckh who, inspired by Herder's writings, founded a periodical called *Bragur, ein literaisches Magazin für deutsche und nordische Vergangenheit,* which was dedicated to the collection and publication of folklore. In the ensuing years others joined the cause. In 1803 Ludwig Tieck published *Minnelieder aus dem Schwäbischen Zeitalter.* From 1805 to 1808 Clemens Brentano and Achim von Arnim[44] published three volumes of folksongs entitled *Des Knaben Wunderhorn:*

*alte deutsche Lieder.* In 1807 Josef Görres published the results of his studies of almanacs and old storybooks. In 1812 Jacob and Wilhelm Grimm edited ancient fragments of the *Hildebrandslied* and the *Weissenbrunner Gebet* and then from 1812 to 1815 published their famous collection of folktales, *Kinder-und-Hausmärchen.* In 1815 they brought out a volume of the Poetic Eddas and from 1816 to 1818 published *Deutsche Sagen,* an analysis of the oldest Germanic epic tradition. Jacob Grimm's attitude toward his material is typical of the period and shows the strong influence of Herder.[45] He wrote:

> Having observed that her Language, Laws and Antiquities were greatly under-rated, I was wishful to exalt my native land. . . . Perhaps my books will have more influence in a quiet happy time which will come back some day; yet they ought to belong to the present too, which I cannot think of without our Past reflecting its radiance upon it, and on which the Future will avenge any deprecation of the olden time.[46]

From the time of the Grimms on, folklore collecting continued unabated and with increasing enthusiasm.

As Herder had hoped it would, the folk poetry revival moved German literature away from the rationalism and cosmopolitanism of the Enlightenment, which Herder believed had led to a sterile uniformity, and based it on the irrational and creative force of the people. He had once said that unless our literature is based on the folk "we shall have no public, no nation, no language, and no poetry of our own. . . . We shall write forever for chamber scholars and disgusting critics from whose mouths and stomachs we get back what we have written."[47] But now the longed-for day had arrived. Men like Novalis and Fichte steeped themselves in folk traditions and wrote literary *Märchen* and ballads. And the young Goethe, who was to set the tone for many others, learned from Herder that German literature, to become great, must derive its inspiration and form from the poetry which had survived from the nation's own past. At Herder's insistence, Goethe even collected folksongs and, as Gillies says, "learned to listen through them to the voice of nature from which they sprang."[48]

The first literary men to follow Herder's footsteps were the members of the *Sturm und Drang* school. Like Herder, they revolted against the authority of the Enlightenment and stressed spontaneity and originality, and, also like Herder, they considered the folk the principal source of genuine poetry. To them creative genius and *Volk* became almost synonymous. Shortly after the turn of the century the Romanticists also focused their attention on the folk. Under the leadership of men like Friedrich Schlegel, who was strongly influenced by Herder,[49] they turned to the literature of the past—to medieval and to folk poetry—to find ideals for the present and future. And on the basis of this material they created a body of literature which—so they believed—once again expressed the national soul, a literature to which a people seeking its national identity could turn for strength and inspiration.[50]

We realize today, of course, that the past to which the followers of Herder turned was, for the most part, a mythic past, that the great and noble nation they wished to re-create was in the main the product of their own fruitful imaginations. But the important point to remember is that the people involved believed that there had once been such a Germany. And believing so, they made it so—that is, they actually created a new nation in the image of what they thought the old one had been. Looking back at this period some fifty years later, T. Benfey assessed the role folklore had played in the creation of this new Germany:

> The recognition of the great value of the German folk song wakened an interest in the other creations and expressions of the German folk soul. With equal zeal, legends, fairy tales, manners and customs began to be investigated, collected, and studied. The influence of the folk soul upon the other fields of human development—law, state, religion, all forms of life—was recognized and traced. From this, assisted by many other factors, there arose not only an entirely new conception of the history of civilization, but above all a reverence and love for our people, such as had long been lost in Germany. The recognition that the individual must be rooted in his own people, that he must feel himself at one with it and with its spirit, and that only on this sod must he ripen to independence, blossomed into full consciousness, into shape and into active life. It became evident where they had erred and what ignominious consequences the lack of patriotism had incurred. The feeling of duty toward the nationality grew strong with the love for it. The whole people became engrossed in the idea of marshalling all its powers to regain the independence so nearly lost and to make secure its nationality by means of the re-establishment of its unity.[51]

The work of Herder had not been in vain.

The seed of nationalism planted by Herder bore fruit in many lands. The concept that each individual nation could contribute to the progress of humanity only by developing on its own cultural foundation was eagerly accepted by underdeveloped ethnic groups in Central and East Europe. It meant "that each could feel a messianic quality within itself."[52] Herder did all he could to engender this feeling and to make these groups nationally conscious, particularly by encouraging them to cultivate their own national literatures. In *Volkslieder* he again set the example by publishing folksongs from many other lands in addition to his German songs. In 1803 he announced his intention to publish a new collection of folk poems which were to be arranged according to nationality and which, he hoped, would further the cause of humanity, but he died before he could complete the project. Throughout his life he insisted on the right of each nation to determine its own destiny in accord with its own innate potentialities.

Perhaps Herder's influence was strongest among the Slavs, whose origins he idealized and whose folk poetry he greatly admired. He frequently urged the collection of this poetry, along with old customs and traditions, that the gap between past and present might be spanned and that the Slavic nations might then go on to a glorious future. Herder's works were published in the Slavic countries in both the original German and in translation and were instrumental in stimulating Slavic patriotism. As

A. Fischel says, Herder is justly called "the real father of the renaissance of the Slavic peoples," for he "was the creator of their philosophy of culture. They saw the course of their historical development up to the present with his eyes, they drew from his promises the certainty of their future high destiny."[53]

The Slavs responded to Herder's call to action with great enthusiasm. A few examples will illustrate. In 1822 the Slovak Jan Kollár, who had studied at Jena and was thoroughly acquainted with Herder's philosophy, preached nationalistic sermons in Budapest. He pleaded for the creation of a common Slavic literature and urged the scattered peoples to unite and fulfill their mission. In 1834 and 1835 he published two volumes of folksongs. From 1823 to 1827 another Slovak, Pavel Josef Šafařík, published folksongs and in 1826 brought out his *Geschichte der slawischen Sprache und Literatur.* In 1822 the Czech František Ladislav Čelakovský, a great admirer of Herder, published a collection of folksongs from the Slavic peoples. Like his teacher Herder, he claimed they expressed the true spirit of the Slavic nationality. In Serbia, folksongs were collected by Vuk Karadžić, and in Poland by Kazimierz Bordziński. Folk poems of the Cashubians, Ruthenians, and Ukrainians were also collected and studied. All this activity led to a literary nationalism which became pan-Slavic in scope.[54] In Slavic lands, then, as in Germany, patriots sought goals for the future in their past; and they sought their past in their folklore.

But Herder's influence was by no means confined to Germany and to the Slavic countries. In Finland, which had become united with Russia in 1809, Herder's philosophy became the guiding light for a small group of patriotic intellectuals who, concerned over the possibility of a forced Russification of their language and culture, turned to their past to find strength for the future. One of this group said, in words that sound as though they were copied directly from Herder:

> No independent nation can exist without folk poetry. Poetry is nothing more than the crystal in which a nationality can mirror itself; it is the spring which brings to the surface the truly original in the folk soul.[55]

Another argued that if Finns would collect their folk poems and work them into an organized whole "a new Homer, Ossian, or *Niebelungenlied*" might be the result; and, "exalted, the Finnish nationality, in the luster and glory of its own uniqueness and adorned with the awareness of its own development, would arouse the admiration of the present and of the future."[56] In 1835 Elias Lönrot fulfilled this prophecy with the publication of the epic *Kalevala,* which he created from his huge collection of folk poems. In the following years, Finnish patriots attempted to restore to the Finnish people, who had been divided and suppressed by years of foreign domination, the national characteristics and cultural values depicted in the epic.

In Norway, during the middle of the nineteenth century, much the same story was repeated. For centuries the country had been under either Danish or Swedish domination. Now it was time, argued a small group of romantic nationalists, for Norwegians to be Norwegians. The influence of the Enlightenment and the infiltration of foreign influences had, they believed, corrupted large sections of the population, causing them to abandon native traditions and to lose contact with the national Idea. Only among the peasants, who were considered the custodians of the national character, could the traditions of the fathers be found. Hence it was to these traditions that the nation must turn for its salvation. Oscar J. Falnes sums up the feeling of the time with phrases that bear the strong imprint of Herder:

> No part of the peasant's heritage gave such adequate expression to nationality as his literary tradition; it was considered preeminent in this respect partly because it was related so intimately to the folk character. The folk tales, it was said, had "grown organically" from within the peculiarity of each people, they were the clearest revelation of the folk spirit. The folk-literature having sprung from the people's "inner-most uniqueness," belonged "to us and to no one else"; in it was enshrined the "soul of the nation."[57]

To recapture this national soul and to put the country back on its own cultural foundation, scholars began seriously to collect and publish folklore. From 1841 to 1844 P. C. Asbjørnsen and Jørgen Moe published their collection of folktales, *Norske Folke-eventyr*. In 1845 and 1848 Asbjørnsen published a collection of fairy tales and folk legends, *Norske Huldre-eventyr og Folkesagen*. And in 1852 L. Lanstad published his famous collection of folk ballads, *Norske Folkeviser*. These works were generally received with enthusiasm, particularly by the press, and helped convince the people that Norway had had a glorious past and that by reviving the spirit of this past the nation could have an equally glorious future. To this task the nationalists dedicated themselves in the years to come.

Though Herder himself is now remembered mostly by specialists, his philosophy of history lives on. The list of nations in which this philosophy has inspired, or is still inspiring, romantic nationalistic movements could be greatly extended, but in each case the story would be about the same. Whenever nations turn to their folkloristic past to find faith in themselves and courage for the future, they are following lines laid down by Herder.

That romantic nationalism is, by definition, a folklore movement should by now be obvious.[58] As we have seen, Herder taught that each nation is by nature and by history a distinct organic unit with its own unique culture; that a nation, to survive as a nation, as well as to contribute to the development of humanity as a whole, must cultivate this national culture, developing it along lines laid down by past experience; that the total cultural and historical pattern of a people—the national soul—is expressed best in folk poetry; and that should the continuity of a nation's development be interrupted the only road to salvation lies in collecting the folk poetry surviving from the time of the break, using it to restore to the nation its national soul, and thus making possible its future development on its own foundation.

Romantic nationalists, then, like English-American folklorists, have studied folklore items as survivals from the past. But while the latter have been content merely to work out historical reconstructions based on these survivals, the former have attempted not only to reconstruct the past, but also to revive it—to make it the model for the development of their nations. Having once achieved their goals, they have often moved on to other endeavors, but their past accomplishments have remained to inspire other dependent nations seeking historical justification for their separatist policies. Consequently the same stirring phrases about glorious national pasts and noble destinies that once moved Europeans to action are today to be heard echoing throughout Africa and Asia. Those who see folklore not just as a body of tradition to be classified and catalogued, but also as a dynamic force in the lives of men would do well to study and learn from the nationalistic movements of the past century; for it appears that for some time to come the story of nationalism will continue to be an oft-told story and that folklore will remain one of its most important chapters.

---

[1]Hans Kohn, "Nationalism," *Encyclopaedia Britannica,* XVI (1961), 149. For more on this same point, see Hans Kohn, *The Idea of Nationalism* (New York, 1967), pp. 3-24.

[2]Carlton J. H. Hayes, *Nationalism: A Religion* (New York, 1960), p. 2.

[3]Carlton J. H. Hayes, *Essays on Nationalism* (New York, 1926), p. 5.

[4]Kohn, "Nationalism," p. 150.

[5]*Ibid.*

[6]The standard summaries of Herder's life and times are Alexander Gillies, *Herder* (Oxford, 1945) and Robert T. Clark, Jr., *Herder: His Life and Thought* (Los Angeles, 1955). The main collection of Herder's works is *Sämmtliche Werke,* 33 vols., ed. Bernhard Suphan (1877-1913; rpt. Hildesheim, Germany, 1967-1968); unless otherwise noted subsequent references to Herder will be by volume and page numbers in the Suphan edition.

[7]Hans Kohn, *Prophets and Peoples* (New York, 1946), p. 2.

[8]Robert T. Clark, Jr., "Herder, Cesarotti and Vico," *Studies in Philology,* 44 (1947), 657-659.

[9]V, 565; XVII, 319; cited in Robert R. Ergang, *Herder and the Foundations of German Nationalism* (1931; rpt. New York, 1966), pp. 218, 252-253.

[10]V, 509.

[11]XIII, 37-38.

[12]XIV, 84.

[13]XIV, 227, 124; XIII, 384. Italics mine.

[14]XIII, 386.

[15]Gillies, *Herder,* p. 87.

[16]XXIII, 160-161.

[17]XIV, 84; V, 505.

[18]XVII, 138.

[19]One of his best definitions is the following: "I wish that I could include in this word *humanität* everything that I have said so far about the noble constitution of man for reason and freedom, finer sense and impulses, the most delicate and most robust health, the realization of the purpose of the world and rulership over it. For man has no nobler word for his destiny than himself, in whom the image of the Creator of our earth lives in that form which could here be made manifest."—Cited in Gillies, *Herder,* p. 80.

[20]Gillies, *Herder,* p. 80.

[21]II, 366; XIII, 159, 343, 346; XIV, 83, 84, 227.

[22]XVII, 212.

[23]Ergang, p. 13.

[24]XXV, 11.

[25]I, 366.

[26]Ergang, p. 232.

William A. Wilson

[27]Clark, *Herder,* pp. 163, 255–257, 269.

[28]Giambattista Vico, *The New Science,* trans. Thomas Bergin and Max Harold Fisch (New York, 1961), p. 270.

[29]*Ibid.,* p. 269.

[30]XVIII, 137; IX, 532; III, 29; XXIV, 266; IX, 530. These passages are all cited in Ergang, pp. 220, 198. It was this idea of Herder's that gave rise to the *das Volk dichtet* doctrine on the origin of folk poetry. It was later expressed in phrases like A. W. Schlegel's *"Das ganz Volk hat es gedichtet,"* Jacob Grimm's "Es dichtet sich selbst," and Uhland's *"Es ist nicht blosse Redeform, das die Völker dichten."*—See Albert B. Friedman, *The Ballad Revival* (Chicago, 1961), p. 250.

[31]Cited in Gillies, *Herder,* p. 105. By emphasizing originality and spontaneity in literature, Herder helped create both the *Strum und Drang* School and the Romantic Movement which followed it.

[32]*Ibid.,* p. 28.

[33]III, 202.

[34]II, 114.

[35]II, 246.

[36]I, 2, cited in Kohn, *The Idea of Nationalism,* pp. 432–433. See also I, 366; II, 13, 19; XVII, 286.

[37]XVII, 58.

[38]Clark, *Herder,* pp. 144, 194–195.

[39]For a good discussion of this point, see Alexander Gillies, "Herder's Essay on Shakespeare: 'Das Herz der Untersuchung,'"*Modern Language Review,* 32 (1937), 262–280.

[40]IX, 528.

[41]Gillies, *Herder,* p. 52.

[42]V, 159–207.

[43]IX, 530–531.

[44]At the very mention of "my poor, poor Fatherland," Arnim once wrote, "tears flow from my eyes and from those of my readers."—Hans Kohn, *The Mind of Germany* (New York, 1960), p. 56.

[45]For the influence of Herder on the Grimms, see *Deutsche Vierteljahrschrift für Literaturwissenschaft und Geisteschichte,* VI (1928), 516.

[46]Jacob Grimm, *Teutonic Mythology,* trans. James Stephen Stallybrass, III (London, 1883), lv.

[47]IX, 529.

[48]Gillies, *Herder,* p. 19.

[49]How thoroughly Herder's ideas about history and folk poetry influenced the Romanticists is indicated by a quotation from Schlegel. Speaking of national memories, Schlegel said that they are "often lost in the darkness of time, but preserved and enhanced by poets. Such national memories, the most wonderful heritage that a people can have, are an advantage which nothing else can replace; and if a people finds itself in its own feelings elated and, so to speak, ennobled by the possession of a great past, of memories from prehistoric times, in brief by the possession of poetry, it will be raised by this very fact in our judgment to a higher plane. Memorable deeds, great events, and destinies alone are not sufficient to keep our administration and to determine the judgment of posterity; a people must also gain a clear consciousness of its own deeds and destinies. This self-consciousness of a nation which expresses itself in reflective and descriptive works is its history."—Cited in Kohn, *The Mind of Germany,* p. 62.

[50]For a good overview of the period under discussion, see Ralph Tymms, *German Romantic Literature* (London, 1955).

[51]T. Benfey, *Geschichte der Sprachwissenschaft und orientalischen Philologie in Deutschland* (Munich, 1869), p. 318; cited in Ergang, pp. 211–212.

[52]Gillies, *Herder,* p. 129.

[53]Cited in Ergang, p. 261.

[54]For treatments of this movement, see M. Murko, *Deutsche Einflüsse auf die Anfänge der böhmischen Romantik* (Graz, 1897) and A. Fischel, *Der Panslawismus bis zum Weltkrieg* (Berlin, 1919).

[55]Cited in John H. Wuorinen, *Nationalism in Modern Finland* (New York, 1931), p. 69.

[56]Karl Aksel Gottlund, *Svensk Literatur-Tidning* (1817), p. 394; cited in A. R. Niemi *Kalevalan kokoonpano*, Suomalaisen Kirjallisuuden Seuran Toimituksia, No. 90 (Helsinki, 1898), p. 35.

[57]Oscar J. Falnes, *National Romanticism in Norway* (New York, 1933), p. 250.

[58]In such movements, as F. M. Barnard says, the belief gained ground that in setting national borders, "the assistance of professors of philology and collectors of folklore ought to be enlisted to aid, if not to replace, the modern statesman."—*Herder's Social and Political Thought: From Enlightenment to Nationalism* (Oxford, 1965), p. 62.

# Tradition, Genuine or Spurious

## Richard Handler and Jocelyn Linnekin

*The term "tradition" has played a role in the conceptualization of folklore from the very beginning of the discipline. It has generally been thought of as something definite, some collection of ideas and behaviors handed down through time. One could say that tradition as a concept had been reified; that is, human thoughts, activities, and products were conceptualized as independent of and apart from those humans who created them. This implied that tradition was an entity unto itself, with its own integrity, obeying its own laws. People might modify the tradition, or perhaps reject it outright, but it was a fact with which one had to come to terms.*

*In the following selection, Richard Handler and Jocelyn Linnekin suggest that tradition is not a thing* sui generis *but a symbolic construction—an interpretation and representation of the past made by people in the present. This reconceptualization of tradition has numerous implications. For example, notions of "authenticity" or "genuineness" of tradition would have to be abandoned or reformulated. Handler and Linnekin's concept of tradition is in keeping with the reconceptualization of "self" (Goffman 1959), "community" (Cohen 1985) and "reality" (Berger and Luckmann 1966) as symbolic constructions. For the application of this concept of tradition to contemporary Quebecois and Hawaiians, see the original publication of this article in the* Journal of American Folklore.

Like many scholarly concepts, "tradition" is at once a commonsense and a scientific category. In its commonsense meaning, tradition refers to an inherited body of customs and beliefs. In the social sciences, an ongoing discourse has attempted to refine this understanding of tradition as it has proven empirically and theoretically inadequate. Recent efforts to clarify the concept of tradition, most notably those of Edward Shils, do much to add nuance to our conventional understanding but leave unresolved a major ambiguity: does tradition refer to a core of inherited culture traits whose continuity and boundedness are analogous to that of a natural object, or must tradition be understood as a wholly symbolic construction?[1] We will argue that the latter is the only viable understanding—a conclusion we have arrived at by comparing our independent investigations in two quite disparate ethnographic situations. In our attempts to analyze national and ethnic identification in Quebec and Hawaii we have concluded that tradition cannot be defined in terms of boundedness, givenness, or essence.

---

Rather, tradition refers to an interpretive process that embodies both continuity and discontinuity. As a scientific concept, tradition fails when those who use it are unable to detach it from the implications of Western common sense, which presumes that an unchanging core of ideas and customs is always handed down to us from the past.

As many writers have noted, one inadequacy of the conventional understanding of tradition is that it posits a false dichotomy between tradition and modernity as fixed and mutually exclusive states.[2] M. E. Smith has pointed out that "traditional" and "new" are interpretive rather than descriptive terms: since all cultures change ceaselessly, there can only be what is new, although what is new can take on symbolic value as "traditional."[3] Following Smith's lead, we can see that designating any part of culture as old or new, traditional or modern, has two problematic implications. First, this approach encourages us to see culture and tradition naturalistically, as bounded entities made up of constituent parts that are themselves bounded objects. Second, in this atomistic paradigm we treat culture and its constituents as entities having an essence apart from our interpretation of them; we attempt to specify, for example, which trait is old, which new, and to show how traits fit together in the larger entities that we call "a culture" and "a tradition." The task of a naturalistic science of tradition is to identify and describe the essential attributes of cultural traits, rather than to understand our own and our subjects' interpretive models. The prevailing understanding of tradition, both in our commonsense notion and in scholarly elaborations of it, embodies these premises.

The naturalistic conception of tradition can be traced to a lineage of Western social-scientific thought that dates at least from Edmund Burke and the reaction to the Enlightenment.[4] The 19th-century concepts of tradition and traditional society, used (whether as ideal types or as empirical generalizations) as a baseline against which to understand social change and "modern society," were embodied in such well-known dichotomies as Maine's status and contract, Tönnies's *Gemeinschaft* and *Gesellschaft*, Durkheim's mechanical and organic solidarity, and, into the 20th century, Sapir's genuine and spurious culture and Redfield's folk-urban continuum. In American anthropology, the received understanding of tradition is exemplified by A. L. Kroeber's classic definition: tradition is the "internal handing on through time" of culture traits.[5] Kroeber's definition accords with the commonsense view of tradition as a core of traits handed down from one generation to the next. Kroeber also enunciated premises that have proven tenacious in scholarly discussions of tradition, especially the identification of a society with a particular tradition, and the notion that temporal continuity is the defining characteristic of social identity. Kroeber's concept of tradition found its most logical application in American archaeology, where tradition refers to "single technologies or other unified systems of forms" characterized by "long temporal continuity."[6] The archaeological concept points up the implications of modeling the phenomenon of tradition after natural objects. We would argue that tradition resembles less an artifactual assemblage than a process of thought—an ongoing interpretation of the past.

Richard Handler and Jocelyn Linnekin

In contrast to Kroeber's conception of tradition, the merit of Edward Shils's approach is his insistence that tradition changes continually. Shils acknowledges that the unchanging folk society never existed, and is careful to build variation into his definition of traditional phenomena: "they change in the process of transmission as interpretations are made of the tradition presented."[7] Since Shils recognizes that tradition changes incessantly, it is surprising to find that his understanding of tradition depends nonetheless upon the notion of an unchanging, essential core. He thereby perpetuates the naturalistic paradigm, which defines objects by specifying their temporal, spatial, and/or qualitative boundaries. In spite of his insistence that tradition changes ceaselessly, Shils offers an unambiguous, basal definition: "in its barest, most elementary sense ... it is anything which is transmitted or handed down from the past to the present." To distinguish tradition from "fashion," Shils posits objectively verifiable temporal criteria: "it has to last over at least three genera- tions ... to be a tradition." Change itself is discussed in terms of the accretion of new cultural elements that leave other pieces in recognizably unchanged form. As Shils phrases it, the "essential elements" of tradition "persist in combination with other elements which change, but what makes it a tradition is that what are thought to be the essential elements are recognizable . . . as being approximately identical at successive steps."[8]

The notion of an approximate identity suggests change, however minimal, but if an object changes does it not become something new and different? One way to escape this dilemma is to invoke organic metaphors, to suggest that traditions are like organisms that grow and change while yet remaining themselves. Shils does not resort to this device but, as we will show, the organic analogy is a common element in nationalistic theories of tradition. For the moment we wish only to point out that the notion of approximate identity poses inescapable problems. As David Schneider has suggested, the problem with viewing cultural phenomena naturalistically is that the boundaries of such things are inevitably "fuzzy" for both actors and observers.[9] Having chosen to describe social facts as if they were natural objects, one is embar- rassed to find that one cannot definitively bound them in space and time, although such boundedness is necessary to satisfy our understanding of what a natural object is.

Both the scholarly and commonsense understandings of tradition have presumed that a society is identified by its traditions, by a core of teachings handed down from the past. The very identity of a society rests on this continuity of the past with the present. As Shils writes: "It would not be a society if it did not have duration. The mechanisms of reproduction give it the duration which permits it to be defined as a society."[10] Shils does not claim that the legacy of the past is immutable, but he stresses that an essential identity persists over time throughout modifications. This is the fuzzy boundaries problem writ large. In a section titled "The Identity of Societies through Time," Shils notes that in spite of ceaseless change, "each society remains the same society. Its members do not wake up one morning and discover they are no longer living in, let us say, British society." This unity over time derives from a shared tradition: "Memory leaves an objective deposit in tradition. . . . It is this chain of memory and of the tradition which assimilates it that enables societies to go on reproducing themselves while also changing."[11]

The notion of an "objective deposit" is fundamental to the commonsense understanding of tradition, and it provides a telling contrast to our view of tradition as symbolically constituted. As much as Shils and other scholars have refined the concept of tradition, the one "ineluctable" fact, to use a word that Shils favors, is that the past leaves some objectively definable inheritance, a "substantive content." Shils's discussion of the processes of change in tradition reveals the drawbacks of his paradigm, which in spite of its apparent sophistication bears striking resemblance to Kroeber's historical-particularist model. Shils even invokes the same processes of change identified by Kroeber: addition, amalgamation, diffusion, absorption, fusion.[12]

Shils recognizes that traditions usually have ideological content, and that views of the past may be changed through self-conscious interpretation. He notes that the "perceived" past is "plastic" and "capable of being retrospectively reformed by human beings living in the present." And he recognizes that nationalist movements often change the traditions they attempt to revive. Nonetheless, he differentiates real and "fictitious" traditionality. He contrasts nationalist versions of tradition, for example, with "actually existing syncretic traditions."[13] Shils explores the breadth and depth of the received understanding of tradition. Yet, as in the works of prior theorists, tradition in Shils's framework has the qualities of givenness and boundedness. In spite of Shils's insistence that tradition continually changes, there is no doubt that in his formulation a real, essential tradition exists apart from interpretations of that tradition.

It is at this point that we take issue with the naturalistic conception of tradition. We suggest that there is no essential, bounded tradition; tradition is a model of the past and is inseparable from the interpretation of tradition in the present. Undeniably, traditional action may refer to the past, but to "be about" or to refer to is a symbolic rather than natural relationship, and as such it is characterized by discontinuity as well as by continuity.[14] It is by now a truism that cultural revivals change the traditions they attempt to revive.[15] We should broaden this insight and argue that the invention of tradition is not restricted to such self-conscious projects. Rather, the ongoing reconstruction of tradition is a facet of all social life, which is not natural but symbolically constituted.

---

[1]Edward Shils, "Tradition," Comparative Studies in Society and History 13 (1971): 122–159 and *Tradition* (Chicago: University of Chicago Press, 1981).

[2]S. N. Eisenstadt, *Tradition, Change, and Modernity* (New York: Wiley, 1973); Lloyd I. Rudolph and Suzanne H. Rudolph, *The Modernity of Tradition* (Chicago: University of Chicago Press, 1967); Milton Singer, *When a Great Tradition Modernizes* (New York: Frederick Praeger, 1972); and Dean C. Tipps, "Modernization Theory and the Comparative Study of Sciences: A Critical Perspective," *Comparative Studies in Society and History* 15 (1973): 199–226.

[3]M. Estellie Smith, "The Process of Sociocultural Continuity," *Current Anthropology* 23 (1982): 127–141.

[4]Karl Mannheim, "Conservative Thought," in Paul Kecskemeti, ed., *Essays in Sociology and Social Psychology* (New York: Oxford University Press, 1953), 74–164.

# Richard Handler and Jocelyn Linnekin

[5]A. L. Kroeber, *Anthropology* (New York: Harcourt, Brace, 1948), 411.

[6]Gordon R. Willey and Philip Phillips, *Method and Theory in American Archaeology* (Chicago: University of Chicago Press, 1958), 37.

[7]Shils, *Tradition*, 13, 19.

[8]Ibid., 12, 14, 15.

[9]David M. Schneider, *American Kinship: A Cultural Account* (Englewood Cliffs, N.J.: Prentice-Hall, 1968), 67.

[10]Shils, *Tradition*, 167.

[11]Ibid., 163, 167.

[12]Ibid., 263, 273 ff.

[13]Ibid., 195, 209, 246.

[14]Richard Handler, "On Sociocultural Discontinuity: Nationalism and Social Objectification in Quebec," *Current Anthropology* 25 (1984): 55–71.

[15]Ralph Linton, "Nativistic Movements," *American Anthropologist* 45 (1943): 230–240.

# The Portal Case: Authenticity, Tourism, Traditions, and the Law

## Deirdre Evans-Pritchard

*The analysis of basic folklore concepts is not merely an intellectual exercise demonstrated in the university classroom or scholarly article. Important issues outside the academy hinge on concepts analyzed and debated by folklorists. In Deirdre Evans-Pritchard's description of "the Portal case," a number of these concepts and issues emerge: What is an ethnic group and how is membership within it determined? What is the nature of the relationship between a producer, the techniques of production, and the object produced? What are the effects when select folk practices are "legitimized" or "endorsed" by official legal, cultural, or educational institutions? What is meant by "tradition" and "authenticity" and how do these terms apply to displays for tourists? What roles, if any, should folklorists play when such issues emerge in public discussion, debate, and policy? For another interesting example of the relationship of folklore to public issues see Samuelson (1982).*

Santa Fe, New Mexico, attracts hundreds of thousands of tourists each year because of its picturesque plaza, its historic role as a Spanish imperial capital, its nearby Indian pueblos, its wealth of museums, and its cultural events—and its ski slopes. It has an image as an Old World haven where one can meet the American Other, the unassimilated Native American culture. Perhaps the closest most visitors will get to real Indians is by strolling along the Portal of the Palace of the Governors, the oldest public building in the United States and now part of the Museum of New Mexico. Here, under this covered walkway spanning one side of the central plaza, the Indians display and sell their wares: jewelry, pottery, sand paintings, food, and occasionally other handicrafts. Sitting with their backs to the stuccoed adobe palace wall, they arrange their wares neatly on blankets in front of them. On a busy day 50 or so Indians and myriad tourists are crammed into this long corridor. The Indians, mostly from the nearby pueblos but also from the Navaho, Zuni, and Hopi reservations and further afield, are there every day in the summer. Many even brave the cold winter days and sit huddled in rugs. For the Indian, selling under the Portal is a financial necessity; for the visitors, the Portal provides comfortable surroundings to see and buy genuine Indian crafts from genuine Indian craftsmen, apparently without the distancing factor of middlemen.[1]

Reproduced by permission of the American Folklore Society, from *Journal of American Folklore* 100, no. 397(1987):287–96. Not for further reproduction.

The presence of the Indians under the Portal is a customary part of the traditional life of Santa Fe. Local people have proudly described this, saying, "The Indians on the Plaza have gained such a reputation that they have become a world-famous landmark in Santa Fe" and "The Indians are the largest drawing card in the city. It's the Indians people come to see . . . " and "The Indians have been there ever since I was a boy. It's right for them to be there." [2]

So people were surprised, and many shocked, when this custom was challenged in the law courts. In 1976, some Anglo and Hispanic craftsmen and traders were selling from stalls on the sidewalk in front of Santa Fe's Museum of Fine Arts. The Museum of New Mexico, the authority administering all state museums, objected to the presence of these vendors. After much argument, the museum evicted them with the support of city authorities who cited a municipal ordinance that street vendors must sell 500 feet away from established businesses and stores selling similar merchandise. When the vendors pointed out that the municipal ordinance was not being enforced at the adjacent Portal, the city authorities answered that the Indians under the Portal were on Museum of New Mexico property. When the vendors argued that they too should be allowed to sell at the Portal, they were told that the museum permitted only Indians to sell there. The proceedings received extensive media coverage, contrasting the vendors' complaints of unfairness with Indian claims that "Indian tradition and culture would be eroded if Indians were not allowed to sell their wares in the Plaza area" and if non-Indians were allowed to sell their goods next to the Indians. [3]

At the time, the museum's Indian-only policy for the Portal was not officially formulated. Indians and others had been using the portal as a marketplace for at least a hundred years. After the Museum of New Mexico was created in 1909, its first director, Edgar Lee Hewitt, brought the Pueblo Indians into the museum program and encouraged them to use the Portal to revitalize their crafts. By the 1950s the Portal had become the exclusive domain of local Indian craftsmen. But it was only after the 1976 dispute and a supporting ruling from the Human Rights Commission that the Board of Regents of the Museum of New Mexico adopted a formal Indian-only Portal policy.

Insulted and angry at being denied a place to sell their goods and frustrated because they had failed to find equally lucrative alternative sites, a handful of Hispanics and Anglos spread out their blankets and displayed their wares next to the Indians under the Portal. The Museum authorities, with the help of the police, several times forced these non-Indian vendors to leave the Portal. Tensions mounted between the three groups involved—the Indians, the museum officials, and the non-Indians. The newspapers carried accounts and opinions of the conflict and featured such headlines as "Plaza Discrimination," "Separate Them," "The Battle For The Portal," and "Equality Impossible To Guarantee." Indians collected tourists' signatures on a petition calling for help in this "battle to retain their identity."

The dispute created a long, tangled, and tortuous sequence of lawsuits and appeals to the Human Rights Commission. The key lawsuit was filed by Paul and Sara Livingston against George Ewing, the Director of the Museum of New Mexico. The Livingstons claimed that their constitutional rights were being violated, and that the policy of the Museum of New Mexico which prohibits the exhibition and sale of arts and crafts by non-Indians at the Portal of the Palace of the Governors on the Santa Fe Plaza but permits and encourages such activities by Indians violates the New Mexico Human Rights Act by unlawfully discriminating against the excluded individuals on the basis of race, ancestry, or color.[4]

The Livingstons lost the case, appealed, and lost again. The two courts articulated the following principles: Native Americans have a unique legal position in the United States; it is a state interest to support Native Americans as independent political and cultural entities; the museum's role is to stimulate and protect authentic Indian crafts; the traditional Portal market of Indians, and only Indians, is an important tourist attraction; and the Portal policy is cultural, not racial, discrimination.[5] In the original case, the courts held that the museum had the right to practice cultural discrimination; in the appeal, the Indians intervened and their lawyer, Michael Gross, successfully argued that the Indians were technically employed by the museum and that this complied with a law giving employment preference to Indians living within a certain distance of their reservations. Thus the Portal case was finally won on the basis of a technicality designed to assist the independent economic survival of Native Americans.[6]

It is my contention that while the Livingston case, on the surface, was entered on the issue of racial discrimination and exited on the issue of protecting the Indians economically, it implicitly revolved around the issue of authenticity—that is, around the question of which ingredients must be combined in which ways to establish the authenticity of Indian jewelry.

Let me explain. The court made its tenuous differentiation between racial and cultural discrimination in order to be able to assert that the museum was permitted to be culturally selective for the purpose of educating the public. In making this differentiation, the court was supported by affidavits submitted by folklorists, anthropologists, and others. Barre Toelken wrote that "when we refer to ethnic arts we are not referring to a racial designation, but to a system of expressions shared by members of a self-identified cultural group that perceives itself and is perceived by others as having a unique esthetic tradition."[7]

J. J. Brody, of the Maxwell Museum of Anthropology in Albuquerque, wrote that "a decision to limit eligibility to participate in an exhibit to members of a particular group is a time-honored and perfectly appropriate way for organizing a cohesive and educational exhibit."[8]

Thus, the court held that the Museum of New Mexico was justified in adopting its Indian-only policy for the Portal because it "was the only way the Museum could maintain its own standards of authenticity and historical relevancy."[9] In using the Portal for presenting and preserving New Mexico's multicultural traditions, the museum was able to present an educational, living exhibit of the historical use of the Portal as a marketplace by the Indians. Indeed, the court stated, the Portal presents what remains of a traditional market. If non-Indian craftsmen were there too, it was implied, the authenticity would be lost: "co-mingling the cultures is less instructive because it fails to clarify the lines of historical development."[10] Further, the courts held, because only Indians can make Indian goods, the museum and state were justified in seeking to prevent the influx of non-Indian substitute and imitation jewelry, pottery, and other handicrafts. In other words, not only would non-Indians change the tone of the market, but they might also sell inappropriate, nonethnic goods and thereby make the Portal merely commercial. Although in reality the Portal market is a commercial venture, as the Director of the Museum said, "We are running a museum, not a market."

All these findings use tradition and authenticity to justify cultural discrimination, but they sidestep the original question of racial discrimination. Livingston was kicked off the Portal because he was not an Indian. It is understandable that he should feel discriminated against as an Anglo and seek redress in court, particularly as the Bakke "reverse-discrimination" case was still being nationally debated.[11] Some of the lawyers concerned have privately expressed the sense that in many strictly legal particulars, Livingston had a case and the museum didn't (given this, the court's judgment would seem to place an undue emphasis on the legally tangential issue of authenticity). But the same lawyers, referring to public opinion and the public good, also stress that there was a far more important *moral* dimension to the case. I interpret the court's emphasis on authenticity and tradition as the law's attempt to express this wider concern, that Livingston and his wife posed a threat to traditional Indian culture by copying Indian jewelry and selling it at the Portal.

Paul and Sara Livingston were self-taught, with a little bit of help from local Hispanic craftsmen. Their materials were silver, turquoise, other semiprecious stones and beads, much like all the other jewelry available in Santa Fe. In fact, few people that I asked could tell the difference between Livingston's jewelry and Indian jewelry. Take Livingston away and leave his jewelry laid out on a blanket at the Portal and people would assume that it was Indian-made. On one occasion, a Canadian tourist bought a necklace from Livingston, under the assumption that the necklace was Indian-made, because she knew that Indians sell under the Portal. She was then told by an Indian that it was not Indian-made, and because she had come to the Portal to buy a real Indian souvenir, she tried unsuccessfully to take it back. So the tourist's expectations, the context in which she had seen Livingston's jewelry, and the lack of explicit information to the contrary, all contributed to making Livingston's jewelry appear Indian-made.

Such contextual factors confer apparent authenticity on craft items. Indeed, it is very difficult to distinguish between Indian and non-Indian jewelry anywhere in Santa Fe. It is a place where one expects all the arts and crafts to be Indian. Further, almost any jewelry that combines silver and turquoise is likely to remind one of Indian jewelry, irrespective of design. Not even the experts necessarily get it right. A court case in 1958 challenged the applicability of the Indian Arts and Crafts Law of 1957 by testing several experts (including John Adair) to see if they could distinguish handmade from machine-made Indian jewelry and Indian from non-Indian jewelry.[12] The four witnesses failed to agree on the origin and production technique of *any* of the pieces. So, although Livingston's jewelry is not Indian-made, it *is* Indian style, and a passing tourist—even a passing expert—may never know the difference.

This illustrates the definitional problems concerning the authorship, appearance, and ingredients of Native American crafts: who decides what is authentic Indian jewelry? Karen Duffek has listed the following four criteria for evaluating contemporary native art: the quality of the item, the ethnicity of the artist, the degree to which the item may be considered traditional, and the purpose for which the item was produced.[13] The *context* of the Santa Fe art market unfortunately blurs the clarity of these distinctions.

New Mexico has a complex pluralistic history, population, and artistic tradition, all of which compound the difficulty in tracing the stylistic origin and manufacture of a craft piece. No art has a pristine unilineal tradition, and much southwestern art is a conglomeration of Indian, Anglo, and Hispanic designs. As one local painter of Indian themes answered when I asked him if his work was Indian art: "Well, that's a good question. We can paint Indians and I guess they can paint cowboys."[14] Indeed, one might well argue that you cannot copyright ethnic characteristics. Hispanic and Indian artistic traditions are particularly intermixed in Santa Fe. Hispanic New Mexicans have been inspired by Indian designs, and as a letter to the *New Mexican* pointed out, "The Mexicans taught the Indians of the Southwest silversmithing. Atsidi Sani was the first Navaho to learn from a Mexicano named Naki Tsosi (thin Mexican) around 1870."[15]

A local Hispanic jeweler felt that the Hispanic contribution to New Mexican culture was being downplayed by the museum. To the museum's contention that the Indians under the Portal are a "living exhibit," she replied bitterly, "I suppose that makes me a dead exhibit."[16] The intertwining and vitality of the several New Mexican artistic traditions make the definition of what constitutes authentic Indian arts and crafts particularly problematic. Since Indian arts and crafts are primarily made for sale nowadays, it has become increasingly important to the buying public that they know what it is they are buying. Indeed, the Livingston affair is not an isolated case. Such cases have been reported since at least 1935, and there has recently been a comparable case in Albuquerque's "Old Town."

Both the museum Portal policy and New Mexico's Indian Arts and Crafts Sales Act, revised in 1976 during the Portal dispute, take the position that "Indian" means any enrolled member of an Indian tribe as evidenced by tribal records or by records of the Bureau of Indian Affairs. Thus an Indian from anywhere in America can make "Indian" jewelry or trade jewelry and sell it at the Portal as long as he or she is a registered Indian. A Canadian Indian woman sold her crafts there for a while. However, a local Hispanic craftswoman who claims to be half-Tarahumara Indian is not allowed to sell under the Portal.[17]

The Act (1978) and the museum policy define "authentic Indian arts and crafts" to mean "any product which is Indian handcrafted and not made by machine or from unnatural materials, except stabilized or treated turquoise."[18] The restriction to manual production suggests a romantic view of a simple rural Indian lifestyle. As one journalist noted:

> Many of the tourists who come here to buy jewelry are under the mistaken impression that handmade means that the craftsperson went out with a pick and shovel and dug up the raw materials himself. Most Indian and non-Indian jewelers usually buy their stones and silver from traders and wholesalers. Coral, for example, is imported from Italy.[19]

Local gossip (and Paul Livingston) has it that some Portal jewelry is machinemade, and sometimes even made by non-Indians.[20] In reality, Indians have always sold all sorts of things at the Portal, although the commercial aspect of the Portal is often forgotten in defining its "traditionality." Since the boom in Indian jewelry, some jewelry has been manufactured on an assembly line. Such jewelry passes as authentic because all the workers involved are Indians working by hand. Yet this is far from the image of a single Pueblo craftsman and his family fashioning individual jewelry in the folk art tradition, a stereotype central to the everyday functioning of the Portal market as a tourist attraction.[21]

Consciousness of tourist expectations informs much of the Portal Indians' display. They are aware that they must project a particular image for their work to be evaluated as true Indian craft and for them to be able to sell it. They are encouraged to dress "Indian-fashion" at the Portal, and one rarely sees an Indian selling expressionist paintings or sculpture—although the Portal policy would not prevent this.[22] The influence of stereotypical definitions of Indian authenticity demonstrates the importance of tourism as a catalyst in the commercialization of Indian crafts. I surmise that the Portal case would never have arisen if Santa Fe were not such a tourist center with Indian crafts so profitable.[23]

Because there are relatively few Indians, and these craftsmen are working in what is largely perceived as an endangered tradition, their product takes on rarity value that is expressed in high prices. But these prices express more than rarity value. An Albuquerque trader, Robert Zachary, describes the abstract value of authentic Indian jewelry thus:

> There is more than silver, labor and turquoise, more than adornment, more than a monetary investment: there is a story ... the story of a fragile, primitive culture, tenuously coexisting within our technological society. It is a disappearing culture, captured best by its body of art.[24]

Price can seem to distinguish the authentic from the imitation, implying that Indian-made jewelry is inherently "better" than similar, non-Indian-made, jewelry. As Clarence Weahkee, a Cochiti Pueblo Indian, put it, "There's no sense paying $10,000 for a Picasso if it's not a Picasso."[25]

The non-Indian craftsman can charge less for an almost identical piece of jewelry because he doesn't have to charge for any "story." Thus, imitation Indian jewelry, which trades on Indian culture, can undercut the real thing in the marketplace. This is devastating for the Indians. As Tony Tortelita, an Indian trader, said to Livingston, "Listen! You took that culture away from me, see? That's my culture what you're selling, see? Supposed to be. That's my living, not yours."[26]

It seems that, to Livingston, it is a purely invisible attribute that can turn a necklace into an authentic Navaho necklace. If one piece of jewelry can only be distinguished from another by an invisible attribute, then he finds the distinction arbitrary and unfair—particularly in the light of his sense that much of the Portal's Indian jewelry is of inferior quality, not necessarily made by hand or even made by Indians. Livingston would have people judge jewelry on quality and by aesthetic appeal, not by relative authenticity. His position highlights the complexities of achieving a workable definition of authenticity, and it put to the test the legal apparatus for defending tradition.

The law went through hoops to sidestep the merits of Livingston's case. Because Livingston's jewelry was so similar to Indian jewelry, the proceedings dwelt on issues of authenticity as well as racial discrimination. But close analysis of the proceedings reveals the inconsistencies inherent in attempting any objective assessment of authenticity. These inconsistencies suggest that our criteria for authenticity, however usefully they are categorized, boil down to something subjective: ultimately, the authenticity of a piece of "traditional folk art" is an ascribed quality, which depends on who is looking at it, in what context, and for what purpose.

Most people I talked to about the case thought that Livingston and his wife were trading on Indian culture, copying Indian jewelry designs, acting offensively, and behaving immorally in challenging tradition.[27] Drawing on Sally Falk Moore's work on law as process, I think that public opinion was instrumental in deciding the outcome of the case.[28] This processual chain of events that evolved opinion into law was set into motion because Livingston went to court and had to be made to lose his case on moral grounds. It was in the interests of the Indians, the local population, the state, and the tourists that tradition was upheld. As is often the case when conflicting interests clash in the public domain, boundaries emerge where there were once ambiguities. People take stands and clarify their opinions on certain issues. In the Portal case, the issues were not simply aired in public; they were given a legal precedent. (The case established another legal precedent: Michael Gross, the Indians' lawyer, said that this was the first time the state had ever gone to court on the side of the Indians.)

The Portal case turned custom into law. Livingston moved to Albuquerque, trained as a lawyer, and now often takes cases relating to New Mexican arts and crafts. The formalization of the museum's Indian-only policy made even more rigid the regulations on what constitutes authentic Indian craft at the Portal. In early 1987, the director of the Palace of the Governors was planning on narrowing the Portal policy further so that Indians could only sell objects that they themselves have made—cutting out the usual trading in which many of the Indian vendors are involved. There is also now an Indian-staffed Portal Committee empowered to assure that all the crafts sold at the Portal are handmade and Indian-made. Further, stringent labeling requirements have been introduced using these criteria to distinguish authentic Indian jewelry from "imitation Indian jewelry." The Portal market is now much more "authentic"—as the museum and general public see it—than it ever was traditionally. In all this, the influence of the museum and the state legislature on the production of Indian craft has been redefined and increased.

49

Deirdre Evans-Pritchard

The laws and the museum Portal policy are attempts to protect Indian arts and crafts and New Mexico's tourist trade.[29] Public opinion, the media, the law, the museums, and the consumer are joining internal Indian processes in dictating the shape of Indian craft traditions. Where in the past the persuasive force of tradition may have limited the range of invention available to an Indian jeweler, now that limitation is imposed by the persuasive force of the marketplace and external conservationism. Most newly made Indian jewelry is recognizably similar not simply because of common heritage but because these are the things that sell well, because of the expectations of the tourists, and because of the strictures of the law. Given the fact that neither the law nor most tourists make many distinctions between different Indian tribal groups, one can't help but wonder whether this process will lead to a pan-Indian craft style.

Certainly the reinforced protectionism that comes out of the Portal case is restricting the scope and content of Indian crafts in Santa Fe.[30] As noted earlier, touristic stereotypes and marketplace economics tend to freeze overall stylistic development, while the strengthened regulations freeze technological innovation. One potter complained to me that she now could not use a pottery wheel without her pots losing their status as authentic.

In all process there is change, but it would seem that an unforeseen consequence of the Portal case and Santa Fe's tourism may be the straitjacketing of tradition and authenticity by the very factors that keep Indian jewelry production alive at all—the support of the museums and the state, and the public demand for the jewelry.

---

[1] An earlier version of this article was presented at the American Folklore Society meeting in Cincinnati, October 1985, as part of a collection of panels on "Authenticity" coordinated by Barbara Kirshenblatt-Gimblett. My thanks goes to Bess Lomax Hawes for telling me about the Portal case in the first place, and to Charlene Cerny, Edward T. Hall, and Paul Bohannan for their practical, encouraging support. Finally I am grateful to Paul Livingston and Michael Gross for giving me access to the legal documentation necessary for this research. This article does not attempt to represent Native American viewpoints concerning their arts and crafts.

[2] New Mexican, 9 July 1978; Olga Curtis, "The Battle for the Portal," Denver Post, 14 October 1979.

[3] Alan Wilson, "Street Vendors Removed," New Mexican, 4 April 1976.

[4] Memorandum Brief, Livingston v. Ewing, SF 81-1290(m)(1985):1.

[5] Livingston v. Ewing, 601 F.2d 1110 (1979).

[6] Michael Gross feels that he argued his case on an important interpretation of the Civil Rights Act of 1964, namely that under federal law, Indians are recognized as a political and not as a racial group.

[7] Livingston v. Ewing, 455 F. Supp. 825 (1978): 829.

[8] J. J. Brody, Letter to Ms. Patricia Barkin, Civil Rights Specialist, Human Rights Commission, 6 December 1977.

[9] Livingston v. Ewing, (1978): 825.

[10] Ibid., 829.

[11] The Bakke case was a landmark U.S. Supreme Court decision that held that Allan Bakke, a California white man, could not be excluded from admission to a state university merely to make room for disadvantaged minority students. University of California Regents v. Bakke, 433 U.S. 265, 98S.Ct.2733, 57L.Ed2d750 (1978).

[12] Maisel v. Standley, unreported Bernalillo County District Court No. 68768 (5 June 1958).

[13]Karen Duffek, "'Authenticity' and the Contemporary Northwest Coast Indian Art Market," *BC Studies* 57 (1983): 99–111.

[14]Steve Iannacito, personal communication.

[15]Remijio Sandoval, Letter to the Editor, *New Mexican*, 11 April 1976.

[16]Martha Wright, personal communication.

[17]Tom Sharpe, "Street Vendors Shut Down," *New Mexican*, 2 April 1976.

[18]30-33-1 and 30-33-2 NMSA 1978 Comp.

[19]Maria Puente, "Pity Those Poor Tourists Who are Looking for Baubles," *New Mexican*, 30 April 1976.

[20]Paul Livingston claims that the Indians used to sell bows and arrows bought from the Woolworth's across the plaza. Several people have told me that they have seen the Indians buying jewelry from wholesalers to resell at the Portal.

[21]The question of whether the use of modern technology or nontraditional materials taints the authenticity of traditional Indian folk arts has been addressed. Michael O. Jones, "'There's Gotta Be New Designs Once in a While': Culture Change and the 'Folk Arts,'" *Southern Folklore Quarterly* 37 (1973): 43–60.

[22]These informal restrictions of tradition on young Indian artists have been discussed in J. J. Brody, *Indian Painters and White Patrons* (Albuquerque: Museum of New Mexico Press, 1971).

[23]A lawyer involved in the case also speculated that if it had been the Hispanic craftsmen who had brought the case against the museum, the museum would probably have lost (personal communication).

[24]Robert A. Zachary, "Authentic Indian Jewelry," *American Indian Journal* (July 1980): 30.

[25]This extract from a local newspaper continues by saying that the issue of "imitation jewelry" is "a crucial and underlying issue in Santa Fe's vending feud. Is silver and turquoise jewelry 'imitation Indian' because it is fashioned by non-Indians? And is shell craftwork 'authentic Indian' merely because it is sold by Indians?" Dave Steinberg, "'Imitation' Key to Dispute on Plaza Jewelry Vending," *The Albuquerque Journal*, 20 April 1976.

[26]Tony Tortelita, Deposition before the Human Rights Commission for the State of New Mexico, used as Plaintiff's Exhibit in *Livingston v. Ewing* (1979), (HRC #79-1-5-1).

[27]Attitudes toward Paul Livingston can be gauged from some of the language used by the media in its coverage of the case. For example, Indians are called "Indians" in the press, while the Hispanics or Anglos are commonly "non-Indians." Similarly, Indians are called craftsmen, while the others are described as "vendors"—denoting that they have a much more commercial occupation and interest. Livingston's actions were characterized to me as "grotesque," "just not acceptable," and "he had no right to do it." One can infer from the language of these responses to a threat to tradition that there is an implicit consensus about there being a moral aspect to traditionality.

[28]Sally Falk Moore, *Law as Process* (London: Routledge & Kegan Paul, 1978).

[29]Brian Joyce, an Anglo vendor who sold his paintings at the Portal with the Livingstons, suggests that the museum dictates the tenor of the art market in Santa Fe. He wrote:

> We are all aware of the tourist attraction of the Portal Indian market. Visitors come to Santa Fe and the Plaza. They pass through the Portal viewing the Indians and what is offered. They enter the Palace of the Governors and eventually reach the Museum shop. In the Museum shop there is virtually no representation by non-Indians, despite New Mexico's many and racially varied artists, particularly in Santa Fe.... The shop provides what buyers seek, and as Indians are emphasized outdoors, the market indoors is for Indian made goods. ... When tourists leave the Palace and the Plaza they go with little awareness of the other living and working Santa Fe artists who are not Indians. ... Thus the Museum of New Mexico's non-representational Indians-only tourist attraction is drawing a tourist type whose primary interest is not in New Mexican or Santa Fean artists, but only Indian artists. [Letter to Museum of New Mexico authorities, n.d.]

[30]There have, of course, been innovative developments in Indian crafts over the past fifty years, the popular storyteller doll being an example of this.

# II
# Ethnic Groups and Ethnic Folklore

## The Letter in Canadian Ukrainian Folklore
### Robert B. Klymasz

*Although immigrant groupings often develop ethnic consciousness and promote ethnically based action, the immigrant experience may be conceptualized independently of ethnic identities and concerns. One immediate concern of immigrants is their ability to communicate with family and friends in the Old Country. The immigration of Ukranian peasants to Canada toward the close of the nineteenth century imbued the activity of letter writing with new value and importance. Letter writing was not only important as an activity, but as a symbol—a symbol of connectedness to and distance from family and homeland. As such, the letter became a prominent motif in Canadian Ukrainian folksongs, and letters came to be composed in the form of folksong texts.*

*For more on the emigrant letter see Dégh (1978). Klymasz (1973) and Kirshenblatt-Gimblett (1978, 1983) provide further insight into immigrant folklore. For more on Ukrainian folklore in Canada see Klymasz (1980).*

## INTRODUCTION

One of the main functions of speech is to communicate, to establish contact between an addresser and his addressee. If, however, the barriers of time and space are insurmountable, the verbalized message, once emitted, will fail to be received by the intended addressee—unless, of course, some vehicle such as the telephone is available to transmit the verbalized message. Until recently, most peasant societies have had no immediate access to such other vehicles for purposes of long distance, interpersonal communication; they have not usually been able to afford them nor, in most instances, would they find them necessary. Verbal messages as well as oral literature, in peasant cultures, are transmitted in that classic setting which involves a direct, face-to-face, physical confrontation of at least two individuals:  the addresser and his addressee, the narrator or singer and his audience.

Reproduced by permission of the publisher, from *Journal of the Folklore Institute* 6, no. 1(1969):39–49. Not for further reproduction.

## Robert B. Klymasz

This discussion is concerned with the breaking-up of such a traditional setting and its folkloristic implications. The examples used here have been selected from a large collection of Ukrainian folklore materials which I recorded in Canada from 1961 to 1967.[1] They are, then, the materials of an immigrant ethnic group which, in common with other immigrant groups on this continent,[2] found that the letter alone could replace the casual, everyday verbal contacts once enjoyed with friends, relatives and loved ones back in the Old Country.

This transition from one form of communication to another marked a crucial change for the Ukrainian immigrant in Canada who had little personal experience with letter writing. The bulk of Canada's early Ukrainian settlers were illiterate or semiliterate peasants whose desire for long distance communication with the Old Country was frequently frustrated, as reflected in the following excerpt from a lyrical immigrant folksong recorded in Mundare, Alberta:

> My beloved [male] is away in the Old Country
> And I [female], poor soul, am here.
> A cuckoo-bird [female, the singer's messenger] did coo
> On a wide bridge:
> "Come, O come, my beloved,
> At least for a visit!"

This is wishful thinking; the bridge represents the traditional solution to geographical barriers in the old country.

> My head does ache,
> I've nothing to bind it with,
> And there's no one to pass the word
> To my beloved that he may know.

Here there is anxiety and frustration at the realization that no bridge can span the ocean and that verbal communication, direct or indirect, is impossible.

> I shall bind my head
> With a silken kerchief,
> And I'll pass the word to my beloved
> By way of the grey falcon [male, his messenger].

The problem is resolved in terms of another day dream.

The Ukrainian peasant in Canada was not, of course, totally unaware that such things as letters and letter writing existed. Generally speaking, however, these were looked upon as something exclusively reserved for the educated, upper classes: the clergy, the wealthy nobility, and assorted professionals. The peasant knew, for example, that letters could function as powerful instruments in the hands of emperors and tsars whose commands concerning matters of life and death were often communicated by means of letters, as recalled in this stanza from a Ukrainian ballad recorded in Canada:

> The tsar became angry
> And wrote a letter to the executioner:
> "Come, executioner, and decapitate the maiden,
> For she has shown contempt for the tsar!"

Furthermore, although the peasant himself seldom received or wrote letters, he did have the occasional opportunity to hear his local village priest read selections from the Apostolic letters or epistles in the New Testament during mass on Sundays. That God himself chose to communicate to His faithful followers by means of letters was evident in the circulation of the apocryphal, so-called "Letters from God" (*Lyst Božyj*)—copies of which are currently available in Canada for ten cents each at a Ukrainian bookstore in Edmonton.

The Ukrainian peasant, then, exhibited something of an awesome respect for letters and the ability to write them. This was reinforced by a carry-over of the medieval approach to penmanship as a highly sophisticated and intricate graphic art best handled by devoted and talented monastic scribes. In this connection it is interesting to note that one of the constant epithets used in Ukrainian folk literature in reference to letters is the adjective *dribnyj*, meaning "delicate" and "fine," while in Ukrainian folk speech the verb "to write," *pysaty*, can also mean "to draw" and "to ornament" (e.g., Ukrainian *pysaty pysanky*, "To color Easter eggs").

## THE LETTER AS A MOTIF IN CANADIAN UKRAINIAN FOLKSONGS

The introduction of the letter as a popular motif in the Ukrainian folksong tradition was the result of two main factors which, beginning towards the end of the nineteenth century, threatened the fragmentation of the Ukrainian peasant community; these were military conscription and emigration to the New World. The folksong cycles which emerged in association with these events reflect the peasant's urgent desire for long distance interpersonal communication and, for the first time, his open acceptance of and dependence on the letter—not as an authoritative upper-class document, but as a suitable and effective vehicle for the transmission of his own messages.[3] Perhaps an indication of the success of the letter is found in the tears shed by the recipient of a letter, a motif shared by both the so-called "recruit folksong cycle" and the songs of emigration. In a recruit song we find:

> The maiden did not sleep for three nights,
> She did not sleep for three nights and [finally]
>    she wrote a finely written letter,
> She wrote a finely written letter and sent it
>    to the soldier.
>
> The soldier received the letter and read it through,
> He sighed heavily and began to weep profusely.

And in a song of emigration:

Somewhere my beloved is writing a letter to me.

She writes with delicately drawn letters [of the alphabet]
And when I read it through, I washed myself with tears.

O Canada, Canada, how deceitful you are!
Many a man have you separated from his wife!

The acceptance of the letter as a form of interpersonal communication is not only reflected in the newly formed folksong cycles, but also in the older, traditional folksong genres, which began to accommodate incidental references to letters, as found in the following excerpt from a commemorative lament recorded in Manitoba:

O my beloved husband,
O my dear husband,
Why have you left me alone in Canada?
What am I to do alone in a foreign land
Since I have no family?
And you are gone now these long years,
And you haven't come to visit me,
Nor have you written me a letter. . . .

The influence of the letter on the established, traditional genres and cycles could, at times, take on a more significant dimension. A comparison of two variants of a single ballad can serve as an example of a radical shift in the narrative content caused by an attempt to accommodate a new letter motif. The ballad tells of a young Jewish maiden who foolishly decides to abandon her Jewish innkeeper father in preference for the company of three flirtatious and supposedly wealthy kozaks (or, in some variants, dragoons). The kozaks, however, having enticed the maiden away from her home, decide to do away with her. They throw her into the Danube and she drowns. The following excerpt brings the ballad to a close without the use of a letter motif:

They arrived near the Danube
And they took Hajuni by her white sides
And threw Hajuni into the deep Danube.
Themselves they returned to her father's inn,
And they ordered bread and wine.
"Why, O innkeeper, have you become so sad?
You must have buried your daughter this week."
"It's been three weeks now since she left the house,
And since then she's not been seen any more."
"O innkeeper, we were near the Danube
And a Jewess was floating there—just like your daughter!"
"Then it was probably you kozaks, since you were that far!

It was you yourselves who took her there!"
"Had we, O innkeeper, taken her there,
We would not dare to appear at your place again!"

Another variant of this same ballad ends with the help of a letter motif as follows:

They showed her the blue seas;
"There, O Rezja, are our estates!"

They took Rezja by the sides
And flung her into the deep.

As Rezja was sinking
She wrote a letter with her right hand.

She wrote a letter with her right hand
And sent if off to her father:

"Would that father not trouble himself,
Would that he not prepare a dowry for me,

"For I lost my dowry
When I stood with that dragoon

"There under the green oak,
With that young dragoon."

The letter motif in the second variant serves, perhaps, to update the ballad in an unexpected, if not wholly unrealistic manner. At the same time, however, it promotes a shift in the focus of attention from the tense confrontation of the maiden's father and the guilty kozaks in the first variant, to the plight of the individual victim herself in the second variant. This change from dialogue to monologue, from externals to internals, is a reflection of the contemporary trend—at least in so far as the East Slavic narrative folksong tradition is concerned—to reduce objective narrative reportage and to accentuate, instead, the inner conflict of the individual on the lyrical level.[4] In this particular ballad, the humanization of the conflict situation has been accomplished with the aid of a letter motif which provides the formal outlet for the drowning maiden's last words.

The Ukrainian immigrant folksong cycle in Canada is especially rich in references to letters of various kinds. Among the most productive are references to (1) letters received in Canada which beseech the recipient-immigrant to help finance the voyage of some loved one or relative to America; (2) letters sent to the Old Country which inform some individual of the tragic death of a loved one in Canada; (3) letters sent to the Old Country which cover up the immigrant's hardships as a settler in Canada; and (4) references to "poison pen" letters which are both received and sent within the Ukrainian immigrant community in Canada.

Robert B. Klymasz

## FOLKSONGS WHICH FUNCTION AS LETTERS

The impact of the letter on the Ukrainian folksong tradition is not, however, a one way affair limited to incidental references or letter motifs, verbatim quotations, and shifts in textual content. Having recognized the letter's ability to function as a suitable vehicle for interpersonal, long distance communication, the Ukrainian peasant considered it appropriate, on occasion, to compose his letters in the form of folksong texts. The point here is that the relationship between the letter and the folksong is a two way, reciprocal process. The following example is an excerpt from a folksong composed by a Ukrainian immigrant in Canada and mailed to his father and mother in the Old Country:

I sit by the table and think a thought;
I'm sending a letter to my father and mother.

I'll go to the valley and stand o'er the fields;
Fly, fly, O finely written letter, across the blue sea!

Fly, fly, O finely written letter, and do not tarry,
And in two or three weeks return unto me!

I'm writing to you with neither pencil nor ink,
I shall write to you, O my beloved ones, with a real diamond!

A letter such as the above was meant to be sung by the recipient(s) or addressee. The structure of the text, its lilt, is based on the popular and currently productive patterns of versification found in the immigrant's home village in the Old Country. The recipient, if he is a semiliterate peasant, will undoubtedly attempt to read it through *aloud* or have someone else read it aloud to him. Upon reading and hearing the text of the song-letter, the recipient easily recognizes the formal textual features of his own folksong tradition and can begin to sing the text using any suitable and familiar melody which the structure of the text brings to his mind. In effect, the addressee or recipient decodes the letter and reconstructs the living folksong using the verbalized text of the letter as a guide.

Another example of a folksong transmitted via letter is the following excerpt from a ceremonial wedding song which one of my informants composed in honor of her sister in the Old Country who was about to get married. The song was recorded in Manitoba and reflects traditional and popular patterns of versification combined with new imagery which is special to the immigrant's Canadian experience:

A cuckoo flew up and sat on the fence;
You, O sister, have invited me as a guest.

I would be glad to come and be your guest,
But the road is far, and I've not the strength to get there.

The road is far and the sea is wide,
When I think of it—O my God!

I walk and wander through the forest
And search for a road that will lead me to my sister.

I keep searching for a road, a dry road;
Perhaps I'll still get to visit my family.

## THE POETICIZATION OF THE LETTER

Still another aspect of the letter's impact is the effort made to poeticize this new vehicle itself—to give it, as it were, poetic stature. Animation and personification of the letter were achieved, for example, by addressing the letter in a direct manner using the second person for personal pronouns and the vocative case in Ukrainian for the word "letter":

*O my letters, my letters,*
When I think of
How far *you* have come!

*You* have crossed rivers
And that great [body of] water!
How miserable it is for me
To be in Canada without my family!

Other effective devices include the use of verbs which normally depict human-like actions:

O my dear mother,
My grey dove,
Write me a letter
And tell me whether you are well.

Do not, O mother, begrudge the pennies
To buy paper,
For I have money
In Canada to pay for the letter.

For when the letter is not paid for
It *goes* and *wanders* (aimlessly),
But if a letter is paid for,
Then it *searches* for me.

The letter's ability to cross the ocean formed a special problem for traditional Ukrainian folksong poetics which were not geared or "programmed" for the depiction of large bodies of water. A popular solution to this problem was found by borrowing on the traditional image of a bird as a personal messenger, as seen in an excerpt quoted earlier ("Fly, fly, O finely written letter...!"). There was still another and rather novel possibility for the figurative depiction of the letter's ability to cross the ocean. In this case, the letter is seen as traveling *through* rather than over the ocean:

> I shall write a letter to the Old Country
> To learn how my family is doing.
> I'll sit upon a bridge and I'll watch for
> A letter from Ukraine swimming by.
> Many a fish did cross through the water,
> But I didn't see a single one carrying a letter.

The image of a fish carrying a letter represents a marked departure from traditional Ukrainian imagery and must be considered a product of the immigrant experience.

In addition to these and other attempts to formulate appropriate imagery, the letter was also incorporated into the poetics in a more concrete sense; that is, in terms of alliteration, rime, assonance, and parallel grammatical constructions. In both of the following examples, the excerpted couplets are introduced by an idyllic, pastoral setting in the first line which serves as a kind of still or slide over which is super-imposed the reference of the second line to the writing of letters. The second example, however, shows a more successful attempt to bind the two lines of the couplet together in terms of parallel sound texture and grammatical constructions:

(1)  Po vysokij hori / trava sja kolyše,
     [O'er the high mountain / the grass does sway,]

     Des' moja mylen'ka / do mene lyst pyše.
     [Somewhere my beloved / to me a letter writes.]

(2)  *Vitryk povivaje, / lystje kolyše,*
     [The wind blows, / the leaves (it: the wind) flutters,]

     *Bratčyk do sestryčky / dribni lysty pyše.*
     [Brother to sister / fine letter writes.]

## THE LETTER IN FOLK PROSE NARRATIVE

Undoubtedly, the most popular letters in the Canadian Ukrainian prose narrative tradition are those written by an illustrious roster of fictitious immigrant folk heroes, including such names as "Uncle Steve Tobacco" (*Vujko Štif Tabačnjuk*), "Harry Blackbread" (*Harasym Čornoxlib*), "Grandpa Tim Pin" (*Didus'o Tymko Špyl'ka*), and others. Poking fun at the immigrant experience, their letters began to appear in a variety of early Ukrainian immigrant publications shortly before World War I.[5] One of Uncle Steve's "letters" begins as follows and reflects several features found in an excerpt from a folksong quoted earlier ("I sit by the table and think a thought..."):

I sit down to the table, grab my pen and compose a letter to my honorable buddy. Fly, O letter, across the mountains, and when you arrive, bow to the Lord God and to my immortal buddy.[6]

The hilarious situations and exploits depicted in these fictitious letters were quickly absorbed into the oral prose tradition of the Ukrainian immigrant community in Canada. That the names of these folk heroes are still inextricably associated with their letters was revealed to me on one occasion in the field in 1966 when one of my informants, having agreed to reminisce about Uncle Steve Tobacco, turned to my tape-recorder and began his account as follows:

Hello there, Steve!

How's your health? Mr. Steve, I am sorry that I was not able to be there today when you got on board the ship which was all decked out special for you to come to Canada. But never mind, it's a good thing that you got to the ship on time! But Steve, don't forget to write a letter! After you arrive and settle down in a good boarding house, be sure to write a letter about your voyage.

## CONCLUSION

The materials presented here, then, serve once again to emphasize the vigorous interaction between different vehicles and media which are engaged in the transmission of folklore. It is obvious that the letter's primary function as an alternative to, or a substitute for direct interpersonal verbal communication promotes rather than impedes the process of transmission. At the same time, the letter has proven to be in itself a productive agent for the formulation of new motifs, new poetic imagery, and different narrative techniques.

The breaking-up, in our complex civilization, of the old face to face confrontation of the addresser and his addressee, the narrator or singer and his audience, does not mark a degeneration of folkloristic creativity, but rather signals the search for other vehicles and media for the manifestation and transmission of folklore. This process involves much experimentation, "give and take," and the selection of various details and items on many different levels. The result is the continual formation and application of new criteria, a re-evaluation and revamping of the old, and the creation of new, living folkloristic phenomena.

[1]The materials were collected with the support of grants from the Canada Council and contracts with the Folklore Division of the National Museum of Canada. I am grateful to both these institutions for their kind help and encouragement. The original field recordings are on deposit with the latter institution in Ottawa, Canada. A copy of the entire collection of field tape recordings (including the items which have been transcribed and translated for discussion here) is on deposit with the Archives of Traditional Music, Indiana University, Bloomington, Indiana, U.S.A.

[2]See especially William I. Thomas and Florian Znaniecki, "Form and Function of the Peasant Letter," *The Polish Peasant in Europe and America,* 2nd. rev. ed. (New York, 1959), pp. 303-315.

# Robert B. Klymasz

[3]The upheaval of World War II had similar repercussions on the peasant community in Eastern Europe. See Franz Konrad Weber, "Volkspoesie in Briefen kroatischer Bauern," *Festschrift für Max Vasmer*, ed. Margarete Woltner and Herbert Bräuer (Berlin, 1956), pp. 552–559.

[4]See, for example, A. M. Kin'ko, "Balady," *Ukrajins'ka narodna poetyčna tvorčist'* (Kyjiv, 1958), I, 600; and D. M. Balašov, *Narodnye ballady* (Moscow and Leningrad, 1963), p. 37.

[5]See item nos. 152–165 listed in Robert B. Klymasz, *A Bibliography of Ukrainian Folklore in Canada, 1902-1964* (= *National Museum of Canada Anthropology Papers*, No. 21) (Ottawa, 1969).

[6]Stefan Fodčuk, *Dyvni pryhody Štifa Tabačnjuka* [*The Surprising Adventures of Štif Tabačnjuk*] (Vancouver, 1958), p. 21.

# Folk Medicine and the Intercultural Jest
## Américo Paredes

*In this article, Américo Paredes introduces us to a complex layering of Mexican-American folk tradition. First there is* curanderismo, *the system of folk curing. Second there are* casos *or belief tales that center about the practice of* curanderismo. *Third there are the* tallas, *which transform and parody the* casos. *The* tallas *that Paredes recorded were told by bilingual, male, middle-class Mexican-Americans, who play important and successful roles in the social structures of the dominant "Anglo" society but who proudly think of themselves as Mexicans. This sense of double identity creates a sense of ambivalence that is expressed in* talla *performance.*

*For a brief introduction to the system of Mexican folk medicine see Martinez and Martin (1966) or Rubel (1960). Different folk medical systems in the American Southwest can be found in Spicer (1977). For more on the* caso *see Graham (1981). Jordan (1975) indicates how belief narratives may be used to make claims to ethnic group membership. Narratives that parody and thus seem to discredit serious legends have been labeled "anti-legends" (Dégh and Vázsonyi 1971), and Limón (1983) provides a solid discussion of another Mexican-American anti-legend performance. For more on the projections of ambiguous identity in humorous folk narratives see Oring (1981, 1984).*

This paper is a discussion of six jests collected in Spanish at the lower end of the Texas-Mexican border and presented here in English translation. They were part of several hundred texts recorded in 1962 and 1963, during a series of field trips in search of jests and legendary anecdotes that might reveal attitudes of Mexicans and Mexican Americans toward the United States.[1] I will attempt to relate them to Texas-Mexican attitudes toward culture change. They are not peculiar to the group from which they were recorded. Some of them have been collected from other Mexican groups, and their basic motifs are universal. The six were recorded from two informants, one narrator telling five, but I heard the same stories from other people during my collecting. It is the circumstances in which the texts were collected that I believe important, and for this reason I will describe them in some detail.

All six texts were collected on tape during two recording sessions at Brownsville, Texas, a bilingual and bicultural community. Jests of this sort are called *talla* in the

Reproduced by permission of the publisher, from *Spanish Speaking Peoples of the U.S.*, ed. June Helm, Proceedings of the 1968 Annual Meeting of the American Ethnological Society (Seattle: University of Washington Press, 1968), 104–19. Not for further reproduction.

regional idiom, and they are told during regular *talla* sessions. Francisco J. Santamaría, the Mexican lexicographer, lists *talla* as a "Texas-Mexican barbarism" for any narrative anecdote or jest, saying it is derived from the English "tale." This certainly would emphasize the intercultural character of the *talla*, were it not for the fact that Santamaría is wrong. Whatever the origins of *talla*, they certainly are not in "tale," to which it has merely a visual resemblance. Santamaría seems to have known, furthermore, that *talla* is found as far away from Texas as Costa Rica. The term may derive from the verb *tallar*, to rub or to chafe and by extension to tease. The *talla* as it is practiced in South Texas often does have a relationship to the Mexican word play known as the *albur*. Under these circumstances the jests are told as having happened to one of those present, or to one of their close relatives. The victims answer in kind, of course. *Talla* sessions are common occurrences along the border among males of all ages and at occasions varying from wakes to beer-drinking parties. Women rarely are present.

In collecting my first consideration was to recreate as closely as possible the circumstances of a *talla* session in its natural context. In Brownsville the sessions were held at a house just outside of town, which happened to be vacant at the time. A group of men would be invited, enough so that a total of ten to fifteen people were present at one time, including the collector. Sessions began around nine or ten at night and were held outside on the darkened patio or the lawn, with the participants sitting in a circle. Outside the circle was a washtub full of beer and ice. Also outside the circle was the tape recorder, but in a direction opposite to that of the tub with beer and just behind where the collector sat. An empty beer case was placed in the middle of the circle, on which the microphone rested on top of a cushion. The machine was a four-track Revere set at a speed of 3¾ inches per second, recording one hour per track on a 7-inch tape. This made it possible to record four hours on one tape without having to bother with the machine more than three times during the night. Four hours was the usual length of a session, from about ten until two in the morning.

The disadvantages to this method of collecting are the relatively poor quality of the recordings and the extreme tediousness of transcription. A four-hour session might well result in a dozen usable texts. But it is the best method I know for capturing the free, unself-conscious idiom in which the jests are told. The informants knew they were being recorded, of course, but a fairly natural atmosphere could be achieved after the first few minutes. The beer was partly responsible, as was the fact that the microphone was barely visible in the dark, so that the group forgot about it once beer and talk flowed freely. Most important, though, was the presence at each session of one or two assistants planted among the group, whose business it was to make the *talla* session as natural as possible and to elicit the kind of materials I was seeking without having to ask the informants for them. Their first job was to get everybody in the right mood by passing out the beer and making the usual small talk. The main purpose of my collecting, however, was to tape-record jokes and other lore about Anglo Americans. So the "plant" went on to tell some familiar joke on the subject, usually one of the large cycle of jests I have tentatively labeled the "Stupid American" joke. Since those invited were chosen because of their abilities as narrators, they responded with jests of their own, one story suggesting another. The "plant" had one other important function. The party sometimes wandered off in other directions, into small talk or verbal dueling, for example, or into reminiscing and sentimental songs. The "plant" tried to bring things back into line by telling another of his stories, usually texts I had already collected. He could do this as long as he stayed sober himself, something that did not always happen.

The main purpose of my field trip, as has been said, was to collect folklore making covert or direct expression of attitudes toward Anglo Americans and their culture. Materials were recorded in between a series of digressions that the "plants" attempted to control and redirect toward our agreed-on objective. On first examining the transcribable texts I brought back with me, I set aside the six discussed here as belonging with the digressions rather than with the material I was looking for. Americans scarcely appear in them. In No. 6 we do have a character of the "Stupid American" stereotype, but it is the Mexican villagers who appear in a ridiculous light rather than he.

All six of the stories do have in common a general situation: there is a sick person, and a group of people seek a cure for him. It is not the patient himself but his family or the community as a whole that seeks help. A doctor or healer is found, who recommends a cure with varying results. Nos. 1 through 5 all are concerned in one way or another with Mexican folk curing practices. Only in No. 6 is *curanderismo* absent, but the story is a variant of other *curandero* jests known to the collector in which it is the folk healer who recommends the wrong purgative to the patient, or the right purgative to the wrong person. That is to say, all six jests are parodies of a folktale type known to Latin American folklorists as the *caso* and sometimes called the "belief tale" in the United States—a relatively short narrative about miraculous or extraordinary events supposed to have happened to the narrator or to someone he knows. The particular type of *caso* parodied here is based on a formula well known to students of *curanderismo*, a simple pattern pitting the *curandero* against medical science, with science driven from the field in utter confusion.

Somebody falls ill and is taken to a doctor, but the doctor can do nothing for him. The patient gets worse and worse. There may be a consultation attended by several doctors, "a meeting of the doctors," as the *casos* put it, but the men of science cannot find the cause of the disease or recommend a cure. Or perhaps they say the patient is beyond hope of recovery. Again, they may recommend a painful and costly operation requiring a long stay at the hospital. Then someone suggests going to Don Pedrito or Don Juanito or some other *curandero*. The patient's relatives are skeptical at first but they finally agree. The whole group journeys to the *curandero*, who receives them kindly but chides the doubters about their skepticism, which he has learned about by miraculous means even before they arrived. Then he asks a standard question, seemingly unnecessary for his diagnosis but very important to the structured arrangement of the narrative, "And what do the doctors say?"

He is told what the doctors say, and he smiles indulgently at their childish ignorance. Then he prescribes some deceptively simple remedy: an herb perhaps, drinking three swallows of water under special circumstances three times a day, washing at a certain well or spring, or the like. The patient recovers completely. There may be a sequel in which the former patient goes and confronts the doctors. They are surprised, incredible. They visit the old *curandero*, seeking to find out the secret of the cure. The old man tells them nothing, or he will answer in words such as, "God cured him, not I." The doctors leave, chastened and still mystified.

A number of these *casos* have been current in south Texas and northern Tamaulipas for generations, most often in association with the saintly figure of Dan Pedrito Jaramillo, the famed healer of Los Olmos, Texas. Ruth Dodson published a number of stories related to Don Pedrito, first in Spanish and later in English translation.[2] More recently, Octavio Romano has studied Don Pedrito as a charismatic figure.[3] Not all *curandero* belief tales follow the strict pattern of this formula, though it is perhaps the most widely retold. Another important narrative pattern deals with the scoffer who comes to the *curandero* pretending to be ill, merely to ridicule or expose him. The *curandero* punishes him by causing him to have a debilitating and embarrassing case of diarrhea.

The function of the *curandero* belief tale among Mexican folk groups is clear enough. It helps bolster belief in folk medicine; it encourages acceptance by the younger generation of the old traditions, especially when the group must live among an increasingly skeptical majority. This may be equally true whether the Mexican folk group is living in the United States or across the border in Mexico, since Mexican physicians are at times even more intolerant of folk medicine than their Anglo-American counterparts. But this type of *caso* plays an important role among rural and semirural Mexican groups in the United States, who see their folk culture assailed not only by modern science and technology but by the belief patterns of rural Anglo-American neighbors, who may have their own folk beliefs but tend to be contemptuous of those held by foreigners.

It is this type of belief tale that is parodied in jests such as the six we are considering. They quite consciously mock the defenses set up by the *curandero* belief tales, and they express an equally conscious rejection of the folk culture holding such beliefs. On the surface they represent as violent a rejection of Mexican values as that of William Madsen's Mexican American from Hidalgo county, Paul, who wishes he could get the Mexican blood out of his veins and change it for something else.[4]

Pertinent is the fact that parodies of *curandero* belief tales are widespread among Mexican Americans, certainly one of the reasons why these six intruded into a session of "Stupid American" jokes. The earliest printed example I know of appeared in the *Journal of American Folklore* in 1914 in one of Aurelio M. Espinosa's collections of New Mexican folklore. It is a variant of our No. 6, except that it is a *curandero* rather than a veterinarian who gives the purgative to the wrong person. It works, though, so the *curandero* justifies his action, saying, *"Haciendo la cosa efecto, no importa que sieso sea."* ("As long as the thing works, who cares whose ass it was?")[5] In the late 1920s, when the celebrated Niño Fidencio was curing the sick, the halt and the blind in Nuevo León, Mexico, similar stories were circulated along the border about some of his cures. In one he cured a hunchback by breaking his spine. The hunchback screamed, "I'm dying!"

"But you'll die straight," Fidencio replied.

These are, of course, adaptations of other stories ranging much farther in space and time. All six contain universal motifs found in Stith Thompson's *Motif-Index of Folk-Literature*, either under J2450, "Literal fools" or J2412, "Foolish imitation of healing."[6] Nos. 5 and 6 resemble Spanish folktales about the numbskull who is told to bathe his grandmother in hot water and boils her to death instead. Or he is told to clean a child, so he cuts its belly open and takes out the intestines. Nos. 2 and 3, especially No. 2, are based on motifs listed by Thompson under B700, "Fanciful traits of animals." There are several methods by which animals that have introduced themselves into people's stomachs are disposed of. For example, in B784.2.1, reported from Ireland, Italy, and the United States, "The patient is fed salt or heavily salted food and allowed no water for several days. He then stands with mouth open before a supply of fresh water, often a running brook. The thirsty animal emerges to get fresh water." Thompson does not tell us if the animal is then beaten to death. Then there is motif B784.2.1.2, reported from India, about which Thompson tells us, "A husband ties a cock near his wife's feet so that a snake-parasite in her stomach will come out to catch the cock. The snake is then killed by the husband." Thompson does not tell us how the snake comes out of the woman's body, an important omission especially for the psychoanalytically oriented investigator. It might also be worth mentioning that we could find parallels to these jests somewhat nearer at hand; No. 6 is very much like North American sick jokes.

The prevalence of feces and other anal motifs as a source of humor in our jests certainly would interest the psychoanalyst. This characteristic may reflect influence from one type of *curandero* belief tale discussed above, seriously told and believed but causing mirth instead of wonder, when the listener thinks of the discomfiture suffered by the skeptic inflicted with diarrhea. At least, this points to a favorite source of humor among groups telling the same tales. But it is the other *caso* formula—in which the *curandero* vanquishes medical science—that is alluded to in Texts 1 through 5, all beginning very much in the serious belief tale style but becoming *tallas* when the ending takes a ludicrous twist, by means of which the *curandero* and his methods are satirized.

## TEXT I

They tell about an old man who was a *curandero*, that they brought him a patient who was sick in the stomach. And he said, "Give him goat turds."

Said, "But what do you mean, give him goat turds!"

"Yes," he said, "Boiled."

Well, so they did it, and the man got well. And then there was a meeting of physicians. Said, "Listen, man," he said. "We never could find out what was wrong with him. And he got well with goat turds."

So they called the old *curandero*. Said, "Well, why did you give goat turds to this man?"

He said, "It's very simple. Because I knew the ailment he had," he said, "could be cured with some sort of herb. But I didn't know which one," he said. "And since goats eat all kinds of weeds and herbs, I knew the plant that was needed would be there in the shit."

Informant No. 24
Brownsville, Texas
October 20, 1962

Text No. 1 reproduces the sequel following many of the *casos*, when the doctors come to the *curandero* and humbly seek to know the secret of his powers—truly a triumph of folk healing over medical science. But our *curandero* is not reticent about explaining his methods, nor does he attribute his success to divine power. His answer, in fact, has a logic all its own, based on a folkish kind of empiricism one might say. The hit-or-miss character of many folk remedies, their far-fetched sense of causality, and the actual use of drugs in *curanderismo* all come in for ridicule.

## TEXT II

They went to see Don Pedrito about a poor *bracero* who was around there in Hidalgo county, and this poor man got up one night to get a drink of water and he swallowed a spider. Well, he got sicker and sicker, so they took him to the hospital at Edinburg.

And they said, "Who's going to pay?"

"Well, there's no money, I guess."

"All right. Get out!"

"So what can we do?" they said. "Nobody can pay. Let's take him over to Don Pedrito."

Well, so the little old man came and looked him over. "And what happened to him?" he said.

"Well, it's like this." Said, "This boy swallowed a spider."

He said, "And what did they say at the hospital?"

Said, "Oh, no! At the hospital they want money to operate on him."

"No," he said, "don't talk to me about operations. I'll take care of him right now. Let's see, turn him over for me with his ass sticking up, with his butt in the air."

They turned him over.

"Now, pull his pants down." They pulled his pants down.

He said, "But bring him out here in the yard." They laid him down in the yard.

He said, "Do you have some Karo corn syrup?"

"Well, yes. Here's some."

Gave his asshole a good smearing with it. "All right, now," he said, "Everybody stand back." And he picked up a stick.

Said, "But what are you doing, Don Juanito?"

He said, "I'm waiting for the flies to gather," he said. "When the flies start buzzing the spider will come out, and I'll kill it with this little stick."

Informant No. 24

## TEXT III

And then there was this other guy who drank the kerosene, this other poor man living in a tent around there who picked up a glass. And they had a lot of milk bottles there, made of glass, and they had water and kerosene in them. And this poor man picked one of them up and downed half a liter of kerosene. And he was choking, so there they go to the hospital at Edinburg.

And they took him there. "WHO'S GONNA PAY?" [Part in caps said in English.]

"Well, there's no money, I guess."

"All right. Get out, *cabrones!*"

Well, there was no money, so out! So they took him back, and the poor man was choking. He had downed half a liter of kerosene. Said, "Call Don Fulanito."

So the old man came. "What's the matter?" he said.

"He drank half a liter of kerosene."

"All right. So what did they say at the hospital?"

Said, "Well, at the hospital they want money. For the operation."

"Ah, no. There'll be no fuckin operation," he said. "Let's see. Bring him out here for me. Just put him out here and leave him to me." He said, "Don't you have a lantern there?"

"Well, yes."

"Let's see, then. Take the wick out of the lantern." They took out the wick. "Does anybody have a pencil around there?"

"Well, yes. Here's the pencil."

"Now get out of the way," he said. "Pull his pants down." He stuffed the wick in his asshole with the pencil and said, "Let's have a match." He lighted the wick. He said, "All right, now. Everybody stand back. When the fire is gone," he said, "when the wick goes out, then all the kerosene will be out of him."

Informant No. 24

Texts Nos. 2 and 3 are variants of the same tale, based on an old and widely traveled motif, B784.2, "Means of ridding person of animal in stomach." It is significant that they were told by the same informant in the order given, 2 before 3, so that No. 3 is an emphatic restatement of No. 2. This jest includes a good part of the belief tale formula: A man falls gravely ill. He is taken to the hospital, where nothing is done for him.

Hospital personnel recommend an operation, something the unsophisticated Mexican American dreads. Madsen, for example, reports that for his Hidalgo county informants the hospital is the most dreaded place next to prison and that hospitalization "can become a nightmarish experience when surgery is involved. . . ."[7] Frightened by the prospect of an operation, the relatives take the patient to the *curandero*, who asks the formal question, "And what did they say at the hospital?" The hospital wants to operate, but the *curandero* is reassuring. No operation is necessary; he will cure the patient without much trouble. Up to this point the joke and the belief tale follow more or less identical lines, and it is at this point that the ridiculous is introduced.

There are some other features about Nos. 2 and 3 that should be noted before passing on to the other jests, even though they do not pertain to our belief tale formula. The action is set in Hidalgo county though the story was recorded in the county of Cameron. The narrator first calls the *curandero* "Don Pedrito," evidently in reference to the celebrated Don Pedrito Jaramillo, though he forgets later and calls him "Don Juanito." Still later, in No. 3, the *curandero* becomes "Don Fulanito"—Mr. John Doe or Mr. Such-and-Such, making him just any folk healer. More interesting still is the matter of the hospital. According to the belief tale formula the patient's family refuses to put him in the hospital because of their horror of operations, or the American doctors do get him into the hospital but are unable to find a cure. It is different with our *bracero's* friends, who do want him treated there. Nor do they question at this point the ability of the American doctors to make the patient well. The hospital attendants refuse to admit the patient, and it is because of this that he is taken to the *curandero*. If we keep this in mind, the emphatic character of the second variant, Text No. 3, becomes significant. The same pattern is stated, but in stronger terms. The demand for money on the part of the hospital staff is emphasized by putting it into English, "Who's gonna pay?" pronounced in a drawling, decidedly unpleasant tone. The "All right. Get out!" of No. 2 becomes "All right. Get out, *cabrones!*"[8] Even the gentle old *curandero* suffers a change with his, "There'll be no fuckin operation!" The narrator has warmed up to his theme, whatever his theme may be. At least we can be sure that he intends to be more than merely funny.

## TEXT IV

This is something they say happened in Mission or McAllen or somewhere over there, in Hidalgo county, you see? A girl began to feel very sick in the stomach, and they took her to the doctor. And the doctor said, "This girl has appendicitis." He said, "We'll have to take out her appendix, no other way. If she isn't feeling better by tomorrow at ten," he said, "I'll come for her."

So then a woman said, "Look," she said, "Don Pedrito is in town. He's a *curandero*," she said, "and he's a very wise old man."

Said, "What for?"

"He never goes around recommending operations," she said, "and he never makes a mistake."

Well, so they called him. He said, "Let's see, let's see," he said. "What does the doctor say?"

"Oh, the doctor says it's her appendix."

He said, "Oh, no. Those doctors are a bunch of *cabrones*; all they know is about diseases in English. But this little girl is sick in the Mexican way; she has a Mexican disease," he said. "And it can be only one of three things: fled flesh, bruised blood, or a blocked fart."

Informant No. 24

Text No. 4 makes an interesting contrast with Nos. 2 and 3. Again the setting is in Hidalgo county, and again the *curandero's* name is Don Pedrito. But in this story the American doctor is sympathetic; he offers to take the sick girl to the hospital. It is the girl's family who decides to take her to Don Pedrito because he "never goes around recommending operations." Up to this point the jest closely follows not only the usual pattern of the *curandero* belief tale but also certain supposedly factual cases reported by nonbelievers in *curanderismo*, in which Mexican Americans are said to have died of such things as appendicitis rather than go to a hospital. Satire begins when Don Pedrito is shown in anything but a humble or saintly mood; he calls the American doctors a bunch of *cabrones*. His diagnosis of what the doctor has called appendicitis is a parody of such folk diseases as *mollera caída* and *susto pasado* (fallen fontanelle and an advanced case of fright sickness).[9] Also satirized is the belief, often encountered by collectors, that only Mexicans can get "Mexican" diseases like *ojo* and *susto*, though it should be mentioned that one encounters just as often belief tales about Anglo Americans who are healed by *curanderos*. Almost twenty percent of Don Pedrito Jaramillo's cures as related by Ruth Dodson are said to have been done to Anglo Americans.[10]

## TEXT V

Z. P. [narrator names a Mexican-American M.D.] went to call on a patient. He examined him and said, "It's not as bad as all that. I'm going to write you a prescription. But I want you to do exactly what I tell you, and I'll come back tomorrow morning. He'll get well, I assure you. But listen very carefully," he says, "because I want you to do it exactly as I am going to tell you."

"Very well, doctor."

He says, "I want you to give him a sponge bath, all right? Soak the sponge in alcohol and give him a good rubbing all over his body. And before the alcohol can evaporate, cover him with a sheet all the way up here to the neck. Then you take a little bit of ashes and sprinkle them around the bed. Pray one Paternoster and three Hail Marys. Then take a ball and balance it very carefully on his forehead," he says. "I'll come back around six or seven in the morning, and I assure you he'll be perfectly all right by then."

Well, so they did as they were told. Next morning the doctor came. But no, the poor man was already dead. "How's the patient?" he says.

"But he already—he's dead."

"But how could he be dead! It wasn't all—it wasn't a fatal disease. You must have failed to do exactly what I told you."

"Oh, no . . . We did, *señor* doctor."

"Well, did you give him the sponge bath with alcohol?"

"Yes, of course. As soon as you left. And we covered him with the sheet so the effect would not be lost."

"And the ashes?"

"Well, see for yourself there they are. Look there, on the bed; you can still see the ashes there."

"And the ball on his forehead?" he says.

"Well, now there, you see doctor. There's where we had a bit of trouble. We had to call three of the neighbors," he says. "And we tried to do it between us four," he says. "But we couldn't pull it up any farther than his navel."

Informant No. 10
Brownsville, Texas
September 7, 1962

At first glance No. 5 seems to be different from the preceding four jests, but it really is based on one small part of the belief tale formula we have been considering: the actual treatment of the patient by the *curandero*. The rubbing down with alcohol is prescribed by *curanderos* and by old-fashioned M.D.'s alike for any number of ailments. In the original Spanish the doctor prescribes that an egg (*huevo*) be put on the patient's forehead, *huevo* being such a common synonym for "testicle" that many prudish people avoid the word altogether, substituting it with *blanquillo*. The use of an egg and of ashes, however, will be recognized by those familiar with Mexican folk medicine as part of the treatment for diseases like *susto* and *ojo*. Even the doctor's reassurance to the patient's family at the beginning, that "It's not as bad as all that," is part of the *curandero* belief tale formula. Medical science has made a great deal of fuss over the patient's illness, but it will be an easy thing for the *curandero* to make the patient well. It is obvious that the M.D. in this story really is a *curandero* in disguise. The sense of the ridiculous is heightened by having an M.D. playing the part of the *curandero*, or vice-versa, but we must also keep in mind that the doctor to whom the joke is attributed is a Mexican-American. The jest is not identified with any particular doctor, by the way. Even the same narrator will use different names in retelling the story, but the name of a real Mexican-American doctor always is used, most often one that the narrator's hearers know well. I can attest to having heard this same informant tell the same jest downtown, away from a tape recorder, using the name of a different Mexican-American doctor.

## TEXT VI

There was a veterinary out there with the Aftosa, a *bolillo* from around here.[11] And then this little old man was very sick; he had indigestion or I don't know what. So they went. "Here's a doctor from the other side of the border. What more do you want!" So they went to see him.

He said, "Oh, no! Me doctor by the cow. But not by the man. NO GOTTA PERMIT." [Vet's dialogue is in heavily accented Spanish, except part in caps, which is in English.]

Said, "No matter, doctor. What do you give the cows when they are sick in the stomach?"

"Well, *hombre*," he says, "me give a little Epsom salts."

Said, "How much Epsom salts do you give the cow?"

He says, "Oh, by one big cow me give her a pound of salts in one gallon of water."

So then they said, "Now we can figure the dose ourselves." They went home and measured half a gallon of water and a half a pound of Epsom salts. And they made the old man drink it.

Well, so next morning they came. Said, "Oh, doctor, we came to see you."

"How is sick man doing? Is he better?"

"Oh, no, he's dead."

He said, "But how could he be dead!"

"Yes, we came to invite you to the funeral, this afternoon. But don't feel guilty about it, doctor." Said, "It isn't your fault."

He said, "Why you say not my fault?"

Says, "We gave him the salts and the salts worked. He must have died of something else, because even after he was dead he still moved his bowels three times."

Informant No. 24

Text No. 6 does not seem to go with the others at all; as it stands there is no *curanderismo* involved. But a comparison with No. 5 reveals an identical plot structure: a naive group of Mexicans misinterpret instructions for the treatment of a patient, with fatal results for the patient, the ending in both cases being very much like that of the "cruel" or "sick" joke common in North American urban lore. The characters giving medical instructions in the two stories also bear comparison. The American veterinarian is portrayed as a likable simpleton, along the lines of the "Stupid American" stereotype. But he is working for the Aftosa commission, engaged in slaughtering the Mexican peasant's cattle to control the hoof-and-mouth disease, and thus a much resented figure. The Mexican-American doctor, on the other hand, acts like a *curandero* and thus is comically seen as "one of our boys," but he is also a representative of American medical science and American culture and therefore must share some of the resentments generated by inter-cultural conflicts.

It is this double nature of our texts that makes them especially interesting. In the satirizing of folk medicine and *curandero* belief tales they express a mocking rejection of Mexican folk culture; in their expression of resentment toward American culture they show a strong sense of identification with the Mexican folk.

The texts, as has been said, were recorded during two sessions in Brownsville, Cameron County, Texas, a bilingual and bicultural community with an influential Mexican-American middle class including doctors, lawyers, teachers, well-to-do merchants, and individuals in elective and appointive public office. These are for the most part descendants of the old Mexican settlers of the region, people with their roots in a past when Brownsville was a "Mexican" town rather than immigrants or children of immigrants from Mexico. By usual North American standards they would belong to the middle class; according to Madsen's class divisions for Mexican Americans in Hidalgo county, they would be "upper class."[12] The participants in the *talla* recording sessions were bilingual males between the ages of twenty-five and fifty-five. They speak good English and have received advanced education in American colleges and universities. They play important roles in community life, not in the life of a "Mexican colony" but in that of the city and the county as a whole. In other words, they would seem to be completely acculturated, having adapted to American culture and functioning in it in a very successful way. At the same time, when they are away from the courtroom, the school, the office, or the clinic and congregated in a group of their own, they think of themselves as *mexicanos*. Not only will they speak Spanish among themselves, but it is quite obvious that they place a high value on many aspects of Mexican culture and are proud of the duality of their background. They do in a sense live double lives, functioning as Americans in the affairs of the community at large and as Mexicans within their own closed circle.

In each of the two sessions groups of about a dozen individuals of the type described told jests of the "Stupid American" type, in which joking tension and hostility toward the majority culture were expressed in joking situations. The *curandero* parodies were introduced into this context by two of the informants, one at each session. Text No. 5 was told by a lawyer, a friend of the doctor to whom the story was attributed in this particular variant. The doctor was not present at the session. Had he been present the joke might have been interpreted in another way, as part of a verbal duel, with the doctor replying by telling a joke about lawyers in which his friend would have been the main character. This is one way the *talla* is performed, as was said in discussing the probable origins of the word. In this case, however, the doctor's name was used because he is well known and representative. The narrator practices criminal law; his work brings him into contact with many Mexican-Americans of the poorer class, much less acculturated than himself, who are usually in trouble when they come to him. His knowledge of Spanish gains him their confidence, and his Mexican background leads him to identify with them in many ways, but his profession demands that he comport himself in the role of an American lawyer functioning in an American court rather than assuming a "Mexican" role as he does when he is with a group of intimates. Many things repressed in the courtroom find an outlet in the *talla* sessions. The lawyer always has amusing anecdotes to tell within his own group, some of them revealing the comic naiveté of his clients, others showing their folk wit and hardheaded common sense.

Texts Nos. 1, 2, 3, 4, and 6 were told by the same person, one of the best narrators I know. Only a sound recording can show his sense of intonation and mimicry, and even then his gestures are lost. He told all five stories in the same session, but not consecutively since he was alternating with other narrators present. It is quite clear, however, that one tale brought another to his mind. These are not his stories any more than No. 5 belongs to the lawyer alone. They are common property, but this informant is recognized as telling them better than most other people do. He works for a school system somewhere in Cameron County, and his job brings him into contact—at times into conflict—with Mexican-American parents of the laboring classes. He also has his anecdotes about his job: the naiveté of some of the parents he deals with, their lack of understanding of American values, their reluctance to keep their children in school. Often he parodies these people when he is among his own group. Just as often he will become exasperated with his job, complaining that his work shows no results, that he is butting his head against a stone wall. He seems sincerely committed in his efforts to raise the educational level of Mexican-Americans in the county and is emotionally involved in the situation.

The two informants are typical of their group. They are socially conscious members of the middle class, impatient about the slow acculturation of the average Mexican-American and his low economic and social status. At the same time, they reveal a strong feeling of identification with the unacculturated Mexican. They are highly acculturated Mexican Americans who value their ancestral culture in spite of such aspects as *curanderismo*, which they would include among the things the Mexican-American must reject in order to compete successfully in an English-speaking world. But their attitude toward the *curandero* is not a hostile one. They will admit that some of these old men are pretty good psychologists in their own way, and they also point out with evident pride that many Mexican herbs have been put to use by modern medical science. Furthermore, the belief in *curanderismo* is something in their own recent past. Such celebrated *curanderos* as Don Pedrito Jaramillo were patronized a half-century ago not only by the poor and illiterate but by many of the land-owning families of the area. Some of those present during the *talla* session I recorded had been treated by *curanderos* in their early childhood. So there is identification on the part of the group not only with the unacculturated Mexican but with *curanderismo* itself. This is most clearly seen in No. 5, in which the *curandero's* role is given to a highly acculturated Mexican-American physician, an absent member of the group in which the tale was told.

*Curanderismo* for this group is a subject viewed with a good deal of ambivalence, but the ambivalent attitude is anything but rare in jokes. The best dirty jokes about priests and nuns are told by Catholics; to be truly effective, the contemporary "cruel" or "sick" joke has to be told among people who are highly sensitive to human suffering. The *curandero* jests release a complicated set of conflicting emotions ranging from exasperation to affection in respect to the unacculturated Mexican American, coupled with a half-conscious resentment toward the Anglo-American culture. Also involved is a definite element of masochism, often expressed in the proverbial phrase, "¡Ah, que mexicano!" (Ah, what a Mexican!) used to express jesting disapproval of some bumbling or foolish act. We must keep in mind that members of this group are quite explicit in identifying themselves as *mexicanos*, and that the above phrase is used only in Spanish, never in English.

So these jests are not after all intrusions into a session of stories expressing intercultural conflict; they also are expressions of the same kind of conflict. Only in No. 4 does the doctor, representative of American culture, appear in a favorable light. In Nos. 2 and 3 the matter is quite explicit. The poor *bracero* must go to the folk healer because he is refused treatment at the American hospital. The *curandero* asks for so little—a small fee or a gift, something the poorest laborer can pay. One does not have to be a rich man to visit Don Fulanito. Many such incidents are seriously told by Mexican-Americans of the poorer classes. We find the same subject matter here in jokes, told by people who can afford to be treated at hospitals, but the stories are not quite in the comic vein. There is a good deal of emotional involvement, which members of the group would readily acknowledge among themselves, and that gives an edge to the humor. They may tell you, with a kind of self-directed exasperation, about Mexican laborers who died for lack of attention, and it is obvious that these stories arouse their resentment.

Why the events in Nos. 2, 3, and 4 are placed in Hidalgo rather than in Cameron county I am not prepared to say. It may be that Mexican-Americans in Cameron County feel that their people in Hidalgo live under worse conditions than they do. It may be a narrative device, placing the action at some distance from narrator and audience. If such is the case, it is worth noting that the device is not a comic one. The comedian uses the opposite approach, relating his story to familiar events and to people close at hand. The introduction of people in the narrator's audience as characters in his jests has been mentioned as typical of one of the aspects of the *talla* session, when it becomes a verbal contest. Narrators tend to place events some distance away for reasons other than comedy. If characters and events are very far away, in a distant time and a distant land, the effect is one of wonder and romance. But to achieve a feeling of verisimilitude, required in the legendary anecdote, events are placed not too far off—in the next town, the next hollow, or the next county. This again is evidence that these jests are not intended to be as funny as they appear on the surface.

This is not, then, a relatively simple case of second-generation Americans ridiculing the culture of their ancestors and thereby rejecting it. As parodies of the *curandero* type of belief tale the jests do express the Mexican-American's rejection of his traditional culture. But combined with parody is a good deal of resentment against Anglo-American culture, expressed in a stereotypic view of American physicians and hospital attendants as caring little about Mexican patients of the poorer, less educated class.

Since the informants are not poor and badly educated themselves but belong to the middle class, the ambivalence of their attitudes is quite marked. Members of the group telling the jests have not lost the feeling that beneath their Americanized exterior they still are *mexicanos*. There is an underlying conflict between their Spanish-Mexican heritage and an Anglo-American culture they have embraced intellectually without completely accepting it emotionally, in great part because Anglo-American culture rejects part of themselves. The jests help resolve these conflicts brought about by acculturation, involving not only a change from rural to urban values but from a basically Mexican culture to the generalized, English-speaking culture of the majority.

---

[1] My field work was made possible by a fellowship from the John Simon Guggenheim Foundation and a supplementary grant from the University of Texas, which I acknowledge with thanks.

[2] Ruth Dodson, *Don Pedrito Jaramillo: Curandero* (San Antonio: Casa Editorial Lozano, 1934) and "Don Pedrito Jaramillo: The Curandero of Los Olmos," *Publications of the Texas Folklore Society* 24 (1951): 9–70.

[3] Octavio Ignacio Romano, "Charismatic Medicine, Folk-Healing, and Folk-Sainthood," *The American Anthropologist* 67 (1965): 1151–73.

[4] William Madsen, *The Mexican-Americans of South Texas* (New York: Holt, Rinehart and Winston, 1964), 43.

[5] Aurelio M. Espinosa, "New-Mexican Spanish Folk-Lore," *The Journal of American Folklore* 27 (1914): 105–147.

[6] Stith Thompson, *Motif-Index of Folk-Literature*, 6 vols. (Copenhagen and Bloomington: University of Indiana Press, 1955–58).

[7] Madsen, *Mexican-Americans*, 93–94.

[8] *Cabrón, cabrones* (singular and plural). Literally "he-goat"; in formal Spanish usage it is the word for cuckold; in current usage, as in the jests, the term is roughly equivalent to the English "bastard."

[9] In Text No. 4 the *curandero's* diagnosis in the original Spanish is *carne juida, sangre molida o pedo detenido*.

[10] Dodson, *Don Pedrito Jaramillo*, 129–146.

[11] *Bolillo*. One of the many derogatory names for the Anglo American. It seems to have been used originally for the French (*bolillo* is a small loaf of French bread), but later it was transferred to the North American.

[12] Madsen, *Mexican-Americans*, 41-43.

# Carnival in Canada: The Politics of Celebration

Frank E. Manning

*Defining the groups in which you are a member is a process simultaneous with defining those in which you are not a member. Thus the definition of a group and the sense of belonging to it is not something constructed from an essential and enduring quality of sameness but rather from the perception of relative difference. Because circumstances change, perceived differences also change, and consequently the definition of groups and the consciousness of kind.*

*The former British colonies in the West Indies scrupulously distinguish among themselves. Individual island identities are promoted and maintained at the expense of potential ecological, historical, economic, or linguistic unities. Emigrants from these islands, however, discover their island identities to be insignificant in the eyes of the larger population of their new homelands. In order to be recognized at all, these islanders must band together and forge a unified identity. They must attempt to seek new unities within old differences. In theory, the redefinition of groups is simple. But when such redefinition restructures social relationships and demands concerted action in the manipulation of scarce resources, it is difficult.*

*The following essay on the efforts to create a Caribbean festival in Toronto shows just how difficult the redefinition of groups can be. The unity presented to the public belies the divisiveness lying beneath. Nevertheless, the fact that the festival takes place at all, and the manner in which it has developed, also suggest that in the arena of ethnic and cultural display, the perception of difference from the larger Toronto population has stimulated islanders to create an island identity that is more than just theoretical. For some other examples concerning the development and organization of ethnic, religious, and community festival see Byrne, Jr. (1985), Danielson (1974), and Giuliano (1976).*

Celebration often exemplifies one of the central paradoxes of play.[1] From one perspective, it is autotelic and purely expressive, an ideal form of the ludic impulse in the classic sense described by Huizinga.[2] From another angle, however, celebration can be replete with studied political maneuvering and other instrumental stratagems. Their polarity notwithstanding, these two aspects of celebration are dialectically related in the "two-dimensional" process discerned by Cohen.[3] Power relations are represented, negotiated, and acted upon in the arena of celebration, while celebratory symbols derive much of their meaning and dramatic impact from underlying sociopolitical realities. Celebration, then, is both culture and politics. It is a "power play," ambiguous and moving.

---

Reproduced by permission of the publisher, from *The Masks of Play*, ed. Brian Sutton-Smith and Diana Kelly-Byrne (New York: Leisure Press, 1984), 24–33. Not for further reproduction.

I am concerned in this paper with the West Indian tradition of carnival, which has its source in Trinidad but which has diffused throughout most of the eastern Caribbean and, more recently, into several metropolitan areas in the United States, Canada, and Britain where large numbers of West Indians have settled. The politics of metropolitan carnivals are shaped by two distinctive factors: first the involvement of West Indians from many different Caribbean islands, whose cultural identities have traditionally been influenced by a thoroughgoing sense of isolation and alienation from each other; second, the social situation of West Indians as a racial-cultural immigrant minority. The Toronto Caribana, one of the most spectacular West Indian carnivals in North America and possibly Canada's outstanding ethnic celebration, richly illustrates the interpenetration of cultural festivity and political discourse.

## INSULARITY ON THE MAINLAND

Caribana traces its beginning to 1967, when West Indians in Toronto were invited to participate in Canada's centennial observances. An *ad hoc* West Indian group brought to the city a contingent of Trinidadian masqueraders and musicians who were then in Montreal for Expo '67. A carnival-style parade was held downtown, and was reportedly the first major Caribbean cultural performance in Toronto.

Enthused by their success, the organizers constituted themselves the Caribbean Cultural Committee and determined to mount an annual summer festival. From the outset, however, they were deeply and acrimoniously divided along lines of island origin—a pattern that has been apparent in every metropolitan carnival with which I am familiar. To appreciate this archetypal conflict, one must be aware that the social category "West Indian" has had little positive meaning in the Caribbean. People view themselves, primarily and often exclusively, in terms of an island nationality and culture. Insular xenophobia is general and diffuse, but it is also structured hierarchically on the basis of island size. From the perspective of a given island, those from smaller islands are seen as "backward," and thus subject to ridicule, condescension, and contempt. Conversely, those from larger islands are seen as aggressive and domineering, a feeling which evokes a response of resentment, suspicion, and defiance. (The phenomenon is somewhat comparable to departmental isolation and disciplinary chauvinism in universities, but that can't be pursued here. Interestingly, it also parallels Canadian regionalism, the country's most powerful political and cultural force.)

The largest West Indian country, Jamaica, has traditionally been the most reluctant to deal at any level with any other island, and in turn is undoubtedly the most unliked by all the rest. Trinidad, the second largest country, is smugly viewed as a "small island" by the Jamaicans, but it dominates the eastern Caribbean. The remaining eastern Caribbean islands—there are eight principal ones—are relatively small compared to Trinidad, and will occasionally speak with one voice in distinguishing themselves from Trinidad or Jamaica. But this posture is invariably short-lived and ineffectual, as the smaller islands insist on ranking themselves according to size and thus preserving the overall hierarchy. The swift collapse of the West Indies Federation—the government

created in 1958 to unite Britain's Caribbean colonies and lead them to independence—
is only the best known of a litany of dismal failures at social and political integration.
The Commonwealth Caribbean today is a melange of the world's smallest mini-states,
each impotent on its own but unwilling to join forces with the others.

Insularity persists in Canada. Virtually all Caribbean institutions in the Toronto
area—clubs, community associations, artistic groups, even student organizations—are
oriented towards particular islands. Predictably, the most powerful group, numerically
and politically, are the Jamaicans. But as Jamaica lacks a carnival tradition and has
stigmatized that genre by associating it with the smaller islands, Jamaicans have had
virtually nothing to do with Caribana. Their determination to "go it alone" as West
Indians say, is dramatized on Caribana weekend when the Jamaican-Canadian Association runs an alternative celebration, Jamaicafest, in commemoration of Jamaica's
national independence.

The non-involvement of the Jamaicans left the Caribbean Culture Committee,
organizers of Caribana, to the Trinidadians and those from the smaller eastern
Caribbean islands. The Trinidadians, many of them masquerade band leaders, insisted
that the festival should preserve the format of the Trinidad Carnival, and that they
should have the upper hand in running it. The claim was politically motivated, of
course, but it also stemmed from a deeply felt allegiance to the notion that carnival is an
exclusive Trinidadian birthright. As one masquerade band leader told me, "No one
knows Carnival like a Trinidadian. We're born into it. It's in our blood."[4]

The Trinidadian position put the others in a dilemma. Most of their islands of origin
have produced carnival celebrations in which local content and significance have been
creatively incorporated into the basic carnival format.[5] One might reasonably conclude
that this type of response—a carnival that articulated the Canadian experience—ought
to be encouraged in Toronto. Acceptance of that premise, however, would have been
tantamount to accepting Trinidadian leadership. The non-Trinidadians therefore
insisted that the name "Caribana" was meant to indicate a distinctive type of festival in
which carnival items—chiefly street masquerading, calypso shows, and steel band
music—were only one component. The festival as a whole was to have pan-Caribbean
scope and significance, and an overall emphasis on black racial identity. They sought to
broaden Caribana as much as possible, introducing ferry cruises, fashion shows, picnics,
art and craft exhibits, dramatic dance, and singing performances, merchandising
displays, beauty contests, dance balls, and various other social and entertainment
events that had little or no direct connection with the carnival genre.

After four years of embittered controversy, this tension produced an organizational
split. The Trinidadians formed the Carnival Development Association, which ran
what it called Carnival Extravaganza. This included the masquerade parade, a contest
for king and queen of the masquerade bands, the display of prize-winning costumes
from the Trinidad Carnival, a children's carnival, and a number of dances featuring
calypso music played by steel or brass bands and highlighted by top name calypsonians
from Trinidad. Dances, for example, were announced as "jump-ups," and the public
encouraged to "jump," "jam," "wail," and "wine"—Trinidadian terms for dance

movements, most of them erotic. Appropriating the Trinidadian calendar, the night before the masquerade was termed "jouvay," a patois term abbreviating *jour ouvert* (daybreak) and referring to the Trinidadian practice of revelling until the sun rises on the night before the first day of Carnival. Similarly, the concluding day of Carnival, was described as "las lap"—an occasion of reckless, unbridled abandon. As is said in Trinidad, "Las lap, we go make bassa bassa"—the final phrase being a Yoruba term for 'wanton destruction.'[6]

Meanwhile, the small-island remnant of the Caribbean Cultural Committee ran what it called the Caribana festival. The program had conscious symbolic intentions. It began with evening dance cruises, which were meant to represent the familiar eastern Caribbean experience of traveling on small boats. The symbolism here, however, was deliberately januslike, as it included a distinctive Canadian image—the attractive, almost majestic view of Toronto's skyline that looms from a short distance off-shore. Another activity was a Miss Caribana contest in which great care was taken to select candidates from as many islands as possible, and, it was hoped, to rotate among the islands in choosing winners. There were also two major dances, one in honor of Miss Caribana and the other known as the Caribana Ball; both were held in prestige hotels. The popular highlight of the Caribana Festival was a series of picnics, exhibits, and shows spanning several days. This part of the program was held on Olympic Island, an island park in the Toronto Harbor chosen to represent a generalized Caribbean environment—an island with which every West Indian, regardless of origin, could identify. An informant spoke almost poetically about the island symbolism as a reminder of "home":

> I remember that, right from the very beginning, whenever I walked off that hot, steaming ferry, I felt that I was returning home—home meaning to someplace, anyplace in the Caribbean. . . . returning home with a lot of other people who felt the same way, returning home to a very beautiful part of my culture—such as the food, such as the music, such as the laughter, the humor that we grew up with. And it was a day to just forget everything else and pretend that you had never left wherever you had to leave, for whatever reason . . .

## RACE AND CLASS

While the conflict between the Carnival Extravaganza and the Caribana Festival was drawn chiefly along lines of island origin, it assumed in time two other dimensions of significance: race and social class. Like inter-island distinctions, these identities have been articulated in the processual interplay—in the double sense—of symbolic expression and political strategy. Interestingly, it is in this secondary field of conflict that the celebration has been most appreciably affected by Canadian circumstances.

Trinidad is a racially plural society. The largest segments are blacks and East Indians, with smaller numbers of Chinese, Portuguese, Lebanese (called Syrians in Trinidad) and whites (northern Europeans). While carnival was introduced to Trinidad by the white plantocracy, it was taken over by Afro-Trinidadians after their emancipation from slavery in 1834, and it evolved as a black celebration for the next century. Many of its performance items, notably calypso and steel band, continue to be associated almost exclusively with blacks, and the event as a whole is still known jokingly as the "creole (black) bacchanal." Street masquerading, however, has drawn a variety of racial-ethnic groups, particularly at the organizational level where there are prominent Indian, Chinese, and Lebanese bandleaders. And the entertainment industry, like other businesses in Trinidad, is dominated by non-blacks. It is with some justification, then, that contemporary Trinidadian scholars of Carnival describe it as a national, rather than a racial, celebration.[7]

Vestiges of the Trinidadian pattern are seen in Toronto. The masquerade band leaders who made up the Carnival Development Association consisted of blacks and Indians, and the group was led by one of the latter. The Indian bands have attracted numbers of Indian masqueraders, and at least one of those bands has included Caribbean Chinese designers and white Canadian craft specialists. Masquerade aficionados encourage their white co-workers, friends, and neighbors to "play mas"—don a costume and join the street parade. Thus, in several of the bands there are whites, small in number but still noticeable enough to give the Toronto parade a distinction that is lacking in most other metropolitan carnivals.

Carnival epitomizes Turner's sense of *communitas*, and there is no doubt that the recruitment of whites is in part inspired by this exuberant, egalitarian, and embracing ethos.[8] But there are also practical reasons why whites are sought. For one, the bigger the band, the better the chances of winning prizes. For another, the presence of whites and other racial-ethnic groups resonates vibrantly with the Canadian notion of multiculturalism. In 1971 Canada was officially declared a multicultural society. The many and diverse cultural groups were given the right, almost the duty, to preserve and display their heritage. This right, however, was expressed with reference to a higher ideal—the social responsibility to share one's culture and to learn about others as a step towards mutual enrichment and tolerance. Government policy, backed by substantial funding, is to promote this objective by "connecting" cultural groups.[9]

As the public highlight of the Carnival Extravaganza, the masquerade parade was able to capitalize handsomely on its multicultural image. The parade begins near Queen's Park, seat of the Ontario Provincial Government. From there it proceeds along University Avenue, a wide tree-lined boulevard that easily accommodates a crowd of 150,000 persons, many of them whites and tourists. The route is also flanked by several of Toronto's largest hospitals affording patients an opportunity to watch the spectacle. The parade concludes at Harbourfront, a federal park on the shore of Lake Ontario that was first made available in 1976—the year that the Carnival Development Association won a provincial grant of more than $20,000.

Trinidad's preeminent calypsonian, the Mighty Sparrow, described the scene in a 1972 calypso entitled Toronto Mas. The chorus went as follows:

It's mas, Toronto gone wild
It's mas, Trinidadian style

Steel band play
Lord, the sweet music
All the white women
Goin' be 'pon the street

The principal trope of calypso is the double-entendre, oral-aural as well as semantic. When sung, the last line of this chorus sounds deliberately like "honky on the street."

The multicultural popularity of the masquerade parade generated considerable publicity in the print and broadcast media. It also made it relatively easy to obtain commercial sponsorship, much of it from beer companies and from the gravel industry. Finally, the parade has enjoyed an unbroken record of non-violence, which has kept its organizers in the good graces of the police and the public. One year the leader of the Carnival Development Association was ceremoniously transported around the city in a police side-car.

On the other side, the Caribana Festival was differently situated and developed a different image. Most of the eastern Caribbean islands have been essentially monoracial since the collapse of the sugar plantation system in the early 19th century. Not surprisingly, all members of the Caribbean Cultural Committee were black. They saw racial identity as the basis of their own solidarity, and actively promoted it as a cultural counter-force to Trinidadian nationalism. Part of the strategy involved a choreographical tactic of integrating entertainment symbols from different islands in order to stress their underlying social unity. In the shows on Olympic Island, for example, there was typically a balance between calypso and other Caribbean rhythms such as spouge from Barbados and cadence from Dominica. There were also attempts to book top entertainers from as many Caribbean islands as possible. The committee's enthusiasm for black solidarity further prompted them to introduce black American styles and even to import black performers from the United States—a controversial move that incited West Indian entertainers in Toronto to call for tighter immigration laws! More recently there has been added a reggae component, partly because of the music's strong association with blackness, but also, and more pragmatically, because of its box office appeal to Jamaicans, the largest West Indian group in Toronto, and ironically, to a growing constituency of whites drawn by the late Bob Marley, Peter Tosh, and other reggae superstars who have regularly played before sellout crowds in Toronto's largest concert halls.

The Caribana Festival's need to boost gate receipts has been chronic. Unlike the masquerade parade and outdoor costume competition, most Caribana events have been held in commercial premises and other private settings, and thus are dependent on ticket sales rather than government grants. Even on Olympic Island an entrance fee has been charged. Ticket prices have been steep, as West Indians, by their own admission are notoriously bad at managing money and scandalously prone to the leakage of profits. In 1981, for example, a couple who attended seven major events in Caribana faced ticket prices of nearly $175.

These circumstances gave the Caribana Festival an elitist aura, in contract to the populist image of the Carnival Extravaganza. Class tension is strong in Caribbean societies, and, as Wilson[10] has observed, some of it is played out in entertainment. There is, for example, a wide social gulf between public amusements and festivities, and private parties where admission is by fee or by special invitation. The bourgeois image of Caribana was reinforced by its boast of being not simply a "fete," but a more "serious" festival in which the arts were displayed and which had the long range "educational" objective of establishing a strong sense of black racial consciousness that would fuse West Indians into a united, powerful bloc in Canadian society. From this perspective, the Carnival Extravaganza was condescendingly dismissed as little more than a hedonistic outlet for the masses. In the critical words of a West Indian journalist, "As far as I can see, it is simply a time to 'find a party, smoke a wattie, when you finish, drink a Guiness.'"[11] The latter phrase of this verse, which ironically, was borrowed from a calypso, is a sarcastic allusion to the Trinidadian fondness for stout.

The organizational split between the Carnival Development Association and the Caribbean Cultural Committee was formally ended in 1980, when it became apparent that the rift had seriously eroded the efforts of both groups and that neither the West Indian population nor the city of Toronto were willing to support two competing festivals. The Trinidadians rejoined the Caribbean Cultural Committee, but acted within it as a caucus responsible for running the carnival program, even though the celebration as a whole became known again simply as Caribana. But despite the organizational rapprochement, the basic tension between the two modes of festivity is never far beneath the surface, and frequently rises well above it. In 1982, one of Toronto's top calypsonians, Lord Smokey, wrote a song in which he maligned "Mister Committee" for being dominated by "small island men," for promoting reggae instead of calypso, for importing expensive entertainers rather than relying on Toronto-based calypsonians, and for various other practices which he presented as indicative of the committee's inability to run the show. Thus, the fundamental symbolic and political conflict that I have examined here persists, even though some of the institutional structures in which it was once fought have undergone certain changes.

## Made in Canada

Drawing these threads together, we see in this celebration an ongoing controversy along lines of island origin, race/color, and social class. These dimensions intersect and overlap, inextricably at times. But they are conceptually distinguishable, and each of itself is significant.

In the Caribbean, island identities are differentiated in terms of a variety of real or imputed factors. Behavioral norms are the most general consideration, but wealth, political power, education, and other attributes are often introduced to the social taxonomy of the islands. Among West Indians in Toronto, entertainment has become perhaps the most common focus of insular images and identities. This is particularly true for Trinidadians, who tend to see their love of calypso (the music and the "jump up" dancing style) at the core of their unique social personality. Interestingly, in Trinidad the calypso season lasts 6–8 weeks, from New Year's until Carnival. At other times, people listen to a variety of music, notably imported American trends. But in Toronto (and, I gather, in other metropolitan areas),[12] the calypso season is year round. Calypso is invariably the musical lingua franca at any social gathering dominated by Trinidadians. (Contrastingly, reggae has the same role in any gathering dominated by Jamaicans.)

In the Caribbean, race and class are important but shifting reference symbols in a dialectical process that Wilson, borrowing a native metaphor for status climbing, calls "crab antics."[13] Society is seen as a bunch of crabs in a barrel, each striving to climb up and out while the others scramble to pull it down again. High status derives from "respectability," a code of conduct based traditionally on stereotyped middle class values and white lifestyles. With nominal decolonization and the rise of a black elite, however, there has emerged a sense of black respectability which is as fully bourgeois as its white predecessor. As one Caribbean author put it, "Massa Day (elite domination) never ends in the Caribbean. It only grows blacker."[14]

In Toronto, the Caribana Festival assumed the aura of black respectability, consigning the Carnival Extravaganza to the bottom of the social barrel. The Caribbean Cultural Committee's cooption of that position is ironical, as it reverses the hierarchy based on island size. To compound the irony, the Caribbean Cultural Committee has sought symbolic rapport with the Jamaicans, the most aloof and chauvinistic of all "big island" peoples, in order to offset their opposition from the Trinidadians. It is the stuff of which a good calypso could be made, and it could only happen in a metropolitan setting.

These subtle developments, then, have given the Toronto celebration a "made in Canada" quality. The politics of festivity reveal a great deal about how West Indians in urban Canada are going about the contentious business of dealing with each other, as well as about how they are coming to terms with Canadian society and negotiating places for themselves within it.

---

[1]I have done field research on the Toronto Caribana each summer since 1980, and have also been involved in promoting West Indian entertainment in London, Ontario. For financial support of the Toronto study, I am grateful to two sources at the University of Western Ontario: the Dean of Social Science and the Population Studies Centre.

[2]Ronald L. Grimes, *Beginnings in the Ritual Studies* (Washington, D.C.: University Press of America, 1982); Johan Huizinga, *Homo ludens: A Study of the Play Element in Culture* (Boston: Beacon Press, 1955).

[3]Abner Cohen, *Two-Dimensional Man: An Essay on the Anthropology of Power and Symbolism in Complex Society* (Berkeley and Los Angeles: University of California Press, 1974) and "Drama and Politics in the Development of a London Carnival," *Man* 15 (1980):65–87.

[4]This sentiment seems widely current among Trinidadians abroad. Cohen, for example, quotes a Trinidadian in London: "Carnival is in our blood. It is ours and cannot be taken away from us." Abner Cohen, "Drama and Politics," 73.

[5]Roger D. Abrahams, "Patterns of Performance in the British West Indies," in Norman E. Whitten and John F. Szwed, eds., *Afro-American Anthropology: Contemporary Perspectives* (New York: Free Press, 1970); Roger D. Abrahams and Richard Bauman, "Ranges of Festival Behavior," in Barbara Babcock, ed., *The Reversible World: Symbolic Inversion in Art and Society* (Ithaca and London: Cornell University Press, 1978); F. Manning, "Carnival in Antigua: An Indigenous Festival in a Tourist Economy," *Anthropos* 73 (1978):191–204; and K. de Albuquerque, "The Saint Thomas Carnival." Paper presented to the West Indian Association, East Lansing, Mich., 1979.

# Frank E. Manning

[6]Errol Hill, "The Trinidad Carnival: Mandate for a National Theatre (Austin: University of Texas Press, 1972), 99.

[7]Hill, "Trinidad Carnival" and A. Pearse, "Carnival in Nineteenth Century Trinidad," *Caribbean Quarterly* 4(1956):176–93.

[8]Victor Turner, *The Ritual Process: Structure and Anti-Structure* (Chicago: Aldine, 1969).

[9]B. Ostry, *The Cultural Connection* (Toronto: McClelland and Steward, 1978).

[10]Peter J. Wilson, *Crab Antics: The Social Anthropology of English-Speaking Peoples in the Caribbean* (New Haven and London: Yale University Press, 1973), 105–11.

[11]M. Solomon, "Is Caribana a True Reflection of Caribbean Culture?" *Contrast* (3 August 1979):10.

[12]I am told by Linda Basch that Trinidadians in New York are similarly preoccupied with calypso throughout the year. Personal communication, December 1981.

[13]Wilson, *Crab Antics*.

[14]O. Coombs, ed., *Is Massa Day Dead?* (New York: Doubleday Anchor, 1974), xv.

# Spacey Soviets and the Russian Attitude Toward Territorial Passage

Natalie K. Moyle

*Folklorists are not only interested in traditional behaviors but in the patterns of thought that underlie and inform those behaviors. The comprehensive set of assumptions, premises, or postulates that groups hold about themselves, their environment, space, time, and the world and the way that it is ordered is called a "world view" (Weltanschauung). How a people perceive and understand the world will in large measure determine their behavior in it (Kearney 1984:1). A world view, however, is only partly based in formal, explicit systems of philosophical reflection. It mostly consists of implicit concepts, concepts that group members are not aware that they hold and which they could not explicitly articulate were they asked to do so. While formal systems of mythology, religion, and philosophy are important for the delineation of a people's outlook toward the world, it is the unarticulated, abstract, unifying ideas underlying such systems that are at the core of world view.*

*The elements of a world view are usually inferred from the examination of a variety of traits and behaviors rather than any single one. After all, one is attempting to delineate a comprehensive orientation toward the world, not merely a tactical response to some particular circumstance. Natalie Moyle uses folktales, wedding customs, linguistic data, and literature, as well as political policy, to argue that ethnic Russians hold an attitude toward territorial passage that is not always shared by other Soviet ethnic populations. Moreover, this view contrasts dramatically with the American orientation. Perhaps these contrasting attitudes toward territorial passage signal Russian and American differences that are more fundamental than the formal contrasts between the political and economic ideologies of the two nations.*

*Alan Dundes has offered particularly intriguing analyses of folklore as the reflection of American world view (1980:69-85, 86-92, 134-59). For a somewhat different type of effort to grasp the nature of Russian and American difference in orientation, see Inkeles et al. (1958).*

All cultures establish territorial boundaries and assign special powers to boundary-crossers. This has been generally accepted since the days of Arnold Van Gennep and his *Rites of Passage* (1909). It is also widely accepted that the special attributes assigned to any "marked" object or person, such as a boundary-crosser, may be either positive or negative; they need not necessarily be one or the other, just as long as they are "special." This was also articulated as early as the nineteenth century in James George Frazer's numerous discussions of how taboo objects can both heal and destroy, protect and harm. As well-established as these premises may be as theory and as often as they have been refined and restated, such as in the work of Claude Lévi-Strauss, Mary Douglas, and others, they are not always easy to apply in practice.[1] A culture which assigns primarily positive attributes to boundary-crossing tends to assume similar values elsewhere. Thus Americans, to whom frontiers and the crossing of same is almost a national creed, assume similar attitudes in other national groups, such as the Russians. Were they to see the true nature of the Russian perception of crossing boundaries in space, then some of Soviet policy, both foreign and domestic, might be somewhat more comprehensible and predictable.

It is easy to demonstrate that boundary-crossers are something quite wonderful in our culture. The recent popular song, "New Kid in Town" by the Eagles, says so quite explicitly, "Johnny-Come-Lately," the "new kid in town," is someone "everybody loves" until "Somebody new comes along" and Johnny ceases to be interesting. The ideal American man is geographically mobile, be it the cowboy on his horse, the "Easy Rider" of the movie, or the corporate executive who relocates every several years as he moves up the corporate ladder. As a corollary, the epitome of financial and social success is to become a "jet setter." The great American hero, Superman, is not only someone unknown and mysterious, like a "new kid in town," but endowed with wonderful powers, all of which have something to do with motion, for he is "faster than a speeding bullet, more powerful than a locomotive, able to leap tall buildings in a single bound." Of course the most prized personal possession is a "set of wheels," Arab oil crisis not withstanding.

To Americans, travel, crossing territorial boundaries, going to new places, is a favorite form of recreation. Witness the travel advertisements in any mass communications medium and all of the tourist agencies. Travel is a desirable, if not almost essential, part of education. The "junior year abroad" is virtually an institution and universities such as my own invest an enormous amount of time and manpower into their study abroad programs. Even the ideal American home, as in "Home on the Range," is pictured as rather boundary-less and even crosses over into the wild because wild animals, buffalo, deer, and antelope, roam and play there. The ideal country, "America the Beautiful," stretches from "sea to shining sea" and encompasses a variety of possible geographical features, making it, too, seem territorially unrestricted, like the home. On the news media we hear that the 1980 census has established that Americans are the most mobile of all nationalities, with fully half of the country's population changing its place of residence between the 1970 census and the latest one. All of this fits well with Alan Dundes's article on the frontier mentality in American culture.[2]

To Russians, crossing boundaries in space does not have the same positive connotations. Boundary-crossers are special and powerful to be sure, but special and powerful in the negative sense. This can be seen in the rather extensive precautions taken against travelers. In the typical layout of a nineteenth century Russian peasant house, icons were located in the upper left hand corner of the room, opposite the door. In this position, they were supposed to be the first object to catch the eye of anyone entering the household and could thus protect it in case the person coming into the house was evil. Any stranger who did enter a household was fed at a table placed under these icons before he was even asked his name or the purpose of his journey.[3] This was not merely a polite gesture done out of consideration for the comfort of the traveler. This was also an attempt at self-protection. To Russians, food symbolism and food exchange are very important. If a stranger accepted and ate one's food, a double symbolic function would be served. First, by eating human food, the stranger would establish that he was human, and not an "unclean one" or devil. Emissaries of evil, like the undead, are notoriously incapable of ingesting human food, as in our vampire movies where Dracula states, "I don't drink . . . wine." Second, if a stranger accepted one's food, he would establish a bond of indebtedness that would oblige him not to harm the source of the food that he had eaten. Such efforts at testing strangers and insuring their good will would not be necessary if fear of strangers did not exist.

While behavior toward strangers may only hint that Russians associate them with evil, folktales state so quite openly. In fact, folktales add the information that the particular category of evil in which Russians place strangers and travelers is that of the unquiet dead. Any ghoul or other monster is almost invariably a stranger who arrives from out of town. One example is the very frightening story of a girl who goes to a quilting bee. After the girls work for a while, the local village boys bring vodka and music and join the girls in merry-making. Somewhat after this, a handsome stranger walks in and pays particular attention to the heroine. She is delighted and tells her mother, but the mother, who is older, wiser, and knows better about travelers, cautions the girl to observe carefully where the stranger goes after he leaves her. She follows her mother's instructions and catches her suitor eating the flesh of a corpse left overnight in the church before burial.[4] The story is a long one, describing the ordeals the girl must suffer to rid herself of this stranger. Her ordeals include the death of her parents and, later, her husband and child. It cannot be retold here for want of space. The point, however, seems to be clear: any fully acculturated member of Russian society knows to associate strangers and travelers with ghouls.

In Russian folktales, not only are people who come into the village from outside suspect; anyone who has left home and traveled, thus crossing boundaries in space, seems to be incapable of returning to the village except as one of the unquiet dead. An example is the story of a young wife who pines for her husband away from home. She grieves so much that he starts appearing to her at night. She is delighted, but her neighbors notice her growing paler and weaker day by day. Needless to say, the husband turns out to be dead and returned as a vampire, draining his wife of her vital essence in typical vampire fashion.[5] The dead that return home are harmful even if they are not inherently evil and there is no indication of their connection to evil while they were alive. The mere fact of return seems to make the person destructive to the living. This is clearest in stories of the dead who return to do good, such as tales of mothers who come back from the grave to suckle their infants. Anyone who sees such a woman kneeling by her baby's crib at midnight is doomed to sicken and die.[6]

Because anyone who crosses territorial boundaries is as good as dead and those who leave the village cannot return, particularly in memorat type tales, Russian soldier stories are quite different from Western folktales on the same topic. Tales in collections such as Grimm's *Kinder-und Hausmärchen* picture the jolly traveling soldier-trickster. Russian tales of this type are few. Instead, there are several rather pathetic ones which tell of a soldier being released from duty, traveling home and, at the last minute, being way-laid by the devil and never reaching his destination. One man is tricked into playing his fiddle for what seems to be hours, but turns out to be years.[7] Another is talked into drinking three glasses of wine, each of which makes one hundred years pass.[8] Another is tricked into marrying one of the Devil's daughters. He almost disenchants her, but forgets one of the Devil's prohibitions as he begins to relax in her company and disappears.[9] One man makes it all the way back home, but it is now a place that might as well be the land of the dead. His village is completely deserted because it has been taken over by the soldier's grandfather, a wizard who died and came back as one of the unquiet dead and either killed or frightened away everyone in the village.[10] Our assumption that anyone who leaves the village, like a soldier, is as good as dead is confirmed by stories about soldiers' sons. Apparently designating someone a soldier's son is but another way of designating him an orphan.[11]

There is one type of Russian folktale character who can travel and cross boundaries and still not be vulnerable, like the soldier, or death-dealing, like the returning husband or mother. This is the figure of the saint who walks the earth. It is instructive that even saints, although they are substantially different from other boundary-crossers, are, nevertheless, associated with the dead. After all, the saints are themselves dead, at least in their human aspect. Further, they are a part of Heaven and that is the realm of the souls of the virtuous deceased, not the realm of man.

The Russian attitude toward people who are territorially removed can even be exemplified by linguistic means, such as the terminology for nationalities. Only the word for "Russian" is an adjective, modifying the understood noun "human being." All other nationalities are designated by nouns, a grammatical peculiarity that seems to imply that all non-Russians are something other than human. Moreover, the first foreigners encountered extensively on Russian soil in the post-Tatar period, the Germans, are called "nemets" from "nemoi" (deaf and dumb). The implication here seems to be that, since their language was non-Russian, it was essentially non-existent.

With the Russian attitude toward others who crossed territorial boundaries being so negative that they associated travelers with the dead and the non-human, it follows that Russians themselves were very reluctant to make any sort of movement in space. In the Tsarist period, there was a day, called the Day of St. Igor, when serfs were allowed to move from one landowner's property to that of another to improve their lot. Considering the Russian attitude toward territorial passage, this was a safe institution and did not cause a depletion of serfs on the lands of even the cruelest nobleman. There is even a proverb, "Vot tebe babushka i Igorev den'!" Literally, it translates, "Well,

Grandma, that's the Day of St. Igor for you," but it is used to refer to, not so much lost, as unrealized and unrealizable opportunity.[12]

It is no surprise that the great Russian explorers, like the famous Bering after whom the Sea and Strait are named, are not really Russians at all. Bering was an ethnic Swede. A great early Russian ethnographer who traveled extensively among the Siberian Turkic peoples was named Willhelm Radloff. He was German and even wrote his studies in German, although they were sponsored by the Russians and published by them.[13] A folklorist who traveled to the north and became one of the best collectors of Russian epic had the very un-Russian name, Hilferding.[14] The other great nineteenth century collector of epics, Rybnikov, an ethnic Russian, went to the north because he was exiled there, not on his own initiative, and started recording epic by chance.[15]

If one looks through the *Great Soviet Encyclopedia*, a document which tends to claim that the Russians did everything first, discovered everything first, and checks for Russian explorers, the results are amazing. A substantial number are not even of Russian, but of Germanic or Baltic birth. Many are Russian-born, but are not ethnically Russian, coming from immigrant families. The list of explorers in the encyclopedia index is dominated by such non-Russian sounding names as Bell, Bellinghausen, Bergholz, Bering, Gmelin, Hofman, Guldenstaedt, Kolsebus, Krenkel, Kruzenstern, Laksman, Lindenau, Litke, Maak, Matisen, Middendorf, Pallas, and Weber. Some of the more Russian sounding names are listed as pseudonyms with real name and date and place of birth not known. Of the few that were true, ethnic Russians, some were captured and forced to travel; a number were Cossacks, thus already belonging to a liminal group before they made themselves more liminal by traveling. Another group of the ethnic Russians are listed as having moved to Europe and died abroad. Possibly these were people who were not fully in harmony with the Russian world view and thus chose to live elsewhere. The number of ethnic Russians who came from and remained in the Russian mainstream and were also travelers and explorers is small indeed.[16]

Even Russian literature, the province of the gentry who were at least partially under Western influence, articulates a distaste for territorial mobility and perhaps even an inability to travel. In Chekhov's *Three Sisters*, everyone keeps talking about going to Moscow and how this will change everything for the better. But like the peasants who only uttered proverbs about St. Igor's Day but never actually moved, so no one goes anywhere in Chekhov's play. The novelist Goncharov was forced to travel to the East and wrote a book expressing his displeasure with the voyage, *The Journey of the Frigate Pallada*. Goncharov's second and most famous novel, *Oblomov* was, as Mirsky points out, immediately sensed to symbolize one side of the Russian character.[17] Although this side is usually labelled "sloth," it can be argued that Oblomov is not so much slothful, as he is an extreme example of what we have been discussing here: the bond to one place and the inability to budge from it. To give just one piece of supporting evidence, as the novel progresses, Oblomov is restricted, or rather restricts himself, to a smaller and smaller area until he finally just stays in bed. As might be expected, the character in the book who personifies the opposite extreme, who moves and is very active and tries to get Oblomov to do and to be the same, is the very Western, in fact Germanic, Stolz.

The extremely strong Russian bond between person and place may well be the reason for the plethora of Russian place spirits: spirits of the house, the barn, and drying barn, the bath house, and even each river, forest, and field. These were not remnants of ancestor cults, as previously assumed.[18] They were not even anthropomorphizations so much as spirits that embodied the essence of whatever place they inhabited and represented. Their existence shows that Russians saw each locale as a vital entity with which one had an I-Thou, rather than an I-it, relationship, to borrow the Frankforts' terminology.[19]

The Russian attitude toward motion in space, like the Russian attitude toward people who engage in such motion, can be corroborated by examining linguistic phenomena. The Russian verb system is complex, but the system of motion verbs, which exists as a separate category, is doubly so. In addition to the distinction between a single, completed act and an action which lacks these features, characteristic of the regular Russian verb system, motion verbs distinguish unidirectional motion from anything that is not unidirectional, be it random motion or round-trip motion. Since any area where a language makes a number of distinctions tends to be an important one for the corresponding culture, the complexity of the Russian motion verb system indicates that this is just such an area. In addition, the difference between the Russian unidirectional/nonunidirectional distinction and the English one of motion toward the speaker (come, bring) and motion away from the speaker (go, take) shows that Russian and English perspectives on movement in space diverge significantly. To Russians, the crucial factor is not the "to where" of motion, but the "how," and perhaps even the mere fact of movement.

Although Russians may have feared those who crossed territorial boundaries and may have shunned travel, under certain circumstances, they simply could not avoid motion in space. The ritual activity performed on these occasions and for people caught in these circumstances is perhaps the clearest indicator of the Russian attitude toward motion across territorial boundaries. The most striking rituals are the funeral-like marriage rites performed for brides. At marriage, brides left their households of birth to travel and join the households of their husbands. This journey from one household to the other was pivotal to the exogamous social structure and deeply woven into the fabric of the culture. Yet, even though it was so important and indicated the continued successful functioning of the social system, it was treated as an event of great sadness, rather than one of great joy. The death symbolism in the rites for Russian brides goes far beyond the death and rebirth motifs common to all rites of passage. In fact, there is little rebirth symbolism, while the funerary aspects are extensive, including the bride's abstaining from food and work during the period between betrothal and marriage and behaving as a non-functioning member of the household, as if she were dead. On the night before the wedding, there is ritual washing and dressing of the bride, as of a corpse. In fact, a woman wears her wedding dress twice, at her marriage and at her funeral. There are extensive laments by and for the bride. The bride was even taken from the house the same way that a corpse was removed; through an unusual aperture such as a window. The door, which was used for normal human passage, could not be used for brides and corpses.[20]

Further evidence that the bride's movement in space was considered akin to death can be found in the fact that the marriage rites for the groom were negligible. Since the groom also made the transition from single to married status and the one real difference between him and the bride was that he stayed where he was while she moved, it seems that precisely this fact of territorial passage required treatment of the bride as dead. Finally, it is significant that women, having once "died" at marriage, were not given elaborate funerals. These were reserved for normal men who never made any territorial passage away from home until their souls left to journey to the world of the dead. The complimentary distribution of ritual and the relative importance of wedding rites for women and funeral rites for men is mirrored by laments which divide by sex so that most laments for women are sung at their marriage and laments for men, at death. In both cases, the lamenters are married women. In funeral laments, a standard portion is the description of the path to the land of the dead. This description is supposed to guide the soul of the deceased on its journey.[21] If the guide in any ritual observance is someone who has already made the transition in question, then married women must be like the dead, having died at marriage, in order to be able to serve as guides at the funerals of men.

Besides brides and the dead, the other two categories of people who were lamented were recruits and men forced by poverty to go and work on someone else's land. The trait that these two groups share with each other and with brides is movement in space. Laments for recruits may have made sense for reasons other than the association between territorial passage and death. After all, military service was for twenty years and chances really were that sending a son into the army was sending him to his death. Even if a son did return safely from the military, for his family he was as good as dead in the sense that he was not a functioning member of the household for a major portion of his adult life. While the motivation for laments for recruits may be logical, this is not true of laments for laborers. In their case, the primary reason for death motifs seems to be territorial passage. Laments for laborers have been explained by Soviet scholars as a protest against the oppression and exploitation of the poor by the rich, but this is a weak explanation and the territorial passage-death association seems to be a sounder one.[22] For one thing, not all landlords were cruel, or evil, or sought only to exploit. For another, the places where laborers went to work were often not far away enough to preclude contact between the family and its departed member. There was no practical reason for the finality of separation that laments for departing laborers would imply.

Linguistic phenomena can again be used as supporting evidence. There are two Russian words for "good bye." One is the "until I see you again" term common to so many languages (*do svidaniia* or *poka*). The other is the imperative of the verb "to forgive" (*proschchai*). The latter is used for the dead and for the categories discussed above: brides, recruits, and laborers. The implication is that if the departed forgave those whom he or she left behind, all debts would be absolved and there would be no need to return and haunt those left behind. The existence of these two leave-taking terms not only puts boundary-crossers in a special category and links them with the dead; it restates one of the phenomena discussed earlier in connection with fairy-tales: a fear of the return of anyone in the deceased or boundary-crosser categories.

In the present day, Soviet official policy emphasizes rational thought and freedom from unconscious associations, such as that between territorial passage and death. This is one of the reasons why most of the data used here was taken from nineteenth and early twentieth century sources. Nonetheless, crossing boundaries in space remains as terrifying to Russians as ever. It is interesting that the best evidence for this comes, not from ethnographies of daily life, the kind of material used up to this point, but from Soviet government decisions and actions. It is hard to say to what extent the Soviets are consciously aware of what they are doing, but there is no doubt that they use territorial passage, usually termed exile under these circumstances, as a means of punishment. Exile as punishment is a Russian tradition and something the Soviets inherited from the tsars. Virtually everyone from Pushkin to Lenin was exiled, either outside of the country or to non-Russian, mostly Turkic, areas under Russian control. In fact Lenin, the pseudonym under which Vladimir Il'ich Ulianov became famous, was derived in accordance with the tradition followed by Pushkin and Lermontov. They assigned names to the heroes of their novels which were based on the names of rivers in the areas where they were exiled (Onegin from Onega and Pechorin from Pechora). Following this pattern, Lenin took his name from the river Lena.

The exile of Soviet dissidents routinely makes the headlines today. The difference between the American attitude toward this policy and the Soviet one brings us back to the difference in perspectives on territorial passage presented at the beginning of this study. Americans feel that this is a wonderful concession which they have won from the Soviets. They perceive the dissidents not as exiles who are forced to leave, but as beneficiaries of a softening in the Soviet hard line who are given their freedom and allowed to leave. Consequently, they feel that the dissidents should be terribly pleased with their chance to escape to the West and are baffled by the reluctance of many of them to leave. A member of the United States State Department recounted a touching story of a Soviet dissident bound hand and foot and forcibly ejected from a plane in Vienna. The fact that the man had to be coerced to go to the West was incomprehensible to the American audience who heard this story.[23] Americans feel that Solzhenitsyn's talent should flower now that he has the artistic freedom of the West and cannot understand his statements about how be needs contact with Russian soil to write.

Part of the American puzzlement with the reactions of Soviet exiles comes from a belief in the superiority of the American system coupled with the conviction that it would be the preferred mode of life of anyone who had a free choice. But part of the problem is an almost complete lack of awareness of the significantly different value Russians assign to territorial passage. Needless to say, for Soviets, letting dissidents emigrate is not as great a concession as Westerners might imagine and it should be noted that forcible motion in space is routinely used to punish people who are not expelled from the country. In fact, the Soviets seem to sense that while motion over great distances and to non-Russian areas is the most painful, any territorial passage, even over limited distances, is traumatic. Thus Gorky, the place to which Andrei Sakharov is exiled, is not far from Moscow and yet everyone reacts to this relocation of the dissident physicist as a severe punitive act.

Americans may be oblivious to the fact that cultural groups which differ from theirs have different attitudes toward territorial passage. Soviets, however, are also not immune from the same narrowness of perspective and use motion as punishment on both groups that share their concept of boundary crossing and groups that do not. One troublesome ethnic group, the Crimean Tatars, was "relocated" from one geographical area to another that would ostensibly put them closer to other Turkic groups and permit their culture to flourish. Apparently the Crimean Tatars are an ethnic group which shares the Russian dread of territorial passage because this move effectively killed the group off. While the conditions under which the relocation of the Crimean Tatars was accomplished were terrible indeed, with people crowded into railroad cars like cattle and deprived of proper nutrition, sanitary facilities and even enough room to sleep, the real horror that destroyed this group seems to be the horror of territorial passage. This is shown by the fact that among those who survived the trip and were supposedly successfully relocated, reproduction rate was extremely low and mortality extremely high. The Crimean Tatars are said to have suffered a great deal of Soviet persecution. They seem to have endured it up until this forced relocation. This was the final blow. Territorial passage seems to have made them feel that they were as good as dead and destroyed their survival capacity.[24]

A different effect seems to have been achieved in the case of the Jews. The Soviet willingness to let Jews emigrate, reluctant though it be, is at least partially based on the unconscious idea that letting someone travel in space is punishment akin to death. Fortunately, the Jews do not seem to share the Slavic movement in space-death association and Jewish émigrés have not suffered as much as ethnic Russians like Solzhenitsyn.

We have discussed the variety of possible perspectives on marked phenomena, such as territorial passage, and have emphasized the differences between cultures, specifically Russian and American. But, as we do this, we should not forget that both positive and negative reactions occur within a culture, as well as cross-culturally. Thus owning one's own home, complete with picket fence, is as much of an American dream as owning a "set of wheels" or traveling on vacation. The detrimental effect that the relocation of corporate executives can have on their personal lives has not gone unnoticed. Even the boy or girl "next door" may be attractive, not just the "new kid in town." In spite of all these disclaimers, there does seem to be a "core" American attitude toward boundary-crossing and an almost inverse core Russian attitude toward the same phenomenon. To sum up these core attitudes and the contrast between them, we can recount an anecdote from diplomatic circles which describes what happens when an American and a Russian greet each other in a doorway. The American instinctively reaches out across the threshold because this is the proper and polite gesture of welcome. The Russian just as instinctively feels that touching another person across a boundary, such as a doorway, is taboo. Thus he either tries to pull the American over to his side of the threshold or to jump in and join him on the side where he is standing; much to the consternation of the American, of course.

[1] Arnold van Gennep, *The Rites of Passage*, trans. Monika B. Vizedom and Gabrielle L. Caffee (Chicago: University of Chicago Press, 1960); James G. Frazer, *The Golden Bough*, 2 vols. (London 1890); Claude Lévi-Strauss, "The Structural Study of Myth," in his *Structural Anthropology*, trans. Claire Jacobson and Broolre Grundfest Schoepf (Garden City, N.Y.: Anchor, 1967), pp. 202–228; Mary Douglas, *Purity and Danger: An Analysis of Concepts of Pollution and Taboo* (London: Routledge, 1966).

[2] Alan Dundes, "Thinking Ahead: A Folkloristic Reflection on the Future Orientation in American Worldview," *Anthropological Quarterly*, 42(1969), 53–72; rpt. in Alan Dundes, *Interpreting Folklore* (Bloomington: Indiana University Press, 1980), pp.69–85.

[3] Sergei Aleksandrovich Tokarev, *Etnografiia narodov SSSR* (Ethnography of the Peoples of the USSR) (Moscow: Izdatel'stvo moskovskogo universiteta, 1958). See the section on buildings and housing among the East Slavs, pp. 51–71. See also B. E. Blomkvist, "Krestianskie postroiki russkikh, ukraintsev i belorusov" (Peasant buildings of the Russians, Ukrainians and Belorussians), *Vostochnoslavianskii etnograficheskii sbornik* (Ethnography of the East Slavs). Trudy instituta etnografii., Vol. 31 (Moscow: Izdatel's stvo akademii nauk SSSR, 1956), pp. 212–251; and P. I. Kushner, ed., *Materialy i issledovaniia po etnograffii russkogo naseleniia evropeiskoi chasti SSSR* (Materials and studies on the Russian population of the European part of the USSR), same series as above, Vol. 57 (Moscow, 1960), pp. 15–44.

[4] A. N. Afanas'ev, *Narodnye russkie skazki* (Russian Folktales) (Moscow: Gosudarstvennoe izdatel'stvo khudozhestvennoi literatury, 1957), Vol. 3, Tale 363, pp. 121–127.

[5] Afanas'ev, Vol. 3, Tale 373, p. 145.

[6] Afanas'ev, Vol. 3, Tale 361, pp. 122–123.

[7] Afanas'ev, Vol. 1, Tale 154, pp. 345–318.

[8] Afanas'ev, Vol. 3, Tale 358, pp. 120–121.

[9] Afanas'ev, Vol. 1, Tale 154, pp. 345–318. Also 813A Accursed Daughter.

[10] Afanas'ev, Vol, 3, Tale 355, pp. 116–118.

[11] Afanas'ev, Vol, 1, Tale 155, pp. 319–357.

[12] Y. M. Sokolov, *Russian Folklore*, translated by Catherine Ruth Smith (Detroit: Folklore Associates, 1971), pp. 263–264.

[13] Willhelm Radloff, *Proben der Volksliteratur der türkischen Stämme* (Studies in the Folk Literature of the Turkic Tribes) (St. Petersburg; Commissioner der Kaiserlichen Akademie der Wissenschaften, 1866-1907), in 10 volumes.

[14] A. F. Hilferding, *Onezhskie byliny zapisannye letom 1871* (Onega epics collected in the summer of 1871) (Moscow-Leningrad: Akademia nauk SSSR, 1949-51;4th edition), in 3 volumes.

[15] P. N. Rybnikov, *Pesni sobrannye 1861-1867* (Songs collected 1861-1867) (Moscow-St. Petersburg: Akademiia nauk, 1909), in 4 volumes.

[16] *Bol'shaia Sovetskaia Entsiklopediia* (The Great Soviet Encyclopedia), A. M. Prokhorov, ed. (Moscos: Izdatel'stvo Sovetskaia Entsiklopediia, 1970-78), in 30 volumes. See also temporary *Index* to volumes 1-25 of the English translation (New York and London: Macmillian, Collier and Macmillian, 1981).

[17] D. S. Mirsky, *A History of Russian Literature*, ed. and abridged by Francis J. Whitfield (New York: Alfred A. Knopf, 1964), p. 182.

[18] E. V. Pomerantseva, *Mifologicheskie personazhi v russkom folklore* (Mythological characters in Russian folklore) (Moscow: Nauka, 1975). See also A. N. Afanas'ev, *Poeticheskoe vozzrenie slavian na prirodu* (The Poetic Outlook of the Slavs on Nature) (Moscow: Izdanie K. Soldatenkova, 1865-1869), in 3 volumes.

[19] H. and H. A. Frankfort, "Myth and Reality," in Henri Frankfort et al., *Before Philosophy: The Intellectual Adventures of Ancient Man* (Baltimore: Penguin, 1949), pp. 12–16.

[20]Sokolov, *Russian Folklore*, pp. 203–223. See also Tokarev, *Prichitaniia severnogo kraia* (Laments of the northern region), Vol. III (Moscow: Chtenii v obshchestve Istorii i drevnostei pri Moskovskom universitete, 1886).

[21]Barsov, *Prichitaniia,* Vol 1, 1872. See also Sokolov, *Russian Folklore*, pp. 224–234.

[22]Barsov, *Prichitaniia,* Vol. 11, 1882. See also Sokolov, *Russian Folklore*, pp. 235–240.

[23]Igor Belusovich, "The Role of Dissent in Soviet Society," lecture sponsored by the Center for Russian and East European Studies, University of Virginia, September 29, 1980.

[24]Edige Kirimal, "The Crimean Turks," in *Genocide in the USSR: Studies in Group Destruction,* ed. by Nikolai K. Deker and Andrei Lebed (New York: The Scarecrow Press, 1958), pp. 20–29. See also V. Stanley Vardys, "The Case of the Crimean Tatars," *Russian Review* XXX (April 1971), 101–110. Alan Fisher, *The Crimean Tatars* (Stanford: Hoover Institution Press, 1978).

# III
# Religious Folklore

## Brothers and Sisters:  Pentecostals as a Religious Folk Group
### Elaine J. Lawless

*A group with a consciousness of kind inevitably will display its identity. Identity may be performed exclusively within the group for the group (as in the case of secret societies), or it may be performed exclusively for outsiders (as in the case of "Turtles," a club whose entire culture consists of a ritual to make non-members into members [Bauman 1970]). Usually, the performance of group identity involves both signs and displays for outsiders as well as for those within the group.*

*A variety of verbal, behavioral, and artifactual expressions may serve to signal identity. Identity may also be marked through non-behaviors—by the avoidance or omission of certain verbal, behavioral, or artifactual expressions. In this sense, it is the non-performance of certain behaviors that constitutes the performance of identity. For example, it may be part of a Swedish-American's expression of identity to offer a guest a cup of coffee. It may be part of a Mormon's display of identity never to do so.*

*The association of holiness with separation is well established in the Judeo-Christian tradition. In the pursuit of holiness and salvation, various groups have tried to separate themselves from the world. Some groups separate themselves geographically and attempt to minimize their interaction with those around them. Others, such as the group of Pentecostals described below, are determined to maintain a presence within the larger community. They signal their separation by other means; through their dress, language, comportment, and ritual. The ridicule of these behaviors by the larger community further serves to reinforce their sense of separation and to enhance the sense of spiritual kinship and identity. For more on Pentecostals see Lawless (1980, 1983), Kane (1974), and Clements (1981).*

> We go into restaurants and people want to know what kind of religion we are, not because what we look like but because they feel a joy about us.[1]

Reproduced by permission of the California Folklore Society, from *Western Folklore* 42, no. 2(1983):85–104. Not for further reproduction.

Elaine J. Lawless

Pentecostals are acutely aware of the many stereotypes, fears, and apprehensions that non-Pentecostals share about them. They realize that most non-believers find their beliefs and their religious behavior strange at best and abhorrent and primitive at worst. Strong anti-Pentecostal sentiment from outsiders only feeds the fire of Pentecostalism, however, and is proof enough for them that they are a special religious group.[2] The differences between Pentecostals and non-Pentecostals become exaggerated as the in-group strives to establish its identity as different from other groups.[3] In general, the conscious Pentecostal removal from the world, their vehement rejection of it, and their refusal to participate in it establish a convenient boundary between "them" and "us." And, as Max Weber indicates, it is, then, an easy step to making rejection of the world the sure path to salvation.[4] This gives Pentecostals the added benefit of believing they are not only special but are the ones likely to be "saved," while the rest of mankind, happily participating in the world, will eventually suffer an eternity in hell. The various religious behaviors exhibited by Pentecostals are further proof of their specialness and help to stabilize their group identification. This article will examine how the Pentecostal system of traditions operates to maintain boundaries between Pentecostals and the "outside world."[5]

The stereotypes of Pentecostals by non-Pentecostals, and those held by Pentecostals about the rest of the world feed on each other. They are in diametric opposition, as might be expected. In examining the manner in which ethnic groups identify themselves and establish and maintain boundaries between themselves and others, Frederick Barth states that "to the extent that actors use ethnic identities to categorize themselves and others for purposes of interaction, they form ethnic groups in the organizational sense."[6] And he isolates two factors relating to the cultural content of ethnic identities: (1) the overt signs and signals that people look for and exhibit to indicate identity (these include such features as dress, language and life-style); and (2) basic value orientations, the standards of morality and excellence by which performance is judged.[7] Barth's major contention is that if groups are viewed as exclusive units, then it becomes essential that we explore the means of boundary maintenance between these groups. While ethnicity scholars do not recognize religious communities as "ethnic" groups, they do recognize that in many respects they are similar to ethnic groups.[8] Particularly in the case of Pentecostals, where language, dress, behavior and ethics mark them as distinctly different from other groups adjacent to them in the modern American milieu, it behooves us to apply Barth's conceptions of ethnic groups and to recognize the importance of boundary establishment and maintenance for the perpetuation of group identity.

Pentecostals are aware of the stereotype that all Pentecostals are poor, uneducated, and are drawn to a charismatic religion because they have nothing better. This stereotype, as it exists in southern Indiana, is based largely on the way Pentecostals dress. Most of the communities in this area are typical midwestern farming communities. Pentecostals look different from others in the community because of the dress codes they have adopted. In general, their dress can be characterized as reminiscent of fashionable styles of about thirty years ago. Pentecostal women always wear dresses, and the dresses they wear are usually of somber colors, fall well below the knees, have long sleeves and high necklines. Outside the home, Pentecostal women are most likely to wear shoes with heels and nylon stockings. Especially in the hot summer months, Pentecostal dress is easily recognizable. Pentecostal women wear no jewelry or make-up, and because they are not allowed to cut their hair, their hair either falls down their backs or is piled high on their heads in a 1950-ish "beehive" hairstyle. It is evident that modern fashion does not dictate what Pentecostal women wear or what they look like. Similarly, Pentecostal men will have shorter hair-cuts than other men in the community and will be clean-shaven; it is not uncommon for Pentecostal men to sport a "burr" or "flat-top" hair-cut. Their clothing, too, is recognizable, as they are most likely to "go to town" in black pants, a white shirt, white socks and black shoes. Even Pentecostal young men are not likely to wear blue jeans for fashion, although they may actually work in them.

From the outsider's point of view, the Pentecostal manner of dressing is a mark of the lower-class. Pentecostals are associated with poor people everywhere who wear old clothes out of necessity and who do not sport fashionable hair-styles because of a lack of opportunity or sophistication. But for the adherents of Pentecostalism, dress embodies an entire complex of notions about "holiness" and what a Pentecostal man or woman represents to the rest of the world and to fellow Pentecostals.

Being a model for others to see, attaining perfection in this life, and extolling "holiness" were the attributes sought by those involved in the nineteenth-century Holiness Movement.[9] The first edicts John Wesley outlined as necessary for sanctification were adopted and elaborated by the Holiness leaders. The strict doctrines of Christian Holiness specifically forbad drinking, dancing, theatre-going, card-playing, and swearing, and outlined restrictions on the dress of believers, especially the women. The term "holiness" as employed by modern Pentecostals still embodies many of the attitudes embraced by the early Holiness movement. A Pentecostal woman defined what "holiness" means to her:

> And the holiness thing...I don't ever want to offend my brother...I don't ever want to offend anyone. I feel like if my dress sleeves are here [motions to elbow] and it would offend my brother, I would put them down to here [motions to wrist]; that's basically how I feel about it.[10]

Pentecostal dress is also a statement to other Pentecostals that the believer is willing to sacrifice all notions of fashion for notions of "holiness." Long sleeves and a high neckline signal to Pentecostals a woman's knowledge of the Pentecostal doctrines and her sincere effort to abide by them. In this sense, dress acts as a cohesive bond between Pentecostal women. They, too, can recognize Pentecostal believers in the context of a grocery or a restaurant. But dress also serves as a comment on the immoral attitudes and styles of the rest of the community. Long skirts and sleeves and high necklines accentuate the short skirts and shorts on the public streets, the bra-less girls, the daring necklines. Denying the fashions that focus on the female body, and electing, instead, to make a comment for the Lord is seen as the most admirable sacrifice. Non-Pentecostals

Elaine J. Lawless

are not blind to the comments Pentecostals make about the life-style of the rest of the world. Not surprisingly, they become offended and become self-conscious about their own dress and behavior. This is, of course, the intent of the Pentecostals—to draw attention to the dress of others through their own. The medium for their message is most effective. It is difficult to flaunt immodest apparel in front of nuns and Pentecostal ladies.

At the same time that Pentecostals are creating distinctive models for members to follow which will differentiate them from other groups and individuals, they are aware that many outsiders consider their behavior "weird."

> I think the thing most misunderstood about Pentecost people, they, a lot of people, look at them like they are maybe a freak and that they are completely different from other people "in the world." And because of our standards that are set up, the Bible tells us we should be a modest and moderate people and we set a standard that might seem extreme to the "outside world" when actually we feel that it's a moderation in the church.[11]

By creating standards that are extreme to the outsider, Pentecostals create distinctive boundaries between themselves and others. They recognize that these stereotypes often become distorted and create negative images that are difficult to combat. The balance between "different" and "freakish" is not an easy one to maintain. Yet, when others find them weird and extreme, it serves to draw attention to the group as well. In fact, by creating a group image that is so clearly the antithesis of modern America, they are also establishing a mechanism for the defense of the group.

Dress is only one aspect of the Pentecostal comment on and public rejection of the evils of the world. The blanket refusal of Pentecostals to participate in modern American amusements and entertainments is often translated by non-Pentecostals into fear and intimidation. The rejection of such all-American activities as movies, ball games, card playing, liquor drinking, dancing, swearing, and television viewing by Pentecostals causes a good deal of resentment on the part of those who swear, go to movies, love ball games, cards, drinking, and dancing. It is an open attack on American life and a Pentecostal comment on what they view as the debauchery and squalor of most American people's lives. As with their dress, Pentecostals use their own rejection of the ways of the world as a comment on the sad lives of the people "in the world" and as a means of enhancing their own sense of group identity at the same time. Outsiders are often intimidated by the exclusive nature of the Pentecostal community, its devotion to the church, rejection of worldly matters, and the incredible sense of family and mutual support it conveys. Historically, asceticism on any level has elicited admiration for the diligent self-sacrificer as well as enmity, stemming from jealousy and feelings of inadequacy from the non-ascetics.

Pentecostals do not participate "in the world" because they have been given the special status of knowing "the truth" and the promise of salvation. One young Pentecostal articulates how believers manipulate stereotypes to conform to esoteric notions of an elected few:

> Everyone looked at Pentecostals as an uneducated misinformed people, under-privileged. That was what Pentecost was represented as. They were people who had nothing else to go to except this weird religion . . . but God had to find a people that wanted him above anything else . . . and he got that people and he grew them into a beautiful family that would turn around and tell the world what we've got is the message for the end time.[12]

Because Pentecostals have been given an order by God to witness to non-believers and try to convert them before "the end time," dress and deportment take on special significance within the Pentecostal community. The life of a "Saint" (a Pentecostal believer) is a model and a witness to all who might observe that life. Saints have a duty to act like saints at all times. They must be prepared to go out into the world, but they must never join the world or participate in it under penalty of hell and rejection by Jesus. Being a model begins very early for the Pentecostal believer. The following story relates how Pentecostal mothers convey to their children the seriousness of their actions.

> And my first son, probably one of his biggest disappointments was he came in and said, "Well, next week is the prom and I'm going." And I said, "All right, you can. Fine, it's all right. You go to the prom, Tony," and I said, "but I want to talk to you about it a little bit." And I go upstairs and said, "You know you can't go to the prom and play your trumpet in church. Now, you're welcome to go to the prom, but you cannot grace the front of the church, anymore, if you go." And he said, "All right." And he didn't go, and I was real proud of him.[13]

Of course, the boy is not actually "welcome" to go to the dance. He fully understands the implications of what his mother says to him. If he goes, he is not a good model to others and it would be wrong, therefore, for him to "grace the front of the church" and play his trumpet in some sort of pretense that he is a model Pentecostal.

The Pentecostal insistence on conformity of dress and public behavior, control of young church members, and complete devotion of members to the Pentecostal group have led to the stereotype that Pentecostals are somehow dangerous. Pentecostals are acutely aware that many people think of Pentecostalism as a "cult," and in recent times have had to fight what they view as an unpleasant stereotype. The belief that Pente-costals are dangerous is reinforced by the evangelistic nature of their faith. For non-Pentecostals, the constant, public proselytizing of Pentecostals is an affront. Pentecostals are seen as pushy, brash, and intolerant of other viewpoints. For the Pentecostal, however, evangelizing is a duty. Theirs is not a religion to keep under lock and key; it is not possible to sit back and rest serene in the knowledge of sure salvation. For Pentecostals believe they are under direct orders from God to save as many souls as they can. They take this commission very seriously. And they are fully aware of the stereotypes that arise from their persistence. But, again, this only serves to further unite them in their evangelistic mission. "Did you get rejected today by the man at work? Do you tire of the ridicule you receive as you try to spread God's word?" questions a Pentecostal preacher as he reassures his flock that "God knows how hard

we're trying. Bug that guy until you break him down. He'll thank you in the end."
Perseverance in the face of distrust, dislike, and ridicule brings Pentecostals closer
together as a group.

Pentecostal dress, rejection of the world, and persistent proselytizing all contribute
to the "holier than thou" attitude that is difficult for outsiders to accept. Pentecostals
generally cultivate this stereotype with pride within their own ranks. It is, in fact, one
of the most effective means of creating importance for a group. Sacrifice, martyrdom,
self-denial, and abnegation are easy routes to self-aggrandizement and inflated notions
of worth. Verbal discourse to this effect pervades Pentecostal church services and must
be recognized as a primary benefit for persons seeking feelings of self-worth, as well as
for the part this attitude plays in establishing group identity. Even so, Pentecostals are
not unaware of the negative effect this stereotype can have and may try to offset it,
primarily because of the adverse effect it may have on potential converts.

> For a long time people looked at Pentecost and they thought, "Oh, you're too
> holy to touch," but that's not the truth, that's not the way it is.[14]

But more than dress, rejection of the world, and persistent evangelizing, it is
Pentecostal religious behavior that has cultivated the most negative stereotypes and
the most animosity from outsiders. Pentecostal church services are characterized as
wild, frenetic, crazy, unbelievable, immoral, unseemly, vulgar, emotional, uncontrollable, and dangerous, especially when attendance reaches into the hundreds. These
attributes associated with Pentecostals are all the more difficult to comprehend when
placed in juxtaposition with the holy asceticism described above. While their dress and
rejection of the world may have earned for them the "holier-than-thou" accusation,
their charismatic religious behavior has earned them the epithet "Holy Rollers."
Although Pentecostals are aware of the wide-spread use of the term, it is not a term
they have adopted for themselves, even though they openly condone and strive for the
expressive, uninhibited behaviors exhibited in their services.

> People call the Pentecostals "Holy Rollers." It came from when people would
> get converted, you know, some of them, not all of them, rolled on the floor, and
> they called everybody then "Holy Rollers." I definitely resented that. I didn't
> like that. I don't think that maybe everybody don't receive their baptism the
> same.[15]

Yet, this same woman, in describing the conversions of both herself and her husband
told the story below, which seems to uphold the stereotype, even though the narrator's
own conceptions of it as a significant religious experience prevent her from recognizing it as part of the stereotype.

> And they said, "Oh, your husband's getting the Holy Ghost, come down here."
> And when I walked in the room it was just full of light, a radiant light in that
> room and some of the brothers was praying with my husband and when I
> opened the door, I guess God planned this for me to see, but my husband was

just knocked backwards just like somebody knocked him down because the power of God was so strong in that room.[16]

The Pentecostal attraction has been likened to the Moon children brainwashings; suggestions of mass hysteria on any level make people nervous. Furthermore, the possession behaviors and trance-like states of tongue-speakers are associated in many people's minds with primitive religious behaviors and are feared and rejected on that level. Yet, the New Testament basis for tongue-speaking as possession of the Holy Ghost makes a lot of Christians nervous—what if the Pentecostals are right? This accounts for the surging interest in charismatic seeking of "tongues" by many closeted groups within main-line denomination churches. These groups cannot be openly condoned by the hierarchy of the churches, but many non-Pentecostal parishioners and pastors are convinced of the "reality" of the tongue-speaking experience. This does not, however, indicate an improvement of the non-Pentecostal public opinion of Pentecostal behavior. On the contrary, very clear distinctions are made between modern "charismatics" (pentecostal with a small "p") and Pentecostalism. Charismatics generally emphasize the quiet, intellectual nature of their evening meetings, held perforce in different homes rather than in the church proper. The Holy Spirit is gently wooed through quiet individual prayer and testimony; connotations of "Pentecostalism" or loud, raucous conventions are vociferously denied. Pentecostals, of course, view recent trends toward charismatic experience as verisimilar to their own beliefs. Yet, they are conversely critical of the reserved nature of the denominational charismatics and look with disdain upon what they see as elite reluctance to admit emotionalism and irrationality, both of which they feel are necessary components of true religious experience. One Pentecostal woman put it this way:

> I think shouting is great and people on the outside don't understand that because they haven't already received the real joy, and they don't have their eyes set on the eternity that we have a hope for. When you think about it, and you think about what we are going to escape and what we're going to receive, it is a joy and it is something to shout about. People don't think a thing about going to a ballgame and screaming and yelling and getting down on their hands and beating the ground and beating the floor. They think that's all right.[17]

Her point is well taken. Americans have decided that quiet decorum is appropriate for church services and that sports arenas are proper places for exuberant, loud, uninhibited behavior. It is not, therefore, Pentecostal behavior so much that dismays outsiders as the associations that behavior has with religious ecstasy and religious emotionalism. Only in this way is Pentecostal religious frenzy established and maintained as a mechanism for group identity and boundary maintenance.

> What I am trying to say is for so long we walked around like, "Hey, we've got it. We've got the answer for the world." And we've become an unreal people. And it is time for them to see that we have got joy. That we are real people. We act crazy . . . we're nuts for Jesus and we are happy about it.[18]

Elaine J. Lawless

The non-Pentecostal response to Pentecostals has been unflattering. When fear, intimidation, awe, and awkwardness come together in one group's perceptions about another group, the likely outcome will be ridicule and persecution. Although Pentecostals feel the same fear, intimidation, awe, and awkwardness about the non-Pentecostal world, their status is the slighter because they are the minority group. Ever since the advent of emotional revivals and camp meetings, Pentecostals have suffered at the hands of outsiders. Persecution and ostracism are bitter realities for most Pentecostals, and the stories they tell often include incidents where they were made to feel ridiculous, embarrassed, and defensive about their religion. But persecution is also a powerful force for uniting people and facilitating cohesion.[19] Pentecostals decry their persecution and vow their perseverance. Church services resound with the testimonies of believers who have been belittled, and the congregation rallies to their support.

> You know when I sing
> and when I testify
> everybody looks at me
> and they think I'm kind of *peculiar*.
> But you know tonight
> we *are* a peculiar people.
> But you know something?
> I'm not ashamed of Jesus,
> because this is the *Lord,*
> that I sing,
> that I testify for,
> that I stomp my feet for,
> that I clap my hands for,
> It's Jesus Christ.[20]

When the congregation responds with "Amen, yes, Sister," they are in one accord.[21] They, as a group, have been misunderstood and mistreated, but it is exactly that identification as a group which binds them together. They are proud that they are peculiar, for that means they have established a distinct identity.

While Pentecostals may not be completely comfortable with the stereotype of "Holy Rollers," they are quite effective in perpetuating the most stereotyping aspects of their religion. Their own stories about Pentecostal behavior are not told, however, as sensationalized accounts of bizarre behavior, but are rather carefully constructed, nearly formulaic personal experience stories reiterated to contrast an outsider's view with an insider's view. The telling of conversion stories especially serves to define boundaries from an inside point of view and interpret behavior within the context in which it occurs. The effect, then, is to solidify the stereotype only as an esoteric conviction. The stories begin on a definite "outsider" note. The following is typical of how one couple felt about Pentecostals before their own conversion and was told to non-Pentecostals.

> He, my husband, would come in and say, "Well, where do you want to go, let's
> go to church." And I would say, "Well, where do you want to go?" . . . And he
> said to me, "I tell you, I'll go anywhere you want to go but don't expect me to go
> up on that hill . . . don't expect me to go up there. Those people are crazy and
> you do not have to live like that to be a Christian."[22]

But through the insistence of the woman's sister and her husband, this couple ends up
at the Pentecostal church and joins the church within a few nights.[23] Then, the woman
defends Pentecostals; the outsider stance has changed to an insider's—"People think
we are freaks, but really we are not." The "they" has become "we." Their daughter-in-
law describes her first encounter with Pentecostals; the account is typical.

> My girlfriend and I when we first entered into this Pentecostal church, this is
> kinda going back, I remember seeing the people raising their hands and
> speaking in tongues and one little lady shouting and we sat back there and I
> would just laugh, because I thought this was really unreal. . . . And when I seen
> these people clapping their hands and raising their hands to worship the Lord,
> I thought this, you know, this is really out of place for them to do this in church.
> Church is to come and sit still.[24]

Although these graphic descriptions of first encounters with Pentecostals are quickly
followed by the converts' changing attitudes toward what was first perceived, the
account of the first encounter serves a critical function. This part of the conversion
narration is easily empathized with by all the outsiders listening—it describes exactly
how they are feeling as newcomers, observers, and outsiders. In essence, the believer is
announcing—I know how you feel at this moment, and yours is a legitimate feeling; I
felt the same way. The recounting of the conversion then leads the outsider toward an
understanding of what he or she should expect to happen next. Skepticism will recede
as God reveals to each individual the "reality" of what is occurring in the service. Signs
will be sought to prove the legitimacy of the experience. The outsider comes to see that
the people are not freakish at all, but rather have found "the Truth."

> The second night after that I came back because I thought I would laugh again . . .
> and I realized it was more than just watching people that they really did have
> something that they were expressing and that it was real . . . I knew there was
> something there and I knew it was right. How I could reach out and get it, I did
> not know. So I watched these people and after a while I started crying . . . and
> then I received the Holy Ghost and I forgot all about my make-up and forgot all
> about my pride . . . and then I just started praising the Lord.[25]

Once non-believers go through the experience of "receiving the Holy Ghost" and
speak in tongues, they become group members and the benefits are multifold. It is the
public display of tongue-speaking that entitles a person to membership into the
Pentecostal Family.[26]

107

> It's a family. It is just like a family. It really is. And you are concerned for your brothers and sisters . . . you have a desire to help your brothers and sisters, and it is a definite family thing. Really, I think in some of the "denominational" churches, they don't have that closeness and it is the Holy Ghost, the difference is the Holy Ghost that covers that, I think.[27]

There is no tie stronger, more resistent to breakage, more filled with a sense of devotion and loyalty against all odds than the tie of blood-related people. Pentecostals are blood-related to each other, compliments of the blood of Jesus Christ. They are brothers and sisters; they belong to a family. They understand what they do and why they do it, and they stand as a group against a world that does not understand, taking the outsider's stereotypes about them to mold an image that is stronger against opposition.

Finally, much of the Pentecostal belief system, as well as their own perceptions of themselves as a group, is firmly embodied in a specialized language they have developed. Generally, the use of this specialized language by Pentecostals does not create contention or distrust on the part of non-believers, because its use is largely confined to the religious church service and the Pentecostal community. But within that group, the special language functions in a significant manner to establish a group sense of cohesion and special identity and should be examined in any discussion of Pentecostals as a folk group. Words and phrases that have developed naturally within the Pentecostal community are fraught with meaning and carry significance not available to the non-member.

Folk groups and subcultures often develop a specialized language understood only by the members of the group, a language which must be learned as a new member becomes assimilated into the group and which, when artfully and correctly employed, will signify membership to others in the group. Specialized language serves further to mark the group to outsiders, to delineate boundaries that keep groups distinct, and can intensify group cohesion and solidarity.[28] A special language must be close enough to the "mother language" to make sense to the members of the group and simple enough for the novice to pick up fairly quickly. There is no time set aside for the teaching of this specialized language, but its constant and repetitive use in the verbal messages of the group members serves to teach the newcomer what words mean and where and how it is appropriate to employ them. Converts to Pentecostalism are expected to participate fully in church services immediately after their conversion and tongue-speaking experiences; hence, acquisition of the "language" quickly follows initiation.

Pentecostal converts generally come from the community in which the Pentecostal church has firmly established itself. Gerlach and Hine suggest that persons are usually converted due to the "fervent and convincing recruitment along pre-existing lines of significant social relationships."[29] The conversion of area residents will, they point out, stabilize the religion and the community and help it to grow; conversion of loners and drifters will not really benefit the group. In southern Indiana, relatives, close friends, and neighbors of Pentecostal believers acquire familiarity with the Pentecostal "language" long before they join the group themselves. Pentecostal believers tell and repeat many stories and anecdotes which artfully employ the language they have acquired within the religion. Much of the language and its proper use is learned in the context of the church service, but the employment of the specialized language and the accompanying stories go beyond the church into the homes, the stores, the schools, in fact, into the entire community. Therefore, when a community member goes from a potential convert to a convert, the assimilation process is abbreviated because of his or her constant exposure to the world of Pentecostals outside the context of the church.

There is no manual of Pentecostal words and their meanings. Many of the words or phrases common to Pentecostals have originated in the Bible but have come to carry specialized meanings for the people who employ them. Some of the terms serve an esoteric function by their mere use—that is, no one else knows what they mean, for example, when Pentecostals speculate about the impending "rapture" (when Jesus will return to gather up believers). Other terms serve that function, as well as also articulating the difference between Pentecostals and outsiders—for example, in the Pentecostal use of the terms "saint" and "sinner." Interestingly, when Pentecostals talk with non-Pentecostals they assume a common knowledge of their specialized language, or at least they employ it consistently with no pause for explanation. It is such an integral part of their own vocabulary, they seem not aware of the terms that might give an outsider difficulties. The Pentecostal terms that follow and their definitions are strictly emic ones and should be understood in the context in which they occur.[30]

Pentecostals call each other *brother* and *sister*.[31] As explained above, this tradition has especial meaning for Pentecostals. As a group, they do feel they comprise a family, and the group members are brothers and sisters. Although this is not unique to Pentecostals, they have imbued the terms with more meaning than other denominations that may refer to "Brother Jones" or "Sister Smith."

> The Pentecostal church as a whole is a very, is kind of a familial feel. We call each other brothers and sisters and we are brothers and sisters. . . . There is definitely a feeling of kinship among each other.[32]

The most significant esoteric differentiation between Pentecostal group members and nonmembers is the use of the terms *saint* and *sinner*. "Sinners" are people who are out *in the world,* a phrase that is used to describe the world of sin in which Pentecostals do not participate but the rest of the world does. Sinners commit sins; they do things that are *worldly*: these include going to movies, dances, any kind of commercial amusements, paid sports events, bars, in fact any place, including other homes, where the influence of the world might be evident—this includes televisions. Pentecostals call themselves, on the other hand, "saints." They have been *saved,* that is, through their conversion they will be saved from an eternity in hell. The Pentecostal church is made up of saints; often the congregation is addressed as "Dear Saints." Sinners seeking to change their status from sinner to saint and gain membership into the group must do so by first professing their sins in the public context of the church and *tarrying* at the altar, that is, waiting at the altar (on bended knees) for the possession of the Holy

Ghost. Part of the kinesic "language" that accompanies tarrying includes raised arms, waving hands, closed eyes, tears, and eventual disconcern for one's surroundings that implies a trance-state. Possession by the Holy Ghost will be manifested by *speaking in tongues*, a linguistic phenomenon which Pentecostals believe is a true language, understandable to persons familiar with it. The tarrying may take minutes, hours, or the potential convert may have to return night after night trying to *pray through*, that is, reach God. This process can be immediate on the first night or may take years. Members generally attribute the inattention of the Holy Ghost to a *seeker*, the one who tarries, to some lack of faith or indecision on the part of the individual. Seekers are encouraged by saint helpers to *let go* and *go all the way with Jesus*, urging them to get rid of all their inhibitions.

In order to become a saint, sinners must be baptized twice—once with full water submersion, the other with the "spirit," which means they receive the Holy Ghost and speak in tongues. Once a sinner has confessed his or her sins and requested baptism, the pastor of the church will baptize this person with water. Pentecostals baptize by total submersion in water accompanied by a standardized prayer, the quoting of a Bible verse, and often tongue-speaking by the pastor or another church member. *Oneness* Pentecostals, whose name comes from the fact that they believe that the members of the trinity are all one and the same and that Jesus *is* God, baptize with the formula: "I now baptize you in the name of Jesus." This formula is the crux of the Oneness/Trinitarian Pentecostal rift. *Oneness* Pentecostals have rejected the long-standing Christian formula for baptism—"I now baptize thee in the name of the Father, the Son, and the Holy Ghost"—preferring instead to recognize only Jesus as the Godhead incarnate. To other Christians, including other Pentecostals, this seems blasphemous. Membership in the group, based on both baptisms, assures salvation and safety in heaven when the *rapture* comes. The rapture will be when Jesus returns to the earth to claim his saints and all persons will be held accountable for their lives and deeds. Pentecostals believe the rapture is imminent. Because of their rejection of the world, their anticipation of the "better life" after the rapture becomes all important.

> We have so many things to do, realizing that the place that we are at, in these times, coming down to the end, when I really feel the rapture of the church is ready to take place. I expect it tonight, if it doesn't take place tonight, I expect it tomorrow. And there's such a short time that we have to witness to other people to let them know that they can receive and the change that can take place in their lives.[33]

Spontaneous tongue-speaking, at events such as baptisms, is distinct in the Pentecostal mind from that which occurs in a conversion experience. Being able to speak in tongues at will is a *gift* and is generally recognized as a message from God. Saints may possess special spiritual gifts from God. Based on First Corinthians chapter twelve, the nine spiritual gifts include wisdom, knowledge, faith, healing, working of miracles, prophecy, discerning of spirits, divers kinds of tongues, and the interpretation of tongues. Pentecostals interpret these verses to indicate that God decides which (if any)

110

of these gifts will be given to whom. Speaking in "diverse tongues" refers to speaking in tongues at will in various appropriate situations; this ability is seen as a gift and is recognized as different from the spontaneous, but involuntary, tongue-speaking which accompanies a conversion experience, which is believed to be available to everyone and is prerequisite to membership in the group.

> I think, as far as the gifts, receiving the Holy Ghost and speaking in tongues, and then I think there is a gift of tongues which are two separate things altogether. Some people have the gift of tongues and some don't. I feel that probably my husband has a gift of tongues. He has prayed in many other languages that went from one just into another and I don't feel that everybody has that gift.[34]

The *interpretation* of what someone "says" in tongues is thought to be the highest gift of all but is rarely practiced, for it is agreed that interpreting is subject to the greatest risk; the burden of a mistaken interpretation lies with the interpreter, whereas the tongue-speaker is possessed and is not responsible for what is spoken.

In a typical Pentecostal church service, several activities are common, all of which are geared toward helping the group members *get happy* or *get a blessing*, which refers to states where uninhibited behaviors such as crying, *dancing in the spirit* (in possession), jerks, tongue-speaking, and *shouting* can be exhibited. Shouting can take various forms, from shrieking to crying to speaking in tongues. It is viewed as a supranormal utterance and, like spirit dancing, cannot be controlled by the individual. This marks the distinction between these as secular activities and as sacred activities performed in the context of the church service. Under the power of the spirit of God, the saints are not responsible for their acts; performed by choice in the context of "the world," the same acts become desecrated. Participation in congregational singing, dancing, shouting, praying, and tongue-speaking is strongly encouraged; saints long to see the *house on fire* for God, that is, all members actively involved in exalting God and invoking the spirit to move among the members. *Testifying* is one verbal activity that all members are expected to perform within any given church service; members must rise at their pew and give an extemporaneous testimony of their faith in God or his particular goodness to them. Testifying is part of the duty of a good saint in efforts to *witness* to others about the goodness and mercy of God. Personal experience stories serve to witness to the Lord; the act of testifying itself is a witness of the saint's effort to be a good model for others.

Knowledge of the specialized language of Pentecostals is attained in a traditional manner, passed from group member to group member, both in the church and in the community. Many Pentecostals relate stories about growing up in Pentecostal homes and "playing church."

> Most of my friends were people that was in the church. When I was little my parents would go to visit every Saturday night. They would go places or would have people to their homes and we played church. . . . That was part of the

games we played. And one little guy he always did the preaching and he always tried to get me to get the Holy Ghost.[35]

Stories such as this one reveal the pervading influence of the Pentecostal religion on the lives of its adherents. Most of their friends were Pentecostal; friends visited each other's homes in the evenings, the same friends they saw at church on other evenings; children "played church." The language used in these stories suggests that the children were, even at a very early age, cognizant of and competent with Pentecostal terminology and behavior.

In a given community, Pentecostals do constitute a folk group. Their sense of identity as a group is a complex of socio-cultural configurations that have developed naturally, yet which are unconsciously manipulated by the members to solidify group cohesion and maintain distinctions between them and everybody else. Pentecostals have set themselves up as being different from the rest of the world; they have established dress codes and a specialized language to mark that distinction. In their efforts to be recognized as different, they have suffered the consequences of ridicule, misunderstanding and persecution. Their differentness is most often perceived by outsiders as freakish, bizarre, and even dangerous. Yet, most of the stereotypes about Pentecostals create little apprehension for the adherents of the faith, for they have learned to turn a negative stereotype into a positive attribute, a fearful connotation into an exaltation of their God. Unlike the Amish or other isolated religious communities within the modern American milieu, Pentecostals seemingly mingle daily with other groups in their world. Yet, close observation and examination of the attitudes and behaviors of Pentecostals allows that, in many ways, Pentecostals have created many similar marks of distinction and established and continue to maintain socio-cultural boundaries important to their distinctiveness as a group. Like ethnic groups, they have a membership which identifies itself, is identifiable by others, and has a cultural focus on one or more symbolic elements defined as the epitome of their peoplehood.

---

[1]Michael N., 20 August 1980, interviewed in his father's home in Bloomington, Indiana, by the author and Elizabeth Peterson. All the interviews referred to in this article were conducted in 1980 in southern Indiana and represent members of two Pentecostal congregations—one rural and one urban. Names of individuals have been abbreviated and church names changed to insure privacy. Fieldwork in 1980 and 1981 eventually resulted in a television program, *Joy Unspeakable*, produced by Elaine Lawless and Elizabeth Peterson with John Winninger, Radio and T.V. Services, Indiana University. See Larry Danielson, Elaine Lawless and Elizabeth Peterson, "Folklore and Film: Some Questions and Answers about *Joy Unspeakable*," *Western Folklore* 41 (1982): 320–326.

[2]See Luther P. Gerlach and Virginia H. Hine, "Five Factors Crucial to the Growth and Spread of a Modern Religious Movement," *Journal for the Scientific Study of Religion* 7 (1968): 36–7. See also R. A. Schermerhorn, "Ethnicity in the Perspective of the Sociology of Knowledge," *Ethnicity* 1 (1974): 1.

[3]For discussions of what a folk group is and how group identity is established and maintained see Alan Dundes, "What is Folklore?" in *The Study of Folklore*, ed. Alan Dundes (Englewood Cliffs N.J., 1965), p. 2, and William Jansen, "The Esoteric-Exoteric Factor in Folklore," in *The Study of Folklore*, especially p. 45.

[4]Max Weber, *The Sociology of Religion* (Boston, 1922), p. 108.

[5]For a description of ethnic boundary maintenance see Frederick Barth, *Ethnic Groups and Boundaries* (Boston, 1969), p. 7.

[6]Ibid., pp. 13–14.

[7]Ibid., p. 14.

[8]Edwin R. A. Seligman, "Ethnic Communities," in *The Encyclopedia of Social Science,* vol. 5 (New York, 1937), p. 607. Seligman does not elaborate on the following remark: "Purely religious communities such as the Mormons or the Shakers or economic communities, like the New Harmony or Brook Farms groups, do not fall under the term (ethnic) although they are in many respects similar to the groups here discussed."

[9]There are several good works that discuss the emergence of the Holiness Movement. These include Vinson Synan, *The Holiness-Pentecostal Movement in the United States* (Grand Rapids, Mich., 1971); John Nichol, *Pentecostalism* (New York, 1966); and Marvin Dieter, *The Holiness Revival in the Nineteenth Century* (New York, 1980).

[10]Ellen L., 13 August 1980, interviewed in her mother's home in Bloomington, Indiana, by E. Peterson and the author.

[11]Madonna N., 20 August 1980, interviewed in her home in Bloomington, Indiana, by E. Peterson and the author.

[12]Michael N., 20 August 1980.

[13]Ellen L., 13 August 1980.

[14]Mike N., 20 August 1980.

[15]Savannah R., 13 August 1980, interviewed in her home by E. Peterson and the author. "Baptism" here refers to the Pentecostal belief in a spirit baptism, a possession by the Holy Ghost that is usually accompanied by speaking in tongues.

[16]Savannah R., 13 August 1980.

[17]Madonna N., 20 August 1980.

[18]Mike N., 20 August 1980.

[19]See Barth, *Ethnic Groups;* Gerlach and Hine, "Five Factors"; and Schermerhorn, "Ethnicity in the Perspective of the Sociology of Knowledge."

[20]Connie S., 17 May 1980, testimony at Johnson's Creek Church, taped by the author.

[21]For a more complete discussion of Pentecostal women's testimonies as a traditional performance form, see Elaine J. Lawless, "Shouting for the Lord: Women's Speech in the Pentecostal Church," *Journal of American Folklore* 96 (1983): 434–59.

[22]Madonna N., 20 August 1980.

[23]This is consistent with Gerlach and Hine's contention that most Pentecostal recuitment takes place "face-to-face along lines of preexisting significant social relationships," in "Five Factors," 30.

[24]Pam N., 20 August 1980, interviewed in the home of her in laws by E. Peterson and the author.

[25]Pam N.

[26]For a discussion of tongue-speaking as a semiotic sign for the presence of God, see Elaine J. Lawless, "'What Did She Say?' An Application of Peirce's General Theory of Signs to Glossolalia in the Pentecostal Religion," *Folklore Forum* 13, no. 1 (Spring, 1980): 1–23.

[27]Ellen L., 13 August 1980.

[28]See Barth, *Ethnic Groups.*

[29]Gerlach and Hine, "Five Factors," 30. They found that relatives accounted for the recruitment of 52 percent of their total sample and close friends accounted for another 29 percent.

[30]See Alan Dundes, "From Etic to Emic Units in the Structural Study of Folktales," in *Analytic Essays in Folklore,* ed. Alan Dundes (The Hague, 1975), pp. 61–73.

[31]Terms treated in this essay as examples of specialized language have been italicized.

[32]Steve R., 13 August 1980, interviewed in his home by E. Peterson and the author.

[33]Madonna N., 20 August 1980.

[34]Madonna N.

[35]Ellen L., 13 August 1980.

# Ethnicity and Citizenship in the Ritual of an Israeli Synagogue

Shlomo A. Deshen

*No institution exists in a vacuum. Even institutions whose charter is to preserve the past respond to current political, economic, and social forces. Religious institutions and their rituals are often designed to enhance the relationship of worshippers to the deity through the re-creation of some past primal event. Yet even in these matters of ultimate concern, change occurs. Changes may be brought about deliberately and sweepingly, as when King Kamehameha II invited his people to sit and eat with him, and thus abrogated in one event the entire traditional system of religious taboo (Howells 1962:36). More often, however, changes are inadvertent and modest, and merely involve a creative alteration in the use of ritual expressions or objects in some local environment.*

*The following essay illustrates how an ethnic synagogue in Israel can be caught between the forms and values of the old community in Tunisia and those of the modern state. Traditional religious forms in the ethnic synagogue are made to accommodate changing personal and social circumstance and respond to the ideological environment of the new nation. Thus traditional forms are made to serve contemporary needs without denying the validity of either the tradition or the contemporary forces.*

*For other examples of the effects of social change on belief and ritual practice, see Passin and Bennett (1943) or Firth (1960). For more on the effects of modern Israeli life on Jewish immigrants to Israel from North Africa see Shokeid and Deshen (1974).*

One of the characteristic social developments among many first-generation immigrant groups in Western countries, particularly in the United States, has been the emergence of "ethnic churches."[1] In Israel the phenomenon is also common. Of the hundreds, perhaps thousands, of synagogues established in Israel in the recent decades of mass immigration, the majority can probably be characterized as "ethnic synagogues." The synagogue congregations tend to crystallize around a nucleus of individuals who, originating from a particular locality abroad, maintain the particular shade of Jewish ritual tradition they have brought with them, with which they are more familiar, and in which they feel at home. They nurture particular melodies, customs, and sentiments of communality, and among themselves they speak their native language or dialect.

Reproduced by permission of the author and the publisher, excerpt from *Southwestern Journal of Anthropology* 28, no. 1(1972):69–82 [excerpt 69–79]. Not for further reproduction.

The old practices, however, are not adhered to rigidly. In common with the other aspects of life in an immigrant situation, ritual undergoes change. In this study I examine the nature of ritual changes that occur in the ethnic synagogue. Particularly, I am concerned with the relationship between these changes and the tension between citizenship and ethnicity which is a general problem of Israeli society. Israeli society is comprised of people who, to a considerable extent, are rooted in the cultures of the countries from which they originate. People born in a country such as Tunisia have a great deal in common, culturally and socially; similarly, persons originating from a country such as Rumania have much in common. The bonds of common culture and origin are cohesive factors within the ethnic group and separate people of variegated origin. Together with existing bonds of traditional culture there emerge new bonds of Israeli nationhood that bind all these people together, but the two kinds of bonds often seem conflicting on the surface. Israel does not have a clearly articulated ideology that legitimizes cultural pluralism. On the contrary the ideology of "the melting pot" was very potent during the years of peak immigration. It is only in recent years that a more liberal pluralistic approach seems to have become popular, yet ethnic loyalties and adherence to ethnic practices remain uneasy bedfellows with Israeli nationalism, patriotism, and citizenship.[2]

I shall approach the problem outlined above through the detailed analysis of a series of ritual actions in a particular synagogal congregation that I studied as a participant-observer. In the first section of the paper, I present the background of the ritual actions. In the second section the actions themselves are described, and in the concluding parts the actions are analyzed and discussed.

## I.

Many of the immigrants to Israel in recent decades stem from relatively homo-geneous, technologically underdeveloped, and generally traditional societies. Traditional religious values and practices were considered binding as a matter of course in these societies. There were, of course, those who strayed from the norm, but they were considered (and saw themselves) as sinners or deviants. Theoretically at least, tradition was paramount.

Immigration to the dynamic, modern, and young State of Israel was for these people an experience out of all proportion to the actual geographical move involved. This change involved the abrupt disappearance of political and judicial institutions that they had been familiar with. In the spheres of livelihood and education they were also confronted with a novel situation in Israel: only rarely did the immigrants make their living in their new home in a manner reminiscent of that of their country of origin, and in matters of education they had to adapt to new institutions and ideas. The immigrants were confronted with comparatively few new demands in the areas of family and domestic life, and religion. There was no ideology in Israel that called for a drastic change in religion and therefore the immigrants established and attended synagogues of their own special traditional ritual shading wherever they settled in Israel.

Shlomo A. Deshen

Despite the relative continuity in religious and family affairs, the ethnic experience is new and often perplexing to a congregant of an ethnic synagogue in Israel, particularly when he has never migrated prior to coming to Israel—and this is true for a large portion of Israeli immigrants. The ethnic synagogue is one of the fields of social life that gauges change in the immigrant group.

Ethnic synagogues emerged in the course of migration to and settlement in Israel because individuals identified themselves as immigrants from a particular country or a particular locality within a country. In the historical past the social identity of a member of autochthonous Jewish communities living in the midst of Gentile majorities was shaped by two basic factors: his Jewishness and his minority status. Consequently, the internal social organization of people in the form of synagogue communities did not normally follow ethnic lines.[3] In present-day Israel, however, where neither of these factors holds, Jewish society is ethnically and religiously much more differentiated; thus, synagogue organization also tends to follow lines of ethnic origin.

I proceed now to discuss one particular ethnic synagogue, *Tzidkat Hayim*,[4] from which I draw the data for the present analysis. The *Tzidkat Hayim* synagogue is located in Ayara, a provincial Israeli town of about 17,000 inhabitants.[5] Ayara was founded in 1955 and is populated mainly by immigrants who came to the country after that time. Economic opportunities in the town are limited; many of the inhabitants are unskilled manual workers employed in industry or as seasonal agricultural laborers. Many people work on relief projects.[6]

The *Tzidkat Hayim* congregants, originating mainly from North Africa, number 60 households with a total of about 280 persons. The official name of the synagogue, "The *Tzidkat Hayim* Synagogue of Immigrants from Southern Tunisia," is not representative since the congregation is more heterogeneous than the name implies. Of the 60 constituent households, 29 originated in Southern Tunisia, 19 in Northern Tunisia, six in Morocco, four in Tripolitania, and two in Algeria. The Southern Tunisians form the social backbone of the synagogue; they were the founders and continue to provide the leadership and the most active laymen. The Southern Tunisians are themselves internally differentiated according to the main Jewish communities of the region. Seventeen of the *Tzidkat Hayim* congregants were from the island of Djerba originally and 12 came from the town of Gabès and surrounding mainland villages.

The Eastern Maghreb, comprising Tunisia and Tripolitania, consists of a single Jewish cultural region whose members speak a Judaeo-Arabic dialect peculiar to the area. While there was considerable internal migration within the region in the past and the fame of eminent religious leaders of particular communities extended throughout the region, there was comparatively little movement between the Eastern Maghreb and other Jewish cultural areas in the vicinity.

Within the orbit of Eastern Maghreb Jewry the Southern Tunisians are proud of their identity, folklore, and particular customs. In recent years they have been tenacious in their adherence to Jewish orthodoxy and tradition in comparison to other parts of the Maghreb where Jewish practice and scholarship have deteriorated.[7] The active persons of the *Tzidkat Hayim* congregation at its establishment in Ayara in the late

1950s were newly arrived immigrants from the town of Gabès in Southern Tunisia. The synagogue is managed by a committee and offers various cultural and leisure activities which are financed by the congregants despite their modest incomes and stations in life. The atmosphere in the congregation, as I have described it elsewhere,[8] is homey and congenial.

## II.

The problem of the relationship between ethnicity and citizenship will be approached through the description of a series of symbolic actions which took place in the *Tzidkat Hayim* synagogue.

### THE NAMING OF THE SYNAGOGUE

One of the worthiest means whereby the dead are commemorated in Judaism[9] is by establishing a synagogue in their name. Concrete focus and expression is thus given to the religious sentiments of the pious who seek to honor and respect the *Torah* (the revealed divine law) and the scholars of the Holy Scriptures whose moral conduct exemplifies the *Torah*. The synagogue *Tzidkat Hayim* (literally "The Righteousness of Hayim"), founded in the late 1950s, was named in honor of Rabbi Hayim Huri, the deceased last rabbi of the community of Gabès. Calling the synagogue after the Rabbi of Gabès fulfilled the symbolic function of concretely expressing the religious sentiments of the congregants attending at the time and it was a concrete demonstration of the influence and power of the Gabèsans who were the most prominent members of the congregation in the 1950s. When I arrived in 1965, the congregation of *Tzidkat Hayim* had changed. Immigrants from the Island of Djerba (off the Tunisian coast near Gabès) had joined the congregation in increasing numbers and had risen in prominence *vis-à-vis* the Gabèsans; none of the latter remained on the synagogue committee.

By 1965 an anomalous situation had arisen in the *Tzidkat Hayim* synagogue. The Djerbans, now the most prominent and influential members of the congregation, did not have an outlet within the synagogue for the expression of their religious sentiments toward their honored dead. Though they have many notable rabbis whom they revere and respect, the Djerbans were attending a synagogue not called after one of them. The incongruity of the situation was, however, not only with reference to their religious sentiments; it was also a question of social prominence and prestige. The Djerbans and Gabèsans were constantly competing for influence in the congregation; the competition, though mild and tempered by mutual joking, was nevertheless pervasive. An element of dissonance emerged, since the social experience of the prominent Djerbans was incompatible with the absence of symbolism for their religious sentiments. The incongruity could have been resolved in a number of ways. The Djerbans might have attempted to rename the synagogue after one of their own dignitaries. As far as I know this was never suggested. Another possibility was to cease attributing active symbolic significance to the name of the synagogue. This course of action was also not taken. The name remained meaningful to the congregants. Instead, the Djerbans symbolically expressed the changed social situation in the synagogue by interpreting the synagogue's name homiletically.

The Djerban leader of *Tzidkat Hayim,* Perfect Sage Rebee Yosseif, explained to me in 1965 that *Hayim* ("HYYM"—in Hebrew, vowels are not indicated by letters but by signs under the consonants) stands for the initials of four well-known deceased Djerban rabbis: Rabbi *H*uita (Kohen), Rabbi *Y*osseif (Berabee), Rabbi *Y*osseif (Bukhriss), and Rabbi *M*oshe (Khalfon Kohen). One of these was his ancestor. The new interpretation, coexisting with the original meaning of the name that the Gabèsan members of the synagogue continue to attribute to it, extended the connotation of the old name so that it became relevant to and consistent with the Djerban social situation. This particular reinterpretation of a symbol is only one example of a type of homiletic manipulation that is very common in local culture.[10]

The one symbol, now become meaningful to Djerbans and Gabèsans alike, is a vehicle through which both can express their deferential feelings toward their dead and through which they can honor the memories of their respective saintly rabbis. Significantly, the divergent interpretations of the synagogue's name are neither voiced on formal occasions nor in writing. There are no confrontations between these interpretations and the name thus remains ambiguous in its definition. This equivocalness can be understood in functionalist terms, though I am far from suggesting that this is the only way to approach the problem: the various groups within the *Tzidkat Hayim* congregation, especially the Djerbans and the Gabèsans, can thereby express their devotion and adherence to a single house of worship.[11] The symbol itself has become enriched and extended, thereby eliminating a source of friction between the two groups of congregants.

## THE COMMEMORATION OF TWO GALLANT MEN

In Judaism it is customary to commemorate a deceased person on the anniversary of his death as well as on certain occasions during the morning synagogue services. A prayer is recited wherein the deceased is mentioned by name. In the Southern Tunisian rite there is a different prayer formula for rabbis and for laymen. The prayer for a rabbi is an elaborate invocation with reference to his wisdom, learning, and outstanding piety—qualities greatly esteemed in traditional Judaism. In Southern Tunisian Jewish sentiment there is also the feeling that great rabbis are endowed with supernatural powers and local folklore recounts miracles associated with them.[12] The entire congregation usually rises at the commemoration of a rabbi. The memorial prayer for laymen is shorter, lacks the florid introduction, and no one rises in honor of the deceased when it is recited with the possible exception of close relatives, such as sons and grandsons.[13]

Early in 1965 Ayara was struck by tragedy. A *wadi,* the deep dry bed of a stream which flows only at the height of the rainy season, runs through the town. During the rains the river bed is likely to become a turbulent river within a few days. In the winter of 1965 a little girl accidently fell into the stream. A new immigrant to Israel, unaware of the dangers involved, jumped in after the child in an attempt to rescue her. A young soldier who witnessed the incident also tried to save the child. All three lost their lives.

The soldier, the little girl, and the other man were immigrants from Morocco. The father of the soldier at the time was a member of the *Tzidkat Hayim* synagogue, which his son had never attended. When a year had passed and it was time to commemorate the death of the soldier, Rebee Yosseif, who led the prayer service, honored his memory by deliberately and emphatically reading the prayer reserved for the great and the wise. In the prayer he mentioned not only the soldier, whose father was present, but also the other man. Practically none of the congregants, most of them Tunisians, had known either one, yet the memory of these two strangers of alien origin was singularly honored. Neither of the drowned men had been particularly pious or learned, perhaps not even observant of basic ritual, nor were these virtues attributed to them in death. The congregation had wished to acknowledge other virtues—their selfless act of sacrifice. In the eyes of the congregants the two men had acted as paragons of selflessness and as exemplary citizens and Israelis. The congregants' deep respect found expression in the hush in which they commemorated the men as though they had been the most eminent, wise, and pious of Tunisian rabbis. They ignored the fact that the accident underlined only too tragically the lack of wisdom of the deceased, their temperamental characters, and their total subjugation to the forces of nature, qualities which are contradictory to those traditionally attributed to great Tunisian rabbis. Furthermore, normally only rabbinical personalities with whom the congregation is very familiar, either personally or through oral report, are honored as rabbis. In the present instance the congregation granted this honor to alien persons of whom nothing was known other than their one act of sacrifice. The symbol of the memorial prayer was extended to honor socially insignificant persons whose station in life was low, and to encompass virtues beyond the traditionally accepted ones.

The incidents that follow focus on the symbolic changes made by two leaders of the congregation, Rebee Yosseif (who has been mentioned previously) and Rebee Shushan.[14]

## THE CHANGING OF HIGH HOLY DAYS GARMENTS

Perfect Sage Rebee Yosseif, a scion of a rabbinical family in Djerba, is the most popular of the ritual circumcisers *(moheil)* in Ayara. He is invited to officiate in the homes of people of all ethnic categories. A happy 60-year-old extrovert, he races through the town on his bicycle from one ceremony to the next, his silver beard flowing in the wind. Rebee Yosseif spent most of his life in Southern Tunisia, except for a few years before immigrating when he lived in the north. In the circumcision ceremonies that he performs in Ayara, Rebee Yosseif is remarkably receptive to varieties of customs. The ritual is based upon Djerban customs, but he has adopted some northern Tunisian variants as well. He has also borrowed practices and melodies of ethnic groups completely strange to him, e.g., Moroccan customs. On one occasion I observed that he chanted a Moroccan hymn in a Tripolitanian home. From long discussions with

Shlomo A. Deshen

Rebee Yosseif on these matters, I gained the clear impression that he was motivated by a desire to present ceremonies that would be lively, aesthetic, and acceptable to everyone.

Rebee Yosseif's disposition to adapt to his new environment and circumstances expressed itself in a remarkable act—he changed his first (given) name. Although this was not a religious act, it illuminates Rebee Yosseif's general social situation and facilitates the interpretation of the religious changes which he adopted so readily. Rebee Yosseif's original name had been a traditional Djerban Jewish one. In the Judaeo-Arabic spoken by Moroccans, however, it has an ambiguous connotation which is sexually obscene. Rebee Yosseif evinced sensitivity to the culture and language of immigrants from Morocco and, to escape the embarrassment that he now felt, officially changed his given name—a most unusual act in his environment.

One of Rebee Yosseif's most striking religious changes is his public appearance in the synagogue on the High Holy Days. Abroad, it was customary to wear a special white garment on the major festival of New Year and on the Day of Atonement. Rebee Yosseif, like most other immigrants in Ayara, discarded this and other traditional garments soon after immigrating to Israel because, he explained to me, "people laugh at us." For several years after his immigration Rebee Yosseif wore a European-styled black suit on the New Year. In 1966, however, he donned a white suit which he had especially made for the festivals.

The varied customs that this one man adopted are indicative of a desire to communicate with ethnically different people. Rebee Yosseif expressly wishes to be a well-liked circumciser, not only among the Djerbans but among all the inhabitants of Ayara. Therefore he discarded the name that is "obscene" and the garments that are "ludicrous" in the eyes of people of a different ethnic group. On the other hand, Rebee Yosseif wants to continue to adhere to ancient religious symbols, such as wearing white garments on the High Holy Days, without expressing an ethnic identity that he considers unfashionable and embarrassing. The color of the new garments continues to express conventional religious sentiments, but the clothing now also expresses Rebee Yosseif's experience of Israel's varied styles of life and culture.

THE CORRECTION OF MISTAKES DURING SERVICE

The activities of another leader of the congregation, Perfect Sage Rebee Shushan, the teacher of the daily class of religious studies held at the *Tzidkat Hayim* synagogue, provide another example of change in symbolism. A morose and touchy character, he prides himself on his proficiency in modern Hebrew and on his knowledge of the rudiments of French. And, indeed, his correct usage of Hebrew stands out in his social environment. Rebee Shushan is self-conscious about his lack of modern education, and he is convinced that were it not for this weakness he would be much further up the social ladder. He is also convinced that had he immigrated to Israel in his youth, his present station in life would have been much higher socially and economically than it is. He never tires of recounting his abortive attempt to immigrate in his youth. Now, he feels that his life has been wasted. Moreover, though only in his late 40s, Rebee Shushan is a sickly man. His eyesight was failing rapidly at the time of research, and he taught his class without recourse to books. Relying on his excellent memory, he was able to instruct his pupils in the fine details of cantillation that demanded a thorough knowledge of the Hebrew texts.

There was a certain measure of competition between Rebee Shushan and the other two prominent religious figures of the congregation, one of whom was Rebee Yosseif. These two leaders publicly read the *Torah* in the synagogue, while Rebee Shushan could not engage in this act of prestige because of his infirmity.[15] At *Torah* readings during religious services Rebee Shushan's behavior was unusual. He made a point of correcting the slightest mistake in pronunciation by the reader, interrupting the reading frequently and at times delivering lengthy discourses on points of grammar. The interruption of the *Torah* reading in the event of mistakes in pronunciation and in cantillation is legitimate and to an extent even prescribed, but Rebee Shushan much exaggerated this practice. Furthermore, Rebee Shushan's comments and corrections often stemmed from his objections to some of the peculiarities of the Hebrew pronunciation of Southern Tunisians.[16] He claimed that the reading was incorrect, formulating his opinion in terms of social values: the desirability of having a uniform Hebrew pronunciation, and a *nussakh yisraeli* ("an Israeli formula") in prayer and in speech. He claimed that his Northern Tunisian pronunciation was identical with the "Israeli" pronunciation, whereas the Southern Tunisian pronunciation was a local variant that differed from the accepted, normal, and everyday Israeli style. An objective evaluation of Rebee Shushan's linguistic objections is not in place here. Significant for our purpose is the fact that he chose to rationalize in this particular manner his unusual religious behavior.

What did Rebee Shushan achieve by this course of action? By continuously interrupting the men who were reading the *Torah* he staked his claim to part of the honor bestowed on them. Through these acts of scholarly ingenuity he sought to gain a prestige similar to that of the men whom he corrected, and to come to terms with his oncoming blindness. Through his rationalizations of the interruptions Rebee Shushan sought to bridge the difference that he felt existed between himself and Israeli society at large. He sought to divest the reading of the texts of its ethnic particularities and to invest the *Torah* reading act with a "modern" and "Israeli" content. The *Torah* reading act became consistent with Rebee Shushan's other personal problems, his sense of frustration at having failed in life because of his belated immigration to Israel and his limited participation in what he conceived as modern Israeli culture. Rebee Shushan's experience of heterogeneity together with his other personal circumstances caused him to adopt a course of ritual action that implied enhancement and acceptance of the strange and wider general culture.

## III.

The significance of the changes that the religious symbols that I have described have undergone within the field of reference of ethnicity and citizenship will now be

Shlomo A. Deshen

discussed. In all these changes the worshippers give symbolic expression to their new situation, and specifically to the social heterogeneity in that situation. This symbolic expression or act is a means through which the worshipper seeks communion with people of alien ethnic background among whom he now lives, and with the strange society with which he interacts. I trace this principle in the four instances of symbolic change that have been described.

(1) The solution of the Djerbans' problem concerning the name of the synagogue (involving a contradiction between symbol and experience) is indicative of the mutual adaptation and integration of the two main social groups in the congregation. The theoretical possibility of solving the problem by a Djerban attempt to change the name of the synagogue would have resulted in a confrontation between the Djerbans and the Gabèsans and was, as far as I could gather, never considered.

(2) In the commemoration incident the congregation evaluated the persons concerned according to new criteria—universal human virtues—yet bestowed on them the honor vested in the symbol of commemoration whose original reference was the traditional criteria of scholarship and piety. The fact that the congregation did not know the men they commemorated was also disregarded.

(3) Rebee Yosseif's adaptation of the ritual symbol of white color to modern dress is essentially an attempt at bridging the gulf between the norms and styles of living that prevail inside the synagogue and outside of it. It is an effort to align the synagogal style with the mundane Israeli style of living.

(4) Finally, Rebee Shushan's rationalizations for interrupting the *Torah* readings are also attempts at associating the traditional act of *Torah* reading with the culture that he conceives as new, fashionable, and Israeli. He seeks to dissociate the act from undertones that are specific to a particular ethnic subculture that he considers undesirable; in this case, the Djerban subculture.

The substantial content common to all these changes in symbolism is the fact that the actors also express their reaction to the experience of contact with strangers and to life in a heterogeneous society. The effect of these actions is to bring about a symbolic rapport with the wider Ayara society outside the secluded ethnic and religious circle of the *Tzidkat Hayim* people. They are steps in the processes of passing beyond the boundaries of ethnicity and tradition and forging identities as citizens and Israelis.

---

[1] An early version of this paper was presented at the Fifth World Congress of Jewish Studies in Jerusalem, August 1969. It is based on fieldwork carried out during the years 1965–66, financed by the Bernstein Fund for Research on Israel under the auspices of the Manchester University Department of Social Anthropology. I am thankful to friends and colleagues who commented on the draft: Abner Cohen, A. L. Epstein, D. Handelman, E. Marx, M. Shokeid, and S. Weitman. Miss A. Goldberg helped with editing and styling.

[2] See, for example, the discussions in S. N. Eisenstadt, ed., *The Integration of Immigrants from Different Countries of Origin in Israel* [in Hebrew] (Jerusalem: Magnes Press, 1969).

[3] In populous Jewish communities, social differentiation was primarily on ecological and lineage bases; synagogues existed on the basis of neighborhood and/or kinship ties. In Eastern Europe synagogues emerged which were based on a more complex pattern of differentiation: economic (synagogues whose members belonged to different economic strata and had specific occupations), and religious (synagogues of

various sects). For a general discussion of the historical background, see J. Katz, "Traditional Society and Modern Society," *Megamot* 10 (1960) 304-11; and *Tradition and Crisis: Jewish Society at the End of the Middle Ages* (Glencoe, Ill.: Free Press, 1961).

[4]All names in the article, including that of the town, are pseudonyms, except for foreign place names and the names of deceased persons. Elsewhere I have discussed various facets of the congregation. (See S. A. Deshen, "The Ethnic Synagogue: A Pattern of Religious Change in Israel," in Eisenstadt, *Integration of Immigrants*, 66-73; *Immigrant Voters in Israel: Parties and Congregations in a Local Election Campaign* (Manchester: Manchester University Press, 1970); and "The Varieties of Abandonment of Religious Symbols," *Journal for the Scientific Study of Religion* (1972).

[5]The data are true for 1965.

[6]For a detailed account of the socioeconomic setting, see Deshen, *Immigrant Voters*, chapter 2.

[7]A social history of the Jews of Southern Tunisia in recent times is a *desideratum*. Many accessible sources are at hand both in print and in manuscript. For an outline, see S. A. Deshen, "A Case of Breakdown of Modernization in an Israeli Immigrant Community," *Jewish Journal of Sociology* 7(1965):63-91.

[8]Deshen, "Varieties of Abandonment."

[9]For a brief general discussion of Jewish memorialism, see W. Zenner, "Memorialism—Some Jewish Examples," *American Anthropologist* 67 (1965):481-83.

[10]For other examples of the art of homiletic manipulation, see Deshen, *Immigrant Voters*, chapter 7.

[11]E. L. Peters, "The Proliferation of Lineage Settlements among the Bedouin of Cyrenaica," *Journal of the Royal Anthropological Institute* 90 (1965):29-53, discussing the dynamics of genealogies in an analytical context comparable to mine, has used the term "area of ambiguity." See also the application of the concept in an analysis of village politics, M. Minkovitz, *From Lineage to Association: Family Organizations in the Process of Adjustment to the Moshav* (Jerusalem: Hebrew University, 1967), and its development by E. Marx, *Bedouin of the Negev* (Manchester: Manchester University Press, 1967), 192-93. I feel that it might be fruitful for the understanding of the proprieties of sociocultural mechanisms to view such phenomena as rabbinical innovations, on the one hand, and manipulations of Bedouin genealogies, on the other, within the single framework of "areas of ambiguity."

[12]D. Noy, *Jewish Folktales from Tunisia* (Jerusalem: World Zionist Organization, 1966).

[13]I hesitate on this point because the ritual takes place when one of the close relatives stands next to the *Torah* scroll during the public reading. It is then customary for that individual's junior next of kin to cluster around him to receive his blessing and kiss his hand. Thus the deceased's next of kin are likely not to be seated anyway.

[14]I am concerned with understanding the actions of these men phenomenologically, and not with whether they represent their congregations or whether their actions are idiosyncratic. However, the study of individual idiosyncrasies, in terms of the sociocultural locale in which they are enacted, is crucial to an anthropological understanding of that locale. Culture generally is a composite of the actions of individuals, and in the courses of actions of individuals the normative dictates of culture are at times articulated ambiguously, if at all. Therefore I believe that one of the major concerns of the anthropologist of culture should be to discover the existential logic of "idiosyncrasies."

[15]The ritual requires that the text actually be read and not recited orally.

[16]I am not aware of any published studies on the language of Southern Tunisian Jews, but for some relevant information see D. Cohen, *Le Parler Arabe des Juifs de Tunis: Textes et Documents Linguistiques et Ethnographiques* (Paris: Mouton, 1964) and R. Lachmann, *Jewish Cantillation and Song in the Isle of Djerba* (Jerusalem: Hebrew University Press, 1940).

# You Are What You Eat: Religious Aspects of the Health Food Movement

Jill Dubisch

*Religion has usually been defined in terms of the belief in spiritual beings or the feelings evoked by and the practices developed to control the supernatural (Howells 1962:19). It may be possible, however, to conceptualize religious behavior without recourse to concepts of spirits, deities, or supernatural forces. Football games (Arens 1975), Memorial Day ceremonies (Cherry 1969), and neurotic behaviors (Freud 1959:117-27) have all been characterized as religious in nature, and Jill Dubisch, in the following essay, extends the perspective to the health food movement in the United States.*

*Foodways often play a key role in formal religious ritual (the Mass, the Seder) and may serve as basic signifiers of sacred time (feast day/fast day) and space ("A land flowing with milk and honey"). They can also serve as markers of religious belief and identity (Jewish dietary laws, Hindu vegetarianism, Christian temperance). For more on the symbolism of food and foodways see Firth (1973:243-61), Apte and Katona-Apte (1981), and Jones et al. (1983). Further discussion of the religious character of secular events may be found in Moore and Meyerhoff (1977).*

> Dr. Robbins was thinking how it might be interesting to make a film from Adelle Davis's perennial best seller, *Let's Eat Right to Keep Fit*. Representing a classic confrontation between good and evil—in this case nutrition versus unhealthy diet—the story had definite box office appeal. The role of the hero, Protein, probably should be filled by Jim Brown, although Burt Reynolds undoubtedly would pull strings to get the part. Sunny Doris Day would be a clear choice to play the heroine, Vitamin C, and Orson Welles, oozing saturated fatty acids from the pits of his flesh, could win an Oscar for his interpretation of the villainous Cholesterol. The film might begin on a stormy night in the central nervous system. . . .
>
> —Tom Robbins, *Even Cowgirls Get the Blues*

I intend to examine a certain way of eating; that which is characteristic of the health food movement, and try to determine what people are communicating when they choose to eat in ways which run counter to the dominant patterns of food consumption in our society. This requires looking at health foods as a system of symbols and the adherence to a health food way of life as being, in part, the expression of belief in a particular world view. Analysis of these symbols and the underlying world view reveals that, as a system of beliefs and practices, the health food movement has some of the characteristics of a religion.

Such an interpretation might at first seem strange since we usually think of religion in terms of a belief in a deity or other supernatural beings. These notions, for the most part, are lacking in the health food movement. However, anthropologists do not always consider such beliefs to be a necessary part of a religion. Clifford Geertz, for example, suggests the following broad definition:

> A *religion* is (1) a system of symbols which acts to (2) establish powerful, pervasive, and long-lasting moods and motivations in men by (3) formulating conceptions of a general-order of existence and (4) clothing these conceptions with such an aura of factuality that (5) the moods and motivations seem uniquely realistic.[1]

Let us examine the health food movement in the light of Geertz's definition.

## HISTORY OF THE HEALTH FOOD MOVEMENT

The concept of "health foods" can be traced back to the 1830s and the Popular Health movement, which combined a reaction against professional medicine and an emphasis on lay knowledge and health care with broader social concerns such as feminism and the class struggle.[2] The Popular Health movement emphasized self-healing and the dissemination of knowledge about the body and health to laymen. One of the early founders of the movement, Sylvester Graham (who gave us the graham cracker), preached that good health was to be found in temperate living. This included abstinence from alcohol, a vegetarian diet, consumption of whole wheat products, and regular exercise. The writings and preachings of these early "hygienists" (as they called themselves) often had moral overtones, depicting physiological and spiritual reform as going hand in hand.[3]

The idea that proper diet can contribute to good health has continued into the twentieth century. The discovery of vitamins provided for many health food people a further "natural" means of healing which could be utilized instead of drugs. Vitamins were promoted as health-giving substances by various writers, including nutritionist Adelle Davis, who has been perhaps the most important "guru" of health foods in this century. Davis preached good diet as well as the use of vitamins to restore and maintain health, and her books have become the best sellers of the movement. (The titles of her books, *Let's Cook It Right, Let's Get Well, Let's Have Healthy Children*, give some sense of her approach.) The health food movement took on its present form, however, during the late 1960s, when it became part of the "counterculture."

Health foods were "in," and their consumption became part of the general protest against the "establishment" and the "straight" life-style. They were associated with other movements centering around social concerns, such as ecology and consumerism.[4] In contrast to the Popular Health movement, health food advocates of the sixties saw the establishment as not only the medical profession but also the food industry and the society it represented. Food had become highly processed and laden with colorings, preservatives, and other additives so that purity of food became a new issue. Chemicals had also become part of the food-growing process, and in reaction terms such as "organic" and "natural" became watchwords of the movement. Health food consumption received a further impetus from revelations about the high sugar content of many popular breakfast cereals which Americans had been taught since childhood to think of as a nutritious way to start the day. (Kellogg, an early advocate of the Popular Health movement, would have been mortified, since his cereals were originally designed to be part of a hygienic regimen.)

Although some health food users are members of formal groups (such as the Natural Hygiene Society, which claims direct descent from Sylvester Graham), the movement exists primarily as a set of principles and practices rather than as an organization. For those not part of organized groups, these principles and practices are disseminated, and contact is made with other members of the movement, through several means. The most important of these are health food stores, restaurants, and publications. The two most prominent journals in the movement are *Prevention* and *Let's Live,* begun in 1920 and 1932 respectively.[5]

These journals tell people what foods to eat and how to prepare them. They offer advice about the use of vitamins, the importance of exercise, and the danger of pollutants. They also present testimonials from faithful practitioners. Such testimonials take the form of articles that recount how the author overcame a physical problem through a health food approach, or letters from readers who tell how they have cured their ailments by following methods advocated by the journal or suggested by friends in the movement. In this manner, such magazines not only educate, they also articulate a world view and provide evidence and support for it. They have become the "sacred writings" of the movement. They are a way of "reciting the code"—the cosmology and moral injunctions—which anthropologist Anthony F. C. Wallace describes as one of the important categories of religious behavior.[6]

## IDEOLOGICAL CONTENT OF THE HEALTH FOOD MOVEMENT

What exactly is the health food system? First, and most obviously, it centers around certain beliefs regarding the relationship of diet to health. Health foods are seen as an "alternative" healing system, one which people turn to out of their dissatisfaction with conventional medicine.[7] The emphasis is on "wellness" and prevention rather than on illness and curing. Judging from letters and articles found in health food publications, many individuals' initial adherence to the movement is a type of conversion. A specific medical problem, or a general dissatisfaction with the state of their health, leads these converts to an eventual realization of the "truth" as represented by the health food approach, and to a subsequent change in life-style to reflect the principles of that approach. "Why This Psychiatrist 'Switched'," published in *Prevention*, carries the following heading: "Dr. H. L. Newbold is a great advocate of better nutrition and a livelier life style. But it took a personal illness to make him see the light."[8] For those who have experienced such conversion, and for others who become convinced by reading about such experiences, health food publications serve an important function by reinforcing the conversion and encouraging a change of life-style. For example, an article entitled "How to Convert Your Kitchen for the New Age of Nutrition" tells the housewife how to make her kitchen a source of health for her family.[9] The article suggests ways of reorganizing kitchen supplies and reforming cooking by substituting health foods for substances detrimental to health, and also offers ideas on the preparation of nutritious and delicious meals which will convert the family to this new way of eating without "alienating" them. The pamphlet *The Junk Food Withdrawal Manual*, details how an individual can, step by step, quit eating junk foods and adopt more healthful eating habits.[10] Publications also urge the readers to convert others by letting them know how much better health foods are than junk foods. Proselytizing may take the form of giving a "natural" birthday party for one's children and their friends, encouraging schools to substitute fruit and nuts for junk food snacks, and even selling one's own baking.

Undergoing the conversion process means learning and accepting the general features of the health food world view. To begin with, there is great concern, as there is in many religions, with purity, in this case, the purity of food, of water, of air. In fact, there are some striking similarities between keeping a "health food kitchen" and the Jewish practice of keeping kosher. Both make distinctions between proper and improper foods, and both involve excluding certain impure foods (whether unhealthful or non-kosher) from the kitchen and table. In addition, a person concerned with maintaining a high degree of purity in food may engage in similar behavior in either case—reading labels carefully to check for impermissible ingredients and even purchasing food from special establishments to guarantee ritual purity.

In the health food movement, the basis of purity is healthfulness and "naturalness." Some foods are considered to be natural and therefore healthier; this concept applies not only to foods but to other aspects of life as well. It is part of the large idea that people should work in harmony with nature and not against it. In this respect, the health food cosmology sets up an opposition of nature (beneficial) versus culture (destructive), or, in particular, the health food movement against our highly technological society. As products of our industrialized way of life, certain foods are unnatural; they produce illness by working against the body. Consistent with this view is the idea that healing, like eating, should proceed in harmony with nature. The assumption is that the body, if allowed to function naturally, will tend to heal itself. Orthodox medicine, on the other hand, with its drugs and surgery and its non-holistic approach to health, works against the body. Physicians are frequently criticized in the literature of the movement for their narrow approach to medical problems, reliance on drugs and surgery, lack of knowledge of nutrition, and unwillingness to accept the validity of the patient's own experience in healing himself. It is believed that doctors may actually cause further health problems rather than effecting a cure. A short item in *Prevention,* "The Delivery Is Normal—But the Baby Isn't," recounts an incident in which drug-induced labor in childbirth resulted in a mentally retarded baby. The conclusion is "nature does a good job—and we should not, without compelling reasons, try to take over."[11]

The healing process is hastened by natural substances, such as healthful food, and by other "natural" therapeutic measures such as exercise. Vitamins are also very important to many health food people, both for maintaining health and for healing. They are seen as components of food which work with the body and are believed to offer a more natural mode of healing than drugs. Vitamins, often one of the most prominent products offered in many health food stores, provide the greatest source of profit.[12]

A basic assumption of the movement is that certain foods are good for you while others are not. The practitioner of a health food way of life must learn to distinguish between two kinds of food: those which promote well-being ("health foods") and those which are believed to be detrimental to health ("junk foods"). The former are the only kind of food a person should consume, while the latter are the antithesis of all that food should be and must be avoided. The qualities of these foods may be described by two anthropological concepts, *mana* and *taboo*. Mana is a type of beneficial or valuable power which can pass to individuals from sacred objects through touch (or, in the case of health foods, by ingestion). Taboo, on the other hand, refers to power that is dangerous; objects which are taboo can injure those who touch them.[13] Not all foods fall clearly into one category or the other. However, those foods which are seen as having health-giving qualities, which contain *mana*, symbolize life, while *taboo* foods symbolize death. ("Junk food is . . . dead. . . . Dead food produces death," proclaims one health food manual).[14] Much of the space in health food publications is devoted to telling the reader why to consume certain foods and avoid others.[15]

Those foods in the health food category which are deemed to possess an especially high level of *mana* have come to symbolize the movement as a whole. Foods such as honey, wheat germ, yogurt, and sprouts are seen as representative of the general way of life which health food adherents advocate, and Kandel and Pelto found that certain health food followers attribute mystical powers to the foods they consume. Raw food eaters speak of the "life energy" in uncooked foods. Sprout eaters speak of their food's "growth force."[16]

Qualities such as color and texture are also important in determining health foods and may acquire symbolic value. "Wholeness" and "whole grain" have come to stand for healthfulness and have entered the jargon of the advertising industry. Raw, coarse, dark, crunch, and cloudy foods are preferred over those which are cooked, refined, white, soft, and clear. (See chart.)

Thus dark bread is preferred over white, raw milk over pasteurized, brown rice over white. The convert must learn to eat foods which at first seem strange and even exotic and to reject many foods which are components of the Standard American diet. A McDonald's hamburger, for example, falls into the category of "junk food" and must be rejected.[17]

HEALTH FOOD WORLD VIEW

| | HEALTH FOODS | JUNK FOODS | |
|---|---|---|---|
| cosmic oppositions | LIFE NATURE | DEATH CULTURE | |
| basic values and desirable attributes | holistic, organic harmony with body and nature natural and real harmony, self-sufficiency, independence homemade, small scale layman competence and understanding | fragmented, mechanistic working against body and nature manufactured and artificial disharmony, dependence mass-produced professional esoteric knowledge and jargon | undesirable attributes |
| beneficial qualities of food | whole coarse dark crunchy raw cloudy | processed refined white soft cooked clear | harmful qualities |
| specific foods with mana | yogurt* honey* carob soybeans* sprouts* fruit juices herb teas foods from other cultures: humus, falafel, kefir, tofu, stir-fried vegetables, pita bread | ice cream, candy sugar* chocolate beef overcooked vegetables soft drinks* coffee,* tea "all-American" foods: hot dogs, McDonald's hamburgers,* potato chips, Coke | specific taboo foods |
| | return to early American values, "real" American way of life | corruption of this original and better way of life and values | |

*Denotes foods with especially potent mana or taboo.

Just as the magazines and books which articulate the principles of the health food movement and serve as a guide to the convert can be said to comprise the sacred writings of the movement, so the health food store or health food restaurant is the temple where the purity of the movement is guarded and maintained. There individuals find for sale the types of food and other substances advocated by the movement. One does not expect to find items of questionable purity, that is, substances which are not natural or which may be detrimental to health. Within the precincts of the temple adherents can feel safe from the contaminating forces of the larger society, can meet fellow devotees, and can be instructed by the guardians of the sacred area.[18] Health food stores may vary in their degree of purity. Some sell items such as coffee, raw sugar, or "natural" ice cream which are considered questionable by others of the faith. (One health food store I visited had a sign explaining that it did not sell vitamin supplements, which is considered to be "unnatural," i.e., impure.)

People in other places are often viewed as living more "naturally" and healthfully than contemporary Americans. Observation of such peoples may be used to confirm practices of the movement and to acquire ideas about food. Health and long-lived people like the Hunza of the Himalayas are studied to determine the secrets of their strength and longevity. Cultures as yet untainted by the food systems of industrialized nations are seen as examples of what better diet can do. In addition, certain foods from other cultures—foods such as humus, falafel, and tofu—have been adopted into the health food repertoire because of their presumed healthful qualities.

Peoples of other times can also serve as models for a more healthful way of life. There is in the health food movement a concept of a "golden age," a past which provides an authority for a better way of living. This past may be scrutinized for clues about how to improve contemporary American society. An archaeologist, writing for *Prevention* magazine, recounts how "I Put Myself on a Caveman Diet—Permanently."[19] His article explains how he improved his health by utilizing the regular exercise and simpler foods which he had concluded from his research were probably characteristic of our prehistoric ancestors. A general nostalgia about the past seems to exist in the health food movement, along with the feeling that we have departed from a more natural pattern of eating practiced by earlier generations of Americans.[20] (Sylvester Graham, however, presumably did not find the eating habits of his contemporaries to be very admirable.)

The health food movement is concerned with more than the achievement of bodily health. Nutritional problems are often seen as being at the root of emotional, spiritual, and even social problems. An article entitled "Sugar Neurosis" states "Hypoglycemia (low blood sugar) is a medical reality that can trigger wife-beating, divorce, even suicide.[21] Articles and books claim to show the reader how to overcome depression through vitamins and nutrition and the movement promises happiness and psychological well-being as well as physical health. Social problems, too, may respond to the health food approach. For example, a probation officer recounts how she tried changing offenders' diets in order to change their behavior. Testimonials from two of the individuals helped tell "what it was like to find that good nutrition was their bridge from the wrong side of the law and a frustrated, unhappy life to a vibrant and useful one."[22] Thus, through more healthful eating and a more natural life-style, the health food movement offers its followers what many religions offer: salvation—in this case salvation for the body, for the psyche, and for society.

Individual effort is the keystone of the health food movement. An individual can take responsibility for his or her own health and does not need to rely on professional medical practitioners. The corollary of this is that it is a person's own behavior which may be the cause of ill health. By sinning, by not listening to our bodies, and by not following a natural way of life, we bring our ailments upon ourselves.

The health food movement also affirms the validity of each individual's experience. No two individuals are alike: needs for different vitamins vary widely; some people are more sensitive to food additives than others; each person has his or her best method of achieving happiness. Therefore, the generalized expertise of professionals and the scientifically verifiable findings of the experts may not be adequate guides for you, the individual, in the search of health. Each person's experience has meaning; if something works for you, then it works. If it works for others also, so much the better, but if it does not, that does not invalidate your own experience. While the movement does not by any means disdain all scientific findings (and indeed they are used extensively when they bolster health food positions), such findings are not seen as the only source of confirmation for the way of life which the health food movement advocates, and the scientific establishment itself tends to be suspect.

In line with its emphasis on individual responsibility for health, the movement seeks to deprofessionalize knowledge and place in every individual's hands the information and means to heal. Drugs used by doctors are usually available only through prescription, but foods and vitamins can be obtained by anyone. Books, magazines, and health food store personnel seek to educate their clientele in ways of healing themselves and maintaining their own health. Articles explain bodily processes, the effects of various substances on health, and the properties of foods and vitamins.

The focus on individual responsibility is frequently tied to a wider concern for self-sufficiency and self-reliance. Growing your own organic garden, grinding your own flour, or even, as one pamphlet suggests, raising your own cow are not simply ways that one can be assured of obtaining healthful food; they are also expressions of independence and self-reliance. Furthermore, such practices are seen as characteristic of an earlier "golden age" when people lived natural lives. For example, an advertisement for vitamins appearing in a digest distributed in health food stores shows a mother and daughter kneading bread together. The heading reads "America's discovering basics." The copy goes on, "Baking bread at home has been a basic family practice throughout history. The past several decades, however, have seen a shift in the American diet to factory-produced breads. . . . Fortunately, today there are signs that more and more Americans are discovering the advantage of baking bread themselves." Homemade bread, home-canned produce, sprouts growing on the window sill symbolize what are felt to be basic American values, values supposedly predominant in earlier times when people not only lived on self-sufficient farms and produced their own fresh and more natural food, but also stood firmly on their own two feet and took charge of their own lives. A reader writing to *Prevention* praises an article about a man who found "new life at ninety without lawyers or doctors," saying "If that isn't the optimum in the American way of living, I can't imagine what is!"[23] Thus although it criticizes the contemporary American way of life (and although some vegetarians turn to Eastern religions for guidance),[24] the health food movement in general claims to be the true faith, the proponent of basic Americanness, a faith from which the society as a whole has strayed.

## SOCIAL SIGNIFICANCE OF THE HEALTH FOOD MOVEMENT FOR AMERICAN ACTORS

Being a "health food person" involves more than simply changing one's diet or utilizing an alternative medical system. Kandel and Pelto suggest that the health food movement derives much of its popularity from the fact that "food may be used simultaneously to cure or prevent illness, as a religious symbol and to forge social bonds. Frequently health food users are trying to improve their health, their lives, and sometimes the world as well."[25] Use of health foods becomes an affirmation of certain values and a commitment to a certain world view. A person who becomes involved in the health food movement might be said to experience what anthropologist Anthony F. C. Wallace has called "mazeway resynthesis." The "mazeway" is the mental "map" or image of the world which each individual holds. It includes values, the environment and the objects in it, the image of the self and of others, the techniques one uses to manipulate the environment to achieve desired end states.[26] Resynthesis of this mazeway—that is, the creation of new "maps," values, and techniques—commonly occurs in times of religious revitalization, when new religious movements are begun and converts to them are made. As individuals, these converts learn to view the world in a new manner and to act accordingly. In the case of the health food movement, those involved learn to see their health problems and other dissatisfactions with their lives as stemming from improper diet and living in disharmony with nature. They are provided with new values, new ways of viewing their environment, and new techniques for achieving their goals. For such individuals, health food use can come to imply "a major redefinition of self-image, role, and one's relationship to others."[27] The world comes to "make sense" in a light of this new world view. Achievement of the desired end states of better health and an improved outlook on life through following the precepts of the movement gives further validation.

It is this process which gives the health food movement some of the overtones of a religion. As does any new faith, the movement criticizes the prevailing social values and institutions, in this case the health-threatening features of modern industrial society. While an individual's initial dissatisfaction with prevailing beliefs and practices may stem from experiences with the conventional medical system (for example, failure to find a solution to a health problem through visits to a physician), this dissatisfaction often comes to encompass other facets of the American way of life. This further differentiates the "health food person" from mainstream American society (even when the difference is justified as a return to "real" American values).

In everyday life the consumption of such substances as honey, yogurt, and wheat germ, which have come to symbolize the health food movement, does more than contribute to health. It also serves to represent commitment to the health food world view. Likewise, avoiding those substances, such as sugar and white bread, which are considered "evil" is also a mark of a health food person. Ridding the kitchen of such items—a move often advocated by articles advising readers on how to "convert" successfully to health foods—is an act of ritual as well as practical significance. The symbolic nature of such foods is confirmed by the reactions of outsiders to those who are perceived as being inside the movement. An individual who is perceived as being a health food person is often automatically assumed to use honey instead of sugar, for example. Conversely, if one is noticed using or not using certain foods (e.g., adding wheat germ to food, not eating white sugar), this can lead to questions from the observer as to whether or not that individual is a health food person (or a health food "nut," depending upon the questioner's own orientation).

The symbolic nature of such foods is especially important for the health food neophyte. The adoption of a certain way of eating and the renunciation of mainstream cultural food habits can constitute "bridge-burning acts of commitment," which function to cut the individual off from previous patterns of behavior.[28] However, the symbolic activity which indicates this cutting off need not be as radical as a total change of eating habits. In an interview in *Prevention*, a man who runs a health-oriented television program recounted an incident in which a viewer called up after a show and announced excitedly that he had changed his whole life-style—he had started using honey in his coffee![29] While recognizing the absurdity of the action on a practical level, the program's host acknowledged the symbolic importance of this action to the person involved. He also saw it as a step in the right direction since one change can lead to another. Those who sprinkle wheat germ on cereal, toss alfalfa sprouts with a salad, or pass up an ice cream cone for yogurt are not only demonstrating a concern for health but also affirming their commitment to a particular life-style and symbolizing adherence to a set of values and a world view.

## CONCLUSION

As this analysis has shown, health foods are more than simply a way of eating and more than an alternative healing system. If we return to Clifford Geertz's definition of a religion as a "system of symbols" which produces "powerful, pervasive, and long-lasting moods and motivations" by "formulating conceptions of a general order of existence" and making them appear "uniquely realistic," we see that the health food movement definitely has a religious dimension. There is, first, a system of symbols, in this case based on certain kinds and qualities of food. While the foods are believed to have health-giving properties in themselves, they also symbolize a world view which is concerned with the right way to live one's life and the right way to construct a society. This "right way" is based on an approach to life which stresses harmony with nature and the holistic nature of the body. Consumption of those substances designated as "health foods," as well as participation in other activities associated with the movement which also symbolize its world view (such as exercising or growing an organic garden) can serve to establish the "moods and motivations" of which Geertz speaks. The committed health food follower may come to experience a sense of spiritual as well as physical well-being when he or she adheres to the health food way of life. Followers are thus motivated to persist in this way of life, and they come to see the world view of this movement as correct and "realistic."

In addition to its possession of sacred symbols and its "convincing" world view, the health food movement also has other elements which we usually associate with a religion. Concepts of mana and taboo guide the choice of foods. There is a distinction between the pure and impure and a concern for the maintenance of purity. There are "temples" (health food stores and other such establishments) which are expected to maintain purity within their confines. There are "rabbis," or experts in the "theology" of the movement and its application to everyday life. There are sacred and instructional writings which set out the principles of the movement and teach followers how to utilize them. In addition, like many religious movements, the health food movement harkens back to a "golden age" which it seeks to recreate and assumes that many of the ills of the contemporary world are caused by society's departure from this ideal state.

Individuals entering the movement, like individuals entering any religious move-ment, may undergo a process of conversion. This can be dramatic, resulting from the cure of an illness or the reversal of a previous state of poor health, or it can be gradual, a step-by-step changing of eating and other habits through exposure to health food doctrine. Individuals who have undergone conversion and mazeway resynthesis, as well as those who have tested and confirmed various aspects of the movement's prescriptions for better health and a better life, may give testimonials to the faith. For those who have adopted, in full or in part, the health food world view, it provides, as do all religions, explanations for existing conditions, answers to specific problems, and a means of gaining control over one's existence. Followers of the movement are also promised "salvation," not in the form of afterlife, but in terms of enhanced physical well-being, greater energy, longer life-span, freedom from illness, and increased peace of mind. However, although the focus is this-worldly, there is a spiritual dimension to the health food movement. And although it does not center its world view around belief in supernatural beings, it does posit a high authority—the wisdom of nature—as the source of ultimate legitimacy for its views.

Health food people are often dismissed as "nuts" or "food faddists" by those outside the movement. Such a designation fails to recognize the systematic nature of the health food world view, the symbolic significance of health foods, and the important functions which the movement performs for its followers. Health foods offer an alternative or supplement to conventional medical treatment, and a meaningful and effective way for individuals to bring about changes in lives which are perceived as unsatisfactory because of poor physical and emotional health. It can also provide for its followers a framework of meaning which transcends individual problems. In opposing itself to the predominant American life-style, the health food movement sets up a symbolic system which opposes harmony to disharmony, purity to pollution, nature to culture, and ultimately, as in many religions, life to death. Thus while foods are the beginning point and the most important symbols of the health food movement, food is not the ultimate focus but rather a means to an end: the organization of a meaningful world view and construction of a satisfying life.

---

[1]Clifford Geertz, "Religion as a Cultural System," in Michael Banton, ed., *Anthropological Approaches to the Study of Religion*, ASA Monograph No. 3 (New York: Frederick A. Praeger, 1965), 4.

[2]See Barbara Ehrenreich and Deidre English, *For Her Own Good: 150 Years of the Experts' Advice to Women* (Garden City, N.Y.: Anchor Press/Doubleday, 1979).

[3]Richard Harrison Shryock, *Medicine in America: Historical Essays* (Baltimore: Johns Hopkins University Press, 1966).

[4]Randy F. Kandel and Gretel H. Pelto, "The Health Food Movement: Social Revitalization or Alternative Health Maintenance System," in Norge W. Jerome, Randy F. Kandel, and Gretel H. Pelto, eds., *Nutritional Anthropology* (Pleasantville, N.Y.: Redgrave Publishing Company, 1980), 328.

[5]Gail Chapman Hongladarom, *Health Seeking Within the Health Food Movement* (Ph.D. diss., University of Washington, 1976).

[6]Anthony F. C. Wallace, *Religion: An Anthropological View* (New York: Random House, 1966), 57.

[7]See, for example, Hongladarom, *Health Seeking*.

[8]"Why This Psychiatrist 'Switched'," *Prevention* (September 1976).

[9]"How to Convert Your Kitchen for the New Age of Nutrition," *Prevention* (February 1975).

[10]Monte Kline, *The Junk Food Withdrawal Manual* (Total Life, Inc., 1978).

[11]"The Delivery Is Normal—But the Baby Isn't," *Prevention* (May 1979):38.

[12]Hongladarom, *Health Seeking*.

[13]Wallace, *Religion*, 60–61.

[14]Kline, *Junk Food*, 2–4.

[15]"Frozen, Creamed Spinach: Nutritional Disaster," *Prevention* (May 1979) and "Let's Sprout Some Seeds," *Better Nutrition* (September 1979).

[16]Kandel and Pelto, "Health Food Movement," 336.

[17]Conrad Kottack, "McDonald's as Myth, Symbol and Ritual" in *Anthropology: The Study of Human Diversity* (New York: Random House, 1978).

[18]See, for example, Hongladarom.

[19]"I Put Myself on a Caveman Diet—Permanently," *Prevention* (September 1979).

[20]See, for example, Hongladarom.

[21]"Sugar Neurosis," *Prevention* (April 1979):110.

[22]*Prevention* (May 1978):56.

[23]Ibid., 16.

[24]See Kandel and Pelto.

[25]Ibid., 332.

[26]Wallace, 237.

[27]Kandel and Pelto, 359.

[28]Ibid., 395.

[29]*Prevention* (February 1979):89.

# IV
# Occupational Folklore

## Risk and Ritual: An Interpretation of Fishermen's Folklore in a New England Community
### John J. Poggie, Jr., and Carl Gersuny

*Bronislaw Malinowski (1954) first formulated the hypothesis that situations of uncertainty and risk foster magic and ritual. Since technological control is never total, there will always be enterprises with highly unpredictable outcomes. The uncertainty and risk attached to such enterprises generate anxiety—a potentially incapacitating anxiety that could predestine these enterprises to certain failure. Malinowski felt that in the absence of complete technological control, this anxiety was alleviated through the illusion of control afforded by magic. Magic functioned, therefore, to alleviate anxiety and to free individuals to engage in those risky enterprises necessary to the maintenance of their social systems.*

*The following essay is one attempt to test Malinowski's hypothesis. If Malinowski's formulation is sound, enterprises with the greatest uncertainty and risk should be associated with the most rituals (or ritual avoidances—taboos). The hypothesis is confirmed when the superstitions of fishermen and factory workers are compared. However, the relatively equal distribution of superstitious behavior among the different types of fishermen is contrary to expectation, although it does not necessarily invalidate the hypothesis.*

*Vogt (1952) has closely followed Malinowski in his analysis of dowsing in the American Southwest, and Gmelch (1971) found the theory appropriate for explaining the distribution of magical behavior in professional baseball. Yet Radcliffe-Brown (1939) argued that rituals create rather than alleviate anxiety, and Moore (1957) suggested that some magical procedures may further reduce the amount of human control in an enterprise. For a discussion of the explanatory power of functional explanation see Oring (1976). For more on the folklore, particularly the beliefs, of fishermen see Mullen (1988).*

John J. Poggie, Jr., and Carl Gersuny

Among certain groups and in certain behavioral settings in the United States, there is a greater use of ritual magic than is generally characteristic of the whole society.[1] Coal miners and fishermen as well as rodeo performers and gamblers are in occupations and situations that are replete with ritual magic. These groups and situations have in common a high degree of uncertainty associated with them. The "retention" of rituals in these cases, in an otherwise highly secularized society, functions to bridge the gaps of uncertainty. This interpretation is based on the classical theoretical formulation proposed by Bronislaw Malinowski.

Malinowski first related magic to different types of risks; the risks were associated with the interrelationship between technology and habitat in fishing activities among the Trobriand Islanders. Concerning fishing among the Trobrianders he states:

> While in the villages on the inner lagoon fishing is done in an easy and absolutely reliable manner by the method of poisoning, yielding abundant results without danger and uncertainty, there are on the shores of the open sea dangerous modes of fishing and also certain types in which the yield greatly varies according to whether shoals of fish appear beforehand or not. It is most significant that in the lagoon fishing, where man can rely completely upon his knowledge and skill, magic does not exist, while in the open-sea fishing, full of danger and uncertainty, there is extensive magical ritual to secure safety and good results.[2]

It is interesting to note that there are two elements of unpredictability in Malinowski's discussion of magic among Trobriand fishermen. On the one hand, there is the question of certainty or uncertainty of the catch, while on the other hand there is the uncertainty or danger to the fishermen themselves. This same distinction appears to apply to such activities in the United States as gambling and rodeo riding, where the risks are related most predominantly to "production" and "person" respectively. We feel that an important conceptual distinction must be made between these two types of uncertainty involved in "risk taking" activities. The distinction appears to be important in understanding why ritual is more prevalent in certain occupational groups and behavior settings than it is in others.

While it is true that man has continually increased his control over and predictability of the process of production, there has not been a comparable increase in technological control over the elements that endanger his life and limb. Man's cognitive image of his capacity to preserve his mortal self through rational technology can never reach the degree of confidence that he has in his ability to control his environment.

We thus wish to emphasize the distinction between ritual associated with production and ritual associated with protection of life and limb. We are hypothesizing that there is a differential rate of retention of ritual associated with these two types of risk. Production is much more secularized than the contemplation of mortality. This hypothesis applies to those domains of production where man has "allowed" technological innovation to occur. It does not apply to gambling, rodeo riding, or like activities, where the technology is purposely primitive.

Medical science is an example of an area in which great technological innovation has taken place, and the practice of medicine itself is largely devoid of ritual. On the other hand, when medical technology fails, as it always does in the end, it is a ritual practitioner and not the medical doctor who "takes care of us."

We have collected data on ritual from two occupational groups in a southern New England community. These two occupational groups are comparable in most respects, except that one is a high physical-risk occupation and the other a low physical-risk occupation. These are fishermen and textile mill workers respectively. Personal risk is higher among fishermen than among mill workers because of the differences in the environments in which the two types of work are carried out. Fishing is innately more dangerous because it requires a technological coping with a marine environment by a terrestrial-arborial species even to start the work.

Precisely how dangerous fishing is as an occupation can be seen from a comparison of data on fatalities in commercial fisheries and coal mining, the most dangerous of land occupations. In 1965 the commercial fisheries of the United States recorded 21.4 deaths per million man-days, while in coal mining there were 1.04 deaths per million man-hours or 8.3 deaths per million man-days. In marked contrast is the rate of fatal accidents in textile mills in the United States which is 0.8 per million man-days.[3]

A comparison of the rituals of fishermen and textile workers will be the basis of testing the above hypothesis.

## DANGER AND RITUALS OF AVOIDANCE

Let us first briefly review the nature of rituals of avoidance as reported in the literature. Ritual, according to Leach, involves "non-instinctive predictable action . . . that cannot be justified by a 'rational' means-to-ends type of explanation."[4] In dangerous situations, especially where the perils besetting men are not susceptible to abatement by "rational" means, ritual is more likely to be developed than in safe and rationally controllable contexts. Avoidance rituals or tabus are thus an integral part of behavioral response to perceived danger.

Radcliffe-Brown referred to tabu as a "ritual prohibition" whose infraction results in undesirable change.[5] Tabu and danger are closely related, though in some cases the perception of danger arises from the tabu (as in the case of mother-in-law avoidance, perhaps, and certain food tabus), while in others it may be presumed that tabus arise in response to perils for which no technological remedy is known. Danger may thus be either the independent or the dependent variable in connection with tabu.

> So far as ritual avoidances are concerned, the reasons for them may vary from a very vague idea that some sort of misfortune or ill-luck, not defined as to its kind, is likely to befall anyone who fails to observe the taboo, to a belief that non-observance will produce some quite specific and undesirable result.[6]

Steiner also elaborates on the theme of danger in his definition of tabu as follows:

> Taboo is concerned (1) with all the social mechanisms of obedience which have ritual significance; (2) with specific and restrictive behaviour in dangerous situations. One might say that taboo deals with the sociology of danger itself, for it is concerned (3) with the protection of individuals who are in danger, and (4) with the protection of society from those endangered—and therefore dangerous—persons.... Taboo is an element of all those situations in which attitudes to values are expressed in terms of danger behavior.[7]

The perils of the sea, compounded by the hazards of the labors peculiar to fishing, create a context conducive to the survival of tabus even in a society among whose dominant values rationality ranks very high.

## PROCEDURES AND FINDINGS

In order to obtain information on frequency and types of ritual associated with the two occupational groups, we administered an interview schedule asking the following question on superstition, the emic term used by the fishermen and mill workers themselves to describe ritual beliefs and behaviors:

> Practically everyone has some superstitions such as walking under a ladder or knocking on wood. Are there any superstitions that are related to your type of work? If so, please describe as many as you can think of.

The interview schedule was administered to a sample of 27 fishermen and 29 factory workers. The sample of fishermen was a random one, while that of the factory workers was nearly a 100 percent sample of the work force in a small textile mill. Shoreville (pseudonym) is a predominantly "Yankee" coastal southern New England township of some 15,000 residents. The individuals involved in the fishermen and factory worker samples are for the most part local Shoreville people. The two groups are also similar in the sense that they are both blue-collar occupations. In educational attainment and age, the two groups are also quite similar. The mean age for both fishermen and factory workers is 37, while their average number of years of education are 12 and 11 respectively.

There are three main types of fishing technology in Shoreville: pot lobster boats that work during the day, draggers that also return to port each day, and draggers that stay out for several days at a time. We surmised that these types of fishing might vary in risk, pot lobstering being the least dangerous, as it is mainly an inshore, daytime activity, and multiple day-trip fishing being the most hazardous, as it takes the men away from protected waters and involves being out of reach of rapid assistance. One-day dragging would be intermediate because it is carried out in offshore waters but only on a daytime basis. Thus we had the possibility not only of comparing factory workers with fishermen but also of comparing different types of fishermen within the general occupational group. There is no corresponding variation in personal risk among the mill workers.

The results of our interviews are tabulated in the table below. It is of particular significance to note that of the twenty-nine factory workers interviewed only one gave what he considered to be a superstition associated with his work. His response was, "I am afraid of getting my arms caught on something." This particular response appears to be more of an expression of a realistic fear than a ritual avoidance. On the other hand, the fishermen responded with numerous reports of superstitions associated with their work. The types of superstition and their frequency of mention are indicated in the following table. Only one out of twenty-seven fishermen reported that there were no superstitions associated with his work.

### FISHERMEN'S TABUS IN SHOREVILLE
($N = 28$; 6 pot lobstermen, 13 day fishermen, 9 trippers)

| Frequency of times mentioned by all groups | Tabu |
|:---:|:---|
| 23 | Don't turn hatch cover upside down—bad luck<br>9—day; 8—tripper; 6—lobstermen |
| 8 | Don't whistle because it "whistles up a breeze"<br>6—day; 2—tripper; 0—lobstermen |
| 7 | Don't mention "pig" on board<br>4—day; 2—tripper; 1—lobstermen |
| 4 | Don't shave on a trip<br>2—day; 1—tripper; 1—lobstermen |
| 4 | Don't turn against the sun, always into it<br>0—day; 3—tripper; 1—lobstermen |
| 4 | Don't allow a man with a black bag aboard<br>1—day; 1—tripper; 2—lobstermen |
| 4 | Don't serve beef stew aboard; it brings on a gale<br>2—day; 2—tripper; 0—lobstermen |
| 3 | Don't bring women out on a trip<br>1—day; 0—tripper; 2—lobstermen |
| 3 | Don't leave for trip on Friday<br>2—day; 1—tripper; 0—lobstermen |
| 3 | Don't return a knife in any other way than the way it was given, open or closed<br>1—day; 2—tripper; 0—lobstermen |
| 3 | Knock on wood for good luck<br>1—day; 0—tripper; 2—lobstermen |
| 2 | Don't put hat in bunk<br>2—day; 0—tripper; 0—lobstermen |

*Mentioned once by day fishermen:*

Don't wash inside of wheelhouse windows
Don't wear a new hat—bad luck
No two-dollar bills—bad luck
No women on first trip of new boat

---

*Mentioned once by day fishermen:* (continued)

Don't wear yellow southwesters on board
Don't bring pork on board
Don't brag, it brings bad luck

*Mentioned once by trippers:*

Only coil a rope in the direction of the sun's path
Don't change name of boat
Don't leave dock twice in the same day

*Mentioned once by lobstermen:*

Don't wear black sweater
Red sky in the morning—warning of bad weather
Calm before the storm, perfect day—be apprehensive
See rat leaving the boat—don't sail
Never use the number 13 in speech
Thirteen pot trawls—bad luck
Metal boats sink
Always refer to boat as "she"

---

A striking pattern in these results is that the vast majority of the rituals are proscriptive in nature. That is to say, most of the ritual enjoins the avoidance of particular behavior patterns with the implication that misfortune will befall the actor if he does not avoid the proscribed behavior.

## DISCUSSION

The general hypothesis of this research is confirmed in that there is indeed considerably more ritual reported among the high-risk fishermen than among the low-risk textile workers. We argue that these differences are related to the differences in predictability and certainty of bodily integrity associated with these two occupational cultures. The textile workers are operating in a relatively safe environment, while the fishermen are operating in a much more hazardous one.

We have noted in our data that there is a preponderance of proscriptive norms or tabus reported by the fishermen. These beliefs deal with avoiding particular acts and are related to danger coming in the form of harm to the individual or his vessel. This situation is in contrast to prescriptive kinds of magic that prescribe necessary behaviors or acts, in this case in order to catch fish or to produce some other kind of output. Thus, if the general interpretation is correct, the prehistoric paintings of animals on the cave walls at Lascaux are prescriptive magic in that they were to ensure, among other things, the catching of animals. There is no logical connection between the clearly prescriptive types of ritual that were reported by our respondents and predictability in the catch. Rather, the types of ritual reported to us are strictly items that relate to preservation of body and its extensions. In the case of boxing and rodeo participation, even though physical danger is high, we are dealing with a select group of men whose physical self is defined as "all enduring" and where we think the major concern to the actor is more with the outcome (production). We find according to limited sources that magic rather than tabu predominates.[8]

It can be argued that the value system of the larger society in which this fishing subculture operates places great stress on technological rationality. The notion that technology can overcome the environment is pervasive in all sectors of American society. To a great extent this value system is consistent with the reality of technological competence that has been brought to bear on catching fish. The fishermen we have studied have at their disposal such efficient fish-tracking systems as sonar, aircraft for spotting schools of fish, as well as other devices that indicate the presence of particular species. Also at their disposal are the ecological data that deal with distribution of fish populations over the yearly cycle and that make locating fish a relatively predictable operation.

Thus we argue in Malinowski's terms that the uncertainty factor of the catch has been subjected by and large to technological remedies. Although it is possible for a fisherman from Shoreville to return to port after a day's work with few fish, it is unlikely for a fisherman to return with no fish. Furthermore, fishermen who do not come back with a large catch on one day have the prospect of a large catch another day to make up for a deficiency of the bad day. In the course of the year, fishermen do bring home large quantities of fish and realize a relatively high economic return for their efforts, at least in the Shoreville case.

Let us now consider the part of the environment with which the ritual reported to us is associated. Although it can be argued that man has brought ingenuity and technological competence to the task of overcoming the hazards of venturing out into the open ocean, we know that fishermen do lose their lives and do receive injury at a high rate because of their occupation. In contrast to a day with a poor catch, there is no second chance in losing one's life or in sustaining permanent injury. Thus, there is great risk involved in a man's going out onto the water to catch fish—more to his personal self than to his economic self. The risk we are talking about is characteristic of man's utilization of the marine environment. As a terrestrial species man is extending himself considerably by simply going out onto the water to carry out his work activities; in contrast, in a factory man does not need to build an artificial land environment under himself before he can even begin his activities. It is not only the artificial land environment (boat or platform) that man has made, but also the medium in which this artificial land environment operates that presents considerable hazard to the fisherman. Storms, rough seas, obstructions in the water, sudden changes in weather conditions, and other factors of the macro-environment along with the remote location of the work reduce predictability.

We had hypothesized that there would be a distinction between the rituals reported by pot lobstermen and those reported by day fishermen and multiple-day fishermen.

John J. Poggie, Jr., and Carl Gersuny

The results, however, did not confirm this hypothesis. Each of the groups has about the same proportion of ritual beliefs except that there are certain specialized ones for particular types of fishing. Trippers, who are out for several days, have peculiar to their set of ritual beliefs items concerning food serving on board the boat and items related to the sleeping arrangements. The pot lobstermen, who do not usually prepare food or sleep on board, show zero responses to these items.

Although we do not have the data necessary to prove why this pattern occurred, we can suggest that the risk factors involved in each of those types of fishing have been equalized more or less. The pot lobstermen who generally do not venture out as far into the ocean, or stay out overnight in the darkness, are often operating in congested inshore waters devoid of ship-to-shore radio, radar, sonar, and other safety features that are a standard part of day and trip boats. Even though safety technology may tend to equalize risk between inshore and offshore fishing, it does not remove the basic danger, which is, according to our view, the basis of tabu associated with man's occupancy of the sea.

In our interviews with fishermen about their ritual beliefs, there was a degree of embarrassment expressed concerning these superstitions. Many times our respondents would disclaim believing in these superstitions but would often admit that they dared not "break the rule" of the superstitions aboard their own boats. The embarrassment, or ambivalence, as Goffman calls it,[9] associated with reporting about superstitions is, we feel, a manifestation of the divergence between the larger landbound culture that the interviewers represent and the occupational subculture of fishermen. Fishermen who are part of both cultures are sensitive to the values of general secularization that exists in the land setting. Nevertheless, while they are at sea they do observe the proscriptions of the tabus that embarrass them on shore.

It can be argued that the persistence of superstitions among fishermen is a relic of the past, "coming from a time" when fishing was much more hazardous than it is today. The wide distribution of the tabus reported seem to support this hypothesis.[10] However, this particular view of the "persistence of relics" says nothing about the functional nature of sociocultural traits. It can be argued that there is no such thing as a functionless trait and that "relics of the past" have contemporary functions. We have argued that, even though their form may be widespread, the contemporary functions of these rituals that are part of fishermen's folklore operate essentially as they did in the past—to help man cope with the uncertainties of operating in a personally hazardous environment.

---

[1]This research, supported by the Marine Resources Committee and the Sea Grant Program at the University of Rhode Island, is part of a general socio-cultural study of a coastal New England community.

[2]Bronislaw Malinowski, *Magic, Science and Religion* (Garden City, N. Y., 1948), 30–31.

[3]Fatalities in fishing cited in Office of Merchant Marine Safety, *A Cost-Benefit Analysis of Alternative Safety Programs for U.S. Commercial Fishing Vessels* (Washington, D. C., 1971); fatality data in coal mining come from U.S. Bureau of the Census, *Statistical Abstract of the United States*, 91st ed. (Washington, D. C., 1970); data on fatalities in textile mills come from Bureau of Labor Statistics, *Injury Rates by Industry—1969* (Washington, D. C., 1971).

[4]Edmund R. Leach, "Ritual," *International Encyclopedia of the Social Sciences*, vol. 13 (New York, 1968), 520–521.

[5]A. R. Radcliffe-Brown, *Structure and Function in Primitive Society* (New York, 1965), 134.

[6]Ibid., 142.

[7]Franz Steiner, *Taboo* (New York, 1956), 20.

[8]S. Kirson Weinberg and Henry Arond, "The Occupational Culture of the Boxer," *American Journal of Sociology*, 57 (1952), 463–464; personal communication with ex-boxer-cowboy Tony McNevin.

[9]Erving Goffman, *Interaction Ritual* (Garden City, N.Y., 1967), 179.

[10]Compare James G. Frazer, *The Golden Bough* (London, 1890); Richard M. Dorson, *Buying the Wind* (Chicago, 1964); Helen Creighton, *Folklore of Lunenburg County, Nova Scotia* (Ottawa, 1950).

# Tending Bar at Brown's: Occupational Role as Artistic Performance

Michael J. Bell

*Although a number of definitions of folklore hold it to be an artistic expression, such expression has often been conceived in terms of traditional genres such as tale, ballad, joke, proverb, or riddle. But, in one sense, art is a component of any activity, even when the aims of an activity can be described in ordinary and utilitarian terms such as earning money, solving problems, or avoiding conflict. This is because art is a mode of attention: an attention to the form, style, and composition of virtually anything whatsoever. To characterize something as art is not to say that it is good (any more than to call something "business" is to imply that it is good business). Bad art is still art. It is merely to call attention to certain aspects of an activity or its products.*

*Michael J. Bell delineates the artistic nature of the job of barmaid in Brown's Lounge—a Philadelphia bar frequented by middle-class blacks. Bell characterizes the barmaids as artists in the ways that they design and shape the social situation of the bar through the performance of their occupational roles. The activity at the bar can be viewed as a piece of theater, with the barmaids serving as both directors and principal characters. It should be noted that this view of occupational role as artistic performance is not Bell's perception alone, but corresponds with the barmaids' conceptualization of their own activities as well.*

*A fuller description of the activities in Brown's Lounge can be found in Bell (1983). For a similar analysis of another woman's occupational performance see Johnson (1973). The conceptualization of folklore as performance can be found in Ben-Amos and Goldstein (1975), and Bauman (1978, 1986). For a discussion of the relation of aesthetics to craft and work see Jones (1987). Kochman (1972) offers a range of descriptions and analyses of black speech play.*

In the traditional description of the public drinking place, tending bar has largely been characterized as a passive profession.[1] The bartender or barmaid has been seen as the distributor of drinks and as the person ultimately responsible for order. In the enactment of either task, they are usually described as peripheral to the existence of the social world of the bar; as persons who, at best, will listen to your talk or your troubles but never become involved in either. In truth, tending bar is more complex. The bartender stands at the center of societal ambivalence over public drinking. The owner

---

of any establishment is in business to make a profit. In a bar this is accomplished by the sale of as much alcohol as possible. At the same time, the unrestricted sale of alcohol offers the real possibility of serious social and business consequences. No owner wants his patrons to consume so much that they become drunk and give the tavern a bad reputation in the community or at the local police station. Accordingly, the person tending bar must create an atmosphere in which people will keep drinking, thus satisfying the legitimate needs of his employer, and, at the same time, not allow anyone to become so drunk as to constitute a threat to social order. To achieve this, the person behind the bar cannot be just a passive listener and observer waiting until disorder arises to exercise control, but he must be an active participant engaged in creating an orderly world in which patron energy can be appropriately expressed. Tending bar thus involves the strategic manipulation of patron energy into a social order in which encounters may occur without threatening consequences to patron, bar or community.[2] This paper will show that in the case of the black bartender or barmaid the accomplishment of such a process is brought about through artistic performance, and that tending bar may be understood as an artful profession in Afro-American culture.

In particular, this essay will begin by formulating the systematic social knowledge which underlies the adequate fulfillment of the bartending role and which permits bar personnel and patrons to make sense of and accomplish the social world. This system will then be contextualized in terms of the actual practices and practical actions which invest this common social knowledge with existential reality. Finally, these patterns of performance will be examined as stylistically constituted artistic performances aimed at investing the social world with a particular "artful" reality.

The data on which this essay is based were obtained as a part of a two-year research project on the nature of folkloric communication in an urban black bar. The primary data gathering techniques were participant observation and personal interviews with key individuals in the setting. The bar, Brown's Lounge,[3] is located in a middle-class black community near the western border of Philadelphia. Most of its customers are drawn from the surrounding area and they, like their environs, reflect the middle-class status expectations of the American dream. In tandem, the bar and its patrons present a personal front designed to show orderliness and social control to the outside world.

The regular barmaids were Harriet, on the day shift, and Sarah, or "Symphony Sid" as she was commonly called, on the night shift. Both were considered by the community to be fully in command of the bartending role. Another bar owner commented:

> Charlie has got two of the best barmaids in West Philly. Both of them are just golden. Shit, he wasn't doing nothing compared to what he's been doing since he's got them to go behind the bar.[4]

This opinion was reflected both in Charlie's weekly receipts and the general contentment of his patrons. The latter saw both barmaids as actively transforming Brown's into a "lively place":

> You know, Mike, I really enjoy comin' here lately. Since Charlie hired Harriet, this bar's been poppin' full time.

> Sarah works a nice bar. You come in an' sit an' she talk with you whether you drinkin' beer or you drinkin' top shelf. She's friendly even when she's ornery an' lookin' to mess.

The basis of their successful fulfillment of their role stemmed from the awareness that working the bar was a job. In one encounter between herself and Charlie, Harriet expressed this understanding quite vehemently:

> C:  You do know where you're working and for who?
> H:  Do I know I'm workin'? Do I know this! Charles Ulysses Brown, with my feet hurtin' and my back talkin' to me and my ears bent out of shape by you and these suckers. You tell me how I could forget. You find one of these river rats who'd let me.

Though there is much exaggeration in this response, Harriet's spontaneous description of the occupational hazards present in bartending is indicative of her understanding of her presence at Brown's as work. This was substantiated in her description of how she became a barmaid:

> It was right after they passed that law that said women could work behind the bar. It didn't used to be that you could have a woman behind the bar. I started with _____ over in North Philly and I worked for him for five years before I came over here to West Philly. You know, when you're a young girl sittin' on that side of the bar it looks easy. It don't look no different from sitting out on the stoop talking with people or hanging at the corner. But Michael, you learn fast. Cause if you don't, those people will run you ragged till they kill you with their shit. You know I don't drink when I'm behind this bar. If a customer comes in and offers, I always tells him I don't drink on the job. Now that just makes good sense cause you can either be working or having a good time. And ain't nobody paying you to have a good time. They buying your work which you either do or get fired. You got to see that this is a job, nothing more, and then act like it all the time.

Though not as extensively stated, Sarah voiced a similar understanding to a patron who was attempting to monopolize her time:

> You got to understand I ain't doing this for fun. I got more customers than you to take care of. Who you to be wailing about "talk with me" and "forget them for a while." I ain't playing. This is my job which I am paid to do with everybody who sits up at this bar. So you just settle down and don't go messing with me.

Expressed in these descriptions of their roles is the clear understanding that there is a socially constituted frame around the time they spend in the bar. Both saw their activities not as examples of who they were as persons, but rather as reflections of the expectations implicit in their work.[5] Both Harriet and Sarah recognized a distance between their social selves and their occupational roles. From their perspectives, their participation in the social life of the bar was wholly professional.

This professional awareness qualitatively distinguished Harriet's and Sarah's participation in the social order from that of their patrons. The knowledge that one is a patron and, therefore, the knowledge of how to appropriately act as a patron is not normally an aspect of conscious purpose. Being a patron is a *reflexive* involvement in social life. The performance of the patron role follows naturally from being in the bar. Under most conditions, patrons are not self-consciously acting when they participate in the social life of the bar. Their perceptions of their activities are that social life just happens. Bartending, on the other hand, does not just happen. It requires a *reflective* involvement in social life. In contrast to the assumptions underlying patron behavior, Harriet and Sarah knew they were playing a part. They sensed themselves as dramatic personae and their performances as a form of acting. As Sarah described:

> Michael, on this side of the bar I can be using all kinds of language and be acting all kinds of crazy an' not one of them will look up. All's I have to do is to be sitting up next to you and they'll be all over me like bees on honey. Here I work, an', hee hee, hee, there I party.

Treating consciousness of performance as the determining factor in differentiating the bartending role from that of patron is not a denial of the potentially dramatic nature of both roles. The question is not whether both roles are performances—obviously they are—but what kind of performances they are. The performances of Harriet and Sarah were more classically theatrical than those of their patrons. As actors on a stage, they possessed a framework of knowledge which allowed them to tend bar while simultaneously asserting that they were only actors and therefore not culpable for the actions the role caused them to perform.[6] Moreover, this perception of their status as actors altered the taken-for-granted orientation they brought to bear on the accomplishment of social order. Their self-consciousness not only freed them from the moral responsibilities of genuineness incumbent on patrons, but it also permitted them to improvise a reality not wholly consistent with the actual world inside or outside the bar. Both Harriet and Sarah were free to become different people in ways that their patrons were not, to "act all kinds of crazy," without the fear of actually being thought so. The informational effect of this stock of knowledge was that their awareness of the boundary conditions surrounding their role freed them from the necessity of consistency normally associated with role performance. It allowed instead a reflective organization of the needs of social life to predetermined ends. In knowing that they were actors, Harriet and Sarah knew more than their patrons and could be "self-conscious while they [the patrons] remained only conscious."[7] The result was that in knowing the part, and knowing it was only a part, they also knew the probable outcome of the play. Their patrons could only guess.[8]

This advantage of knowledge was reflected in the manner in which Harriet and Sarah enacted their particular course of action behind the bar. Harriet worked the bar in a highly calculated fashion. She viewed the day shift as a naturally quiet time and saw her responsibility in terms of creating life and evoking energy:

> The men who come here during the day are pretty quiet. They aren't all the time talking loud. Mostly, I like to get a little life in them. Get 'm doing something 'stead of just sitting. Now some of them'd be plain drunks if you let them be. Just sit and suck liquor all day. You give 'm someone to talk to an' talk about an' they'll have a good time and not cause trouble.

For Harriet, the focus of her involvement in Brown's was on the construction of social life in which her patrons actively related to each other. Obviously, such an atmosphere was conducive to drinking and thus served the economic purpose of the bar. As important, the creation of a "good time" served the social interests of her patrons by expanding their frame of expectations with regard to bar activity. Freed from the necessity of only drinking by the existence of a viable social life, the patrons were presented with the potential to choose drinking as only one of many available alternative claims on social time. Harriet's focus on action brought patrons together and kept them involved with each other and with their situation rather than solely with alcohol consumption.

This system of action was dependent upon her ability to establish relationships with the regular patrons. She was aware that the construction and maintenance of such a network among the regulars gave her a framework for articulating the stable and continuous social order she felt they needed:

> Most of the customers who come here during the day are looking to bullshit with someone. They aren't out to party like no young boys. If I can get something happenin', they'll play with it an' keep it going. Now, with this group here, I've got a head start. Most of these people know each other so I can use them at each other to get some action.

Harriet's activity involved a manipulation of the already existing structure of patron awareness to create an environment of discourse among those present.

She generated this action with two distinctive forms of role work. The first kind of role work was directed at the building of an information frame[9] supportive to talking shit. Such work was designed to create a firm base line on which to accomplish the aims of social life. The second type of role work was aimed at evoking relevant expressions of play within the constituted frame. This work sought to involve the patrons in the performance of the social definition of situation; to make them become performers in, rather than watchers of, social life. This division of the role work involved in tending bar is not intended to indicate a causal chain. Framework is not preparatory to acting. The image of a supportive frame should not be of a static scaffolding, but of a system of social boundaries developing as an integral part of the unfolding of everyday life. Social frame reflects the communicative intent of the social setting. It is fixed, however, not by this system but rather by the definition of situation as it grows with social life.[10] Neither is the distinction of two types of role work an indication that bartending action is exclusively distributed to either category. It is possible for an individual act to be frame and acting at the same time. Their distinction is based not on what is done but how it is accomplished. The immediate focus is not the activity's manifest goal but whether the dramatic use of self is the means by which the goal is achieved. For example, if Harriet "feeds the jukebox" by depositing the money herself, then her action is framework oriented toward the maintenance of the communicational environment. If she "feeds the jukebox" by calling out to those in the bar "All right you River Rats, I serve you all day, least you can do is keep the music going!" or hands a patron a dollar, tells him to pick some music, and then argues with him over his choice, then she achieves the same goal but does so by involving herself in the flow of social life and manipulating her image to achieve her end. The distinctions, framework and acting, represent methodologies of cataloging self-involvement in social life and not different classes of acts; both reflect processes and not ends.

Harriet spent most of her time interacting. She saw her responsibility as generating action, and thus actively sought to create social life. Framework, for her, was limited to those moments when the bar was empty. During such periods, she always saw that the jukebox was playing and that the barroom was "neat." She said of this activity:

> Michael, you have to give them noise. No one's gonna come into an empty, silent bar. Hell, I'd sooner drink in a morgue than in a dead bar. Same with the cleaning. A bar that's all full up with empty glasses and beer bottles just isn't inviting. I bet you don't like sitting at a dinner table with all them empty plates, now do you?

Once the bar was full, however, she concentrated on acting to gain her ends.

Harriet's techniques for generating action during her shift were aimed at drawing all those present into an interactive web. She was constantly involving herself with patrons, monitoring their needs and conversations in order to draw them out, or draw them into existing interactions. She opened all closed encounters whenever possible. She used her freedom of movement behind the bar to expand the boundaries of conversation by moving away from a speaker or a group while maintaining conversational contact. Thus, she would move to the far end of the bar while still talking to a patron, increasing the volume of talk as she moved. The effect was to draw the conversation open to all other patrons. Likewise, she would perch herself on a stool in the farthest corner from the entrance so that all interactions with her were carried on at maximum distance and volume. This effectively meant that all interaction with Harriet was public interaction regardless of its form. From greeting to exit, what you said to her and she to you was the conversational property of the community.

A central aspect of this interactional net was her manipulation of herself as image through her raps.[11] She was considered to be "a woman who raps like a man," and she took this description quite seriously. Several patrons commented on her argumentativeness and how it was hard to talk to her:

> She'll fight about anything. You start to have a conversation with her and the next thing she's rapping at you. She's telling you, you don't know anything and you better listen to her. And she won't talk no shit if you tell her otherwise. She is a hard woman.

Most recognized her words as just that and responded accordingly. They knew that she was "just messing," as one informant put it, and enjoyed the opportunity to rap back. With Harriet you always knew where you stood:

> It's cool, you know? She'll put you through some changes but she won't fuck with your mind. When she rap, you rap, and when she won't you don't. It's as simple as that.

Thus, a shift with Harriet was one in which she was both the center and source of much of social life; one marked by a high degree of energy being directed from her to those present:

> I guess I come cause I know something will always be happening. She'll be after Teddy or Charlie or someone and it's fun to watch, you know. It's never dull with Harriet behind the bar. She keeps the place jumping with noise.

In contrast to Harriet's performance, Sarah's was directed more towards framework. Sarah saw her responsibilities as polar opposites to those of Harriet:

> The people who come here at night don't need me to tell them to party. They wouldn't be here lessen that was a part of their program. Nah, my problem is slowing their roll.

Sarah perceived the night shift as one in which the social universe was committed to action and her job as requiring her only to maintain that action, and to see that it did not break through its naturally evolving boundaries. Her performance as bartender was quiet and direct and subdued when compared with Harriet:

> Mostly I just talk to 'em when they come in until they get settled. Then I can leave 'em alone. They let me know when they want me. Until then I just lets them be an' have a good time.

This low-keyed approach was reflected in her verbal interplay as well. Sarah's conversations were usually short in duration and more clearly phatic.[12] They served to maintain contact and to mark tempo and tenor, rather than to invite involvement. This is not to suggest that they were not meaningful to the maintenance of the system or imply that they were superficial. They were extremely functional, in the communicational sense, in that they allowed her to observe social life without disrupting its natural flow. She acted to preserve the frame that the patrons had come to create rather than formulate one for them:

> When they're having a good time, it don't make no sense for me to be sticking myself or my two cents in. They can take care of themselves just fine.

Her conscious acts to remain outside of social life did not reflect an attempt to withdraw from the event. She was by no means a mechanical doll dispensing drinks. Her involvement, however, was not as intensely within the flow of social life as Harriet's. For example:

> Sarah was dancing quietly in the area near the beer cooler. Her movements were slow and languid and directed toward the far wall. A patron observing her said: "You're sure moving good. How about I come over and you and me drag." Sarah, still dancing, replied: "Be cool now an' enjoy your drink—I'd be too much for you." A ripple of laughter flowed down the bar and another voice said: "Too much to handle, huh Sarah?" and she answered: "I'd be too much for all of you. You have troubles just watching." She finished her dancing with the end of the song and moved off to serve a customer.

Whereas Harriet could have used the playing to initiate a verbal contest, Sarah treated it as a closed exchange. Her responses framed the incident into a routine "cracking"[13] relationship rather than a public rap. Such acts of closure were characteristic of her performance style. Sarah was present to social life but not wholly within it. She acted to entertain by performance, not to create social life.

Her overall detachment from acting as a mechanism for generating social interaction did not prevent Sarah from the active maintenance of social frame. The bulk of her time was given over to insuring an adequate level of noise[14] in the bar. She "fed the jukebox" not only to keep the music flowing but also to create an appropriate mood in the setting. She would juggle the sounds of the music so that it would balance good interactions or lead patrons into good interactions:

> A patron who had been sitting alone at the bar walked to the jukebox, selected about five songs and went back to his seat. The first two were slow, mournful ballads of lost love. As the third song, another ballad, started, Sarah said: "Is that all you played? You must be out of it. Ricky, go play some music. We'll see if we can't get this man out of his mood. Cause if we don't he'll have us all crying in our beers, ain't that right?" She then pushed the reject button until all his songs were off the box and said "Buy that man some happiness on me. I ain't workin' no sad-eyed shift tonight. Tonight we all party, hee hee hee.

Such acts were not uncommon, but mood was usually maintained by asking someone to play a specific song while he was at the jukebox, as "Punch out 3-9-7 will ya, baby" or the like. Sarah also monitored each patron's drinking so as to always be ready to refill their glasses when necessary. As one patron said:

> You gotta watch Sid, you know, She'll have you drinkin' all night if you'd let her. She's not all the time loud talkin' at you: "Do you want another or are you just takin' up space." She just gets the job done by fillin' your glass. You put it down an' turn your head an', wham bam, there's a full glass where your empty was. Hee hee hee. Or she's got your beer glass under that thing.... [Sarah broke

153

> in and, smiling, said: "Spigot. 'Thing', you got less sense than this glass."] . . .
> an she's saying: "You did want another, right?" She's real pretty doing it,
> though, you know.

A shift with Sarah was one in which the flow of social life was maintained by regulation of social boundaries rather than by the forceful use of self-information within interaction. Sarah accomplished social life through subtle direction; action she left to her patrons.

The fulfillment of the bartending role by both Harriet and Sarah exemplifies the model of appropriate involvement articulated earlier. The activities of each are examples of reflective responses to the inherent tensions of the role and of effective methods of structuring social life to insure the maintenance of social order. Their accomplishment of the role represented the kind of active work necessary to protect the social universe. Their actions exhibit a sense of the institutional requirements for control. Both actively sought to keep the flow of social life under their watchful eye. Although their individual styles were different, the results were the same. Both barmaids were intent on being the prism through which social life was refracted into its appropriate spectrum. Both held tight rein on how it would proceed, yet neither did so as policemen outside the ongoing event. Each, in their own way, acted as an aspect of social life appropriate to the definition of situation.

Within this universe of theatricality, there existed a further technique for enacting social order in the form of patterned routines, or raps, between the barmaids and the other available bar personnel, Charlie, the owner, and Teddy, the porter.[15] These raps on Teddy and Charlie were a regular part of the process of tending bar,[15] and served as a device to further structure and organize social life. Stored as recognizable, repeatable events in the communicative system, they served as a ready-made and viable mechanism for concentrating patron energy and interest on the behavior of bar personnel.

> It was ten o'clock in the morning. There were five customers, all regulars, in
> the bar. They were seated at one end talking and drinking, with the jukebox
> playing softly as background. Teddy, who had just finished with the trash, sat
> down next to, but not with the group, and waited. Harriet looked up and said:
> "What you want? You taking a coffee break? Get off that stool, you ain't a
> customer." Teddy smiled at the five heads turned in his direction and replied:
> "Woman give me a drink. I have worked an' now I will rest." "Worked?"
> Harriet replied, "You haven't worked a day since you started suckin' up gin. An'
> who you callin' woman? I ain't your woman. And if I was, you'd be dead cause
> I'd kill a sucker like you. Any woman'd kill you, you so full of gin one good shot
> an' you'd be dead." Teddy answered: "No way, woman, I got enough for any
> woman, 'specially you." This "argument" continued with varying intensity for
> about five minutes and then died only to flare into action in about half-an-hour
> when social life had begun to quiet down. The bar was nearly full but the
> general atmosphere was subdued. Sarah looked at Teddy cleaning up behind
> the far end of the bar and said: "Do you believe Teddy? He's so skinny if he'd
> turn sideways he'd disappear. You just look at him, skin and bones. If he ain't

the raggedy-ass man I ever seen. Shit, if he get you between them legs he'd cut you in two." "Who you shootin' off at, woman? You want to see som'thin' you jus' let me get you up to the back, back booth an' I'll give you lovin' like you never got," Teddy replied. The argument lasted most of the shift with patrons regularly joining in to take sides.

These incidents exemplify the basic pattern of the barmaid-porter interchanges. In each case their effect was to focus interactive energy on a public performance, a performance, moreover, which was bar- rather than patron-centered, and therefore, "safe energy."

Similar in structure and function to the barmaid-porter interchanges were those between Harriet or Sarah and Charlie. These exchanges had the routine quality, in the performance sense, of those cited above. Their only noticeable difference was content. These contests centered around Charlie's alleged tightness or his basic failures as an employer. In their process of accomplishment they were no different than the others:

> Charlie sat up at the bar and ordered a drink. Harriet poured it and said: "That'll be ninety-five cents." Charlie turned to Tookie Brooks, a regular, and said: "Took, did you hear that? My bar, my whiskey, and she wants me to pay for my drink." Harriet cut in: "Charlie, I don't wanna rap. Just pay me my money, you sucker." "You watch your mouth, Harriet, or I'll hafta take you to the back booths for a lesson," continued Charlie. Harriet said again, "Just give me my money—you be here at the end of the day wantin' to know how many free drinks of your whiskey did I give away. Well you ain't gonna be one of them. Now pay up." They continued for fifteen minutes during which the assembled patrons followed the encounter closely. At its conclusion, one remarked: "That Harriet. Watchin' her give it to Charlie's worth the price of these drinks."

Both sets of routines point up the essential nature of social control as stored in the social structuring of staff. In the performance of their various roles, Harriet and Sarah actively work to generate an orderly social universe for patron interaction. In so doing, they create a world in which energy is free to express itself and because its boundaries are continually being established and ordered, they build a world into which chaos cannot penetrate and overwhelm everyday life.

What I have attempted in this essay has been to discuss the role of the black barmaid in creating and organizing the social order of a black neighborhood bar. This has been done by examining the social knowledge and the patterns of performance of two barmaids as they are reflected in the artful accomplishment of tending bar. I have shown that both Harriet and Sarah were aware of a specific set of occupational expectations and that their actualization of this role work was aimed at the maintenance of a social environment in which patrons can fully interact without violating the moral order of their social world. Further, it has been demonstrated that the accomplishment of this self-conscious process of tending bar in Brown's is artful work, and hence folkloric in nature.

Michael J. Bell

It has been my intent to argue that within the black experience certain occupational roles are best understood as extended artistic performances and their fulfillment as artistic action by highly conscious actors. It is a further corollary of this argument that folklorists should not only be concerned with the folklore of occupational groups and the folklore surrounding work and workers, but also with working itself as a folkloric form and process. If it is true in general, as has been shown in particular cases of black bartending, that occupational roles can be artistic as well as social, then it is of the greatest importance that those trained to see art and artful practices in everyday life participate fully in their analysis. To do otherwise, to leave occupations to sociologists and anthropologists alone, is ultimately to reduce our own contributions to the better understanding of human beings, and to reduce the unique contributions of those human beings themselves.

---

[1]For example, see Sherri Cavan, *Liquor License: An Ethnography of Bar Behavior* (Chicago, 1966); B. E. Macrory, "The Tavern and the Community," *Quarterly Journal of Studies on Alcohol* 13 (1956):319–414; and Mass Observation, *The Pub and the People* (London, 1943). An interesting exception to the pattern is E. C. Moore, who wrote: "The saloon keeper is the only man who keeps open house in the ward.... His place is the common meeting ground of his neighbors—and he supplies the stimulus which renders social life possible." "The Social Value of the Saloon," *American Journal of Sociology* 3 (1897):7–8.

[2]Such a manipulation is not necessarily an active process in which the person tending bar forces himself into the forefront of every encounter occurring in the environment. Strategic manipulation can just as easily be effected by no action as by intense interaction. Rather, the strategic aspects of the profession involve knowing when and how to act and when and how *not* to act. It is a profession of placement of self in the right place, with the right action at the right time.

[3]Brown's Lounge is a pseudonym, as is its location. All other names in the text have similarly been altered.

[4]Unless otherwise noted, all conversational data is drawn from field notes and taped interactions.

[5]This differentiation between self and performance has been extensively dealt with by Erving Goffman in *The Presentation of Self in Everyday Life* (Garden City, New York, 1959), 17–76, particularly 30–34.

[6]For a discussion of the nature of such theatricality, see Elizabeth Burns, *Theatricality, A Study of Convention in the Theater and in Social Life* (New York, 1972).

[7]Edmund Husserl, *Cartesian Meditations: An Introduction to Phenomenology*, trans. D. Carins (The Hague, 1964), 105.

[8]Such guesses are, of course, not random. They occur in a fairly stable social and moral order. Thus, regular patrons possessed of a reasonable understanding of the boundary conditions surrounding social life were able to accurately predict the unfolding of the stream of behavior. Thus, the degree of social control held by the barmaids in the open system of social life is not absolute, but only relatively greater than that possessed by the patrons.

[9]The concept of frame is drawn from the writings of Gregory Bateson, *Steps to an Ecology of Mind* (New York, 1972), 184–193, 315–321.

[10]According to Bateson: "The network is not bounded by the skin but includes all external pathways along which information can travel. It also includes those effective differences which are imminent in the 'objects' of such information." *Steps to an Ecology of Mind*, 319.

[11]According to Thomas Kochman: "Rapping, while used synonomously to mean ordinary conversation, is distinctively a fluent and lively way of talking characterized by a high degree of personal narration." "Towards an Ethnography of Black-American Speech Behavior," *Afro-American Anthropology: Contemporary Perspectives*, eds. J. Szwed and N. Whitten, Jr., (New York, 1970), 146. See also Roger D. Abrahams, "Rapping and Capping: Black Talk as Art," *Black America*, ed. J. Szwed (New York, 1970), 132–142.

[12]The term "phatic" is taken from B. Malinowski, "The Problem of Meaning in Primitive Languages," *The Meaning of Meaning*, eds. C. K. Ogden and I. A. Richards (New York and London, 9th Ed., 1953), 296–336.

Roman Jakobson defined phatic communication as those messages "Primarily serving to establish, to prolong, or to discontinue communication, to check whether the channel works ("Hello do you hear me?"), to attract the attention of the interlocutor or to confirm his continued attention, ('Are you listening?') or in Shakespearean diction, ('Lend me your ears!'—and on the other end of the wire 'Um-hum!')." "Closing Statement: Linguistics and Poetics," *Style in Language,* ed. T. A. Sebeok (Cambridge, Mass., 1960), 335.

[13]In Brown's, cracking, sometimes called signifying, woofing, or sounding, is a ritualized insult often taking the form of a left-handed compliment. For other more formalized definitions, see Roger D. Abrahams, "Playing the Dozens," *Journal of American Folklore* 75 (1962):209–220; John Dollard, "The Dozens: Dialect of Insult," *American Imago* 1 (1939), 3–25; Thomas Kochman, 145–162; Claudia Mitchell-Kernan, "Language Behavior in a Black Urban Community," *Monographs of the Language Behavior Laboratory,* 2 (1971); and finally, William Labov, "Rules for Ritual Insults," in *Language in the Inner City: Studies in Black English Vernacular* (Philadelphia, 1972).

[14]In Brown's, the concept of noise does not refer to interference in the informational sense. Rather, it describes a necessary supportive level of sound which underlies patron interaction. For a further analysis of this phenomena, see Michael J. Bell, "Running Rabbits and Talking Shit: Folkloric Communication in an Urban Black Bar" (Ph.D. diss., University of Pennsylvania, 1975), 106–112.

[15]During fieldwork, informants made a general distinction between "rapping with" and "rapping on." The former defined a conversational encounter in which the exchange of information, though lively, was never aimed at bringing an unequal outcome between participants. In such rapping events, the goal was only to "put down" your opponent. The latter described a verbal interaction in which one participant attempts to dominate and devastate the other. In such cases, the goal is to "cap bad" on the other participant. Accordingly, such "raps on" represented highly dangerous interactions in which the outcome had the potential to overwhelm and destroy social life. The performer who undertook such a rap was expected to know how to act appropriately, and it was not surprising that in Brown's such raps were restricted to well-defined performers in the setting and to bar staff.

# The Last Forty-Niner: The Uses of History in the Mother Lode

Russell Frank

*An occupation may put its stamp on an entire region. The whalers who embarked from the coastal cities of New England and the cowpunchers who drove the herds out of southeast Texas to the Kansas railheads conditioned, to some extent, the perception of these regions both locally and nationally. The imprint of the forty-niners who swept through the California goldfields in the middle of that same century also remains. But the nature of this imprint is not always a matter of consensus, even for the local population of the region. Russell Frank shows that, within the gold country itself, there are competing perspectives on the forty-niners and their occupational endeavors; indeed, that there are alternative relationships to and conflicting uses of the past.*

*The nineteenth century was a period of economic transformation in the United States. New resources were tapped, new industries were developed, and new systems of transportation and communication were put in place. Occupations were born and died along with their folklore and culture. Some sense of this transformation is presented in Richard M. Dorson (1973:123–250). William Ivey (1970) also explores the relationship of the occupational past to the life and lore of a rural community.*

> The newcomer doesn't know. To them mining is '49, you know, the old bearded man with the gold pan out in the stream with his jackass. That's what they think of mining.[1]
>
> —Carlo DeFerrari
> Tuolumne County Historian

In a cabin on a little peak east of Tuolumne City, California, lives "The Last Forty-Niner." At least, that is what a San Francisco television station dubbed him in a five-minute segment of a magazine-format program about "real people."

If Ben Fullingim were really the last forty-niner, his participation in the California Gold Rush, as fascinating as that would be, would have to take a backseat to his being "The Oldest Man on Earth." Since the last forty-niner could not be much younger than 160 years old in 1988 it appears that what was meant was that Old Ben is "The Last Person Living in the Manner of the Forty-Niners."

With his chewed-up hat and his chest-length beard, his donkey named Nugget and his rusted picks and pans, Ben Fullingim certainly looks the part. But with his truck and his generator, his radio and telephone and his counterparts in every town in the Sierra Nevada, even this more modest claim must be withdrawn. If it were accuracy the producers were after, they would have come up with something like "One of the Last People Who Sometimes Lives in a Manner Similar to the Forty-Niners."

Not very catchy, or even worth mentioning since we are all so familiar with the use of superlatives as attention-getting devices that such claims as "first," "fastest," and "longest-lasting" no longer impress or convince. The distortion that remains after we cut through the hype of "The Last Forty-Niner" is the suggestion that the gold miner is a vanishing breed. Try telling that to Ben's partner Chuck Roberts, who is in his thirties, or to any of the men and women who hold one of the two thousand or so mining claims on file at the Tuolumne County recorder's office.

If this number comes as a surprise—and one supposes it would to the producers of "The Last Forty-Niner"—it might be because, knowing that the Gold Rush ended, we assume that the gold ran dry. To my literal mind the term "Gold Rush" conjured up a mustachioed horde that streamed into California from land and sea, picked the gold fields clean, and streamed back out again, like cartoon ants making quick work of a picnic.

The forty-niners were almost that quick, but not nearly that thorough. They went for the easy stuff—the nuggets and concentrations of dust that could be plucked or panned out with a minimum of stooping in a cold creek. There wasn't much to go around: gold is too heavy to be plentiful on the surface. Hence the "rush."

Once the easy pickings had been skimmed—a phrase that belies how much work was involved in even the early days—treasure hunting yielded to mining, the two immutable laws of which are: (1) it takes a lot of earth-moving to find a little bit of gold, and (2) it takes a lot of money to move a little bit of earth.

Only three years after James Marshall's discovery of gold on the American River in 1848, *The San Francisco Alta Californian* foresaw the changeover. There's still plenty of gold in the central Sierra foothills, the Alta reported, "but to get the gold ... we must employ gold. The man who lives upon his labor from day to day must hereafter be employed by the man who has in possession accumulated labor, or money."[2]

When word spread east that mining was no different from most jobs—hard work for low pay[3]—the Gold Rush was over. There were plenty of ways to get rich slowly without wallowing in mud and breaking your back.

The family men returned to the States.[4] The restless moved on to the next big bonanzas—the Comstock in Nevada, the Klondike in Canada. The entrepreneurs who made killings selling supplies to the miners built railroads and banks, San Francisco and Sacramento. And the new Californians drifted off to fulfill the promise of the land with its "four or five hundred miles of seacoast with several good harbors; with fine forests in the north; the waters filled with fish and the plains covered with thousands of herds of cattle ... and with a soil in which corn yield from seventy to eighty fold."[5]

One need only glance at a map and an AAA guidebook to see that the mining camps that had become towns did not then become ghost towns. For those who stayed, there was still mining and there were the industries that began by providing what the mines needed.[6] In good times, you farmed, ranched, logged or hauled. And on spring and summer weekends you took your boy and did a little work on your claim. That way you and he were ready when things were not so good.

Mining booms when everything else goes bust. When jobs are scarce and the prices of equipment and supplies are low, mining pays. The records of the state division of mines show increased gold production during the hard times of the 1880s and in the mid-teens of this century.[7] Bub Dambacher, whose great-grandfather came to the gold fields in 1852, recalled the gold boom of the depression years.

> In the thirties, without gold there would have been nothing to eat in this county. Every stream had villages along 'em, cardboard shacks, tarpaper roofs. If they made a dollar's worth of gold a day they had enough to buy beans and bacon. They did a lot of mining from '33 on, a regular gold rush.

The production figures gathered by the state bear Bub out. The outputs for the years 1938–1941 were the largest since 1862. Then the war came and War Production Board Limitation Order L-208 shut the mines down.

> They just had 'em into production [Bub recalled], just starting to produce, when World War II broke out and all this had to be shut down, left here to rot. All these crews of men, all that expensive machinery, new gallis frames, new hoists, new compressors, new mills and everything.

When the war ended the moratorium was lifted, but the moment had been missed; while costs rose, the price of gold remained fixed at $35 an ounce.

> After World War II [Bub said], you couldn't make a living at it. That's when the prices started going up. You couldn't come out of it with anything at $35 an ounce. You couldn't pay several hundred dollars a ton for mining rails when it'd take eight-ten rails to the ton. Your drill and drill bits, an inch, inch-and-a-half carborundum bit costs $60. I paid $25–$30 apiece seven, eight years ago. I can remember back in the thirties, a box of powder, you could go to any little country store and buy a box of powder at $3.50, $4.00 for 120 sticks. You get your caps for a penny apiece, your fuse for a cent a foot. After World War II and the '50s, it kept goin' up.[8]

By 1968, hitching the world economy to the stability of America and its dollar no longer seemed like a very good idea. The world went off the gold standard and the free market price of gold began to rise, hitting its $850 apogee in 1980 just before I began spending time in the gold country.[9] At that price there were plenty of people interested in putting as much money as they could spare into moving as much earth as they could, to find the little bit of gold it would take for them to make a profit on their investment.[10]

The rush was on. Instead of converging on a new discovery, as their nineteenth-century predecessors did, the twentieth-century argonauts returned to the familiar ground of the Mother Lode. But when they went to reopen old claims or stake new ones they found that reviving the industry that had settled the county was going to be difficult in ways that had nothing to do with the hardness of rock or the cost of equipment. The unquestioned right to range freely over the land, digging holes, uprooting trees and rerouting streams had become a privilege conferred by the government and was subject to the strictest controls.

The change hardly occurred overnight. As far back as 1901, a brochure published by the Tuolumne County Progressive Association identified "picturesque spots . . . fast gaining popularity among pleasure seekers who are desirous of spending a few weeks vacation during the summer."[11] Yosemite National Park began drawing visitors into the county in the 1920s. Skiing became popular after World War II. And the Gold Rush centennial was marked by publication of guides to the old towns and mines of the Mother Lode and the opening of the state historic park in Columbia.

This was a new kind of gold rush. If pumping gas or slinging hash didn't suit you, you could run pack trips or prospecting tours or go to work for one of the two outfits that owned all the recreation land in the mountains—the state or federal governments. The easiest pockets to mine were the ones in the tourists' pants. And as long as the price of gold remained at $35 an ounce, few people objected that lawmakers—goaded by a growing conservation, then environmentalist movement—were becoming more zealous in protecting this land from the depredations of those who would mine its wealth.

> In 1872 [said Bub], you could prospect anywhere, dig your hole. If you wanted to, you could fill it up. If you didn't want to, you just went on—if it didn't pan out. You don't know if it's gonna be there or not. You have to prospect, have it sampled. Just a lot to it today, that's all there is to it. The Western Mining Council and other mining organizations, *California Mining Journal*, all fighting to get where you can mine like you used to.

The Tuolumne County chapter of the Western Mining Council meets once a month in Jamestown's Community Hall to commiserate, to stay informed of changes in mining law and plot collective courses of action. The members are a diverse lot—male, female, young, old, recent refugees from the wage-earning life in Stockton, Los Angeles or San Jose, or descendants of forty-niners like Bub—but what they have in common is a stubborn belief that all persons should have the right, in the words of mining council president George Bedford, "to go on the public domain to search out and claim valuable minerals."

Technically, the miners have that right. As the sign at the entrance to the Stanislaus National Forest says, "Land of Many Uses"—including mining. But these days, the principal uses of the forest are for recreation and timber. In 1976, Congress passed the Federal Land Policy and Mangement Act. In addition to prospecting, discovering, assaying, developing, extracting and processing—all expensive and time-consuming steps in themselves—there was now the reclamation step, the requirement that one reshape "land disturbed by operations to an appropriate contour and, where necessary, revegetate disturbed areas so as to provide a diverse vegetative cover."[12] As far as mining council secretary NaDean Bedford was concerned, they may as well have declared mining on public lands illegal.

> You can't go out and dig in the ground and not leave a hole. You can't take something out that the good Lord put there and not leave a hole 'cause you got to dig a hole to fill that hole and there's still a hole. This is the kind of legislation that they're trying to do, saying we have to fill up our hole.

The miners I met didn't deny there are some who, left to their own devices, would ravage the landscape. But most, they insisted, have what George Bedford called "a special feel for the earth," and do their work with care, pride, even love. To be sure, you can't mine without having some kind of impact on the environment, but in their view, getting the minerals and the right to get them are more important than leaving the wilderness in pristine condition for the "flatlanders" who use it one or two weekends a year.

> In our opinion [George said], we can't see why it should be locked up for any one group of people like the Sierra Club or others where they want to lock it up strictly for their own personal use. It's limited to such a few people when you put it into a wilderness area. They claim less than two percent of the public ever uses that portion of the public domain, so it seems ridiculous for legislation to be passed to put it in wilderness.

To the environmentalist ideal of a landscape free of the taint of man, the miners counter with a land-use aesthetic that sees natural beauty as enhanced by signs that income is being generated for those who live in the region all year round. The permanent scars inflicted by hydraulic mining do not help their cause. Hills reduced to fields of limestone boulders attest to the popularity of this particularly violent method of mineral extraction during the nineteenth century. As former Sonora city councilwoman Sharon Marovich observed, "I'm not sure the Gold Rush could have happened if we had CEQA (the California Environmental Quality Act) at that time."

But for the sake of fairness, there are a couple of things that should be pointed out. First, hydraulic mining has been outlawed since 1884 (one of the first pieces of environmental legislation ever passed), so you can't blame present-day miners for that kind of damage. And second, as for the "scars" themselves, if one did not know they were man-made, one might find they make for an interesting landscape. One might even admire that landscape for its "ruggedness." Or, knowing that the landscape is the result of mining, one might appreciate its historical significance in the same way that one appreciates the nineteenth-century look of Mother Lode towns and the mining relics that now stand as monuments to the Gold Rush era. The 1901 Progressive Association brochure shows that soon after the Gold Rush the appetite for ruins took hold.

> As one rides along, the old deserted placer diggings are most interesting to behold, and the ancient, tottering ruins of log cabins and rock chimneys that are

still in view call plainly to the senses the echoes of the past. On approaching the mineral-bearing section, stamp-mills and hoists are seen here and there ... and the first thought of the stranger is, that he is undoubtedly in a busy mining section.[13]

Ben Fullingim, "The Last Forty-Niner," had an old two-stamp mill that Chuck Roberts was using to crush the rock that comes out of a small gash in the side of a mountain near Tuolumne City. Until his death in 1981, Bill Dodd used a chipmunk jaw crusher to pulverize rock that came out of his nearby claim. To these men, such machines were not eyesores.

> This particular stamp mill [Chuck Roberts said] was made about 1860 and that engine, that was made about 1890. One's a little over 100 years old and the other one's almost. You'll no longer find stamp mills in use unless it's a little mill like this. Stamp mills are too slow. They've got big ball mills now that do three hundred tons in eight hours. So these went to the wayside and they went to bigger and better things. But this is pretty much a classic example of the older mining and hopefully we'll make enough expense money to pay for newer machinery and put this in a museum somewhere, put it to final rest where I don't have to pull on the flywheel to get it to start for half an hour.

Dodd spent the better part of a morning trying to demonstrate how his crusher works. He never lost patience and he never quite got it to work right. When he showed us his mine that same day, there was no place I'd rather have been. It was about 110 degrees outside, but only about half that down in the mine. He showed me what had been done and what needed to be done.

> So it kind of gives you an idea of what these old miners did back in the early days with some of the very crudest of tools. They were able to mine this hard rock and get in places where you really have to bellycrawl to get your ore out. It's kind of interesting the equipment they used to build. Those old miners were pretty ingenious people.

You can imagine how it galls these people to see the merchants and realtors exploit the Gold Rush flavor of the Mother Lode while turning their backs on those who are bearing the Gold Rush heritage into the present. While guys like Bill Dodd and Chuck Roberts salvage old machines from weeds and rust and tinker them back into operating condition, the city fathers of Jamestown, Sonora, and every other historic mining town in the Mother Lode install the same old machines in the parks and at the gateways to their towns. While miners like Sam Hilburn pack their gear into the back country, stake claims, pitch camp, and sample the rock, visitors sign up for pan-your-own-gold bus tours of the abandoned mines. While clean-shaven prospectors in baseball caps like George Bedford drive their pickups on Highway 49, images of bearded prospectors in slouch hats riding donkeys, jumping for joy, or panning streams bedeck the signposts and storefronts of every other motel, restaurant, RV park, realtor's office, and antique store along the Golden Highway.

Prospectors Pizza, The Miners Motel, Gold Rush Mobile Home Park, Forty-Niner Thrift Shop—the Yellow Pages list no fewer than thirty-six businesses in the

Tuolumne-Calaveras County area with Gold Rush-related names. When I came back from a two-year absence I was disappointed to find that the Nugget Gas Station's sign with its points of light emanating from a nuggety-looking yellow shape had fallen victim to Sonora's tough new sign ordinance. A change in name and ownership had brought down the sign across the street that pictured a prospector with a frying pan with two fried eggs in it, sunnyside up. These losses were offset somewhat by the giant billboard of townhomes in a gold pan; I used it as a landmark when I gave people directions to my house.

How can we read the signs along the Golden Highway? Dean MacCannell, in *The Tourist*, consigns such things to "the touristic front region, decorated with reminders of back region activities: mementos, not taken seriously, called 'atmosphere.'"[14]

I'm glad he put in that "not taken seriously." You wouldn't want to say that the guy who owns the Nugget Gas Station is enticing motorists to fill up at his place with the promise of some kind of authentic Gold Rush experience. After all, you've got to name your business something. A Gold Rush name or logo is as good as any other and better than most inasmuch as it mediates between the authenticity your clientele seeks and the inauthentic services and conveniences it is unwilling to do without.

Where then, is the back region, the mining industry from which the commercial images are derived? There are a couple of indications that, to the county's business people at least, the back region is located in time and not space. You can't get there from here, except imaginatively, via contemplation of mythic representations of the past.[15] One such indication, one such mythic representation is the prospecting tour, an activity that uses the glamor of "hands-on" experience to present itself as back region. "The Gold Rush is on," says the brochure, but it really has the staged quality of the front region.

Another indication that the back region is in historical deep freeze is the peculiar status of our friend Ben Fullingim. Though not representative of the modern miner, he is the perfect symbol for modern Tuolumne County. For years, he and his donkey Nugget led the Mother Lode Roundup parade through downtown Sonora. The beard is real but he confided that he keeps it for the school kids he takes prospecting on the Tuolumne River. He knows how to pack a mule, but he does so more often posing for postcard and phonebook cover photos than for prospecting expeditions. Yet his collection of rough-hewn cabins on Mount Eaton are neither stage sets nor relics. He built them in the 1950s. One of them he calls "The Museum."

How far can Old Ben trace his history in California? To 1949, the Gold Rush Centennial, the year Columbia ceased to be a town and became a park, the dawn of the age of tourism, subdivisions and gridlock in once "sleepy" Tuolumne County.[16]

What's at play here are two conflicting views of history, two vested interests,[17] each with its own version of the Gold Rush myth. Following Fernand Braudel, we can call the merchant-realtor use of the past the event-centered version, and the miners' use of the past the "longue-durée" version.[18]

The event-centered version, which is the one that dominates history writing about California, sees the Mother Lode as launching pad: all eyes are on it until the rocket that is the Golden State takes off. Then all eyes follow the rocket. The idea that the

Gold Rush is over and done with is what underpins the presentation of history to the tourists. While the Mother Lode joins the world of malls, video rentals, and health spas, certain features have been deliberately taken out of the path of change, features that "say" they are out of the past by how different they look from things of the present.

Without markers, without sharp distinctions between what is past and what is present, the tourist has no way of knowing what is worthy of his contemplation. You would not enshrine a Model A Ford in the town square if there were plenty of them still on the street, or sell old Coca-Cola bottles in an antique shop if the Coca-Cola Company had not changed the design of its bottle, or try to tell people they are taking a step back in time if you'd tacked twentieth-century facades on nineteenth-century buildings.[19] Contemporary miners blur that boundary. With their "Model A" stamp mills, their persistent use of pick and pan, their refusal to be relegated to the nineteenth century, they belie the very pastness of the past.

If, like Bub Dambacher, you are the fourth generation of a Mother Lode family, who grew up hearing about the strength and resourcefulness of the oldtimers, who ran a sluice box in the thirties and are now trying to get the family claim back into production, you do not see the Gold Rush as an event that is over and done with, or as raw material to be worked up into an entertaining and profitable "living history" package, but as a continuity to which you are heir, a tradition to which you have recourse in justifying the reopening of the claim and recovering lost social status. Sam Hilburn stated the case plainly enough.

> A lot of people say, Oh, you want to go over here and see this old mine. I don't want to see an old mine, I want one of my own, I want a brand new one. Instead of sightseeing, I'm down here splitting out bedrock, trying to find a little bit of gold. Now to me that's fun and exciting. Wandering around looking at what someone did a hundred years ago, that's the past.

In other words, it is not the miners who are nostalgic. When guys like Chuck Roberts and Bill Dodd spend half a morning trying to get their old machines to work, they know too well what their predecessors had to contend with to be sentimental about the good old days. The purpose of all this looking backward—and it is the folklorist's purpose as well—is not, in Charles Briggs's words, "to romanticize the past,"[20] but to cull and recommend its sustaining values. As Wallace Stegner writes, "If you have any desire to understand and thus to help steer a civilization that seems to have got away from us, then I think you don't choose between the past and the present; you try to find the connections, you try to make the one serve the other."[21]

The miners know that change means loss.[22] They also know that living is believing that what's been lost can be regained. The Gold Rush may be a historical event to us; to present-day miners it is not just the way things were but the way things ought to be, a story about the past that resonates in the present, the golden-age myth by which they live.

---

[1]The passages of quoted speech in this paper are excerpted from interviews recorded on audiotape or videotape between 1980 and 1985.

²Quoted in Donald Dale Jackson, *Gold Dust* (Lincoln: University of Nebraska Press, 1980), 314. See also Robert V. Hine, *The American West* (Boston: Little, Brown & Co., 1973), 119; Neil Morgan, *The California Syndrome* (Englewood Cliffs, N.J.: Prentice-Hall, 1973), 166; and Otis E. Young, Jr., *Western Mining*, (Norman: University of Oklahoma Press, 1970), viii.

³"To be a miner in 1860 was to have given up any hope for wealth and to accept wages or returns roughly equivalent to those for unskilled labor." Ralph Mann, *After the Gold Rush* (Stanford: Stanford University Press, 1982), 84.

⁴J. S. Holliday writes that the California Gold Rush was unique in the westward movement in that most of the participants did not bring their families and had no intention of settling in the West: "The goldseekers' jackpot psychology had blinded them to California's potential." *The World Rushed In: The California Gold Rush Experience* (New York: Simon & Schuster, 1981), 354.

⁵Richard Henry Dana's prophetic assessment of the potential of the land in *Two Years Before the Mast* (New York: New American Library, 1964), 163.

⁶"Lumbering, building, stone quarrying, cement kilns, the tourist trade and farming have replaced gold extraction as a means of livelihood," (over) stated a pamphlet put out by the State Division of Mines, *Geologic Guidebook Along Highway 49*, 1948, p. 91.

⁷See Henry H. Symons, *California Mineral Production and Directory of Mineral Producers for 1942* (California State Division of Mines Bulletin No. 126, 1942).

⁸Gold mining in the pre- and post-World War II period is summarized in California State Division of Mines Bulletin No. 191, p. 183.

⁹A good outline of the sequence of events is to be found in *Gold Prospectors News*, 1980, p. 9.

¹⁰"The early day miners took millions of dollars in gold and silver from these areas; working under the most adverse conditions, employing rudimentary and often very crude tools and equipment. And this during a period when gold brought $20 to $35 per ounce and silver ran 50 cents to $1. These stalwart pioneers barely scratched the surface. They took the easy pickings; God bless 'em. Geologists have estimated the take of these hardy souls at somewhere around 10 percent of the extractable minerals contained in the hills and streams of the Mother Lode. The rest of it is still there. What the hell are we saving it for?" from Bill Dodd, "An Open Letter to President Reagan," *Poke of Gold* (Mariposa, Calif.: Western Mining Council/United Mining Counties, June 1980), 5.

¹¹*Illustrated Historical Brochure of Tuolumne County, California* (The Progressive Association, 1901), 11.

¹²Federal Land Policy and Management Act, sec. 3809.0-5(j) (1976).

¹³*Illustrated Historical Brochure*, 80.

¹⁴Dean MacCannell, *The Tourist* (New York: Shocken Books, 1976).

¹⁵"The creation of the mental domain of phantasy has a complete counterpart in the establishment of 'reservations' and 'nature parks' in places where the inroads of agriculture, traffic, or industry threaten to change the earth rapidly into something unrecognizable. The 'reservation' is to maintain the old condition of things which has been regretfully sacrificed to necessity everywhere else." Sigmund Freud's *General Introduction to Psychoanalysis* is quoted in Leo Marx, *The Machine in the Garden: Technology and the Pastoral Ideal in America* (New York: Oxford University Press, 1964), 8.

¹⁶Morgan does a little then-and-now number on the Mother Lode: "Then it was everything: raucous, new, lusty, intense, determined, courageous. Now it is gentle and sleepy, too corporeal to be thought of as a ghostland, but so nebulous in focus that it is difficult to imagine it as the catalyst of modern California." *The California Syndrome*, 166.

¹⁷The reference is to Edmund Leach, "Myth as Justification for Faction and Social Change," in Robert A. Georges, *Studies on Mythology*, (Urbana: University of Illinois Press, 1968), 184–98.

¹⁸Fernand Braudel, *On History* (Chicago: University of Chicago Press, 1980), 27.

¹⁹"It is perfectly true that to restore part of a town to its mid-19th century appearance is not in fact to restore it to its original form. But anthropologists tell us that, in the thoughts of most peoples, primal time—the golden age, that is to say,—begins precisely where active memory ends—thus about the time of one's great grandfather. Perhaps this accounts for our present fascination with the 1870s and 1880s. That was in fact a period of great change, but it is now remote enough to be perceived as part of the old days and in consequence to be the theme of countless small town restorations." J. B. Jackson, *The Necessity for Ruins* (Amherst: University of Massachusetts Press, 1980), 101.

[20]"The elders do not romanticize the past, asserting it perfect in every way. They are quick to point out that 'the elders of bygone days used to work like mules'." Charles Briggs, "Treasure Tales and Pedagogical Discourse in Mexicano, New Mexico," *Journal of American Folklore* 98 (1985):309.

[21]Wallace Stegner, *The Sound of Mountain Water* (New York: E. P. Dutton, 1980), 200.

[22]The reference is to Richard Hugo's poem "Letter to Matthews from Barton St. Flats": "Then the war took everything, farm, farmers and my faith that change (I really mean loss) is paced slow enough for the blood adjust." *Selected Poems* (New York: W. W. Norton, 1979), 143.

# V
# Children's Folklore

## The Lore and Language of Schoolchildren
### Iona and Peter Opie

*Folklore is often transmitted from one "generation" to another, but that genera-
tional transmission only occasionally flows from parent to child. In fact, the transmission may not be from adult to child at all, but from slightly older child to slightly
younger child. Indeed, adults may make little or no contribution to the stock of
children's folklore. Children's lore is thus to a great extent independent of the
teachings and wishes of parents and their surrogates.*

*In the following excerpts from the remarkable collection of children's folklore by
Iona and Peter Opie, we can get some sense of this independence of children's culture.
In those moments in which they constitute their own groups free from the supervision
of adults, they have recourse to a variety of mechanisms—contractual, judicial, penal,
legislative, economic, and communicative—in the conduct of their affairs. One striking
quality of this lore, from an adult perspective, is its extremism. Children swear on their
lives, their friendships are forever, they exact strict and immediate punishment for
wrongdoing, and their communications are not merely private but highly encrypted.
For a more thorough description of the lore of children see this and other works by
Opie and Opie (1969, 1973, 1985) and Knapp and Knapp (1976). Also see the essays
and bibliography in Grider (1980).*

### AFFIRMATION

Children reinforce the truth by swearing upon their honour, their heart, their Bible,
their own life, or, preferably, their mother's. Spitting, linking fingers, holding their
hand up to God, and making crosses upon their body accompany their declarations.

If this catalogue seems impious it should be emphasized that the asseverations in the
following pages (mostly collected from ten- and eleven-year-olds) are not treated

lightly by those who use them. An imprecation such as 'May I drop down dead if I tell a lie' is liable to be accorded the respect of its literal meaning, and distinct uneasiness may follow its utterance, even when the child concerned is fairly certain that he has not departed from the truth. He has very probably heard the tales his fellows tell of violent death instantly overtaking those who have dared to defy an oath; and it may well be that he believes these tales, however strange they sound to adult ears, for childhood is on nodding terms with the supernatural. A Somerset writer for instance has recalled that, in his day, schoolboys had a story in which a sinner was not only immediately struck dead when he perjured himself but became rooted to the spot where he stood 'so that no power on earth—not even a team of horses attached by ropes and chains— could move the body, which stood (like Lot's wife) as a terrible warning to other men and women.'[1]

>—<

*Drop down dead.* 'May I drop dead here, if I tell a lie', 'God let me drop dead this minute', 'God strike me stiff and blind', and suchlike imprecations are apparently hazarded almost everywhere. Sometimes, as in Ruthin, two oaths are metrically combined:

> Cross my heart and hope to die,
> Drop down dead if I tell a lie.

In Penrith a girl chants 'to show I am telling the truth':

> God send the lightning to strike my tree,
> And God send the lightning if I tell a lee.

The following has been reported only from Swansea. Two girls link their little fingers and cry 'Pull the dying oath'. From the same school this has also been reported as 'Pull oath', 'Die on oath', 'Dianothe', and 'Diamond oath', an interesting trail of corruption.

The children's practice of staking their parent's well-being on their truthfulness is very general, and almost anywhere they are liable to exclaim: 'On my mother's life!' 'On my mother's death bed!' 'Across my mother's dead body!' or, 'If I tell a lie my mother will die' (Cornwall), 'Mother's death, father's death, I'm not telling a lie' (Glamorgan), 'Mother, Father, will die, if I tell a lie' (Fife). 'You have to tell the truth', warns a 10-year-old, 'otherwise it's your mother's death.'[2]

In the north-west, that is in Cumberland, Westmorland, the West Riding, Lancashire, Cheshire, north Derbyshire, and in the north of Wales, spitting plays a prominent part in their attestations. A child, when questioning the veracity of a statement, will demand 'Spit your death' or 'Spit your mother's death', whereupon the challenged one will repeat the words demanded of him and, according to local custom, will spit and cross his throat, or spit over his wrist or little finger, and perhaps cross his throat as well, or, in Liverpool, link little fingers and spit, or, in the West Riding, spit on the ground and declare, 'If I tell a lie may I die on the spot where I spit'.[3]

*Cut my throat.* Of the oaths current today this is the one which was the most documented in the nineteenth century, perhaps because it is the most dramatic;[4] and it is general throughout the English-speaking world. It is another instance in which the special properties of spittle is recognized. A child moistens his finger and shows it, and says:

'My finger's wet.'

He wipes it—usually in his armpit—and shows it, and says:

'My finger's dry.'

He tilts his head back, draws his finger across his throat, and says:

Cut my throat if I tell a lie.'

Only the most depraved will tell an untruth after repeating such a formula, which is made not a whit the less startling by the miniature stature of some of its practitioners. The wording varies only slightly from one place to another:

Wet my thumb,
Wipe it dry,
Cut my throat
If I tell a lie.

*Farnham, Surrey*

I wet my finger,
I wipe it dry,
I cut my throat
If I tell a lie.

*Lydney*

My finger's wet,
My finger's dry,
God strike me dead
If I tell a lie.

*Hull*

That's wet,
That's dry,
I hate God
If I tell a lie.

*Kirkcaldy*

Sometimes the oath is taken on the blade of a boy's penknife, which is first spat upon: 'See it's wet, see it's dry, cut my throat if I tell a lie' (Bishop Auckland). Sometimes, less elaborately, they say, 'Cut my throat and may I die, if I ever tell a lie' (Scarborough), or 'If I tell a lie, cut my throat and let me die' (Welwyn). In north Devon, more cautiously, 'Cut my mother's throat'. Also 'Slit my throat if I lie' (Croydon), and 'Split my neck' (Lydney). And sometimes there are no words, just a significant gesture across the wind pipe.[5]

># <

## ORDEALS

The following ordeals, or ones similar, appear to be common to many schools in Britain.

Iona and Peter Opie

*Sending to Coventry.* 'When someone does something most of the class disagrees with, we send that person to Coventry which means we never speak to them. Sometimes one or two people hold their noses with their fingers and say that the place smell where they have been. Another name for this is "giving them a cold shoulder".'—Girl, 10, Birmingham.

Sending to Coventry is often preceded by a class committee, which deliberates the length of time the person should stay in Coventry, and enforces the sentence. Nobody may speak to the child, 'not even the person's best friend', except during class, and if anybody does he is liable to be put in Coventry himself; and care is taken to ensure that two people in Coventry do not get talking to each other. In Aberdeen the punishment is also known as 'Solitary'.

\*\*\* The phrase 'to send to Coventry' became proverbial in the second half of the eighteenth century. Its origin is unknown, but it may come from a one-time Parliamentarian practice, mentioned by Clarendon in his *History of the Rebellion* (vi, § 83), of sending Royalist prisoners to Coventry for safe keeping. The punishment is referred to in many school tales, e.g. in Maria Edgeworth's story 'Eton Montem' in *The Parent's Assistant* (1795), in *Tom Brown's School Days* (1857), *Jack Harkaway's Schooldays* (1871), and in *Vice Versâ* (1882).

*Bumps.* The 10-year-old Birmingham girl quoted above, says of 'Bumps': 'This is also for someone who is unpopular. Two pretty hefty people get hold of the person's legs and arms and bump them on the ground. The boys mostly do this, and the girls are "sent to Coventry".' The operation, in Camberwell carried out with the cry 'Bounce him, boys', in Alton called 'bumpers', and in Scotland generally known as 'dumps' or 'dumping' (a term which also embraces thumping a person on his backside with the bent knee), is also ritually inflicted on children's birthdays (q.v.). In Newcastle 9- to 11-year-olds have a rhyme, when either bumping or ducking:

> Bump, bump, salty water,
> Give the dog a drink of water,
> One, two, three, *drop*!

\*\*\* Compare Edward Moor, who was at school in the 1770's: 'The punishment of a schoolboy for telling tales or for any act of treachery, coming immediately under the summary jurisdiction of his peers, is *bumping*: and this is performed by prostrating the coatless culprit on his back, in the immediate vicinity of a large block of wood, or of a wall. A strong boy seizes the right ankle and wrist, another the left, and lift him off the ground; and after a preparatory vibration or two to give a due momentum, he comes in violent contact with the block, *a posteriori*. This is repeated six or eight more times, according to the enormity of the offence, or the just resentment of the executioners.'—*Suffolk Words*, 1823, p. 53. Around Halifax, *c.* 1900, this practice was termed 'free-bumming' (correspondent).

*Running the Gauntlet.* Although well known by this name, the ordeal is also termed the 'House of Whacks' (Camberwell), 'Under the Arches' (Enfield and

London), and, very generally, 'Under the Mill' or 'Through the Mill'. A Knottingley lad, aged about 13, writes:

> 'When boys are not agreeable and are bullies they are put through the mill. This is a kind of torture, and about twenty boys or less, as the case may be, put their hands flat on the wall, with arms outstretched to form a tunnel. The bully has to go through the mill four times. The first time he has *rain*, this is a good slap from each boy. The second time he gets *lightning*, this is a rabbit-punch. The third time he gets *thunder*, this is a prod with the knee. Fourth time he gets *hailstones*, this is a very hard punch in the back. I can assure you the bully will behave after this.'

The mill may also be made by two lines of boys facing each other, making an arch with one hand, and inflicting punishment with the other. Or the offender may be given a 'frog march' along the line of boys, that is to say be forcibly conducted along the line with his arms twisted behind his back.

In less severe form Running the Gauntlet is inflicted on the loser in such games as Bad Eggs and Donkey, as part of the game.

\*\*\* Pieter Brueghel the Elder (1525?–1569) depicts children making one of their playfellows run the gauntlet in his famous picture *Kinderspiele*. Running the gauntlet was at one time a regular military punishment, and was made a legal punishment in America in 1676.

*Frog Marching*. This can be and, indeed, usually is inflicted independently of Running the Gauntlet. 'The person is marched backwards with his arms locked by two boys. He is marched through mud, puddles, bushes, &c.'

*Stretching Board*. 'Four boys get the bully, two grab his arms and two grab his legs, and they pull.' Alternatively, in a classroom, and more painfully, 'Stretch the body on desk with boys pulling each end of the boy.'—Brentwood, Camberwell, Peterborough, and Pontefract.

*Wylums Torture*. This punishment, said to be 'popular in Langholm', is in a sense the opposite of the Stretching Board. Thus a 12-year-old: 'You lay them on the ground stomach downwards. Then put one hand under their chin and with the other hand lift their legs so that their legs touch their head. It usually takes more than one to do it.'

*Piling On*. This is done either 'to hurt a person if he has done wrong', after he has been forcibly thrown to the ground, or, as opportunity occurs, during rough play, when somebody accidentally falls, and one of the company jumps on top of him, yelling 'Pile on', a summons readily obeyed by everybody else rushing up and adding their weight on top of the fallen one. The summons 'Pile on' seems to be understood everywhere from Guildford to Golspie, but in Liverpool the usual cry is 'Piley on', and in Lydney 'Pile on sacks'.

\*\*\* In New Zealand the common call is 'Sacks to the mill', a formula which was known in Oxfordshire until the end of the nineteenth century *(English Dialect Dictionary)*, and which goes back more than 300 years. In Mabbe's translation, 1622, of Aleman's novel *Guzman de Alfarache* appears the passage: 'When there was nothing to be done at home, your Lackies . . . would . . . fright me with Snakes, hang on my backe, & weigh me downe, crying, More sackes to the Mill.' Biron, in *Love's Labour's Lost*, (IV. iii), may also be referring to the sport when he exclaims, 'More Sacks to the myll. O heavens I have my wish.'

*The Chamber*. 'One boy is put between the door and the wall, then damp leaves are thrown over him.'—Boy, 13, Laindon, Essex.

><

## SECRET LANGUAGES

By using slang, local dialect, a multiplicity of technical terms, word-twistings, codes, and sign language, children communicate with each other in ways which outsiders are unable to understand, and thus satisfy an impulse common to all underdogs. In fact children use esoteric speech more commonly than is generally supposed. Rhyming slang, for instance, which they call 'Crooks' language': 'almond rocks' for socks, 'apples and pears' for stairs, 'turtle doves' for gloves, and so on, normally associated with cockneys, is neither confined to the metropolis, nor to the shift-for-a-living class. As far away as Newcastle respectable children can be heard saying they are 'going for a ball of chalk' when setting out for a walk, and accusing someone of being a 'tea-leaf' when they mean a thief.

Perhaps the most common secret vocabulary children use is a modification of back-slang, although 'Eggy-peggy' and 'Arague' language are also popular and seem to predominate in some areas, or it may be with some classes of children. Back-slang proper, sometimes employed by barrow-boys and hawkers, and indigenous to certain trades such as the greengrocer's and the butcher's, where it is spoken to ensure that the customer shall not understand what is being said ('*Evig reh emos delo garcs dene*'— Give her some old scrag end) consists simply of saying each word backwards, and when this is impossible saying the name of the letter instead of its sound, usually the first or last letter, thus: '*Uoy nac ees reh sreckin ginwosh*' (You can see her knickers showing). An Enfield master reports that he found 'at least half a dozen boys who could talk it quickly'. But what most children colloquially refer to as 'back-slang' is either a simplification in which the final sound is moved to the front of the word, 'Shba uyo fi uyo tedon teshu aryou petray' (Bash you if you don't shut your trap), or a slightly more complicated and very popular form, sometimes known as 'pig Latin', in which the first consonant or double consonant (e.g. *br* and *th*) is transferred to the end of the word and *ay*, or less frequently *e*, is added thereafter, thus: 'Unejay ithsmay isay igpay' (June Smith is a pig); and the 'Bash you' threat becomes 'Ashbay ouyay ifay ouyay ontday utshay ouryay aptray'. This has been spoken by children since before the First World War, and is sometimes given a high sounding name such as 'Sandy Hole Gaelic' (Wood Green, 1938).

In contrast to turning the words, they sometimes disguise what they are saying by inserting one syllable, or occasionally two, before each vowel. In Scarborough teenage girls are reported to have 'thageir agown pagattager' which they call pidgin English or double talk, putting *ag* before each vowel, a peculiarity said to have been first practised in that town at the beginning of the century, and then known as 'stage slang'.[6] In Watford, Hertfordshire, and Barry, Glamorganshire, girls report that *eg* is introduced before vowels.[7] In Worcester it is, or was, 'Aygo-paygo language'. In Chelmsford and Manchester boys use 'Arague Language'. Thus:

> Taragoo baraged, saragays slarageepy haragead,
> Taragarry ara wharagile, saragays slaragow,
> Paragut aragon tharage paragot, saragays grarageedy garagut,
> Waragell saragup baragefaragore warage garago,

which turns out to be:

> To bed, says sleepy head,
> Tarry a while, says slow,
> Put on the pot, says greedy gut,
> We'll sup before we go.

And this secret juvenile pattern is another item which is not only old but adult in origin, for, by an ironic twist, it seems formerly to have been used when adults did not want children to know what they were talking about. The following passage appears in the privately printed autobiography of Elizabeth Grant of Rothiemurchus, and refers to the year 1808:

> 'There had been a great many mysterious conversations of late between my mother and aunt Mary, and as they had begun to suspect the old *how-vus do-vus* language was become in some degree comprehensible to us, they had substituted a more difficult style of disguised English. This took us a much longer time to translate into common sense. "Here*thegee* is*thegee* a*thegee* let*thegee* ter*thegee* from*thegee*," etc. I often wondered how with words of many syllables they managed to make out such a puzzle, or even to speak it, themselves. It baffled us for several days; at last we discovered the key, or the clue, and then we found a marriage was preparing—whose, never struck us—it was merely a marriage in which my mother and my aunts were interested.' (*Memoir of a Highland Lady*, reprint 1898, p. 73.)

>—◄

## MAKING AND BREAKING FRIENDS

In general children's friendships are far from placid. Perhaps because of the gregariousness of school life they make and break friends with a rapidity disconcerting to the adult spectator. Two girls will swear eternal friendship, arrange signs and passwords, exchange necklaces, walk home together from school, invite each other to tea, and have just settled down together, so it would seem, when suddenly they are very 'black' with one another and do not speak any more. They seek a new friend, and have no sooner found one than they are with their old pal again. And they may be well aware of their fickleness. 'I like Jean,' says a 9-year-old, 'because if we break friends it is only for a day or two.' 'Brian and I don't like each other now as he bosses me about and I boss him,' says another 9-year-old, 'but we will be friends again soon I hope.'

The finger of friendship is the little finger. They link the little fingers of their right hands and shake them up and down, declaring:

> Make friends, make friends,
> Never, never break friends.

They quarrel, and their friendship is ended with the formula,

> Break friends, break friends,
> Never, never make friends,

repeated in a like manner, but, in Croydon, with the little fingers moistened, and in Portsmouth with linked thumbs. They make up again, intoning,

> We've broken before,
> We break now—

and they separate their little fingers,

> We'll never break any more,

and they intertwine their little fingers again, squeezing tightly (Weston-super-Mare). Alternatively, in places as far apart as South Molton and Cleethorpes (and commonly in the London area), they say,

> Make up, make up, never row again,
> If we do we'll get the cane,

and thereupon they slap hands or smack each other. In Radnorshire they hook little fingers, touch thumbs, and then turn hands over and clap.

Sometimes the reunited friends merely shake hands with a formal expression of goodwill: 'Shake, bud', 'Always shake, never break', 'Let bygones be bygones', 'Put the quarrel down the drain'. In Glasgow when they shake hands they have a third person who brings his hand down between them, saying 'Cut cheese'. Romantically minded, some children solemnize the rite by pricking each other's fingers and mixing the blood so that they become 'blood brothers'. In Dublin girls employ an intermediary. She walks over to the person they are not talking to, and asks:

> Are you spin, spout, or blackout,
> Falling in or falling out?

Should the reply be 'blackout' it means the girl does not want to make up. 'Ahem to the dirt!' exclaims the rejected one. But if they make up they swear friendship: 'You're the lock and I've the key', and customarily, as a token of their restored friendship, they go out shopping together.

[1]A. S. Macmillian, *Word-Lore* (1926), 1:59. A number of instances of supernatural retribution following upon the telling of a lie have been formally documented. The fate of Ruth Pierce on 25 January 1753 was inscribed on the Market Cross of Devizes, Wiltshire, 'as a salutary warning against the danger of impiously invoking the Divine vengeance.' According to the inscription she protested that she had paid her full share for a sack of wheat she was buying with three other women, and said she might drop down dead if she had not. 'She rashly repeated this awful wish, when, to the consternation of the surrounding multitude, she instantly fell and expired, having the money concealed in her hand.' In a report of the Coroner's inquest in *The Western Flying Post,* 29 January 1753, the further detail is added that the amount Ruth Pierce was concealing in her hand was three pence.

Similar stories, some of them grisly, may be found the *The Taunton Courier,* 22 April 1857; *The Western Flying Post,* 1 March 1813; *Aris's Birmingham Gazette,* 12 September 1796; and *The Sherborne Mercury,* 21 April 1741. For details see first reference.

[2]How seriously such oaths are regarded by adults also, in some levels of society, may be seen in the police court report on a sixteen-year-old Dorset boy accused of murder. It was his mother who asked: 'Will you swear over my dead body you did not do it?' The boy replied: 'I tell you I didn't. I swear over your dead body.' *News of the World,* 14 February 1954, p. 2.

[3]The juvenile practice of making an oath more terrible by spitting was noticed in the eighteenth century by the antiquary John Brand of Newcastle in his *Popular Antiquities* (1777), 101 n.: 'Boys have a Custom *(inter se)* of spitting their Faith, or as they also call it here, their Saul (Soul), when required to make Asseverations in a Matter of Consequence.'

[4]See G. F. Northall, *English Folk Rhymes* (1892), 336 and S. O. Addy, *Household Tales* (1895), 127.

[5]During the proceedings of the Lynskey Tribunal held in London in 1948 to inquire into abuses at the Board of Trade, Mrs. John Belcher, wife of the ex-Railway Clerk, Parliamentary Secretary to the Board of Trade, won the sympathy of everyone present with her frank evidence as she twice licked her fingers and crossed her throat in this schoolgirlish affirmation of honesty.

[6]*Scarborough Evening News,* 14, 25, and 28 October 1954; *Scarborough Mercury,* 5 November 1954.

[7]This must be the most 'U' of secret languages being spoken by members of high society in Nancy Mitford, *Love in a Cold Climate* (1949), chapter 3: 'Lady Montdore led me to the table and the starlings went on with their chatter about my mother in "eggy-peggy", a language I happened to know quite well. "Egg-is shegg-ee reggealleggy, pwegg-oor swegg-eet."'

# Transformations: The Fantasy of the Wicked Stepmother

## Bruno Bettelheim

*At the beginning of the twentieth century, Sigmund Freud proposed a theory of dreams and a method for their interpretation. It was a small step for him to recognize a similarity between dreams and folklore. Folklore was but a collective dream, amenable to the same type of analysis and interpretation. The psychoanalytic interpretation of folklore offered startling new perspectives on the meaning and motivation of myths, beliefs, and tales. Rapacious wolves, friendly woodcutters, glass slippers, and wicked stepmothers were not as fantastic as they first appeared. Behind these fairytale images lay realities that were frighteningly familiar.*

*Folktales are not strictly children's folklore. Rarely do children tell folktales to one another. Folktales are usually told to, read to, or edited for children by adults. Nevertheless, folktales often do capture the imaginations of children and they may have significant and enduring effects (Freud 1958:12: 279-87). In the following excerpt, Bruno Bettelheim brings a psychoanalytic perspective to the folktale image of the wicked stepmother. He attempts to show the sense of this image in the psychology of the child, and he evidences his interpretation with material from clinical practice.*

*Freud wrote readable introductions to psychoanalysis (1961:15:15-239; 1963:16: 243-496) which have appeared in paperback editions, and Jones (1930) demonstrated the application of psychoanalytic theory to folklore. For contemporary interpretations of folklore from a psychoanalytic perspective see the essays of Alan Dundes (1980, 1987). While Bettelheim believes very strongly in the positive psychological value of fairytales for children, there is no consensus on this issue. A survey of some of the views to the contrary can be found in Stone (1981).*

There is a right time for certain growth experiences, and childhood is the time to learn bridging the immense gap between inner experiences and the real world. Fairy tales may seem senseless, fantastic, scary, and totally unbelievable to the adult who was deprived of fairy story fantasy in his own childhood, or has repressed these memories. An adult who has not achieved a satisfactory integration of the two worlds of reality and imagination is put off by such tales. But an adult who in his own life is able to integrate rational order with the illogic of his unconscious will be responsive to the manner in which fairy tales help the child with this integration. To the child, and to the adult who, like Socrates, knows that there is still a child in the wisest of us, fairy tales reveal truths about mankind and oneself.

In "Little Red Riding Hood" the kindly grandmother undergoes a sudden replacement by the rapacious wolf which threatens to destroy the child. How silly a transformation when viewed objectively, and how frightening—we might think the transformation unnecessarily scary, contrary to all possible reality. But when viewed in terms of a child's ways of experiencing, is it really any more scary than the sudden transformation of his own kindly grandma into a figure who threatens his very sense of self when she humiliates him for a pants-wetting accident? To the child, Grandma is no longer the same person she was just a moment before; she has become an ogre. How can someone who was so very kind, who brought presents and was more understanding and tolerant and uncritical than even his own mommy, suddenly act in such a radically different fashion?

Unable to see any congruence between the different manifestations, the child truly experiences Grandma as two separate entities—the loving and the threatening. She is indeed Grandma *and* the wolf. By dividing her up, so to speak, the child can preserve his image of the good grandmother. If she changes into a wolf—well, that's certainly scary, but he need not compromise his vision of Grandma's benevolence. And in any case, as the story tells him, the wolf is a passing manifestation—Grandma will return triumphant.

Similarly, although Mother is most often the all-giving protector, she can change into the cruel stepmother if she is so evil as to deny the youngster something he wants.

Far from being a device used only by fairy tales, such a splitting up of one person into two to keep the good image uncontaminated occurs to many children as a solution to a relationship too difficult to manage or comprehend. With this device all contradictions are suddenly solved, as they were for a college student who remembered an incident that occurred when she was not yet five years old.

One day in a supermarket this girl's mother suddenly became very angry with her; and the girl felt utterly devastated that her mother could act this way toward her. On the walk home, her mother continued to scold her angrily, telling her she was no good. The girl became convinced that this vicious person only *looked* like her mother and, although pretending to be her, was actually an evil Martian, a look-alike impostor, who had taken away her mother and assumed her appearance. From then on, the girl assumed on many different occasions that this Martian had abducted the mother and taken her place to torture the child as the real mother would never have done.

This fantasy went on for a couple of years until, when seven, the girl became courageous enough to try to set traps for the Martian. When the Martian had once again taken Mother's place to engage in its nefarious practice of torturing her, the girl would cleverly put some question to the Martian about what had happened between the real mother and herself. To her amazement, the Martian knew all about it, which at first just confirmed the Martian's cunning to the girl. But after two or three such experiments the girl became doubtful; then she asked her mother about events which had taken place between the girl and the Martian. When it became obvious that her mother knew about these events, the fantasy of the Martian collapsed.

During the period when the girl's security had required that Mother should be all good—never angry or rejecting—the girl had rearranged reality to provide herself with what she needed. When the girl grew older and more secure, her mother's anger or severe criticisms no longer seemed so utterly devastating. Since her own integration had become better established, the girl could dispense with the security-guaranteeing Martian fantasy and rework the double picture of the mother into one by testing the reality of her fantasy.

While all young children sometimes need to split the image of their parent into its benevolent and threatening aspects to feel fully sheltered by the first, most cannot do it as cleverly and consciously as this girl did. Most children cannot find their own solution to the impasse of Mother suddenly changing into "a look-alike impostor." Fairy tales, which contain good fairies who suddenly appear and help the child find happiness despite this "impostor" or "stepmother," permit the child not to be destroyed by this "impostor." Fairy tales indicate that, somewhere hidden, the good fairy godmother watches over the child's fate, ready to assert her power when critically needed. The fairy tale tells the child that "although there are witches, don't ever forget there are also the good fairies, who are much more powerful." The same tales assure that the ferocious giant can always be outwitted by the clever little man—somebody seemingly as powerless as the child feels himself to be. Quite likely it was some story about a child who cleverly outwits an evil spirit which gave this girl the courage to try to expose the Martian.

The universality of such fantasies is suggested by what, in psychoanalysis, is known as the pubertal child's "family romance."[1] These are fantasies or daydreams which the normal youngster partly recognizes as such, but nonetheless also partly believes. They center on the idea that one's parents are not really one's parents, but that one is the child of some exalted personage, and that, due to unfortunate circumstances, one has been reduced to living with these people, who *claim* to be one's parents. These daydreams take various forms: often only one parent is thought to be a false one—which parallels a frequent situation in fairy tales, where one parent is the real one, the other a step-parent. The child's hopeful expectation is that one day, by chance or design, the real parent will appear and the child will be elevated into his rightful exalted state and live happily ever after.

These fantasies are helpful; they permit the child to feel really angry at the Martian pretender or the "false parent" without guilt. Such fantasies typically begin to appear when guilt feelings are already a part of the child's personality make-up, and when being angry at a parent or, worse, despising him would bring with it unmanageable guilt. So the typical fairy tale splitting of the mother into a good (usually dead) mother and an evil stepmother serves the child well. It is not only a means of preserving an internal all-good mother when the real mother is not all-good, but it also permits anger at this bad "stepmother" without endangering the goodwill of the true mother, who is viewed as a different person. Thus, the fairy tale suggests how the child may manage the contradictory feelings which would otherwise overwhelm him at this stage of his barely beginning ability to integrate contradictory emotions. The fantasy of the wicked stepmother not only preserves the good mother intact, it also prevents having to feel guilty about one's angry thoughts and wishes about her—a guilt which would seriously interfere with the good relation to Mother.

While the fantasy of the evil stepmother thus preserves the image of the good mother, the fairy tale also helps the child not to be devastated by experiencing his mother as evil. In much the same way that the Martian in the little girl's fantasy disappeared as soon as Mother was once again pleased with her little girl, so a benevolent spirit can counteract in a moment all the bad doings of an evil one. In the fairy tale rescuer, the good qualities of Mother are as exaggerated as the bad ones were in the witch. But this is how the young child experiences the world: either as entirely blissful or as an unmitigated hell.

When he experiences the emotional need to do so, the child not only splits a parent into two figures, but he may also split himself into two people who, he wishes to believe, have nothing in common with each other. I have known young children who during the day are successfully dry but who wet their bed at night and, waking up, move with disgust to a corner and say with conviction, "Somebody's wet my bed." The child does not do this, as parents may think, to put the blame on somebody else, knowing all the while that it was he who urinated in the bed. The "somebody" who has done it is that part of himself with which he has by now parted company; this aspect of his personality has actually become a stranger to him. To insist that the child recognize that it *was* he who wet the bed is to try to impose prematurely the concept of the integrity of the human personality, and such insistence actually retards its development. In order to develop a secure feeling of his self, the child needs to constrict it for a time to only what is fully approved and desired by himself. After he has thus achieved a self of which he can be unambivalently proud, the child can then slowly begin to accept the idea that it may also contain aspects of a more dubious nature.

As the parent in the fairy tale becomes separated into two figures, representative of the opposite feelings of loving and rejecting, so the child externalizes and projects into a "somebody" all the bad things which are too scary to be recognized as part of oneself.

The fairy-tale literature does not fail to consider the problematic nature of sometimes seeing Mother as an evil stepmother; in its own way, the fairy tale warns against being swept away too far and too fast by angry feelings. A child easily gives in to his annoyance with a person dear to him, or to his impatience when kept waiting; he tends to harbor angry feelings, and to embark on furious wishes with little thought of the consequences should these come true. Many fairy tales depict the tragic outcome of such rash wishes, engaged in because one desires something too much or is unable to wait until things come about in their good time. Both mental states are typical for the child. Two stories of the Brothers Grimm may illustrate.

In "Hans, My Hedgehog" a man becomes angry when his great desire for having children is frustrated by his wife's inability to have any. Finally he gets carried away enough to exclaim, "I want a child, even if it should be a hedgehog." His wish is granted: his wife begets a child who is a hedgehog on top, while the lower part of his body is that of a boy.*

In "The Seven Ravens" a newborn child so preoccupies a father's emotions that he turns his anger against his older children. He sends one of his seven sons to fetch baptismal water for the christening of the infant daughter, an errand on which his six brothers join him. The father, in his anger at being kept waiting, shouts, "I wish all the boys would turn into ravens"—which promptly happens.

If these fairy stories in which angry wishes come true ended there, they would be merely cautionary tales, warning us not to permit ourselves to be carried away by our negative emotions—something the child is unable to avoid. But the fairy tale knows better than to expect the impossible of the child, and to make him anxious about having angry wishes which he cannot help having. While the fairy tale realistically warns that being carried away by anger or impatience leads to trouble, it reassures that the consequences are only temporary ones, and that good will or deeds can undo all the harm done by bad wishing. Hans the Hedgehog helps a king lost in the forest to return safely home. The king promises to give Hans as a reward the first thing he encounters on his return home, which happens to be his only daughter. Despite Hans's appearance, the princess keeps her father's promise and marries Hans the Hedgehog. After the marriage, in the marital bed, Hans at last takes on a fully human form, and eventually he inherits the kingdom.† In the "Seven Ravens" the sister, who was the innocent cause of her brothers being turned into ravens, travels to the end of the world and makes a great sacrifice to undo the spell put on them. The ravens all regain their human form, and happiness is restored.

These stories tell that, despite the bad consequences which evil wishes have, with good will and effort things can be righted again. There are other tales which go much further and tell the child not to fear having such wishes because, although there are momentary consequences, nothing changes permanently; after all the wishing is done,

---

*The motif that parents who too impatiently desire to have children are punished by giving birth to strange mixtures of human and animal beings is an ancient one and widely distributed. For example, it is the topic of a Turkish tale in which King Solomon effects the restitution of a child to full humanity. In these stories, if the parents treat the misdeveloped child well and with great patience, he is eventually restored as an attractive human being.

The psychological wisdom of these tales is remarkable: lack of control over emotions on the part of the parent creates a child who is a misfit. In fairy tales and dreams, physical malformation often stands for psychological misdevelopment. In these stories, the upper part of the body including the head is usually animal-like, while the lower part is of normal human form. This indicates that things are wrong with the head—that is, mind—of the child, and not his body. The stories also tell that the damage done to the child through negative feelings can be corrected, through the impact of positive emotions lavished on him, if the parents are sufficiently patient and consistent. The children of angry parents often behave like hedgehogs or porcupines: they seem all spines, so the image of the child that is part hedgehog is most appropriate.

These are also cautionary tales which warn: Do not conceive children in anger; do not receive them with anger and impatience on their arrival. But, like all good fairy tales, these stories also indicate the right remedies to undo the damage, and the prescription is in line with the best psychological insights of today.

†This ending is typical for stories belonging to the animal-groom cycle.

things are exactly as they were before the wishing began. Such stories exist in many variations all over the globe.

In the Western world "The Three Wishes" is probably the best known wish story. In the simplest form of this motif, a man or a woman is granted some wishes, usually three, by a stranger or an animal as reward for some good deed. A man is given this favor in "The Three Wishes," but he thinks little of it. On his return home his wife presents him with his daily soup for dinner. "'Soup again, I wish I had pudding for a change,' says he, and promptly the pudding appears." The wife demands to know how this has happened, and he tells her about his adventure. Furious that he wasted one of his wishes on such a trifle, she exclaims, "I wish the pudding was on your head," a wish which is immediately fulfilled. "'That's two wishes gone! I wish the pudding was off my head,' says the man. And so the three wishes were gone."[2]

Together, these tales warn the child of the possible undesirable consequences of rash wishing, and assure him at the same time that such wishing has little consequence, particularly if one is sincere in one's desire and efforts to undo the bad results. Maybe even more important is the fact that I cannot recall a single fairy tale in which a child's angry wishes have any consequence; only those of adults do. The implication is that adults are accountable for what they do in their anger or their silliness, but children are not. If children wish in a fairy tale, they desire only good things; and chance or a good spirit fulfills their desires, often beyond their fondest hopes.

It is as if the fairy tale, while admitting how human it is to get angry, expects only adults to have sufficient self-control not to let themselves get carried away, since their outlandishly angry wishes come true—but the tales stress the wonderful consequences for a child if he engages in *positive* wishing or thinking. Desolation does not induce the fairy-tale child to engage in vengeful wishing. The child wishes only for good things, even when he has ample reason to wish that bad things would happen to those who persecute him. Snow White harbors no angry wishes against the evil queen. Cinderella, who has good reason to wish that her stepsisters be punished for their misdeeds, instead wishes them to go to the grand ball.

Left alone for a few hours, a child can feel as cruelly abused as though he had suffered a lifetime of neglect and rejection. Then, suddenly, his existence turns into complete bliss as his mother appears in the doorway, smiling, maybe even bringing him some little present. What could be more magical than that? How could something so simple have the power to alter his life, unless there were magic involved?

Radical transformations in the nature of things are experienced by the child on all sides, although *we* do not share his perceptions. But consider the child's dealings with inanimate objects: some object—a shoelace or a toy—utterly frustrates the child, to the degree that he feels himself a complete fool. Then in a moment, as if by magic, the object becomes obedient and does his bidding; from being the most dejected of humans, he becomes the happiest. Doesn't this prove the magic character of the object? Quite a few fairy tales relate how finding a magic object changes the hero's life; with its help, the fool turns out smarter than his previously preferred siblings. The child who feels himself doomed to be an ugly duckling need not despair; he will grow into a beautiful swan.

183

# Bruno Bettelheim

A small child can do little on his own, and this is disappointing to him—so much so that he may give up in despair. The fairy story prevents this by giving extraordinary dignity to the smallest achievement, and suggesting that the most wonderful consequences may grow out of it. Finding a jar or bottle (as in the Brothers Grimm's story "The Spirit in the Bottle"), sharing a piece of bread with a stranger ("The Golden Goose," another of the Brothers Grimm's stories)—such little everyday events lead to great things. So the fairy tale encourages the child to trust that his small real achievements are important, though he may not realize it at the moment.

The belief in such possibilities needs to be nurtured so that the child can accept his disillusionments without being utterly defeated; and beyond this, it can become a challenge to think with confidence about an existence beyond the parental home. The fairy tale's example provides assurance that the child will receive help in his endeavors in the outside world, and that eventual success will reward his sustained efforts. At the same time, the fairy tale stresses that these events happened once upon a time, in a far-distant land, and makes clear that it offers food for hope, not realistic accounts of what the world is like here and now.

The child intuitively comprehends that although these stories are *unreal*, they are not *untrue;* that while what these stories tell about does not happen in fact, it must happen as inner experience and personal development; that fairy tales depict in imaginary and symbolic form the essential steps in growing up and achieving an independent existence.

While fairy tales invariably point the way to a better future, they concentrate on the process of change, rather than describing the exact details of the bliss eventually to be gained. The stories start where the child is at the time, and suggest where he has to go—with emphasis on the process itself. Fairy tales can even show the child the way through the thorniest of thickets, the oedipal period.

---

[1]Sigmund Freud, "The Family Romance of the Neurotic," *The Standard Edition of the Complete Psychological Works* (London: Hogarth Press, 1953ff), vol. 10.

[2]"The Three Wishes" was originally a Scottish tale, reported by Katherine M. Briggs, *A Dictionary of British Folk Tales,* 4 volumes (Bloomington: Indiana University Press, 1970). As mentioned, with appropriate variations the motif is found all over the world. For example, in an Indian tale a family is granted three wishes. The wife desires great beauty and uses the first wish to gain it, after which she elopes with a prince. The angry husband wishes her changed into a pig; the son must use the third and last wish to restore her as she was originally.

# Strategy in Counting Out: An Ethnographic Folklore Field Study

Kenneth S. Goldstein

*The socialization of a child to a large extent involves the mastering of rules—rules of language and discourse, rules of interaction and etiquette, even rules of play and fantasy. On the one hand, many of the rules that children internalize are implicit; they are never explicitly taught or consciously regarded as having been learned. For example, in the United States many children learn that it is impolite to employ a utensil to pick up food that is to be returned to the plate. A utensil should carry food to the mouth, not away from it. Food that may be picked up with the hands, however, can be returned to the plate. On the other hand, children learn many explicit rules that they can easily describe and explain, such as the impropriety of using certain language in the presence of adults or looking both ways before crossing the street. Although the term "rules" connotes constraint and restriction, there is considerable creativity involved in the use of rules. Even the most explicit system of rules requires some degree of interpretation in its application to the real world.*

*Folklorists have been particularly concerned with rules of games. In the following essay, Kenneth S. Goldstein explores the role of rules in a preliminary to games—the procedures for "counting out." Goldstein shows that beyond the ordinary rules for counting out there are other rules, sanctioned by tradition, that may be optionally invoked in order to achieve satisfactory outcomes. Indeed, some individuals employ private higher-order rules in order to manipulate the public traditional ones.*

*The manipulation of game is not always done in order to win. Burridge (1957) provides an interesting example of how different the goals of game may be in another culture. For a discussion of the effects of game rules on player success and failure see Gump and Sutton-Smith (1955). For more examples of counting out rhymes see Bolton (1969), Gardner (1918), Gregor (1972), and Abrahams and Rankin (1980). Further discussion of the prosody of the counting out rhyme can be found in Arleo (1980).*

Though considerable attention has been paid to game activities by travellers, historians, antiquarians, and numerous others for almost two centuries, much of the scholarship of such pastimes, until well into the twentieth century, consisted of little more than gathering and publishing descriptions and the related texts.[1] A few scholars attempted interpretation and analysis,[2] but the majority were content to present their texts and descriptions in regional and national collections with occasional comparative references to analogous items among other peoples.[3]

It is no wonder, then, that so little attention of any serious nature was paid to this folklore genre until after World War II. When this new interest finally manifested itself, it was more through the work of social and behavioral scientists than of folklorists that this previously "minor" genre was raised to the status of an area of prime interest and importance. The work of Huizinga and Caillois in defining the nature of play,[4] the social-psychological insights into children's play activities of Piaget and Erikson,[5] and, more recently, the work of Roberts, Arth, Bush, and Sutton-Smith in relating games to other aspects of culture,[6] have written new chapters in game scholarship. Among folklorists the recent work of Robert Georges with his interest in the relevance of behavioral models for the analyses of traditional play activities, of Alan Dundes and his interest in the structural analysis of games, and of Roger D. Abrahams and his application of rhetorical models to the performance of folklore, show promise of removing game scholarship from the arid and sterile domain of description and comparativist annotation along historical and geographical lines.[7]

Folklorists, moreover, have the means to make a still larger contribution to the study of games by the application in their field work of the concept which has come to be known as the "ethnography of speaking folklore," or the study of folklore "texts in their contexts" for the purpose of determining the rules which govern any specific folklore event.[8] Since much of the recent research and scholarship on games involves correlations of game types to other aspects of culture (e.g., social systems, religion, child training, etc.),[9] the classification of games can be crucial to the findings. And the accurate classification of games by types calls for better understanding of play events and the rules which govern those events. Folklorists whose field research is directed at developing ethnographics of games may find the work rewarding not only to their own better understanding of the mechanics by which folklore is expressed, performed, transmitted, circulated, and used, but to the development of closer interdisciplinary ties between folklore and the behavioral sciences.

The prospect of doing such ethnographic studies of games is especially intriguing because of all the genres of folklore the games genre is one of the few for which rules of performance are consciously recognized by the participants and are sometimes overtly expressed. The opportunity thus presents itself to study the manner in which the stated rules relate to the actual rules which operate in playing the games. Any attempt at doing an ethnography of a game could serve not only as a model for the collecting of data concerning game events, but also as a base for evaluating the reliability of earlier descriptions of games and thus of effecting criticism of research in any way involving game classification based on such descriptions.

This paper is an attempt at an ethnographic study of the game activity known as "counting-out." The game was selected because all previous studies of this game type had consisted of descriptions of the manner in which certain rhymes were used, of their poetics, music, rhyme, and rhythm patterns, or attempts at devising a classification system for its many texts.[10] Nowhere, however, was there any description of the rules actually at work in "counting-out."

My field work was carried out in a six block area in the East Mount Airy section of northwest Philadelphia between January 1966 and June 1967. The area, a racially integrated middle class neighborhood, contains young whitecollar workers, professionals, and businessmen, mainly homeowners with larger than average size families. Their children use the mostly tree-shaded, exclusively residential streets as their playgrounds.

My informants consisted of 67 children between the ages of four and fourteen, who comprise eight separate, independent, and essentially non-overlapping play groups. As might be expected these groups were peer-oriented according to age. The eight groups consisted of four pairs of age groups, the first containing larger pre-school and kindergarten children whose ages ranged from four to seven, the second pair of school children from six through eight, the third of children from eight through twelve, and the fourth from eleven through fourteen. The first two pairs, containing the youngest children, had both boys and girls, though one group in each age category was predominantly male and the other mainly female. The members of each of the oldest groups were exclusively male or female. The groups were selected from among the many to be found in the neighborhood because of their age and sex composition after an initial survey indicated these were the major factors contributing to their own sense of group identity and awareness.

Collecting methods employed in obtaining data for this paper consisted of observations made both in natural and induced natural[11] contexts, followed first by non-directed and then by directed interviewing, the latter including hypothetical situation questioning.[12] Interview data were then checked by additional observations, reinterviewing of the same informants over time, and interviewing informants from one group on information obtained from other groups.

## GENERAL DATA

"Counting-out" is used for selecting personnel for two other kinds of game activities: for games for which an "it" figure must be chosen, and for games for which sides must be chosen. "Counting-out" is introduced to younger children in the first age group (four through seven years) by older members of the group who report learning it from siblings and from contacts with members of the second age group (six through eight years) on the street and in school play. The rhymes are learned first (as early as two years of age) and the activity later (at four or five). It is less frequently used by both sexes in the final age group (eleven through fourteen), with other selection methods employed in its place (e.g., coin tossing, bat holding, drawing lots, and spinning bottles). Girls employ "counting out" more frequently for choosing sides than for determining who shall be "it," with boys reversing this pattern. Though size of the play group employing "counting out" may theoretically vary from two to quite large numbers, in actual play conditions it was never used when the group numbered more than ten. At such times (and such cases were only among boys), selection was made by "odds or even" coin tossing or finger matching, though there were no "rules" against the use of "counting-out" in such instances.

## STEPS INVOLVED IN "COUNTING-OUT"

1. One member of a group suggests playing a specific "it" game or one for which sides must be chosen.
2. A number of others verbally agree (sometimes a majority of the group, at other times only one or two with the others silently acquiescing).
3. The method of selection is determined by the first suggestion made.
4. If "counting-out" is suggested the counter is appointed by one of the following methods:
   a. The person who suggests the game announces himself as counter.
   b. A recognized leader of the group assumes the role without asking or being asked.
   c. A suggestion is made by one member of the group that some other member should do the counting, with the others agreeing verbally or silently.
5. The other members of the group gather in a circle around the counter or are lined up by him in specific order.
6. The counter begins, sometimes with himself and at other times with the nearest person on his left. The direction of counting is clockwise.
7. Counting continues until the counter indicates who is "it," or until sides have been chosen.

The steps previously outlined follow in the order given. After the counter has been selected (step 4), the alternative forms of succeeding steps are left completely to his choice.

## REASONS FOR USING "COUNTING-OUT" AS THE METHOD OF SELECTION

When queried as to why "counting-out" rather than some other method was employed in the task of choosing "it" or in determining the composition of sides, the answers given were as follows:

| | | |
|---|---|---|
| equal chance ................ 90% | (Typical answers: "Everybody has the same chance." "It's more democratic.") |
| removal of friction ......... 18% | (Typical answers: "We don't fight about it." "Less trouble.") |
| supernatural decision ...... 8% | (Typical answers: "Fate decides." "God does the choosing.") |

(The percentages add to more than 100 because some children gave more than one answer.)

The answers given would appear to clearly indicate that the great majority of the children queried considered "counting-out" to be a game of chance. It should be noted that this is also the opinion of those scholars who have tried their hand at classifying games; Roger Caillois and Brian Sutton-Smith, among others, refer to "counting-out" as a game of chance.[13] It is, however, precisely on this matter that my field work resulted in my finding that for a large number of the children involved "counting-out" is far from being a game of chance. It is, rather, a game of strategy in which the rhymes and movements of the players are manipulated to limit or remove chance as a factor in selection.

## THE STRATEGY OF COUNTING-OUT

What we find here is that children—like their parents—do *not* in fact do or believe what they *say* they do or believe. As stated earlier, more than for any other folklore genre, rules are an essential part of games at an overt and sometimes verbalized level. But the rules which are verbalized by informants and which are then presented by collectors in their papers and books for our analysis and study are an idealized set of rules—they are the rules by which people *should* play rather than the ones by which they *do* play. The field results presented in the remainder of this paper indicate that for games we may have to know *two* sets of rules: the ideal ones *and* those by which the ideal rules are applied, misapplied, or subverted.

Only a few of the children were at first willing to admit that "counting-out" rhymes, player movements, or both were manipulated by certain of their peers. By using the hypothetical situation interview technique, I was able to discover how, by whom, and when manipulative strategies were applied, and through later observations and reinter views I confirmed earlier collected data as well as adding several strategies employed by the children in the groups I studied:

## EXTENSION OF RHYME

If the counter finds that the rhyme ends on a child whom he does *not* wish to be "it," he may add one or more phrases or lines to the rhyme until it ends on the one whom he wishes to be "it." In the following example, when the "Eenie, meenie, meinie, mo" rhyme was used in a group of six children, the final word ended on player 4. The counter wanted someone else to be "it" and extended the rhyme so it ended on player 5. He could similarly extend it still further to have it end on 6, or carry it out to end on any one in the group including himself. Controlling selection of "it" by extending the rhyme is the most common "counting-out" strategy, with better than fifty per cent of both boys and girls in the two oldest age groups employing it.

Kenneth S. Goldstein

## Position of Players

| 1 | 2 | 3 | 4 | 5 | 6 |
|---|---|---|---|---|---|
| Eeenie | meenie | meinie | mo, | Catch | afeller |
| by the | toe; | If he | hollers | let him | go, |
| Eenie | meenie | meinie | mo.# | (My | mother |
| says | that | you | are | it.) # | (But |
| I | say | that | you | are | out.) # |

(John J., age 10)

## SPECIFIC RHYME REPERTORY

In order to insure the selection of himself when he wishes to be "it," the counter may employ one of a special set of rhymes, the specific rhyme to be used depending upon the number of players involved. Each of the rhymes has a different number of stresses, and the counter knows which of the rhymes to apply in any specific group numbering up to eight players so that the final stress will end on himself. In the example given below the informant had a fixed repertory of four rhymes, including ones of seven stresses, eight stresses, nine stresses, and sixteen stresses. If there are three players in the group she may employ either the seven or sixteen stress rhyme; for four players she would use the nine stress rhyme; for five players the sixteen stress rhyme; for six players the seven stress rhyme; for seven players the eight stress rhyme; and for eight players the nine stress rhyme. Conversely, if the counter wanted to be sure she was *not* "it," she would select a rhyme—again according to the number of players—in which the final stress would fall on someone other than herself.

*Seven* stresses:   Andy / Mandy / Sugar / Candy //
Out / Goes / He.#

       Counter is "it" when there are 3 or 6 players; not "it" when there are 4, 5, 7, or 8 players.

*Eight* stresses:   Inka / Bink / A bottle / Of Ink //
I / Say / You / Stink.#

       Counter is "it" when there are 7 players; not "it" when there are 3, 4, 5, 6, or 8 players.

*Nine* stresses:   Apples / Oranges //
Cherries / Pears / And A Plum //
I / Think / You're / Dumb.

       Counter is "it" when there are 4 or 8 players; not "it" when there are 3, 5, 6, or 7 players.

190

*Sixteen* stresses:   Eena / Meena / Mina / Mo //
                        Catch / A Tiger / By The / Toe //
                        If He / Hollers / Let Him / Go //
                        Eena / Meena / Mina / Mo.

Counter is "it" when there are 3 or 5 players; not "it" when there are 4, 6, 7, or 8 players.

(Sarah M., age 11)

Use of specific rhyme repertory to control "counting-out" was employed by three children, all girls in the eight through twelve age group. Each of the girls employed a different set of rhymes, and each was aware that the others employed a similar strategy.

## SKIPPING REGULAR COUNTS

To insure against his being "it," the counter will skip over himself on the second and successive times around. In the example given below, in which five players were involved, the counter simply passed by himself each of the last three times. Normally the rhyme would have ended on the counter, but by omitting himself he arranged for it to fall on someone else.

Back / Side / Front / Side //
1       2       3       4

Looking / For A / Little / Ride; //
5       2       3       4

In / And Out / And Up / And Down //
5       2       3       4

Goes In / Red / And Comes Out / Brown.
5       2       3       4

The numbers below the text indicate the positions of the players on whom each of the words fall.

(Jerry B., age 9)

The children employing this strategy have no idea whether any particular rhyme will end on them and, when they don't wish to be "it," will use this strategy with any "counting-out" rhymes they perform. Skipping regular counts is the second most popular form of strategically manipulating "counting-out;" one-third of all informants have done it at one time or another. It should be noted that while other strategies were considered "clever," this one was frowned upon as being "dishonest" and "against the rules!"

Kenneth S. Goldstein

## STOPPING OR CONTINUING

The first person "counted-out" may be designated "it" or the counter may continue by repeating the rhyme until all but one player has been "counted-out" and that player is "it." In the case of the "one potato, two potato" rhyme, the "potatoes" are the fists which the players extend for counting. The fist which the counter points to on the word "more" is withdrawn. The counter repeats the rhyme until both fists of one player have been withdrawn and that person may be designated "it" or, if the counter wishes someone else to be "it," he may continue repeating the rhyme until there is one player left who has not been "counted-out" and that player is "it." If, for example, there were five players, the first to be counted out would be number three; if the counter continued the rhyme he himself would be the last remaining person counted. The informants who used this strategy (with the one exception of the case cited in 5, below) did so without knowing on which players the first or last "out" would fall. They were merely shifting the chance factor from first to last but not to any specific player. The choice of stopping or continuing was employed by twenty children, evenly distributed between sexes in the six through eight and eight through twelve age groups.

## CHANGING POSITIONS

The counter, using the "One Potato, Two Potato" rhyme mentioned above [eight stresses, two-fisted play, continuous counting beginning with counter—ED.], had memorized the "first out" position for any number of players from two through ten. After each player was counted out, he would start the rhyme again from his own position after first moving to a new position either himself or the next player he wanted to count out, according to the memorized list of "first out" positions for the specific number of players remaining. In the example given below, involving ten

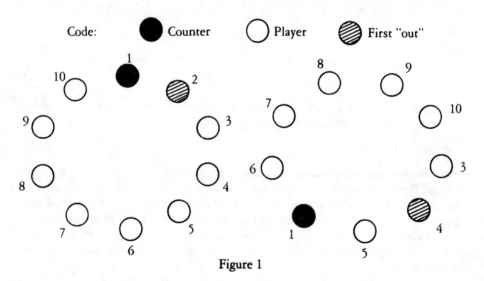

Figure 1

players, the counter wanted a specific player to be counted-out first. He therefore placed that player in the second position. The next player whom he wished to count-out was originally in the fourth position; he therefore shifted his own position so that player would be in the eighth position and would be counted-out next.

In addition to employing this strategy for choosing sides, the informant also employed a variation of it together with the "stopping or continuing" strategy for electing "it." By memorizing both the "first out" and the "last remaining" position for any number of players through ten, he could always place himself relative to any other player so as to be able to completely control the selection according to his whim.

In the table given below, for use with the "One Potato, Two Potato" rhyme, the positions of the players are those in relation to the counter who is in position number 1. The first column indicates the number of players. The second column refers to the position of the first player to be counted "out" and the third column refers to the position of the "last remaining" position for any number of players through ten.

| | Position of Player | |
| :---: | :---: | :---: |
| Number of Players | First Out | Last Remaining |
| 10 | 2 | 1 |
| 9 | 8 | 3 |
| 8 | 8 | 4 |
| 7 | 7 | 4 |
| 6 | 6 | 3 |
| 5 | 3 | 1 |
| 4 | 3 | 2 |
| 3 | 1 | 3 |
| 2 | 1 | 2 |

(Samuel G., age 9)

The "changing position" strategy was used by one extremely precocious nine year old boy who was considered somewhat of a mathematical genius at school. One member of his play group, who was aware that some kind of manipulation was going on without knowing exactly what it was, would frequently thwart the change of position of the counter by changing his own position in the remaining group. Eventually, the precocious boy who had worked out the strategy began to count out the other youngster first so he would be free to make his further manipulations without interference.

## RESPITE BY CALLING OUT

When a child wished to remove himself from the possibility of becoming "it" or to thwart any of the strategies indicated above, he could do so by calling out "safe" (in one group), "free" (in another group), or "in-or-out" (in a third group). This could be done only after counting began, and only one child in any instance of "counting-out" would be permitted to do so. What is surprising is that despite the fact that all eight groups had respite or truce terms for other game activities only three had specific terms for removing oneself from a "counting-out" situation.

From the data given in this paper it is readily apparent that at least for some children "counting-out" is a game of strategy rather than of chance. If games serve as mechanisms through which children are prepared for adult roles in life, as some social psychologists maintain, then identifying a game as one of chance when it, in fact, is one of strategy may complicate any attempt at relating the end result of a socialization process with prior childhood activities. Similarly, if one sees in the play activities of children a mirror of the real adult world and its values, concepts, tendencies, and ways of thought, then incorrect classification of a society's games may result in a wholly reversed or otherwise inappropriate or false picture of that world.

If we are to fully utilize the great store of information imparted to us in the cross cultural game studies of Roberts, Arth, Bush, and Sutton-Smith,[14] in which game types have been correlated with other facets of culture and from which various generalizations have been made as to the involvements of individuals and groups in games, the cultural and social functions of games, and the cultural evolution of games, then a clear and precise classification and identification of games must be made before such correlations may be entirely trusted.

Though carefully selected, my sample was a small one and may be viewed by some as inadequate for making any generalization other than that some children in Northwest Philadelphia play "counting-out" as a game of strategy.[15] If, however, the reclassification of *one* game results from an intensive ethnographic study of the manner in which it is played, then it should certainly prove profitable to reexamine other games employing the same methods.

---

[1]See, for example, Joseph Strutt, *The Sports and Pastimes of the People of England*, London, 1801, and numerous later editions; the many editions of John Brand's *Observations on Popular Antiquities*, Newcastle, 1777, London, 1810, itself based on Henry Bourne's *Antiquitates Vulgares*, Newcastle, 1725, and later revised and edited by Henry Ellis, London, 1813, two volumes, culminating in a completely new edition in dictionary form by W. Carew Hazlitt under the title *Faiths and Folklore*, London, 1905, two volumes.

[2]A prime example is William W. Newell in his *Games and Songs of American Children*, New York, 1883, new edition 1903. Many of Newell's speculations and theories, especially those concerning games as "survivals" of earlier times and places, were popular with other collector-scholars for many years before being challenged and discarded.

[3]For example, James O. Halliwell, *The Nursery Rhymes of England*, London, 1841, with later editions; Robert Chambers, *Popular Rhymes of Scotland*, Edinburgh, 1925, though the important edition for our purpose is the third edition of 1842 and its later reprintings; Alice Bertha Gomme, *The Traditional Games of England, Scotland and Ireland*, London, 1894, 1898, two volumes; G. F. Northall, *English Folk Rhymes*, London, 1892; continental works of the same order were Eugène Rolland, *Rimes et jeux de l'enfance*, Paris, 1883, and F. M. Böhme, *Deutsches Kinderlied und Kinderspiel*, Leipzig, 1897.

[4]J. Huizinga, *Homo Ludens: A Study of the Play Element in Culture*, English translation, London, 1949, New York 1950; Roger Caillois, *Man, Play, and Games*, Glencoe, Ill., 1961.

[5]Jean Piaget, *The Moral Judgement of the Child*, New York, 1965, and *Play, Dreams and Imitation in Childhood*, London, 1951; Erik H. Erikson, *Childhood and Society*, 2nd revised and enlarged edition, New York, 1963.

[6]John M. Roberts, Malcolm J. Arth, and Robert R. Bush, "Games in Culture," *American Anthropologist* 61 (1959), 597–605; Brian Sutton-Smith, "Cross Cultural Study of Children's Games," *American Philosophical Society Yearbook,* 1961, 426–429; John M. Roberts and Brian Sutton-Smith, "Child Training and Game Involvement," *Ethnology* I (1962), 166–185, and "Cross Cultural Correlates of Games of Chance," *Behavior Science Notes* 3 (1966), 131–144.

[7]Robert A. Georges, "The Relevance of Models for Analyses of Traditional Play Activities," *Southern Folklore Quarterly* 33 (1969), 1–23; Alan Dundes, "On Game Morphology: A Study of the Structure of Non-Verbal Folklore," *New York Folklore Quarterly* XX (1964), 276–288; Roger D. Abrahams's work on rhetorical models in folklore is a continuing project, and its application to games is in preparation at the time of this writing.

[8]Alan Dundes and E. Ojo Arewa, "Proverbs and the Ethnography of Speaking Folklore," *American Anthropologist* 66 (1964), No. 6, part 2, 70–85.

[9]See note 6.

[10]For some of the more important works on "counting-out" see Henry C. Bolton, *The Counting-Out Rhymes of Children,* London, 1888; Emil Bodmer, Empros oder Anzählreime der französischen *Schweiz,* Halle, 1923; Jean Baucomont, Frank Guibat, Tante Lucile, Roger Pinon and Philippe Soupault, *Les Comptines de langue française,* Paris, 1961, containing an extensive international bibliography on "counting-out." I am grateful to Roger Pinon for making the latter two works available to me.

[11]For a description of the induced natural context technique, see Kenneth S. Goldstein, *A Guide for Field Workers in Folklore,* Hatboro, Penna., 1964, 87–90, and "The Induced Natural Context: An Ethnographic Folklore Field Technique," *Essays on the Verbal and Visual Arts" Proceedings of the 1966 Annual Spring Meeting of the American Ethnological Society,* Seattle, 1967, 1–6.

[12]The hypothetical situation is described in Melville J. Herskovits, "The Hypothetical Situation: A Technique of Field Research," *Southwestern Journal of Anthropology* 6 (1950), 32–40.

[13]Roger Caillois, *Man, Play, and Games,* Glencoe, Ill., 1961, 36; Brian Sutton-Smith, *The Games of New Zealand Children,* Berkeley and Los Angeles, 1959, 89–90.

[14]See note 6.

[15]After the presentation of this paper at the American Folklore Society Meeting in Toronto, November, 1967, several members of the audience informed me they knew of similar and, in some cases, other strategies employed in "counting-out" in other parts of the United States, Canada, Europe, and Africa. To my knowledge none of these has been reported in print.

# VI
# Folk Narratives

## The Structure of the Turkish Romances
İlhan Başgöz

*Structure is a conceptualization of how parts are related—to one another and to the whole they comprise. To say that a genre has a particular structure is to argue that the ways in which the parts of different texts are arranged are in some basic respects similar. There are several perspectives that have been applied to the analysis of folk narrative structure. Most have centered either on plot structure (Propp 1968) or thematic structure (Lévi-Strauss 1963b, 1967). The structures of the component parts themselves can also be analyzed, such as the relations that govern the elements in a particular story scene (Olrik 1909).*

*Most folklorists have been content merely to identify narrative structures. Fewer have attempted to interpret them. In the following essay, İlhan Başgöz not only attempts to outline the plot structure of Turkish romances, but he goes on to character-ize a relationship between that structure and the Turkish minstrels (ashiks) who perform them. For more on plot structure in folk narrative see Dundes (1963) and the response by Georges (1970). Further discussion of structuralism and folklore can be found in Dundes (1976), Hendricks (1970), and Waugh (1966). Some other examples of the relationship of folklore to individual psychology may be found in Burns with Burns (1976), Jones (1975:34-103), and Oring (1984).*

## I.

A structural study of folk narrative that challenged type and motif oriented research was designed by Vladimir Propp.[1] In his analysis of the Russian magic tale, Propp identified the functions of the dramatis personae as the most constant aspect of tales. My study is an attempt to outline the apparent structure, the compositional structure, of the Turkish romance of the minstrel (*ashik*) by means of basic plot actions. I will not

Reproduced by permission of the Indiana University Board of Trustees, from *Folklore Today: A Festschrift for Richard M. Dorson,* ed. Linda Dégh, Henry Glassie, and Felix Oinas (Bloomington: Indiana University Press, 1976), 11-23. Not for further reproduction.

be content, however, with the delineation of the romance structure in isolation from the socio-cultural milieu, but I will explore the meaning for the teller within the Ottoman-Turkish culture.

The data on which our analysis is based came from nine romances, some of them existing in several variants.[2] Though limited, the material is representative of this genre which narrates the life story of the *ashik* in prose interspersed with song.

The plots, motifs, and characters, as well as the historical and geographical settings of the romances, vary considerably, but all nine exhibit a compositional unity, which persists despite the changes introduced by the individual tellers or by temporal or spatial distribution. The romances of the *ashik* arise, I believe, from this unique romance pattern which can be outlined in three parts, consisting of a limited number of basic units of plot action, six altogether:

## A. THE DISINTEGRATION OF A FAMILY

### *Plot Action 1:* Crisis.

Following some introductory songs, which are a traditional part of story-telling but have no connection to the plot, the romance begins with what Propp called the "initial situation." Here a family is introduced in a particular social milieu within a historical and geographical setting.

The teller strives to convince the audience that such a family really existed at a historical time in a certain area. The social and economic standing of the family is briefly described, and the names of the members are given. These temporal-spatial elements of the romance are all variable except for the pseudonym (*mahlas*) of the hero. The romance takes its title from this unchanging *mahlas*, which is usually paired with the name of the heroine. The title of the story of Kerem and Asli is an example.

The first plot action consisting of one of the following crises comes after the initial situation:

a. The father dies (romance 1, 2, 3).
b. Both parents (the mother, then the father) die (romance 5).
c. The couple has no child (romances 7, 8).
d. The family escapes from their native land for fear of persecution (romances 4, 9).
e. One of the members of the family is cursed by an old woman to lead a tragic life (romance 6).

No matter what the individual nature of the crisis is, it destroys the equilibrium of the family structure and after that the happy family unity will never be restored. If the crisis is childlessness, however, it is temporarily solved, following the "childlessness" pattern of Propp's tabulation,[3] except that in the Turkish romances two families are involved and later each has a child, one a boy and the other a girl. The children are betrothed prenatally by their parents. The real crisis in such a romance appears later, when the boy and girl reach maturity and one of the families breaks the engagement vow.

The disintegration of the family order, which has meant security, love, and affection for the young boy hero soon becomes a psychological crisis for him and reaches an intolerable point following a failure—a physical or spiritual ordeal, or some social blame being placed upon the hero. This always happens when he is at puberty, between fourteen and seventeen years of age, and introduces the second plot action.

### *Plot Action 2:* Transformation.

The young boy (hero) is transformed during this sequence into an adult-lover-artist.

In all romances, this transformation takes place in an ecstatic dream and contains the main elements of an initiation ceremony. The boy is visited in the dream by a holy figure (the future protector) who offers him a love potion and introduces a young girl to him. After seeing the girl and drinking the love potion from her hands, the infantile personality of the hero dies and he becomes a God-inspired minstrel who can sing, compose poems, and play a musical instrument beautifully. This is the rebirth of an adult-lover-artist with a new name (*mahlas,* a pen name used in his poetry), which is given him in the dream.

This transformation is the most important action of the romance for several reasons. The passionate love of the romance emerges from this ecstatic experience. Here the young man is also unmistakenly established as the main figure of the plot: his song and adventures become the main attraction of the narrative. New characters such as the holy protector and the heroine are also introduced in this sequence. It is only after this action that the hero, as a mature person, dares to leave his family to follow his own destiny and establish a new family of his own. This is the final blow for the little family unity that remains. No longer can anyone prevent the minstrel from finding and marrying his "dream" girl. The whole dream, which includes the main characters of the romance, the romantic love, and a short description of the plot by the holy figure, is in fact the core of the romance in micro-form.

### B. The Struggle to Establish a New Family

### *Plot Action 3:* Search.

Following the dream, the hero gets a musical instrument and sings his first song in which he describes what happened in his dream and then reveals his resolution to leave the family in search of the young girl. His decision upsets his family, especially his mother who begs him not to leave them alone. But his decision is unalterable and he sets out, taking his *saz* (a musical instrument) and nothing else, in search of the city and the house of the heroine. In romances where childlessness is involved, this takes the form of a pursuit since the two had previously been together and the heroine was taken away by her parents. As soon as the hero leaves his family, obstacles (Plot Action 4) arise to make the journey difficult. Nevertheless, the young lover manages to locate the heroine and meet with her. The meeting takes different forms depending upon the

İlhan Başgöz

individuality of the teller and the nature of the audience. When they meet, the two just talk, or they make some advances and hug and kiss each other, or they go to bed and sleep with each other—without the proper marriage ceremony. Then, with the arrival of Plot Action 4, they are separated.

*Plot Action 4:* Obstacles.

This action overlaps with the previous one; actions 3 and 4 then follow each other in alternation until the end of the story. The teller may increase the number of obstacles, extending the plot as much as he wants. It can readily be seen, then, that this segment of the romance opens conveniently to variation. When one of the obstacles is overcome, the narrator can introduce another. Sometimes a set of obstacles is repeated, utilizing different characters and geographical settings each time. For example, in Romance 4, when a set of obstacles which revolve around Shah Abbas[4] is overcome and the hero is about to marry, the same obstacles are repeated around a new character, Emir Kugu Khan, this time not in Isfehan but in Tabriz.

The following table is a list of these obstacles. To facilitate their identification, the agent who introduces the obstacle, the motivation of the agent, and the nature and consequences of the obstacle are selected as descriptive components. The Roman numerals identify the romance, while the others indicate the number of the obstacle. (That is IV-1 means the first obstacle in Romance 4.)

The Agent Introducing the Obstacle:

The father of the heroine: I-3, VI-2, VII-2, VII-8, VIII-2,3, IX-2; The mother of the heroine: III-2, VIII-2,4; The brothers of the heroine: IV-7; The father of the hero: IV-1; A rival: (the heroine's nephew) I-4; The rival's mother: II-5,6; The hero himself: V-8, VII-6; The forces of nature: I-2, VII-4, VII-5; A ruler: (Bey, Pasha, Shah, Governor, Vezir) IX-1, II-2,4, VI-2, II-7, IV-9, III-6, The Shah Abbas: III-3,5, IV-5,6; The men or policemen of a ruler: IV-8, V-7; An Armenian youth: V-6; A Negro: (the heroine's relative) VI-3; A cafe owner: VIII-5; An Imam: VII-3; The daughter of a ruler: VII-7.

The Motivation of the Agent:

To prove superiority: I-1, I-5, II-3, III-1, V-1,2,3,4,5, IV-1,2,3; To prevent the marriage of the heroine to: a poor *ashik*, I-3, III-2, IV-7, VI-7, VI-1, VIII-1,2, a Muslim, VIII-2; To marry the heroine: I-4, III-3, IV-4, IV-9; Wickedness (no other motivation): II-1; No motivation (perhaps God's will): I-2, VI-3; A mistake on the hero's part: VII-4,5; To punish the hero who: wants to marry the Shah's daughter, II-2, beats the Shah's daughter in a contest, II-4, VIII-3, sleeps with the heroine, V-8, has acted badly, IV-8, breaks his promise, VII-2, VIII-3; To prevent the marriage of the hero: II-5,6, II-7, 8, VII-8, VIII-4; To get rid of the hero: III-4; To test the hero's talent as a true *ashik*: III-5, III-6, IV-5, IV-6, VII-7; Racially motivated revenge: V-6; To protect the honor of a girl and of the heroine: V-7, IX-2; To be able to see the heroine a little more: VII-6; To save his business from bankruptcy; VIII-5; To put an end to the troubles caused by the hero's father: IX-1.

The Nature of the Obstacle:

A ballad-riddle contest: I-1, I-5, II-3, III-1, V-1,2,3,4,5, IV-1,2,3, VII-1, VIII-3, VIII-6; A flooded river: I-2, VII-4; A storm in the mountains: VII-5; Asking too much money for the bride (from the hero): I-3; Spreading false news: (the death of the hero) I-4, II-8; Spending the hero's share of the inheritance: II-1; Ordering the execution of the hero: II-2,4, VI-2, VIII-4; A test (a difficult question or a hidden situation to solve): II-5, III-5, IV-5, VII-3; Giving the hero and the heroine a drink to put them to sleep: II-6; Planning a meeting between the hero and the heroine to inform the police: III-2; Informing the heroine's father of her secret meetings with the hero: VIII-4; Separating the heroine from her home by sending forces to take her: III-2; Throwing the hero into a well: III-4, VIII-5, or into a dungeon: IV-8, IX-2; Forbidding the marriage of his daughter to the hero: VI-1; Giving the hero a glass of poison: III-6; Sending a girl to the hero's bedroom: V-6; Getting the heroine pregnant: V-8; Kidnapping the heroine: IV-4,7, VII-2; The consequences of the hero's being seen in the heroine's bed: VI-3; Thirty-two of the hero's teeth are pulled: VII-6; The heroine is clad in a magic robe which cannot be removed: VII-8; Exiling the hero's family: VIII-1; Attempting to murder the hero: VIII-2; Sending the hero's father to his death: IX-1.

The Consequences of the Obstacles:

The hero wins the contest and the support of influential people: I-1,5, II-3, III-1, V-1,2,3,4,5, IV-1,2,3, VII-1, VII-7, VIII-6; The obstacle is eliminated through the Hizir's ("Saint's") or God's help: I-2, II-4, III-4, VII-5, VIII-5; The hero's song eliminates the obstacle: VII-4; The hero leaves for 7 years to make money: I-3; The rival is engaged to the heroine: I-4; The hero's family becomes poor: II-1, VI-1; The hero is beaten: II-2, V-6,7; The hero passes the test: II-5, III-5, IV-5, VII-3; The hero is banished to an uninhabited island: II-6; The hero is saved by luck: II-7; The hero attempts suicide: II-8; The hero escapes out of the trap: III-2; The heroine (or hero) is separated from the hero (or heroine): III-3, IV-4,7, VI-3, VII-2; The hero survives the poison: III-6, IV-6, VIII-1,2; The hero is wounded: V-8; The hero is saved by a person: IV-8,9, IX-2; The hero is forgiven: VI-2; The hero magically gets his teeth back: VII-6; The hero is burned to death: VII-5; The hero flees the country: VII-4; The father is saved by a friend: IX.

*Plot Action 5:* Resolution.

At the end of the romance, the recurring obstacles raised by the different agents to prevent the marriage are successfully eliminated by the hero. He is helped to succeed by the holy protector seen in his dream, by his own talent—magical or artistic (both of which were obtained during the initiatory dream), and by various individuals. He wins all contests, answers the most difficult of questions, survives the deadliest poisons. His songs have the power to stop a flooding river or to control the weather. His actions transform his adversaries into his helpers.

İlhan Başgöz

## C. THE ESTABLISHMENT OF A NEW FAMILY

### Plot Action 6: Union.

The romance ends in the bridal chamber. Following their long and dangerous ordeal, the hero and the heroine "reach their earthly goals" and marry and have a family of their own.

### Variation

The structural uniformity of the minstrel's romance is surprisingly strong with regard to the number of plot actions. However, there is important variation in the last action of the romance, union and marriage. The ending can be sad or happy. The story of Kerem, a Muslim boy, and Asli, a Christian girl, ends with the death of both in the bridal chamber. This ending is traditional for that plot. However, in variant 2, God helps Kerem in the bridal chamber—the forty magic buttons of the girl's dress are unbuttoned and Kerem and Asli reach their earthly goal; a happy end prevails. The romance of Abbas of Tufargen and Peri ends in marriage in all the variants I have found except variant 3, where the hero is bitten in the bridal chamber by a snake sleeping between the breasts of the heroine. In variants 6 and 8, Emrah, the hero of the romance, "Emrah and Selvi," dies at the end, while in all others he is united with Selvi and marries her.

The variation of the last action reveals an important social force operative in the formation of romance structure. According to the oral history of the romances, a hundred and fifty years ago they all ended tragically. The romance audience was not pleased when tragedy struck the hero they liked, and they expressed their feelings on various occasions, sometimes very effectively indeed.

A mighty Bey, for example, once rose during a performance of the story of Kerem and Asli and, when the hero was nearing his tragic death, pointed a gun at the teller and said, "Look here! If you kill Kerem then I will kill you!"[5] The teller, after ending the story traditionally, had a saint intervene and bring Kerem back to life again. Observing the demands of the audiences (even when they were not expressed in such a violent manner) the romance narrators came together and decided to end the romances happily.[6] Even the story of Kerem and Asli, which usually ends with the death of the hero due to the religious differences between the boy and girl, did not remain unaffected by this audience impact. In areas where a sizable Armenian community does not exist or where hostility between the two races is not strongly felt, the ending pattern is transformed into a happy one in keeping with the audience's wishes.

## II.

The heroic epic tradition of the Turkic peoples provides a close parallel to the structural pattern of the *ashik's* romance. It is the theme of "the heroic quest for a bride"—whose Oguz-Turk variant, the story of Bamsi Beyrek, is found in the Dede Korkut Epic.[7] The origin and historical and geographical development of this quest for a bride, as well as its relation to the nomadic and feudal society, has been studied.[8] If we ignore the lack of romantic love and the emphasis given to the heroic fight, the Bamsi Beyrek story is structurally similar to the romance pattern. Crisis, transformation (the hero becomes not a lover but a fighter), search for a bride, obstacles and marriage (to two women), are also the basic actions of the epic story. However, there is an important difference which greatly facilitates the romance analysis. The crisis in the epic does not destroy family unity. The boy does not act independently of the will of his father in his search for the girl. In fact, the father arranges the marriage, finds the girl, pays for the bride, and at the end the boy joins his father's family, erecting another tent next to his. The family unity of the nomadic tribe is invincible in all but one of the Dede Korkut stories, not only in Bamsi Beyrek.

This fact reflects the social reality of the nomadic-pastoral society. Strongly inter-dependent social relations in the nomadic society cannot be broken by an individual. There is no conflict between an individual's aspirations and those of society.[9] Devia-tion and individualistic pursuit are not tolerated.[10] The epic teller conforms to the rules of the nomadic-tribal society; he would never narrate an epic in which a son would leave his father, revolting against his authority.

Here a sharp contrast arises between the epic and the romance. The whole action in the romance—that is, the wish to break the family, to search for a girl who is not selected by the parent, to establish a new family far away from home—is composed of individualistic aspirations in opposition to communal norms. The hero strives to fulfill this individual passion. Does this mean that a boy of fourteen can leave his family for an individualistic adventure in Turkish society? It seems not. The boy in the Turkish family seldom leaves his father's household even after his marriage.[11]

## III.

It is my hypothesis that the romance pattern is a frame which combines the sexual fantasies of an adolescent boy with revolt against his father's authority.

The narrator of the romance is an *ashik*, but he is not only the transmitter of the tradition; he is the author-creator of the genre. The romance as a whole, in prose as well as poetry, is written (or orally composed) by an *ashik*. Some of them are still remembered as the author of a romance; others are forgotten when the romance begins its own life in oral transmission.[12] The romance structure survives as long as the tale is told by an *ashik*. What makes the romance-*ashik* interrelation more complex is that the hero of the romance is also an *ashik*. This means an *ashik* creates the narrative, transmits it, and makes himself the hero of the plot. The *ashik* consequently is the key to the study of the origin, development, and structure of the romance.

For this reason I will take the life story of Ashik Sabit Müdami (1918-1968), a famous romance teller and the author of three romances,[13] as an example for the analysis of the romance-*ashik* interrelation.

Born in a northeastern Anatolian village, Varizna (now Demirdöğen) in 1918, Müdami lost his mother in 1921. His family moved to Ardahan in 1925. His father was

İlhan Başgöz

a village *imam* who made his son memorize the Koran at a very early age—when he was four years old. "I feared my father like mice fear a cat," he tells us. Like all other Orthodox Muslim *imams*, his father was strongly opposed to playing musical instruments, singing songs and narrating romances. ("The *imams* and the *ashiks* cannot get along with each other at all.") He says, "when my father told me to study the Koran, I felt like Atlas with the weight of the earth on my shoulders and, although I could not read it, I could not refuse him due to fear." Müdami began attending elementary school at age seven, completing three years of public education and learning the Roman alphabet together with the Arabic alphabet, which was taught to him by his father.

When he was seven a very important incident took place in Müdami's life. On a Friday, the Moslem holy day, his father went to a mosque and gave Müdami a strict order to stay home and study the Koran. Hearing the joyful noises of the children in the street, Müdami joined them as soon as his father left home. When his father returned several hours later, he found the boy in the street, playing with the other village boys. He then gave Müdami a thorough beating, lasting until blood ran from the boy's mouth and nose. Müdami says, "I was so scared that I was unable to utter a single word. I then felt great anger not toward my father who had beaten me, but rather toward my stepmother because she had not protected me and spared me from the beating. My heart was ready to explode like an atom bomb."

Müdami fell asleep early that day and had a dream. In this dream the prophet Mohammed and the two khalifs Osman and Ali showed him a chapter from the Koran and said, "Read it, Müdami." Müdami obeyed. Then an old *ashik*, holding a *saz* in his hand, introduced Müdami to a young girl and betrothed them. Next, he offered them a glass of sherbet (a sweet drink) as part of the engagement ceremony. Müdami drank this sherbet and was given the pen name Müdami and shown a book containing his own poetry.

The next morning when Müdami awakened, all the books, including the Koran, "began to speak to him." He could now read the Koran better than his father, and he memorized the holy book in a very short time.

At the age of fourteen, Müdami had the same dream for the second time. In it he fell in love with the girl, began to write and sing his poetry, and played the *saz*. According to him, it was only after this dream that he really dared have a *saz* and practice on it. At this point he realized the meaning of love.

Müdami's reported dream has a pattern similar to the visionary dreams of the Muslim mystics[14] on the one hand, and to the initiatory dreams of the Asian shaman on the other.[15] The mystics discover the realm of divine love in a similar dream and the shaman is initiated into the healing profession through this ecstatic experience. It is for this reason that I interpret this reported dream (which has been reported by many other *ashiks*) as the aspiration of the *ashik* and as the expression of some wish, and not necessarily as a real dream. The role and the function attributed by Müdami to this culturally patterned dream are important because the *ashik* reveals some aspects of his personality using this pattern as a vehicle.

Müdami says that he was seven years old and very afraid of his father, a forbidding and domineering man, when he had the first dream. He memorized the whole Koran and learned the Arabic alphabet in the dream; thus the dream achieved what his father had asked for and had ordered the boy to do. Although he strongly resented having a traditional education like this, he had no courage to stand before his father's authority, and no one else in the family protected him. Consequently, he had to bow before the patriarch and follow his orders. The first dream represents fear, submission, and obedience to authority; this is a part of Müdami's personality.

Müdami had the same dream for the second time at age fourteen, but this time it expressed something totally different. In the dream he fell in love, and obtained the artistic gifts of composing poetry and playing a musical instrument. It was immediately after the dream that Müdami managed to get a *saz* and began practicing it. Knowing that his father would oppose the idea, he hid the musical instrument at his uncle's house and practiced it when his father was not home. Müdami thus did what his father had strictly forbidden. So, through "the dream" he expressed a protest, a revolt, and a challenge to his father. This reflects another facet of Müdami's personality.

The two different functions of the same dream clearly manifest the personality conflict in a Turkish boy: fears and submission to authority; aggressiveness and revolt against authority. This conflict is not an individual one; it is rooted in the Turkish family and social structure.[16]

Müdami is unique in reporting two dreams. The other *ashiks* always talk about one dream as the source of their love and artistic talent—the dream which expresses the challenge and revolt, or the beginning of the young boy's struggle to assert himself as an individual. This is the dream which is the micro-form of the romance.

No matter what specific form it takes in Turkish folklore, a universal revolt which occurs at the age of puberty can easily be identified in "the dream." At the age of puberty the adolescent boy becomes rebellious toward his father's authority. Freud calls this change "the most painful psychic accomplishment of puberty."[17]

The association of this challenge of puberty with love and artistic power in the dream are its most important and culturally specific elements. Why is the challenge expressed in connection with love and the image of a girl? Why does the *ashik* need this female image to express his protest? A possible explanation can be found in my early discussion where I identified the girl in the dream as the female protector spirit who symbolized the Goddess, lover, mother, and protector of the Turkish shamans.[18] Her support provides the boy with the courage and self-confidence necessary in his challenge of his father. Henry Corbin, who studied the similar dreams of the Muslim mystics, called this female symbol the "anima,"[19] which Jung identified as the female part of the man, and to which he attributed divine qualities: "Such impressions have immense power, since they release forces, both in the child and the man, which in their irresistible and absolutely compelling nature, merit the title divine."[20]

I do not intend to investigate further the origins of this female symbol in human psychology. The data collected from Turkey, however seem to relate to Jung's concept. The girl in the dream is given a divine origin by all *ashiks*. The vocabulary and the symbols used by the *ashik* in reporting the dream, as well as the appearance of a holy figure in it, are undoubtedly connected with the divine love concept of Muslim mysticism. Furthermore, the meeting of the young boy with this female symbol in the dream releases tremendous energy which had remained hidden until that time. This is the force which makes an artist, a lover, and a rebel out of the young boy.

The counterpart of this archetypal image, the subject of the erotic fantasy of the *ashik*, can be found in the life of our romance tellers. The *ashik* idealizes a neighbor girl and makes her the subject of his fantasy or dream. When he was fourteen, Ashik Ishak Kemali (1915–1970), a romance teller from Erzurum, used to see a "Persian girl" of his age with beautiful eyes, in the neighborhood. Sometime later this girl began to appear in his dreams, and the appearance was repeated several times. His love and talent were awakened by this dream. In real life nothing happened between the girl and him; she left the neighborhood sometime later and Ishak Kemali married someone else. But at the age of fifty-two, he still remembered the beautiful eyes of this "dream girl."[21]

Ashik Ilyas (b. 1918) of Çildir gives us another interesting account of such a girl. "I had a friend in our village of Gereşin (Çildir-Kars) when I was a child. Her name was Selvinaz and she was the daughter of a rich neighbor. We used to play together in the meadows, we went to the forest and visited the fountains. When we drank water from the spring, she used to offer me the cup and say, 'Take it, this is my love potion!' At the age of twelve or thirteen, I had a dream in which I met a girl of my age whose eyes, eyebrows, figure, hair color and dress were similar to my friend Selvinaz's. The holy Hizir who introduced this girl to me in the dream told me, however, that her name was not Selvinaz but Selatin. Selatin was from a far away land called Çin Maçin where I could not go and find her. He instead suggested that I should marry Selvinaz in my village because she was the counterpart (similar) of Selatin."[22] Ashik Ilyas attributes the origin of his love and artistic gift to the "dream." Six months after the dream, Ashik Ilyas had his first nocturnal emission and became aware of his sexuality.

The two girls, the objects of inspiration and passionate love on the part of the minstrels, were in reality two girls in their neighborhoods, two real beings. The moral codes which prohibited the boy and girl from meeting and being together (a social factor), or the sexual fantasies of puberty in object selection[23] (a psychological factor), make the *ashik* transform the real girl into an idea and make her the subject of idealization, fantasy, and perhaps sometimes, a real dream.[24]

An ordinary village girl thus became a heavenly creature, an ideal beauty who does not exist anywhere except in the boy's mind. She is an inaccessible symbol of love.

It is in this stage of life that the adolescent revolt against parental authority takes place. On the one hand, the revolt and the ensuing self confidence lead to fantasizing a girl, but on the other, the image of the beauty encourages revolt and makes family life intolerable for the boy. Now, more than at any other time in his life, he wants to leave his family, find the girl of his own selection, marry her, and establish a separate family. The image of beauty and the revolt against parental authority form an integrated unity—two inseparable facets of a complex emotion. The basic plot actions of the romance are the literary expression of this pattern in human psychology.

[1]Vladimir Propp, *Morphology of the Folktale* (Austin: University of Texas Press, 1968).

[2]Romances and Variants:

*Romance No. 1.*

Ashık Garip and Shah Sanem. A manuscript dated 1836, probably recorded in Istanbul. In the Turkish Folklore Archive (TFA), Department of Uralic and Altaic Studies, Indiana University, Bloomington, Indiana.

Variant I.

Ashık Garip and Shah Sanem. Tape recorded from Dursun Cevlani in 1958. In the Music Department of the National Library of Turkey, Ankara.

Variant II.

Ashık Garip and Shah Sanem. A manuscript which is dated 1830. In Inkilap Kütüphanesi, Muallim Cevdet Yazmalari, No. K. 556, Istanbul.

Variant III.

Ashık Garip and Shah Sanem. Collected from Dursun Cevlani by Pertev Boratav in 1944. In Boratav's personal archive.

Variant IV.

Muharrem Zeki Korgunal, *Aşık Garip* (Istanbul: Bozkurt Matbaası, 1939).

*Romance No. 2.*

Kurbani and Perizat. Tape recorded from Ashik Sabit Müdami in 1967. Recording and typescript in TFA.

*Romance No. 3.*

Abbas of Tufargan and Perizat. Tape recorded from Ashık Sabit Müdami in 1956. Recording and typescript in TFA.

Variant I.

Abbas of Tufargan and Perizat. Tape recorded from Dursun Cevlani in 1957 in Ankara. In the Music Department of the National Library of Turkey, Ankara.

Variant II.

Abbas of Tufargan and Perizat. Collected from Ibrahim Mutluer in 1946. In Boratav's personal archive.

Variant III.

Abbas of Tufargan and Perizat. Tape recorded from Kurban Gezer by Muhan Bali in 1961. In the personal archive of Muhan Bali.

*Romance No. 4.*

Emrah and Selvi. Tape recorded from Ashık Sabit Müdami in 1956. Recording and typescript in TFA.

Variant I.

Murat Uraz, *Ercişli Emrah* (Istanbul: Maarif Kitabevi, 1937).

Variant II.

Emrah and Selvi. Tape recorded from Behçet Mahir by Muhan Bali and published in Muhan Bali, *Ercişli Emrah ile Selvi Hikayesi* (Ankara, 1973).

Variant III.

Ihsan Ozanoglu, *Ercişli Emrah* (Istanbul, 1958)

Variant IV.

Ercişli Emrah. Collected from Ashık Sabit Müdami in 1944 by Pertev Boratav. In Boratav's personal archive.

Variant V.

Fethi Tevet, "Ercişli Emrah", *Yücel* 6, no. 108 (Istanbul, 1938):19.

Variant VI

Fuat Köprülü, *Erzurumlu Emrah* (Istanbul, 1929):27.

Variant VII.

Ercişli Emrah. Collected from Ashık Muharrem of Kars in 1944. The manuscript in TFA.

Variant VIII.

Ali Rıza Yalgın, "Ercişli Emrah," *Türk Sözü* 22 March 1940 (Adana), a series of 12 articles.

Variant IX.

Ercişli Emrah and Selvi. Tape recorded from Dursun Cevlani in 1957. Recording in TFA.

# İlhan Başgöz

*Romance No. 5.*
Mahiri and Mahitaban. Manuscript collected from Ardahan by Adil Özder. In TFA.

*Romance No. 6.*
"Karacoğlan," in V. Radlov, *Proben der Volksliteratur der Turkischen Stamme* 7 (St. Petersburg, 1896):297–323.

*Romance No. 7.*
Kerem and Aslı, *Tevatür ile Meşhur Kerem ile Aslı Hikayesi* (Istanbul: Ikbal Kitaphanesi, 1941).
Variant I.
Kerem and Aslı. Ahmet Serdar manuscript dated 1850. In Boratav's personal archive.
Variant II.
Kerem and Aslı. Eflatun Cem Güney manuscript. In Boratav's personal archive.
Variant III.
Kerem and Aslı. Raif Yelkenci Manuscript. In Boratav's personal archive.

*Romance No. 8*
Asüman and Zeycan. Tape recorded from Ashık Sabit Müdami in 1956. Recording in TFA.

*Romance No. 9.*
Eşref Bey. Recorded in 1944 from Ashık Latif Yılmaz of Kars. In TFA.

[3] Vladimir Propp, *Morphology*, p. 120.

[4] Shah Abbas I (Abbas the Great 1588–1629), Shah of Persia.

[5] Pertev N. Boratav, *Halk Hikayeleri ve Türk Halk Hikayeciliği* [Folk Stories and Folk Story Telling Tradition in Turkey] (Ankara: Milli Eğitim Basimevi, 1943), p. 103.

[6] Pertev N. Boratav, *Halk Hikayeleri*, p. 104.

[7] *The Book of Dede Korkut*, trans. Geoffrey Lewis (Middlesex: Hazell Watson and Viney, Penguin Books, 1974).

[8] Victor Zhirmunsky, "The Epic of Alpamish and the Return of Odysseus," *Proceedings of the British Academy* 12 (1966):261–85.

[9] Victor Zhirmunsky and T. Zarifov, *Uzbeksy Narodny Geroicesky Epos* [Uzbek Heroic Folk Epics] (Moscow, 1947), p. 302.

[10] Guillaume Frederic Le Play, *Family and Society*, trans. C. Zimmerman (New York: D. Van Nostrand Co., 1935), p. 244.

[11] Paul Stirling, *Turkish Village* (New York: John Wiley and Sons, 1965), p. 100.

[12] Ashık Şenlik (1853-1913) is known as the author of three romances "Latif Shah," "Sevdager," and "Salman Bey."

[13] The life story was told us in 1967 by Ashık Sabit Müdami himself. The recording in TFA.

[14] Henry Corbin, "The Visionary Dream in Islamic Spirituality," in *Dream and Human Society*, ed. Gustav von Grunebaum and Roger Collins (Los Angeles: University of California Press, 1960), p. 400.

[15] İlhan Başgöz, "Dream of Motif and Shamanistic Initiation," *Asian Folklore Studies* 1 (1966):1–18.

[16] Gökçe Cansever, "Psychological Effect of Circumcision," *British Journal of Medical Psychology* 38 (1965):329.

[17] Sigmund Freud, *Three Contributions to the Theory of Sex*, trans. A. A. Brill (New York: Dutton Paperback, 1962), p. 83.

[18] İlhan Başgöz, "Dream Motif."

[19] Henry Corbin, "The Visionary Dream."

[20] C. G. Jung, *Psychological Types*, trans. H. Godwing (London: Baynes, 1923), p. 277.

[21] The life story of Ashık Ishak Kemali was tape recorded in 1967. The recording in TFA.

[22] Süleyman Kazmaz, *Aşhik Ilyas Anlatıyor* [Ashık Ilyas Narrates] (Ankara, 1946.)

[23] S. Freud, *Three Contributions*, p. 82.

[24] Ashıks try to have such dreams. Ashık Mahzuni, for example, told me that he used to drink a glass of salt-water before going to bed hoping to be offered love potion in his dream to quench his thirst.

# The Wife Who Goes Out Like a Man, Comes Back as a Hero: The Art of Two Oregon Indian Narratives

Jarold W. Ramsey

*The oral literature of another culture is often difficult to penetrate. The reader (since this literature is invariably encountered in printed translation) may be overwhelmed, on the one hand, by what seems to be an abundance of needless repetition, yet stymied on the other by brevity and conciseness that borders on the cryptic or nonsensical. What we often lack is access to the complex matrix of assumptions, associations, conventions, and understandings that inform that literature and are immediately available to almost every member of the culture. Despite the difficulties, such literature can be made accessible through careful and informed reading. Of course, this accessibility may be more a hypothesis than a definitive accomplishment; nevertheless, something may be gained from the attempt.*

*Jarold W. Ramsey leads us through several variants of a Northwest Indian narrative. Starting with the informed commentaries of Jacobs (1959, 1960) and Hymes (1981), Ramsey presents these stories as a literature that can be analyzed and discussed in literary terms. Tedlock (1972) has done much of the original work on the representation of oral literature, particularly native American literature, in print. Further discussion of native American literature can be found in Kroeber (1981), Ramsey (1977, 1983), Swann (1983), and Toelken (1969).*

One of the few stories in a North American Indian repertory to receive genuine analysis from more than one writer is a brief, starkly horrifying text in the late Melville Jacobs's collection of Clackamas Chinook literature from Oregon—titled "Seal and Her Younger Brother Dwelt There"[1]—with full and penetrating commentaries on it by Jacobs himself and by Dell Hymes, and illustrative references to it in an important essay on the nature of fiction by Frank Kermode. "Seal and Her Younger Brother" might be said to have "arrived," critically.[2] My intention here is not so much to add to its understanding and fame (it is still a long way, I imagine, from inclusion in a freshman literature anthology) as to draw on the attention given it by Jacobs and Hymes in order to introduce another, closely related, Northwest myth-narrative, and, in discussing *it*, to raise some issues about our long overdue reclamation of native American literature.

---

Jarold W. Ramsey

About that literature, the reader is reminded here at the outset that in general terms it is an oral, formulaic, traditional, and anonymous art form; that ultimately its engagement with reality is mythic and sacred; that what survives of it comes to us at two removes, translated from an oral-traditional mode into print and from a native language into English; that it flourished through public performance (generally during winter religious festivals) by skilled recitalists whose audiences already knew the individual stories and prized not plot invention but rather the recitalists' ability to exploit their material dramatically and to weave stories into sequences and cycles. Indian myth-narrative, being dramatic in conception and performance, inevitably strikes us as a highly *tacit* expression; motivation and emotional states are generally implied rather than directly specified. And Indian literature is likely to seem all the more terse, even cryptic, to us for being the verbal art of highly ethnocentric, tribal people, whose infinitely diverse cultures we still don't know much about. An elderly Papago singer said to Ruth Underhill by way of commenting on this difficulty: "The song is so short because we understand so much."[3]

Our two Oregon narratives are indeed short and concentrated, and yet, with some ethnographic help, we can hope to understand and appreciate them as instances of native American literature. First the text of "Seal and Her Younger Brother," as narrated by Mrs. Victoria Howard in Oregon City, Oregon, in 1929 and transcribed and translated by Jacobs, with corrections by Hymes:[4]

> They lived there. Seal, her daughter, her younger brother. I do not know when it was, but now a woman got to Seal's younger brother.
>
> They lived there. They would go outside [to urinate] in the evening. The girl would say, she would tell her mother: "Mother! There is something different about my uncle's wife. It sounds like a man when she 'goes out'."—"Don't say that! [She is] your uncle's wife!"
>
> They lived there like that for a long time. They would 'go out' in the evening. And then she would tell her: "Mother! There is something different about my uncle's wife. When she 'goes out,' it sounds like a man."—"Don't say that!"
>
> Her uncle and his wife would 'lie together' in bed. Some time afterward the two of them 'lay' close to the fire, they 'lay' close beside each other. I do not know what time of night it was, but something dripped on her face. She shook her mother. She told her: "Mother! Something dripped on my face."—"Hm . . . Don't say that. Your uncle [and his wife] are 'going'."
>
> Presently again she heard something dripping down. She told her: "Mother! Something is dripping, I hear something."—"Don't say that. Your uncle [and his wife] are 'going'."
>
> The girl got up, she fixed the fire, she lit pitch, she looked where the two were lying. Oh! Oh! she raised her light to it. In his bed her uncle's neck was cut. He was dead. She screamed.
>
> She told her mother: "I told you something was dripping. You told me: 'Don't say that. They are 'going.' I had told you there was something different about my uncle's wife. When she 'goes out,' it sounds like a man when she urinates. You told me: 'Don't say that!'" She wept.

210

> Seal said: "Younger brother! My younger brother! They [his ornamental house-posts] are valuable standing there. My younger brother!" She kept saying that.
>
> But the girl herself wept. She said: "I tried in vain to tell you. My uncle's wife sounds like a man when she urinates, not like a woman. You told me: 'Don't say that!' Oh! Oh! my uncle!" The girl wept.
>
> Now I remember only that far.

Despite the raw imaginative power of this story—its sinister convergence of aberrant sexuality and apparently motiveless homicide, the vivid evocation of darkness, liquids dripping, and screams, the sense of horror obliquely rendered and thereby intensified—one might in rereading it conclude that it is manifestly only a fragment of something longer and draw back from full appreciation of its art on the grounds that, however engaging they may be, fragments and oddments ought not to be interpreted into occult masterpieces. To do so is of course a familiar form of literary sentimentality—what is lacking or incomprehensible in a work, especially if it comes from a remote culture, becomes in such a reading a covert virtue of the work.

But although they acknowledge the possibility of fuller, more explicit versions, both Jacobs and Hymes emphatically argue that the story has its own effective unity of parts and can be understood and appreciated as it stands. Summary and paraphrase cannot do justice to their interpretations, and the reader is urged to turn to them as models of two very different ways of proceeding with native literary texts. It will have to suffice here to say, on the one hand, that Jacobs's interpretation proceeds along characteristic psychosocial lines: he concludes that "the myth is . . . a drama whose nightmarish horror theme, murder of one's own kin by a sexually aberrant person who is an in-law, causes profound fear and revulsion as well as deep sympathy. The tension around in-laws [which Jacobs finds to be a feature of Clackamas literature generally] is basic to the plot." In the case of this story, the trouble begins when "a woman [gets] to "Seal's wealthy younger brother, the master of the household, and he brings her home as wife apparently without the formalities that should attend such an important transaction. In Jacobs's view this sinister "wife" is a homosexual who, as the main actor, murders her husband so as to "avenge herself on a family the daughter of which casts aspersions upon her manner of urinating, that is upon her sexuality."[5] In effect, however unwittingly, the daughter occasions the murder.

On the other hand, Hymes, employing a modified form of the structural analysis of Claude Lévi-Strauss, engages the verbal text of the story in the context of related Chinookan narratives and finds a unity in it very different from that of Jacobs. In simple terms, the story belongs not to Seal's brother and his homicidal "wife," but rather to Seal herself and especially to her young daughter, whose perspective on the action we most attend to and who is in fact the "heroine." Following Lévi-Strauss's method, Hymes sets up a systematic analysis of the way the story's structure unfolds; in the process he discovers that it effects a complex mediation between preservation of Social Norm, at one pole, and awareness of Empirical Situation, at the opposite pole.

In summary, the analysis, which goes beyond Lévi-Strauss's practice into considera- tion of imagistic and verbal elements, reveals that "the leading theme of the myth is the conduct of Seal. The behavior of the girl is not a device to express the horror of an ambiguously sexed and hateful 'female' in-law, but rather, an ambiguous 'female' is a device to express the failure of a proper woman to relate to a danger threatening one she should protect. The myth uses a stock villain [Hymes means a Trickster in disguise, common in Northwest Indian stories] to dramatize a relationship subtler than vil- lainy" (Hymes, pp. 184, 191).

The two readings, then, are mutually exclusive, differing on the fundamental interpretive point as to what and whom the story is about. In my view, at least, Hymes's reading opens "Seal and Her Younger Brother" to a literary understanding much more fully; in its careful attention to structure and texture and in the effort it makes to relate this one Clackamas story to general patterns in native literature from the region, it points to a viable way of engaging such work *as* literature, and indeed it suggests possibilities for interpreting Indian verbal art and ours together, as dissimilar as they are in mode, subjects, and artistic conventions.

For example, Hymes's emphasis on the stylized conflict in the story between two goods, preservation of social propriety versus alertness and openness to the situation immediately at hand, might remind us that, although our literature is not "tribal," it often dramatizes such conflicts, too—"The Emperor's New Clothes" being just one obvious comic example. In fact, most of our fiction dealing with children and youthful initiations into experience centers on such a conflict between the formal, received "way" of society and the tentative and untutored ego-way of the young protagonist. By way of illustration, it would be interesting to consider Hemingway's Nick Adams story, "Indian Camp," alongside "Seal and Her Younger Brother." Beyond the strange resemblances, centering on the mysterious cutting of an Indian husband's throat, there is Nick's predicament: he is caught (like Seal's daughter) between a set of adult norms and stock responses, as embodied in his father and uncle, and his own raw, immediate registering of experience. Happily no one's life depends on how Nick's conflict is resolved. Whereas Seal's daughter ends her story in bitter lamentation, a sort of tragically valid "I told you so" to her mother, Hemingway allows Nick to conclude with a child's naïve joy—he has made it through a terrible, "grown-up" experience involv- ing violent birth and death; his faith in his father's powers remains unshaken; with his hand in the lake water he is so richly alive in the moment that he feels he "will live forever." It is tempting to ask which represents a higher literary realism: the dramati- zation by writers like Hemingway of such romantic illusions, with heavy irony, or their simple exclusion from Indian myth-narratives like the one under discussion?

Now we have seen how Hymes devalues Jacobs's emphasis on the "wife" as a principal actor, identifying "her" instead as merely the catalyst of the crucial action between Seal and her daughter. Arguing that it is beside the point of the story to seek for psychosocial motives for the murder, Hymes supposes that the sinister "wife" is in origin not a murderous homosexual or transvestite, but a Trickster (pp. 184–85). That is, a conventionalized being like Coyote or Raven (or Loki in Nordic myth) who "travels around" and who, by acting habitually without restraint or any motives beyond those of greed and appetite, and short-term cleverness, creates *possibility* (mainly disorder, confusion, imbalance, crisis!) in the plots of myth-narratives.[6] As Radin, Jung, Róheim, and others have pointed out, the Indian Trickster figure seems to serve a wide variety of psychological and social purposes at once: Hymes reminds us that, in addition, the Trickster may simply be an indispensable plot agent: he makes things happen for the narrator. With this in mind, Hymes glances at some analogous stories about mysterious domestic murders from various Northwest Coast tribes, and concludes that as a disguised Trickster (Raven) is responsible for those killings, so too with the slaying of Seal's younger brother. According to the conventions of the Northwest Trickster, no special purpose or provocation for killing is necessary; it follows that Seal's daughter does not trigger or provoke her uncle's murder.

This seems to be indisputable, and once it is granted, it is hard not to admire the narrative artistry by which means the ostensible primary action (the deception and killing of the husband by his "wife") is muted and left obscure so as to bring the apparent secondary action (the interplay of Seal and her daughter) into the foreground. Yeats speaks of Shakespeare's similar practice of leaving the rational motives and purposes of some of his protagonists unclear (as with Richard, Leontes, Hamlet himself) so as to rivet our attention on the play of tragic emotions themselves.[7]

So here, against the sinister enigma of the "wife's" actions, the little heroine and her mother play out their immediate and unresolvable conflict of consciousness. At the end, Seal's lament for her dead brother is characteristically decorous and conventional, not expressive of what has actually happened; her daughter, having been painfully open to experience throughout the story, is transfixed by feelings of helplessness, frustration, horror, and grief—

> Seal said: "Younger brother! My younger brother! They [his ornamental house-posts] are valuable standing there. My younger brother!" She kept saying that.
> But the girl herself wept. She said: "I tried in vain to tell you. My uncle's wife sounds like a man when she urinates, not like a woman. You told me: 'Don't say that!' Oh! Oh! My uncle!" The girl wept.

But now I want to turn to another Northwest Indian myth—from the Coos people, who lived along the southern Oregon coast about 200 miles from the Clackamas and spoke a different language. This story, titled "The Revenge against the Sky People" (narrated by Jim Buchanan to Harry Hull St. Clair in 1903 and translated by Leo J. Frachtenberg)[8] is at first sight much more accessible than "Seal and Her Younger Brother," because it is more detailed, especially in terms of character and motivation, and because it conforms more closely to our conventional expectations of fictional art. What is immediately striking about it is that it contains within its hero-tale structure a version of "Seal and Her Younger Brother"!

213

Jarold W. Ramsey

A man lived in Kiweet. He had an elder brother, who was always building canoes. Once he was working on a canoe, when a man came there to him. "What do you do with your canoe after you finish it"—"I always sell my canoes." He kept on working, with his head bent down, while the man was talking to him. Alongside the man who was building lay his dog. All at once he [the stranger] hit the neck of the man who was building, and cut off his head. He took his head home.

The man who was building did not come home, and they went out looking for him. They found him lying in the canoe, dead, without a head. The little dog was barking alongside the canoe. The dog would look upwards every time it barked. Straight up it would look. So they began to think, "Someone from above must have killed him!" Then the next day the man's younger brother looked for him. The young man shot an arrow upwards, and then he would shoot another one. He was shooting the arrows upwards. Every time he shot, his arrow would stick in the one above, and as he kept on shooting that way, the arrows soon reached to him.

Then he climbed up there. He went up on the arrows. He saw people when he climbed up, and he asked, "From where do you come?" They were taking home a man's head. "We danced for it," they said. They were taking home his elder brother's head. They said to the young man, "At a little place [nearby] the wife of the murderer is digging fern-roots. Every forenoon she digs fern-roots there." So he went there. He did not go very far. Suddenly, indeed, [he saw] a woman digging fern-roots. There was a big river.

So he asked the woman, "Do you have your own canoe?"—"Not so."— "Who ferries you across the river?"—"My husband ferries me across."— "What do you do when he ferries you across?"—"He does not land the canoe. I usually jump ashore."—"What does he do afterward?"—"He usually turns back. Then, when it is almost evening, I go home. Again he comes after me. A little ways off he stops the canoe. I jump in with that pack. I get in there all right."—"What do you do with your fern-roots?"—"I usually dry them."— "What do you do with your fern-roots after they are dry?"—"I usually give some of them to all the people who live here. A little ways off in the next house, there lives an old man and an old woman. I never give them any fern-roots."— "What do you usually do?"—"Then I cook them in a big pot."—"What do you do then?"—"I stir them with my hands."—"Doesn't your hand get burned?"— "Not so, it does not hurt me."—"What does your husband do when you lie down?"—"I lie a little ways off from my husband."—"Does your husband usually fall asleep quickly?"—"He usually falls asleep quickly."

Now he asked her all [these] questions, and then he killed her. He skinned the woman, and put on her hide. Indeed, he looked just like the woman. Then he took her load and packed it. He saw the husband there as he arrived. The husband was crossing back and forth. A little ways off in the river he stopped his canoe. Thus [the young man] was thinking, "I wonder whether I shall get there if I jump! I will try it from this distance." He packed the load and jumped. One leg touched the water. He pretty nearly did not get there. Thus spoke the man, "Is that you, my wife?" Thus he spoke: "I am tired, this is the reason why

I almost did not get there. My pack is heavy." [The husband] did not think any more about it.

Whatever the woman had told him, indeed, the young man did it that way. He made only one mistake. He gave fern-roots to those old people. He opened the door. The two old people saw him when he entered. They did not take the fern-roots which he held in his hands. [They] shouted, "Someone from below gives us two something!" They did not hear it [in] the next house.

When the thing he was cooking began to boil, he stirred it with his hands. "Ouch! It burned my hand!" The husband heard it. "What happened to you?"—"My finger is sore, this is the reason why I said so." And he was looking at the head that was fastened to the ceiling. It was his brother's head. He cried there when he saw his elder brother's head. Thus spoke the husband: "You seem to be crying."—"There is so much smoke, my eyes are sore." [The husband] no longer paid any attention to it.

Now it got to be evening. The woman was going upstairs. Thus spoke the little brother-in-law. "My sister-in-law looks like a man!" Thus his grandmother said to him, "The women from there look just like men! You must keep quiet!" Nobody thought about it. From everywhere people came there to the murderer to help him. They were dancing for the head. For it they were dancing. Blood was dripping from the head that was hanging there.

Then it got to be evening, and they all went to bed. When they went to bed she had a big knife under the pillow. The husband went to bed first. The woman was walking outside. So she bored holes in all the canoes in the village. Only in the one in which she intended to cross she did not bore a hole. As soon as she got through, she went inside. Then she went to bed a little away from her husband. At midnight the husband was asleep. She got up on the sly. She cut off the head of the husband, and seized her eldest brother's head. Then she ran away, and crossed alone in the canoe.

[The husband's] mother was lying under the bed. The blood dripped down on her, and the old woman lighted a torch. "Blood! Blood! What have you done? You must have killed your wife!" She heard nothing. So everybody woke up. They saw the man lying under the bed, without a head. His wife had disappeared, and the head that was hanging from the ceiling was gone. "The woman must have killed her husband."—"It was not a woman."

Then they followed him. Other people shoved the canoes into the water, but they kept sinking, and they could not follow him.

Then [the young man] went down on his arrows, on which he had climbed up. Then he returned there. He brought back his elder brother's head. He assembled all his folks. Now, it is said, they were going to join his elder brother's head. Now they commenced to work. A small spruce tree was standing there. Alongside of that small spruce tree, they were joining his head. Then they danced for it. His head climbed up a little bit, and fell down. Four times it happened that way. His head would go up a little bit, and then fall down again. The fifth time, however, his head stuck on. Then thus [the young man] said to his elder brother, "Now you are all right." Then he came down from the spruce tree.

> None of those people from above could come down, and none could take his revenge.
>
> These are the Woodpecker people; this is the reason why their heads are red today. The blood on the neck, that's what makes the head red. Thus one said to them, "You shall be nothing. You shall be a woodpecker. The last people shall see you."

Now one might very well get the impression on reading this rousing story that it "explains" everything that is obscure in "Seal and Her Younger Brother," and go on to conclude that that story is in fact no more than an interesting fragment, now that the "true" version has been found. But both the impression and the conclusion would be wrong. Indian mythology, like all oral literature, relies on narrative motifs and situations that may be current in differing combinations over a wide area, through intensive borrowing. The story analogues and parallels produced by dissemination are certainly worth studying, but (as Lévi-Strauss points out) such study should aim at gaining knowledge of relationships between myths, not at somehow discovering "the *true* version" behind them all.[9] As Hymes has demonstrated, the story of Seal and her younger brother has its own artistically sophisticated unity of parts; and keeping that particular unity in mind as we take up a different narrative unity involving the same parts—in the Coos text—should help us to understand both stories better.

"The Revenge against the Sky People" is a genuine hero story, a fast-paced thriller in which the younger brother's fidelity to a code of vengeance on behalf of his slain brother propels him through a series of desperate adventures—or *tests*, really—his triumphant passing of which reveals him to be not only faithful, but also remarkably courageous, quick-witted and alert, and self-controlled. Whereas the slayer in the Clackamas story is, as Hymes observes, mainly a means to an end, the younger brother is unambiguously the protagonist here; from his ascent of the arrow-ladder (a very widespread Indian narrative motif), his perspective is *ours*, and, although what Melville Jacobs says about the tacit dramatic nature of most native American storytelling—"the feelings of the actors remain wholly the task of the audience to project and devise"[10]—is true here also, the clues as to our hero's feelings are so vividly dramatized throughout that our empathy with him is, I think, unusually rich.

In his analysis of "Seal and Her Younger Brother," Hymes concludes that that story is of a tragic type, in which social norms are upheld, but at the expense of failing to reckon with an empirical situation: Type Two (+ –) in the Lévi-Straussian code of bipolar permutations in myths. He then observes that Type One (+ +), in which social norms are upheld *and* the empirical situation successfully reckoned with, is not common in the Clackamas collection: "I suspect that myths told aboriginally by males might have had more examples of male heroes to whom the type would apply" (Hymes, pp. 189–90). ("Seal and Her Younger Brother" was told by a woman, who in turn had her repertory from three generations of female raconteurs; there seems to have been special male and female subrepertories amongst Western tribes.)

Now, discounting the fact that "The Revenge against the Sky People" is from a different tribal literature, we can claim it as the missing but predicted Type One (+ +)

story par excellence. That is, the young avenger is able to uphold his people's social norm of loyalty-in-revenge precisely because he is so successfully in command of the empirical situation, so alert and nervily resourceful as an improviser in his disguise. That perspicacity will be important in the story is established very early, in fact: negatively, when the canoe builder carelessly converses with the stranger "with his head bent down," and positively, when even before the hero appears the victim's people quickly interpret the eldritch clue of his little dog barking "straight up"—at the sky. And the placement within the Coos story structure of an analogue to the Clackamas story—the child who observes something sinister about his "sister-in-law" but is shushed by his grandmother out of an adult's regard for propriety and ethnocentric wisdom ("The women from there look just like men," declares the grandmother)—is, surely, a brilliant stroke of counterpointing, perfectly setting off the hero's keen-eyed and canny exploits at the expense of his unwitting hosts. (I am not suggesting, of course, that the Coos storyteller or his audience necessarily knew the Clackamas story as a separate item, only that *our* knowing it helps us to understand how its analogue functions in the Coos narrative.)

The central conflict of "The Revenge against the Sky People" is "located" with unusual dramatic intensity (as already noted) in the mind of the hero.[11] Will he make it? Can he possibly be resourceful and composed enough to maintain his desperate disguise, or will he slip up, or break down, and be found out? The creation of a high degree of psychological tension in a narrative is never a casual happenstance, as devotees of the thriller know; by turning now to the text of the Coos story, perhaps we can see the narrative art of the story for what it is and look beyond it to some features of Indian narrative art generally.

From the direct opening sentence, the translated verbal style of the piece is simple, unobtrusive, "linear," and in general highly serviceable for oral narration of a "thriller": in the original Coos-language text, sentences very frequently begin with *Tso*—"Then...,"—leading the action on its way. Though unadorned, the style is not as sparse or paratactic as that of the Chinook narrative, and although there seem to be fewer verbal cues for mimicry, gesture, and "sound effects" on the part of the narrator than in other Coos stories (especially those with humorous content), there are some cues—as in the hero's conversations in disguise with his various Sky Country hosts and in the final ritual to restore the brother's head to his body. In general, like the best of his contemporaries, Frachtenberg seems to have aimed in his translation at a literal, readable accuracy, and probably not much more. As so often with American Indian texts, it is hard to say much more than this: without fluency in the native language, of the all too rare sort that informs Jacobs's and Hymes's commentary on "Seal and Her Younger Brother" and indeed their translation of it, we are obliged to bypass matters of diction, word-play, and other elements of verbal texture in favor of larger stylistic elements that constitute the story's narrative artistry per se, the cunning of its telling.

The teller opens his tale, then with a small but effective bit of *foreshadowing*—of all storytelling devices the most frequently used in native literature, in part I suppose because narrators could count on audiences knowing their stories in outline and thus being able to respond to narrative anticipations. The murderer from Above inter-rogates the elder brother at his work before decapitating him—just as eventually the younger brother interrogates the murderer's wife while she is digging fern-roots, at greater length and for more obviously practical reasons. In turn, of course, this second interrogation serves, as it often does in native stories, to outline roughly and fore-shadow the ideal course of events from this point on in the story: each of the younger brother's questions to the unsuspecting woman reveals habitual actions on her and her husband's part that, we guess, the young hero will have to imitate in the course of his most unhabitual mission in disguise. The overall effect of such foreshadowing, I imagine, is to deepen the tense imaginative bond between the hero and the listeners (or readers): we come to share a detailed secret knowledge that will be for the hero the basis of highly risky actions and for us the basis of highly dramatic expectations.

In these terms, the younger brother's momentary lapses of attention are heart-stopping, and his improvised excuses are all the more impressive because of what we know. When he forgets what he has learned about local customs and offers the two old pariahs some fern-roots, we are reminded forcibly that he is after all in a strange, alien country in the sky, where such a norm as kindness to the aged is apparently not honored (Sky and Undersea are frequently separate "worlds" in Coastal stories, culturally as well as physically set apart from earthly life). Here our hero's adherence to a point of Coos etiquette is dangerously at odds with his adherence to the empirical situation. But although the old couple recognize and point him out with apparent vindictive glee, the danger passes, and he moves on into the scene of greatest risk, the house of his brother's murderer, where he must play the part of "wife."

Here a second major foreshadowing occurs, in the gruesome dancing of the Sky People around the elder brother's bleeding head. Presumably, the dance is intended to help the killer obtain its spirit power, as in the practice of most Western Indian groups: according to the Coos custom concerning killings, for example, "the inhabit-ants of the village in which the murderer lived danced for a number of nights (usually five) in a dance called *saat*—the murderer dance."[12] In our story, the Sky People's *saat* is ultimately interrupted: the measure of their defeat and the younger brother's triumph is taken at the end in his successful dance with his people to revive the elder brother and restore his head to him.

The crises now come pell-mell. First the younger brother cries out against the physical pain of the boiling water on his hand, and then, as if one level of torment has prepared for a deeper one, he cries out in implied grief and outrage as he recognizes his brother's gory head hanging from the ceiling and yet must improvise an excuse for his tears. The scene is starkly effective, like a piece of highly economical stagecraft; and we may recall Jacobs's view that the art of Indian myth-narrative is in general best considered and appreciated as a dramatic art.[13] Especially so in the present scene, of course, with the hero's very survival dependent on his skill as a self-conscious "actor."

Now comes the story's convergence on the incidents in "Seal and Her Younger Brother"—and what a difference! Despite the earlier assurances of the murderer's wife that her husband "usually falls asleep quickly," there is clearly the possibility of a violent sexual encounter and unmasking of the younger brother (in the Alsea form of the story, the husband, already in bed, actually calls out for intercourse: "Come up here: make war upon me!"[14]). The first thought of the mother after the murder (empirically wrong, predictably), that her son "must have killed his wife," underscores this implicit threat of sexual violence against the false "wife," our hero. As for the little boy who warns that "My sister-in-law looks like a man," the story seems to allow him a distant sympathy; he is given the last word on the matter, at any rate—"It was not a woman." Following Hymes's idea that "Seal and Her Younger Brother" is profoundly a Chinookan woman's story, told by women, with a sensitive young girl as its heroine, we might say the "The Revenge against the Sky People" is complementarily a man's story in these respects, as in others, that it was told by a man, that the unheeded discoverer of the killer is a sharp-eyed *boy* (a faint counterpart of the hero himself), and that it is his mother, one of the heedless female adults, and not the boy himself, who is made to feel the drops of blood and actually discover the murder.

But we have gotten a little ahead of the narrator's strategy, which takes a surprising turn just at the outset of the murder scene. "Now it got to be evening. *The woman* was going upstairs. . . . When they went to bed *she* had a knife under the pillow. The husband went to bed first. *The woman* was walking outside." (Emphasis mine.) Whatever Percy Lubbock and James himself might say about such a drastic shift of pronominal point of view, clearly it works here. We have been brought into so full an engagement with the younger brother's predicament and the secret trial of his attention and composure that now the narrator can afford to reverse the perspective, calling the hero "the woman," just as he is known to his victim and his household, and thereby preparing to render the hero's grisly revenge from the standpoint of those who discover and suffer it. So complete is the reversal, in fact, that the victim's brother is referred to by the narrator as "the little brother-in-law."

The effect is to deepen the horror through a kind of double vision of the climactic action—we know the actor now called "the woman" for what he is, but at the same time that we are (presumably) wishing him well, we perforce find ourselves in a world of nocturnal household terror and helplessness that is much like the world that the heroine of "Seal and Her Younger Brother" herself inhabits. It is a notable and sophisticated strategy; Shakespeare does something like it in *Macbeth,* after all, in dramatizing Duncan's murder and the events leading to its discovery from an "inside" and then an "outside" perspective. Even after he has given us back the hero's perspective, as he returns safely to his home and successfully revives his brother, the narrator returns once more to the victims' point of view—"None of those people from above could come down, and none could take his revenge."

According to our own narrative conventions, the story ought to end at this point, with an unusually perfect revenge heroically concluded (the initial victim is even living again) and with the possibility of counterrevenge precluded. Part of the power of "Seal and Her Younger Brother," of course, derives from the utter finality of *its* ending. Here, instead, the narrator goes on to translate the entire action into simple mythic terms—the hero and his folks constitute the Woodpecker people: "The blood on the neck, that's what makes the head red. Thus one said to them, 'You shall be nothing. You shall be a woodpecker. The last people shall see you.'" After the tensely dramatic action of the younger brother's mission, this seems regrettably anticlimactic, especially the promised reduction of the hero—"You shall be nothing"; students with whom I have discussed the story have generally responded, "Shucks, is *that* all it means?" Even admitting a certain logic in the creation of woodpeckers out of a man who at the first of the story is a canoe maker, a worker in cedarwood, and, beyond that, noting that the Coos prized woodpecker feathers as tokens of sexual prowess,[15] it is hard not to agree with the students' dissatisfaction.

Still, it is possible to assert the functional integrity of this conclusion, I think, although not necessarily according to the rules of our fiction, especially those dictating strong, programmatic endings. In both the Clackamas Chinook and Coos repertories, and others in the West, mythic explanatory endings like this one are common, often sounding similarly "tacked-on."[16] Specifically, the Alsea and Tillamook versions of "The Revenge against the Sky People" also end with the woodpecker motif. What is involved, perhaps, is a native generic convention, a set of formal storytelling options. Although we might not have guessed it from the relatively realistic quality of much of the action, the story of the younger brother's revenge is implicitly set, like the great majority of Northwest Indian narratives, in the "Myth Age," a time before Time when the world was unfinished and ungoverned by precedent, and inhabited by freaks and monsters as well as beings with human form. Ultimately, the Myth Age gives way to an era of Transformation, in which the *lusus naturae* are cleared away, usually by an itinerant Transformer (often a Trickster), and the Myth Age beings are transformed one by one into the various natural creatures, according to their personalities and conduct—all of this in preparation for the coming of the *real* People, i.e., the Clackamas or the Chinook, if you belonged to one tribe or the other.

Now such a "historical" context or matrix would surely exert heavy pressure on the formation of individual stories and, during their recitation in cycles, lead at their conclusions away from localized events in the Myth Age to the transformations and precedents, great and minor, that produced the "real world" as it is today. In the preface to his collection of Coos myths, Melville Jacobs observes that when finishing his narration of a folktale or myth involving a Myth Age being, "the raconteur would usually close with a conventional phrasing something as follows, 'When the people next to come (the Indians not yet here in the land but soon to arrive and make their home here) see you, you will run, whenever you see a person.'"[17] Likewise, to take a somewhat farfetched modern example, there is clearly a strong tendency in the historical novel to shift at the end of its narrative of a historical continuum into the reader's own time reality—"And here's how it turns out ultimately." Indeed, as T. T. Waterman argued long ago in a classic essay on the instability of etiological elements in Indian stories, what appears to be mythic explanations of the "Just So" variety may actually constitute a narrative device whereby the story asserts its cogency and "truth" to the audience—as if the Coos narrator were to say on behalf of his completed story, in effect, "Now then, if you don't believe it, just look at the woodpeckers' heads!"[18]

The fact that "Seal and Her Younger Brother" does *not* end with an explanatory mythic foretelling, unlike a number of other stories in the Clackamas Chinook literature, suggests to me that the Indian raconteurs worked with options, not ironclad generic rules; and in this case and others like it the exclusion of all mythic consequences from the narrative probably indicates some sort of special strategy, perhaps aimed at intensifying the story's immediacy. In terms of cultural purposes, perhaps we can suppose (following a footnoted hint from Hymes, p. 197) that the bare drama of "Seal and Her Younger Brother" was especially recast by Mrs. Howard or one of her recent female predecessors so as to dramatize, in the era of white contact and native deculturation, the insufficiency of traditional social norms and the corresponding importance of keeping your eyes and ears open and your tongue at the ready, as the little heroine tries to do. In Edgar's formula at the end of *King Lear,* with the elders dead and the old way crumbling: "Speak what we feel, not what we ought to say."

As for "The Revenge against the Sky People," as anticlimatic as the etiological "coda" may seem to us still, it does accomplish a certain graceful distancing of the main action. Not only is it promised that the heroes of this horrendous story will become the familiar woodpeckers of today, but the listeners themselves are drawn explicitly into the action, as myth gives way to here-and-now "reality." The actors are told: "The last people [meaning us, the present knowers of such inherited stories] shall see you." So we do. And such distancing—which might very well have had special value for an audience including small children, allowing for the dissipation of their awakened fears—*is* prepared for, before the end. The younger brother's ritual dancing, with its magic-formulaic five repetitions leading to his brother's revival, points beyond the "improvised," that is, dramatic, action of the main story; as does, more subtly, the narrator's one self-conscious comment just as he turns his tale to ritual and transformation for posterity—Now, *it is said,* they are going to join his elder brother's head."[19] (Emphasis mine.) So, having framed his gripping and well-made story as a traditional Coos "saying," the narrator concludes his performance of it.

In the mid-1830's a Protestant missionary named Samuel Parker surveyed the Clackamas Chinook homelands along the Willamette River in Oregon for possible converts and, regarding native mythology, reported: "I am far from believing the many long and strange traditions with which we are often entertained. It is more than probable, that they are in most instances the gratuitous offerings of designing and artful traders and hunters to that curiosity which is ever awake and attentive to subjects of this description. The Indians themselves would often be as much surprised at the rehearsal of their traditions, as those are, for whose amusement they are fabricated."[20]

Fortified with hindsight, one winces at the opportunities for studying Indian literature firsthand thus wasted on an educated observer who could not even bring himself to accept the fact that the Indians had a genuine oral literature and that "the many long and strange traditions" (he offers no examples) represented authentic native art, not the idle coinage of white visitors. One ought to wince all the more, then, in realizing that although our libraries contain a wealth of carefully transcribed and translated Indian texts from all over Western America, collected by men like

Jarold W. Ramsey

Melville Jacobs and other students and followers of Franz Boas, the literary significance of this wealth is still, forty to seventy-five years later, virtually unknown. Such opportunities as we have we have so far ignored.

There are serious obstacles to our study of America's first literatures, to be sure—ignorance of original languages, incomplete ethnographic information, difficulties with the oral basis of the material, academic biases, and so on. But as the work of Jacobs and Hymes demonstrates, and as I hope this essay has at least suggested, the art of native storytelling is worth trying to elucidate, both for itself and for the light it may shed on the literature we call our own.[21]

[1] *Clackamas Chinook Texts*, Pt. II, Text No. 37: Publication Eleven of the Indiana Univ. Research Center in Anthropology, Folklore, and Linguistics (1959), 340–41.

[2] Melville Jacobs, *The People Are Coming Soon* (Seattle: Univ. of Washington Press, 1960), pp. 238–42. This book of explications and Jacobs's *The Content and Style of an Oral Literature,* Viking Fund Publications in Anthropology No. 26 (New York: Viking, 1959), constitute the fullest treatment yet made of a native literature *as* literature. Dell Hymes, "The 'wife' Who 'goes out' like a Man: Reinterpretation of a Clackamas Chinook Myth," *Social Science Information,* 7, No. 3 (1968), 173–99. Kermode, "The Structure of Fiction," *Modern Language Notes,* 84 (1969), 891–915.

[3] Underhill, "The Autobiography of a Papago Woman," *Memoirs of the American Anthropological Association,* 46 (1936), 23. For a thorough and lucid description of the storytelling context of one Western tribe, see Theodore Stern, "Some Sources of Variability in Klamath Mythology," *Journal of American Folklore,* 69 (1956), 1–9, 135–46, 377–86.

[4] I give Hymes's lightly revised text, as printed in his essay, pp. 177–79.

[5] Jacobs, *The People Are Coming Soon,* 242–43.

[6] I have adapted this idea from an excellent essay by J. Barre Toelken, "The 'Pretty Language' of Yellowman: Genre, Mode, and Texture in Navaho Coyote Narratives," *Genre,* 2 (1969), 221. See commentaries by Paul Radin and Karl Jung in *The Trickster* (New York: Philosophical Library, 1956), and Géza Róheim, "Culture Hero and Trickster in North American Mythology," in Sol Tax, ed., *Indian Tribes of Aboriginal America* (Chicago: Univ. of Chicago Press, 1967).

[7] W. B. Yeats, "The Tragic Theatre," *Essays and Introductions* (London: Macmillan, 1961), 240–44.

[8] Frachtenberg, *Coos Texts, Columbia University Contributions to Anthropology,* 1 (1913), 149–57. Another version is in Melville Jacobs, *Coos Myth Texts, University of Washington Publications in Anthropology,* 8, No. 2 (1940), 235–37.

[9] Claude Lévi-Strauss, "The Structural Study of Myth," in *Structural Anthropology* (Garden City: Doubleday, 1967), p. 213. There are in fact forms of "The Revenge against the Sky People" in the recorded mythology of the Alsea and Tillamook tribes, both from the Oregon coast, and the Quileutes of the central Washington coast have a more distant analogue. See Frachtenberg, *Alsea Myths and Texts, Bureau of American Ethnology Bulletin,* No. 67 (1920), pp. 141–49; Franz Boas, "Traditions of the Tillamook Indians," *Journal of American Folklore,* 11 (1898), 136–38; Elizabeth Jacobs, *Nehalem Tillamook Tales* (Eugene: Univ. of Oregon Books, 1959), pp. 24–28; Manuel Andrade, *Quileute Texts, Columbia University Contributions to Anthropology,* 12 (1931), 69–71.

[10] Jacobs, *The People Are Coming Soon,* p. 218.

[11] For another instance of internal conflict dramatized with complete "behavioristic" objectivity and with great power see "Coyote and Badger Were Neighbors" and Jacobs's interpretation in *The Content and Style of an Oral Literature,* pp. 27–36.

[12] Frachtenberg, "Traditions of the Coos Indians of Oregon," *Journal of American Folklore,* 22 (1909), 25. For additional ethnographic information on the Coos, see Jacobs, *Coos Ethnologic and Narrative Texts, University of Washington Publications in Anthropology,* 8, No. 1 (1939), and H. G. Barnett, *Culture Element Distributions VII: Oregon Coast Anthropological Records,* 1, No. 3 (1937), 155–203.

[13] Jacobs, *The People Are Coming Soon,* ix–xi et passim.

[14]Frachtenberg, *Alsea Myths and Texts*, p. 145.

[15]Jacobs, *Coos Ethnologic and Narrative Texts*, p. 74.

[16]E.g., see the mythic ending of an otherwise highly realistic Wasco tale, "A Wasco Woman Deceives Her Husband," in Edward Sapir, *Wishram Texts, Publications of the American Ethnological Society*, 2 (1909), 248-52.

[17]Jacobs, *Coos Myth Texts*, p. 129.

[18]T. T. Waterman, "The Explanatory Element in the Folktales of North American Indians," *Journal of American Folklore*, 27 (1914), 1-54.

[19]When, at the end of a Myth Age narrative, the raconteur thus directed the story's long-ago action at his listeners, "The people are almost here," what *did* they feel? Solidarity, a sense of historical continuity, and therefore, perhaps a sense of responsibility as the People? Ignoring all sorts of obstacles to such a comparison, there is something of this effect at the conclusion of Shakespeare's history plays, notably *Richard II* and *Henry VIII*: the Shakespearean audience was made to see itself as "coming soon," in the accession of Henry VII and in the birth of Elizabeth.

[20]*Journal of an Exploring Tour beyond the Rocky Mountains* (Ithaca, 1838), p. 235.

[21]These issues are discussed more fully in my forthcoming anthology of Indian literature from the Oregon country, *Coyote Was Going There* (Seattle: Univ. of Washington Press), and in a remarkable essay by Dell Hymes on the prospects of American folklore, "Folklore's Nature and the Sun's Myth," *Journal of American Folklore*, 88 (1975), 345-69.

# Family Misfortune Stories in American Folklore
Stanley H. Brandes

*Although stories of personal and family experience are embedded in specific inter-actions, such stories may be conceptualized and analyzed as a class. Stanley H. Brandes collected reports of stories told about family "missed fortunes" and categorized them thematically. After examining these stories in the light of American attitudes toward success, Brandes hypothesizes possible psychological and rhetorical functions that family misfortune stories may fulfill in conversation. Framing Brandes's analysis is a comparison with legends of serendipitous fortune that seem to predominate in Latin cultures and correlate with peasant values and attitudes toward wealth and station (Foster 1964).*

*For an introduction to the study of family folklore see Yocom (1982). A broad survey of the forms and themes of family folklore can be found in Zeitlin et al. (1982). Personal and family experience stories that focus on a single theme or stem from a single event have been discussed by Kalčik (1975), Wachs (1982), and Zeitlin (1980). Folklore suggesting that the American belief in the availability of boundless wealth may be changing is discussed by Baer (1982).*

Whatever their culture, people have always sought to understand why some individuals live in better circumstances and have greater access to the good things of life than others.[1] Generally, scholars have found that explanations for differential living standards are not infinitely diverse and idiosyncratic, but rather that they are neatly patterned into stories and tales which revolve around well defined themes. These stories are sensitive cultural barometers. They not only reflect the way people perceive economic opportunities and social structure, but also indicate how particular individuals rationalize or justify their own position within that structure. For any full comprehension of a society's world view, we must turn to its explanations of socio-economic variation as embodied in tales of success, misfortune, and failure.

Two seemingly opposite types of explanation have proven to be particularly prevalent objects of study. The first characteristic of Mediterranean Europe and Latin America, among other places, emphasizes the role of luck. In this explanation one's social position and economic well-being are attributed primarily to chance or to having been born under certain circumstances over which one had little or no control. Accordingly, dramatic improvements in a person's life situation are frequently explained in local stories as resulting from the discovery of treasure, success in the lottery, the unexpected beneficence of a patron, or some other radical reversal of fortune.[2] It is largely because people in these cultures perceive social structural arrangements as fixed and immutable, and the material pie as limited in quantity and unequal in distribution, that they believe that mobility can only be attained through luck, not individual manipulation and effort.

By contrast, scholars have found that American explanations of socioeconomic variation rest on individual personality characteristics and motives. According to the so-called "American myth of success,"[3] with which we are all familiar, economic achievement and social position are dependent upon a person's intelligence, hard work, thrift, and a judicious mixture of similarly oriented qualities usually associated with the Protestant ethic.[4] Those who exhibit the opposite traits are left behind. As a number of recent ambitious studies have shown,[5] the reliance on inherent personality characteristics to explain success or failure is deeply rooted and pervasive within the American popular imagination. Benjamin Franklin, Norman Vincent Peale, and the Horatio Alger stories have merely crystallized and articulated in literary form what the mass of our people have already known and orally expressed in a wealth of family and local tales. Such popular notions, moreover, have been bolstered by concomitant faith in a seemingly high rate of social mobility and an apparently boundless supply of wealth, ideas which recent political developments have only barely begun to undermine.

Not surprisingly, in the effort to define and elaborate the crucial Protestant strain in American thought, and distinguish it from its Latin counterpart, scholars have overlooked other equally important motifs in American folklore concerning socioeconomic status. Perhaps the most prominent of the heretofore ignored themes has been the family misfortune story. Lacking codified, traditional form as well as a localized social base, these stories are in no sense legends. Nor can they be termed memorates, for in general they concern events outside the actual experiences of the tellers. They are loosely structured narratives, almost always known and told only within particular families. They usually concern family figures of two or three generations past and are transmitted orally from parents to children.

I call these narratives misfortune stories because they are literally stories of missed fortune or of aborted opportunities to gain fabulous wealth. In my experience, each family has its own variant of the misfortune story, though, taken as a whole, the stories manifest a surprisingly limited range of prominent themes. Throughout this paper I will attempt to explicate these themes by giving illustrative examples and will then analyze the possible function misfortune stories play in American life.

I first identified and became interested in family misfortune stories through informal conversations with friends and relatives. For several months I simply recorded such stories whenever they casually occurred during the course of discussion. I quickly found that eliciting misfortune stories can be readily done, for usually the mere mention of one is enough to evoke the recollection of others. After I had collected approximately thirty stories in this manner, I actively sought to amass a greater

Stanley H. Brandes

number so as to uncover as much of the full variation as possible. Using the students in several introductory anthropology classes at Michigan State University, East Lansing as informants, I elicited over a hundred and fifty additional stories.

Most of the students and other informants are from cities and small towns in Michigan, though a good number come from other parts of the eastern and midwestern United States as well. In fact, in one of the few essays extant on family stories, Boatright relates three clear examples of what I have termed misfortune stories, all of them collected in Texas.[6] Though Boatright's stories concern oil, silver mines, and other typically western motifs, they are definite examples of our overall theme. I suspect that misfortune stories are found throughout the United States.

The stories seem to be told with about equal frequency by both rural and urban families. There is, however, a curious ethnic dichotomy. Family misfortune stories of the types described here seem to be restricted almost exclusively to whites, particularly those from working and lower middle-class backgrounds. When I described my project in class, black and Mexican American students, with few exceptions, adopted a posture which can only be described as a mixture of apology and defiance. They stated sincerely that they wanted to help, but that their families never had serious illusions or hopes of amassing wealth, so that stories of success or failure were never told. This ethnic dichotomy will become clearer in the analysis, following the description of the stories themselves.

I found that about eighty percent of the stories could be grouped into six discernible themes. As in the case of all such categorization, some stories seem appropriate to several themes, and inclusion under one or the other heading is largely arbitrary. In most instances, however, a story will fit most certainly within a particular category. The attempt here is not to establish an exhaustive, tightly compartmentalized scheme, but rather to provide some idea of basic consistency and similarity among the wide range of particular family stories.

## THEME ONE: LOSS OF LEGITIMATE INHERITANCE

Reminiscences dealing with inheritance form one of the most prominent kinds of misfortune stories. Typically, the stories concern an ancestor two or three generations back who was supposed to inherit a fortune, but who was, through various circumstances, cheated out of his or her just property. In some cases the potential heir foolishly rejects the money himself. The storyteller, a direct descendent of the would-be heir, tries to impart the idea that the money might have been his or hers had the inheritance taken proper effect. The following examples serve to illustrate this point.

> A. *Man, age 18, Detroit.* Although my father is not a very solemn gentleman, and one can never tell whether he is serious or not, he insists on this story being the truth. My father is of English descent on his mother's side. It is said that his mother's great-great-grandmother (or something along that line; how many generations exactly is unknown) was the daughter of one of the three or four richest nobles in the English hierarchy. It is said that she ran away with the stableboy and was disowned by her father.

B. *Man, age 20, Oregon.* Supposedly my maternal great grandfather had a brother and sister in England who amassed a fortune in the shipping trade about 1830–40. This money had evidently not come from strictly legal sources; perhaps opium. When they both died approximately the same time, the fortune was left to my great grandfather, as neither his sister nor brother had married. The old man, being a Puritanical old guy, wouldn't take what he called their 'tainted' money, and it reverted to the English government. I am not sure of the magnitude of the fortune but according to my father his mother estimated it as approximately five million pounds.

C. *Woman, age 67, Chicago.* My great aunt (that is, my father's father's sister) was married to a well-to-do businessman in hardware. The couple had no children, so he willed all his money in trust to his wife, to be divided among the nieces and nephews on *his* side of the family. These nieces and nephews already had a lot of money of their own, and anyway didn't treat him properly. Just before he died he wanted to change his will so that the nieces and nephews on his wife's side, that is, my side, would inherit, eliminating all the others from the will entirely. He changed it in his own hand, but caught pneumonia and died within the next few days, before being able to bring it to a lawyer. The altered will would have stood up in a court of law, but his widowed wife, being a proper lady, didn't want to be involved in lawsuits with the original heirs. So they got the inheritance, while the sons and daughters of my great aunt's siblings were excluded entirely.

## THEME TWO: VICTIMIZATION BY RELATIVES

A common misfortune theme concerns the underhanded attempts of relatives to cheat each other out of money or opportunities for financial gain. Typically, the details of these stories, as with so many others, are vague even when they recount relatively recent events.

A. *Man, age 19, Detroit.* My father and his father were partners in a house building construction company in the early 1950s. The company only lasted for two years. My grandfather, after becoming tired of the business, left with all the company's profits. He died shortly afterward, leaving money to my aunts and uncles but none to my father. I've heard this explanation of our financial condition since early childhood. My father never forgave his father for this. He now works for an architectural firm in Southfield, Michigan, as head of the construction department.

B. *Man, age 22, Armada, Michigan.* My grandfather at an early age left home to see how well he could do. When he returned home several years later, his two brothers had convinced their father (my great grandfather) that my grandfather was no good. So when my great grandfather died my grandfather inherited no land. Years later oil was discovered on this land and my grandfather's brothers are well off.

C. *Woman, age 21, Traverse City, Michigan.* During the time when France was trying to colonize North America, the King of France gave an uncle on my father's side a large grant of land in the area that is now Quebec. I believe the year was 1617 and my uncle's name was Louis a'Bauer, although I am not sure on either account. Our family seal and relics are in a convent in St. Anne de Beaupré, which is just outside of Quebec. I have personally seen this seal when I visited the convent a few years ago. Somehow we lost the land and my ancestors came to Traverse City to go into logging. How we lost the land we are not sure, but according to family lore if the rest of our relatives had not been 'horse thieves' we would now own Quebec, Canada.

## THEME THREE: LACK OF ENTREPRENEURIAL SPIRIT

This type of story usually involves an unambitious or financially naive ancestor, distant or recent. The ancestor had either money or the opportunity to earn it, but lacked interest in the possibilities presented by the situation.

A. *Woman, age 21, Charlevoix, Michigan.* At one time my grandfather used to run the Ironton ferry that goes back and forth between Ironton and Breezy Point. He of course met during this time many wealthy men—Charlevoix was a millionaire's resort in the '20's. If he had taken up half the stock market tips, land deals, etc., that had been offered to him, he would have been a millionaire.

B. *Woman, age 19, Flint.* My family would have been considerably wealthy if my father had listened to his father-in-law and chosen the occupation he suggested. Instead, much to my mother's distress, Dad stayed close to his mom and settled for a lesser job. Ten years ago he passed away and my mother was left in debt. The family has not had the opportunity to accumulate wealth because of this.

The absence of entrepreneurial spirit is further reflected in a number of family stories about relatives who were inventors but who failed to seize the economic opportunities offered by their creativity.

A. *Man, age, 21, Marshall, Michigan.* My great grandfather, a dentist, supposedly invented a material which was used to fill teeth which was much cheaper than gold or silver. He used it himself and let any other dentist who wanted it to use it. But he never told anyone how he made it. This story was just told to me by my parents and then by a local dentist who knew my great grandfather and used the material. According to him, if my great grandfather had patented the material, we would all be rich as a result.

B. *Man, age 20, Watervilet, Michigan.* My grandfather from East Bethany, New York, a very small rural community in western New York, invented a milk cooler. This machine and ones similar to it were the predecessors of the modern day refrigerator. Were he to have patented his machine and had sufficient backing, there is a great likelihood that our modern-day Frigidaire would bear his name rather than the one we see today, and therefore we would be immensely wealthy. He was a brilliant craftsman, but a man who held no particular desire for wealth. We have a drawing and advertising sheet dated years before any such milk cooler became popular which prove his having invented and sold the mechanism.

## THEME FOUR: LACK OF BUSINESS ACUMEN

This is the single most common type of misfortune story in my sample. Unlike the stories in the preceding theme, which concern complacent or unambitious souls, these stories involve ancestors who actually try to make it, but fail. Though the precise source of the failure varies widely, it almost always results from some gross inability to calculate future business trends. There are several prominent subthemes within this category, the most frequently cited of which recounts poorly timed land deals.

A. *Man, age 32, East Lansing.* Many years ago my great grandfather traded the land where Marshall Field is located in Chicago for land in a little town in Wisconsin called Union Grove. Union Grove was supposed to be the site where canals linking Chicago, Milwaukee, and Minneapolis would meet. The canals were never built.

B. *Woman, age 67, Chicago.* Just before the Civil War my great grandfather was offered a piece of marshy property alongside the Chicago River in return for his horse and wagon. He didn't think it was a good buy, and therefore didn't make the deal. The property is under where the Wrigley Building now sits.

C. *Woman, age 23, Grayling, Michigan.* My grandfather was offered about a hundred acres of lake frontage for about twenty-five dollars an acre in the 1920s. He said no, that he needed land for his pine trees to start a nursery. If we had that property now, we would be quite wealthy.

Another prevalent theme reflecting lack of business ability concerns poorly managed investment transactions or opportunities.

A. *Man, age 21, St. Clair Shores, Michigan.* My family would have been wealthy if my great uncle had not sold his Ford Motor Company stock. At one time he owned about one quarter of the stock when the company first got started.

B. *Man, age 18, Cheboygan, Michigan.* My grandmother has told us about the time when Henry Ford, or a man working with him, I'm not sure which . . . anyway, when this person came to my grandmother trying to raise money to start Ford Industries. He offered 10 percent of the profits if my granddad would invest $5000. My grandfather did have the sum, and was willing, but was persuaded not to by my grandmother, who wisely proclaimed, 'these things (cars) will never sell; they scare the horses too much.' Thus they lost their chance at a fortune.

C. *Man, age 18, Menominee, Michigan.* My grandfather owned a large bowling alley in the Detroit area before pinsetter times. Well when Brunswick Corporation was very small they approached him. Flew him out to New York to look over their equipment and offered him large amounts of stock if he would put them into his lanes, but he thought that they would never catch on.

## THEME FIVE: SPURNED OPPORTUNITY THROUGH LOVE OR PRIDE

In many families misfortune has resulted from the conscious rejection of wealth in deference to some higher goal. The most frequently cited goals include either the obligation to a loved one or the maintenance of self-esteem or pride. Most, though certainly not all, of these stories impart less of a sense of bitterness and defeat than do those concerning other themes.

A. *Woman, age 25, Detroit.* This story concerns my grandfather. He was a very talented pianist. He had the opportunity to study under a famous pianist in France, but he fell in love with my grandmother and married her and gave up concerts and took a job working in the city. If he had continued his talent, he would have been very famous now and very rich. He was born in Atlanta, Georgia, and married my grandmother in Detroit where they still live. He is still a very gifted man.

B. *Man, age 20, St. Joseph, Michigan.* When I was born my grandfather owned a small hardware store in St. Joseph. It was the only store of this type and the community liked it. The town was smaller than it is today and so the store would have definitely grown with the town. My dad worked at the store and, I suppose, he eventually planned to own it. One day he was offered a job in a big plant. He had only a high school education, but this job would have a chance for high positions. Then my grandfather had a stroke. My dad gave up the opportunity for the good job to try to bring my grandfather to health while running the store. In the end they had to sell the store. He missed his good opportunity and now we're really screwed up. He works for the Post Office and is too old to change jobs now.

C. *Woman, age 18, Detroit.* My mother almost married the owner of Strohs brewing factory; but she fell in love with my dad and married him instead.

## THEME SIX: THE DEPRESSION OR OTHER UNFORESEEN DISASTER

Many families trace their financial situation to the Great Depression or to other equally unpredictable and uncontrollable misfortunes, especially those related to health.

A. *Woman, age 18, New York City.* My grandfather built up a profitable law practice in the '20's and early '30's and made huge investments which made him very wealthy. He lost his fortune, however, much real estate and houses, etc., because of the Depression, and the family became rather poor.

B. *Woman, age 30, Bay City, Michigan.* My great grandfather was co-owner and partner in the lumbering firm of Allen and Light, located in the

Harrisville-AuSable area of northeastern Michigan. They owned many hundreds and hundreds of acres of what is now *prime* tourist land. My grandfather once told me that his dad traded a forty acre farm to get him a pony. In the early part of this century the whole place burned to the ground (a great fire swept through that part of the state), destroying the lumber mill and the town of AuSable and Harrisville. The firm of Allen and Light never got back on their feet. My great grandfather became a broken man, ran away from home, and was not heard from for many years. When he came back my great grandmother wouldn't let him in the house; he slept in the barn for the rest of his life. All the valuable timber land was sold for taxes. All that land is now worth millions in the summer recreation land market.

C. *Woman, age 20, Muskegon, Michigan.* My paternal grandfather owned the largest coal/wood/coke yard in town. My father had a French governess and traveled extensively throughout the country. During the Depression he got a new sports car every year. My grandfather's money was lost in two ways, as far as I know: my grandmother was quite ill for many years, and *her* mother lived in a private room in a hospital for fifteen years.

## ANALYSIS

Family misfortune stories reflect a basic paradox in American explanations of success, stagnation, and failure. On the one hand, we are inclined to place almost total responsibility for socioeconomic status on personality characteristics inherent in the individual. Our culture imposes upon us the view that we will almost surely succeed given certain favorable attributes such as intelligence, energy, wise financial management, and the ability to get along with colleagues. Correspondingly, as Richard Sennett and Jonathan Cobb have astutely pointed out, "There is . . . indifference to those who do not move ahead. Failures and static people . . . are seen as having undeveloped personalities. . . ."[7] In the United States, unlike England, a move downward more often than not has moral overtones. Horatio Alger stories, as well as contemporary success manuals of the same ilk, portray failure as an inability to survive in the great competitive marketplace and as a reflection of the weakness of a person's talents.[8]

On the other hand, we encounter quite a different attitude expressed in the family misfortune stories. Here, for the most part, it is the behavior and personality of other people, specifically one's ancestors, that are called upon to explain economic immobility or decline. In some instances, the storyteller, speaking either for himself or for his parents, lays the blame for economic hardship squarely on the relative, who is said to have bungled his clear and easy opportunities. In other cases the accusation is implicit and can be gleaned only from the context in which the misfortune story is told. Usually these stories are recounted spontaneously in response to tales of success. Another family's financial boons will be the main subject of conversation, only to recall to the storyteller's mind the tale of the bygone opportunities of his own family. The storyteller's underlying message is that, given the ancestor's shrewd economic management, he, the storyteller, would have had a significant head start in his own struggle for the good things in life. As it is, states the narrator implicitly, he or his parents had to start out virtually from scratch.

To understand why misfortune stories concerning ancestors are so prominent in a society which places the main burden of success on the individual, let us recall Sennett and Cobb's notion of the "hidden injury of class."[9] In America, these sociologists point out, we are all considered responsible for our own fate, for the course of our careers, and for the financial circumstances and opportunities we provide to our families. The possibility of failure is an ever present concern. "This fear of being summoned before some hidden bar of judgment and being found inadequate," write Sennett and Cobb, "infects the lives of people who are coping perfectly well from day to day; it is a matter of hidden weight, a hidden anxiety in the *quality* of experience, a matter of feeling inadequately in control. . . ."[10] This terrible burden, the knowledge that we will be measured by our degree of success, a success over which we are supposed to have virtual control but over which in actuality we do not, is the hidden injury of class.

The injury is hurtful because, even though we have internalized the familiar Protestant-derived values and criteria for personal evaluation, we know that success is largely a matter of ascribed status and opportunities. Henry Ford notwithstanding, it is clear to us all that social class is not solely dependent on individual achievement. Thus, Robert Lane, in an intensive analysis of fifteen working and lower middle class whites in New Haven, found that most of his subjects accepted the view that America opens up opportunities for all people, if not in equal proportions then at least enough so that a person must assume responsibility for his own status. Yet Lane also discovered the concurrent belief that subordinate socioeconomic positions result largely from birth and class, matters over which the men knew they had no control.[11] In their study of one hundred and fifty working class Boston whites, Sennett and Cobb encountered the same view. These workers, despite their nagging anxieties of inadequacy, felt that "they could be just as strong, just as free, as anyone else if they had the chance."[12] Indeed, their opinion is borne out by a National Opinion Research Center study which shows that only eighteen out of every thousand sons of manual laborers in this country enter the professions.[13] The ideology of mobility and equal opportunity with which we are burdened is controverted by the realization of relative social class rigidity.

This realization does nothing, however, to relieve a person's persistent fear that, given higher intelligence or different personality endowments, he might have done better. He suffers from this diffuse kind of anxiety while at the same time resisting the implications of personal inferiority imposed upon him by the standards of the wider society. Total capitulation to these standards could only result in deep self-hatred, guilt, and resentment, such as that embodied in the familiar literary figure of Willy Loman, who becomes so crippled by these feelings that he can no longer act normally.[14] The blame for defeat must be deflected away from the self onto someone else.

It is this crucial deflection of blame for one's position onto one's ancestors that family misfortune stories provide. Particularly the stories subsumed under the first four themes, loss of legitimate inheritance, victimization by relatives, lack of entrepreneurial spirit, and lack of business acumen, perform this function, and do so through a subtle recognition of both ascription and achievement. On the one hand, the storyteller reassures himself and his audience, typically his children, that his own position and opportunities were severely limited by that which was bequeathed him. He thereby consciously resorts to the notion of unequal opportunity to explain his status and dismisses to himself and others, the terrifying possibility of inferior capabilities as an explanation. At the same time, however, the storyteller speaks of his own ancestors as if they had total control over their destiny. Through incompetence, absence of economic realism, or emotionally unstable qualities, and not because of bad fortune or low birth, one's ancestors experienced less of a rise than they should or might have. It seems that we reserve little of the ameliorating sympathy for others that we shower upon ourselves.

Generally, it is in only two of the six misfortune themes, those concerning spurned opportunity and unforeseen disaster, that storytellers blatantly look to their own experiences (as told and reported here, in many cases, by their children) as the source of financial stagnation. In the one instance, spurned opportunity, the protagonist foregoes material luxury for the achievement of higher rewards. In the other instance, unforeseen disaster, financial ruin in no sense emanates from the inherent personal deficiencies of the actor. These explanations threaten neither the positive self-image of the storyteller nor the child's favorable concept of his parents. It is almost, as Sennett and Cobb say, as if, "there is no room for failure in our schemes of respect, unless the failure is found to result from some cataclysmic event like the Great Depression."[15]

Of course, we might be tempted to dismiss these stories as simple but perceptive reflections of reality. Perhaps several generations ago, or more, the opportunities for mobility and economic achievement *were* greater for the common man. Perhaps our ancestors *should* be blamed for acting stupidly or irrationally when confronted by such financially favorable circumstances, while we and maybe our parents, constrained by a considerably tighter class system and restricted economic milieu, are justified in attributing stagnation or failure to ascribed factors. In deciding whether or not the stories reflect reality, however, we would do better to view them from a social interactionist perspective, that is, as an attempt on the part of the storyteller to impart to his audience a certain image of self. Of everything that we know about the experiences of ourselves and our families, we select only certain items for oral transmission. This selection is not random, but rather is based, at least in part, upon a screened impression which we wish to relay to our audience. Through the misfortune story a person can neatly absolve himself of essential responsibility for disabilities and mediocrity.

In adopting this interpretation of family misfortune stories we may perhaps understand why they seem to be limited, at least in our admittedly restricted sample, to whites. For, as blacks and Mexican Americans consistently relate, there was never any expectation of great financial opportunities in their families, hence no development of stories concerning how such opportunities were undermined. Neither blacks nor Mexican Americans have considered themselves to have the same possibilities as whites. To the contrary, and unlike most whites, they have been firm in their conviction that the American class system is rigid and that it inherently limits contention for the good things in life. For these minorities the explanation of financial stagnation clearly lies in their ascribed ethnic affiliation, never in the bumbling economic tactics of ancestors. We may speculate, however, that the enhanced educational and economic opportunities of these groups in recent years might within several generations yield the creation of misfortune stories similar to those presently found among whites.

Finally, we must ask whether these misfortune stories may legitimately be considered within the domain of folklore. Surely, as Brunvand and Honko have said, narratives like family stories are in most cases highly unstructured, and therefore difficult to distinguish from simple musings or occasional reminiscences.[16] Yet even such reminiscences have a tendency to become codified over time. As Bascom points out, ". . . they may be retold frequently to acquire the style of verbal art and some may be retold after the characters are no longer known at first hand. They are accepted as truth and can be considered as a subtype of the legend, or a proto-legend."[17] It seems to me that such stories or reminiscences, especially when they may be grouped into prominent themes such as those related here, deserve recognition as a critical and often-neglected form of folklore.

Garrett has told us that "family folklore, like other folklore, not only mirrors the group's habits, motivations, and aspirations, but also acts as a cement that welds individual members of one group together in time as well as space."[18] Misfortune stories fully perform these functions in the lives of a good number of Americans. They are a critical product and barometer of the social psychology of our people.

---

[1] The research on which this study is based was supported in part by a grant from the All-University Research Funds at Michigan State University. I wish to thank my colleagues Loudell F. Snow and John Hinnant for stylistic comments on an earlier verson of the paper.

[2] See, for example, Edward C. Banfield, *The Moral Basis of a Backward Society* (New York, 1958), pp. 64–65, 175–179; N. T. Colelough, "Social Mobility and Social Control in a Southern Italian Village" in F. G. Bailey, ed., *Gifts and Poison: The Politics of Reputation* (New York, 1971), pp. 220–225; and George M. Foster, "Treasure Tales and the Image of the Static Economy in a Mexican Peasant Community," *Journal of American Folklore* 77 (1964):39–44.

[3] Richard Weiss, *The American Myth of Success: From Horatio Alger to Norman Vincent Peale* (New York and London, 1969).

[4] Max Weber, *The Protestant Ethic and the Spirit of Capitalism*, tr. Talcott Parsons (New York, 1958).

[5] John G. Cawelti, *Apostles of the Self-Made Man* (Chicago and London, 1965); Moses Rischen, ed., *The American Gospel of Success: Individualism and Beyond* (Chicago, 1965); and Weiss, *The American Myth of Success*.

[6] Mody Boatright, "The Family Saga as a Form of Folklore," in Mody Boatright, *et al.*, *The Family Saga and Other Phases of American Folklore* (Urbana, Illinois, 1958), pp. 2, 15–16.

[7] Richard Sennett and Jonathan Cobb, *The Hidden Injuries of Class* (New York, 1972), p. 183.

[8] Richard Sennett, *Families Against the City: Middle Class Homes of Industrial Chicago, 1872–1890* (Cambridge, 1970).

[9] Sennett and Cobb, *The Hidden Injuries of Class*.

[10] *Ibid.*, pp. 33–34.

[11] Robert E. Lane, *Political Ideology: Why the American Common Man Believes What He Does* (New York, 1962).

[12] Sennett and Cobb, *The Hidden Injuries of Class*, p. 182.

234

[13]*Ibid.*, p. 225.

[14]Arthur Miller, *Death of a Salesman* (New York, 1949).

[15]Sennett and Cobb, *The Hidden Injuries of Class*, p. 183.

[16]Jan Harold Brunvand, *The Study of American Folklore: An Introduction* (New York, 1968), p. 93 and Lauri Honko, "Memorates and the Study of Folk Beliefs," *Journal of the Folklore Institute* 1 (1964):12.

[17]William Bascom, "The Forms of Folklore: Prose Narratives," *Journal of American Folklore* 78 (1965):5.

[18]Kim S. Garrett, "Family Stories and Sayings," *Publications of the Texas Folklore Society* 30 (1961):273.

# Personal Experience Narratives: Use and Meaning In Interaction

Barbara Allen

*In addition to the highly structured and dramatic narrations of heroes and their exploits recounted in myth and tales, folklorists are concerned with briefer, more loosely organized accounts of personal experience. These stories are often embedded in conversation and may be conceptualized and conveyed by their tellers as "information" rather than "art."*

*These kinds of stories often depend heavily upon the social context of interaction for their sense and meaning. They are rarely monologues but are rather constructed in and around conversational exchange. When removed from that immediate context they may prove pointless and eminently forgettable. Barbara Allen illuminates some of the ways in which such personal experience narratives function in conversation. Using examples from specific interactions, she discusses how these stories can work to define, maintain, enhance, or transform a social situation.*

*For more on personal experience narrative see Abrahams (1977) and Stahl (1977a, 1977b). For studies involving the close analysis of narration in context see Bennett (1986), Bauman (1986), and Sacks (1974).*

Personal experience narratives have recently begun to attract the attention of folklorists, although there is no general consensus on the admission of such narratives into the canon of traditional folklore genres.[1] Up to now, studies of personal experience narratives have tended to concentrate on structure and content in efforts to identify what they have in common with traditional narrative forms. In this paper, I would like to make a few observations about the distribution and use of personal narratives in conversation, based on the assumption that, as forms of communication, such narratives do not occur in an interactional vacuum, but that they are responses to, and receive responses from, surrounding interaction.

A number of definitions proposed for folklore have emphasized its nature as verbal art and/or communication.[2] Yet folklorists have tended to neglect the immediate interactional or conversational contexts in which folklore is used. This is partially due to the methodological difficulty of encountering and recording "natural context," especially for traditional conversational genres such as proverbs, superstitions, taunts, boasts and charms,[3] and partially because of an emphasis in folkloristics on the collection of "important" forms, such as the folktale and folksongs, through interviewing. As a result, folklorists have done relatively little systematic study of folklore in interaction.[4]

My purpose here is to demonstrate first, that personal experience narratives are carefully shaped and precisely positioned for rhetorical effect in their conversational settings, and, second, that the meaning of any personal experience story derives in large part from its use in a particular interactional matrix. At the end of the discussion, I will point out some implications that the interactional analysis of personal experience narratives may have for the study of narrative and of folklore in general.

The relative neglect of personal experience narratives by folklorists seems to be due to a number of factors. First they are not traditional in content and so afford little opportunity for the comparison of analogues. Second, telling personal experience stories, while governed interactionally by a number of delicate and complex constraints, requires no specialized or esoteric knowledge; anyone can and, if socially competent, does tell such stories. Third, a certain reverse ethnocentricity may be at work: if personal narratives are so common among ourselves, they must not be very important. Finally, when extracted as "texts" from their interactional settings, these kinds of narratives often seem incoherent and unstructured. Perhaps more than any other narrative form, personal experience stories live only in the telling.

The importance of the immediate conversational context to the telling of personal experience narratives can be seen in the fleeting relevance of any given example. Most of us, for instance, have had the experience of a conversation in which someone tells a story for which we have the perfect follow-up, but someone else tells his or her follow-up story first, steering the conversation in another direction. In cases like this, the chance to tell one's story may be permanently lost, unless the conversation can be manipulated back to an appropriate point for telling it. This quality of context-relevance reveals why personal experience narratives look naked as collected texts. Their meaning, like the funniness of some events, depends on the situation in which they occur. Frequently, "you had to have been there" to see why something was funny or why a story was to the point. In being specifically formulated for context relevancy, personal experience narratives can be seen as "strategies for the encompassing of situations."[5] Not only do they dramatically characterize or "encompass" a situation in narrative form, but they also are shaped for, and told in, particular interactional situations for specific rhetorical purposes: "Stories, generally . . . are formed up for just the audience and just the occasion for their occurrence."[6] The best way of demonstrating this is to look at the specific distribution and use of personal experience narratives in conversation.

Personal experience narratives tend to occur in clusters or rounds; that is, they frequently appear as "second stories" in response to other personal narratives. Such clusters of stories are linked by similarities in topic or theme. A story about a physician is not likely to be immediately followed by an account of a vacation trip, unless there is some topical link between the two, such as an encounter with a physician on the trip or an experience on the trip similar to the previous speaker's experience with the physician.

But the fit between succeeding stories is often closer than just that of topical. According to Michael Moerman's analysis of second stories, "the teller of the second story stands in the same relation to the events and other characters of his story as the teller of the first did in his."[7] Thus, the distribution of personal narratives in conversation is directly related to their use, for the narrator of a second story chooses that story in order to express sympathy with the first speaker. This point is clearly illustrated in the following example.[8]

> V At the end of the summer the greatest thing happened. I was ready to go back to school and this man came in [to the restaurant in which she worked]. You know, the last two weeks are so great 'cause you can tell the customers all the things you've wanted to tell them all summer. And you can't get fired. You know, you've only got two more weeks. Well, this man came in and he was with a group of men that came in all the time, but he didn't usually come in. And it was for breakfast. And this one man, in the group, that I knew, who was really nice, says, "Oh, are you going to leave and go back to school?" I said, "Yeah," you know. And this other guy goes, "Well, I think I'll just go to school and be one of you college students supported on welfare and just have this easy life."
>
> M Oh!
>
> V I said, "Oh yeah? I'd like to see you live on what I live on a month. Nobody supports me but me and I have a job at school. If you want to live on forty bucks a month for food which is what I do, you might lose fifty pounds!"
>
> M Fantastic!
>
> V "And you'd look so much better if you did!"
>
> M You didn't say that!
>
> V I did too.
>
> M What did he say?
>
> V Nothing.
>
> M What was the look on his face?
>
> V It was just [makes appropriate face].
>
> M Oh, Virginia!
>
> V And the thing—I was really—I was almost scared after I finished, but I was so mad at him. I mean I work my butt off at school and the government doesn't give me jack shit. And so then this other man that I know said, "Yeah, you just shut up." This poor guy. He didn't come in again before I left.
>
> M I bet he didn't.
>
> B Oh, boy.
>
> V He made me so angry.
>
> M Terrific. That's like the time—I'm sure I told you—over at McKenzie Bridge. I'd gotten on the bus in Springfield and they'd changed the busing system—the stop—so that it was out in the open for a while until they got new things—did I tell you about it?
>
> B Hunh-uh.

M  So it was out in the open in the hot sun and the rain and everything else. And of course a lot of old people take the bus system down there. So I was standing there and some other woman—really nicely dressed woman— came up and she started telling me how she's been to the welfare offices here and now ni—didn't I tell you this?

B  No. I don't remember.

M  Oh, and how she'd just gotten back from California. Uch, you know, those welfare people down there, just gave her hell, you know, but she could come up here and get whatever she wants. She's originally from this area, mind you.

B  Oh, no.

M  And she said, she can get whatever she wants and they don't question her and they just give it to her, by golly.

B  Oh, god.

M  And just beautifully dressed, I mean right down to the T. You wonder what she's riding the bus for, you know? And anyway . . .

V  Her Mercedes is in the shop.

M  Really! That must have been it.

B  Oh, no, welfare people drive Cadillacs.

M  Yeah, 'course. So anyway, after telling me all the benefits of Oregon welfare as opposed to California welfare, we got onto the subject about the bus system and I was saying, you know, "It's really a shame—" it was kinda inconvenient 'cause there were no seats there. "It's really too bad they changed this before they got places set up," I says, "especially the old people that have to sit out here in hot sun and rain." She goes, "Oh!" she says, "You know, you'd never hear a California kid say that. None of those people— but up here everybody's—" So I turned to her and I said, "I am from California," and I turned around. I was pissed.

B  I don't blame you.

M  You know—but that's the attitude up here.

While Mary's story displays an understanding that Virginia's story was about telling someone off (and not about school or work or welfare), and is thus topically linked to Virginia's, what specifically makes Mary's story a second to Virginia's is that her reason for telling off the woman at the bus stop is the same as Virginia's for telling off the customer. Both were angry at having imputed to them something that was not true, the imputation being made in each case on the basis of an assumption about a group (student or Californian) of which each is respectively a member. Thus, second stories can function as a particularly effective and appropriate means of expressing an understanding of, and agreement with, the point of the first speaker's story.

Another example of this confirmatory use of a personal narrative as a second story occurs in the following excerpt from the same conversation:

V  I was so disappointed. You know at eleven o'clock or ten o'clock all the church bells rang [for the Bicentennial Fourth of July]. I was working at Bob's. Did I hear anything? Clunk.

B   I know. I missed it too.

M   That's okay. I didn't hear anything. I was really sick Fourth of July.

B   Oh, really?

M   And there was nothing going on in McKenzie Bridge anyway. I mean nothing.

B   Didn't ring the dinner bell or anything?

M   No. Anne and Harry—I told them, "Go for a walk, find out if anything's happening." So they walked around McKenzie Bridge and said [shakes her head] no.

Here Mary offers a consoling account of her Fourth of July, after Virginia and Barbara have complained about theirs. But a personal experience narrative can also, at least theoretically, be chosen to align the second speaker against the first, by characterizing an experience similar to the first in topical terms, but one in which the speaker plays an opposing role. What interactive effect such a story might have is revealed in Moerman's hypothetical example of a response to a first story in which the speaker witnesses a roadside accident. The second speaker "would have been insulting, embarrassing or otherwise discomfiting [the first speaker] had she told of an accident in which she was also not a witness, but a victim annoyed by witnesses gawking at her."[9]

This "matching up" of speakers' roles in personal experience narratives told as second stories seems to be related to what Peter Seitel has called the correlation process in selecting proverbs.[10] According to Seitel, an appropriate proverb is chosen by correlating the relationship between the terms in the proverb with the relationship between interactants in the situation to which it is applied or in which it is used. In Barbara Kirshenblatt-Gimblett's study of the telling of a parable, it is clear that her informants made this same kind of correlation between the roles of the characters in the parable and the people in the situation in which it was told.[11] Through this correlation mechanism, personal experience narratives can convey a meaning beyond that of their content by commenting on, offering an evaluation of, or revealing an attitude toward, a situation without making a direct statement about it.

While not all personal experience narratives are told as second stories, they are always responses of some sort to the ongoing interaction. Beneath the topical and correlational levels already discussed, personal experience narratives are responses to the nature of the social setting as mutually recognized and defined by the participants (e.g., cocktail party, rap session, business conference) and to the relationships that exist between the participants, both inherently (parent-child) and situationally (host-guest). Recognition of the social setting and relationships among participants is generally shown through "appropriate" behavior—wearing the proper clothes, using the correct forms of address. In conversation, this can be done through telling the right kinds of stories, and, when personal experience stories are appropriate, by telling just the right one.

While social situations and relationships are usually conceived of by folklorists as contextual aspects of a folkloric "event," it is important to remember that these factors are individually perceived by interactants. Thus "inappropriate" behavior, such as telling a dirty joke to the wrong audience, can be seen as either (1) a failure to perceive the situation correctly, i.e. as everyone else sees it; or (2) as a deliberate manipulation of the situation for the speaker's own purposes, such as effecting a redefinition of the social situation or altering the relationships between speakers. Through careful selection, positioning, and correlation of personal experience narratives, speakers can engage in this kind of manipulation by obliquely expressing sympathy with, or disapproval of, other speakers.

A speaker is thus faced with a series of choices in telling a personal narrative. First, he or she must select out of the continuum of experience one occurrence that seems characterizable in narrative form, on the basis of a certain structural or logical coherence. Second, the speaker must choose an experience that is appropriate to the conversation with respect to the definition of the social situation, the relationships among the participants, and the topic at hand. Third, in telling a personal experience narrative as a second story, the narrator must correlate the role he or she plays in the story according to a desire to express solidarity with, or opposition to, other speakers. Finally, irrelevant details must be omitted and significant ones highlighted to make the story's pertinence and situational appropriateness as clear as possible to the audience.

In making these choices, the narrator shapes the story into something more than a news account—shapes it rhetorically—so that the telling of the experience in that particular form will indicate to the audience some of the meaning of the original experience for the narrator, his or her attitude toward why it is being recounted at this point in the conversation. Narrators frequently state the point of a story or their attitude toward the experience explicitly, to keep the level of ambiguity at a minimum. Both Virginia and Mary, for example, end their stories with this kind of evaluative statement: Virginia says, "He made me so angry" and Mary says, "I was pissed."

A number of other observations can be made about personal experience narratives as they are told in conversation. For example, the distribution of personal experience narratives in rounds—like the organization of conversation into turns—seems to put pressure on all those present to contribute; everyone is expected to perform. For example, after Virginia and Mary each tells her story of telling someone off, Barbara has no appropriate example to contribute and so "passes" on her turn by saying to Virginia, "Did you tell Mary about that time at Arturo's?" Barbara remarks when that story is over, "Nothing like that ever happens to me," simultaneously offering an excuse for not telling a similar story and letting Virginia's story stand as a surrogate for her contribution.

Another constraint put on the use of personal experience narratives in conversation is that a story should not be repeated to an audience which has heard it before. Several remarks already cited illustrated this, such as Mary's repeated asking if the other two have heard her bus story before, and Barbara's eliciting of Virginia's Arturo story by asking if she has told it to Mary. In this latter case, Mary gives Virginia permission to tell it again by saying, "Oh, you did, but tell me again because I can't remember." Later in the conversation, reference is made to a story about the "Drano woman":

> V  Well, John was telling us—Remember the woman that was living next
>     door to John? . . .
> M  Oh, Oh, yeah. The Drano woman?
> V  Remember that?
> B  That was so funny. How anybody can grow up—
> M  Y'know, I have told people that story but I don't think they really believed
>     me.
> V  Well, who would?
> B  Oh, dear. That was so funny.

In this case, the story does not get retold, presumably because, by making comments about it, all the participants display their familiarity with it. Violations of this principle of non-repetition are, of course, regularly made, when a personal experience story is felt to be the most appropriate example to offer in a given situation. Such repetitions may be forestalled by the remark, "You've already told me that," or repetition may be cut short and the story referred to by a catch phrase (such as "the Drano woman"). Such references are what Susan Kalčik has called "kernel" narratives[12] and seem to be used most frequently among people who interact with each other on a regular basis.

The sensitivity to the audience in telling personal experience narratives is also shown by changing a story in mid-course to accommodate a listener's reactions:

> V  Oh, the parking. Remember the Fourth of July, the parking was so insane.
> M  Why? . . . Who was there Fourth of July?
> V  Xavier's car was there. Barbara's car was there.
> B  That wasn't this Fourth of July?
> V  Yeah, it was.
> B  Oh, it was, wasn't it?
> V  There were so many—Scott's car was there . . . and every time—
> M  Uch! I don't want to talk about it. I keep finding out all these good things
>     I've missed out on.
> V  Oh, it wasn't that great, actually. All we did was move cars all day.
> B  That was it, really.

In response to Mary's complaint, Virginia offers a depreciating assessment of the account she and Barbara have been giving of the Fourth of July celebration at which Mary was not present. The focus of their story changes from a list of those present to a difficulty with parking cars.

It seems to me that the interactional study of personal experience narratives has several implications both for the study of narrative and for folkloristics in general. First, personal narratives, used as second stories, can be seen as framing devices which distance the speaker both from the event being characterized and the situation to which it is addressed. Through interactional analysis of different kinds of narratives, it might be possible to distinguish between types of situations in which different kinds of stories appear. For example, in particularly tense or delicate situations, a narrative with relatively more "distance," such as a parable, might be a more appropriate and effective form to use than a personal experience narrative.

Secondly, we have seen that a large part of the meaning of personal experience narratives seems to derive from their use in specific interactional settings. As Moerman says:

> The point of the story is not objective and pre-existent: it is an interactive accomplishment in which the teller of the second story lends a hand. We, the readers of the transcripts, come to know what the first story was about in part because of what the teller of the second successfully took it to be about.[13]

Through interactional analysis, we may begin to see how meanings associated with traditional items of folklore, such as proverbs, take on a particular pertinence in being used in specific situations.[14]

---

[1] Sessions on personal experience narratives were presented at the 1975, 1976, and 1977 meetings of the American Folklore Society. The papers from the 1975 meeting have been published as a special issue of the *Journal of the Folklore Institute*, 14 (1977), 5-126. In addition, personal experience narratives were the subject of a recent Ph.D. dissertation in folklore at Indiana University: "The Personal Experience Narrative as a Form of Folklore," Sandra Stahl, 1975.

[2] See, for example, William Bascom, "Folklore, Verbal Art, and Culture," *Journal of American Folklore*, 86 (1973), 374-381; Dan Ben-Amos, "Towards a Definition of Folklore in Context," *Journal of American Folklore*, 84 (1971), 3-15.

[3] Roger D. Abrahams, "A Rhetoric of Everyday Life: Traditional Conversational Genres," *Southern Folklore Quarterly*, 32 (1968), 44-59.

[4] An outstanding example of an international study of folklore materials is Barbara Kirshenblatt-Gimblett's "A Parable in Context: A Social Interactional Analysis of Storytelling Performance," in *Folklore, Performance and Communication*, ed. D. Ben-Amos and K. Goldstein (The Hague, 1975), 105-130.

[5] Kenneth Burke, *The Philosophy of Literary Form: Studies in Symbolic Action* (Baton Rouge, 1941). Revised edition: New York, Vintage Books, 1957, 3.

[6] Michael Moerman, "The Use of Precedent in Natural Conversation: A Study in Practical Legal Reasoning," *Semiotica*, 9 (1973), 208.

[7] Moerman, 207.

[8] This and the following transcriptions were made from a tape-recorded conversation among three sisters in March 1977.

[9] Moerman, 207-208.

[10] Peter Seitel, "Proverbs: A Social Use of Metaphor," *Genre*, 2 (1969), 143-161.

[11] Barbara Kirshenblatt-Gimblett, "A Parable in Context: A Social Interactional Analysis of Storytelling Performance," in *Folklore: Performance and Communication*, ed. D. Ben-Amos and K. Goldstein (The Hague, 1975), 105-130.

[12] Susan Kalčik, "... like Ann's Gynecologist or the Time I Was Almost Raped: Personal Narratives in Women's Rap Groups," *Journal of American Folklore*, 88 (1975), 3-11.

[13] Moerman, 206.

[14] Roger D. Abrahams and Barbara A. Babcock, "The Literary Use of Proverbs," *Journal of American Folklore*, 90 (1977), 414-429.

# VII
# Ballads and Folksongs

## A Model for Textual Variation in Folksong
### Thomas A. Burns

*Oral transmission often promotes variation to such an extent that some folklorists have made the process of variation basic to their definitions of folklore (Brunvand 1986: 9, Dundes and Pagter 1975: xvii). For those scholars who conceptualized folklore primarily as "oral" or "unwritten tradition," the versions and variants of folklore texts became a major object of investigation. This was particularly true for the study of ballads, folksongs, and other poetic and musical forms.*

*Thomas A. Burns provides a helpful overview of the concepts and terminology of change employed by scholars in their study of ballad and folksong. However, his model, which depends upon conceptualizing change in terms of the addition, subtraction, and rearrangement of elements, may prove too limited for conceptualizing the full range of song variation. Although a song parody is the result of some subtraction, some addition, and some rearrangement, this characterization misses the important and deliberate connections that exist between the parody and old song upon which it has been modeled. When one performs a parody one is highlighting relationships between songs. In essence, one is presenting two songs at the same time. Song variation based on such relationships may not be adequately captured by the model. Burns, however, is fully aware that models and classifications are not ends in themselves, and that a model of song variation is only a first step in the understanding of the forces that bring that variation about.*

*Examples of folksong variation can be found in Abrahams and Foss (1968:12-60). Goldstein (1960) produced an extremely useful phonograph record illustrating many of these types of variation. A study that involves the close comparison of the versions of a single ballad is Long (1971). Greenhill (1987) provides an interesting discussion of change as it pertains to popular printed verse. For an experimental approach to variation and memorization that influenced folklore research see Bartlett (1920). Dundes (1965:243-47) and Oring (1978) both comment on the relationship of experimental to natural situations of transmission and variation.*

Reproduced by permission of the author and the publisher, from *Folklore Forum* 3, no. 2(1970):49-56. Not for further reproduction.

Thomas A. Burns

## I. INTRODUCTION

The purpose of this paper is to present a model for textual change in folksong. It is hoped that the model will be useful as a device in at least three ways: first, to bring together the various concepts dealing with textual variation which have been advanced by scholars; second, to clarify the relationships among different types of textual change; and third, to suggest possible types of changes which might otherwise be overlooked. To the degree that textual changes exhibited in folksong are paralleled by changes in oral narratives, the model may also be useful in the study of variation in narrative materials.

## II. PREVIOUS SCHOLARSHIP

D. K. Wilgus, in the section of his *Anglo-American Folksong Scholarship Since 1898* devoted to variation in folksong texts, indicates that while the ballad war "stimulated the study of oral transmission, the intensity of the dispute hampered careful study."[1] The fact of the matter is that those scholars concerned with variation tended not to focus on the process of variation itself but to utilize the evidence of variation to advance their causes as degenerationists, diffusionists, or "Emersonians." Interpreting the fact of variation rather than exploring the process or types of variation was what interested these scholars. Thus, while there exist, for example, several superior historical geographical studies of certain individual ballads—studies based on the analysis of a great many variants of a single ballad—there are few studies which either treat in depth the process of change or attempt to systematically identify and order types of textual variation in folksong.

The first work to focus on textual variation as significant in itself was Tristram P. Coffin's *The British Traditional Ballad in North America* (1950).[2] In the chapter of this book devoted to "A Description of Variation in the Traditional Ballad of America," Coffin defines, discusses, and illustrates most of the major types of textual change and suggests the forces which lie behind them. However, Coffin's division of change into textual alteration (minor changes) and story variation (changes affecting the mood or plot of a song) is rather artificial and tends to obscure the basic similarity of the changes at both levels. It should be noted that while Coffin's division of change is artificial from the point of view of the study of process, it is useful to his real purpose in the chapter which is to indicate his criteria for differentiating story variants in the bibliographic survey of ballads which follows.

Most scholars who have considered the general subject of textual variation in Anglo-American folksong in the past fifteen years have added little to what Coffin had to suggest. Malcolm Laws in his chapter "American Ballad Forms and Variants" in his *Native American Balladry*[3] recognizes the various types of textual change and the forces which lie behind them, but he stresses the basic stability of most songs and tends to view most change as degenerative.[4] Laws does make one important contribution to the study of variation by indicating the significance of the internal nature of the song to the possibility for change. Laws discusses and illlustrates the fact that the more loosely structured the contents of a song are, the more likely it is to undergo change.[5]

The most recent work to consider the matter of textual variation is *Anglo-American Folksong Style* by Roger Abrahams and George Foss.[6] Besides more fully illustrating the various types of textual change in folksong, Abraham's and Foss's contribution to the study of variation is to indicate the bi-polar direction of change (dramatization vs. lyrication[7] and localization vs. universalization[8]).

What the study of textual change in folksong seems to lack is a basic framework within which all of the specific change concepts developed by various scholars can be seen and understood. In Dundes's terms, it is for the purpose of liquidating this lack that the model in this paper is presented.

## III. WHY TEXTUAL VARIATION?

Before elaborating the model of types of textual change, it is necessary to consider briefly the principal forces causing change. One of the problems of previous scholarship on variation has been the confusion of types of change with the causes of change. For instance, forgetting is sometimes cited along with localization as a type of change. Other problems have arisen due to the confusing ways in which the causes for change have been handled. Coffin, for instance, identifies three forces for variation: the personal factor, trends in folk art, and print.[9] Such a listing suggests that trends in folk art and print are autonomous or superorganic forces for change apart from the performer. The fact of the matter is that trends in folk art (aesthetic trends) and print (one vehicle for transmission) are simply two elements influencing change at the personal level. If we are to come to an understanding of why textual change takes place, we must focus on the individual and reckon with the forces which exist within him and impinge upon him to bring about change.

Most of those who have considered the matter of textual variation have pointed out the importance of a performer's mishearing, misunderstanding or forgetting as forces for change. Some important factors which in turn influence mishearing, misunderstanding and forgetting are: (1) limited mental capacity, (2) duration of exposure, (3) the inherent nature of the song and its parts, and (4) the personality of the performer (included in this last category are the social and cultural values operative in the individual). It seems that regardless of an individual's desire he may not have the ability to comprehend parts or remember the whole of a song text considering the given degree of his exposure. Likewise, a song text which is loosely structured or which contains words or actions foreign to the individual's understanding or whose tune and text are estranged at points,[10] may affect a performer's ability to understand or retain certain materials of a song. Personal idiosyncracies or the working out of social pressures or cultural values in the individual may well make for the conscious or unconscious rejection of or attraction to (Coffin's emotional core) specific song text elements. Like the awareness of other oral versions of a song, the knowledge of the text of a song in print is another aspect of the performer's experience which may affect the song he finally produces.

It should be pointed out that while mishearing, misunderstanding and forgetting are essentially passive or largely unconscious causes for textual change in folksong, creation (composition, recreation, recomposition) is for the most part a conscious act on the part of an individual.[11] Creation or recreation tends to be a particularly important cause of textual change in traditions which value originality or improvisation. In the highly "creation" conservative Anglo-American tradition, creation or recreation exists as a force for change more at the level of the substitution of words and phrases than at the level of stanza additions or complete reworking of a piece. It seems that in Anglo-American tradition textual changes resulting from the more extensive forms of recreation have most often been the product of literary tradition. Whether conscious or unconscious, textual changes are affected by the individual and it is to this individual's limitation, idiosyncracies and socio-cultural experience that we must look for the causes of these changes.

## IV. THE MODEL

The following model is built upon the simple assumption that there are only three basic types of textual change that are possible. In short, material can be taken away (Subtraction), material can be added (Addition) and material can be rearranged (Rearrangement). A specific type of textual alteration may involve any one or combination of these three basic changes. For example, a common type of textual change involves the substitution of portions of the text from one song for portions of another. This type of textual alteration is the product first of Subtraction and the Addition of material. With three variables (Addition, Subtraction and Rearrangement) there exist seven possible ways to characterize textual variation (each variable alone—3, paired combinations—3, and all three variables together—1). The three basic change types and their combinations can be represented by the intersection of three circles as in Figure 1. What will become apparent shortly is that nearly all concepts developed by Anglo-American folksong scholars to deal with the subject of textual variation fall within the bounds of Addition or Subtraction, or Subtraction and Addition (Substitution). The implications of this fact will be discussed later.

Before we consider the specific concepts of textual variation that have been defined by analysts and how these concepts are placed according to the model, it is necessary to emphasize that by textual variation is meant change at all levels of song material. Thus, Subtraction as a basic type of change describes the loss, for whatever reason, of textual material from a word through phrases, line, lines, stanza, stanzas to the point where perhaps only a title or tune is retained. Textual change is not being used here as Coffin employs the term to mean minor changes which do not significantly affect mood or story.

A brief survey of the literature on textual variation in folksong has revealed nineteen different types of change with which Anglo-American folksong scholars have been primarily concerned. All but four of these concepts refer to changes involving Addition or Subtraction or Addition and Subtraction. These types of variation are differentiated

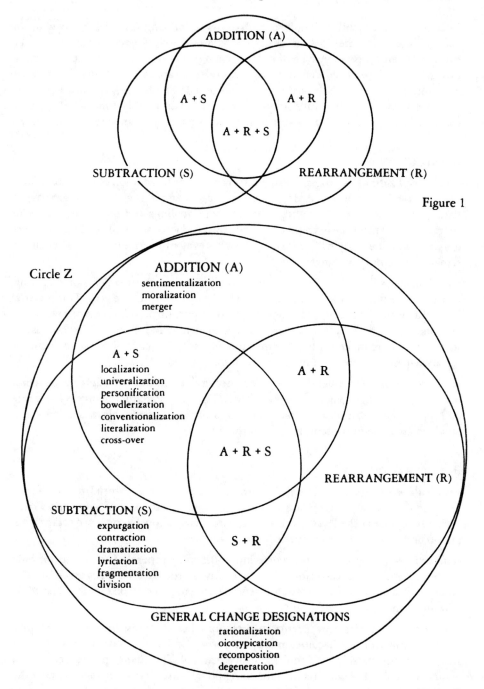

Figure 1

Figure 2

from one another by the kind, level and/or degree of song material involved in the change. The four other change designations are of a very general nature and can conceivably encompass any type of possible change. What follows is a brief consideration of each of these specific change concepts under the appropriate model heading, i.e. Addition, Subtraction, Subtraction and Addition (Substitution). The concepts are arranged within these headings according to the level of material to which the change concepts refer from least to most inclusive (i.e., word or phrase to several stanzas).

## A. ADDITION

*sentimentalization*—a process usually associated with the addition of song material at the stanza level throughout a song text. The added material is generally descriptive in nature and functions to heighten the listener's feelings toward an act, scene or character. That this type of change is largely the product of social or aesthetic pressure is apparent, but exactly why this change is so prevalent in American ballad tradition remains something of a mystery.

*moralization*—the addition of material, usually a stanza at the conclusion of a song, which states explicitly the lesson supposedly to be learned from the song. This material is often addressed directly to the audience or some portion of it. It is perhaps fair to say that one reason moralization arises as a type of change in folksong is in response to social pressure to make explicit the meaning of a song which is no longer evident for the audience and therefore cannot be taken for granted.

*merger*—the process whereby two songs become one either through simple compounding or through fusion of their elements. This type of textual change is fairly rare in Anglo-American folksong tradition and is likely to occur only when the songs involved are close in content, mood and theme.

## B. SUBTRACTION

*expurgation*—the deletion by the performer of selected song material, usually bawdy or obscene material, in response to social pressures. This form of subtraction most often takes place at the level of the stanza, particularly a concluding bawdy stanza, but can occur at the level of phrases or lines.

*contraction*—(compression, concentration)—the most general of the terms for Subtraction, "contraction" can refer to the loss of any type of material at any level. Usually, however, it is implied that materials essential either to plot or mood are retained while peripheral material is shed.

*dramatization*—refers to a particular direction that compression takes wherein a single or climactic act becomes more and more the focus of attention due to the shedding of peripheral action and descriptive material. This change process most often occurs at the level of the loss of stanzas. Although this form of change is generally associated with Subtraction, there seems to be no reason that at the same time peripheral action and descriptive detail is lost, the focal action cannot be somewhat elaborated through the addition of dramatic material.

*lyricization*—change opposite to that of dramatization and involving the progressive loss of all kinds of action elements while detail capable of eliciting a particular mood or emotion is retained. Here, as in dramatization, there seems to be no reason that the loss of action components cannot be accompanied by the addition of appropriate descriptive detail in new stanzas.

*fragmentation*—refers to an extreme state of contraction wherein the loss of material (either of action or mood) becomes so extensive that what remains of the song text is no longer considered a complete piece.

*division*—a process which occurs infrequently in Anglo-American tradition and which is characterized by a song splitting into two or more songs. Such a change process is most likely to occur among songs which are episodic, lengthy and loosely structured.

## C. Subtraction Plus Addition (Substitution)

*localization*—the process whereby details of a folksong, particularly those of person, place and time, are replaced by local counterparts which account for the song's special local relevance. The process of localization is considerably aided when local events attached to local names and places at least loosely parallel the events and characters in a song.

*universalization*—a process exactly counter to localization. Change in this instance involves the substitution of generalized categories (the three sisters) or common names (John) for specific designations (Emilou, Adelade and Marge; Egbert). Whether the change that is brought about is one of localization or universalization, the result is much the same—to make identification with the contents of a song easier and more intense for an audience.

*personification*—change which involves the substitution of the first person for the third person point of view in a song. The usual effect of such a change is to place the performer in the role of the song's major character, thereby bringing the performer and his specific performance more to the attention of the audience. Personification represents one of the first intrusive steps by the performer as an interpretive agent into the song.

*bowdlerization*—the substitution of socially acceptable words, phrases or stanzas for song material considered too coarse to be related, given the social situation of the performance.

*conventionalization*—a process whereby familiar, almost formulaic words or phrases (clichés) are substituted for forgotten original counterparts.

*literalization*—textual changes which accompany the substitution of a literal meaning for a figurative one in a phrase, line or stanza of a song text. It is possible to consider literalization as a kind of fallacious rationalization, an attempt which misfires to make sense of a passage which is not understood.

*cross-over*—a process whereby because of similarities in content, mood, theme or tune, material at any level passes from one song to another. Although cross-over usually is a matter of substitution, it may also occur as a phenomenon under Addition. Particular types of materials, lyric elements, refrains and stanzas of generalized or common action, are especially subject to this type of movement. When the cross-over of materials from one song to another is viewed negatively, the change is termed *contamination*.

## D. FOUR INCLUSIVE CHANGE DESIGNATIONS

*rationalization*—textual changes which result from the imposition of the criteria of reason or probability on the contents of a folksong. Rationalization may result in certain materials being deleted, substituted or added. Although I know of no instance that has been pointed out, there seems to be no reason that rationalization of material might not also be effected through the rearrangement of materials.

*oicotypification*—the process whereby song materials are adapted to a particular cultural or subcultural environment, i.e., the acculturation of a song text. Clearly this process encompasses all the basic change possibilities and their combinations.

*recomposition* (limitation, recreation)—although any conscious change in a song text, however slight, might be considered recomposition, this term is usually reserved to refer to the more or less complete revamping of song materials. In this more comprehensive sense, the process of recomposition, like oicotypification, may involve any type of basic change or combination of changes possible in the model.

*degeneration*—this concept refers to any change at any level of song material which is viewed negatively.

## V. THE COMPLETED MODEL

In the second graphic representation (Figure 2) specific types of textual change are located within the three basic circles and their areas of overlap. General change designations which may involve any one or combination of the three basic types of change are located within the circle Z which encompasses the three basic circles.

## VI. CONCLUSIONS: WHAT THE MODEL INDICATES

1. Scholars concerned with textual variation in Anglo-American folksong have been almost exclusively concerned with Addition or Subtraction or Substitution changes.

2. Rearrangement as a type of textual change has been very little considered as a factor in variation[12] perhaps because such a change is not prevalent in the Anglo-

American ballad tradition that has been the focus of most scholarly attention. Rearrangement as a factor in textual change in the Anglo-American folksong tradition is possibly rather slight; but, from what little work has been done with the American Negro song traditions in which improvisation is highly valued, we might assume Rearrangement to be a much more significant factor of textual change in these traditions.

3. It may well be that certain genres of folksong exhibit particular types of textual change and not others. For instance, textual variation in the ballad may be characterized for the most part by changes of Addition, Subtraction and Substitution, as has been indicated for Anglo-American tradition. Textual variation in lyric and descriptive song on the other hand may prove to be primarily the result of changes of Rearrangement or Rearrangement in conjunction with Addition and/or Subtraction. Likewise, different song traditions may be characterized by different types of textual changes. If so, then the reason for these differences should be traceable to different cultural sets which permit or sanction different types of behavior by the performer with regard to his use of song texts. Textual changes may vary with time as well as with genre and culture. Viable, on-going song traditions may exhibit either different types of variation or broader ranges of variation than do waning song traditions. Comparative studies of textual changes, both cross genre and cross cultural, are needed to shed light on these matters. Such studies are predicated, of course, on a renewed interest by folksong scholars in the area of process.

---

[1] New Brunswick, New Jersey, 1959, p. 277.

[2] Philadelphia, 1950, revised 1963.

[3] Philadelphia, 1957, revised 1964.

[4] Laws, *Native American Balladry*, pp. 71–77.

[5] *Ibid.*, pp. 77–82.

[6] Englewood Cliffs, New Jersey, 1968.

[7] Abrahams and Foss, *Anglo-American Folksong Style*, p. 24.

[8] *Ibid.*, pp. 29 ff.

[9] Coffin, *The British Traditional Ballad in North America*, p. 1.

[10] Wilgus, *Anglo-American Folksong Scholarship*, p. 279.

[11] Abrahams and Foss, *Anglo-American Folksong Style*, pp. 24–25.

[12] Coffin, *The British Traditional Ballad in North America*, p. 9. Coffin briefly suggests that shifting of lines, phrases and stanzas within ballads often occurs.

# Oral Formulas in the Country Blues

## John Barnie

*In an effort to discover whether the* Iliad *and* Odyssey *originated as written literature or began as oral compositions, Milman Parry set out to record the living oral tradition of contemporary South Slavic epic singing. Yugoslav epic singers sang epics composed of tens of thousands of metrical lines. Parry and his student Albert Lord discerned that these enormous poems were not memorized as wholes, but that individual singers learned the structure of the songs, the sequences of incidents and episodes, and a large vocabulary of verbal* formulas—*poetic phrases and expressions—appropriate to the description of these incidents and episodes. In effect, when a singer came to sing, he recomposed his song as he sang it, utilizing his knowledge of the organization of incidents and descriptions and his large stock of poetic formulas. Analysis of recorded Yugoslav songs revealed striking similarities with the Homeric texts, thus suggesting the oral origins of Greek epic poetry (Lord 1960).*

*Parry and Lord's oral formulaic composition theory reconceptualized oral expression as a creative act. In oral cultures, the production of oral poetry is not a matter of rote memorization and mechanical recall. Composition, performance, and transmission must be conceived as a single phenomenon. These ideas were soon brought from epic to the analysis of poetic expressions that ranged from the ballad (Buchan 1972:51–173) to the sermon (Rosenberg 1970, Davis 1985). In the following essay, John Barnie applies them to the analysis of the blues.*

*For more on the techniques of blues composition see Evans (1974). Blues texts can be found in Oster (1969), Oliver (1963), and Taft (1983). Further textual, musical, social, and cultural analyses of blues can also be found in Charters (1963), Titon (1977), and Evans (1982) as well as in the journal issue in which Barnie's article originally appeared. For a history of oral composition theory see Foley (1988).*

Anyone listening to a number of country blues songs will have noticed that they share certain basic linguistic and thematic features. Most noticeably, half-lines, lines, and stanzas will be found to recur in the songs of a great many singers. These may be modified, sometimes radically so, but they bear a recognizable relationship to lines and stanzas in other songs within the tradition. A similar correspondence exists at the thematic level, since the country blues singer develops a comparatively limited range of themes. Yet it is rare to find one singer reproducing *exactly* the blues of another. A

Reproduced by permission of the publisher, from *Southern Folklore Quarterly* 42(1978):39–52. Not for further reproduction.

close relationship exists between many blues, but it is not that of a copy (even an imperfectly remembered one) to its original.

An explanation for these features may be sought in the theory of oral-formulaic composition, first propounded by the American classical scholars Milman Parry and A. B. Lord in relation to the Homeric poems and Jugoslav folk epics.[1] The results of their research have received a wide currency in recent years, and the theory has been applied with varying degrees of success to such diverse material as Old English alliterative poetry and black American chanted sermons.[2] Its relevance to the blues, however, is only now being appreciated by scholars in the field; and unfortunately, with the exception of Jeff Titon's exposition in *Early Downhome Blues* and the important research-in-progress of Michael Taft,[3] most attempts to apply the Parry-Lord thesis in this area have been far from satisfactory.

William Ferris, Jr., for example, refers to the theory in *Blues from the Delta*, but fails to take into account the difficulties caused by the lyric rather than narrative structure of the blues.[4] Likewise, John Fahey, in his study of blues singer Charley Patton, alludes to Parry and Lord's thesis, but is confused as to the nature and significance of formulas in Patton's blues. He identifies formulaic lines which he refers to as "traditional commonplaces," but goes on to assert that, "In no case does the use of a particular commonplace play an integral or even especially important part in one of Patton's texts."[5] Yet in a later characterization of his blues Fahey claims that they are "an extreme case of oral-formulaic creativity in which the singer, if he does not (and Patton probably did not) actually make up the stanzas at the time of the performance, simply selects stanzas and verses at random from a large storehouse of them in his mind."[6] Unfortunately, Fahey never defines exactly what he means by a formula in the blues.

The uncertainties and contradictions in these two studies are indicative, I think, of some of the problems involved in adapting the oral-formulaic theory to the blues. For while it is clear that the country blues singers were working within a tradition similar to that described by Parry and Lord, there are fundamental differences which must also be taken into account. The most important of these relates to genre. Parry and Lord developed their ideas from the study of Jugoslav folk epic: poetry which is essentially narrative, sometimes extending into thousands of lines. The blues, on the other hand, is lyric insofar as it can be equated with any Western poetic genre. It is a crucial difference, which I will return to later.

Briefly, the Parry-Lord thesis is that the singer of epic verse in a pre-literate society creates his songs in the act of performance, largely, though not exclusively, with the aid of an extensive repertoire of formulas: a formula being in Parry's definition, "a group of words which is regularly employed under the same metrical conditions to express a given essential idea."[7] The oral poet is able to draw on a large store of such formulas, some of which will be common to the tradition as a whole, others limited to a group of related singers, and yet others unique to the songs of a particular singer. Such formulas should not be thought of as clichés, for as Lord has pointed out, they are "capable of change and are indeed frequently highly productive of other and new formulas."[8] Nor does a formula necessarily involve word-for-word repetition. Elements in a given formula may vary, providing they meet the demands of metre and the "given essential idea." Extensive variation, however, results in the formation of a "formulaic system" which is defined by Parry as: "a group of phrases which have the same metrical value and which are enough alike in thought and words to leave no doubt that the poet who used them knew them not only as single formulas, but also as formulas of a certain type."[9]

In applying this concept to the blues, one is at once confronted with a problem of definition: what is the basic metrical unit of the blues and hence the basic unit of the formula? With most work in recent years concentrating on the stanza as a unit of *meaning*, it is a problem which has received little attention.

Several writers have emphasized the non-narrative structure of the country blues, which consists typically of a series of discrete stanzas which may collectively evoke a particular mood or experience.[10] Such stanzas correspond more or less to the "themes" of oral epic poetry, defined by Lord as "the repeated incidents and descriptive passages in the song."[11] To this extent therefore, William Ferris, Jr., is right to argue that "any relevant study of the blues must focus its attention on the verse (sic) as the basic unit."[12] It is misleading however to claim, as he does in the same sentence, that "the verse [stanza] is the only textual unit which remains structurally intact." For while a singer *may* adopt a stanza wholesale, he is more likely to borrow lines and in particular half-lines which he recombines into stanzas of his own. At one level, therefore, it is the line and half-line which should be considered the basic "textual unit" of the blues, and upon which any discussion of oral formulas must concentrate.[13]

I would suggest that the metre of such lines is accentual, based on a comparatively free patterning of stressed ($/$), half-stressed ($\backslash$), and unstressed ($\wedge$) syllables.[14] Certain normative features are discernible however. Usually a metrical line will consist of 4 to 6 stresses, with most singers I have analyzed showing a preference for 5 or 6.[15] It is divided by a caesura, with a tendency towards an equal distribution of stressed syllables if the line is composed of 6 stresses, and towards a 2/3 ratio in a 5-stress line. Half-stress is quite common, while unstressed syllables, though in theory unlimited, rarely exceed 3 to 5 in any given line. Thus, for example, "Júdge pléase dôn't kìll mé | Î wón't bê bád nô móre."[16] It should be noted that the caesura is often heavily emphasized in performance, since it serves the dual function of breath pause and formula boundary.

An accentual structure of this kind centers on the distribution of stressed and, to a lesser extent, half-stressed syllables; while unstressed syllables may vary in number without necessarily affecting the basic metre of a given half-line. Superficially, this structure is reminiscent of the accentual verse of the Anglo-Saxons, much of which is oral-formulaic in origin.[17] One major difference, however, is that in Old English verse a *particular* stress pattern forms an integral part of any given formula from which little or no variation is permissible. But in the blues, for a number of reasons, it is not possible to define the metrical basis of the formula (or indeed its verbal components) so precisely. An example will make this clear.

A widely disseminated formula is based on the "given essential idea" of the singer's *going away*. With few exceptions, it is a formula of the first half-line of verse one (1ᵃ), and is sufficiently generalized to allow a range of formulas or non-formulaic phrases in the second half-line (1ᵇ). In the examples I have collected, however, there are four apparent "variants" of this formula which need to be considered.

The simplest consists of a bare statement of the "given essential idea" which may be shortened by the omission of the personal pronoun and auxiliary verb, as in:

> Î'm góin' âwáy
> Góin' âwáy.[18]

It will be noticed that in both examples, accent is placed on the two key words "going'" and "away," and although there are exceptions to be discussed later, metrical stress usually reinforces the key words of the formula in this way.[19]

Most singers expand the half-line, however, by the addition of tags placed either at the beginning or the end of the formula proper, or both. As is well known, tags such as "Lord," "mama" and "honey" are ubiquitous in the blues, so much so that they are frequently ignored by scholars who do not always transcribe them when establishing texts. This is regrettable, for tags often serve the dual function of heightening the dramatic element in a blues and (I would suggest) of satisfying the singer's innate preference for a particular pattern of stresses within the half-line. They are far from being mere ornamentation.

For example, the *I am going away* formula is most frequently used with reference to a woman whom the singer has decided to leave. The insertion of "baby," "honey" or "mama" after the formula addresses the singer's words directly to the woman, emphasizing her personal involvement in the stanza. It also provides the singer with the possibility of a 2½ or 3 stress half-line which is the commonest of the metrical variants open to him:

> Î'm góin' âwáy bábŷ
> Î'm góin' âwày bábe.[20]

More rarely, the singer *may* retain the 2 stress pattern by emphasizing the concluding tag at the expense of the initial stress on "goin'." The second syllable of "away," however, always receives stress or, very occasionally, half-stress:

> Î'm gôin' âwáy mámâ
> Î'm gôin' âwáy bábŷ.[21]

A third variant involves the addition of a tag such as "says," "well," "and" or "Lord" before the formula (examples 22–30). With the exception of "Lord," however, these are almost always unstressed and so do not affect the given stress pattern of the formula. They seem to serve an introductory function, allowing the singer to signal a new stanza by a prefatory interjection which is often omitted in the second verse (examples 24-6, 29, 30, 33, 34). "Lord," on the other hand, always receives half-stress and occasionally stress: an indication of its relative importance as an intensifier of the singer's intention as expressed in the formula (examples 30-2, 35).

As one might expect, the largest single group (examples 31-42) contains initial and concluding tags, since this allows the singer to fulfill all the conditions noted above: the preference for a half-line of 3 or 2½ stresses; the desire to heighten the content of the formula dramatically; and the need to mark off the first verse of a new stanza with an interjection.[22]

A related function of tags should also be noted. It is a direct result of the unusual structure of the three-line blues stanza, in which the second line is essentially a repetition of the first. Through the addition or subtraction of tags, the singer is able to modify the stress pattern of the line, thus providing a degree of variation in a potentially monotonous verbal repetition.[23]

However, while the stress pattern may be altered by the introduction of tags, it can be argued, I think, that the "given essential idea" is not. There is a significant difference, for example, between "I'm goin' away *mama*" and "I'm goin' away *to leave you*" (examples 43-5). In the latter, the singer has modified the formula to such an extent that it must be considered a different formula within the larger system based on the idea of going away. In the first example, however, "mama" represents so slight a modification to the main idea of the formula that the singer may choose to delete it in the second, repeated line. "I'm goin' away" and "I'm goin' away mama" clearly represent minor variations of a single formula, although the metrical pattern is not the same. In this respect, oral formulas in the blues are quite distinct from those in Old English verse or Jugoslav folk epic, where the formula is integrated with a particular and largely inflexible metrical unit. It should be noted however that significant limits are placed on the singer's use of stressed tags by the prevalence in the blues of a half-line of two or three stresses, two of which *generally* correspond with the key words of the formula.

In the examples I have collected, four major themes are developed in line 1^b. These are concerned with: (1) the duration of the singer's absence, (2) his motive for leaving, (3) the real or imagined reaction of his woman, and (4) the assertion that he is leaving *soon*. A larger sample would undoubtedly reveal others. They are expressed through a variety of formulas and non-formulaic phrases, although a glance at the appendix makes it quite clear that formulas predominate.[24]

Four blues songs in the sample incidentally confirm that the singers worked with half-line units when composing their blues in performance. In the examples below, the singer uses the *I am going away* formula in two separate stanzas, followed in each case by a different formula in 1^b:

A st.3 Wêll Î'm góin' âwáy mámâ | wón't bê baćk tîll Fáll
   st.7 Sâys Î'm góin' âwáy | máke iî lónesôme hére

B st.2 Î'm góin' âwáy | bábŷ añd iî wón't bê lóng
   st.6 Lórd Î'm góin' âwáy | hónêy hôw cán Î stáy?

C st.1 Sàid I'm̂ góin' âwáy mámâ | wéar yôu óff mŷ mínd
   st.2 Sàid I'm̂ góin' âwáy bábŷ | cátch tĥe Hóllŷwoòd líne

D st.5 Sâys I'ṁ góin' âwày mámâ | bábŷ dón't yòu cŕy
   st.7 Sàys I'ṁ góin' âwày mámâ | Î aṁ góin' tô stáy.[25]

In C it should be noted that the singer substitutes what appears to be a non-formulaic half-line in st.2, 1[b]. Thematically however it is closely related to the formulaic system based on the idea of catching a specified train or riding a specified line.

As I will suggest, a singer may show a preference in his blues for a particular collocation of formulas in 1[a] and 1[b], but it is clear that the tradition as a whole provides a wide range of formulas for 1[b] which the more inventive singer may vary at will.

An important but so far unresolved problem relating to oral-formulaic composition in the blues, concerns those factors which influence a singer's choice and juxtaposition of formulas. It is beyond the scope of this paper to discuss the problem in detail; it would seem, however, that rhyme words play an important part in determining the progression of formulas within a stanza. This becomes evident when a singer either makes a mistake or deviates for some other reason from the more usual collocations of rhymed formulas. As an example, one may take the following stanza from "Court Street Blues: by Stovepipe No. 1:

Góin' âwáy | aín't cômîn' báck tîll Fáll
I'ṁ góin' âwáy | aín't cômîn' báck nô móre
Wêll tħe blúes ôvêrtáke mê | Î aín't cômîn' báck nô móre.

1[a] and 1[b] represent a familiar collocation of formulas. In the second line, however, the singer substitutes the closely related formula *ain't comin' back no more.*[26] This places him in a dilemma, since the formula he sang in 1[b] is almost always associated with *won't be back at all* in 3[b], with its logical progression underpinned by the rhyme on "Fall" and "all." Conversely, the formula in 2[b] is normally associated with the *hang crepe on your door* formula in 3[b], with which it shares the rhyme on "more" and "door."[27] Unable to resolve his dilemma, Stovepipe No. 1 compromises weakly by repeating *ain't comin' back no more* in 3[b], even though this formula is most often reserved for lines 1 and 2.

It is perhaps not possible to talk with certainty of a "mistake" on the singer's part here, although he was certainly aware of the Fall/all progression which he uses in st.4. But the unusual substitution in 2[b] highlights the way in which rhyme words act as a determining factor in the collocation of formulas, helping to ensure the inner logic and narrative consistency of the stanza. Through his inattention to the progression of rhyme words, Stovepipe No. 1 has sacrificed both.

A detailed study of similar stanzas in which the singer either makes a mistake or deviates radically from the more usual collocations, could add to our understanding of the process of oral-formulaic composition in the blues.

In this paper, in common with Michael Taft and Jeff Titon, I have taken the half-line as the basis of oral-formulaic composition in the blues. But there are complicating factors which Parry and Lord did not encounter in their study of Jugoslav epic poetry and which arise from the lyric as opposed to the epic structure of the blues. Even in the most favourable 'field' conditions, a blues song never achieves the length of an oral epic, and narrative complexity is essentially alien to the tradition. As Ferris, Jr., and others have observed, the thematic unit of the blues is a discrete three-line stanza. It is hardly surprising therefore that a singer will often find one coupling of half-line formulas particularly to his liking, with the result that in *his* songs the two formulas invariably appear linked together. In many instances the positioning of the caesura makes it clear that the singer is thinking from the beginning in terms of a completed line and not half-lines. For example:

Cryin' Lord I wonder will I | ever get back home.
Some people say the | Green River blues ain't bad.[28]

Where the singer is composing through the medium of half-line formulas, the caesura acts as a formula and syntax boundary. Here however, the singers ignore syntax in the positioning of the caesura: a certain indication that they are thinking in terms of a *line* unit rather than basic half-line formulas.

Similarly, there are many stanzas which tend towards a set form. A singer who begins with "The sun's gonna shine in my back door some day" will almost invariably conclude with "The wind's gonna rise, blow my blues away." It should be noted, however, that the formulaic basis of such stanzas does allow an inventive singer to substitute other half-line formulas for the more conventional collocation.

No doubt the widespread dissemination of blues via gramophone records hastened this process of ossification; but it is probably inherent in the lyric structure of the blues itself, which makes it easy and natural for memorable lines and stanzas to achieve a set form. Many of these still retain the aura of the formulas from which they undoubtedly derived, but although they may be considered "formulaic" they are not themselves formulas. Perhaps the closest analogy is with similar lines and stanzas in ballad tradition; and indeed, one difference between blues singers and Jugoslav epic singers is that the former usually include a range of other secular and religious songs in their repertoires which, unlike their blues, have been learnt by heart. Composing and singing within an oral-formulaic tradition *and* something approaching a literary song tradition must have hastened the process whereby the blues lost its pure oral-formulaic character—if indeed it ever had one.

## APPENDIX

Note: with the exceptions of examples no. 32 and 42 (available on a Library of Congress LP), all records indicated in parentheses are 10″ 78s.

1. Big Boy Cleveland, "Goin' to Leave You Blues" (Gennett 6108, 1927), st. 2.
   I'm góin' âwáy | tô wéar yòu óff m̂y mínd (3)
   Keep me worried bothered all the time.

2. Elizabeth Johnson, "Sobbin' Woman Blues" (OKeh 8789, 1928), st. 8.
   I'm góin' âwáy | jùst tô wéar yôu óff m̂y mínd
   Góin' âwáy | tô wéar yòu óff m̂y mínd (2)
   Keeps me worried bothered all the time.

3. Papa Charlie Jackson, "Ash Tray Blues" (Paramount 12660, 1928), st. 8.
   Î'm góin' âwáy | wón't bê lóng
   You look for me I'll be gone . . .

4. Lottie Beaman, "Going Away Blues" (Brunswick 7147, 1929), st. 1.
   Î'm góin' âwáy | ît wón't bê lóng
   I know you'll miss me even singing this lonesome song
   Î'm góin' âwáy | ît wón't bê lóng
   And then you'll know you must have done me wrong

5. Charlie Kyle, "Kyle's Worried Blues" (Victor 21707, 1928), st. 2.
   I'm góin' âwáy | bábŷ añd ît wón't bê lóng (2)
   You mistreated me and I'm gonna lay my hat at home

6. Henry Thomas, "Don't Leave Me Here" (Vocalion 1443, 1929), st. 6.
   I'm góin' âwáy | añd ît wón't bè lóng
   Just [    ] you train lovin' baby I'm Alabama bound.

7. Charley Patton, "Down the Dirt Road Blues" (Paramount 12854, 1929), st. 1.
   Î'm gôin' âwáy | tó thê oñe Î knów (2)
   I'm worried now but I won't be worried long.

8. Charley Patton, "Green River Blues" (Paramount 12972, 1929), st. 7.
   I'm gôin' âwáy | gónnâ máke ît lónesôme hére
   I'm gôin' âwáy bábŷ | tô máke ìt lónesôme hére
   Yês I'm góin' âwáy | tô máke ìt lónesôme hére.

9. Blind Lemon Jefferson, "Struck Sorrow Blues" (Paramount 12541, 1927), st. 1.
   Î'm góin' âwáy | hónêy dón't yòu wánt tô gó?
   Î'm góin' âwáy bábŷ | dón't yoù wánt tô gó?
   I'm goin' to stop at a place I haven't never been before.

10. Stovepipe No. 1, "Court Street Blues" (OKeh 8514, 1927), st. 1.
    Góin' âwáy | aín't cômiñ' báck tîll Fáll
    Î'm góin' âwáy | aín't cômiñ' báck nô móre
    Well the blues overtake me I ain't comin' back no more.

11. Blind Blake, "Doing a Stretch" (Paramount 12810, 1929), st. 7.
    Góin' âwáy | hòw háppŷ Î wîll bé
    If I know you still love me . . .

12. Charley Patton, "Circle Round the Moon" (Paramount 13040, 1929), st. 4.
    I'm goin' away make it lonesome here (2)
    I'm goin' away babe to make it lonesome here.
    (Note: I have not heard this song. The text is taken from Fahey, *Charley Patton*, p. 107.)

13. Tom Dickson, "Happy Blues" (OKeh 8590, 1928), st. 6.
    I'm góin' âwáy bábŷ | sée whât yóu gôin' dó
    I'm góin' âwáy bábŷ | sée whât yóu goîn' dó
    I done all I could can't get along with you.

14. Furry Lewis, "Big Chief Blues" (Vocalion 1133, 1927), st. 1.
    Î'm gôin' âwáy bábŷ | táke mê sév'n lòng moñths tô ríde (2)
    January February March April May June July.

15. Charley Patton, "When Your Way Gets Dark" (Paramount 12998, 1929), st. 6.
    Î'm gôin' âwáy bábŷ | (dón't yôu wánt tô gó?) *spoken*
    Î'm gôin' âwáy bábŷ | dón't yôu wánt tô gó?

16. Charley Patton, "Devil Sent the Rain Blues" (Paramount 13040, 1929), st. 6.
    Î'm gôin' âwáy mámâ | dón't yôu wánt tô gó?
    Î'm gôin' âwáy mámâ | dón't yôu wánt tô . . . (2)

17. Henry Thomas, "Bull Doze Blues" (Vocalion 1230, 1928), st. 1.
    Î'm góin' âwáy bábe añd ît wón't bê lóng
    Î'm góin' âwáy | añd ît wón't bê lóng
    Î'm góin' âwáy añd ît wón't bê lóng

18. Blind Lemon Jefferson, "Lonesome House Blues" (Paramount 12593, 1927), st. 2.
    Î'm gôin' âwáy mámâ | jûst tô wéar yôu óff ṁy mínd
    Î'm gôin' âwáy prèttŷ mámâ | jûst tô wéar yôu óff ṁy mínd
    Gonna find a lady in Chicago murder is gonna be my crime.

19. Roosevelt Sykes, "Single Tree Blues" (Paramount 12827, 1929), st. 4.
    Góin' âwáy mámâ | cómiñg hére nô móre
    Góin' âwáy bábŷ | cómiñg hére nô móre
    You know you sure is mean you thrown my trunk out-door.

20. Walter Taylor, "Thirty-Eight and Plus" (Gennett 7157, 1930), st. 6.
    Góin' âwáy prèttŷ mámâ | wón't bê báck tîll Fáll
    If I don't get back then I won't be back at all.

21. Hi Henry Brown, "Skin Man" (Vocalion 1692, 1932), st. 3.
    Well it's skins oh skins | skin skin skin skin
    Well it's skins it's skins | skin skin skin
    I'ṁ gôin' âwáy ôld skín bût I'm | cómìn' báck âgáin.

22. Henry Thomas, "Don't Leave Me Here," st. 5.
    Sâys I'ṁ gòin' âwáy | ánd ît wón't bê lóng
    Just as sure as the train leaves out of the yard
    She's Alabama bound.

23. Lewis Black, "Rock Island Blues" (Columbia 14429-D, 1927), st. 7.
    Said mmm-well-mm-well-well I'm | máke ît lónesôme hére
    Sâys Î'm góin' âwáy | máke ît lónesôme hére
    Sâys Î'm góin' âwáy mámà máke ît lónesôme hére.

24. Lonnie Coleman, "Old Rock Island Blues" (Columbia 14440-D, 1929), st. 5.
    Wêll Î'm góin' âwáy | aîn't cómîn' hére nô móre
    Î'm góin' âwáy | aîn't cómîn' hére nô móre
    [      ] hang crepe on your door.

25. Tommy Johnson, "Bye-Bye Blues" (Victor 21409, 1928), st. 3.
    Wêll I'ṁ góin' âwáy | wón't bê báck tîll Fáll
    I'm góin' âwáy Lórd | bábŷ wón't bê báck tîll Fáll
    If I meet my good gal then baby won't be back at all.

26. Otto Virgial, "Little Girl in Rome" (Bluebird B6213, 1935), st. 3.
    Wêll Î'm góin' wáy-âwáy tô | wéar yôu óff m̂hy mínd
    'Cause you keep me worryin' bothered all the time
    Î'm gòin' wáy-âwáy tô | wéar yôu óff m̂hy mínd

27. Papa Charlie Jackson, "Shave Em Dry" (Paramount 12264, 1925), st. 3.
    Nòw Î'm góin' âwáy | tô wéar yôu óff mŷ mínd
    You keep me broke and hungry mama all the time . . .

28. Kid Cole, "Hey Hey Mama Blues" (Vocalion 1186, 1928), st. 5.
    Añd Î'm góin' âwáy | â-prèttŷ mámâ cŕyin' ît wón't bê lóng
    Añd Î'm góin' âwáy | prèttŷ mámâ crýin' ît wón't bê lóng (2)
    Get your typewriter mama and type the [    ] days I'm gone.

29. Kid Cole, "Hard Hearted Mama Blues" (Vocalion 1187, 1928), st. 7.
    Añd Î'm góin' âwáy | lîttle bábŷ crýin' ît wón't bê lóng
        Lórd ît wón't bê lóng
    Î'm góin' âwáy | lîttle bábŷ crýin' ît wón't bê lóng
    Said take your bible pretty mama and read the days your daddy's gone.

30. Charlie Kyle, "Kyle's Worried Blues," st. 6.
    Lórd Î'm góin' âwáy | hónêy hôw cán Î stáy?
    Î'm góin' âwáy | hónêy hôw cán Î stáy?
    I can't be downhearted mistreated this-away.

31. Papa Charlie Jackson, "The Faking Blues" (Paramount 12281, 1925), st. 4.
    Lórd Î'm gôin' âwáy mámâ | b'líeve mé ît aín't nô stáll (2)
    'Cause I can get more women that a passenger train can haul.

32. Son House, "Low Down Dirty Dog Blues" (Lib. Congress AAFS L-59, 1942), st. 4.
    Mmmm Lòrd Î'm góin' âwáy bábŷ | I'm̂ gôin' stày â gréat lóng tíme
    Ohhhhhh | Î sày Î'm gôin' stáy â gréat lóng tíme
    You know I ain't comin' back now honey oooh-babe until you change your mind.

33. Jabo Williams, "Fat Mama Blues" (Paramount 13130, 1932), st. 5.
    Sâys Î'm góin' âwày mámâ | bábŷ dón't yòu cŕy
    Î'm góin' âwày mámâ | dón't yòu cŕy Lòrd
    Î'm góin' âwày mámâ | plèase dón't yòu cŕy
    Î'm góin' âwày mámâ | bábŷ dón't yòu cŕy
    I will be back by and by.

34. Jabo Williams, "Fat Mama Blues," st. 7.
    Sàys Î'm góin' âwày mámâ | Î âm góin' tô stáy
    Î âm góin' âwày mámâ | góin' tô stáy Lòrd
    Î'm góin' âwày mámâ | góin' tô stáy
    Them big legs baby gonna keep me away
    Them big legs goin' keep me away.

35. Cannon's Jug Stompers "Springdale Blues" (Victor 21351, 1928), st. 1.
    Sàid Î'm góin' âwáy mámâ | wéar yôu óff mŷ mínd
    Lòrd Î'm góin' âwáy mámâ | wéar yôu óff mŷ mínd
    You keep me worried and bothered baby lordy all the time.

36. Cannon's Jug Stompers, "Springdale Blues," st. 2.
   Sàid Ỉ'm góin' âwáy báby̆ | cátch tħe Hólly̆wòod líne
   Sàid Ỉ'm góin' oût hére nòw | cátch tħe Hólly̆wòod líne . . .

37. Kid Cole, "Sixth Street Moan" (Vocalion 1186, 1928), st. 4.
   Aħd Ỉ'm góin' âwáy mámâ | báby̆ swéar ît wón't bê lóng
   —Oh doany don't you want to go along?—
   Aħd Ỉ'm góin' âwáy brównskìn | hónêy ît wón't bê lóng
   And I swear you goin' miss your Kid Cole baby baby when I'm gone.

38. Lewis Black, "Rock Island Blues," st. 3.
   Wêll Ỉ'm góin' âwáy mámâ | wón't bê báck tîll Fáll
   Sây̆s Ỉ'm góin' âwáy mámà | wón't bê báck tîll Fáll
   And if I get kind of lucky won't be back at all.

39. Mooch Richardson, "T and T Blues" (OKeh 8554, 1928), st. 4.
   Wêll Ỉ'm gòin' âwáy brównskìn | Ỉ aìn't gônnâ côme bâck hêre bêfôre nèxt Fáll
   Wêll Ỉ'm gòin' âwáy brównskìn Ỉ | áin't cômîng bâck hêre bêfôre nèxt Fáll
   If I don't get no good brown I ain't comin' back in this town at all.

40. Skip James, "Cyprus Grove Blues" (Paramount 13088, 1931), st. 2.
   Wêll Ỉ'm góin' âwáy nòw | góin' âwáy tô stáy (2)
   That'll be alright pretty mama you gonna need my help some day.

41. Tommy Johnson, "Maggie Campbell Blues" (Victor 21409, 1928), st. 4.
   Wêll Ỉ'm góin' âwáy Lórd | wón't bê báck tîll Fáll | wón't bê | báck tîll Fáll
   Wêll Ỉ'm góin' âwáy Lórd | wón't bê báck tîll Fáll
   And if I meet my good gal mama won't be back at all.

42. Son House, "Special Rider Blues" (Lib. Congress AAFS L-59, 1942), st. 1.
   Wêll Ỉ'm góin' âwáy hónêy | Ỉ wón't bê báck nô mόre
   When I leave this time I'm goin' hang crepe on your door.

43. Roosevelt Sykes, "As True As I've Been to You" (Victor 23286, 1931), st. 4.
   Ỉ'm gôin' âwáy tô leáve yóu | Ỉ knòw tħe mén wîll bê glád íf Ỉ dó (2)
   Because as long as I'm round here they can't get a fair break at you.

44. Curley Weaver, "Oh Lawdy Mama" (Champion 50077, 1935), st. 8.
   Gòin' âwáy t'leáve yòu | crýin' wôn't máke mê stáy
   —Oh lawdy mama great God almighty—
   Gòin' âwáy t'leáve yòu | crýin' wôn't máke mê stáy
   I may be back in June baby may be back in first of May.

45. Furry Lewis, "Mr. Furry's Blues" (Vocalion 1115, 1927), st. 5.
   Some of these mornings baby listen to what I say (2)
   Ỉ'm góin' âwáy tô léave yòu | ît wíll bê tôo láte tô práy.

46. Blind Lemon Jefferson, "Broke and Hungry" (Paramount 12443, 1926), st. 3.
   You miss me woman why count the days I'm gone
   You miss me woman count the days I'm gone
   I'm góin' âwáy tô búild mè â | ráilròad ôf my̆ ówn

47. Lewis Black, "Gravel Camp Blues" (Columbia 14291-D, 1927), st. 1.
 . . . góin' oùt ón thê cúe
 Sâid Î'm gòin' âwáy tômór' mámâ | góin' oût ón tĥe cúe
 And if I find anything comin' back after you.

48. Frank Stokes, "What's the Matter Blues" (Victor V38531, 1928), st. 3.
 Añd Î'm góin' dòwn tówn | gònnâ stày rôund thére tîll Fáll
 Añd Î'm góin' dòwn tówn gónnâ stáy roûnd thére tîll Fáll
 Don't get the gal I want I don't want no girls at all.

---

[1] See A. B. Lord, *The Singer of Tales* (1960, rpt. New York: Atheneum, 1968). Parry's pioneering studies are collected in *The Making of Homeric Verse*, ed. A. Parry (Oxford: Oxford Univ. Press, 1971).

[2] For the latter see Bruce A. Rosenberg, *The Art of the American Folk Preacher* (New York: Oxford, 1970).

[3] Jeff Titon, *Early Downhome Blues: A Musical and Cultural Analysis* (Urbana: Univ. of Illinois Press, 1977), ch. 5. I am most grateful to Titon and Taft for generously allowing me to read their work in typescript and for their detailed criticisms of an earlier draft of this paper.

[4] *Blues from the Delta* (London: Studio Vista, 1970), pp. 34ff.

[5] *Charley Patton* (London: Studio Vista, 1970), p. 58f.

[6] Ibid., p. 65. Paul Oliver, *Screening the Blues* (London: Cassell, 1968), p. 18 observes: "Often a single line rather than a verse reappears in numerous contexts; sometimes even a single phrase. Maverick lines that move from blues to blues are given new rhymes and new meaning by their juxtaposition with other ideas, while they retain the quality of surprise." He is describing, without apparently being fully aware of it, the process of oral-formulaic composition.

[7] M. Parry, "Studies in the Epic Technique of Oral Verse-Making," in *The Making of Homeric Verse*, p. 272.

[8] *The Singer of Tales*, p. 4.

[9] Parry, "Studies," p. 275.

[10] See, e.g., Ferris Jr., *Blues from the Delta*, pp. 34, 36; Oliver, *Screening the Blues*, pp. 17f.

[11] *The Singer of Tales*, p. 4.

[12] Ferris Jr., p. 34. He is presumably using "verse" here in the sense of "stanza" rather than "metrical line" since on p. 36 he writes: "The stanzas . . . are the fundamental unit of black song, and it is through their study rather than through patterns of narrative development that black song style can be understood." Cf. Samuel Charters, *The Poetry of the Blues* (New York: Oak, 1963), p. 14 who makes the same claim.

[13] Michael Taft, "I WOKE UP THIS MORNING: A Transformational-Generative Approach to the Formulaic Structure of Blues Lyrics" (Unpubl. paper deliv. at the annual meeting of the American Folklore Society, Austin, Texas, 1972), and Titon, *Early Downhome Blues*, ch. 5, demonstrate this clearly. Ferris Jr., *Blues from the Delta*, pp. 34ff and 58 has asserted that formulas are closely related to tunes. This is based on his assumption that the unit of the formula is the stanza. The argument seems to me invalid however if the basic unit of the formula is the half-line. Formulas such as *I woke up this morning* and *I'm going away* are too widely distributed within the blues tradition to be discussed meaningfully in the context of tune patterns.

[14] The blues are certainly not composed in iambic pentameters as Oliver casually remarks in *Screening the Blues*, p. 18.

[15] It should be noted that the distinction between stress and half-stress is at times a difficult one, and is bound to be arbitrary to some extent.

[16] Barefoot Bill, "Bad Boy" (Columbia 14526-D, 1930) st. 2. For an extended use of unstressed syllables see appendix, example 39, 1[b].

[17] For a convenient description see T. A. Shippey, *Old English Verse* (London: Hutchinson, 1972), pp. 101ff and, on the oral-formulaic theory, pp. 89ff.

[18] Big Boy Cleveland, "Goin' to Leave You Blues," st. 2; Stovepipe No. 1, "Court Street Blues," st. 1. See also examples 1–12 in the appendix.

[19] In a written communication, Titon has suggested to me that the demands of the tune may sometimes cause the singer to "wrench stress away from a normally accented syllable and place it on a normally unaccented syllable." Whether or not one agrees with this depends on one's definition of the essential components of stress in language; but if Titon is correct, its relevance to the metrics of oral formulas in the blues is obvious. The problem is a complex one however, beyond the scope of this paper, and I would refer the reader to Titon's account of the phenomenon in *Early Downhome Blues*.

[20] Tom Dickson, "Happy Blues," st. 6; Henry Thomas, "Bull Doze Blues," st. 1. See also examples 13–20 and 31–42.

[21] Blind Lemon Jefferson, "Lonesome House Blues," st. 2; Charley Patton, "When Your Way Gets Dark," st. 6. See also examples 14 and 16. This is a metrical variant favoured by Patton, which may explain his unusual adoption of a single stress half-line in "Down the Dirt Road Blues" (example 7). This is extremely rare. In the vast majority of cases, two stresses represent an obligatory basis for the formula.

[22] Examples 43–7 represent different formulas within the larger system based on the general idea of going away. 43–6 are interesting in that the basic idea is expanded to include an account of the singer's motive in leaving: something which is normally expressed in 1$^b$.

[23] I am aware of course that there are other ways in which the singer may do this.

[24] (1) *won't be back till Fall* 10, 20, 25, 38, 39, 41, 48; *coming here no more* 19, 24, 42; *going to stay* 34, 40; *possible non-formulaic phrases* 14, 21, 32. (2) *wear you off my mind* 1, 2, 18, 26, 27, 35; *make it lonesome here* 8, 12, 23; *possible non-formulaic phrases* 7, 11, 36, 46, 47. (3) *don't you want to go?* 9, 15, 16; *possible non-formulaic phrases* 30, 31, 33, 44, 45. (4) *won't be long* 3, 4, 5, 17, 22, 28, 29, 37.

[25] A. Lewis Black, "Rock Island Blues," B. Charlie Kyle, "Kyle's Worried Blues," C. Cannon's Jug Stompers, "Springdale Blues," D. Jabo Williams, "Fat Mama Blues."

[26] Cf. examples 19, 24 and 42.

[27] Fall/all 20, 25, 38, 39, 41 (cf. 48). More/door 24, 42 (cf. 19).

[28] Tommy Johnson, "Cool Drink of Water Blues" (Victor 21279, 1928), st. 2; Charley Patton, "Green River Blues (Paramount 12972, 1929), st. 4.

# The Battle of Harlaw
## Francis James Child, Editor

*Between 1882 and 1898, Francis James Child published what he considered to be a definitive collection of English and Scottish ballads. He included only those ballads he felt to be "popular"; that is, anonymous, old, narrative songs that were orally composed and transmitted. Child was not a fieldworker, so he relied on old manuscript collections, printed texts, and reports from various individuals who transcribed texts directly from singers for his ballad sources. His collection aimed toward completeness and included three hundred and five ballad types with their known variants.*

*Below is the A text of the one hundred and sixty-third ballad in Child's collection, which concerns the battle fought at Harlaw. For an overview of the nature of the traditional ballad see Gerould (1957). Wilgus (1959) provides a detailed history of the folksong scholarship that was initiated or stimulated by Child's opus. Analyses of traditional ballads as well as contemporary oral poetry can be found in Renwick (1980).*

*a.* Communicated by Charles Elphinstone Dalrymple, Esq., of Kinaldie, Aberdeenshire, in 1888, as obtained from the country people by himself and his brother, fifty years before.
*b.* Notes and Queries, Third Series, VII, 393, communicated by A. Ferguson.

1    As I cam in by Dunidier,
        An doun by Netherha,
    There was fifty thousand Hielanmen
        A-marching to Harlaw.
    Wi a dree dree dradie drumtie dree.

2    As I cam on, an farther on,
        An doun an by Balquhain,
    Oh there I met Sir James the Rose,
        Wi him Sir John the Gryme.

3    'O cam ye frae the Hielans, man?
        An cam ye a' the wey?
    Saw ye Macdonell an his men,
        As they cam frae the Skee?'

Reprinted from *English and Scottish Popular Ballads*, Vol. 3, ed. Francis James Child (New York: Dover Publications, 1965), 318–19.

4 'Yes, me cam frae ta Hielans, man,
    An me cam a' ta wey,
An she saw Macdonell an his men,
    As they cam frae ta Skee.'

5 'Oh was ye near Macdonell's men?
    Did ye their numbers see?
Come, tell to me, John Hielanman,
    What micht their numbers be?'

6 'Yes, me was near, an near eneuch,
    An me their numbers saw;
There was fifty thousan Hielanmen
    A-marchin to Harlaw.'

7 'Gin that be true,' says James the Rose,
    'We'll no come meikle speed;
We'll cry upo our merry men,
    And lichtly mount our steed.'

8 Oh no, oh no,' says John the Gryme,
    'That thing maun never be;
The gallant Grymes were never bate,
    We'll try phat we can dee.'

9 As I cam on, an farther on,
    An doun an by Harlaw,
They fell fu close on ilka side;
    Sic fun ye never saw.

10 They fell fu close on ilka side,
    Sic fun ye never saw;
For Hielan swords gied clash for clash,
    At the battle o Harlaw.

11 The Hielanmen, wi their lang swords,
    They laid on us fu sair,
An they drave back our merry men
    Three acres breadth an mair.

12 Brave Forbës to his brither did say,
    Noo brither, dinna ye see?
They beat us back on ilka side,
    An we'se be forced to flee.

13 'Oh no, oh no, my brither dear,
    That thing maun never be;
Tak ye your good sword in your hand,
    An come your wa's wi me.'

14 "Oh no, oh no, my brither dear,
    The clans they are ower strang,
An they drive back our merry men,
    Wi swords baith sharp an lang.'

15 Brave Forbës drew his men aside,
    Said, Tak your rest a while,
Until I to Drumminnor send,
    To fess my coat o mail.

16 The servan he did ride,
    An his horse it did na fail,
For in twa hours an a quarter
    He brocht the coat o mail.

17 Then back to back the brithers twa
    Gaed in amo the thrang,
An they hewed down the Hielanmen,
    Wi swords baith sharp an lang.

18 Macdonell, he was young an stout,
    Had on his coat o mail,
An he has gane oot throw them a',
    To try his han himsell.

19 The first ae straik that Forbës strack,
    He garrt Macdonell reel,
An the neist ae straik that Forbës strack,
    The great Macdonell fell.

20 An siccan a lierachie
    I'm sure ye never saw
As wis amo the Hielanmen,
    When they saw Macdonell fa.

21 An whan they saw that he was deid,
    They turnd an ran awa,
An they buried him in Leggett's Den,
    A large mile frae Harlaw.

Francis James Child

22  They rade, they ran, an some did gang,
        They were o sma record;
    But Forbës an his merry men,
        They slew them a' the road.

23  On Monanday, at mornin,
        The battle it began,
    On Saturday, at gloamin,
        Ye'd scarce kent wha had wan.

24  An sic a weary buryin
        I'm sure ye never saw
    As wis the Sunday after that,
        On the muirs aneath Harlaw.

25  Gin ony body speer at you
        For them ye took awa,
    Ye may tell their wives and bairnies
        They're sleepin at Harlaw.

# History and Harlaw

David D. Buchan

*On July 24, 1411, Donald of the Isles and his force of Highlanders moved on Aberdeen. They were stopped eighteen miles to the northwest, at Harlaw, by a force of Lowlanders under the Earl of Mar. Over four hundred years later a ballad was written down and published in Scotland. To what extent does this ballad text reflect events that took place at Harlaw on that day? Francis James Child felt that the ballad was a more recent Lowland composition (Child 1965: 3:317) with little historical value. In his essay, David D. Buchan suggests that Child and others may have dismissed the ballad account too readily, with the ballad perhaps being more historical than previously imagined.*

*The historicity of oral tradition in general and of individual texts in particular has been vociferously debated by a number of scholars over the years. Lowie (1917) and Raglan (1956:3–44) have been particularly hostile to the idea that oral traditions may be considered in any way a trustworthy historical source. Vansina (1965) has argued, however, that an oral account is like any other purportedly historical document. All documents need to be individually examined and evaluated according to explicit scientific criteria. Montell (1970) is a folklorist who has valued the historical potential of oral traditional sources. One overview of the debate over the trustworthiness of oral tradition can be found in Dorson (1972).*

*The position of many folklorists on the relationship of folklore and history is represented by Wilson (1973). For other inquiries into the historical basis of particular ballads see Fife (1953), Hoffman (1952), and Wachs (1978).*

In the introduction to the ballad numbered 163 in his collection, Francis James Child wrote, "A ballad taken down some four hundred years after the event will be apt to retain very little of sober history."[1] And with this view most critics have concurred. In fact, it has even hardened into an axiom and on occasion has produced the paradoxical situation where ballads which are untrustworthy as history are reckoned, ipso facto, trustworthy as ballads, and ballads which are trustworthy as history are looked at askance as probable fabrications. At any rate, that statement of Child's expresses our general attitude toward the historical ballads: they are not to be taken seriously as history. A consideration of one particular historical ballad would suggest, however that a too easy acceptance of such an attitude would be rather rash. The ballad in question is

Reproduced by permission of the publisher, from *Journal of the Folklore Institute* 5, no. 1 (1968):58–67. Not for further reproduction.

David D. Buchan

"The Battle of Harlaw," which is dismissed by Child as a "comparatively recent" production, a view which has become standard among subsequent editors and critics.

As the *A*-text of this ballad, Child prints what amounts to one version, which originated from Charles Elphinstone Dalrymple of Kinaldie; this version would have been recorded just before 1840. As his *B*-text he prints the three stanzas in the 1823 "Thistle of Scotland," which was compiled by the Aberdeen printer and chapman, Alexander Laing. Child's rather meager haul was expanded greatly when Gavin Greig's collection was published, for it includes no fewer than nine more versions, all, like the previous, from Aberdeenshire. The editor of the Greig collection, Alexander Keith, reinforces the Child viewpoint: "Amid all the variations in the already printed versions and in our records, there is a distinct and unusual correspondence of stanza with stanza, whereas long tradition should have left more and greater changes in so many versions." The ballad of the Battle of Harlaw, says Keith, is "largely unhistorical."[2]

The battle itself was fought in Aberdeenshire in 1411, and in its way was a battle of no little importance. An older generation of Scottish historians used to see it as a battle for the domination of Scotland, the battle which determined once and for all whether Lowland Scotland was to be predominantly Celtic or predominantly Anglo-Saxon, but this opinion has been modified by modern historians. They are inclined to see it in more medieval terms as the result of a feudal squabble over land, specifically, the Earldom of Ross. The major claimant for this earldom was Donald, Lord of the Isles, who, fearing the rapacity of the then Regent of Scotland, the Duke of Albany, collected a large army of Highlanders and set out to occupy the earldom's lands in the Northeast. The people who had most to lose from this incursion were the burgesses of Aberdeen who, fearing the rapacity of Donald and his caterans, helped organize a large body of Lowlanders under the leadership of Alexander Stewart, Earl of Mar, to protect the Northeast. The provenance of the troops, and the edict, customary after a battle of national importance, that the heir of any man killed at Harlaw was to receive his ward, relief, and marriage free from the king, would seem to suggest that the struggle, if not for the domination of Scotland, was viewed by contemporary Lowlanders as a more than local defense of Lowland Saxon prosperity against the onslaught of Highland barbarism. The battle, later known as "Red Harlaw," was bloody and lasted an entire day with, at the end of it, no apparent result. The next morning, however, the Highlanders were nowhere to be seen, so victory lay technically with the Lowlanders.[3]

Child's objections to the historicity of the ballad rest on three major counts. Firstly, there are stanzas 15 and 16:

> Brave Forbës drew his men aside,
>   Said, Tak your rest a while,
> Until I to Drumminnor send,
>   To fess my coat o mail.
>
> The servan he did ride,
>   An his horse it did na fail,
> For in twa hours an a quarter
>   He brocht the coat o mail.

These, says Child, "have a dash of the unheroic and . . . may fairly be regarded as wanton depravations." Secondly, there are stanzas 21 and 22, which, contrary to the known facts, describe the Highlanders as being routed:

> An whan they saw that he was deid, [Macdonell]
>    They turnd an ran awa,
>
> . . . . . . . . . . . . . . . . . . . . . . . . . .
>
> They rade, they ran, and some did gang,
>    They were o sma record;
> But Forbës an his merry men,
>    They slew them a' the road.

The next stanza, with disconcerting inconsistency, says what does accord with the known facts, that "at gloamin, / Ye'd scarce kent wha had wan." And thirdly, there is the prominence of the Forbeses. Child comments:

> The ignoring of so marked a personage as Mar and other men of high local distinction that fell in the battle in favor of the Forbeses, who, although already of consequence in Aberdeenshire, are not recorded to have taken any part in the fight, is perhaps more than might have been looked for, and must dispose us to believe that this particular ballad had its rise in comparatively recent times.

Any consideration of the battle, and consequently of the ballad, is complicated by the dearth of relevant records, but the foremost historian of the Northeast of Scotland, Dr. Douglas Simpson, has, on the basis of the material available, reconstructed the campaign and the battle in his book *The Earldom of Mar*. This reconstruction sheds much light on the problems raised by Child. To take the last objection first: Dr. Simpson points out that the Forbeses were the Earl of Mar's most powerful vassals in the Northeast, and that, given the nature of feudal obligations, it would be inconceivable that they would not play a significant part in the campaign. This belief is reinforced by a long-standing family tradition among the Aberdeenshire Forbeses that they rendered signal service to Mar on this occasion.[4] It can be safely assumed that the Forbeses took part in the battle. What then of the other two objections? How do we account for the leader of the Lowlanders breaking off the fighting to send to Drumminor, the head seat of the Forbeses, for a coat of mail that take two hours in the coming, but on arrival makes the crucial difference between defeat and victory?

    Dr. Simpson indicates that though Mar knew Donald's destination, the burgh of Aberdeen, he would not know Donald's approach route, whether he would come through the Garioch or through the Rhynie Gap into the Glen of Brux. As Mar could not cover both approaches by falling back on the city without leaving the Lowlands open to the ravages of the caterans, he would have to try to block both the approach routes at the points where the Highlanders would debouch on the Lowlands. He stationed himself, as we know, at Harlaw, to block the first route. The second route, through the Rhynie Gap, would bring Donald out at the lands of Brux, and these lands belonged to the Forbeses. So the obvious thing for Mar to do would be to leave his strongest vasals on their own land to block this second route. When Mar realized that Donald had chosen the first route he would have to send a messenger to the Forbeses to bring them hotfoot to Harlaw. They would, of course, arrive late, but ready for the second stage of the battle, and could claim, like Blucher a few hundred years later, that their extra numbers had made the decisive difference in the outcome of the battle. This falls into two stages, and why the sending to Drumminor had such a crucial effect on the way the battle went. It would also dissolve the remaining objection of Child by explaining away the apparent incongruity of stanzas 21, 22, and 23. The ballad was obviously composed from a Forbes viewpoint, that is, it deals largely with the part played by one section of the Lowland army. If this section arrived at the battlefield with the advantage of surprise and comparative freshness it would probably have the upper hand over the wearied wing of the enemy that it attacked. This, at Harlaw, would give us stanzas 21 and 22, in which the Forbeses rout their immediate opponents. This victory on one wing would satisfactorily relieve the pressure on the rest of the army, but, as the rest of the army was in dire straits, it would not automatically produce a large-scale victory. What we have, in effect, in stanzas 21 and 22, and then 23, are two camera shots: the close-up of the Forbes victory on one wing and the long shot of the battle as a whole. Ironically, then, the points which Child adduced as evidence of the ballad's youth are in fact the points which would indicate that the ballad reflects with a fair degree of accuracy the actual pattern of events, as far as we can ascertain what that pattern was, in the battle itself.

Though Child's objections are the major ones, other details in the ballad have evoked sceptical responses. The sceptic would say that the entire first scene is quite out of tone with the rest of the ballad. Instead of preparing us for a cataclysmic encounter, it concentrates on burlesquing a Highlander's attempt to speak Scots, an effect reinforced by the refrain which imitates the skirl and drone of the pipes. Again, the sceptic can point to the fact that the opponents of the Highlanders are referred to at some place in most of the records as "redcoats," an anachronism of a few hundred years, and declare the ballad merely an unhistorical palimpsest. Now if, instead of dismissing the whole thing as a farrago, we accept the basic premise that the ballad does reflect, although sometimes in a Hall of Mirrors fashion, the actual pattern of events in the battle, and look at the unhistoricities in the light of this, there is a chance that we might find out something about the nature of the folk imagination and the ways it operated upon its material.

To understand the nature of the two peculiarities, the burlesquing and the redcoats, one must first consider the relations between the Highlands and the Northeast Lowlands. It is a fact insufficiently recognized outside its borders that Scotland has contained for much of its history two nations, with different social organizations, different customs, different languages, and a mutual distrust. The Northeast was a border region, abutting the Highlands, which naturally brought the folk of the Northeast into contact, mainly warlike but sometimes commercial, with the Highlanders. In the eyes of the northeasterner, the Highlander was to be feared because of his depredations, but he was also looked upon as a rather comic fellow, wild yet courteous, proud yet naive, whose comic side became very pronounced when he tried to grapple with the foreign tongue of Lowland Scots. The Lowland attitude is eloquently summed up in the Scots word for the John Hielanman stereotype—he is a "tyeuchter." This dual view of the Highlander as at once a feared raider and a comic figure runs right through Scottish literature from Dunbar to Fergusson. I need only mention the famous poem from the Bannatyne Manuscript, "How the First Hielandman was Made by God of ane Horse Turd," with its incisive quatrain:

> God turned owre the horse turd with his pykit staff,
> And up start a Hielandman black as ony draff.
> Quod God to the Hielandman, "Where wilt thou now?"
> "I will doun in the Lawland, Lord, and there steal a cow."[5]

This is the attitude that is reflected in the first scene of the ballad, which, while burlesquing John Hielanman, uses a number of repetitive devices to remind us that the Highlanders are "A-marchin tae Harlaw." In short, the first scene is, *inter alia*, a correlative for the Lowland folk's emotional attitude to the Highlanders.

What about the redcoats? It would appear that the folk had conflated two incursions of Highlandmen more than three hundred years apart, in 1411 and 1745. Can we, however, just leave it at that? What were the reasons for this conflation? These two incursions were alike in being exceptional; they were no mere forays, but of national as well as regional importance. And yet this explanation is far from being satisfactory. There was one large difference between the two incursions: in 1411 the Northeast was united in arms against the Celts, but in 1745 the Northeast was comparatively passive, watching a struggle between Charles's Highlanders and the Government's redcoats, more than half of whom were Hanoverian mercenaries. The Highlanders were unpopular, but the Government levies were equally disliked. This difference is interestingly reflected in Greig's *A*-text, recorded at the beginning of this century. In most versions of the ballad the opening stanza runs something like this:

> As I cam in by Dunidier,
>   An doun by Netherha,
> There was fifty thousand Hielanmen
>   A-marching to Harlaw.

It is followed by a series of stanzas designed to give an impressionistic effect of the Hielanmen's march forward. In Greig's *A*-text, however, the opening stanza reads:

> As I cam in the Geerie lan's,
>   An' in by Netherha',
> I saw sixty thoosan redcoats
>   A' marchin to Harlaw.

and is followed five stanzas later by:

> O yes, me was near them,
>   An' me their number saw;
> There was ninety thoosan Hielanmen
>   A' marchin to Harlaw.

This repetition effectively suggests a disengagement, a watching of two armies. The way in which this new view of the battle, as a fight between Highlanders and redcoats rather than Highlanders and Lowlanders, was infiltrating the old can also be seen in Dalrymple's version. His stanza 11 reads:

> The Hielanmen, wi their lang swords,
>   They laid on us fu sair,
> An they drave back our merry men
>   Three acres breadth an mair.

He gives as a variant for the third line, "An they drave back our merry men," "An they drave back the redcoats." Here again, emotional commitment to one side against the other gives way to objectivity.

There is a shift in the emotional attitudes implicit in the ballad. It would seem that a ballad dealing with the 1411 encounter was in the process of being altered to a ballad dealing with the 1745 encounter. Why should this have happened? After the 1745 rebellion and the breakup of the clan system by the Heritable Jurisdictions Act of 1747, relations between the Northeast and the Highlands altered decisively. The Highlanders were driven by economic necessity to come to social terms with the Lowlanders, and, though it took a considerable time, the old barriers of suspicion and distrust were gradually broken down. In brief, the attitude of the Lowland folk to the Highlanders changed, and the ballad reflects the change in attitude. The earlier event was a suitable correlative for the earlier attitude of the folk to the Highlanders, but unsuitable for the later attitude; the newer event, however, was a suitable correlative for the new, more neutral attitude. The supersession of the one event by the other is not merely gratuitous; it answers the folk's need for different correlatives for different emotional attitudes.[6]

The ballad, then, despite the initial impression it is likely to give, is historical in a rather extraordinary way. If reflects, although in blurred fashion, what is reckoned to be the actual pattern of events in the battle, and this pattern, it is worth remarking, is not recorded in any known document, but only in the ballad. What appears to be the ballad's largest unhistoricity actually reflects the kind of historical truth that normally never finds its way into the documents, the nature and quality of the folk's emotional purposes, the raw material of historical event.

Child's objections can now be seen in perspective, but there still remains Keith's argument that if the ballad were really old there would be much greater variation in the recorded versions. To solve this problem one must trace a hypothetical history of the ballad. The ballad was composed soon after the events of 1411 and must have gained some acceptance, for in 1549 the *Complaynte of Scotland* mentions it, and references to the tune crop up in various places in the seventeenth and eighteenth centuries. It was first recorded in the early 1820's by Alexander Laing; and with Laing we have the key to the problem. Laing made his living both as printer and as chapman. In his latter capacity, he traveled round Aberdeenshire selling pins, ribbons, and chapbooks and prints to the farm servants, and while on his travels he would pick up from his customers some of their songs, which, on his return to Aberdeen, he would print up, publish, and sell back to his rural clientele; it was a cycle for everybody's benefit. Laing, we know, was the first man to collect the ballad. He would print only three stanzas of this "burlesque" in the *Thistle of Scotland* because the book was for him a prestige publication, a genteel and scholarly production, but he also, I suggest, would prosecute his normal practice and hawk the ballad in printed single-sheets round the farm servants of Aberdeenshire. The versions of the ballad which we have, then, are not versions of a ballad composed near 1411, but versions of the one record of that 1411 ballad collected by Laing and disseminated in his usual fashion through Aberdeenshire.

The historical ballad, it would appear, is perhaps more historical than it has been given credit for. But is "The Battle of Harlaw" an isolated case? A brief glance at another Aberdeenshire ballad, "Edom o Gordon," would suggest not. After careful consideration of the historical authorities, Child decided that Towie castle had been the scene of the event described in the ballad, in which choice he has been followed by every editor. Dr. Douglas Simpson, however, has shown that the locale could not have been Towie castle as it was not built until the seventeenth century, and that the scene was in fact Corgarff castle. Scrutiny of the five local versions of the ballad would lead one to the same locale. Not one of the five refers to Towie castle. Child *E* has Cargarff, and Greig *B* and *C* both have Corgraff. Grieg *B* has also a reference to Cragie, while Child *H*, collected from the Southwest, speaks of Craigie North. These two words, "Cragie" and "Craigie", are probably contracted and metathesized renderings of Carriegill, or Corriehoul, the demesne lands of Corgarff. The confusion has presumably arisen from misinterpretation of phrases like the one that occurs in Greig *A*—"Towie's hoose." In the Northeast of Scotland it is still customary in rural districts to refer to a man by the land he owns or farms rather than by his surname; after this fashion, Geordie Smith, the tenant-farmer of Cairnmore, is normally referred to as "Cairnmore." The phrase "Towie's hoose" does not, therefore, pertain to an actual edifice named Towie, but simply to the residence of Towie himself, or, to give him his full due, John Forbes of Towie. In locating the event at Corgarff, the Northeast versions of "Edom o Gordon" are in accordance with the findings of modern research. Again it would seem that a historical ballad can be more accurate historically than we generally anticipate.[7]

The historical ballads, we would all agree, are no "documents," but the evidence just presented would indicate that they can be much nearer to the truth than is normally realized. They can contain factual truths that are not found in the often scanty records, and they can contain emotional truths, the attitudes and reactions of the ballad-singing folk to the world around them. Given the nature of these emotional truths, it might prove fruitful to investigate historical ballads along joint aesthetic and sociological lines, since this ballad has shown how a historical event is made to serve as an aesthetic

David D. Buchan

correlative, an aesthetic correlative which fulfills a certain sociological function in that it focuses the emotional conceptions of a particular culture. Given the nature of the factual truths, the moral in general would seem to be: "Gyang cannily, and look closer." At any rate, we can no longer hold it as axiomatic that "the historical ballads fly in the face of all history."

---

[1] *The English and Scottish Popular Ballads*, III (Boston, 1888), p. 317. All subsequent allusions to Child's versions of, or comments on, "Harlaw" refer to III, 316–320.

[2] *Last Leaves of Traditional Ballads and Ballad Airs* (Aberdeen, 1925), p. 102. Two other versions that I know of have been recorded for the School of Scottish Studies by Hamish Henderson, and the other is the version recorded by Kenneth S. Goldstein from the singing of Lucy Stewart and available on Folkways FG3519.

[3] W. C. Dickinson, G. Donaldson, and I. A. Milne, *A Source Book of Scottish History*, I (Edinburgh, 1958), 168–170; W. C. Dickinson, *From the Earliest Times to 1603, A New History of Scotland*, I (London, 1961), pp. 202–203.

[4] (Aberdeen, 1949), pp. 49–53. Two recent historians, Dickinson, p. 202, and Fenton Wyness, *City by the Grey North Sea: Aberdeen* (Aberdeen, 1965), p. 129, state, though without indicating their sources, that the Forbeses took part in the battle.

[5] M. M. Gray, ed., *Scottish Poetry from Barbour to James VI* (London, 1935), p. 243.

[6] For relations between the Northeast and the Highlands see William Watt, *A History of Aberdeen and Banff* (Edinburgh, 1900); James Allardyce, ed., *Papers Relating to the Jacobite Period 1699-1750*, 2 vols. (Aberdeen, 1895-96); and the relevant parish accounts in Sir John Sinclair, ed., *The Statistical Account of Scotland*, 21 vols. (Edinburgh, 1791-97), and J. Gordon, ed., *New Statistical Account of Scotland*, 18 vols. (Edinburgh, 1843). One coincidental factor which could have facilitated the ballad's shift in historical focus was the association in the popular mind of the Forbeses with the established government; from 1715 to 1745 the foremost adherent of the Hanoverian house in the North of Scotland was a Forbes, Duncan Forbes of Culloden.

[7] III, 424–428; Simpson, pp. 145–146; Greig, pp. 110–112.

# VIII
# Riddles and Proverbs

## "Wine, Women and Song": From Martin Luther to American T-Shirts

Wolfgang Mieder

*Although any folkloric expression is a unique occurrence in time and space, that expression is never a creation* ex nihilo. *Something always comes from something else. Folklorists are aware that every expression is conditioned by antecedent models and forces. In turn that expression will likely have some impact upon future forms of the expression. At one time the aim of the folklore discipline was to discover the histories of particular folklore items. Energies were directed toward gathering and scrutinizing all the known versions and variants of a tale, song, proverb, or game in an attempt to reckon its likely period and place of origin as well as to infer its probable paths of dissemination (see Brewster 1942; Thompson 1953). In the past several decades this approach has largely been abandoned. The effort in amassing and analyzing the data often exceeded the certitude and ultimate worth of the results. The recent emphases on folklore context have made the delineation of the historic and geographic peregrinations of a tale or song an endeavor of more dubious significance.*

*Nevertheless folklorists have not lost their interest in comparative inquiry. Even historic-geographic studies have not been abandoned altogether, although they are generally reduced and restricted in scope (e.g. Brunvand 1977). In the following essay, Wolfgang Mieder traces a part of the history of a contemporary proverbial expression. His purpose is not to ascertain ultimate origins, nor to merely document the persistence of a tradition. What he really hopes to illustrate is the creativity that a traditional expression evokes through time.*

*For examples of other comparative proverb studies see Taylor (1966), Mieder (1981), or articles in* Proverbium, *a journal exclusively devoted to the study of the proverb. Recent discussion of the historic-geographic approach can be found in Goldberg (1984) and Dégh (1986).*

---

Reproduced by permission of the publisher, from *Kentucky Folklore Record* 29, no. 3–4 (1983):89–101. Not for further reproduction.

Wolfgang Mieder

There exists a long tradition which claims that Martin Luther coined the common proverb "Who loves not wine, women and song, remains a fool his whole life long." Even though the proverb appeared in print for the first time in the year 1775 in Germany, scholars and others have continued to attribute it to Luther.[1] But nobody has been able to locate this Epicurean proverb anywhere in Luther's voluminous works. The closest statement that Luther ever made was in one of his so-called "Table-Talks" which was recorded between October 28 and December 12, 1536. Here Luther discusses the overindulging of the Germans in drinking and concludes his macaronic German and Latin comments with: "wie wollt ir jetzt anders einen Duedschen vorthuen, denn ebrietate, praesertim talem, qui non diligit musicam et mulieres"[2] (how else would you characterize a German, because in his drunkenness [he is] chiefly such a one who does not choose music and women). The reference to drinking, music and women is somewhat reminiscent of the proverb, but it is still a far cry from the actual proverb text.

Besides, Luther might only be alluding to one of the many classical and medieval Latin or German proverbs which follow the basic triadic structure of "Wine, women and X" in various sequences, as for example:

Nox, mulier, vinum homini adulescentulo.[3] (classical Latin)
(Night, woman, wine are for the adolescent man.)

Alea, vina, venus tribus his sum factus egenus.[4] (medieval Latin)
(Dice, wines, love are three things that have made me destitute.)

Drei Dinge machen der Freuden viel:
Wein, Weib und Saitenspiel.[5] (German)
(Three things made much joy: Wine, women and strumming.)

The many variants of such proverbs in Latin and German are clear indications that "Wine, women and X" was a very popular proverbial formula, one that was doubtlessly known to Martin Luther as well. Considering his detailed knowledge, appreciation and use of German folk speech which went so far as to putting together his own proverb collection around 1536,[6] it would not at all be surprising that this skillful linguist and poet had coined the rhyming German proverb "Wer nicht liebt Wein, Weib und Gesang, der bleibt ein Narr sein Leben lang" (Who does not love wine, woman and song, remains a fool his whole life long). But then the proverb might also have been current already at his time as only one further variant of the many texts based on the well-known triad of "Wine, women and X." Alas, since the proverb appears nowhere in Luther's works, it is impossible to ascertain his possible authorship and, as Archer Taylor points out in regard to this proverb, "all ascriptions to definite persons [of a proverb] must be looked upon with suspicion."[7] There is, however, no doubt that folk tradition has declared the down-to-earth reformer to be its author, and to this day books of quotations, proverbs and phrases continue to associate this proverb with Luther, making it his most famous apocryphal statement.

The proverb appeared in print for the first time in Germany on May 12, 1775 as part of a small poem ascribed to the poet Johann Heinrich Voss:

Wer nicht liebt Wein, Weib und Gesang,
Der bleibt ein Narr sein Lebelang,
Sagt Doctor Martin Luther.[8]

The same author included the proverb again as a small epigram in a thin volume of poetry that he edited in 1777,[9] and he also cites it in a longer poem "An Luther" (To Luther) which he wrote on March 4, 1777.[10] All of this has led some scholars to consider Voss as the originator of the proverb, but once again there is no certain proof of that.[11] Voss never admitted to having written the short poem or the epigram, and in his own longer poem he quotes the proverb as having been used already by Martin Luther as do the anonymous authors of the two shorter texts. Considering also the large popularity of the triad "Wein, Weib und Gesang" which appeared in print the first time in a German folksong recorded in 1602, one cannot help but question Voss's authorship.[12] Most likely he is only quoting a proverb which was already current for a considerable period of time, possibly since or before Luther even.

Many German folksongs, particularly drinking songs, lighthearted love poems and, of course, folk literature as well as serious literary works by none less than Thomas Mann abound with references to the proverb and to Martin Luther after its first appearance in 1775. The proverb and Luther seem to be permanently coupled to each other in the German language, even though the longer proverb text is of late often reduced to a mere "Wein, Weib und Gesang." This truncated version is applicable to numerous situations, it satisfies modern people's desire for short statements, it is based on the popular number three, and it has dropped the archaic relative clause of the "Narr" (fool). Nevertheless, there will hardly be a German native speaker who will not connect this sensuous triad with the reformer, who, as legend has it, was quite the lover of the good life himself.

How, then, did this very German "Luther-proverb" enter the Anglo-American realm? Just as in German, there were early English proverbs of the sixteenth century and later which are vernacular versions of the classical and medieval Latin originals: "Weemen, dise and drinke, lets him nothing" (1576),[13] "Play, women and wine undo men laughing" (1660),[14] "Women, wine, and dice will bring a man to lice" (1732).[15] Such gloomy proverbial pessimism is surely alluded to by Robert Burton in a chapter concerning the dangers of Epicureanism in his *The Anatomy of Melancholy* (1621): "Who wastes his health with drink, his wealth with play, The same with womanfolk shall rot away."[16] How much more does the "carpe diem" mood of a short song out of John Gay's *The Beggar's Opera* (1728) remind us of the pleasure-seeking German proverb:

Fill ev'ry glass, for wine inspires us,
And fires us
With courage, love, and joy.

> Women and wine should life employ.
> Is there aught else on earth desirous?
> Fill ev'ry glass, etc.[17]

Another hundred years later we find a similar short poem by John Keats with the title "Give me women, wine, and snuff" (1817), which certainly is but another variation of the triad of "Wine, women and X".

> Give me women, wine and snuff
> Untill I cry out 'hold, enough!'
> You may do sans objection
> Till the day of resurrection;
> For, bless my beard, they aye shall be
> My beloved Trinity.[18]

And finally George Byron wrote the following verses in his *Don Juan* (1819) in which he expands the triad by a fourth element:

> Few things surpass old wine; and they may preach
> Who please,—the more because they preach in vain,—
> Let us have Wine and Women, Mirth and Laughter,
> Sermons and soda-water the day after.[19]

All of these proverbs and literary texts do not contain as a third element "Gesang" (song), but they are ample proof that triads of the pattern "Wine, women and X" were indeed popular in England as well. It took, however, until the year 1857 for the German proverb to appear in English print. Henry Bohn, one of England's greatest paremiographers, had discovered it in Karl Simrock's proverb collection *Die deutschen Sprichwörter* (Frankfort 1846) and printed it in German with an English translation in his valuable collection *A Polyglot of Foreign Proverbs* (London 1857): Wer nicht liebt Wein, Weib und Gesang, der bleibt ein Narr sein Lebelang. Who loves not women, wine, and song, remains a fool his whole life long.[20] With this entry the proverb found its way into English paremiography, even though Bohn erroneously reversed the order of "wine" and "women" and also changed "woman" to the plural "women." Such variants exist in German as well, but the normal sequence is in both languages today: "Wine, woman (women) and song" (Wein, Weib [Weiber] und Gesang).

Yet a scholarly proverb collection is hardly the medium to help a foreign proverb gain currency in another culture. Who, after all, reads proverb collections and tries to remember hundreds of translated proverbs as assembled in Bohn's book of Danish, Dutch, French, German, Italian, Portuguese and Spanish proverbs? Much more important is that William Makepeace Thackeray went to Germany from 1830 to 1831, where he came in touch with German literary figures and works, possibly even with Voss's poem "An Luther." He subsequently translated four poems by German romanticists which appeared in his works under the collective title of "Five German Ditties."[21] The fifth poem, entitled "A credo" is, however, no translation but rather a poem written by

Thackeray himself which also appeared in slightly different form with the title "Doctor Luther" in his novel *The Adventures of Philip*(1861–1862):

## DOCTOR LUTHER

'For the soul's edification
Of this decent congregation,
Worthy people! by your grant,
I will sing a holy chant.
    I will sing a holy chant.
If the ditty sound but oddly,
'Twas a father wise and godly,
Sang it so long ago.
    Then sing as Doctor Luther sang,
    As Doctor Luther sang,
    Who loves not wine, woman, and song,
    He is a fool his whole life long.

'He, by custom patriarchal,
Loved to see the beaker sparkle,
And he thought the wine improved,
Tasted by the wife he loved,
    By the kindly lips he loved.
Friends! I wish this custom pious
Duly were adopted by us,
To combine love, song, wine;
    And sing as Doctor Luther sang,
    As Doctor Luther sang,
    Who loves not wine, woman, and song,
    He is a fool his whole life long.

'Who refuses this our credo,
And demurs to drink as we do,
Were he holy as John Knox,
I'd pronounce him heterodox
    I'd pronounce him heterodox.
And from out this congregation,
With a solemn commination,
Banish quick the heretic.
    Who would not sing as Luther sang,
    As Doctor Luther sang,
    Who loves not wine, woman, and song,
    He is a fool his whole life long.'[22]

Wolfgang Mieder

Before quoting this poem, Thackeray gives a hint of where he got the idea for its composition: "Then politeness demanded that our host should sing one of his songs, and as I have heard him perform it many times, I have the privilege of here reprinting it: premising that the tune and chorus were taken from a German song-book, which used to delight us melodious youth in bygone days." Thackeray must be referring to a song which he heard and perhaps sang as a student in Cambridge or while he was in Germany, and he now quotes the chorus from memory while writing his own poem.

After much search I have been able to locate the "German song-book" that Thackeray mentions. It is Albert Methfessel's *Allgemeines Commers- und Liederbuch* (Rudolstadt 1818) which contains a student song by L. von Lichtenstein and notes by Methfessel with the predictable title "Wein, Weib und Gesang":

Wo der geistge Freudenbringer,
Wo der starke Grillenzwinger,
Wo der wein mit Götterkraft
Jugendliches Leben schafft;
Wo die vollen Becher schäumen,
Wo die Dichter trunken reimen,
    Fühlt die Brust
    Lebenslust!
Drum singt wie Doctor Luther sang,
Wie Doctor Luther sang:
Wer nicht liebt Wein, Weib und Gesang,
Der bleibt ein Narr sein Leben lang!

Wo ein Weib mit süßem Triebe
Liebe tauscht um Gegenliebe,
Wo Die Höchste gern gewährt,
Uns der Minne Glück beschert,
Strahlet aus verklärten Blicken
Vollgelohnter Lieb' Entzücken,
    Wallt im Blut
    Wonn' und Glut;
Drum singt etc.

Wo des Weins, der Liebe Leben
Im Gesang wird kund gegeben,
Blüht der köstlichste Verein,
Leben, Brüder! Denn, wo Wein,
Wo Gesang und Liebe thronen,
Müssen gute Menschen wohnen,
    Füllt das Herz
    Glück und Scherz;
Drum singt etc.[23]

[English translation]:

Where the spiritual bringer of joy,
Where the powerful banisher of bad moods,
Where the wine with its divine power
Creates youthful vitality;
Where the full mugs foam,
Where the poets drunkenly rhyme,
> There the breast
> Feels the joy of life!
Therefore sing as Doctor Luther sang,
As Doctor Luther sang:
Who does not love wine, woman and song,
Remains a fool this whole life long!

Where a woman with sweet desires
Exchanges love for love,
Where the noblest love gladly grants
And presents us with love's fortune,
The delight of fully requited love
Shines forth from the transfigured gaze,
> There seethes in the blood
> Rapture and passion;
Therefore sing etc.

Wherever the vitality of wine and love
Is proclaimed in song,
There blossoms the most agreeable company,
Let's live, Brothers! Because, where wine,
Where song and love hold sway,
There good people must reside,
> There the heart is filled
> With happiness and jest;
Therefore sing etc.

Thackeray's chorus is a precise translation of the German original, while his three stanzas are a free rendition for English readers (see his reference to John Knox). Thackeray's poem is also more a statement about Luther while the German poem is a drinking song which has as its motto "Wine, women and song." But the fact that Thackeray also brings Luther in connection with the joyful attitude of life helped to associate Luther with this proverb in the Anglo-American world (Bohn made no reference to Luther in his proverb collection!). And since the triad "Wine, women and X" already existed in a number of English proverbs and literary texts, this loan translation of a German proverb fell on receptive ears and was easily acceptable as just another variant, this time at least one that stresses the enjoyable aspects of life to boost.

Thackeray's poem was clearly more influential in spreading this new proverb among English speakers than was Bohn's slightly earlier translation. But there was also the famous waltz *Wein, Weib und Gesang* which Johann Strauss composed in 1869 and which conquered London, then England, and eventually the entire United States with the English title *Wine, Women and Song*. By the end of the nineteenth century this waltz title had become so popular that the American author Eugene Field used it as a fitting title for an ironic love and drinking song (1892):

## WINE, WOMEN AND SONG

> O Varus mine,
>    Plant thou the vine
> Within this kindly soil of Tibur;
>    Nor temporal woes,
> Nor spiritual, knows
> The man who's a discreet imbiber.
>    For who doth croak
>    Of being broke,
> Or who of warfare, after drinking?
>    With bowl atween us,
>    Of smiling Venus
> And Bacchus shall we sing, I'm thinking.
>
>    Of symptoms fell
>    Which brawls impel,
> Historic data give us warning;
>    The wretch who fights
>    When full, of nights,
> Is bound to have a head next morning.
>    I do not scorn
>    A friendly horn,
> But noisy toots, I can't abide 'em!
>    Your howling bat
>    Is state and flat
> To one who knows, because he's tried 'em!
>
>    The secrets of
>    The life I love
> (Companionship with girls and toddy)
>    I would not drag
>    With drunken brag
> Into the ken of everybody;
>    But in the shade
>    Let some coy maid

With smilax wreathe my flagon's nozzle,
> Then all day long,
> With mirth and song,
Shall I enjoy a quiet sozzle![24]

Only seven years later John Addington Symonds published a collection of translated student songs with the title *Wine, Women and Song, Medieval Latin Student Songs* (Portland, Maine 1899) which also helped to popularize the proverb since the entire proverb with reference to Luther is placed as a motto at the beginning of the collection. Many songs deal with wine, women and song, but only the one that contains the triad "wine and love and lyre" comes close to that contained in the proverb.[25] Surely this book, Thackeray's poem, and Strauss's waltz were influential in getting people acquainted with the actual proverb, but one must also consider the many German immigrants who translated their proverbs into English, of which some were obviously picked up by English speakers in due time.[26]

By the end of the nineteenth century, the short version of the proverb was equally current in England as can be seen from the poem "Villanelle of the Poet's Road" (1899) by Ernest Christopher Dowson. Almost every stanza contains the "wine and woman and song" motif whose pleasurable and sensuous tendency is, however, negated by a second leitmotif of "yet is day over long." Thus the poet contrasts the "carpe diem" and the "memento mori" throughout his short stanzas:

Wine and woman and song,
> Three things garnish our way:
Yet is day over long.

Lest we do our youth wrong,
> Gather them while we may:
Wine and woman and song.

Three things render us strong,
> Vine leaves, kisses and bay;
Yet is day over long.

Unto us they belong,
> Us the bitter and gay,
Wine and woman and song.

We, as we pass along,
> Are sad that they will not stay;
Yet is day over long.

Fruits and flowers among,
> What is better than they:
Wine and woman and song?
> Yet is day over long.[27]

The reduction of the proverb text to a mere "Wine, women and song" appears to be even more prevalent in modern Anglo-American usage than in German. A 1938 book was entitled *Wine, Women and Song* (Del Rio, Texas 1938), for example, but it was nothing but a trick by members of the temperance movement to get people to read their tirades against alcoholism. One of the chapters is appropriately called "Wine, Women, Irreverence and Ruin," and it depicts a not at all positive image of "Wine, women and song."[28] A convincing indication of how the short triad is preferred to the longer proverb text is also Helen T. Lowe-Porter's translation of a passage in Thomas Mann's novel *Doctor Faustus* (1948). While the German original has the complete proverb "Wer nicht liebt Wein, Weib und Gesang, der bleibt ein Narr sein Leben lang,"[29] Lowe-Porter renders it by a mere "Wine, Women, and Song."[30] Obviously the translator was of the opinion that this shortened form was more acceptable to the Anglo-American reader, even though a more direct translation of the entire proverb would have been no serious problem.

In the meantime the shortened expression "Wine, women and song" has become so common that it has replaced the longer and somewhat awkward older version which never gained a large currency in the English language. Due to its popularity it is also often parodied in caricatures, headlines, slogans or on T-shirts. From the American journalist and humorist Franklin Pierce Adams stems, for example, the funny statement: "In the order named, these are the hardest to control: Wine, Women and song."[31] Perhaps President Harry S Truman also alluded to this Epicurean motto when he exclaimed: "Three things can ruin a man—money, power, and women. I never had any money, I never wanted power, and the only woman in my life is up at the house right now."[32] As a third and considerably earlier American bonmot we can also add J. A. McDougall's quadriple alliterative remark out of his Senate speech in February 1861: "I believe in women, wine, whiskey and war."[33]

But finally a few truly modern references: The *Playboy* magazine printed the following party joke in the sixties: "Advice to the exhausted: When wine, women and song become too much for you, give up singing."[34] The same magazine included in 1977 a caricature in which a doctor gives the following advice to a homosexual: "All right, then, you'll have to give up wine, men and song for a while."[35]

Also on this sexual plane is a very recent caricature from the *New Yorker*. It depicts a gentleman getting out of a limousine about to enter an establishment on whose marquee are inscribed the suggestive words "Wine, Women & Song."[36] Another cartoon from the same magazine shows two deceased men as angels on a cloud in heaven who are obviously bored with their life after death. The accompanying caption questions ironically: "For this I gave up a lifetime of wine, women and song?"[37] The use of the word "lifetime" permits the assumption that the cartoon also refers to the second part of the actual proverb, namely "remains a fool his whole life long." And, finally, the famous triad appears on a T-shirt, where "wine and women" are, however, brought into connection with a materialistic goal: "Wine, Women & Porsches, not necessarily in that order."[38]

Further references could certainly be found, and many will continue to appear in literature, magazines, advertisements and caricatures. The proverb also continues to be popular in oral speech, and there can be no doubt that the shortened version of this German loan proverb will survive in modern Anglo-American language usage. The longer original proverb with its association with Martin Luther will, however, most likely fall more and more into disuse, while the triad of "Wine, women and song" will remain an often cited expression in our modern pleasure-seeking society.

---

[1] For a review of the German literature on this proverb see Wolfgang Mieder, "Wer nicht liebt Wein, Weib und Gesang, der bleibt ein Narr sein Leben lang." *Muttersprache* 93 (Sonderheft 1983):68–103.

[2] Ernst Kroker, ed., *D. Martin Luthers Werke. Kritische Gesamtausgabe* (Weimar: Hermann Böhlau, 1914). *Tischreden*, 3:344.

[3] August Otto, *Die Sprichwörter der Römer* (Leipzig: Teubner, 1980; reprint, Hildesheim: Georg Olms, 1971), 372 for further examples of proverbs based on the triad "nox, amor, vinum."

[4] Hans Walther, *Lateinische Sprichwörter und Sentenzen des Mittelalters* (Göttingen: Vandenhoeck & Ruprecht, 1965), vol. 1, 88 (No. 72). See also nos. 64, 71 and 73.

[5] Karl Friedrich Wilhelm Wander, *Deutsches Sprichwörter-Lexikon* (Leipzig: F. A. Brockhaus, 1867; reprint, Darmstadt: Wissenschaftliche Buchgesellschaft, 1964), vol. 1, col. 616 (No. 322). Wander lists literally dozens of such proverbs attesting to the popularity of expanding the alliterative binary formula of "wine and women" by a third element, many of them also starting with a "w."

[6] For a critical edition of this proverb collection see *Luthers Sprichwörtersammlung*, ed. Ernst Thiele (Weimar: Hermann Bühlau, 1900).

[7] See Archer Taylor, *The Proverb* (Cambridge: Harvard University Press, 1931; reprint, Hatboro, PA: Folklore Associates, 1962), 38.

[8] Matthias Claudius, ed., *Wandsbecker Bothe* (Freitag, den 12. Mai 775), No. 75.

[9] Johann Heinrich Voss, ed. *Musen Almanach fur 1777* (Hamburg: L. E. Bohn, 1777), 107.

[10] Johann Heinrich Voss, *Sämtliche Gedichte* (Konigsberg: Friedrich Nicolovius, 1802; reprint, Bern: Peter Lang, 1969), 4:58–60.

[11] See for example Bernard Darwin, *The Oxford Dictionary of Quotations* (Oxford: Oxford University Press, 1953), 321; Burton Stevenson, *The Macmillan Book of Proverbs, Maxims, and Famous Phrases* (New York: Macmillan, 1968, 2526 (No. 4); John Bartlett, *Familiar Quotations* (Boston: Little, Brown, 1980), 399.

[12] The song is included in *Herders sämtliche Werke*, Carl Redlich (Berlin: Weidmann, 1885), 25:21–22.

[13] F. P. Wilson, *The Oxford Dictionary of English Proverbs* (Oxford: Clarendon Press, 1970), 296.

[14] Morris Palmer Tilley, *Elizabethan Proverb Lore in Lyly's "Euphues" and in Pettie's "Petite Pallace" with Parallels from Shakespeare* (New York: Macmillan, 1926), 248 (No. 491).

[15] G. L. Apperson, *English Proverbs and Proverbial Phrases: A Historical Dictionary* (London: J. M. Dent, 1929; reprint, Detroit: Gale Research Co. 1969), 706 (No. 43).

[16] Robert Burton, *The Anatomy of Melancholy*, ed. Holbrook Jackson (London: J. M. Dent, 1972), 291.

[17] John Gay, *The Beggar's Opera*, ed. Edgar V. Roberts (Lincoln: University of Nebraska Press, 1969), 32.

[18] *The Poems of John Keats*, ed. Jack Stillinger (Cambridge: Harvard University Press, 1978), 47.

[19] *The Works of Lord Byron*, ed. Ernest Hartley Coleridge (London: John Murray, 1903), 6: 132, verse CLXXVIII.

[20] Henry G. Bohn, *A Polyglot of Foreign Proverbs* (London: Henry G. Bohn, 1857; reprint, Detroit: Gale Research Co., 1968), 184.

[21] See *The Complete Works of William Makepeace Thackeray* (Boston: Houghton, Mifflin, 1895), 20:297–299. None of the editions give a date for these translations.

[22] Thackeray, vol. 17, part 1, 199–200.

[23] Albert Methfessel, *Allgemeines Commers- und Liederbuch enthaltend ältere und neue Burschenlieder, Trinklieder, Vaterlandsgesänge, Volks- und Kreigslieder, mit mehrstimmigen Melodien und beigefügter Klavierbegleitung* (Rudolstadt: Hof-, Buch- und Kunsthandlung 1818), 102–104. The translation is my own.

[24] *The Poems of Eugene Field* (New York: Charles Scribner's Sons, 1912), 390–391.

[25] See John Addington Symonds, *Wine, Women and Song. Medieval Latin Student Songs Now First Translated into English Verse with an Essay* (Portland, ME: Thomas B. Mosher, 1899), 147–148.

[26] See as an example Wolfgang Mieder, "'Der Apfel fällt nicht weit von Deutschland': Zur amerikanischen Entlehnung eines deutschen Sprichwortes," *Der Sprachdienst*, 25 (1981):89–93.

[27] *The Poems of Ernest Christopher Dowson*, ed. Mark Longaker (Philadelphia: University of Pennsylvania Press, 1962), 110. A "Villanelle" is a short poem of French origin consisting usually of five stanzas of three lines each and a final stanza of four lines. It has only two rhymes throughout.

[28] See Sam Morris, *Wine, Women and Song* (Del Rio, TX: William McNitzy, 1938), 58–69.

[29] See Thomas Mann, *Doktor Faustus*, (Frankfurt: S. Fischer, 1947), 149.

[30] See Thomas Mann, *Doctor Faustus*, translated from the German by Helen T. Lowe-Porter (New York: Alfred A. Knopf, 1948), 97.

[31] Franklin Pierce Adams, *Book of Quotations* (New York: Funk & Wagnalls, 1952), 848.

[32] Leo Rosten, *Infinite Riches. Gems from a Lifetime of Reading* (New York: McGraw-Hill, 1979), 510.

[33] See H. L. Mencken, *A New Dictionary of Quotations on Historical Principles from Ancient and Modern Sources* (New York: Alfred A. Knopf, 1960), 1303.

[34] Quoted from A. K. Adams, *The House Book of Humorous Quotations* (New York: Dodd, Mead, 1969), 331.

[35] *Playboy* (September 1977), 234.

[36] *New Yorker* (8 August 1983), 62. I owe this reference to my graduate student, Leesa Guay.

[37] *New Yorker* (4 February 1980), 58.

[38] *Der Stern*, No. 39 (17 September 1981), 142.

# "Wise Words" of the Western Apache

## Keith H. Basso

*Proverbs and riddles are formulaic verbal expressions whose sense often assumes an ability to comprehend a metaphor—an ability to perceive a concealed relation between two objects or events that are otherwise dissimilar. In fact, most of the communications that scholars have come to call "folklore" depend upon a capacity to encode and decode metaphor. In the following essay, Keith H. Basso introduces us to the world of Apache metaphor. Beginning with a discussion of what metaphors are and how they are constructed, he pursues the particular characteristics of Apache "wise words." In the course of his analysis, he also provides a glimpse of the process by which ethnographers are instructed by their informants. The implications of metaphorical speech for contemporary linguistic theory are broached by Basso in the original version of this essay.*

*Further discussion of the nature and function of metaphor may be found in the journal* Critical Inquiry *(1978:1-197). It was once thought that proverbs, and particularly riddles, were not genres indigenous to native American cultures (Parsons 1936). Although this is no longer thought to be true, such traditions have only occasionally been described (Scott 1973; McAllester 1974). Other works by Basso (1979, 1984) address language creativity among the Western Apache. For essays and a bibliography focusing on the creative use of language in specific cultures see Kirshenblatt-Gimblett (1976).*

## METAPHOR AS SIMILE

The most salient characteristic of metaphor consists in a blatant violation of linguistic rules that results in the expression of a proposition that is either logically false or, in Rudolf Carnap's terminology, "conceptually absurd."[1] Walker Percy has put the matter nicely: a metaphor "asserts of one thing that it is something else" and is therefore inevitably "wrong."[2] At the same time, of course, a metaphor is also "right" because, semantic disobedience not withstanding, the proposition it expresses can be construed as containing a truth. Interpreted one way, Thomas Brown's metaphor, "Oh blackbird, what a boy you are," is utter nonsense since it is simply not the case that blackbirds are boys, or vice versa. On the other hand, this statement can be taken to mean that despite numerous differences there is some sense in which boys and

---

blackbirds are alike—in their penchant for loud noise, for example, or in their propensity for energetic play. Herein lies a dilemma: how is it that a metaphorical statement can be at once both true and false?

This question is most commonly answered by asserting that metaphor is simile in disguise, a view which rests upon the more basic claim that an analytic distinction can be drawn between semantic features which compose the *designative* or *literal* meanings of words and features which compose their *connotative* or *figurative* meanings. Designative features are relatively few in number and serve as a set to specify the necessary and sufficient conditions for membership in the class of objects referred to by the word in question.[3] Connotative features are much more numerous, are nondefining in the sense just described, and consist of any and all "associated commonplaces" or "contingent facts" which the designative meaning(s) of the word call(s) to mind.[4]

If designative meanings are relied upon to interpret a metaphor, the reasoning goes, the proposition it expresses will be understood as false or, at worst, contradictory. However, if the metaphor is construed as a covert simile, it will be understood as expressing a noncontradictory proposition whose truth value can be assessed—and, for those in a position to do so, established—on the basis of connotative meanings. The trick to interpreting a metaphor, then, is to reject it as a declarative proposition (e.g. Blackbirds are boys), interpret it as a comparative proposition (e.g. Blackbirds are *like* boys), and confirm the truth of the latter by adducing at least one valid similarity between the classes of objects being compared (e.g. Blackbirds are like boys *by virtue of* a shared fondness for whooping it up).

This theory has two important implications. One of these is that the same metaphor may be interpreted in different ways—as many, in fact, as there are features of connotative meaning shared by the metaphor's main constituents.[5] We have interpreted Thomas Brown's metaphor on the grounds that blackbirds and boys share the attribute of being raucous, but other similarities could easily be adduced—liveliness, playfulness, an inclination to hide things, and so forth. It would be arbitrary, then, to insist that a metaphor has one "best" or "proper" sense; to the contrary, as many writers have noted, it is the special virtue of metaphor that it is capable of gathering unto itself several senses any one (or two, or three, or more) of which can serve as a basis for interpretation. This is a significant point because it accounts for the empirical fact that interpretations of a metaphor may exhibit wide variation even within the same speech community.

The theory before us also implies that the interpretation of a metaphor is ultimately grounded in an ability to form a concept (or two, or three, or more) which serves to establish an equivalence between the metaphor's main constituents, and of which, therefore, the constituents become exemplars par excellence.[6] In other words, if X and Y are the constituents equated in a metaphor, interpretation requires the formation of a concept that subsumes both X and Y and thus defines the terms of their identity. Our interpretation of Brown's metaphor presupposes and derives from a concept that may be glossed as 'animate objects that are raucous'. It is essential to assume both the possibility and validity of such a concept. Otherwise, there would be no way to account for our particular interpretation of the metaphor, or to explain the fact that it can be readily understood by others.

The concepts required to interpret a metaphor are not expressed by the metaphor itself. Rather, they may be said to underlie it and must be *discovered* through the adduction of shared features of connotative meaning. It is this act of discovery, coupled with the sometimes puzzling search that precedes it, that can make the interpretation of metaphor an original and personal experience. And it is this same act of discovery—this "finding" of a meaning that resolves the puzzle—that endows metaphor with the capacity to cause surprise, to structure the perceptions of individuals in unanticipated ways, and to make them "see" associations they have never seen before. Thus, as Herbert Read has written, "A metaphor is the synthesis of several units of observation into *one commanding image*; it is an expression of a complex idea, not by analysis, or by abstract statement, but by a sudden perception of an objective relation" (italics added.)[7]

This brings us back to where we began. The meaningful interpretation of metaphor rests upon an ability to discern some element of plausibility or truth in a statement that asserts an implausibility or falsehood. It is clear, I think, that if we can characterize this ability—or, more precisely, if we can determine how the concepts that underlie the interpretation of metaphor are formed—we will have learned something interesting about metaphor itself. We will also have learned something interesting about cultural symbols and the way they work to impose order and meaning on that elusive entity sometimes known as the "real world."

## 'WISE WORDS' AS SIMILES

The class of Western Apache metaphors that will concern us in this essay takes the form of simple definitional utterances which represent expressions of a single surface syntactic type: subject + predicate + verb. In every case, the subject is a term designating some category of animate natural phenomena (e.g. *hadaditl'a'*: 'lightning'; *kaage čo:* 'raven'; *koyiłčoože:* 'carrion beetle'), the predicate is a term designating some human category (e.g. *'iitsaa:* 'widow'; *'iškįįn:* 'boy'; *'indaa':* 'whiteman'), and the verb is a copula (*'at'ee:* 'is'; 'are'). In every case, too, a semantic rule is violated; subject and predicate do not agree. To put it more precisely, the subject possesses designative features that are incompatible with designative features possessed by the predicate. As a result, a proposition is expressed which is contradictory and therefore always false. Eight of these metaphors are presented below:

(1) a. *hadaditl'a' 'iškįįn 'at'ee* ('Lightning is a boy')
   b. *kaage čo 'iitsaa 'at'ee* ('Ravens are widows')
   c. *koyiłčoože 'indaa' 'at'ee* ('Carrion beetle is a whiteman')
   d. *gooše čaɣą́ą́še 'at'ee* ('Dogs are children')
   e. *mba'tsose 'indee 'at'ee* ('Coyotes are Western Apaches')
   f. *doole č'ikii 'at'ee* ('Butterflies are girls')
   g. *doole 'izeege 'at'ee* ('Butterflies are sweethearts')
   h. *toołkaiyee saan 'at'ee* ('Burros are old women')

Metaphors of this type are identified by Western Apaches as prime examples of what they call 'wise words' (*goyąąʾyo yaiti'*), a distinctive speech genre associated with adult men and women who have gained a reputation for balanced thinking, critical acumen, and extensive cultural knowledge. These persons, who form collectively a kind of intellectual elite, are typically well along in years and because of their advanced age are not expected to participate in the full round of daily activities that occupy most younger members of Western Apache society. Consequently, they have plenty of time for visiting and talking, especially with one another, and it is in the context of these conversational settings, called *baiyan diidała'at'ee* ('old people talking together'), that 'wise words' are used most frequently.

When an Apache—or an ethnographer—encounters a metaphor he does not understand, he may request an interpretation of it. The appropriate form of such a request is XY *haago 'at'eego dałęlt'ee?* (X and Y, how are they the same?), where X stands for the subject of the metaphor and Y stands for the predicate. The appropriate response is an explanatory paraphrase that describes one or more ways in which the referents of subject and predicate are alike. I recorded sixty-four of these explanatory paraphrases—one for every metaphor listed in (1a–h) from each of eight Western Apache consultants—of which the following are representative:

> (2) a. *Metaphor: hadaditl'a' 'iškįįn 'at'ee* ('Lightning is a boy')
>
>    *Interpretation:* Yes, young boys are the same as lightning. They both dart around fast and you just can't tell what they are going to do. They both act unpredictably. They never stay still. Both are always darting around from place to place. They will shoot aimlessly, too. They will both shoot anywhere, not aiming away from people's camps, not caring what they hit. That is why they both cause damage.

> (2) b. *Metaphor: kaage čo 'iitsaa 'at'ee* ('Ravens are widows')
>
>    *Interpretation:* Ravens are widows, these people say. They say that because ravens and widows are poor and don't have anyone to get meat for them. That is why sometimes these women will stand near your camp and wait like that until you give them food. It is the same way with ravens. They stand around near roads so they can eat what is killed there; they just wait like that until some car hits something and kills it. That's what ravens are doing when you see them standing near roads. They are waiting to get fresh meat.

> (2) c. *Metaphor: koyiłčoože 'indaa' 'at'ee*
>          ('Carrion beetle is a whiteman')
>
>    *Interpretation:* Well, there is this way that carrion beetle reminds us of whitemen—they waste much food. Carrion beetle, when he is young and before he starts to eat meat, just eats a little hole in a leaf and then moves on to eat a little hole in another. He leaves plenty

of good food behind him. It is like this with some white people, too. Another way they are the same, these two, is that in the summer they only come out from where they live when it is cool. You only see carrion beetles early in the morning and again in the early evening. It is the same with some white people. In the summer they always want to stay some place where it is cool.

(2) d. *Metaphor: gooše čaʼyąąše ʼatʼee* ('Dogs are children')

*Interpretation:* I think this way about what that means. Both of them, children and dogs, are always hungry. They like to eat all the time, and when they don't get food they come to a place where someone is cooking. There is this way, too. Both of them get into everything and don't leave anything alone. So you have to shoo them away. If you don't, they might break something or soil it so you can't use it anymore.

These explanatory paraphrases, like all of the others I recorded, focus pointedly upon the specification of attributes in terms of which the referents of the constituents in a metaphor can be considered the same. Consequently, it seems safe to conclude that Western Apache metaphors of the type presented here are intended to be construed *as if* they were similes, and that failure to construe them in this manner will render interpretation extremely difficult, if not impossible. Of course, this does not explain how the concepts underlying particular interpretations are formed, or why some interpretations are judged more appropriate than others. I turn now to a consideration of these problems.

## METAPHORICAL CONCEPTS: DESIGNATIVE FEATURES

The concepts that underlie interpretations of Western Apache metaphors consist of one feature of connotative meaning and one or more features of designative meaning. The connotative feature is criterial, is openly described in explanatory paraphrases, and may be viewed as the "outcome" of a search and selection procedure. The designative features are noncriterial and are not described in explanatory paraphrases; they are contingent upon—and therefore must be inferred from—the position in lexical hierarchies of the semantic categories labeled by the metaphor's constituents.

Consider the following example. In paraphrase (2c) an equivalence is drawn between carrion beetles (*koyiłčooše*) and whitemen (*ʼindaaʼ*) on the grounds that both 'waste food' (*-ʼiitʼan donaodi yodawołsida*). 'Waste food' is a feature of connotative meaning since it does not state a necessary condition for membership in either of the categories 'whiteman' or 'carrion beetle'. But 'waste food' is only one component of the metaphorical concept. The other components consist of two features of designative meaning that together define a superordinate category to which both 'whiteman' and 'carrion beetle' belong, namely, *niʼgostsangolįįhi* ('living things that dwell on or below

295

the surface of the earth'). Thus the complete metaphorical concept, defined by the features 'living thing' + 'earth dweller' + 'waste food', is *ni'gostsangolįįhi 'iitan donaodi yodawołsida* or 'living earth dwellers that waste food'.

The designative features of a metaphorical concept are always those features which the metaphor's constituents share by virtue of membership in the same semantic domain. As shown by the hierarchy presented in Figure 1, the referents of 'carrion beetle' and 'whiteman' do not become members of the same domain until the node labeled by *ni'gostsangolįįhi* ('living earth dwellers') is reached. At this point, they become exemplars of a single category, thus overcoming and resolving the semantic conflict—or, in Geertz's phrase, the "semantic tension"—that distinguishes them at subordinate levels.[8] It follows that a metaphorical concept will always be *more inclusive* than either of the categories labeled by the metaphor's constituents. The concept 'living earth dwellers that waste food' is more inclusive than either 'carrion beetle' or 'whiteman'; it must be because it subsumes them both.

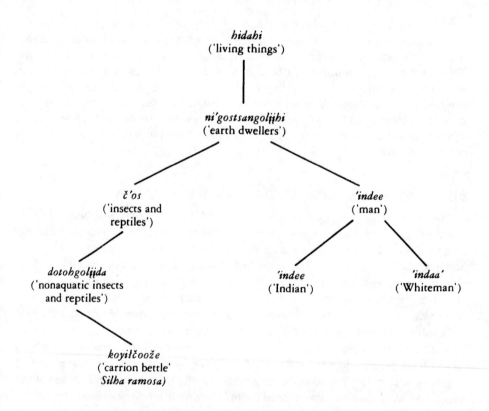

Figure 1. Lexical Hierarchy Showing Location of Western Apache Categories 'Carrion Bettle' (*koyiłčoože*) and 'Whiteman' (*'indaa'*)

The hierarchical level at which the categories labeled by a metaphor's constituents are incorporated into the same domain is also the lowest level at which features of connotative meaning can be adduced. This is because shared connotative features must be compatible with designative features *shared by both constituents,* a condition that can only be satisfied when the referents of the constituents become exemplars of a single category. In terms of our example, this simply means that any connotative feature adduced to establish a similarity between carrion beetles and whitemen must be compatible with features that define 'carrion beetle' and 'whiteman' as 'living earth dwellers'. Any connotative feature that fails to meet this requirement (e.g. 'never die', 'cause snowstorms', 'make good cooking pots') will be prohibited.

This claim is supported by empirical evidence which will be presented later in the chapter. For the moment, however let us agree with R. A. Waldron who has observed that:

> Metaphor is by no means carried out in total contravention of the rules [of a language] but in part by courtesy of the system itself. . . . Linguistic categorization involves classification on the basis of similarity of attributes. Metaphorical categorization is only an extension of normal linguistic activity; it is exceptionally *wide classification* [italics added].[9]

The rules to which Waldron refers in this passage are what transformational grammarians commonly call "selection restrictions."[10] These rules define the conditions under which the semantic features of a language can cooccur, and therefore determine which combinations are allowable and which are not. We have hypothesized that Western Apache metaphorical concepts do not violate selection restrictions and therefore are defined by allowable combinations of semantic features.

## METAPHORICAL CONCEPTS: CONNOTATIVE FEATURES

The connotative features of Western Apache metaphorical concepts are chosen in compliance with a set of sociolinguistic principles which specify the *kinds of attributes* that can be adduced to establish equivalences between the referents of a metaphor's constituents. From the point of view of the individual Apache hearer, these principles constitute a heuristic strategy or plan that guides and simplifies the search for shared similarities.[11] Simultaneously, they serve to define the criteria in terms of which the appropriateness of his interpretation will be assessed by other members of the speech community. The principles may be stated as follows:

A. To be appropriate, an interpretation of a Western Apache metaphor must specify one or more *behavioral attributes* which the referents of the metaphor's constituents share in common.

B. (Corollary) Interpretations that are based upon other types of attributes—such as size, shape, color, habitat, and the like—will be rejected as inappropriate.

Keith H. Basso

C. To be appropriate, an interpretation of a Western Apache metaphor must specify one or more behavioral attributes that are indicative of *undesirable qualities* possessed by the referents of the metaphor's constituents.

D. (Corollary) Interpretations based upon attributes indicative of desirable qualities will be rejected as inappropriate.

The validity of principles A and C was given strong empirical support by regularities in the corpus of sixty-four explanatory paraphrases provided by my Western Apache consultants. Close examination of these statements revealed that principle A was never violated. In other words, all the paraphrases I recorded concentrated upon the identification of behavioral similarities and none adduced similarities of other kinds. Principle C was violated only twice, both times by the same consultant, and on each occasion his interpretation was challenged by other Apaches on the grounds that it "spoke too well" of the referents of the constituents of the metaphor in question.

Principles B and D were upheld by the Apaches' consistent rejection of metaphorical interpretations that violated the conditions defined by principles A and C. Discussions centering upon the reasons for such rejections were of special interest because, as shown by the three excerpts presented below, they yielded valuable information concerning the Apaches' own conceptions of how 'wise words' should be interpreted. The first excerpt, which describes an exchange between myself and two consultants, deals with the central importance of adducing behavioral similarities. So does the second, which presents a portion of a conversation between one of my consultants and his eleven-year-old daughter. The third excerpt, involving three consultants and myself, is from a discussion concerning the requirement that behavioral similarities be chosen which reflect unfavorably on the referents of a metaphor's constituents.

(3) a. *Consultant 1:* Butterflies are girls—try that one.

*Ethnographer:* Well, this is what I think of that one—they're both the same because they're pretty, brightly colored, like the dresses the girls wear.

*Consultant 2:* [Laughter] You could say that, but it sounds wrong to us . . . like when you said ravens are widows because they wear black. [More laughter] Maybe they are the same that way, but to us it doesn't mean anything.

*Ethnographer:* Why not?

*Consultant 1:* [Long pause] It doesn't mean anything because it doesn't tell us what they *do*, these things in the 'wise words'. You have to think about how they are the same in what they do—not what they look like. Think about how they act the same. That way you'll understand it. Butterflies are girls because sometimes they act mindlessly, just chasing around after each other having a good time when they should be working, helping out with chores and younger children. What they look like doesn't matter, it's how they *act* that makes them the same.

(3) b. *Consultant 1 (to daughter):* Who said it to you: carrion beetle is a whiteman?

*Daughter:* X's wife. She said it yesterday at her camp.

*Consultant 1:* What did you say?

*Daughter:* Nothing. I didn't know what she meant.

*Consultant 1:* Wise words. That old woman likes to talk that way. She wanted to know if you knew how they were the same— whitemen and carrion beetles. Do you know how they are the same?

*Daughter:* No.

*Consultant 1:* Think.

*Daughter:* Because there are many of them.

*Consultant 1:* [Laughter] No. Think about what they do, those two—like leaving clear tracks so they are easy to follow, or like the way they waste food.

*Daughter:* But there *are* many of them.

*Consultant 1:* Yes. But when old people talk like that, using 'wise words', they want you to think about how carrion beetle acts . . . then they want you to think about whitemen that same way. So you have to watch both of them, and then you will see how they are the same. It's what they *do* that matters. Now, do you understand?

*Daughter:* [Pause] I think so.

(3) c. *Ethnographer:* Yesterday I was talking about 'wise words' with Y, the medicine man's wife, and she said something I didn't understand. Maybe you could help me out.

*Consultant 1:* What did she say?

*Ethnographer:* She said these old people use 'wise words' when they want to say something bad about someone.

*Consultant 1:* What made her say that?

*Ethnographer:* Well, she asked me why coyotes are Apaches and I said because they knew all about this country and were very smart.

*Consultant 2:* [Loud laughter] Maybe what you said about coyotes is true, but is doesn't sound right to us. Coyotes are like some Apaches who don't stay at home and roam around from place to place. Even at night they don't stay at home where they should be. They roam around from place to place and make lots of noise, yelling at night so you can't sleep. Some Apaches do like that, too, and it's no good; they should stay at home at night and keep quiet. That way they will stay out of trouble.

*Consultant 3:* It is true what that old woman told you. Those old people use 'wise words' when they don't like what someone has done. But they don't want to come out and use that person's name because that way he might hear about it and get angry. So they just say something like coyotes are Apaches and that is enough—everyone knows what they mean and who they are talking about.

*Ethnographer:* So when you are thinking about coyotes and Apaches you look for *bad* ways that make them the same? You look for what they do that is *no good?*

*Consultant 2:* Yes. I thought you knew that. It's the same for all 'wise words'. . . . One time when we were talking you said butterflies were girls because they were both pretty. That was wrong because it's good to look nice. I don't think butterflies are pretty, but you do, and that made us laugh. It's because they chase around after each other, like they had no work to do, that makes them the same. And that's no good.

*Consultant 3:* Let me tell you a story. One time my mother was sick and went to the hospital in Whiteriver. It was before my older sister got married. She was supposed to look after us, cook for us. She did all right, but then one day she took off with my two [female] cousins and they went to where some people were getting ready for a dance. They stayed there all morning. Then they went to another camp to drink beer with some boys. Then they went to another camp. At night they went back to the dance. Finally, they came home. My grandmother had come to take care of us, and I guess she knew that my sister had been running around. When my sister came in my grandmother didn't say anything at first. Then she said to my older brother, "Butterflies are girls and one of them just flew in." My sister knew what it meant, I guess, because she started feeling bad. . . . That's how they use 'wise words', these old people—when they want to say something bad about someone.

It should now be apparent that the principles which govern the selection of connotative meanings are closely related to what Western Apaches conceive to be the proper use of 'wise words' in ordinary conversation. As the material presented above suggests, metaphors of this type are regarded by Apaches as vehicles for the expression of mild personal criticism. It is criticism of a highly oblique sort, however, and the identity of the person (or persons) being denounced can only be inferred from other kinds of information. This is a complex and often extremely subtle process whose analysis falls beyond the scope of the present study. What is significant here is that the requirement to select behavioral attributes—and, more specifically, behavioral attributes indicative of undesirable qualities—arises directly from the purposes 'wise words' are designed to serve and the objectives they are intended to accomplish in the course of social interaction.

[1]Rudolph Carnap, *Philosophy and Logical Syntax* (Routledge and Kegan Paul, 1955), 47.

[2]Walker Percy, "Metaphor as Mistake," *Sewanee Review* 66 (1958):79–99.

[3]Harold W. Scheffler and Floyd G. Lounsbury, *A Study in Structural Semantics: The Siriono Kinship System* (Englewood Cliffs, N.J.: Prentice-Hall, 1971), 4 and Harold W. Scheffler, "Kinship Semantics," in Bernard J. Siegel, ed., *Annual Review of Anthropology* (Palo Alto, Calif.: Annual Reviews, 1972), 1:309–28.

[4]Max Black, *Models and Metaphors* (Ithaca, N.Y.: Cornell University Press, 1962), 32 and Jerrold Katz, *Semantic Theory* (New York: Harper and Row, 1972), 285.

[5]Warren A. Shibles, *Metaphor: An Annotated Bibliography* (Whitewater, Wis.: Language Press, 1971); I. A. Richards, *The Philosophy of Rhetoric* (Oxford: Oxford University Press, 1948); Black, *Models;* and Herbert Read, *English Prose Style* (London: G. Bell and Sons, 1952).

[6]Roger Brown, *Words and Things* (Glencoe, Ill,: Free Press, 1958); I. A. Richards, *Interpretation of Teaching* (London: Routledge and Kegan Paul, 1938); Wilbur Marshall Urban, *Language and Reality* (London: George Allen and Unwin, 1939); Scheffler and Lounsbury, *Structural Semantics.*

[7]Read, *English Prose Style,* 23.

[8]Clifford Geertz, "Ideology as a Cultural System," in David E. Apter, ed., *Ideology and Discontent* (Glencoe, Ill.: Free Press, 1964), 59.

[9]R. A. Waldron, *Sense and Sense Development* (London: Andre Deutsch, the Language Library, 1967), 174.

[10]Jerrold Katz and Jerry A. Fodor, "The Structure of a Semantic Theory," *Language* 39 (1963):170–210; Thomas G. Bever and Peter S. Rosenbaum, "Some Lexical Structures and Their Empirical Validity," in Danny D. Steinberg and Leon Jacobvits, eds., *Semantics* (Cambridge: Cambridge University Press, 1971), 586–99; and Katz, *Semantic Theory.*

[11]G. A. Miller, E. Galanter, and R. Pribram, *Plans and the Structure of Behavior* (New York: Holt, Reinhart and Winston, 1960), 159.

# "The Land Won't Burn": An Esoteric American Proverb And Its Significance

James P. Leary

*In the following essay, James Leary gives us an account of the origin and use of a proverb by the members of a family in the upper Midwest. The meaning of the proverb is explained with a family story that probably is as traditional as the expression itself. Although the proverb appears in none of the proverb indexes, it may still not be unique to the Russell family. Ideas similar to that expressed by the proverb can certainly be found. ("I had heard my father say that he never knew a piece of land [to] run away or break"—John Adams, Autobiography; "It is a comfortable feeling to know that you stand on your own ground. Land is about the only thing that can't fly away"—Anthony Trollope, The Last Chronicle of Barset; "But that land—it is one thing that will still be there when I come back—land is always there"—Pearl S. Buck, A House Divided.) Whether the proverb was indeed peculiar to the Russell family is not really at issue. The important point in the following discussion is that family members considered it to be a unique family expression. Furthermore, the proverb was more than an idiosyncratic figure of speech. Rather, it served as a sober commentary on the bonds of kinship, the forces that threaten them, and the importance of their rootedness in the land. The behavior of the family members suggests that this proverb both summarized and evoked ideas and feelings concerning their sense of place and purpose in the world.*

*While folklorists and anthropologists have repeatedly noted the important role of proverbs in African formal and informal speech, this role may have been somewhat overstated (Yankah 1986). Since Leary's essay first appeared, observations by Arora (1988) and Georges (1981) suggest that proverbs hold a more prominent and serious place in the speech of urban Americans than was previously imagined. For another study of proverbs in context see Jordan (1982).*

In recent years folklorists have urged the abandonment of solely text-oriented approaches to their disciplines.[1] Theoretical articles have demanded that various folkloristic genres be seen as vehicles of communication appearing naturally in social contexts.[2] Not surprisingly, much discussion has focused on that most prevalent of verbal genres, the proverb. Proposed methodologies for collection have emphasized the importance of recording age, sex and status of proverb-users as well as the specific contexts in which proverbs are used.[3] Sociological relationships between proverbs and

---

other minor verbal genres have been scrutinized,[4] and structural models have been formulated in an attempt to link the use, meaning, and function of proverbs with specific social situations.[5] Common to all of these studies is the assumption that proverbs involve "strategies" which most frequently "confront and attempt to control recurrent anxiety situations by giving them a name."[6] In other words, proverbs suggest a course of action through a wise and aphoristic traditional statement.

Unfortunately, almost no studies have been undertaken implementing the methodologies and testing the proposed hypotheses. This neglect is particularly apparent with regard to the United States. Following the example of functional anthropologists,[7] scholars of proverbs have confined their contextual descriptions to "traditional" societies whenever they have ventured beyond the realm of theory.[8] The paucity of contextual studies of proverbs in the United States may be merely attributable to lack of interest; however, it may also indicate some basic problems hindering such a project. If so, what might they be?

To begin with, we must realize that the structures of traditional and modern societies differ radically. As Redfield has pointed out, the traditional society

> is small, isolated, nonliterate, and homogeneous, with a strong sense of group solidarity. The ways of living are conventionalized into that coherent system which we call "a culture." Behavior is traditional, spontaneous, uncritical, and personal. . . . Kinship, its relationships and institutions, are the type categories of experience and the familial group is the unit of action. The sacred prevails over the secular; the economy is one of status rather than of the market.[9]

In contrast modern society is the antithesis of traditional society: our society is large and marked by rapid communication and literacy; it is heterogeneous and individualistic; behavioral patterns are subject to periodic change, social relations are usually more impersonal, and the secular often prevails over the sacred. This total situation has affected the significance of proverbs in American society.[10] Various examples should effectively illustrate this.

Whereas in Africa proverbs play a vital role in the instruction of youth,[11] no one has yet produced evidence indicating proverbs are widely used with comparable intent and rigor in the United States. Whereas proverbs are integrally and formally utilized in the settlement of disputes in Africa,[12] they are not so universally employed or valued by Americans. A mother may tell her child "haste makes waste," but she is just as likely to rely on "Sesame Street" for the conveyance of this insight, or perhaps she may forget about it altogether. A lawyer may caution an adversary by warning him not to count unhatched chickens, but this would be merely to embellish an argument founded on knowledge of legal statutes, not verbal wisdom. Such a lack of formalized situations in which proverbs are both used and regarded as important tends to reduce their social meaning in the United States.

The potential significance of a proverb is further reduced by the frequently disparate backgrounds of speakers and auditors. Hence, Americans are often unaware of the original or intended meanings of proverbs to the extent that the utterance of a specific proverb in a given social context may well be interpreted in varying ways by those to whom the proverb is addressed.[13] Even if a proverb's meaning is understood, its appearance is generally seen as a witty or pedantic, as opposed to a wise or sacred, pronouncement. Furthermore, the prevalence of contradictory proverbs and the numerous parodies of proverbs[14] indicate that they are regarded within the context of American society as quaint old things to play with rather than as words to live by.

The foregoing suggests that any successful contextual study of proverbs in America must limit itself to examining only the verifiably significant proverbs of individuals or small groups.[15] By examining an esoteric proverb in the possession of one family I hope to show that a proverb may not only fulfill a variety of functions, but that these functions multiply and crystallize as the size of the group possessing the proverb decreases.

It was mid-afternoon and sunny as I sat with George Russell, a retired bachelor farmer, in his tiny kitchen in Brill, Wisconsin, on August 21, 1974. Yellowed photographs of relatives and bright holy cards were intermingled with a Home Gas calendar and a clipping of grocery specials on the white walls around us. George poured his 82 years of experience into my tape recorder, while I poured his brandy down my throat. "You know," he said to me, "I own this house and I own land." His arm swept broadly in a kind of benediction over his surroundings. "My mother always said, in fact, we all said it, but she made it up: 'the land won't burn.' And I'll tell you a little story about that saying. . . ."[16] What followed was the complex explanation of an esoteric proverb.

When George Russell told me that he owned land and that his mother had said "the land won't burn,"[17] it was not his intention to be either clever or obscure. Rather he was making a complex and compressed statement about himself, his family, and basic beliefs they had held in common. His utterance was immediately recognizable as a proverb—it was a complete sentence stating some kind of truth; it was binary in structure and could be typologically described as expressing negative equivalence[18]— yet I was unable to penetrate its meaning. Fortunately, George's explanation rapidly followed.

In 1870 Irish-born Patrick Russell moved from Ontario, Canada, to Oak Grove, Wisconsin, to become one of the pioneer settlers of an agricultural township located northeast of the lumbering community, Rice Lake.[19] On land which he had purchased, Russell built a farm home, and it was there that George was born in 1892. In the second decade of the twentieth century two of George's older brothers decided to leave home. Rather than invest in land, they planned to buy timber in Idaho and ship it for sale in midwest markets. As George tells it:

> They were going to make a little money with that Idaho pine, 'though it isn't so good as our Wisconsin white pine. They had the timber all piled up and ready to ship out on railroad flatcars, but lightning struck it and everything burned up. They came back home to the farm, and my mother told them, "You should've bought land with the money; the land won't burn." After that, we'd use that saying among ourselves.[20]

Thwarted in the outside world, the boys stayed with the farm. George, himself, left briefly to work with the Canadian railroad, but returned home before the First World War. By 1928, the Russell farm was "one of the finest in Barron County."[21]

The Russells' farm continued to prosper until, unable to work it any longer, they sold it in the early 1950's and moved to a smaller place southeast of Rice Lake. By this time the parents were long dead; dead too was one brother. Another brother had married, while a Russell girl had joined a convent. But the remaining core of the family—two bachelor sons and three spinster daughters—continued to live together. Today—the others having died one-by-one—only George is left.

Given this knowledge of the Russell family and of their proverb's etymology, it is readily apparent that a great many things might be said about the proverb's function. Chronologically, the proverb appeared in a variety of social contexts:

(1) *"The Land Won't Burn" as Mrs. Russell's creative expression.* The proverb Mrs. Russell coined that day her sons returned from Idaho was no mere witticism; rather, it was a poetic effort to "name" and "control" an anxious situation. As was the case with many midwestern farm families in the early twentieth century, the Russells were on the verge of splintering as a family unit. Patrick Russell had died in 1912 and briefly it had appeared that two of the boys might leave. By saying "the land won't burn" Mrs. Russell was, first of all, implying that anything which was not the land—which was not, in fact, the farm—would burn, disintegrate, vanish. Secondly, Mrs. Russell was rhetorically pressuring her sons to remain at home. Consequently, Mrs. Russell's proverb not only stressed the dangers attending ventures into the outside world and her faith in the timeless security of the farm home, but it also argued the need for familial unity.

(2) *"The Land Won't Burn" as family expression.* As George tells us—"we'd use that saying among ourselves"—Mrs. Russell's proverb was taken up and utilized by other family members both previous to and long after her death in 1939. The fact that so many of the sons and daughters remained together until death suggests that the proverb was interpreted and used by family members as both a mechanism for maintaining and validating familial cohesion and as a charter for future actions.[22] This latter function is exemplified by the fact that after selling the large family farm the Russells invested in a smaller farm rather than buying or renting an apartment in town as other retired farm families commonly do. Furthermore, the proverb was esoteric; it belonged to the Russells and to no one else. Even if others heard it, they could not know the depth of its meaning without being told by a Russell.

(3) "The Land Won't Burn" as George Russell's personal expression. When George Russell spoke the proverb to me, he was not only acting as a historian in recalling the circumstances surrounding its emergence and its subsequent use within his family, but he was also consciously employing the proverb to both commemorate his past and justify his present. As the last Russell, he had sold their second farm, but, true to his mother's maxim, he had purchased a small house with some land. Thus, with a

James P. Leary

single—and apparently simple—statement, George simultaneously evoked three distinct contexts and many more functions for "the land won't burn." As a proverb in the possession of a single speaker, "the land won't burn" achieved its fullest complexity.

Accordingly, it seems that in America as a group becomes more esoteric the chance of confusion or ambiguity over the meaning of a proverb decreases, while the possibility of its fulfilling multiple functions increases. This is certainly true in the case of the Russells.

As we parted George told me of his efforts to fix up the family plot before he passed on. All the Russells are buried together in the town of Oak Grove, and George is the last one alive. I asked to take his picture. He said "yes," put on his hat and coat, and led me outside. Directing me to a point at the lawn's far edge, he posed stiffly and proudly before his small house, surrounded by land he owned.

---

[1] See Richard M. Dorson, "Concepts of Folklore and Folklife Studies," in *Folklore and Folklife* (Chicago, 1972), 45–47.

[2] For example, see Roger Abrahams, "The Complex Relations of Simple Forms," *Genre*, 2 (1969), 105–128; Alan Dundes, "Texture, Text, and Context," *Southern Folklore Quarterly*, 28 (1964), 251–265; and Dan Ben-Amos, "Toward a Definition of Folklore in Context," *Journal of American Folklore*, 84 (1971), 3–15.

[3] E. Ojo Arewa and Alan Dundes, "Proverbs and the Ethnography of Speaking Folklore," *American Anthropologist*, 66, No. 6, Part 2 (1954), 70–85; and Roger Abrahams, "On Proverbs and Proverb Collections," *Proverbium*, 7 (1967), 181–184.

[4] Roger D. Abrahams, "A Rhetoric of Everyday Life: Traditional Conversational Genres," *Southern Folklore Quarterly*, 32 (1968), 44–54.

[5] Peter Seitl, "Proverbs: A Social Use of Metaphor," *Genre*, 2 (1969), 143–161; Richard Priebe, "The Horses of Speech: A Structural Analysis of the Proverb," *Folklore Annual of the University Folklore Association* (Austin, Texas), No. 3 (1971), 26–32; and Heda Jason, "Proverbs in Society: The Problem of Meaning and Function," *Proverbium*, 17 (1972), 617–23.

[6] Kenneth Burke, *The Philosophy of Literary Form* (New York, 1957), pp. 3–4 and 253–55; Abrahams, "A Rhetoric," p. 47.

[7] For example, Raymond Firth, "Proverbs in Native Life, With Special Reference to Those of the Maori," *Folk-Lore*, 37 (1926), 134–53, 245–70; George Herzog, *Jabo Proverbs From Liberia* (London, 1936); Saul H. Riesenberg and J. L. Fisher, "Some Ponapean Proverbs," *Journal of American Folklore*, 68 (1955), 9–18; John Messenger, "The Role of the Proverb in a Nigerian Judicial System," *Southwest Journal of Anthropology*, 15 (1959), 64–73; and George M. Foster, "Character and Personal Relationships Seen Through Proverbs in Tzintzuntzan, Mexico," *Journal of American Folklore*, 83 (1970), 304–317.

[8] Arewa and Dundes investigate the Yoruba; Seitl examines the Ibo; Abrahams, "On Proverbs and Proverb Collections," draws his inferences from fieldwork in the Carribbean. A notable exception is Richard Bauman and Neil McCabe, "Proverbs in an LSD Cult," *Journal of American Folklore*, 83 (1970), 318–324.

[9] Robert Redfield, "The Folk Society," *Journal of American Sociology*, 7 (1947), 293. The criticisms and modifications of George M. Foster—"What is Folk Culture?" *American Anthropologist*, 55 (1953), 159–173—notwithstanding, Redfield's ideal model remains useful in illustrating what are basic contrasting features.

[10] Robert B. Klymasz, in an article treating the Ukrainians of Western Canada—"From Immigrant to Ethnic Folklore: A Canadian View of Process and Transition," *Journal of the Folklore Institute*, 10 (1973), 131–139—outlines the various processes by which old world folklore is modified to accommodate the complexities of modern civilization. He contends that "The specifics of the Old Country folklore complex are forgotten, unknown, or blurred"; thus when forms such as the proverb appear in the new world, they seldom possess the deep significance they bore in times past.

[11] Dundes and Arewa; Seitl; Ruth Finnegan, *Oral Literature in Africa* (London, 1970), 413–414.

[12] Messenger; Finnegan, pp. 408–410.

[13] This problem is discussed briefly in Alan Dundes, "Metafolklore and Oral Literary Criticism," *The Monist*, 50 (1966), 505–516.

[14] C. Grant Loomis, "Traditional American Wordplay: The Epigram and Perverted Proverbs," *Western Folklore*, 8 (1949), 348–357; see also Jan Brunvand, *The Study of American Folklore* (New York, 1968), p. 45.

[15] This has been done by Bauman and McCabe; proverbs used by a small group are also briefly touched upon in Mary Ellen Lewis, "The Feminists Have Done It," *Journal of American Folklore,* 87 (1974), 85–87.

[16] Tape-recorded interview, August 21, 1974.

[17] Although it is possible that Mrs. Russell's proverb is not unique, it was considered as such. Investigation of standard reference works yielded no parallel example.

[18] For a recent comment on the structure of proverbs, see Roger D. Abrahams, "Proverbs and Proverbial Expressions," in *Folklore and Folklife,* pp. 119–121; see also Matti Kuusi, *Towards an International Type-System of Proverbs,* Folklore Fellows Communications, No. 21 (Helsinki, 1972).

[19] Russell's account is corroborated in Katharine Leary Antenne, *A Saga of Furs, Forests, and Farms* (Rice Lake, 1955), p. 32; see also Newton S. Gordon and Franklyn Curtiss-Wise, *History of Barron County, Wisconsin* (Minneapolis, 1922), pp. 334–335.

[20] Tape-recorded interview, August 21, 1974.

[21] Rice Lake *Chronotype,* September 12, 1928.

[22] Here I am borrowing from William Bascom, "Four Functions of Folklore," in Alan Dundes, *The Study of Folklore* (Englewood Cliffs, New Jersey, 1965), 290–295.

# Totemism and the A.E.F. Revisited
Elliott Oring

*Figurative or connotative meanings underlie most, if not all, expressions that we have come to label "folklore" (Edmonson 1971:1-6). Metaphor is one prominent figure in which an object or event is likened to another by virtue of some structural, functional, or qualitative similarity. Metonymy is another figure in which a part comes to stand for the whole (as a crown may signify monarchy or a tooth dentistry). The relevance of metaphor and metonym to the analysis of riddles, proverbs, and other artistic forms of expression has been amply demonstrated. The following essay extends the analysis of these relations to the non-artistic realm of folk belief and ritual practice.*

*"Totemism" was a term used to characterize a variety of practices and beliefs including: the belief that the members of kinship groups (lineages, clans) are related to and descended from a particular species of plant or animal or class of natural objects; prohibitions against killing, eating, or touching one's totem species; employment of the totem as a name or emblem of the group; rituals focused around the totem. Because such beliefs and practices were found among certain technologically primitive groups, totemism was thought to be the very earliest form of religion. Today anthropologists regard totemism as a process of mind rather than as a specific set of beliefs and practices—the process of classifying social groups in terms of objects in the natural world (Lévi-Strauss 1963a). Totemism, in this sense, can be found operating in all human groups. Since totemism is fundamentally concerned with relations, the analysis of metaphor and metonym should contribute to the understanding of this process.*

*For a discussion of metaphor and metonym in the context of a theory of symbols see Leach (1976). The difference between metaphoric and metonymic relations is at the root of Sir James George Frazer's distinction between homeopathic magic (1963: 12-43) and contagious magic (43-52). For other examples of folklore from the Vietnam War see Tuso (1971, 1972) and Dewhurst (1988).*

In 1924, Ralph Linton called attention to the curious development of a "pseudo-totemic complex" among the members of the 42nd division of the American Expeditionary Force stationed in France during the First World War.[1] The 42nd division (it was said) had been named the Rainbow Division by higher officials because it comprised units from an assortment of states whose regimental colors were as variegated as a rainbow. After the division arrived in France, non-division personnel persisted in referring to division members as "Rainbow" and individual division members would identify themselves as such. Several months after the use of this name became prevalent, a feeling of sympathy developed between the divisional organization and its namesake:

> It was believed that the appearance of a rainbow was a good omen for the division. Three months later it had become an article of faith in the organization that there was always a rainbow in the sky when the division went into action. A rainbow over the evening's lines was considered especially auspicious, and after a victory men would often insist that they had seen one in this position even when the weather conditions or direction of advance made it impossible.[2]

Because of contact with other divisions who had emblems, the rainbow later developed as a divisional emblem, individualistically and surreptitiously painted upon various kinds of divisional equipment; until after the armistice, when a standardized design was officially permitted. A similar development took place with an individual shoulder insignia. Linton postulated that this and other similar behavior-belief complexes that developed in the A.E.F. were fully as rich as complexes that had been designated totemic for many primitive societies.

Lévi-Strauss cites Linton's article as a contribution to the American anthropological indifference to the totemic problem; for what had been made eminently clear since the writings of Boas and Goldenweiser in the early decades of this century was that there was no stable complex of traits that could be delimited by the term totemism. In reality, exogamous clan organization, the use of plants, animals and other natural phenomena as names or emblems, the belief in a relationship (often of descent) between clan and species, and killing and eating taboos only rarely coincide, although each of these traits is often encountered in the absence of the others.[3] Lévi-Strauss, consequently, denies the reality of any institution that might properly be labeled totemism and characterizes most of the scholarship on totemism as the investigation of an "illusion."[4] But where Lévi-Strauss is unwilling to grant totemism institutional existence, he is willing to recognize it as a process of the human mind; as a "classificatory device whereby discrete elements of the external world are associated with discrete elements of the social world."[5]

It is under this radically reformulated definition that we propose to extend our catalogue of contemporary totemisms. The two cases we intend to present derive from the more recent experiences of American "expeditionary forces" in Vietnam. It is hoped that in reporting these recent cases, we may begin to appreciate the diversity of forms generated by the totemic process and to evaluate the applicability of extant theory in accounting for these phenomena.

The first case developed in 1967 and 1968 among the members of an Airforce Para-Rescue Squadron who were functioning as military police securing the perimeters of American air bases in Vietnam. Generally, they would undertake night and day patrols in teams of twelve men to intercept North Vietnamese regulars and Viet Cong that were operating in the area. On one occasion while on patrol, the team was involved in a major firefight that developed between the 101st Airborne Brigade and some North Vietnamese regulars. There was extensive small arms and mortar fire and the team was pinned down in trenches awaiting the arrival of support gunships and rescue. During the heaviest part of the fight, however, the men noticed that some distance off to one side of the trench, a mongoose was attacking a large snake (not a cobra). Despite all that was taking place, the men became fascinated with the progress of this mini-battle in the world of nature. As it turned out, the mongoose was victorious, and after the firefight ended, the team returned to base bringing the mongoose with them. When one of the men suggested that the mongoose had been instrumental in turning the tide of battle, the notion was generally disputed. But once the idea had been planted, it was not so easily dismissed:

> A lot of guys scoffed at it. I myself kind of thought about it, laughed about it and
> forgot about it until the next time around. When we were pulling security, and
> when you are alone and when you are worried about being wounded or killed,
> you know, you begin to think about things like that.[6]

Shortly, though not immediately, after the firefight, security teams began to take the mongoose with them on patrol. It was on one of these patrols, led by the mongoose on a little leash, that another transformation in the group's attitude toward the mongoose occurred. A Viet Cong had planted grenades and dug himself in alongside the trail awaiting the passage of American troops. It would have been possible for the lead men to have overlooked his presence but the hairs on the mongoose's back went up and it started jumping up and down. Because of the antics of the mongoose, this Viet Cong "zapper" (as he was called) was spotted.

Because of these incidents, the mongoose began to assume a more important place in the thinking and behavior of the group.

> We really came to rely on the mongoose to come through. It's like we turned off
> our own senses and relied on the mongoose's alone. A lot of guys really
> dropped their guard. They figured that depending [upon] how the mongoose
> would react while we were on patrol was how we would fare.[7]

Subsequently, the mongoose's senses were extended not only to the presence of the enemy and the imminence of a firefight, but to prediction of the outcome of the fight as well. The mongoose would remain comparatively passive in what would turn out to be small scrimmages; but in fights where it became necessary to call in army units or air support, his behavior would appear much more frenetic.

This relationship between the group and the mongoose had reached a level that one can only characterize as "mystical." It was a relationship that my informant found difficult to express:

I feel that we established a closeness with the mongoose. I mean closer than you can get with a typical domestic pet. I don't really know how to put it into words—I mean it seems kind of ridiculous to say a oneness—but I really thought that the mongoose was looking out for us and we were looking out for the mongoose.[8]

Members of this squadron eventually came to be known by other groups as "Mongoose." Trucks were painted with mongoose figures and some squadron members even had themselves tattooed. By the time my informant left Vietnam, this complex of behavior closely resembled that described by Linton for the 42nd Division.

The second case involving the totemic process varies considerably from the first. It developed among a platoon of approximately twenty infantrymen in 1969 and 1970. The skull of a Vietnamese was dug up by platoon members while routinely exploring a fresh grave site for possible caches of enemy arms and ammunition. Skulls seem to have been in demand in the infantry. Infantrymen would keep them while they were in Vietnam and then try to smuggle them out of the country. They were usually unsuccessful because skulls never got through the mail. This particular skull, however, was not claimed by any individual and became a group possession. It was named Bruce, given a hat, sunglasses, a combat infantry badge and even a pair of pants, and was mounted on the top of a stake. Whenever the platoon moved from one encampment to another, Bruce moved with them. The stake would be planted in the ground to serve as an identification marker for the platoon. Within the platoon encampment, whenever there were parties or guys would get together drinking, or if group pictures were being taken, someone always would make sure Bruce was involved. When on the move through Vietnamese villages, Bruce would often be brandished in order to intimidate the local populations. The members of the platoon implied that the skull on the pole was a fate that uncooperative Vietnamese could expect. The more contemptuous the reaction elicited from the Vietnamese, the greater the hilarity of the men.

The platoon in general was committed to the aggravation of all but other combat infantry. In fact, anyone who was not combat infantry was considered a *Rimp*. Rimp is a phonetically pronounceable shift from R-E-M-F which is the acronym for *rear eschelon motherfucker*. Combat infantry were known as *Grunts*.[9] Rear eschelon people had a very easy tour of duty from the point of view of combat infantry. They accumulated more money, had less rigorous assignments, received quicker promotions and didn't have to do any dirty work (since they had the South Vietnamese population to do everything for them). They were the object of a great deal of hostility and antagonism (to the extent that occasional shots were fired at them). Whenever the platoon would enter or leave a base, they would yell and curse and throw things at the rear eschelon people. Those who tried to be friendly towards them would meet with rejection. If someone gave them the peace sign they would give him the "finger". If anyone shouted "peace" they would yell "war" and suggest they "shouldn't knock something until they tried it." All peace slogans and hymns were revised with "war" and "aggression" substitutes. With all of this they would brandish Bruce about at the end of his pole.[10]

Elliott Oring

According to Lévi-Strauss's definition of the totemic process which we cited above, both behavior-belief complexes that we have described should qualify as totemisms. Each involves a classificatory act by which elements of the natural world are associated with elements of the social world. Admittedly, the principles of association differ. The mongoose stood in some sort of mystical relationship to the airforce para-rescue squadron; Bruce, however, was considered a member of the infantry platoon. Nevertheless, both could serve as emblems to represent the entire social group.[11]

Current theory tends to view totemic representations as a code. The choice of representations is not arbitrary but rather is designed to convey messages about social realities utilizing symbols drawn from the world of nature organized in a series of contrasts and oppositions.[12] The natural species are often chosen as symbols not because they are "good to eat" (as Radcliffe-Brown proposed in his first theory of totemism) but because they are "good to think."[13] This general perspective is not without value in the analysis of our contemporary data, although modifications in some of its specific corollaries will be necessary.

The elevation of the mongoose to significance for the para-rescue squadron is based upon a "thinkability" that is emotionally charged and contextually derived. It is only in the context of a particular life and death struggle with the enemy that the opposition between mongoose and snake becomes a "significant thinkable." Given all the possibilities of stimuli received by the security team during the firefight, it is only the stimulus of the mongoose fighting the snake that is accorded significance because of its structural similarity to the social reality of the moment. It must have been viewed by the team members in terms of a Lévi-Straussian homology: *we are to the enemy as the mongoose is to the snake.* It is only the temporal coincidence of conflict in the social and natural worlds that accords the mongoose its special status. It is important to note that a lasting identification develops between only one set of terms in the homology; the security team and the mongoose. No permanent association develops between the enemy and the snake, for the enemy is never faunally characterized. The structure as a whole does not persist. Furthermore, the identification with the mongoose required additional reinforcement for its stabilization. This reinforcement came when the mongoose proved instrumental in saving the team from ambush. After that incident, the identification with the mongoose was firmly established.

When the mongoose began to be employed as an emblem and members of the squadron were referred to as "Mongoose" we must note that this identification has achieved autonomy. It is no longer dependent upon the original homology for its significance. Nor can it be understood at the level of the social system. There is no way to contrast "Mongoose" with the "Wolf Hounds" (an army unit that was operating at the same time) and understand the mongoose as a symbol. The process by which the mongoose achieved symbolic significance is not relevant to the differentiation of military units from one another. When they are viewed from the perspective of social differentiation, these totems may be regarded as arbitrary.

Unlike the case with the mongoose, skulls already possessed what Radcliffe-Brown has called "ritual value"[14] prior to the elevation of Bruce to a group emblem. The value of skulls at the individual level, however, is directly related to the significance of Bruce as a group symbol. The combat infantry saw themselves as markedly distinct from all other American groups. They were the only ones that were actively engaged on a day-to-day basis in a deadly shooting war. Members of the platoon anticipated being killed or maimed in combat. Rimps, on the other hand, though nominally a part of the Vietnamese War, were ensconced in safety and comfort. They were the very antithesis of what the real war was all about. They represented all the values, attitudes and behaviors alien to a theater of war. The combat infantryman inverted all of these values, and these inversions were most clearly reflected in platoon songs: "Red roses for a blue lady" became "Red tracers for my M-16"; "All we are saying is give peace a chance" became "All we are saying is give war a chance"; "And we'll all feel gay when Johnny comes marching home" became "We'll all be dead by Christmas of this year." If we wished to phrase the relationship between combat infantry and rear eschelon personnel formally it might read: *Rimps are to grunts as living men are to dead men.* The realization of this abstract formula is the recruitment of a dead man into the platoon. Bruce was a platoon *member.* He possessed elements of infantry uniform, he appeared in platoon pictures and he was listed in unofficial platoon rosters.

Despite the differences between the behavior-belief complexes described in our two examples above, we believe that they are both classifiable as totemisms. Moreover, it would appear that elements of current theory are useful in illuminating the dynamics of both totemic processes. Each may be expressed in terms of a homology that provides an insight into the nature of the relationship between species[15] and social group. Nevertheless, questions arise regarding the applicability of other aspects of Lévi-Strauss's analysis; most notably, his contention that totemism involves a homology

> not between social groups and natural species but between the differences which manifest themselves on the level of groups on the one hand and on that of species on the other. They are thus based on the postulate of a homology between *two systems of differences,* one of which occurs in nature and the other in culture. . . . This structure would be fundamentally impaired if . . . the entire system of homologies were transferred from relations to terms.[16]

In our examples from Vietnam however, it is an analogy of terms that is fundamental. The para-rescue squadron is like the mongoose; the combat infantry platoon is like the skeleton Bruce. Systems of difference play no part here, only the establishment of a relationship between terms.

In any event, we have no reason at this time to challenge Linton's basic hypothesis that:

> the A.E.F. complexes and primitive totemism are results of the same social and supernaturalistic tendencies. The differences in the working out of these complexes . . . readily . . . [being] accounted for by the differences in the framework to which they have shaped their expression.[17]

313

# Elliott Oring

There was a time when psychological and sociological theories suffered from the exclusive dependence upon the data of Western civilizations. Anthropologists infiltrated the societies of the world in an effort to gather the relevant cross-cultural data by which these theories might be confirmed, amended or discarded. But the immersion of anthropologists in exotic cultures led them to formulate new theories of thought and behavior. Now, it seems that the wheel has come full turn, and it remains for us to scrutinize these new theories in their applicability to the substance of our own behavior and belief.

---

[1] Ralph Linton, "Totemism and the A.E.F." in *Reader in Comparative Religion*, eds. William A. Lessa and Evon Z. Vogt, 2nd edition (New York, Evanston and London, 1965), 286–289.

[2] Ibid., 286.

[3] Alexander Goldenweiser, "Totemism," in *Reader in Comparative Religion*, 275–276.

[4] Claude Lévi-Strauss, *Totemism*, trans. by Rodney Needham (Boston, 1963), 15.

[5] Claude Lévi-Strauss, "The Bear and the Barber" in *Reader in Comparative Religion*, 294.

[6] A. H., personal communication, 3 March 1972.

[7] Ibid.

[8] Ibid. For an analogous (though not identical) relationship with a rooster see, Yehoshua Granot, "Fouad's Rooster" in *Written in Battle*, ed. Mordekhay Barkai (Tel Aviv, n.d.), 197–210.

[9] The term "grunt" was originally restricted to Marines but later became extended to combat troops in general. Michael Herr "200, Sir," *Esquire*, 84 (November 1975):100. There are two traditional connotations to the term "grunt" that make it relevant to combat soldiers: (1) a pig, [as in "grunter"], (2) a habitual grumbler or a complaint. See John S. Farmer and W. E. Henley eds., *Slang and Its Analogues: Past and Present* (New York, 1965), and Lester V. Berry and Melvin Van Den Bark, *The American Thesaurus of Slang* (New York, 1942).

[10] S. M., personal communication, 14 May 1975.

[11] Current structuralist terminology would distinguish between the mongoose as *metaphor* and Bruce as *metonym*. See Edmund Leach, *Culture and Communication* (Cambridge, London, New York and Melbourne, 1976), 14.

[12] Lévi-Strauss, "The Bear and the Barber," 182.

[13] Lévi-Strauss, *Totemism*, 89.

[14] A. R. Radcliffe-Brown, "Taboo," in *Reader in Comparative Religion*, 113.

[15] Note that dead men are not a social group but a natural species. The mongoose may also be considered as the representative of a species rather than as an individual since it never acquired a name. It was simply referred to as "the mongoose".

[16] Claude Lévi-Strauss, *The Savage Mind* (Chicago, 1970), 115.

[17] Linton, 289.

# IX
# Folk Objects

## The Nebraska Round Barn
### Roger L. Welsch

*The study of folk architecture, largely the province of folklife researchers and cultural geographers, has primarily focused on the classification, measurement, distribution, construction, and modification of rural material forms (e.g. Petersen 1976). In the following essay, Roger L. Welsch briefly sketches the history of the round barn but turns to the contemplation of its potential functional advantage in the environment of the Plains. While most of these advantages can be inferred from the structural characteristics of the form itself, some advantages can only be recognized through use. It is the behaviors that occur in and around a barn, and the ideas that are expressed about it, that situate this object from the past in contemporary folklife.*

*Glassie (1968) provides a useful survey of the patterns and distribution of architectural and other material forms in the eastern United States. Beyond historical, geographical, and functional issues, questions concerning the symbolism, psychology, grammar, and ideology of folk architecture have been explored (Cunningham 1964; Welsch 1976-77; Glassie 1975). For more on the traditional architecture of the Plains see Welsch (1968, 1970, 1976).*

*Round barns*—henceforth in this paper a generic term used for both round and polygonal barns—are a traditional feature of American folk architecture, a feature which has been now and again reinforced by extrinsic, sophisticated architectural fashions. In a forward to a New York State Historical Association pamphlet entitled "Octagon Buildings in New York State"[1] Carl Carmer remarks that though Orson Fowler's 19th century architectural polemics for the octagon certainly encouraged the construction of late 19th century polygons, the ultimate provenience of round and polygonal structures antedates Fowler by some years. Indeed, in Marguerite Marigold's article "Hayfield"[2] in the journal of the Historical Society of Fairfax County, Virginia, it is noted that George Washington had a sixteen-sided barn. In *Les Granges du*

Roger L. Welsch

*Québec*,[3] Robert Lionel Seguin speculates that the round barn entered American agriculture around 1830, during a period of extensive experimentation with farming techniques. Eric Sloane also supports this contention: "The famed octagon house of 1850 was preceded by the octagon and circular barn of 1830,"[4] but other substantial errors by Sloane in regard to round barns cast suspicion on this conclusion too. At any rate, round barns have been a part of rural architecture since the Revolutionary War. Beyond this I have not yet been able to find European antecedents; although many of the builders of Indiana, Iowa, Wisconsin, Pennsylvania, and Nebraska barns were Germans, this may only be a reflection of the predominance of German farmers in these areas; that is, many midwestern barns, regardless of configuration, were built by Germans.

In 1854 Orson Squire Fowler's octagon gospel, *A Home for All*, was published.[5] Fowler was a phrenologist and some of his reasons for designing an octagonal house were mystic; others were surprisingly practical. Besides the natural advantages of the polygon, which I shall catalog later in this paper, he devised an efficient system for central heating, indoor plumbing (including hot and cold running water), and gas lighting. His ideas caused some impact on Victorian, neo-Gothic architecture, and houses in his style were built all across the country—including Nebraska. Though his designs were principally for houses, most of the general, theoretical advantages of the octagon are also valid for the barn and, even though it is not a certain fact, it does seem likely that his influence extended to rural architecture, especially in light of the new favor round barns found in the later years of the 19th century and the frequent mention of Fowler in farm journals of the time. The question is, however, did Fowler strike on the octagon independently or did he discover and elaborate on the already extant tradition? Was his an external or internal impetus to the tradition?

Shortly after Fowler's work, in the years from 1890 to 1915, farm journals and magazines began to publish occasional articles on round barns—but rarely did they present theoretical considerations for the ideal barn; instead they used photographs and sketches of existing barns. The *Breeder's Gazette* manual entitled *Farm Buildings*,[6] for example, shows photographs and drawings of ten extant round barns in Iowa, Indiana, Pennsylvania, Wisconsin, and Illinois. This suggests that the sophisticated concern was a product of the tradition rather than the reverse. Furthermore, the barns are common enough to constitute a tradition; they are neither isolated nor unique. In Nebraska there are at least 35 such barns and the fact that most have been reported to me by only one informant suggests that many others have not been reported at all. Almost every Nebraska round barn is within 25 miles of another, but in spite of this, few people have noted them, and they are usually viewed as curiosities. Even Richard Perrin, an architecture scholar of some stature, says in his book *Historic Wisconsin Buildings*,[7] "A wood-frame barn unique to Wisconsin is the octagonal type."

It is difficult to establish the historical context of the round barn in Nebraska because of the limited history of the State. (Statehood was granted in 1867.) All Nebraska round barns were built from 1885 to 1922, but then almost *all* Nebraska barns were built during these years. However, evidence from other states—including a survey by

Couser barn, rural Cedar County, Nebraska. *Photograph by D. Murphy, Nebraska State Historical Society.*

Starke Brothers/Rasser round barn, rural Webster County, Nebraska. *Photograph by John Carter, Nebraska State Historical Society.*

Roger L. Welsch

Henry Glassie, an eastern folk architecture scholar—indicates that the "Golden Age of Round Barn Building" was indeed from about 1875 to 1920.

The distribution of the 35 barns in Nebraska promises—dependent upon a more definitive collection—to provide more information about the development and diffusion of the round barn in the State. For example, south of the Platte River, the most formidable physical feature of the State, are concentrated those round barns that are round rather than polygonal, those containing silos and lofts, and the bank barns. Furthermore, almost every builder I have been able to interview reports contact with another builder or owner. Variation of structural details within a general form and this established "oral" tradition verifies that the Nebraska round barn is a part of traditional, not sophisticated, farm architecture.

A common, though not universal, feature of traditional architecture is practicality; patently inefficient structures are quickly eliminated from traditional architecture. It seemed a reasonable course of action to determine the functional advantages of round construction, and the answers were so striking that I now must ask why barns were ever built rectangular.[8]

At this point I would like to catalog briefly the advantages of the round and polygonal barn:

1. A square barn with four forty-foot sides and ten-foot high walls contains 16,000 cubic feet. An octagon with eight twenty-foot sides (the same wall space as the square barn) ten foot high holds 19,314 cubic feet. A round barn with ten-foot walls and a circumference of 160 feet contains 20,382 cubic feet. In the lumber-poor areas of the plains this kind of economy was of capital importance.

2. Also of importance to the plains farmer was the fact that cylindrical structures resist side pressures more successfully than do cubic ones. One farmer told me that Nebraska barns seldom have wind vanes, for you can tell which way the wind is blowing by observing which direction the barn is leaning. To my knowledge, however, no Nebraska round barns have been blown down; one has lost its roof to a tornado and another was knocked down when a silo was blown over on it, but none has been directly damaged by the wind.

3. A parenthetical comment by Perrin offers another very important fact that I had sensed but never previously been able to pinpoint. Most of the barn lofts are astonishingly vast. They seem enormous and cathedral-like. Perrin says, ". . . the plates upon which the rafters rest are tied together with angle irons to make a continuous ring of the plate, thus converting the lateral thrusts of the roof into vertical loads upon the outside bearing walls."[9] Gambrel roofs need stretchers from the ridge beam to the plate; the gable roof needs stretchers from plate to plate to form the chord of the triangle (and these stretchers then form the joists for the loft floor). If the rafter span is at all long—and a barn is after all usually a large structure—there are additional vertical or horizontal members. Thus the space between the rafters and the floor of the loft is often obstructed by these stretchers. The loft is therefore reduced to a triangle, or near-triangle, the corners of which are the roof ridge and the meeting points of the

roof, the walls, and the loft joists. In the round barn, however, the plate, itself serves as the stretcher, for it is a solid, inseparable ring. Although the stretchers are sometimes also added, the floor can now be dropped several feet below the plate or omitted entirely, for the joists no longer serve as stretchers, only as floor bearers.

4. This "balloon" construction transfers all vertical stress to the walls and eliminates the need for heavy internal timbering—again an advantage on the barren plains. Most round barns have no members larger than a two-by-four.

5. About one third of the Nebraska barns have a silo in the center. This serves as a support for the roof and offers obvious ease in feeding animals. Perhaps it should be noted here that there is no difficulty in partitioning the barn. The center section, if there is no silo, can be cut into any size or shape desired and the animal stalls near the outer edges of the barn are, for all practical purposes, square, thereby discounting Sloane's fatuous, patently false statement that "... the idea was good but the proof was poor. Hay storage requires complicated devices for loading and the pie-shaped stalls would have been best only for pie-shaped animals."[10] Indeed, cows *do* require pie-shaped areas and as long as the stalls face the center the stall shapes are ideal. The two main disadvantages of the round barns are, contrary to Sloane's statements, sheathing of the cone-shaped roof and the carpentry of other than right angles.

6. Few barn owners, however, have given the above reasons. Indeed, most have no reason to offer, but then few of them have built the barns they are using. Of two explanations I have gotten from builders, the first was offered in jest: "I built the barn when the travelling salesmen were travelling about the countryside and I figured they could never corner my daughter there." The second was offered in all sincerity (although I hesitate to say in all honesty) and it is clearly related to my first point concerning the increased volume of the round barn in relation to wall area. In Nebraska all taxes are based on property and a farmer's hay is liable to taxation. In a square barn the volume can easily be calculated and local assessors are equipped to handle this; but because of the surprising increase in volume in a round structure the assessors have inevitably underestimated by at least one-fourth this farmer's hay supply and he feels that in its 44 years it has saved enough in taxes to pay for itself.

---

[1] Ruby Rounds (!), Compiler, *Octagon Buildings in New York State*. Information and photographs by Stephen R. Leonard, Sr. (Cooperstown, 1954), p. 3.

[2] Marguerite Marigold, "Hayfield," (journal of) *The Historical Society of Fairfax County, Virginia*, volume 9 (Vienna, Virginia, 1964–1965), p. 52.

[3] Robert Lionel Seguin, *Les Granges du Québec* (Ottowa, 1963), p 82.

[4] Eric Sloane, *American Barns and Covered Bridges* (New York, 1954), pp. 76–77.

[5] Orson Squire Fowler, *A Home for All, or the Gravel Wall and Octagon Mode of Building, New, Cheap, Convenient, Superior, and Adapted to Rich and Poor* (1854).

[6] *The Breeder's Gazette. Farm Buildings* (Chicago, 1911), pp. 27–28, 50, 51–52, 133–134, 146, 363, 370, 378.

[7] Richard Perrin, *Historic Wisconsin Buildings, Milwaukee Public Museum Publications in History*, no. 4 (Milwaukee, n.d.), p. 43.

[8] I am indebted to Warren Roberts of the Folklore Institute, Indiana University, for suggesting this consideration.

[9] Perrin, p. 43.

[10] Sloane, p. 77.

# The Palauan Story-Board: The Evolution of a Folk Art Style

Roger Mitchell

*As traditional societies were contacted by agents of Western civilization, their folklore and cultures changed. Ancient technical processes were often abandoned in favor of Western tools and machines; oral, social, and ritual traditions disappeared or went underground in response to both missionizing and secularizing forces. When folklorists and anthropologists came to describe these societies, they wrote down the words to the old tales and songs, elicited reports about the old rituals, photographed the traditional technical processes, and collected old artifacts in their efforts to document and preserve an image of the lore and culture that had existed prior to contact. In their zeal to reconstruct this image, they at first overlooked the adaptation of the old to the new.*

*Roger Mitchell traces the development and transformation of a Micronesian art form through a series of contacts and colonizations. He notes the early tie of story-boards to the institution of the bai or men's house. But with the destruction of the bai, the art form did not disappear. The marketing of handicrafts provided a major impetus to the survival and development of the form. Tourists became the new audience for story-board art, and consequently influenced its performance.*

*Folklorists have frequently viewed a market economy generally and tourism specifically as inimical to the maintenance or development of folk arts. The term "tourist art" is often used pejoratively to connote the inauthentic and inferior arts that have come to replace the traditional ones. Yet as Mitchell points out, the Palauans are not perturbed by the changes in story-board art. They do not dismiss it because it is no longer an outgrowth of bai decoration. Nor is there any objective basis for characterizing recent story-board art as inferior. What then is the folklorist to make of contemporary story-board production?*

*Similar changes in the traditional arts have been reported for Pueblo ceramics (Babcock et al. 1986) and Hmong textiles (Peterson 1988). Graburn (1976) provides a perspective on the development of ethnic and tourist arts worldwide.*

It is not unusual in academic circles to hear deprecatory remarks about "airport art" when the locals cluster about the newest influx of tourists, hawking their carvings, shell necklaces, and other assorted twentieth century facsimiles of artifacts once vital to

Reproduced by permission of the publisher, from *Midwestern Journal of Language and Folklore* 1, no. 2(1975):40–51. Not for further reproduction.

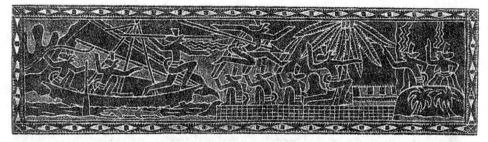

STORY-BOARD A—A man and his brother are fishing and they observe a shark swimming upside down. This means that the man's wife is committing adultery. He hurries home. Knowing that one of the men on the stone jetty must be guilty, he brandishes his spear and threatens the group. The adulterer runs and is speared. The murderer presents his case to the chief and is forgiven, for the chief admires his cleverness. The chief's wife then tells him to consider the weakness of women and to forgive his wife. (The jagged lines indicate speech.)[1]

STORY-BOARD B—A woman who cannot be satisfied sexually is taken by her sons to a man famous for his long penis. He instructs them to paddle out to the end of his penis. The woman is thrown to her death by the force of his ejaculation. (Note the increase of detail in this modern carving. People have eyes, nipples, and navels. The bai itself is carefully decorated in the traditional fashion, including a sitting woman, which indicated that prostitutes were kept within).[2]

aboriginal ceremony and ritual. Indeed, the exuberant purchaser is fortunate if his joy in his recent acquisitions is not dampened by some purist's studied opinion that native art is on the decline, prostituted to the lack of taste of the uninitiated and the cupidity of Westernized natives who know far better the value of a dollar than the studied skills of their forefathers.

I have no intention of developing here a brief for the usual kind of native handicraft picked up by the casual visitor and toted home to gather dust on a shelf as solemn witness to an excursion to some exotic part of the globe. Yet before condemning such efforts *in toto,* one should take into consideration certain truisms. Culture is dynamic, and those aspects of culture having sufficient vitality and flexibility will seek new functions and live on, even if in attenuated form. There is also a matter of identity.

Roger Mitchell

Through these contemporary art forms, the craftsmen maintain contact with their cultural past and avoid being submerged completely in the rising tide of Westernization.

As for the visitor, if he would but abjure the curio shop bargain and search diligently, he would find excellent examples of native handicraft well worth the price and display space. With similar diligence, the specialist can learn a great deal about culture change in a study of the evolving process by which aboriginal art has been modified to fit the demands of the marketplace. As for the crude copies, they serve both the immediate needs of the casual visitor and the shrewd native entrepreneur seeking the means by which to satisfy his desires and needs for introduced goods that have become part of his definition of the good life.

Certainly I have found this less stuffy approach to local handicraft rewarding during two decades of contact with Micronesia in which I have busied myself in collecting both folklore and handicraft.[3] It was in this part of the Pacific following the United States' assuming of control over Japan's Micronesian possessions at the end of World War II that I first became acquainted with that art form called by Americans the story-board (see illustrations).

Story-board art is limited to the Palau Islands in Western Micronesia and consists of carving in bas-relief a series of important episodes from oral traditions. These carvings are then painted and serve to illustrate for the people of a village their mythological and legendary past. Traditionally, the carvings themselves were executed on the boards closing in the gable ends of the village men's house (called *bai*) and also on the exposed ceiling rafters within the bai. In this paper I will trace this art form in its journey from the men's house to the curio shop.

If history has not been kind to the Palauans, neither has it been dull. Beginning with Spanish claims associated with Magellan's 1521 landing on Guam, the Palau Islands along with the most of Micronesia have been successively claimed, governed, and exploited by Germany (following the Spanish-American War), Japan (post-World War I), and lastly the United States as the aftermath of victory over Japan in World War II. Through it all the Palauan story-board has survived. Languishing, being revived, taking new directions in technique and function—but nevertheless surviving as a viable art form.

The earliest reported contact with the Palau Islands (1710) by Spanish missionaries from Manila resulted in little more than a brief skirmish with the natives. The quest for souls was aborted and a new group of islands was added to the sailing charts.[4] The first sustained contact was less well planned. In 1783 the East India Company packet, the *Antelope*, went aground, and the crew established friendly relations with the islanders while building a new ship to carry them to Canton, China.

During their several months enforced sojourn, the English became well acquainted with their hosts, aided them in their inter-village feuds, visited in their villages, and observed in depth the Palauan way of life. Curiously enough, while describing tattooing, canoe decoration, and sundry carving—even a discussion of the men's houses on which story-board art was lavished—no mention was made of the decoration of these houses.[5] Indeed, one might well assume from this omission from the first major report on the Palau Islands that the steel tools which the marooned sailors left for their hosts might have had a direct effect on the developing of the story-board tradition itself.

Fortunately, it is not necessary to indulge in this kind of speculation, for a supplement to this popular first account soon followed. Drawing from interviews with the captain of the ill-fated *Antelope* and from journals of a second (and intentional) voyage to the Palau Islands in 1791, this addendum referred specifically to the men's houses (or *bai*):

> The pyes, or public buildings, are the most astonishing fabrics that we ever beheld, considering the tools and the workmen that constructed them.... The inside of this house was most curiously worked and ornamented with various flowers and figures; the ends had much the appearance of Gentoo temples.[6]

In addition to these pointed references, there are two sketches, side and front, of a men's house, and adorning these sketches are faces, roosters, trees, and stylized sun disks, motifs that are still to be found in contemporary story-board art.[7] While this early source does not state that these assorted carvings were a form of narrative in wood, it seems safe to assume that these early voyagers were indeed describing the Palauan story-board and its associated carvings and paintings.

Nearly a hundred years pass before one again encounters any sustained reference to men's houses and story-boards. This does not mean that contact with the Palau Islands had ceased but rather that the reporters apparently did not consider the carvings and paintings worth discussing. Even the enterprising German, Albert Tetens, who left a chatty, even garrulous, account of his stay in a trading station on Palau, ignores the men's houses and their well-executed art. Rather, Tetens seems much more concerned with projecting himself as an astute trader, brave warrior, and accomplished ladies' man.

However, fortunately for those interested in the arts, Tetens' countryman, Karl Semper, also appeared on the scene; and we can turn to Tetens for an assessment of Semper's powers of observation:

> ... he filled me with admiration in undergoing the hardships and privations of his life and his persistence in the service of science.... Nothing escaped him; he grasped the political, economic, and social conditions with unusual clarity and explained the smallest happenings scientifically.[8]

Tetens describes Semper well, for although he was a natural scientist (and suffering from an infected foot), he responded to the art and function of the story-board. In his discussions with the old men and chiefs, Semper learned that the carvings on the gable ends and rafters of the bais represented myths and legends and that when the houses became old and were rebuilt anew, the same tales were etched into the woodwork of the new edifice. According to Semper's informants, some of the carvings were so old that the stories behind them had been forgotten. Yet some chiefs insisted that only the old tales and motifs be used in bai decoration, even though they knew that in some village bais ships and their English crews were included in the pictorial representations of events old and recent.[9]

Roger Mitchell

From these early English and German accounts, it emerges that Palauan story-board art was an aboriginal cultural trait and that the first century of contact had not destroyed it as a functional art form. It also appears from Semper's book that while some Palauans were purists when it came to the traditions to be carved on the bais, others were quite flexible and were willing to include carvings honoring recent events.

Karl Semper in his *Die Palau-Inseln im Stillen Ocean* bequeathed neither photographs nor sketches to posterity. But this omission was soon to be rectified. As was common among nineteenth century men of wealth, Johannes Godeffroy, a German merchant of Hamburg, took great interest in the natural sciences. He indulged this predilection by supporting his own private museum, journal, and ethnographer-natural scientist. Godeffroy made a fortunate choice when he employed for this task a Polish exile, Johann Kubary, as his envoy to Micronesia.[10] Kubary spent the greater part of his life there, and among his several excellent reports on Palau he included a careful study of the bai and its carved and painted oral traditions.[11]

Thorough scholar that he was, Kubary gave a painstaking account of the bais and their construction, along with many references to the myths and legends used in the decoration of the gable ends and rafters. All this is backed up with fifty-five plates of etchings and colored sketches that vividly portray the story-board technique. He notes, too, that with the coming of European traders, some traditional motifs such as the bat have been replaced in some bais by representations of Western sailing vessels. He also agreed with Semper that the subject matter of some of the old carvings was no longer understood the Palauans.[12] All this is of historical interest in understanding the development of story-board art; for it means that before Western powers assumed active control of the Palau Islands, the tradition was a flexible one. Tales were carved and painted, forgotten in part as time passed, reinterpreted, added to with a fresh infusion of new motifs and narrative incidents, all a part of cultural dynamics.

Important to our understanding of Palauan art and culture, the next major shift in Micronesian politics allowed a continuation of the thorough German scholarly approach. Following the Spanish-American War, the United States decided to claim only the island of Guam, and Germany bought out Spanish claims to the rest of Micronesia. The area was brought firmly under German control, which was to have grave import for the future of the bai and its highly developed art. As a men's house, the bai was a central focus for Palauan political activity, and this often included raids and counter-raids. All this was outlawed, and the Germans took active control of politics, economics, and through missionaries, even religion. Add this to the depopulation already brought about by new diseases and firearms, and one can see that the bai and its associated activities were soon to go into a well-documented decline.

The German government early decided to fund a broad ethnographic study of its new colony, and a direct outcome of this was a hefty volume by Augustin Krämer, which dealt extensively with the oral traditions carved and painted on the Palauan bai.[13] Like Semper and Kubary before him, Krämer's work was largely descriptive. In addition, he kept in contact with a literate informant of the 1908–1910 period and documented the rapid disappearance of the bai and its carving. The loss was especially great in 1926 and 1927 when severe earthquakes and typhoons toppled many men's houses which were never rebuilt in their original forms. In one aside Krämer illustrates well the Palauan willingness to include recent events in the traditional story-board art. He introduced his opening chapter with a story-board that immortalized Krämer and his wife at work with their informants along with a domestic scene that included the Krämer family's dog.[14]

Thus far the record reveals a tradition that was losing its vitality in direct proportion to the degree that aboriginal Palauan culture was undergoing drastic change. With the advent of the Japanese era, a new direction was added to a flagging art. The Japanese had made Palau the administrative center of their Micronesian colony, and a booming wage economy sprang up. Unlike many Micronesians in other districts, the Palauans entered this new economy with gusto. Culturally they were oriented toward money and the accumulation of wealth as one way to prestige and power, having had an aboriginal kind of money based on glass beads and ancient pieces of ceramics; and many of the tales carved on the bais celebrated the important role that this money played in Palauan life.[15]

This new impetus arrived in the person of Hisataku Hijikata (or Hisakatso Hidikata, according to some recent translations of his work).[16] Both a folklorist and an artist, Hijikata came to Palau to study the melding of art and oral traditions in the bai carvings. In the process and over a period of years, he trained a group of young Palauans in the dying art of the story-board. He also promoted the carving of stories on small boards that could be sold to the many Japanese in residence on the islands and to the many more who came as tourists. Thus was spawned an active handicraft industry that promises to outlive the vanishing story-board as applied to the traditional bai, also an endangered species.

While Hijikata has been described as a purist,[17] one can see by comparing the carvings of his students with the plates in Kubary's major study that Hijikata introduced several major changes. The shift from building decoration to a portable art form is a great functional leap, and to this he added a good deal more. True, he insisted on the aboriginal colors obtained from ochres, burnt lime, and soot, and kept the subject matter within the realm of traditional narratives; but the narratives themselves were greatly limited in numbers. As McKnight has pointed out, the Hijikata-trained artists rarely carved tales beyond the twenty that they learned to carve under their mentor.[18] Moreover, there has been a great compression of style. Tales that I have seen worked out in a series of scenes filling a twenty-foot ceiling rafter are accommodated on a board of two to three feet. The figures were stylized with the men wearing loin cloths and the women grass skirts, whereas in Kubary's plates there is more variation in human representation. In addition, the men regularly appeared naked and often with oversized, spear-shaped penises. There has also been a reduction in representation of mythological creatures. Finally, a border was added to each board. As carved aboriginally on the rafters, there were no borders, for this was a feature of gable decoration.

This shift to a handicraft industry did not mark the end of bai art, but the tradition was weakening. As more and more Palauans moved to the district center and became involved in a wage economy, fewer bais were built and kept up; and when they fell, they were often not rebuilt. If they were, it was in a combination Japanese-Western style with the carving often left in abeyance.

Japanese influence in Palau came to an abrupt halt with the end of World War II. All Japanese nationals returned to their homeland, and the pre-war economy was left in ruins. This included the handicraft industry. Many Palauans immigrated to Guam to seek their fortunes there in the thriving post-war American economy. As for the story-board, it responded to the times. As American administrators replaced Japanese, they were faced with getting island societies moving again. One measure was to encourage the production of handicraft, and on Palau this meant that Hijikata's students had found a new audience. Although Americans never came in large numbers to the islands as did the Japanese, an outlet for Micronesian handicraft was opened on Guam; and since World War II, a stream of story-boards seeking an American market has reached the island.

As one would expect, Palauan culture has undergone further change during this American period. The traditional bai, the wellspring of Palauan art, has virtually disappeared. A lonely survivor stands in the district center where it has become, appropriately, the Palau Museum. In the villages the bai has become more a community house, with only whispers of its past remaining. The last one I visited (1971) was a board structure with a galvanized metal roof. Gone were the high gable ends with their medley of carving and paint. Inside the ceiling rafters displayed village traditions, which on closer inspection revealed that the scenes were not in bas-relief. Paint alone sufficed. And many community houses do not even have the paintings.

However, the Hijikata-inspired portable story-board shows no signs of malaise. One of Hijikata's students, Osiik, secured a loan from the Trust Territory Economic Development Loan Fund and set up a handicraft shop, where he now employs several men.[19] An Osiik story-board signed on the back by the master craftsman himself is a guarantee of quality. Prices have increased with the times. One of my first story-boards (A) cost ten dollars. A more recent acquisition (B) carried a price tag of seventy dollars.

Other more subtle changes are to be noted. The border introduced by Hijikata has moved from the traditional black and white geometric pattern in Item A to simpler patterns that can be executed with a curved chisel as in Item B. The simple stark colors of Item A have been replaced by a broad spectrum of colors that illustrate the artist's choice (Item B). Some boards have been carved and finished in the natural wood favored by many Americans. And the functional rectangular shape inherited from the gable boards and rafters of the bai has been replaced in many cases by irregular pieces sawed from unsquared logs. A further variation has been to shape the board in the form of a fish with pearl inlay eyes (a technique borrowed from a mother-of-pearl inlay style once lavished on the carving of ceremonial bowls). In some of the fancier boards the carving is very deep, so that the figures are high relief rather than the traditional bas-relief.

At this point one might well ponder the future of the Palauan story-board as an art form. Obviously, it is less than it once was. On contact it was an able handmaiden to oral tradition, fixing in wood and paint a village's important traditions and at the same time advertising the skills of the village carvers. Today with the virtual disappearance of the traditional bai, many of the oral traditions have passed into a similar oblivion; and the story-board has become portable art dependent on outside sales.

Yet I would argue that in the process the story-board has gained a new stature, even in the diminution of its narrative content. It has become a symbol of Palauan culture. The art form has been worked into such diverse Palauan public buildings as community centers, assembly buildings, and schools. On Guam, a Japanese hotel has been erected which displays both the decorated gable ends and the decorated interior beams. A widely read column in a Guam newspaper, "Notes on Micronesia," has as its masthead a stylized story-board. In a series of supplementary readings for the Palauan public schools, traditional myths and legends were illustrated using techniques and narratives borrowed from story-boards.[20]

That the Palauans still judge the story-board to be a valued part of their cultural heritage is to be seen in a recent development. Palau is the locale of the only major non-Christian religion to be found in contemporary Micronesia, the Modekgnei cult. Modekgnei attempts both to maintain a distinctive Palauan way of life and at the same time to prepare Palauan youth for living in a changing world; and to further this goal, the cult's adherents have founded a new school. In a recent interview, the Modekgnei leader, Ngirchobeketang, stressed the goal of self-sufficiency, saying:

> The overriding goal of the school is to teach our students to live as Palauans in the modern world. . . . Everyday we see our culture being replaced by another culture, and we want to assist in preserving what is good in Palauan culture.[21]

The villagers raised the bulk of the money to build their school, and the course work stresses learning usable skills rather than the emphasis on Western education found in American-supported public schools. The carving of story-boards is included as part of the Palauan cultural emphasis. Aiding in this endeavor is an American artist-administrator on loan from the University of Guam. This individual, William Vitarelli, is quite blunt in stating that survival in the modern world includes the need to make money (to which I would add that the Palauans have long been known for their economic orientation).

In the selection of Vitarelli as program advisor, story-board art has been given another dimension. Since income is desired, the carvings are destined to become part of the handicraft industry, and recent story-boards offered for sale at the Micronesian Product Center illustrate Vitarelli's personal contribution. Bas-relief carving has been reduced and painting has been replaced by staining. One such board was recently sent to me from Guam. The result is aesthetically pleasing to the American eye, and I am willing to predict that American customers will buy it eagerly, thus causing such craftsmen as Osiik to expand their techniques to meet this new artistic and economic challenge.

To the academic folklorist trying to squeeze cultural practices into theoretical molds, the evolution of the Palauan story-board presents some nice conundrums. Folk art has

Roger Mitchell

become divorced from traditional function and subordinated to economics. The art form itself owes its survival and many of its innovative techniques to alien craftsmen and foreign tastes. Yet the Palauans themselves do not appear perturbed that arguments concerning folktale as text or as performance have been made superfluous. To them the carving is the thing.

[1] See Mitchell Collection, Folklore Institute Archives, Indiana University, Motif Q241. "Adultery punished," Variant 3, for a complete version of this tale.

[2] See Roger E. Mitchell, *The Folktales of Micronesia, Asian Folklore Studies,* XXXIII (1973), pp. 190–191, and Mitchell Collection, Folklore Institute Archives, Motif H1570. "Miscellaneous tests [sexual contest]," Variants 2, 3, 4, for full versions of this tale.

[3] Most of Micronesia has been administered since World War II as the Trust Territory of the Pacific Islands.

[4] Andrew Sharp, *The Discovery of the Pacific Islands* (London, 1962), pp. 94–95.

[5] George Keate, *An Account of the Pelew Islands* (Paris, 1789), pp. 304–306.

[6] John P. Hockin, A Supplement to the Account of the Pelew Islands (London, 1803), pp. 20–21.

[7] Hockin, *A Supplement*, p. 20.

[8] Albert Tetens, *Among the Savages of the South Seas: Memoirs of Micronesia,* trans. Florence Spoehr (Stanford, 1958. First published 1888), p. 8.

[9] Karl Semper, *Die Palau-Inseln im Stillen Ocean* (Leipzig, 1872), pp. 157, 202, 334.

[10] Roger E. Mitchell, "Kubary: The First Micronesian Reporter," *Micronesian Reporter,* XIX, No. 3 (1971), 43–45.

[11] Johann S. Kubary, "Die Pelausche Baukunst," *Ethnographische Beitrage zur Kenntnis des Karolinen Archipels* (Leiden, 1895), pp. 221–306. Plates 1–55.

[12] Kubary, "Pelausche Baukunst," pp. 242–247.

[13] Augustin Krämer, *Palau.* II. Ethnographie: B. Mikronesien. Band 3. 4. Teilband. Abteilung VII: *Geschichten und Gesänge,* in *Ergebnisse der Südsee-Expedition 1908-1910,* ed. Georg Thilenius (Hamburg, 1929).

[14] Krämer, *Palau,* p. 1.

[15] Robert E. Ritzenthaler, *Native Money of Palau,* Milwaukee Public Museum Publications in Anthropology No. 1 (Milwaukee, 1954).

[16] Hisakatso Hidikata, *Stone Images of Palau,* Micronesian Area Research Center Publication No. 3 (Guam, n.d. First published 1956).

[17] Robert K. McKnight, "Palauan Story Boards," *Lore,* XVII, No. 3 (1967), 82–88.

[18] McKnight, "Palauan Story Boards," 82.

[19] Elizabeth Udui, "Palauan Craftsmen Produce Many Beautiful Forms of Art," *Micronesian Reporter,* XIV, No. 2 (1966), 14–15.

[20] Moses Sam, Dengelei Sechalraimul, and Donicio Ngirakelbid, "A Tragic Legend of Palau," Legend Book Series No. 3 (Koror, Palau Islands, 1962).

[21] Joan King, "Palau's School of Self-Reliance," *Pacific Daily News* (Guam), April 19, 1975, p. 31.

# Objects of Memory: Material Culture as Life Review

Barbara Kirshenblatt-Gimblett

*Most folklorists who have studied material culture have focused on objects as reflections of a cultural past. Those folklorists who do look at objects in relation to individuals have focused almost entirely upon artisans, upon creators. Yet throughout life, every person—whether as producer, admirer, distributor, or consumer—is necessarily involved with a myriad of objects. Many of these involvements leave little or no impression; others, however, become fundamental in conceptualizing and symbolizing the self. In the following essay, Barbara Kirshenblatt-Gimblett explores the role of objects as the correlatives of memory. She reviews the situation and organization of objects in everyday life and discusses the ways objects encode memories and stimulate life review. Through the making, arranging, and remaking of objects, she suggests people can make, arrange, and remake themselves.*

*Relationships between individuals and their lore have been explored by a number of folklorists; for example, see Erdész (1961, 1963), Glassie et al. (1970), Ives (1978), and Bronner (1985). For more on the role of objects in the construction and presentation of self see Csikszentmihalyi and Rochberg-Halton (1981).*

Though in the history of folkloristics, biography has served primarily to illuminate folklore, recent work has reversed the relationship to show the extent to which folklore can serve as a primary medium for recovering a life. Traditional singers appreciate the powerful associations of songs with the circumstances of their acquisition and performance because they so vividly remember learning their songs from particular individuals and performing them in specific contexts. The songs continue to carry these associations over the years and to evoke memories each time they are performed. Though folklorists have utilized reminiscence to illuminate the songs, they have yet to understand how music shapes memory.

Repertoires, whether of songs, tales, or other expressive forms, are examples of accumulations made over a lifetime. Their powers of evocation derive from the associations that accumulate with them. One elderly man who participated in the *minyan* (prayer quorum) of a Philadelphia synagogue had this to say about the *kaddish* (prayer for the dead):

> Last week after I recited the *kaddish* for my father, for some reason I was
> reminded of the time I recited *kaddish* for him at the *kotel* [Western Wall

Barbara Kirshenblatt-Gimblett

in Jerusalem] soon after the Yom Kippur War. Then my mind raced back to the time just after my *bar mitzvah* [confirmation at age thirteen] to my father's first *yortsayt* [anniversary of death] and I was wearing my corduroy knickers and was in a little *shtibl* [house of prayer] in South Philadelphia. My thoughts wandered back even more to my father reciting *kaddish* for his father in Belz, Bessarabia. In no kind of order at all I thought of my brother's description of the *minyan* he organized of G.I.'s in May 1945, so that they could recite *kaddish* for a pile of corpses in Dachau. Then I remember a *minyan* of Jews in Russia secretly reciting a *kaddish* for a fellow Jew. Do you think I'm *meshuge* [crazy]? But I felt as if I were in all those places with all those Jews myself.[1]

This account reveals how aware individuals can be of the extraordinary power of a prayer, or other expressive form, to call up in paradigmatic fashion memories of the many contexts in which a prayer or song has been performed.[2]

The same holds for artifacts, a topic generally neglected in studies of the expressive life of the elderly.[3] In the words of Marcel Proust, "The past is hidden . . . beyond the reach of the intellect—in some material object." But folklorists, though they have long studied how people make things, have yet to explore how people save, collect, and arrange their possessions in ways that are profoundly meaningful through the life span. Clues to the significance of this subject, particularly in relation to memory, are suggested by Hannah Arendt:

> The whole factual world of human affairs depends for its reality and its continued existence, first, upon the presence of others who have seen and will remember, and second, on the transformation of the intangible into the tangibility of things. Without remembrance and without the reification which remembrance needs for its own fulfillment and which makes it, indeed, as the Greeks held, the mother of all things, the living activities of action, speech, and thought would lose their reality at the end of each process and disappear as though they had never been.[4]

Distinctions among types of objects, their relations to the past, and the ensembles they form can illuminate the interaction among objects, memory, and the life review process.

Domestic interiors are often filled with things that have aged with their owners. These *material companions* to a life are valued for their continuity. A wooden spoon stirred to a stub is still used despite the fact that almost nothing is left but the handle; with a chuckle, Lina Auckett, now in her eighties, will talk of the years of use the spoon has seen. Such objects are not "saved"; they are allowed to grow old and, however humble, they accumulate meaning and value by sheer dint of their constancy in a life. Their continuous and quotidian presence parallels the ongoing life of the owner and makes them powerful, if diffuse, stimuli for reminiscence. They are generally incorporated into daily life, rather than set aside for display, and bring reverie to the most mundane tasks.[5]

330

In contrast, *souvenirs and mementos,* as the terms themselves imply, are from the outset intended to serve as a reminder of an ephemeral experience or absent person. Because mementos tend to signify particular events, people, and experiences, they are more highly focused stimuli for reminiscence. They too are rooted in the history of a life and are generally valued more for what they signify, for the larger biographical whole of which they are a part, than in themselves; they are of "sentimental value." As a result, bric-a-brac, folk altars, mantles covered with snapshots, scrapbooks and albums, and china cabinets filled with family heirlooms give to domestic interiors their intensely personal character: such environments offer access to the interior of the lives they signify, and as such constitute a kind of autobiographical archeology. The objects are fragments awaiting the autobiographer to repair the damage of time.

Some individuals create *memory objects* as a way to materialize internal images, and through them, to recapture earlier experiences. Whereas souvenirs are saved prospectively, with a sense of their future ability to call back memories, memory objects are produced retrospectively, long after the events they depict transpired. After her husband died, Mrs. Ethyl Mohamed started embroidering pictures of moments and scenes of her life in Mississippi. As she explained: "You know, the thing I would rather do than anything in the world is relive my life again."[6]

Consider the approach to life review in the paintings of Ray Faust. Born in 1901 in Tomashow, Lublin District, in Central Poland, Mrs. Faust came to New York in 1920. The shock of the Holocaust precipitated a heightened sense of discontinuity and intensified her desire to paint what she remembered from the early part of her life. Not only was her childhood gone, but now the communities themselves had been destroyed. Mrs. Faust is quite explicit: "I am painting a life that is lost when I am painting Jewish life."[7] In her paintings, which are complemented by her oral and written memoirs in prose and poetry, Mrs. Faust focuses on the enduring and recurrent, rather than on the unique, moments in her childhood: she paints scenes of her home, the market, the house of study, and annual holidays and life cycle celebrations. Just as she repeats and varies her oral accounts, she creates versions and variants of paintings, sometimes as many as five, for she will not relinquish an image, which she characterizes as "*a kapitl fun mayn lebn*" (a chapter of my life), until she has painted a replacement. These paintings and their multiple versions fill every nook and cranny in Mrs. Faust's small apartment—they hang on the walls and lean up against the furniture. She has thus made discrete moments in the past simultaneously present by saturating her immediate environment with images of her own fashioning.

Mrs. Faust's approach is like that of Bella Chagall, whose memoir is also confined to her childhood years in Vitebsk, Russia, and organized, *not* chronologically from her birth, but according to the sequence of annual holidays.[8] In their "struggle to recover a whole and undamaged world upon which time has no hold,"[9] Ray Faust and Bella Chagall have chosen to focus on the enduring, recurrent, and collective aspects of their childhoods, rather than on unique events that shaped or changed the direction of their individual lives. In both cases, the individual recedes, as Bella Chagall and Ray Faust present themselves in their works as a child witness to a way of life, rather than as the protagonist of a life's journey. Though these childhood experiences in East European towns occupy about a quarter of a lifetime, they expand to fill almost the totality of the memoir.

Ray Faust and Bella Chagall understand that one way to transcend the limits of linear, biographical time is to focus on what is enduring and recurrent, on what is paradigmatic about their remembered past. Like the salvage anthropologist, they too inscribe culture on the threshold of its disappearance; they even go so far as to appropriate the ethnographic mode as the vehicle for their life review. So too does Vincent Ancona, a Sicilian living in New York, who recreates scenes of his childhood out of telephone wire. According to Joseph Sciorra, "Describing the activities he portrays in wire, Ancona often uses the Italian word *tramontato*, which can be translated as 'faded,' 'vanished,' 'outmoded,' or 'forgotten.'"[10] Speaking of the baskets he used to weave out of cane, palm, willow, and olive branches, Ancona adds: "After the war, other materials were introduced to make these things. Plastic destroyed everything. This art is dead. This doesn't exist anymore, even in Sicily where it was born. Now, only the old people know of these things."[11] This statement vividly conveys what might be called cohort awareness. Members of a cohort derive a sense of enlarged time and significance through forging links between their individual lives and a larger whole, in this case, a lost way of life.[12]

Individuals such as Mrs. Faust fill their interiors with memory objects, and through the metaphor of their home as a museum, come to think of themselves as 'curators' of their own lives. Vincent Ancona, whose home is filled with scenes of his childhood in Western Sicily woven out of multi-colored telephone wire, declared: "If you want to see a living museum, come here!"[13] Ironically, Ancona uses industrial waste to salvage an agrarian past. After Lenon Holder Hoyte filled her Harlem home with the five thousand dolls she had collected, she declared the premises a museum and opened it to the public.

*Collectables* differ from companion objects, souvenirs, and memory objects by virtue of how they are acquired and the ensembles they form.[14] They too enjoy a special relationship to time. Whereas the souvenir authenticates the past and is a tool for remembering, the collectable is authenticated by the past.[15] Objects in a collection have a history prior to the moment of their acquisition, the point at which they insert themselves into the life of the collector. However, the activity of collecting is future-oriented: the agenda includes the possibility of new acquisitions.[16] Many objects are rendered collectable by the disjuncture that comes with a shift in context, a process that relates collecting to both autobiography and ethnography. Objects that are no longer usable or useful, fashionable or readily available, or connected to an originating context, become collectable; they are liberated for semiotic retooling.

Collections create their own frame of reference and offer the pleasures of control, order, and relative closure within a hermetic universe. The criteria for collecting and the principles governing the internal order of the collection are at the discretion of the collector. Objects lifted from a prior context become significant in relation to other objects in the collection and the process of collecting: as Walter Benjamin, an avid book collector suggested, "the systematic collection of objects can be a mode of structuring memory."[17]

*Ensembles* are as revealing as particular objects, whether the ensemble is a loosely assembled collection, carefully arranged tableau, new synthetic object, or entire environment.[18] Recipe notebooks, rag rugs, quilts, and collections of miniatures are among the many tangible ways that lives are gathered together and reviewed. Whether scribbled in a notebook or on scraps of loose paper, recalled in conversation, or preserved in the more formal medium of privately printed booklets, recipes and the dishes prepared from them have long served as a medium for life review. *Mamoo's Soggy Coconut Cake, Mrs. Wartik's Recipes from the Personal Collection of her Granddaughter Barbara Fingerman Melamed,* and *The Grandmothers' Cookbooks ... Where They Grew Up and How They Lived* are among many examples of food being used as a medium for recalling a life.[19] Such volumes often include in addition to recipes, genealogical charts, family snapshots, letters, entries from diaries, local history, and reminiscences. Many of the recipes will be cherished more as texts connected to lives than as instructions to follow, for with changing food preferences, old recipes rich in eggs and animal fat and time-consuming to prepare often serve more as food for thought than for eating. Even in the most extreme conditions, while starving to death in the Terezín Concentration Camp in Czechoslovakia during World War II, several women devoted the pages of a precious notebook to recording what they remembered of recipes for the elegant and luxurious dishes that signified the fullness of their former lives.[20]

Indigenous forms of life review are the *projects* referred to by Jean Paul Sartre: "One does not possess one's past as one possesses a thing one can hold in one's hand, inspecting every side of it; in order to possess it I must bind it to existence by a project."[21] On their fiftieth wedding anniversary, Viola and Elmer Hanscam of Oregon retired from their family store, and Mrs. Hanscam determined to undertake such a project:

> All I could think of was it is our fiftieth anniversary. Why not put the years down on stair rugs? I cut up those old coats and dresses—starting on our first year of marriage—to the fiftieth. Children coming home can see where we were and [what we were] doing when they were born.[22]

Each stair marks a key moment such as a wedding, birth, or new home. The choice of stairs, a series of rising steps, as the format for this life review and the recycling of materials drawn from the life remembered are characteristic of the density of meaning achieved in these tangible projects. Significance is wrested not only from iconography but also from format and medium. The recycling of materials is a common method of embedding tangible fragments of the past in an object that reviews and recaptures the experiences associated with those fragments. The metaphor of stairs for the stages of life is also an old convention, and appears in popular prints of the ages of man.

Perhaps the quintessential example of the synthetic memory object is the quilt. The scraps are literally parts of a life and are often used to recall the larger whole. They are ordered, however, not with regard to any story or linear development, but according to repetitive visual patterns that structure attention somewhat in the manner of a mandala. In contrast with rag rugs, where the recycled fabrics are amalgamated beyond recognition, the patches used to make quilts retain their identity. As one quilter reported:

> Now I have some ten big scrap bags. If someone else were to see them, they would seem like a pile of junk, but I've got all my pieces sorted according to color. . . . Different ones of my family are always appearing from one of these bags. Just when you thought you'd forgotten someone, well, like right here. . . . I remember that patch. That was a dress that my grandmother wore to church. I sat beside her singing hymns, and that dress was so pretty to me then. I can just remember her in that dress now.[23]

The key to the way quilts work is in the tension between the abstract principles of visual organization ("I've got all my pieces sorted according to color") and the metonymic nature of the pieces themselves ("Different ones of my family are always appearing from one of those bags"). Scraps are literally parts that stand in a contiguous relation with larger wholes. But most quilts are assembled, not in terms of the memories evoked by particular pieces, but according to abstract principles of color and geometry and repetitive patterns such as stars, wedding rings, log cabins, or flower baskets. This process of construction, while it results in a highly structured visual statement, randomizes the associative possibilities. The potential for reminiscence is left wide open.[24]

*Miniatures,* and their arrangement in tableaux, offer still other possibilities for life review. In their extreme iconicity and radical smallness, miniatures offer an economy of scale coupled with a plenum of detail. The careful mapping of a world remembered is another instance of rescuing culture on the threshold of its disappearance: "When in his seventies Joe Reid found he could no longer build boats as he used to, he began to build miniature garveys. 'It kind of takes me back to my childhood,' he commented. 'I'd like to make a model of every kind of boat they used to use around here'."[25] At the subway museum in New York, one elderly man donated models he has made of the many types of subway trains that once hurtled through the tunnels and on the elevated tracks of the city. In California, there is a club of train buffs who have not only miniaturized the trains, and the landscape through which they run, but also the train schedules, on a scale of so many minutes of miniature train time to so many hours of real train time. The trains actually run, and the men are constantly creating scenarios in the train landscape, and incorporating each other, to scale, into the miniature world.

Doll houses are subject to similar extremes of iconic detail:

> One doll house owner had a working fish tank—with fish—in his house; another would light miniature cigarettes and place them in ash trays. Electrifying a doll house so that each room will have its own switches is taken for granted by serious owners. Working toilets, kitchens full of wares, cupboards stocked with brand-name packages, working doors and windows must all be in place. This extends even to the unseen. To open a cupboard and find its shelves bare is a violation of form and the doll-house reality. The rule of thumb: if it exists in the real world, it *must* exist in the doll-house world.[26]

Who lives there? Doll house owners disagree on whether or not dolls should be included in the doll house. According to Linda Lehrhaupt, some feel that a house without 'people' in it is dead, whereas others "want to put themselves in the house, and dolls get in the way."[27]

Like the collection, the miniature tableau offers the pleasures of a hermetic universe, autonomous and controllable, where connoisseurship is a quest for the perfect fit, a goal that can never be fully achieved no matter how many and how accurate the details. As Susan Stewart notes:

> This tendency of the description and depiction of the miniature to move toward contextual information and away from narrative also transforms our sense of narrative closure, for in the miniature we see spatial closure posited over temporal closure. The miniature offers a world clearly limited in space but frozen and thereby both particularized and generalized in time—particularized in that the miniature concentrates upon the single instance and not upon the abstract rule, but generalized in that the instance comes to transcend, to stand for, a spectrum of other instances. The miniature offers the closure of the tableau, a spatial closure which opens up the vocality of the signs it displays.[28]

Miniatures also have the effect of freezing time. Doll houses of interest to adults are often in the style of an earlier period, in contrast with children's doll houses, which are often miniatures of the contemporaneous adult world. Similarly models are usually of obsolete tools, vehicles, and technology.

Models are appealing not only because the objects they miniaturize may no longer exist or may be too expensive and large to collect, but also because the process of making models is a way of crafting memory. Tools that were once instrumental extensions of the body, now extend their makers imaginatively into the past and socially into the world. Objects that were once good to work with are now good to think with, particularly in collaboration with others in the same cohort:

> Joe Reid, as a memory wright for his cohort, was asked to make a scale model of a garvey he'd built for a man who could no longer work the bay, but wanted to keep the boat as a memento. Reid replicates the process he uses for building full-size boats in his miniature, which he builds, "by eye" on a miniature form in a room in his house. And Reid himself was one of Ed Hazelton's memory clients, agreeing to trade a miniature garvey for a miniature sneakbox.[29]

Such objects are a medium of exchange and focus of interaction—a talking point.

Memory objects, whether models of boats or embroidered scenes, are in the words of Ethyl Mohamed a "conversation piece."

> When I first started doing this embroidery, I was kind of ashamed of it. So I didn't show it to anyone but the children, just for conversation. I'd make a picture, like "The New Baby," or something they did when they were little. When they'd come in for a cup of coffee or something, I'd say, "Does this make you think of us? Is this right? How's this?" You know, everybody would laugh.

It was a conversation piece with us. . . . I do not sell my pictures; I love them too much. But I love to show them and share them with others. This gives me great pleasure.[30]

Provoked by the grief she felt when her husband died, Mrs. Mohamed, who described herself at that time as a ship without a rudder, took hold of her life by recovering her memories. The embroidered images were her way of materializing internal images and focusing conversation about past experiences. She exemplifies the richness of indigenous modes of life review, their centrality to everyday life, and their complex relations to time.

Ironically, folklorists have typically studied precisely the kinds of subjects immortalized by the elderly in their memory projects—folkways of a bygone era—but have had difficulty assimilating the memory objects themselves. Strictly speaking, these artifacts fail to meet the criteria of traditionality associated with folk art. They are too "personal." Mrs. Mohamed did not learn to stitch pictures from her mother. Mr. Ancona did not learn to weave wire scenes from his father. They, and others like them, proudly take credit for their personal discovery of a medium and form for recasting their lives. They have forged distinctly individual solutions to common needs: in the process they affirm the creative potential in the expressive culture of the elderly and the centrality of life review to this period in the life course. From such indigenous modes of life review, folklorists have much to learn about the social construction of the self through time and the transformation of experience through materials readily at hand. Such insights have the potential to reshape the boundaries of our discipline.

---

[1] Maxine T. Segal, "Musings and Memoirs of Men in the Morning *minyan*: An Ethnographic Account," paper written for Folklore 564: Folklore, Culture, and Aging, University of Pennsylvania, Spring 1979, 23.

[2] Many other examples could be cited. Barbara Myerhoff, *Number Our Days* (New York: Dutton, 1978), 22, describes the ceremoniousness with which Basha ate her modest dinner: "Before eating, she spread a white linen handkerchief over the oilcloth covering the table, saying: 'This my mother taught me to do. No matter how poor, we would eat off clean white linen, and say the prayers before touching anything to the mouth. And so I do it still. Whenever I sit down, I eat with God, my mother, and all the Jews who are doing these same things even if I can't see them.' Such a meal is a feast, superior to fine fare hastily eaten, without ceremony, attention, or significance."

[3] Recent attempts to address this topic include E. Sherman and E. S. Newman, "The Meaning of Cherished Personal Possessions for the Elderly," *Journal of Aging and Personal Development* 8, 2 (1977-78):181-92; Adele Wiseman, *Old Woman at Play* (Toronto: Clarke, Irwin & Company, 1978); Mihaly Csikszentmihalyi and Eugene Rochberg-Halton, *The Meaning of Things: Domestic Symbols and the Self* (Cambridge: Cambridge University Press, 1981); Simon J. Bronner, *Chain Carvers: Old Men Crafting Meaning* (Lexington: University of Kentucky Press, 1985); Brenda Danet and Tamar Katriel, "Books, Butterflies, Botticellis: A Life-Span Perspective on Collecting," paper prepared for the Sixth International Conference on Culture and Communication, Philadelphia, 9-11 October 1986; and Mary Hufford, Marjorie Hunt, and Steven Zeitlin, *The Grand Generation: Memory, Mastery, Legacy* (Washington, D.C., and Seattle: Smithsonian Institution Traveling Exhibition Service and Office of Folklife Programs, and University of Washington Press, 1987).

[4] Hannah Arendt, *The Human Condition* (Chicago: University of Chicago Press, 1958), 95.

[5] See Arendt, *Human Condition*, 137: "The things of the world have the function of stabilizing human life, and their objectivity lies in the fact that . . . men, their ever-changing nature notwithstanding, can retrieve

their sameness, that is their identity, by being related to the same chair and the same table. In other words, against the subjectivity of men stands the objectivity of the man-made world rather than the sublime indifference of an untouched nature. . . . Without a world between men and nature, there is eternal movement, but no objectivity."

[6]Hufford, Hunt, and Zeitlin, *Grand Generation*, 44.

[7]Quoted in Gloria Pleskin, "Sign and Structure in the Anthropological Study of Art: Analyses of Works by the Naive Artist Rachel Ray Faust," unpublished paper, New York University, 1978, 20.

[8]Bella Chagall, *Burning Lights* trans. Norbert Guterman (New York: Schocken Books, 1962).

[9]Eugene Ionesco, quoted by Simone de Beauvoir, *Old Age,* trans. Patrick O'Brian (Harmondsworth, England: Penguin, 1972), 419.

[10]Joseph Sciorra, "Reweaving the Past: Vincenzo Ancona's Telephone Wire Figures," *The Clarion* (Spring/Summer 1985); 52.

[11]Sciorra, "Reweaving the Past," 49.

[12]Mrs. Faust and her paintings are discussed in greater detail by Barbara Kirshenblatt-Gimblett, "In Search of the Paradigmatic: Ethnic Symbol Building among Elderly Immigrants," paper presented at the International Symposium on Ethnic Symbol Building, Hungarian Academy of Sciences and American Council of Learned Societies, Budapest, July 1982. Mrs. Faust considers herself an authority on the Jewish folklore of her region: she refers to herself as a folklorist and to her papers as an archive, and she frequently admonishes me for not learning enough from her.

[13]Hufford, Hunt, and Zeitlin, 66.

[14]The following discussion of collections is indebted to Susan Stewart, *On Longing: Narratives of the Miniature, the Gigantic, the Souvenir, the Collection* (Baltimore: Johns Hopkins University Press, 1984) and Danet and Katriel, "Books, Butterflies, Botticellis." See also the discussion of the customizing of mass culture in relation to collections on pages 214–20 in Barbara Kirshenblatt-Gimblett, "The Future of Folklore Studies in America: The Urban Frontier," *Folklore Forum* 16, No. 2 (1983):175–234.

[15]Stewart, *On Longing,* 151.

[16]Danet and Katriel, 17.

[17]Ibid., 6.

[18]Accumulators frequently outgrow their living rooms, take over the entire living space, build on additions to their homes, and extend out into gardens and yards to accommodate their assemblages. Much has been written about such total environments. See *Spaces: Notes on America's Folk Art Environments*, a newsletter published by Spaces: Saving and Preserving America's Folk Art Environments, Los Angeles.

[19]Guy Miles, Frances Hurley, and Faye Miles, *Mamoo's Soggy Coconut Cake* (Maryville, Tenn.: L. & M. Printing and Miles Documentary, 1979); [Barbara Fingerman Melamed], *Mrs. Wartik's Recipes from the Personal Collection of her Granddaughter, Barbara Fingerman Melamed* (Scarsdale, N.Y.: Barbara Fingerman Melamed, nd); Mrs. Sydney L. Wright, *The Grandmothers' Cookbooks: Letitia Ellicott Carpenter [Mrs. William Redwood Wright, "Muz"], Anna Wharton [Mrs. Harrison S. Morris, "Mama"], Where They Grew Up and How They Lived* (Newport: Wiseman's Printing, 1977).

[20]I am grateful to Annie Stern for making her mother's recipe notebook available to me, and to Dalia Carmel for her help in locating the document. The gastronomic memoir or autobiography is a well-established genre, though as yet unstudied: among the better known examples are the volumes of M. F. K. Fischer, Joseph Wechsberg, and Ludwig Bemelman. In this genre, there is often a convergence of diary, memoir, travel accounts, cookbook, and food ethnography. Though frequently written by professionals (chefs, restaurateurs, wine specialists, food journalists, and *becs-fins*), life review through food also occurs among ordinary people.

[21]Quoted by Hufford, Hunt, and Zeitlin, 41.

[22]Ibid., 48.

[23]Patricia Cooper and Norma Bradley Buferd, *The Quilters: Women and Domestic Art* (Garden City, N.Y.: Doubleday & Company, 1977), 75.

[24]There are many varieties of quilts. Not all of them are made from recycled fabrics or abstract in design. Ina Grant of Chelsea, Vermont, took seven years to complete a "memory quilt" made up of 172 embroidered blocks, each of them a scene from her life. She depicted the houses in which family members were born, recurrent scenes of ploughing, planting, and tapping maple sugar, cherished leisure moments such as

dancing, and favorite farm animals and pets. Her quilt is described by Hufford, Hunt, and Zeitlin, 48–49. Recently, the Names Project in San Francisco has initiated a nationwide project to create a quilt that memorializes those who have died of AIDS (Acquired Immune Deficiency Syndrome). As of April 1988, more than four thousand panels have been created by friends and relatives of those who have died, and the quilt was almost large enough to cover two football fields. Panels are constantly being added.

[25] Hufford, Hunt, and Zeitlin, Interview, Grand Generation Project.

[26] Linda Lehrhaupt, "It's a Small World: Doll Houses and Miniaturization," paper prepared for Performance Studies 1040: Aesthetics of Everyday Life, New York University, Spring 1983, p. 12.

[27] Lehrhaupt, "Small World," 16.

[28] Stewart, 48.

[29] Hufford, Hunt, and Zeitlin, 65.

[30] Ethyl Wright Mohamed, *My Life in Pictures* (Jackson: Mississippi Department of Archives and History, 1976), 12.

# X
# Documenting Folklore

## Mediating Structures and the Significance of University Folk
Jay Mechling

*As folklore fieldwork projects are generated by students working within constraints imposed by an academic quarter or semester, they tend to be carried out within groups and environments that are a part of everyday student experience: student residence units, special interest clubs, student arts and political organizations, or student occupational settings. The focus on these university environments mostly has been a matter of mere convenience rather than theoretical interest. In fact, students often do not perceive these environments to be worthy of serious investigation. Faculty often support such perceptions when they distinguish between the university environment and what they often call the "real world."*

*Although the university engages in much social and cultural research, very little of that research is directed at itself. But the university is a real world and its culture merits serious consideration. In the following essay, Jay Mechling characterizes a dimension of university environments that makes them significant in understanding the larger society. For Mechling, student folklore projects can be more than heuristic exercises in fieldwork or entertaining collections of youth idiom and expression. They can document the processes by which modern plural societies are constructed and maintained.*

*The small literature on the folklore of the academy has been growing in recent years. None of this literature, however, approaches academic lore from the perspective described by Mechling. The existence of a lore of the academy was discussed by Dorson (1949) and Toelken (1986). Particular traditions within the academy have been studied by Leary (1978), McGeachy (1978), Wise (1977), Eschholz and Rosa (1970), and others. More recently, a short film of a fraternity tradition on the Pennsylvania State University campus was produced (Hornbein et al. 1982).*

Triviality stalks folklore studies like an ugly family secret. The everyday use of the term "folklore" as a synonym for "false belief" or "superstition" is a difficult enough prejudice to overcome. But folklore inquiry lends itself to "fun" topics, and a culture that sustains the work/play dichotomy as strongly as does ours tends to devalue work that seems too much like play. Folklore genres such as children's games or drinking songs or proverbs, for example, seem unimportant when compared with a novel or an opera.[1] And, worse, the folklorist studies these genres in settings and among groups that are peripheral and marginal to those that really "count" in our society. Add to these characteristics some folklorists' penchant for violating the revered scientific norm of objectivity, and we can see the problem professors of folklore face daily, as they attempt to explain and justify their research to colleagues in history, economics, chemistry, and literature.

It is with some wariness, therefore, that my students launch folklore fieldwork projects in a ten-week academic quarter. For most students at a residential university, the natural groups for study are living groups (dorm, apartment, fraternity, or sorority), occupational groups (academic departments, food services, the library, student government, or local businesses), voluntary organizations (clubs, athletic teams, religious organizations, the campus newspaper, or musical groups), and those groups that coalesce in occasional, though traditional, social environments (a bar or a party, for example). These groups become the objects of study, however, not for their theoretical significance, but because they are local, available, and cooperative.

Accustomed to term paper topics in literature or political science, students are a bit incredulous that their residence hall or softball team can be the subject of a serious term essay. Students who have reached the university generally know that an appropriate term paper topic sounds something like "The Uses of Visual and Olfactory Imagery in Stephen Crane's *Maggie, A Girl of the Streets*," and naturally suspect the acceptability of a term paper entitled "The Evolving Slang of an Intramural Softball Team." Absent are all the landmarks and cues that persuade students that they are doing something legitimate and important.[2] The students' nervousness increases as they learn that there is likely very little published scholarship on their topic (a trivial one, after all) and that they will not be able to employ the formulaic approach of reading the secondary literature on a topic and presenting the professor with a well-edited summary of that scholarship, interspersed with liberal quotations from the experts. Students don't quite believe me when I tell them that often they are the experts on the groups and the lore they are studying.

The usual way of justifying a piece of folklore research is to cast it as a case study of a larger idea or theory. As a case study of a theory or as an application of a methodology, a particular folklore inquiry can enter into a dialectic with a larger idea; the larger idea informs the case study and the empirical details of the case study may confirm, falsify, or modify our understanding of the larger idea. The importance of the case study depends, accordingly, upon the importance of the idea it tests.

This is the traditional, academic justification for case studies in scholarly communities, and it is not a bad goal for the work of both faculty and students. But I want to suggest in these pages an important, additional justification for doing folklore field-work in the university setting. The study of the slang of an intramural softball team may be every bit as important as more traditional topics of inquiry in the university once we see that folklorists are studying not the trivial behavior of marginal groups but institutions and processes that are absolutely vital to the continuation of the American experiment in plural, democratic society.

This perspective raises the stakes of the folklore research conducted by students. Intellectualizing about folklore, studying folk traditions, and writing analytical essays linking the ideas and the case studies are profoundly important political activities. The most common sites for student fieldwork in folklore are precisely those where, in daily, face-to-face practice, Americans are working through what it means to be a "citizen" of a pluralistic society. This is not merely an abstract, intellectual matter, but one of praxis, of connecting and reconciling "private troubles with public issues."[3]

The key concept in this approach is that of *mediating structures,* a term introduced in 1976 by sociologist Peter L. Berger and Lutheran pastor and culture critic Richard John Neuhaus. Mediating structures are *"those institutions standing between the individual in his private life and the large institutions of public life."*[4] The concept of mediating structures is not new; it has forebears in Edmund Burke's "small platoons," de Tocqueville's "voluntary organizations," and Durkheim's "mid-range institutions." The Berger and Neuhaus contribution further refines our conception of this special category of American institution to help us understand how crucial these institutions are to the future of the American democratic experiment.

The forces of modernization, marked in large part by the confluence of technology and bureaucracy, result in a dichotomy in modern life. On the one hand is the *public world,* consisting primarily of large-scale, bureaucratic institutions, what Berger and Neuhaus call "megastructures." The university in its institutional totality is one such megastructure. Most universities are large, far beyond the size conducive to face-to-face interaction. More important, the twin forces of technology and bureaucracy determine the institutional character of the university. The megastructure prizes efficiency, specialization, "moralized anonymity," procedural justice, orderliness, impersonality, and a host of other values.[5] The norm of universality in megastructures pays no heed to human particularities of gender, race, ethnicity, and so on. This makes it possible (in theory, at least) for the bureaucracy to treat all members as equals. In modern societies one is always bumping into world views, life styles, and moralities different from one's own, and the megastructure provides the most likely venue for this encounter with pluralism.

Put differently, the university has a shared "public" culture. What is "shared" is a public set of symbols, procedures, and meanings; there need be no assumption of shared values.[6] The students' private lives are of no concern to the university so long as students conduct themselves "as if" they agreed with the values of the institution. There is no requirement that the student's "cognitive map" match the map of the university's public culture. All that is required is that students know what behaviors the university expects of them. It makes little difference to the university, for example, whether the student refrains from cheating on a test because of deeply held ethical values or because of a fear of getting caught. Conformity with the institution's norm satisfies the institution.

These characteristics of megastructures make them seem *alienating*. The university as experienced in lines at the registrar's office or in large lecture classes is often not humanly satisfying. It lacks a human scale. We feel detached, "alienated," from the institution. Contributing to this alienation is "reification," the process whereby institutions lose for us their "human-madeness" and acquire a kind of facticity or givenness against which we feel powerless.[7]

Opposed to the megastructure is the *private world*, the intimate "home world" of particular (as opposed to universal) values and traditions. Sometimes we are willing to endure the alienation of our society's megastructures because we have the "home world" as our shelter, as our "haven in a heartless world."[8] To the institution of the university students bring a constellation of values, meanings, and beliefs acquired from family and close friends in their home worlds.[9]

The individual's experience of home world folk groups is essentially one of homogeneity; the individual has sustained interaction with people who matter the most to the individual and who likely share (indeed, they formed) the individual's ethos and world view. The conditions of the home world and of the "primary socialization" one undergoes in the home world, therefore, work in favor of *shared values*.[10] Accordingly, the folklore of the home world tends to stress performances of sameness, of cohesion, of confirmation, and of celebration, from family foodways through the verbal routines of intimate dyads.[11]

When students come to a residential university, their ties to the home world weaken. They often must work hard to sustain home values, and they must effect a reconciliation of their values with those brought from other home worlds and with those of the institution itself. This has more than just the making of an individual's identity crisis, argue Berger and Neuhaus. The present condition amounts to a political crisis of large proportions. "Without institutionally reliable processes of mediation" between these two worlds, they write, "the political order becomes detached from the values and realities of individual life. Deprived of its moral foundation, the political order is 'delegitimated.' When that happens, the political order must be secured by coercion rather than by consent. And when that happens, democracy disappears."[12]

The special feature of mediating structures is that they are mid-range institutions lying between the home world and the alienating megastructures. They "mediate" between these two worlds with a face toward each. "Such institutions have a private face, giving private life a measure of stability, and they have a public face transferring meaning and value to the megastructures."[13]

Now we are prepared to see the role of mediating structures in the university. In the mid-range would be the residential groups, occupational groups, voluntary organizations, and similar face-to-face groups that are the home groups to which students belong or with which they relate. These mediating structures are "public" in the sense that they are organized within and sanctioned by the megastructure, but as mid-range institutions they create groupings closer in size and experience to the groups of the home world.

Some of these mediating structures enjoy the high-context symbolic culture we come to expect in the home world. Fraternities and sororities, for example, employ at least two strategies for enhancing shared meanings. First, they are able to practice selectivity in their membership, exercising the particularity and exclusivity we associate with home world institutions. As a megainstitution, the university officially avoids such particularism as discrimination, but the bureaucratic, technocratic public culture only rarely presumes to tell home world institutions they cannot be particularistic in their membership.

The second device available to some mediating structures for creating a high-context culture is socialization. Berger and Luckmann call "alternation" those cases of secondary socialization that attempt to recreate the qualities of primary socialization (the original socialization) taking place in the family.[14] Thus, fraternities and sororities often employ techniques perfected by the military, by cults, and by religious seminaries. These organizations may literally strip the recruits of their clothes and cut their hair in order to "invest" them with clothes and an appearance appropriate to their new identities. They may disorient the initiates by moving them around in the dark, by making them tired and hungry, and by making them transfer their affection and dependence from previous significant others to members of the organization. The socialization is sealed by a highly symbolic and ritualistic ceremony announcing the new identity.

This "alternation," though never as successful as the original primary socialization, succeeds to the extent that the groups create and sustain a high-context culture. It is no accident that fraternities and sororities use the vocabulary of the family—"brothers," "sisters," "little sisters," and "house mothers"—which is the institution in which primary socialization established the "home reality" against which all others are somewhat alien.

The processes of alternation are often folklore processes. They are designed to establish a private, home-like world in a world away from home. Like the folklore of the home world, these processes aim at creating a distinctive group culture and a sense of common identity. Fraternity songs, foodways, costumes, and celebrations frequently help define and solidify the group. Even the seemingly humiliating and divisive initiation rituals are ultimately designed to turn "green" outsiders into "true blue" members of the group.

But mediating structures have their public face as well. Groups in the mid-range interact with other groups, and folklore participates in these interactions. In fact, it is at these borders between cultural groups that the most visible folklore performances occur. Unlike the private rituals that promote sameness, these border performances tend to emphasize difference. Intramural contests, campus festivals, jokes, pranks, graffiti, shouting matches, demonstrations, sit-ins, riots, and numerous other genres of folk performances on a university campus all exhibit the *agonistic* quality characteristic of rituals of difference.[15]

Thus, mediating structures actually mediate. In the university, students bring to these structures meanings and values particular to their home worlds. This may be their first encounter with values from different home worlds. In such circumstances students are forced to negotiate their own values as part of the process of confronting the values of others and creating a new home world. Yet, the new home world must accommodate the bureaucratic, technocratic values of the megastructure. The essence of the mediation, then, is that private values move into the public realm, while very public values become more privatized. Mediating structures, therefore, are likely arenas for the conflicts and contradictions between public and private worlds. How and whether these conflicts are resolved, and the role of folklore in the process, are far from trivial questions.

The conflicts between the home world and the megastructure become more visible in the "public square." I urge my students to think of our central campus quadrangle (a designated "free speech" area) as the university community's literal "public square" where public and private realms collide. But there are figurative "public squares," as well, such as the campus newspapers, the bulletin boards, the athletic fields, the radio station, and so on. The home world contributes to the public square particular values that are religious, ethical, moral. The public university contributes universalistic values inherited from eighteenth-century French and English liberal political theory and deposited in our Constitution and in two hundred years' worth of interpretation of that text. The university's contribution to the public square, in other words, is the unique blend of Protestant Christianity and English liberal political theory that has come to be called, variously, America's "public religion," "public philosophy," or "civil religion."[16] An important dimension of this American civil religion is that it is also a "religion of civility"; that is, the rules of discourse in the public square demand a certain civility in the free contest of private values in the public arena. (In fact, some folklore works to teach and sustain these rules, such as the proverbial phrases, "Everyone's entitled to an opinion" and "Your freedom of speech stops at my nose.")

In essence, the university really may be the laboratory for democratic pluralism that its rhetoric sometimes asserts, and students doing fieldwork projects in the university, rather than merely studying convenient folk groups, are actually in an excellent position to contribute to an understanding of modernity and pluralism.[17] Some concrete examples will help illustrate the role of folklore in the encounter between private and public worlds of the university. The first instance involves a residence hall party, and the second a public fund-raising event sponsored by a fraternity.

Michael Moffatt studied one floor of a residence hall in an East Coast university.[18] The floor was divided into two "sections," one composed of thirty black students who elected to live together to foster cultural awareness and black solidarity, and the other composed primarily of white students randomly assigned to the floor. What distinguished this floor from other floors in the residence hall was its total lack of a shared folk culture. In fact, the two sections on the floor developed separate and mutually hostile folk cultures. The "Secret Santa" gift exchanges at the end of the first semester, normally activities shared by an entire floor, were celebrated separately by the whites and blacks. Minor pranking, normally tolerated and enjoyed on other floors, was generally avoided. However, when carried out by a few of the blacks, pranking was resented by the white students, whose verbal joking then became extremely hostile. Efforts to organize floor parties, the common folk event of residential units, repeatedly failed. By all measures, the folklore of the floor reflected division, rather than cohesion. The source of this division can be understood largely in terms of conflicting home world cultures. Each section seemed unwilling or unable to negotiate with the other to create a shared folk culture.

The white students had come from their home worlds with various values and expectations. Among these were the values of "friendliness" and the individual freedom to choose. These two values are closely related, as friendliness connotes friendship, the single most important social relationship predicated upon individual choice. The white students viewed black solidarity as a challenge to freely chosen relationships with individuals. Furthermore, white students felt a strong injunction to be "friendly," even toward casual acquaintances. When they failed to perceive reciprocal signs of friendliness from the blacks, they regarded the blacks as unfriendly. This is why the pranking by blacks provoked such hostility in the white section; pranking is harmless only when performed by people who are friends or, at least, "friendly." The blacks, on the other hand, did not think of themselves as unfriendly. However, they saw friendship as more like kinship, a serious and enduring relationship. In fact, the black section on the floor was created specifically to cultivate and maintain friendships within a black "kinship" group. They found it more difficult to be friendly with those outside that group.

This division between the sections made life on the floor uncomfortable, especially as they shared basic facilities and could not avoid one another. But more importantly, a residence hall floor is an important stage for the spontaneous expression of individual identity within a bureaucratically structured university. All of the students had a stake in creating an environment that could promote individual expression. The desire for such an environment, however, was not sufficient to bring it into being.

Only when the conflict on the floor entered the public square were the students motivated to examine and overcome their differences. A black reporter from the student newspaper got wind of the "problem" on the floor, investigated the scene, and wrote a front-page article attacking the racism in both sections. The article stimulated a series of floor meetings in which a letter was drafted denying the charges made in the article. The members of both sections signed the letter. Both groups had an interest in defending the reputation of the floor against outside criticism, particularly in publicly denying that the division on the floor was the result of racist feelings on the part of either group. Although it was a conflict of home worlds that created the problem on the floor, the students wished to affirm their commitment to those public values that denied racial difference as a legitimate basis for hatred or discrimination.

A few days after the letter was sent to the campus newspaper, a floor party was organized. The party was small and a bit awkward, but it was friendly and people from both sections sat and talked together. However, there was no bi-racial dancing and students danced only when "their" music was played. The party reflected simultaneously the newly created social unity and the ongoing cultural differences between the two sections. It was a complex folk ritual that attempted to reconcile the conflict between public and private values, between the demands of the megastructure and the values of home worlds.

Whereas the residence hall example illustrates how public values may forge a unity out of underlying home world differences, in the following example public values recast home world unity into an expression of division. Most fraternities and sororities "adopt" a charitable cause and raise money during the year for that cause. The Greek "slave auction" is a public fund-raising event in which fraternity members offer themselves to be auctioned to the highest bidder. The slaves are supposed to perform whatever services (presumably legal and moral) the purchaser demands for a fixed period of time. The auction is simply a "themed event" consistent with the ancient Greek symbolic frame that pervades the formal and informal folk cultures of fraternities and sororities throughout the nation. In this frame, "Greeks" have "slaves" which may be bought and sold.

This auction ran into trouble on my own campus, however, when one of the fraternity men being auctioned was black. The resonances of a black man being auctioned as a slave were too much for some of the audience, both white and black, who did not share the "Greek" frame for the event and, instead, understood slave auctions as a particularly insensitive reference to the enslavement of Africans in the New World. This public reaction resulted in a protest that moved into the halls of the Interfraternity Council, the office of the Vice Chancellor for Student Affairs, and onto the pages of the campus newspaper. Again, it took a public forum to try to mediate the conflict.

The fraternity members, including the black member, were puzzled by the outcry. The fraternity was integrated and, indeed, united in conducting this event. To have excluded the black member from participating in the auction would have been discriminatory in the eyes of the fraternity members. Where the fraternity had miscalculated was in its assumption that it could move a ritual from the relatively high-context, private world of the folk group into the public realm of strangers who did not share the group's intimacy or their frame for interpreting the ritual. The fraternity learned the hard way that public understandings cannot be taken for granted. What the fraternity took to be an expression of solidarity was interpreted as racist and divisive.[19]

Interestingly, another conflict of interpretations occurred on campus, only with the sides reversed. Some white students observed the subservient behavior and mild hazing of pledges to a black sorority and expressed shock at the stereotypical behavior, worrying that the pledging rituals were fostering harmful racial stereotypes. The black sorority members countered that the white audiences were misinterpreting the behavior. What the white students were taking as slave-like subservience was, within the frame of the sorority, an expression of black pride and solidarity. Once again, a folk event safe in its home world became problematic when performed before strangers in the public square.

In these controversies over theme parties and slave auctions and sorority pledging, one supposes that the Greek organizations involved must have had some sort of internal conversation about such issues. After all, festivals and ritual doings require planning and effort. A student folklorist with privileged entree into the organization is in a position to chronicle the full life cycle of such events, noting (among other things) how the folk group consciously or unconsciously uses its traditions to handle or to ignore the group's problems.[20]

Of course, not every floor party, public forum, newly invented "tradition," or similar folk event in the mediating structures at the university will reflect so obviously these efforts to reconcile public and private values. I offer these examples only to illustrate that the folk cultures one encounters in the university can be instructive models of the society as a whole. Members of the university community slip easily into talking about institutions outside the university as "the real world," as if the university really were an "ivory tower" isolated and protected from the historical, social, and economic forces that govern other institutions. But this is a false picture of the university. The university often contains all the ethnic, gender, political, religious, and other differences that characterize American experience. While no university is a true microcosm of America, it may be useful to treat universities as laboratories for the study of many of the forces, values, and conflicts that characterize the civilization. Americans never experience abstract "American culture." Rather, Americans experience the public culture as it is mediated through mid-range and smaller institutions.[21] They experience not "freedom of the press," for example, but a concrete argument as to whether a third-world campus newspaper should lose its student government funding. They experience not "competitive individualism" but the problem of fellow students cheating on examinations and laboratory experiments. They perceive not "racism" but blacks being sold by whites as a part of a fraternity stunt.

The study of folklore forms, content, and processes in mediating structures at the university may help us understand American culture as Americans actively create and modify it in their everyday lives. This perspective on mediating structures is not the only way to understand the university, but it is one productive way of conceptualizing university folklore and culture as serious business. Moreover, if this approach should encourage folklorists and their audiences to confront normative issues of good or bad mediating structures, of healthy or unhealthy ones, of humanly nourishing or humanly degrading ones, then so much the better. Questions of value cannot be divorced from questions of fact. Once and for all we can banish triviality from the study of folklore and commit ourselves to the intellectual work that matters most.

---

[1]Alan Dundes addresses the issue of trivial genres in his "Some Minor Genres of American Folklore," *Southern Folklore Quarterly* 31 (1967):20–36. See also Brian Sutton-Smith, "Psychology of Childlore: The Triviality Barrier," *Western Folklore* 29 (1970):1–18.

[2]Barre Toelken's essay, "The Folklore of Academe," in Jan Harold Brunvand, ed., *The Study of Folklore*, 3d ed. (New York: Norton, 1986), 502–28, still serves as the best survey of folklore genres and processes in the university, but Toelken makes no larger claim for the importance of such study.

[3]C. Wright Mills, *The Sociological Imagination* (London and New York: Oxford University Press, 1959).

# Jay Mechling

4Peter L. Berger first introduced the ideas for this project in his essay, "In Praise of Particularity: The Concept of Mediating Structures," *The Review of Politics* 38 (1976):399–410. More fully describing the rationale for the project is Peter L. Berger and Richard John Neuhaus, *To Empower People: The Role of Mediating Structures in Public Policy* (Washington, D.C.: American Enterprise Institute for Public Policy Research, 1977). This definition is from Berger and Neuhaus, 2; emphasis in original.

5Peter L. Berger, Brigitte Berger, and Hansfried Kellner, *The Homeless Mind: Modernization and Consciousness* (New York: Vintage/Random House, 1973).

6On the meaning of cultural "sharing," see Anthony F. C. Wallace, *Culture and Personality*, 2d ed. (New York: Random House, 1970), 22–24. Wallace would say that public culture is "shared" to the extent that it is a strategy for "the organization of diversity," not the "replication of uniformity." As Richard Bauman puts this same point to folklorists, "folklore performance does not require that the lore be a collective representation of the participants, pertaining and belonging equally to all of them. It may be so, but may also be differentially understood." See his "Differential Identity and the Social Base of Folklore," in Américo Paredes and Richard Bauman, eds., *Toward New Perspectives in Folklore* (Austin: University of Texas Press, 1972), 38.

7Peter L. Berger and Thomas Luckmann, *The Social Construction of Reality: A Treatise in the Sociology of Knowledge* (Garden City, N.Y.: Anchor/Doubleday, 1966), 89–92.

8Christopher Lasch, *Haven in a Heartless World: The Family Besieged* (New York: Basic Books, 1977) and Richard Sennett, *Families Against the City* (Cambridge: Harvard University Press, 1970).

9Of course, this is an idealized picture of the home world. Often the home world is "underinstitutionalized," as Berger might say, and is in poor shape to provide the institutional anchor for values and meaning in a broader public world. Disordered, chaotic, weak home worlds lead to *anomie*, as Durkheim called the modern feeling of detachment. Unlike the student who comes to the mediating structures of the university from a strongly institutionalized home world and must negotiate a personal set of values out of the materials of both the private and public world, the student from a weak home world must construct an entirely new value system within the public institution. While the construction of a value system is of great theoretical interest, I shall not pursue the point in this essay.

10Berger and Luckmann, 129–37, discuss "primary socialization." The sort of cultural sharing we find in the home world tends to be what Wallace would call "the replication of uniformity."

11On family folklore, see Steven J. Zeitlin, Amy J. Kotkin, and Holly Cutting Baker, *A Celebration of American Family Folklore: Tales and Traditions from the Smithsonian Collection* (New York: Pantheon Books, 1982). On the folklore of couples, see Elliott Oring, "Dyadic Traditions," *Journal of Folklore Research* 21 (1984):19–28.

12Berger and Neuhaus, 3.

13Ibid.

14Berger and Luckmann, 157.

15Roger D. Abrahams, "Shouting Match at the Border: The Folklore of Display Events," in Richard Bauman and Roger D. Abrahams, eds., *And Other Neighborly Names* (Austin: University of Texas Press, 1981), 303–21.

16See Robert N. Bellah, "Civil Religion in America," *Daedalus* 96 (1967):1–21; John F. Wilson, *Public Religion in America* (Philadelphia: Temple University Press, 1979); and William M. Sullivan, *Reconstructing Public Philosophy* (Berkeley: University of California Press, 1982).

17Another way of saying this is that folklore fieldwork in the university contributes to the sociological study of American beliefs and values as they are actually constructed, interpreted, and employed in social interaction. See Norma Haan, "The Interactional Morality of Everyday Life," in N. Haan, R. M. Bellah, P. Rabinow, and W. M. Sullivan, eds., *Social Science as Moral Inquiry* (New York: Columbia University Press, 1983), 218–50.

18Michael Moffatt, "The Discourse of the Dorm: Race, Friendship, and 'Culture' among College Youth," in Hervé Varenne, ed., *Symbolizing America* (Lincoln: University of Nebraska Press, 1986), 158–77.

19The student folklorist will find similar scenes and processes on any university campus. Fraternities and sororities at the University of California, Davis, for example, have followed a tradition of creating "theme parties," of creating an ethnic motif that carries through the party's advertisements, costumes, foods, drinks, and decorations. But problems arise when the themes "borrow" ethnic cultures and make them the target of caricature and humor. One fraternity's theme party, "Sombreros and Cervezas," outraged the campus

Chicano community, who protested the party's stereotypes about alcoholism and laziness in Mexican society. Similarly, a "Godfather Night" party featured stereotypes offensive to some Italian students. Increasingly public conflicts over the offensive theme parties led student leaders from the Greek organizations and from the ethnic organizations to stage a public open forum for the campus to discuss these parties and the issue of public sensitivity to the home cultures of others.

[20] Barbara Babcock-Abrahams provides an excellent discussion of five strategies for dealing with ambiguity: (1) settling upon one interpretation or another; (2) physically controlling the ambiguity; (3) creating and enforcing rules of avoidance; (4) labelling anomalous events as dangerous; and (5) using ambiguous symbols in ritual "to enrich meaning or call attention to other levels of existence." The student folklorist might find one or more of these strategies operating in a university group forced to deal with an ambiguous or anomalous event. See Barbara Babcock-Abrahams, "Why Frogs are Good to Think and Dirt is Good to Reflect On," *Soundings* 58 (1975):167–81.

[21] Interestingly, Richard M. Dorson at one point wrote about folk groups in terms similar to the language of the mediating structures idea. In his 1972 essay on "History of the Elite and History of the Folk" in *Folklore: Selected Essays* (Bloomington: Indiana University Press, 1972), 241-42, he wrote:

> Folk history is not however simply a matter of oral traditions. By history of the folk I have in mind the history of the structures in which individuals play active roles, of what psychologists call 'vital circuits.' . . . This is not state and local history, an alternative to national history which simply reduces the governmental unit but does not necessarily involve the individual any more deeply. What are these structures that involve the individual? Well, schools and colleges involve most of us. The great sports—football, baseball, basketball—absorb large sectors of the American public. Ethnic, racial, regional affiliations engender tribal loyalties, but within small groupings: not the Italians, but the Apulians; not the blacks, but blacks from the Mississippi delta; not the Kentuckians, but the residents in the creek bottoms of Pine Mountain. The factory, the shop, the neighborhood, the family, the office, all have their histories, and a representative history of one would do service for its innumerable counterparts.

What is missing in Dorson's formulation is the midrange character of these structures, as they face in both directions, drawing from and contributing to both home worlds and large-scale public worlds.

# The Study of Folklore in Literature and Culture: Identification and Interpretation

## Alan Dundes

*The benefits of a comparative perspective are clearly revealed in the following essay. Alan Dundes describes two cases in which the understanding of folklore must extend beyond the immediate social and cultural contexts of its performance. In the first case, Dundes selects a riddle from James Joyce's* Ulysses *to illustrate the identification of traditional sources of folklore in literature. Dundes then goes on to show that an understanding of folklore sources is basic to establishing the significance of a folk expression in a literary work. In the second case, Dundes uses a Native American tale that he collected to show how a comparative perspective permits the folklorist to glimpse something of the transformation that takes place when stories cross social or cultural boundaries.*

*Many of the early studies of folklore and literature were limited to the mere identification of folklore in literature, and such essays have not entirely disappeared (e.g., Moorehead 1981). Since Dundes's essay, however, interpretation has become the primary endeavor. For some examples of contemporary perspectives see Danielson (1975) and Mitchell (1981). Recent work has gone beyond the interpretation of elements embedded in folklore to the consideration of the interplay of folk and literary genres. See particularly de Caro (1978), Stanley (1979), Singer (1984), and Feintuch (1987).*

Many of those outside the discipline of folklore and even some of those within tend to divide folklorists into literary or anthropological categories. With this binary division comes a related notion that each group of folklorists has its own methodology appropriate for its special interests; hence there is thought to be a method for studying folklore in literature and another method for studying folklore in culture. Looking at this dichotomy from the viewpoint of a professional folklorist, one can see that it is false; moreover it is a dichotomy whose unfortunate persistence has tended to divide unnecessarily scholars working on similar if not identical problems. The basic methodology of studying folklore in literature and studying folklore in culture is almost exactly the same; in other words, the discipline of folklore has its own methodology applying equally well to literary and cultural problems.

There are only two basic steps in the study of folklore in literature and in culture. The first step is objective and empirical; the second is subjective and speculative. The first might be termed identification and the second interpretation. Identification essentially consists of a search for similarities; interpretation depends upon the delineation of differences. The first task in studying an item is to show how it is like previously reported items, whereas the second is to show how it differs from previously reported items—and, hopefully, why it differs.

Professional folklorists who are usually skilled in the mechanics of identification are apt to criticize literary critics and cultural anthropologists for failing to properly identify folkloristic materials before commenting upon their use. And folklorists are quite right to do so. Naive analyses can result from inadequate or inaccurate identification. Plots of traditional tale types might be falsely attributed to individual writers; European themes in a European tale told by American Indians might be mistakenly considered to be aboriginal elements. However, folklorists themselves might be criticized for doing no more than identifying. Too many studies of folklore in literature consist of little more than reading novels for the motifs or the proverbs, and no attempt is made to evaluate how an author has used folkloristic elements and more specifically, how these folklore elements function in the particular literary work as a whole. Similarly, listing the European tales among the North American Indians does not in itself explain how the borrowed tale functions in its new environment. The concern of folklorists with identification has resulted in sterile study of folklore for folklore's sake and it is precisely this emphasis on text and neglect of context which estranged so many literary critics and cultural anthropologists. The text-without-context orientation is exemplified by both anthropological and literary folklore scholarship. Folklorists go into the field to return with texts collected without their cultural context; folklorists plunge into literary sources and emerge with dry lists of motifs or proverbs lifted from their literary context. The problem is that for many folklorists identification has become an end in itself instead of a means to the end of interpretation. Identification is only the beginning, only the first step. A folklorist who limits his analysis to identification has stopped before asking any of the really important questions about his material. Until the folklorist is prepared to address himself to some of these questions, he must be resigned to living on the academic fringe in a peripheral discipline. As illustrations of how interpretation must follow initial identification in the study of folklore in context, the following brief discussion of a folktale found in James Joyce's *Ulysses* and a European tale found among the Prairie Band Potawatomi is offered.

In Joyce's *Ulysses,* one finds many different kinds of folklore, including tale types, nursery rhymes, tonguetwisters, folksongs, mnemonics, palindromes, and children's games.[1] Joyce's keen interest in folklore is further attested by his use of one of the minor characters, Haines, as an English folklorist come to Ireland to collect Irish folklore. Of all the examples of folklore in *Ulysses,* I have selected the riddle Stephen Dedalus asks his class to demonstrate the techniques of identification and interpretation. After reciting the opening formula and first line of a well-known riddle for writing, Stephen asks his class this riddle:

Alan Dundes

> The cock crew
> The sky was blue:
> The bells in heaven
> Were striking eleven.
> 'Tis time for this poor soul
> To go to heaven.

The first riddle that Stephen recites in this situation—"Riddle me, riddle me, randy ro / My father gave me seeds to sow"—has been identified by scholars as the first part of riddle number 1063 in Archer Taylor's great compendium, *English Riddles from Oral Tradition,* and also has received interpretive examination (Weldon Thornton says, for example, that Stephen's suppression of the last part of the riddle may be an admission of his failure as a writer)[2]—but so far as I know, no one has correctly identified the riddle Stephen puts to his class. Stephen's students are as much in the dark as the literary critics, though he gives them the answer, "the fox burying his grandmother under a hollybush." Work has been done on the problem of identification, since because of Joyce's frequent allusions to it throughout the book it is obviously of some importance to the interpretation of the book itself.[3] Several scholars have pointed out the similarity of Joyce's riddle with one in P. W. Joyce's *English as We Speak It in Ireland*:[4]

> Riddle me, riddle me right
> What did I see last night?
> The wind blew
> The cock crew,
> The bells of heaven
> Struck eleven.
> 'Tis time for my poor *sowl* to go to heaven.

> Answer: the fox burying his mother under a holly tree.

P. W. Joyce did not identify the riddle and he even commented upon what he called "the delightful inconsequences of riddle and answer." Yet a trained folklorist knows immediately that the riddle is closely related to a subtype of an international tale type, Aarne-Thompson 955, The Robber Bridegroom. In this subtype, which is very popular in Anglo-American oral tradition, the villainous suitor is frequently named Mr. Fox. Mr. Fox plans to do away with his betrothed and often the frightened girl, hidden in a tree, actually watches Mr. Fox digging her grave-to-be. Later at a large gathering the girl recites the riddle describing the villain's actions and thus unmasks the villain and reveals his nefarious plot. The folklorist can tell from the riddle text alone that there is a reference to the whole folktale, but there is additional evidence that Joyce himself knew the tale. In the memorable Circe chapter, the mob shouts derisively at Bloom as a disgrace to Christian men, a vile hypocrite, and the like: "Lynch him! Roast him! He's as bad as Parnell was. Mr. Fox!"[5] This very last allusion is what T. S. Eliot calls an objective correlative in that the mob scene in the folktale is evoked, a scene in which all those present cry out at the evil designs of the wicked Mr. Fox. So much for the identification of Stephen's riddle. What about the interpretation?

All previous interpretations of the significance of the riddle and fox imagery have been made without the benefit of a correct initial identification. William M. Schutte, for example, suggests that Stephen thinks of himself as a fox in that the fox as the wily foe of the hounds employs the weapons of silence, exile, and cunning. Schutte also says that the fox must be Stephen who killed his mother without mercy and who cannot stop scratching at the ground where she is buried.[6] However, in terms of the folktale the fox only plans to kill his sweetheart; he does not actually commit the crime. The fox is judged by his thought rather than by his act. In the novel Stephen did not kill his mother, but he judges himself in thought: "I could not save her"; earlier Buck Mulligan had spoken of Stephen killing his mother.[7] Of even more interest is the fact that in most versions of the tale Mr. Fox's victim is his bride-to-be, whereas in the Joyce variant the fox's victim is a mother. If the mother is equivalent to a sweetheart, then this would be part of the extensive Oedipal aspect of Stephen's character which I have discussed elsewhere.[8] In this light, Stephen the fox kills his mother instead of marrying her as she expected. If the P. W. Joyce text of the riddle was the source for James Joyce, then Stephen's changing the mother of the original to grandmother in the answer he gives the class also points to Stephen's Oedipal problem, for it is clear that in Stephen's own mind the fox's victim is a mother, not a grandmother.

The folktale source also clarifies the puzzling association of the fox and Christ. "Christfox" is described as a "runaway in blighted treeforks."[9] The latter description suggests not only a crucifixion but also the striking scene in the tale when the girl victim, hiding in a tree, looks down upon Mr. Fox digging her grave. The accompanying phrase "women he won to him" could allude to the Bluebeard Mr. Fox plot as well as to Christ and His faithful females. Stephen as "Christfox" is both victim and villain, both innocent and guilty. The point is, however, that unless the reader understands Joyce's skillful use of the riddle from the tale type as an objective correlative, he cannot appreciate the paradox.

One could proceed in similar fashion to identify and interpret other folkloristic elements in *Ulysses*. For example, one might examine Joyce's ingenious adaption of the riddling question "Where was Moses when the light went out?"[10]—or the impact of Stephen's singing the anti-Semitic ballad "Sir Hugh" or "The Jew's Daughter" (Child 155) at that point in the novel when the Gentile Stephen has been invited to stay the night at the home of the Jew Bloom, who has a marriageable daughter;[11] but these and other examples would only demonstrate the point made here in the exegesis of the Fox riddle.

So the literary critic without proper knowledge of folklore can go wrong in identification and consequently in interpretation—but so can the anthropologist who knows only the basic tools of his discipline's trade. In April of 1963 I collected a fine example of folklore in culture from William Mzechteno, a 74-year-old Prairie Band Potawatomi in Lawrence, Kansas. Here is the raw story as I transcribed it, with myself identified by the initial D and my informant with the initial M.

Alan Dundes

M. Well there was once, there was a little boy. There was always a little boy, you know, and he had a name, his name was ah—[pause of six seconds' duration]—P'teejah. His name is P'teejah, and ah—

D. P'teejah?

M. Yeah. And he, he had a little, let's see now—[pause of three seconds' duration]—oh, he had a little tablecloth, you know. He can eat, you know, there's food every time he spreads that tablecloth on the ground or anywheres; he name many food, any kinda food he wants. It'd just appear on the, right on the tablecloth and was eaten. Well, all he had to do to clean up, you know, is just shake; everything was disappear, you know, into thin air. And he was goin' long the road one time, he met a soldier, he had a cap on. Uniform caps, you know, those soldiers wear. And the soldier was hungry. [The boy asked] "You got anything to eat?" [The soldier answered] "Oh, I got this hard bread." It's all he had. [The boy said] "Let's see that bread," he told him, "oh, that's hard, that's no good, not fit to eat," he told him. He throw it away. [The soldier said] "Mustn't do that, it's all I got to eat." [The boy said] "I'll give you something better," he told him. He pull out his tablecloth, and spread it on there, on the ground. "You name anything you want, ANYTHING! So he, ah, he named all he wanted to eat, Soldier, he was real hungry. "So, if you want any of that red water, you can have that too," he told him, whiskey.

D. Red water?

M. Yeah, they call it red water [laughing].

D. Who called it red water?

M. The Indian boy. They called it red water.

D. Yeah?

M. Yeah, 'cause it's red, you know. He didn't call it fire water.

D. This is an Indian boy?

M. Yeah, yeah, And, oh the soldier enjoyed his meal; he filled up, you know, and "Well, I got something to show you," he told me. He [the soldier] took his cap off, you know, and he throwed it on the ground and said, "I want four soldiers." And sure enough, four soldiers, there, well armed, stood there at attention. "It's pretty good," he [the boy] told him, "but you can go hungry with those four soldiers," he told him [laughing]. So, he put on his cap, you know. Course the soldiers disappeared, and he start to go and then the soldier said, "Say, little boy, how you like to trade? I'll give you this cap for that cloth." Naw, he wouldn't trade. "I'd go hungry without it." Oh, he got to thinking, you know. He said, "Well soldiers could get me something to eat," he thought, I guess. So, he traded, fair trade. He kept looking back, the little boy, you know. He had that little cap on. He thought about his tablecloth. He sure hated to lose it. So he, come to his mind, you know, "I'll get it." He took off [laughing] that cap and throwed it on the ground. "Four soldiers," he told 'em. Soldiers come up, you know, stood up right there and [he] says, "See that man goin' over there. He took my tablecloth away from me," he told 'em, "you go and git it [giggling laugh]." So they went [laughing] after that man; he fought 'em like everythin'. "You belong to me," he said, "No [laughing] we belong to him over there," they said. So then he got his tablecloth and the boy got it back. And he had the cap too. That's where.

D. The boy was, you say, an Indian boy?

M. Yeah.

D. But the soldier was a white man.

M. Yeah.

D. So the Indian boy was fooling the white man.

M. Yeah, [laughing] he put it on him.

D. In a trade, too.

M. Yeah, it was a fair trade but he was using his noodle [laughing].

D. That's very nice. I didn't know it was an Indian boy.

M. Yeah.

D. I see.

M. Yeah.

D. Well, that's good, that's a fine story.

In order to analyze this tale in terms of Potawatomi culture, one must first identify the tale not as an indigenous Indian story, but as a European tale type. From the detail of the magic food-providing tablecloth (Motif D 1472.1.8), the professional folklorist can easily identify the tale as a version of tale type 569, The Knapsack, the Hat, and the Horn. Moreover, from internal evidence one can without difficulty demonstrate that the tale was borrowed originally from a French source. The Indian boy's name is P'téejah and the long pause before the utterance of the name shows the narrator's praiseworthy concern with getting the name right. P'téejah is a recognizable corruption of the French folktale character of Petit-Jean. As a matter of fact, Franz Boas in his essay "Romantic Folk-Lore among American Indians" observed that the name of this French figure had been taken over by a number of American Indian groups.[12] Another trace of French culture is the allusion to "red water" which is probably wine although the narrator interpreted it as whiskey. So the tale has been identified: It is a borrowing from a French version of Aarne-Thompson tale type 569 and certainly not an aboriginal tale type. But the statement that it is a European tale does not answer such questions as what have the Potawatomi done with the tale?—how have they changed it and how do these changes tell us something about present-day Potawatomi culture? As a general rule European tales among American Indian groups can be used as indexes of acculturation. If the European tale is little changed, then it is probable that the borrowing Indian culture is waning if not defunct. If on the other hand the European tale is reworked and adapted to fit American Indian rather than European values, then it is more than likely that the American Indian culture in question is still a going concern. What about this Potawatomi tale?

First of all, the hero has been changed from a French character to an Indian boy. The narrator was questioned repeatedly about the identity of P'téejah and each time he insisted that P'téejah was an Indian boy. Secondly, the magic cap which belonged to the white soldier worked magic in American Indian symbolic terms rather than in European. Four soldiers were produced, not three; four is the ritual number of the Potawatomi as of most American Indian groups. Thus the magic soldier-producing hat (Motif D 1475.4) operates in American Indian terms and this in a sense is precisely what the whole tale does. In the tale the soldier offers to make a trade—protection in exchange for food, an exchange not unusual in the light of American colonial history. One senses that the exchange is unfair and that the adult European soldier is tricking the young Indian boy into giving up his only source of food. But in this folktale the Indian boy gets the best of the trade, the "fair trade" proposed by the white man. Although the hero does not appear to have planned his actions in advance, the narrator commented after telling the tale that the boy had "used his noodle," that is, he had out-thought the white man. In this tale of wish fulfillment, the Indian boy has sufficient force to overpower the European soldier antagonist and to regain his original abundance of food.

In the cultural phenomenon which anthropologists term nativistic movements, it is common for the borrowing, dominated culture to dream of taking over the dominating culture's artifacts without the presence of members of that culture.[13] In this tale the Potawatomi has control of European artifacts; it is the Indian boy who is able to offer the soldier "red water" rather than soldier offering the Indian liquor—it is the Indian boy who uses the white man's object to defeat the white man. One can see even from these few comments why this particular European tale could easily have been accepted by Potawatomi raconteurs and audiences. A few deft changes made it a tale with considerable appeal for most Potawatomi. One can see from a "mistake" made by the narrator that he identified with the Indian boy. After the soldier finished eating, he told the boy he had something to show him. At this point, Mr. Mzechteno said "Well, I got something to show you," he told *me*. This use of "me" instead of "him" strongly suggests that the story was in some sense about Mr. Mzechteno and perhaps other Potawatomi. This detail plus the informant's frequent laughter demonstrate his enjoyment of and involvement with the tale.

The study of Joyce's use of a riddle and the study of a Potawatomi adaptation of a European tale appear to be distinct, but the methodology employed in both studies was the same. Identification was equally necessary. Failure to identify the Mr. Fox riddle in *Ulysses* could result in one's being unable to appreciate fully Joyce's use of this folkloristic element and accordingly limiting in a small way one's comprehension of the novel; failure to identify the Potawatomi tale as a standard European folktale might have made it difficult to determine just what changes the Potawatomi had introduced. One might have assumed, for example, that it was a Potawatomi idea to cast the dupe as a soldier, but in fact the soldier is frequently the dupe in European versions of the tale. But identification though necessary was only the first step, a prerequisite for interpretation. If it is true that folklorists too often identify without going on to interpret whereas literary critics and anthropologists interpret without first properly identifying folklore, then it seems obvious that some changes are needed. Either folklorists are going to have to educate their literary and anthropological colleagues in the mechanics of identifying folklore or they will have to undertake some of the problems of interpretation themselves. Ideally, both alternatives might be effected so that the study of folklore could become something more than a scholarly series of shreds and patches or a motley medley of beginnings without ends and ends without proper beginnings.

---

[1] Page references to *Ulysses* are from the Modern Library edition. For a sample of Joyce's use of folksongs see Mabel P. Worthington, "Irish Folk Songs in Joyce's *Ulysses*," *PMLA*, LXXI, 3 (June, 1956), 321–39.

[2] Weldon Thornton, "An Allusion List for James Joyce's *Ulysses*, Part 2, 'Nestor,'" *James Joyce Quarterly*, I, 2 (Winter, 1964), 3.

[3] *Ulysses*, 47, 60, 191, 288, 480, 544, 545, 557.

[4] Scholars who have noted this source include Joseph Prescott, "Notes on Joyce's *Ulysses*," *Modern Language Quarterly*, XIII (1952), 149, and William M. Schutte, *Joyce and Shakespeare: A Study in the Meaning of* Ulysses (New Haven, 1957), 102, note 4.

[5] *Ulysses*, 482.

[6] Schutte, 103. W. Y. Tindall also remarks on Stephen's identification with the cunning fox, but he equates the buried grandmother with Stephen's mother, the Church, and the Poor Old Woman (Ireland) in his *James Joyce: His Way of Interpreting the Modern World* (New York, 1950), 23.

[7] *Ulysses*, 46.

[8] Alan Dundes, "Re: Joyce—No in at the Womb," *Modern Fiction Studies*, VIII, 2 (Summer, 1962), 137–47.

[9] *Ulysses*, 191.

[10] *Ulysses*, 714.

[11] *Ulysses*, 674–76.

[12] Franz Boas, *Race, Language and Culture* (New York, 1940), 517. See also Alanson Skinner, *The Mascoutens or Prairie Potawatomi Indians, Part III—Mythology and Folklore, Bulletin of the Public Museum of the City of Milwaukee*, VI, 3 (January, 1927), 400–2.

[13] Sometimes the dominating culture's artifacts may be used as weapons against it. In this instance the Potawatomi have borrowed a European folktale and successfully employed it to attack Europeans. For another example of Potawatomi borrowing of European folktales in which the tales are used as vehicles for Indian superiority over whites, see Gary H. Gossen, "A Version of the Potawatomi Coon-Wolf Cycle: A Traditional Projection Screen for Acculturative Stress," *Search: Selected Studies by Undergraduate Honors Students at the University of Kansas*, IV (Spring, 1964), 8–14.

# Documenting Folklore: The Annotation

## Elliott Oring

*Folklore courses commonly include some kind of fieldwork component. Students may be directed to a close examination of the traditions of an individual or group, or instructed to collect from a variety of people a range of folklore genres, which then may be deposited in an archive. In both cases, accurate renderings of texts and reports of behaviors, along with detailed contextual information, constitute the major portion of these projects.*

*There is another facet of folklore documentation that may properly accompany field-oriented projects; the commentary on the relations of a particular item of folklore to other texts, ideas, behaviors, and events—i.e., annotation. Annotation attempts to lift a folklore expression out of the immediate context of its performance and situate it in a world of expression. While the task of annotation characterizes no single theoretical perspective, it does presuppose the value of identifying folklore's connections beyond their immediate social and communicative environments. The following essay advocates the search for these kinds of connections as a worthwhile adjunct of introductory field projects.*

Every event, each human behavior, is a unique occurrence brought about by the interaction of particular objects, in particular places, at particular times, and under particular conditions. Since objects, time, place, and circumstance continually change, no two events are ever identical. Everything is utterly singular and new. The human mind cannot comprehend such a world, however. Concepts serve to rob events of their uniqueness by making them members of more general classes. The human mind is forever perceiving analogies, similarities, identities, and hierarchies, or otherwise recognizing *relations* between events. Were it not for our categorizing and classifying propensities, we would be hopelessly overpowered by the relentless novelty of the world.

Each folklore expression is in some sense a unique occurrence as it is part of a fabric of unique experience. In documenting folklore, folklorists are asked to capture something of this uniqueness through their descriptions of context. A thorough description of the social, cultural, and individual contexts of folklore, in some measure, is an attempt to situate an expression within the flow of individual and group experience. But folklorists must also perceive relations. They must be alert to those similarities, analogies, and identities that cause an otherwise unique expression to be transformed into an element of a more general class. For even designating a particular linguistic expression a "tale," or a particular occurrence a "storytelling event," affirms its similarity to a host of expressions and events from other times and places. To regard a tale as a version of "Little Red Riding Hood" or a storytelling event as "joketelling" asserts even more specific relations to a subset of expressions and events within the general class.

Thus the folklorist must maintain two perspectives: one that is local, contextual, and descriptive: and another that is broad, comparative, and theoretical. Throughout *Folk Groups and Folklore Genres: An Introduction,* notions of context were discussed and methods of reporting context were illustrated. Text and context must be recorded by an observer in the field. It is difficult, perhaps impossible, to adequately reconstruct text and context. The phraseology and intonation of a tale, for example, and the details of the interaction in which narration is embedded are unlikely to be accurately recalled after the fact.

However, the relations of a recorded tale to the world of narrative may be traced at anytime by anyone. Given the text of an oral tale (or proverb, riddle, joke, dance, etc.), anyone may peruse the published literature for reports of similar tales recorded in other times and places. It is a matter of search and research. One can construct an *annotation* of the tale, i.e., a commentary on the relations of the tale, its structure, content, theme, and phraseology to other literary, historical, and cultural documents.

Such commentaries have been a part of folklore research from its inception. In 1822, the Brothers Grimm appended a volume of comparative notes to *Kinder- und Haus-märchen* to indicate that the tales were Indo-European rather than distinctly Germanic in character.[1] Later in the century, evolutionists employed a broadly comparative approach to identify primitive survivals and discover their original significance.[2] By the end of the nineteenth century a methodology had developed to map the versions of an item of folklore, deduce its probable date and geographical point of origin, and trace the routes of its dissemination.[3] This methodology involved amassing all known published or archival analogues of the item and subjecting them to rigorous examination, comparison, and classification. In the twentieth century, psychoanalysis made extensive use of analogues to uncover associations that might be brought to the interpretation of a difficult text.[4] In other words, all these perspectives relied heavily upon broad textual comparison, despite fundamental differences in their theoretical orientations.

Folklorists are no longer interested in reconstructing primitive philosophies or tracing paths of diffusion, and psychoanalytic interpretation has only a few devoted practitioners. Today, folklorists tend to focus on the folklore of particular groups in a particular environment. Nevertheless, a comparative perspective can still be of value, for the following reasons.[5]

(1) A comparative perspective may serve as a buffer against cultural parochialism. In focusing upon a single individual or group, it is easy to regard every expression as idiosyncratic, peculiar, or unique. For example, as part of an experiment, anthropologist

David Maybury-Lewis submitted to two other anthropologists and a folklorist four versions of a tale that he collected among the Sherente Indians of Central Brazil for blind analysis. The tale itself was a transformation of the story of Adam and Eve in the book of Genesis. Eve had so many children she couldn't make clothes for them all. She was ashamed and hid the naked ones in the jungle. When Jesus came to baptize her children, those hidden in the jungle were overlooked. They became the ancestors of the Indians, while the baptized children became the ancestors of civilized peoples. The anthropologists were quick to argue that the transformation of the biblical tale reflected values and conditions peculiar to Sherente society. The folklorist pointed out, however, that the transformation of the biblical narrative in the Sherente tales was well-known in the Old World (Aarne and Thompson Type 728, which even appears in the Grimms' collection) and probably had been introduced into Sherente society by Europeans. In other words, whatever the particular plots and motifs of these tales might mean for the Sherente, they could not be regarded as unique Sherente innovations. If one is to speak of Sherente adaptations of European narrative traditions, one needs to know what narrative elements they were in fact modifying and what adaptations they were actually making.[6]

(2) A comparative perspective is also necessary in identifying socio-cultural change. For example, Roger Abrahams argued that the badman had replaced the trickster as the most popular hero in black-American narrative tradition. The subservient and childlike characteristics of the trickster in the tales of the Old South were displaced in contemporary tales in the urban North by naked aggression and revolt. As part of his evidence, Abrahams produced a Brer Rabbit tale that had been published by Joel Chandler Harris in 1883 and a version of that tale from urban black tradition of the late 1950s. Chandler's crafty yet childlike hero had been replaced in the urban tale by one that was angry and cruel.[7] Did such urban tales reflect a more aggressive black identity opposed to accommodation with the existing social order? This question may not be definitively answered from comparative data alone, but in the absence of these kinds of data, such questions cannot even be framed.

(3) Any effort to suggest the psychological or sociological importance of certain themes or values in folklore needs to be supported by quantitative data. How often do these structures, themes, or values actually emerge in the tales, songs, or superstitions of a group? Although the significance of such data is often skewed in folklore research (collecting is not random sampling), the building of even a modest argument based upon quantitative data involves amassing analogues.

How does one go about annotating a text—writing a commentary on its folkloric, literary, and historical relations? What should it look like? How long should it be? When is it finished? There are no absolute answers to these questions. The search for analogues could theoretically go on forever. For historic-geographic studies, the accumulation of the comparative data for one text could take months or years. Evolutionists and psychoanalysts were generally content to identify a few salient parallels with no aims of bibliographic completeness. For introductory students, the task of annotation is primarily an exercise—an exercise designed to illustrate that the folklore materials they collect in the face-to-face encounters at home, in the dormitory, or at work are often related to traditions that have been reported by other collectors in other times and in other places. The purpose is to acquire some sense of this web of relations, rather than to attempt some kind of definitive "study" of the item in question.

Annotation involves detective work, and detective work depends upon skill, perseverance, and luck. The availability of adequate library or archival resources is also a factor. Without access to Archer Taylor's *English Riddles From Oral Tradition* (Berkeley: University of California Press, 1951), an otherwise straightforward annotation of an English riddle may turn into a complicated and laborious affair. There are always some basic sources that one checks first, but if these don't lead anywhere, one must become more resourceful and even creative. But there is also the possibility that the materials collected are idiosyncratic, so that no closely related materials may be found and consequently there can be no annotation. In the sample annotations that I provide below, this likelihood is greatly reduced because the scope of potential relations is quite wide. Furthermore, negative results are also considered appropriate for inclusion in the commentary. (That is, *not* finding an analogue after searching a major source also merits comment.)

In my folklore classes, I have regularly collected sample texts from students in order to demonstrate that what is called "folklore" is not merely the property of others, for we are all "folk," and we all have "lore." But I would then go on to transcribe one or two of the items I collected and then research them and write them up for the next class meeting to provide some sense of the annotative possibilities. Each of the three annotations below originated as one of those specimen exercises. They required between three and six hours to research. These annotations are in no sense complete, but are meant to illustrate what might be accomplished within the designated time frames.

## SPECIMEN 1:

The following tale was collected from a student in 1985. She was born in South Africa, and while living in the United States had married an Iranian.

> *Text:* This is a Persian folktale my husband and I, we tell it to my son and we're going to tell it to my daughter. It has to do with the cunningness of women. And there's a famous poet-scientist, lived hundreds of years ago in Persia: his name was Sa'di. And he always wrote books about every subject you could imagine. So, one day he was going to write a book on the cunningness of the women. So he was going to go from one door to the other and ask them a question. So, he finally gets to this one door and he's got his notebook in his hand, and pencil, and he asks the woman, "Yes, could I come in and ask you some questions to find out the secrets?" So the woman says, "Come on inside," and she closed the door. So she said, "I don't want you to write this book. I don't want you to." And he says, "I want to and I'm going to." So there's a knock on

the door and she says, "Oh my God, it's my husband." Now Middle Eastern men tend to be very jealous and so she said, "Quickly hide and come inside this [pause] *somar* [?]"; and it's like a chest that they have, a huge chest, and they put everything in it. So she makes him go and hide and she closes the lid on it and everything. So the husband comes in and she says, "Oh, you can't believe it. There was this man here and I think he was going to rape me." And he says, "Oh yeah" and he grabs a knife. He says, "Let me kill that son-of-a-gun. Just wait until I find him." And she says, "He's over there in the *somar*." And he says, "Oh, I'm going to kill him." And all of a sudden she starts laughing. "Hehehehe." And he says, "Why are you laughing?" And she says, "You stupid fool! Eh! I'm just joking you. Do you think there is somebody here?" Now poor Sa'di, inside, he'd already died. He wet his pants and everything and he felt this guy was going to kill him. So then the husband said, "Okay, then, so she was joking me. I'm not going to kill him." So he leaves and later on Sa'di comes out of the thing. He says, "Why did you do that?" She says, "You can never find the secrets of women. She can always trick the husband or anybody that's around. You can't write a book on woman's cunning."

Certainly there are many questions one could ask concerning the social, cultural, and individuals contexts of this tale. On what occasions is this tale told? What is the cultural identity of the family and how is it negotiated? How does this identity inform upon the eduction of the informant's children in general, and the telling of this tale in particular? What ideas concerning the statuses of and relations between men and women does this informant hope to communicate to her children through this tale, and what messages are actually received by them? These and many more questions are immediately stimulated by the encounter with such a text, but these are not the kinds of questions that are directly addressed by annotation. The annotation lifts the text from its immediate environment and relates it to broader streams of culture, history, and literature. The following annotation begins with a perusal of the major indexes of plots and motifs, briefly explores thematic aspects of the story frame, which leads to a discussion of the historicity of the tale protagonist, and finally concludes with the examination of particular collections of tales.

*Annotation:* Although this tale concerns a poet-scientist who seeks to discover the secrets of women, it seems related to tales in which a paramour is hidden (in a chest or other container) from a jealous husband. No specific type in Antti Aarne and Stith Thompson's *The Types of the Folktale,* Folklore Fellows Communication LXXV, No. 184 (Helsinki: Suomalainen Tiedeakatemia 1964) corresponds to all the features of this text, yet several types concern the hiding of suitors. Type 1358B: *Husband Carries Off Box Containing Hidden Paramour* is one, but our story lacks the escape of the suitor through the unwitting aid of the husband. Type 1419K*: *Lover Hidden in Chest, etc.* is more relevant but also more general. The protagonist of our tale is a scholar and poet, perhaps even a religious figure, and Type 1725: *The Foolish Parson in the Trunk,* and Type 1730: *The Entrapped Suitors* demonstrate that there is a well-established tradition of putting respectable members of the clergy in trunks or hiding them from jealous husbands.

Numerous motifs from Stith Thompson, *Motif-Index of Folk-Literature* (Bloomington IN: Indiana University Press, 1966) seem appropriate to our tale. Many are very general such as J2301: *Gullible husband* or J1112: *Clever wife*. Our tale seems especially concerned with a series of "deceptions" by the wife that would seem related to Motifs K1500: *Deceptions concerned with adultery* and K1510: *Adultress outwits husband* but nothing specifically relating to our tale can be found under these headings. The most appropriate motif categories seem to be those that come under K1213: *Terrorizing the paramour*: more specifically, K1213.1: *Woman dares husband to try his sword on a pile of clothing in which hides her paramour*. She stops him just in time. Also see K1213.1.1: *Adultress frightens paramour with cries of "rape!"*. Then she removes her husband's suspicion by feigning a fit. Both motifs culminate with the retribution of the paramour, who later exposes the woman naked (except for her face) to his friends. This latter element is absent from our tale. Thompson cites D. P. Rotunda, *Motif-Index of the Italian Novella* (Bloomington IN: Indiana University Press, 1942), for both of these motifs. Rotunda's index is organized after Thompson's and under these motif categories are cited works by Ser Giovanni, Matteo Bandello, and Celio Malespini. Also in Thompson and Rotunda are K1218.1.4: *Importunate lover (priest) is forced to hide in chest* (although the lover/priest's release is again different than in our tale), and K1521.2; *Paramour successfully hidden in chest*. All in all, it would seem that we might find the closest European parallels to our tale in Italian Renaissance novella. None of these types or motifs appear in Ernest W. Baughman, *A Type and Motif-Index of the Folktales of England and North America* (The Hague: Indiana University Folklore Series No. 20, 1966), although Type 1419: *The returning husband hoodwinked*, which concerns a lover hiding in a pot and being carried out of the woman's home by a second lover, is cited.

There are numerous proverbs and aphorisms in world tradition that concern the characteristics of women. T. F. Thistleton-Dyer cites two "Oriental" proverbs. "None knows the wily tricks of a woman" and "Women's wiles and thieves' tricks cannot be fathomed" in his *Folklore of Women* (Chicago: A. C. McClurg & Co., 1906), p. 4. "An Evil woman in a good man's home; It is as if in this life Hell were come," is an assessment of evil women made by Shaikh Saadi and listed in *The World Treasury of Religious Quotations*, comp. and ed. Ralph L. Woods (New York: Hawthorn Books, 1966) p. 1060. The Sa'di in our narrative probably refers to one of the greatest figures of Persian literature, Mosleh Od-Din Sa'di, or Mosharref Od-Din, who lived in the thirteenth century. Born in Shiraz, he travelled widely in the Middle East and North Africa. Two of his best-known books are *Bustan* [The Orchard (1257)] and *Golestan* [The Rose Garden (1258)]. The former is entirely in verse while the latter is in prose and verse. Both consist of stories that are designed to illustrate virtues, offer advice, and engage in philosophical reflection. A brief glance at translations of these works did not turn up any analogues to our tale, however. It is possible that it is because Sa'di is famous for his parables and anecdotes that our tale has been attached to him [*The New Encyclopaedia Britannica* s.v. "Sa'di"].

The works of the Persian poet Jalal al-Din Rumi (1207–73), who was a contemporary of Sa'di, contains a tale that bears some resemblance to our example. The *Masnavi*, which contains some 25,000 rhyming couplets, includes tales and fables that are employed as religious parables and allegories. A. J. Arberry has translated the greater number of these stories into prose in *Tales from the Masnavi* (London: George Allen and Unwin, 1961) and *More Tales from the Masnavi* (1963). In the latter work I found a tale of Goha, who persuades his wife to seduce the Cadi so they can blackmail him. When the Cadi comes to visit the wife, Goha returns and the Cadi hides in a coffer. The Cadi manages to inform a porter to call for his deputy. Goha feigns reluctance, but finally consents to sell the coffer, unopened, to the deputy for a goodly sum. The next year he and his wife try the same trick on the Cadi, but he recognizes them (pp. 230–33). Although this tale contains elements that are similar to our text, it may represent a different type.

A much closer parallel to our tale is found in Sir Richard Burton's edition of the *Thousand and One Nights*. This work is a composite work with materials added in different places and periods. The earliest reference to the work is in the ninth century. In the next century it is referred to as the Persian *Hazar Afsanak* [Thousand Tales]. A translation into French in the early eighteenth century was the first published edition. The first Arabic edition was published a century later in Calcutta [*The New Encyclopaedia Britannica*, s.v. "Thousand and One Nights"]. Burton's translation was published in 1885 with six supplemental volumes following in 1886–88. Our tale is designated, in the supplemental tales, as the one begun on the seven hundred and forty-first night. It is entitled "The Tailor and the Lady and the Captain." It concerns a tailor who persists in admiring the beauty of a married woman whose house is across from his shop. Although she is offended by his attentions, he persists. She sends a slave girl to invite him over. The woman serves him and converses with him until the woman's husband returns. She then hides him in a cabinet. When the husband comes in, she tells him that her lover is hiding in the closet. The tailor wets his pants when he hears the husband threatening to kill him and demanding the closet key from his wife. Finally the wife bursts out laughing and claims to be mocking her husband. The husband is persuaded and abandons his pursuit. Although this tale lacks the framing idea of a scientist seeking to understand the cunningness or secrets of women, it otherwise seems to parallel our collected tale quite closely. See Richard F. Burton, *Supplemental Nights to the Book of the Thousand and One Nights with Notes Anthropological and Explanatory*, 5:196–202.

Because this tale is a fiction that involves the deception of men by women, and involves a traditional triangle that resembles that of wife-lover-husband, I anticipated locating some appropriate references in the type and motif indexes. Nevertheless, I had no specific familiarity with this tale. I was unfamiliar with the person or works of Sa'di, unaware of the translation of the prose excerpts of the *Masnavi*, and I did not know that a close analogue was to be found in the *Thousand and One Nights*. The link to Sa'di was first discovered while investigating the theme of "women's trickery" and the fortuitous citation of Sa'di which led me to look into this historical character more thoroughly. Discovering an analogue to our tale in *More Tales of the Masnavi* led me to suspect that a version might be found in the *Thousand and One Nights*. It was sheer luck, however, that I located the analogue, since there was no time to really scrutinize the Burton edition and the abridged editions that I first consulted revealed no evident parallels. Certainly, the title "The Tailor and the Lady and the Captain" provides only slight clues of the story's contents. As it turns out, there is a guide in French to the themes and motifs of the *Thousand and One Nights* as well as two German dissertations on Arabic folktale types.[8] These works are rare and difficult to obtain, and I was unaware of their existence when I set out to annotate the tale for the class.

Thus our individual tale can be viewed as more than the verbal report of a behavior uniquely occurring at a single point in time and space. The story is one of a set stories that have been documented over several hundred years. Exactly how this particular instantiation of a tale type came to be would require more investigation of what is clearly an old and probably widespread type. What is clear is that the basic elements of this tale are not the products of idiosyncratic fantasy (not even in such minor and optional elements as Sa'di wetting his pants). Nor is the narrator's characterization of her tale as "Persian" a purely subjective attribution. As the protagonist of the tale is a famous Persian historical figure, and as analogues to plot and motif appear in early Persian sources, we may, in part, understand how the narrator may regard this tale as a vehicle for symbolizing an Iranian identity and instilling a sense of Iranian culture and history in her American-born children.

## SPECIMEN 2:

The following material was offered by a student in 1983. Unlike the fictional tale reported above, this account is offered as a purportedly true account of events during the American Civil War.

> *Text:* I'll tell you about where I was born and where I was raised down around Birmingham, Alabama, in a part called Bessemer. . . . It is really a town that doesn't exist much anymore. That's what the story is about. It was a steel-making town. It probably would have been where Birmingham is now if it hadn't been for the Civil War. It was destroyed in the Civil War. Anyway, it was a Southern steel-making center which was important strategically to the South during the Civil War, 'cause they didn't have much industry; it was all agricultural. So I lived there, and I think the area still is, I haven't been there in a long time. It was pretty rich in lore about the Civil War and. . . . This particular story; how can I describe it? The steel works now are on a place called Red Mountain which is in Birmingham. And Birmingham has all the train connections and Birmingham grew up to be a fairly large city. In the South I guess it's rivaled only by Atlanta and maybe New Orleans. I don't know how many people it has; maybe close to a million. Anyway, Bessemer was a town that during the Civil War was very important because it had a steel mill, and the railroad lines went

into the town. I don't know the different campaigns, but anyway, shortly after Richmond had fallen and the capital had moved to Mobile, the Northern Forces decided they were going to make a sweep down to Mobile and destroy Bessemer which was where they were making the cannons and all the steel which was used in fabricating the industrial support for the Confederacy.

They were getting most of their cannons from the North. There was even a joke about that. You ever hear the joke about the Confederate prisoner-of-war who is on the ramparts and he says, "God! You guys have about as many USA cannons as we do." So they were getting most of their cannons out of capturing them, black market, and I don't know, whatever. Anyway, this steel works was real important. The Southern army was really a very effective army, I guess, considering the equipment. It's pretty amazing, I think, that the South did as well as they did. They were very under-equipped. I think historically soldier for soldier they were considered to be superior soldiers; at least better shots.

Anyway, the South was falling apart. I don't know the year; sixty-four, sixty-three and the North made a sweep into Alabama from the north. This was the battle of . . . [hesitates] Shiloh. Shiloh I think was the turning point. Anyway, a contingent of Alabama militia, I think each state had a different army in the Confederacy. It wasn't a federal army. I guess it was a federal army but they had state militias anyway. Anyway, these Alabamans decided they were going to defend Bessemer; which was where they were making steel. It was one of those Alamo-type situations. Their wives went up there with them. Anyway, they all died fighting. They held out for a long time too and against great odds. Whatever. Then the North took the iron plant and destroyed it.

It's still there. It was really an interesting place to play as a little kid because all the walls . . . you could see where the soldiers they . . . the train tracks that went into the steel mill. The Northerners melted the tracks and wrapped them around oak trees. I mean they destroyed it and they wrecked the . . . they did a lot to destroy the railway. That was very important. Anyway they wrapped, I don't know if they melted them, but anyway they wrapped them. Anyway, the train tracks go up a tree which is kind of funny. And they did a lot to destroy the towers and everything to make sure that the industrial part of Alabama was destroyed. Anyway, that place is a very interesting place to play, but you leave at night because it's haunted and that's the basis of the story.

That it's still haunted and on the anniversary of the defeat of the garrison you can still hear the screaming and the spectral visions of their wives who were melting down their silverware to make musket balls. They were still using black powder I guess in those days. Anyway, the tale is that they melted down whatever metal they could find to make musket balls and these guys and their family fought and died. I guess rather horrible . . . fire . . . from the North, northern soldiers. And it's still supposed to be haunted. . . .

Well, there's supposed to be cries in the night. That's a common assumption of the haunting. And lights that move behind the ramparts. It really wasn't a fort. You've got to understand that this was a factory, but the walls or whatever where they defended the thing. Or outside of the factory. Anyway, the location where this happened. You know, what do you call these things that you carry in the night? A lantern! Lantern lights. And screams of dogs barking. These people apparently took their families up there. And certainly it has an eerie feeling.

Most of this account might be regarded as folk history—a native account (rather than a formal scholarly account) of historical events and processes. The account is said to be recalled from childhood. It begins to approach local legend as it describes the haunting of the battlefield. Yet both the description of the battle and of the haunting of the battlefield are reported rather than dramatically rendered.

The following annotation focuses upon the correlation of the folk historical account with those from written records of the time. Although they are closer in time and place to the events that purportedly occurred, it is not necessary to conceptualize the early written account as "right" and the later oral account as "wrong." Rather, they may be viewed as *different* accounts, each with its own point of view, its own validity, and its own sphere of influence. The latter part of the annotation focuses upon the classification of supernatural motifs.

*Annotation:* The town of Bessemer lies to the southeast of Birmingham and has a population of 31,729 people [*The World Almanac* 1982]. However, Bessemer was only founded in 1887 by a local coal baron who built the first steel plant in the area [*The New Encyclopaedia Brittanica*, s.v. "Bessemer"]. Birmingham's population is currently 284,413 and not the million estimated by the informant, but it is not uncommon for children to remember places as being larger than they were. Birmingham also was founded after the Civil War, in 1871. The area was first settled in 1813, and Elyton became the seat of Jefferson County in 1821. Elyton later became a part of modern-day Birmingham [s.v. "Birmingham"]. The incident described in the informant's account would seem to correspond to that reported as taking place in March and April 1865 during the Union Army's invasion of Alabama. General James Harrison Wilson with three cavalry divisions marched through Alabama from Chicasaw in the northeast to Girard on the Georgia border. His forces captured Selma and Montgomery which were their major objectives. Around Elyton, a force under General John Croxton was dispatched to the west to attack Tuscaloosa. On March 29, 1865, large iron works six miles south of Elyton were burned. These were the McIlvain and Red Mountain Iron Works, and these might be those referred to in the informant's account. Several other ironworks further south were destroyed the following day. These published sources suggest that no pitched battle at the Red Mountain works took place as they describe resistance to Wilson's advance as light. But these sources do describe the US forces as destroying all the ironworks they encountered as well as rail linkages. It does seem unlikely that the families of the Confederate soldiers would be present at a battle. [See Malcolm C. McMillan, *The Alabama Confederate Reader* (University AL: University of Alabama Press, 1963), pp. 404–8; Donald B. Dodd, *Historical Atlas of Alabama* (University AL: University of Alabama Press, 1974), p. 53; *The War of Rebellion: A Compilation of the Official Records of the Union and Confederate Armies*, 1st Serial, XLIX Pt. 1 (Washington, DC: Government Printing Office, 1897), pp. 471–72].

367

Elliott Oring

It would seem that the story of a pitched battle and subsequent haunting were attached to the ruins of the Red Mountain Iron Works sometime after the events of March and April 1865. The nature of the haunting seems traditional and various related motifs can be found in Stith Thompson, *Motif-Index of Folk-Literature* (Bloomington IN: Indiana University Press, 1966) B733.2: *Dogs howling indicates death;* E231.3: *Ghost light hovers over hiding place of murdered person;* E334: *Non-malevolent ghosts haunt scene of former misfortune, crime, or tragedy;* E421.1.3: *Ghosts visible to dogs alone;* E502: *The sleeping army: Soldiers killed in battle come forth on occasions from their resting place;* E722.1.3; *Soul as point of light;* F1961.4: *Flame indicates place where innocent person was murdered.* For a tale involving ghost lights see *The Frank C. Brown Collection of North Carolina Folklore.* ed. Newman Ivey White (Durham NC: Duke University Press, 1952), 1:684. For a survey of Alabama ghost stories see Ray B. Browne, *A Night with the Hants, and Other Alabama Folk Experiences* (Bowling Green OH: Popular Press, n.d.).

The narrator had been born and raised in Alabama, but he was relating his account to a university class in California. The purported reason for relating this account was the haunting of the battlefield that appears at the very end ("because it was haunted and that's the basis for the story"). This was the "folklore" that the student was ostensibly reporting to the class. The description of the disposition of forces and military events was offered as a factual account of what transpired, meant to introduce the report of the haunting of the battlefield. The haunting was only tentatively offered for belief ("It's *supposed* to still be haunted"), although the student included elements to encourage the entertainment of this belief ("And certainly it has an eerie feeling"). The purportedly historical introduction to the account of the haunting seems designed to emphasize the military and moral superiority of the Confederate soldiers, despite the Union victory. The emphasis of the "Alamo-type" situation of the defending soldiers, the stealing of Union cannons and the melting down of silverware for musket balls in the face of a superior Northern technology, and the death of all the defenders together with their families all seem to symbolize the righteousness of the Southern cause. Interestingly, the supernatural motifs at the conclusion reinforce this interpretation of the account. Ghosts often appear at the scene of a misfortune, crime, or tragedy. Flames and ghost lights are traditionally associated with the murder of *innocents*. The account of the haunting of the battlefield may serve as supernatural confirmation of the terrible tragedy or crime that had befallen the defenders of the Red Mountain Iron Works specifically, and the South generally—a tragedy so great that the dead still cannot rest.[9]

## SPECIMEN 3:

A belief, embedded in narrative, is our final example of annotation. Part of the material was recorded and transcribed verbatim and is subsumed under the heating of "Text." The remainder, however, was based upon notes and is reported in the section "Notes." Occasionally a direct quotation from the informant is included in the notes section. It was reported by an African student in 1977.

*Text:* This is a story about reincarnation. There used to be a girl who lived around us, that is, in Nigeria, my native home. She had a real big scar on her upper lip, and that scar was real deep. Deep. And I asked my dad, "How did this girl get that mark?" He told me that the father of this girl on numerous occasions had a . . . [indecipherable]. Anytime she was born, she would live up to about three years and then die. And she came about five times. Now the sixth time, she lived up to about six years. And she was very pretty and very beautiful. And the fellow was so annoyed, and so he took a knife and sliced up the upper lip. [Collector: "On the dead child?"]. Yes. On the dead. The last time she was born she was born with that mark.

*Notes:* The informant said he remembers asking his father about the girl's scar when he was seven years old. The informant used to play with the child, saw the mark on her lip, and asked her father about it. He never asked the girl herself about the scar. He stated that he believed the explanation his father provided. The informant did not recall the girl being different from any of the other children except that her speech was somewhat affected by her condition. The informant stated that children who died were often reborn to the same parents. The purpose of the mutilation by the father was to discourage the girl from returning again and being born to the same parents. The informant indicated that he still tends to accept his father's explanation of the scar, "A child cannot just be born with a natural injury like that; a natural mark."

Knowledge of other instances of reincarnation and mutilation were known to the informant. His uncle (father's younger brother) was believed to have been born several times but "didn't stay" until about the third time. When he was born the last time, he stood up and started walking at the age of five months without having gone through a previous crawling stage. It appeared the informant was implying that his uncle had already learned to walk in a previous incarnation. The informant recalled that there was a special word for these kinds of children but he couldn't recall it.

*Annotation:* Reincarnation or metempsychosis (the transmigration of souls) is an old and widespread belief central to many religions, past and present. The Pythagorean and Orphic cults of Greece believed in the purification of the soul through reincarnation, and Hindus today believe that it is through successive reincarnations that the soul eventually reaches extinction in the Absolute, *nirvana.* [See *Funk and Wagnall's Standard Dictionary of Folklore, Mythology, and Legend,* ed. Maria Leach, 2 vols. (New York: Funk and Wagnall, 1949), s.v. "nirvana," "karma," "reincarnation"].

Rebirth, reincarnation, and mutilation are all common motifs in folk literature, although there is nothing that quite parallels the informant's report. According to Thompson's *Motif-Index,* reincarnation may serve as a punishment, Q584.3: *Reincarnation form fitted to crime,* or the reincarnation may be of a recently deceased person, T589.5: *New-born child reincarnation of recently deceased person,* which is somewhat closer to our example. There are also motifs E728.1.1: *Evil spirit cast out of person by killing and resuscitating;* M375.3: *Child mutilated to avoid fulfillment of prophecy;* and H56.2: *Mutilation of children's bodies for identification* although these

369

seem only vague approximations of our example. The overcoming of spirit possession through assaulting the body is reflected by F405.8: *Spirit overcome by driving stake through body it inhabits*. The precocious infant is identified in T585.8: *Child stands (walks) at birth*. For an example of an African tale in which the infant hero walks shortly after birth see Melville and Frances Herskovits, *The Dahomean Narrative* (Evanston: Northwestern University Press, 1958), p. 156.

Among the Yoruba of Nigeria, the term *abiku* (literally: that which possesses death; i.e. predestined to death) designates the spirits of children who die before puberty. It also designates a class of spirits that cause the children to die. It is believed that there exists a whole host of forest spirits to whom no sacrifice is made. Consequently, they are always hungry and thirsty. They compete for the possession of the body of a child, enter the child, and divert the child's nourishment to themselves and to other *abiku* who have not succeeded in finding a human dwelling. When a child is fretful it is believed that outside *abiku* are hurting him in order to get the indwelling *abiku* to give them more to eat.

There are various methods to exorcise the *abiku*. If the child dies, however, if the corpse is buried at all it is buried without ceremony. "Often the corpse is simply thrown into the bush, to punish the *Abiku*, say the natives. Sometimes a mother, to deter the *Abiku* which has destroyed her child from entering any other infant she may bear in the future, will beat, pound, and mutilate the little corpse, while threatening and invoking every evil upon the *Abiku* [who] . . . is believed feel the blows and wounds inflicted on the body, and to hear and be terrified by the threats and curses." [A. B. Ellis, *The Yoruba Speaking Peoples of the Slave Coast of West Africa* (The Netherlands, 1966 [orig. 1894]), pp. 111–14]. Babatunde Lawal relates Yoruba notions of immortality, reincarnation, possession by *abiku* to their art in "The Living Dead: Art and Immortality Among the Yoruba of Nigeria," *Africa* 47(1977):50–61. For tales involving *abiku* see Herskovits & Herskovits, pp. 300–305.

A similar belief is known among the Ibo, the northern neighbors of the Efik. The informant identified himself as Efik. A child who repeatedly dies and returns to its mother to be reborn is called *ogbanje*. It is impossible to bring up an *ogbanje* child without it dying unless its *iyi-uwa* (a stone that links the *ogbanje* to the spirit world) is discovered and destroyed. These Ibo beliefs are dramatically portrayed by the Nigerian author Chinua Achebe in the ninth chapter of his novel *Things Fall Apart* (New York: Obolensky, 1959). This chapter includes mention of the mutilation of the child's corpse so that the *ogbanje* will not return to the mother's womb.

The Efik are an offshoot of the Ibibio and number about 25,000 persons. Traditional Efik religion includes beliefs in a supreme creator God, various spirits, sorcery, witchcraft, and reincarnation, although most today are Christians. [*The New Encyclopaedia Britannica*, s.v. "Efik"]. For a description of Efik death and burial customs see P. Amaury Talbot, *The Peoples of Southern Nigeria* (London, 1969 [orig. 1926]), 3:513–16.

Each of the above annotations has a different emphasis. The annotation of the tale primarily explored its literary relations, the account of the Civil War battle emphasized its relation to other historical accounts, while the annotation of the belief focused upon its relations to systems of belief in various West Africa cultures.

I was not particularly knowledgeable about any of this lore before beginning the annotation process. I simply set out to discover what I could within a limited time frame. The annotations are in no sense definitive or complete, and much might be appended or emended with further research. Nevertheless, I believe that even this circumscribed investigation can broaden perspectives and permit the formulation of new questions and inquiries. For example, most Efik today are Christian, yet my student informant claimed to continue to hold traditional ideas about reincarnation and *ogbanje*. (He recollected the term after reading the annotation.) Is this characteristic of other Efik? Which traditional religious ideas were first abandoned by the Efik after their adoption of Christianity, and which persisted long after their conversion? Which, for example, persist in the face of the modern secularism of an American university? What principles might describe the transformation of Efik beliefs, and are these principles applicable to the changes in other religious systems as well? These are not the kinds of questions that are likely to be posed merely on the basis of scrutinizing an individual performer in a particular social context. They depend upon an awareness of the relation of a particular expression or behavior to a much wider range of expressions and behaviors.

Where does research for the annotation begin? In the space of this essay, it is not possible to list even the basic resources available to aid the student in this enterprise. As a rule of thumb, however, the annotation of collected materials should commence with a perusal of the relevant folklore indexes, dictionaries, and encyclopaedias. These volumes exist for folklore in general, myth and folktale, legend, riddle, proverb, superstition, children's rhyme, ballad, folk speech, and gesture. Some of the works are transparent and simple to use. Others may require some study before they become truly useful (particularly indexes of types and motifs).

After consulting these works, the next step would be to turn to the major genre, national, and regional folklore collections. These sources are often useful even when the material to be annotated seems geographically distant from the areas of the regional collections. For example, two of the volumes of the *Frank C. Brown Collection of North Carolina Folklore* are devoted to the classification and arrangement of thousands of superstitions. This collection is useful in annotating superstitions collected far beyond the boundaries of North Carolina. After the major collections, there are numerous scholarly articles that describe as well as analyze a great variety of genres, groups, objects, events, and processes.

Ethnographies, histories, and biographies are also useful sources. However, the perusal of these sources may require significant expenditures of time, particularly if they are not well indexed. But these sources can also provide analogues accompanied by rich descriptions of social and cultural context.

Folklore archives can be found on a number of university campuses in the United States. They are primarily the repositories of folklore collected by students in fulfillment of class assignments. A university with an active folklore program is likely to have a folklore archive. Since folklore students often collect folklore locally, archives may be particularly useful in developing some idea of the local distribution and importance of an expression.

There are also numerous popular culture and literary sources that can be used in annotating collected materials. Joke books, riddle books, song books, short stories, novels, newspapers, comic books, and movies employ many of the same plots, motifs, and themes as folklore. For example, a number of nineteenth-century American short stories and twentieth-century horror films make use of the folk legend. Such literary and popular culture analogues may well deserve comment in an annotation.[10]

The question remains as to how to find one's way to the analogues which are then commented on in the annotation. What bibliographies can aid in this process? Perhaps the most useful bibliographic resources, for American folklore materials at least, are found at the conclusion of each chapter in Jan Harold Brunvand's *The Study of American Folklore* [3d ed. (New York: W. W. Norton & Co., 1986)]. Because the chapters of this book are organized by genre, it is relatively easy to find bibliographic clues to appropriate sources. Major indexes and collections, as well as individual studies in the genre, are listed and described in sufficient detail to give students a point of departure for their research. Brunvand also provides some introduction to the organization of Antti Aarne and Stith Thompson's *The Types of the Folktale*, Stith Thompson's *Motif-Index of Folk-Literature* (after which virtually all other type and motif indexes are modeled), and the indexes of Anglo-American balladry, as well as the classification of superstitions in the *Frank C. Brown Collection of North Carolina Folklore*. Unfortunately, Brunvand's volume is primarily limited to American sources. Brunvand's *Folklore: A Study and Research Guide* (New York: St. Martin's Press, 1976) also provides a useful overview of folklore bibliography.

For students collecting from foreign students, immigrants, or members of ethnic groups, it may also be worthwhile to consult sources more specifically focused on the lore of these peoples. A recent bibliography by David S. Azzolina, *Tale-Type and Motif-Indexes: An Annotated Bibliography* (New York: Garland Press, 1987) lists and describes the full range of type and motif indexes available. This bibliography was published by Garland Press, which has issued a number of other folklore bibliographies (e.g., ethnic folklore, Italian folklore, folklore and literature) under the general editorship of Alan Dundes. Charles Haywood's *A Bibliography of North American Folklore and Folksong* (New York: Dover Books, 1961 [1951]), although dated and incomplete, may still prove a useful guide to sources. The periodicals *Journal of American Folklore, Western Folklore, Journal of the Folklore Institute, Kentucky Folklore Record, Tennessee Folklore Society Bulletin,* and *Folklore Forum* all have special index volumes that permit access by genre and topic, and a number of folklore journals are regularly indexed in *The Humanities Index* and in the *MLA International Bibliography*. Of course, the very best guide to sources can be the folklore instructor, who may be able to offer informed recommendations based on a review of a student's collected materials.

I have tried different term projects for my folklore students over the years. Often I have required my introductory students to collect and annotate folklore. It is an assignment well within the capabilities of introductory folklore students. Annotation can become totally engrossing. There is a certain exhilaration in the chase and a measure of joy in the discovery of parallels to the lore one has collected. While on occasion I have had to urge some students to do more research on their annotations, I have also had to convince others that perhaps they had done enough, and that they might reserve some of their energies for other projects and other courses. Annotating is a worthwhile assignment for introductory students and should accompany those collecting assignments that emphasize contextual description. Student collecting should not be designed to fill archives, but to teach students something about the expressions they record. Annotation promotes an awareness that expressions recorded in specific face-to-face encounters can often be related to broader streams of culture, history, and literature. In a fundamental sense, this is what humanistic inquiry is all about.

---

[1] The notes to the tales first appeared as a special volume in 1822. For a translation of these notes see Margaret Hunt, trans., *Grimms Household Tales*, 2 vols. (Detroit: Singing Tree Press, 1968), 1:337–453, 2:373–583. The Grimms' annotations were later expanded by Johannes Bolte and Georg Polívka into the 5 volume *Anmerkungen zu den Kinder- und Hausmärchen der Brüder Grimm* [Commentaries on the Children's and Household Tales of the Brothers Grimm] (Leipzig, 1913–32).

[2] For example, Edward Burnett Tylor, *Primitive Culture,* 2 vols. (London: John Murray, 1871); James George Frazer, *Folklore in the Old Testament,* 3 vols. (London: MacMillan & Co., 1919), 1:vii–xi.

[3] See Kaarle Krohn, *Folklore Methodology,* trans. Roger Welsch (Austin: University of Texas Press, 1971).

[4] Ernest Jones, "Psychoanalysis and Folklore" in *Jubilee Congress of the Folklore Society: Papers and Transactions* (London, 1930), 220–37, reprinted in Alan Dundes, ed., *The Study of Folklore* (Englewood Cliffs N.J.: Prentice Hall, 1965), 87–106.

[5] I am referring to a broadly comparative approach to texts from different cultures and historical periods, not simply to the kind of comparison that characterizes all research—indeed all life. See Robert A. Georges, "The Folklorist as Comparatist," *Western Folklore* 45 (1986):1–20.

[6] Alan Dundes, Edmund R. Leach, Pierre Maranda, and David Maybury-Lewis, "An Experiment: Suggestions and Queries from the Desk, with a Reply by the Ethnographer," in Pierre Maranda and Elli Köngäs Maranda, eds., *Structural Analysis of Oral Tradition* (Philadelphia: University of Pennsylvania Press, 1971), 292–324.

[7] Roger D. Abrahams, *Deep Down in the Jungle: Negro Narrative Folklore from the Streets of Philadelphia,* 1st rev. ed. (Chicago: Aldine Publishing, 1970), 69–74.

[8] Nikita Elisséeff, *Thèmes et motifs des Mille et une nuite: essai de classification* (Beyrouth, 1949); Ursula Nowak, "Beiträge zur Typologie des arabischen Volksmärchen." (Diss., Freiburg im Breisgau, 1969); Fadel Ayten, "Beiträge zur Kenntis des arabischen Märchen und seiner Sonderart" (Diss., Bonn, 1978).

[9] Of course, the elaborate history would also contribute to the credibility of the account of the haunting, for legends must be grounded in a rhetoric of credibility. In this particular case, however, I believe that the legend serves more to moralize the history, than the history serves to legitimize the legend. Certainly the informant was much more tentative about the legend than the history. Indeed, his explicit tentativeness about the supernatural account would enhance his credibility as an objective historian.

[10] For examples see Daniel R. Barnes, "The Bosom Serpent: A Legend in American Literature and Culture," *Journal of American Folklore* 85 (1972):111–22 and Larry Danielson, "Folklore and Film: Some Thoughts on Baughman Z500-599," *Western Folklore* 38 (1979):209–19.

# References Cited

Abrahams, Roger D. 1977. The Most Embarrassing Thing That Ever Happened: Conversational Stories in a Theory of Enactment. *Folklore Forum* 10:9–15.

————, and George Foss. 1968. *Anglo-American Folksong Style*. Englewood Cliffs, NJ: Prentice Hall.

————, and Lois Rankin. 1980. *Counting-Out Rhymes: A Dictionary*. Austin: University of Texas Press.

Apte, Mahadev L., and Judit Katona-Apte. 1981. The Significance of Food in Religious Ideology and Ritual Behavior in Marathi Myths. In *Food in Perspective*, ed. Alexander Fenton and T. M. Owens, pp. 9–22. Edinburgh: John Donald Publishers.

Arens, William. 1975. The Great American Football Ritual. *Natural History* 84:72–80.

Arleo, Andy. 1980. With a Dirty, Dirty Dishrag on Your Mother's Big Fat Toe: The Coda in the Counting-Out Rhyme. *Western Folklore* 39:211–22.

Arora, Shirley L. 1988. "No Tickee, No Shirtee": Proverbial Speech and Leadership in Academe. In *Inside Organizations: Understanding the Human Dimension*, ed. Michael Owen Jones, Michael Dane Moore, and Richard Christopher Snyder, 179–89. Newbury Park, CA: Sage Publications.

Babcock, Barbara, Guy Monthan, and Doris Monthan. 1986. *The Pueblo Storyteller: Development of a Figurative Ceramic Tradition*. Tucson: University of Arizona Press.

Baer, Florence E. "Give me . . . your huddled masses": Anti-Vietnamese Refugee Lore and the "Image of Limited Good." 1982. *Western Folklore* 41:275–91.

Bartlett, F. C. 1920. Some Experiments on the Reproduction of Folk Stories. *Folklore* 31:30–47 [reprinted in Dundes 1965:243–58].

Basso, Keith H. 1979. *Portraits of "The Whiteman": Linguistic Play and Cultural Symbols among the Western Apache*. Cambridge: Cambridge University Press.

———— 1984. "Stalking with Stories": Names, Places, and Moral Narratives among the Western Apache. In *Text, Play, and Story: The Construction and Reconstruction of Self and Society*, ed. Edward M. Bruner, pp. 19–55. 1983 Proceedings of the American Ethnological Society. Washington, D.C.: American Ethnological Society.

Bauman, Richard. 1970. The Turtles: An American Riddling Institution. *Western Folklore* 29:21–25.

———— 1978. *Verbal Art as Performance*. With supplementary essays by Barbara Babcock et al. Rowley, MA: Newbury House.

———— 1986. *Story, Performance, and Event: Contextual Studies of Oral Narrative*. Cambridge: Cambridge University Press.

Bell, Michael J. 1983. *The World from Brown's Lounge: An Ethnography of Black Middle-Class Play*. Urbana: University of Illinois Press.

Ben-Amos, Dan, ed. 1976. *Folklore Genres*. Austin: University of Texas Press.

# References Cited

_____, and Kenneth S. Goldstein, eds. 1975. *Folklore: Performance and Communication.* The Hague: Mouton Publishers.

Bennett, Gillian. 1986. Narrative as Expository Discourse. *Journal of American Folklore* 99: 415–34.

Berger, Peter L., and Thomas Luckmann. 1966. *The Social Construction of Reality: A Treatise in the Sociology of Knowledge.* New York: Anchor Books.

Bolton, Henry C. 1969 [1888]. *The Counting-Out Rhymes of Children.* Detroit: Singing Tree Press.

Brewster, Paul G. 1942. Some Notes on the Guessing Game, How Many Horns Has the Buck? *Bealoideas: Journal of the Folklore of Ireland Society* 12:40–78 [reprinted in Dundes 1965: 340–68].

Bronner, Simon J. 1985. *Chain Carvers: Old Men Crafting Meaning.* Lexington: University Press of Kentucky.

_____ 1986. *American Folklore Studies: An Intellectual History.* Lawrence: University of Kansas Press.

Brunvand, Jan Harold, 1977. "The Lane County Bachelor": Folksong or Not? *Heritage of Kansas: A Journal of the Great Plains* 10:3–20 [reprinted in Brunvand 1979:289–308].

_____, ed. 1979. *Readings in American Folklore.* New York: W. W. Norton.

_____ 1986. *The Study of American Folklore: An Introduction.* 3d edition. New York: W. W. Norton.

Buchan, David. 1972. *The Ballad and the Folk.* London: Routledge & Kegan Paul.

Burns, Thomas A. with Inger H. Burns. 1976. *Doing the Wash: An Expressive Culture and Personality Study of a Joke and Its Tellers.* Norwood, PA: Norwood Editions.

Burridge, Kenelm O. L. 1957. A Tangu Game. *Man* 57:88–89.

Byrne, Jr., Donald E. 1985. The Race of the Saints: An Italian Religious Festival in Jessup, Pennsylvania. *Journal of Popular Culture* 19:119–30.

Charters, Samuel. 1963. *The Poetry of the Blues.* New York: Oak Publications.

Cherry, Conrad. 1969. Two American Sacred Ceremonies: Their Implication for the Study of American Religion. *American Quarterly* 21:739–54.

Child, Francis James, ed. 1965 [1884–98]. *The English and Scottish Popular Ballads.* 5 volumes. New York: Dover Publications.

Clements, William M. 1981. Ritual Expectation in Pentecostal Healing Experience. *Western Folklore* 40:139–48.

Cocchiara, Giuseppe. 1971 [1954]. *The History of Folklore in Europe.* Translated by John N. McDaniel. Philadelphia: Institute for the Study of Human Issues.

Cohen, A. P. 1985. *The Symbolic Construction of Community.* Chichester, Sussex: Ellis Horwood and London: Tavistock Publications.

Csikszentmihalyi, Mihaly, and Eugene Rochberg-Halton. 1981. *The Meaning of Things: Domestic Symbols and the Self.* Cambridge: Cambridge University Press.

Cunningham, Clark E. 1964. Order in the Atoni House. *Bijdragen tot de Taal-, Land- en Volkenkunde* 120:34–68 [reprinted in Lessa & Vogt 1972:116–35].

Danielson, Larry. 1974. Public Swedish-American Ethnicity in Central Kansas: A Festival and Its Functions. *The Swedish Pioneer Historical Quarterly* 25:13–36.

——— 1975. The Uses of Demonic Folk Tradition in Selma Lagerlöf's *Gösta Berlings saga*. *Western Folklore* 34:187–99.

Davis, Gerald L. 1985. *I Got the Word in Me and I Can Sing It, You Know*. Philadelphia: University of Pennsylvania Press.

de Caro, Francis A. 1978. Proverbs and Originality in Modern Short Fiction. *Western Folklore* 37:30–38.

Dégh, Linda. 1978. Two Letters from Home. *Journal of American Folklore* 91(1978):808–22.

———, ed. 1986. *The Comparative Method in Folklore*. *Journal of Folklore Research* 23:77–232.

———, and Andrew Vázsonyi. 1971. Legend and Belief. *Genre* 4:281–304 [reprinted in Ben-Amos 1976:93–123].

Dewhurst, C. Kurt. 1988. Pleiku Jackets, Tour Jackets, and Working Jackets: "The Letter Sweaters of War." *Journal of American Folklore* 101:48–52.

Dorson, Richard M. 1949. The Folklore of Colleges. *American Mercury* 48:671–77.

——— 1966. The Question of Folklore in a New Nation. *Journal of the Folklore Institute* 3:277–98.

——— 1968a. *The British Folklorists*. Chicago: University of Chicago Press.

———, ed. 1968b. *Peasant Customs and Savage Myths: Selections from the British Folklorists*. 2 vols. Chicago: University of Chicago Press.

——— 1972. [1968]. "The Debate over the Trustworthiness of Oral Traditional History." In *Selected Essays*, by Richard M. Dorson, 199–224. Bloomington: Indiana University Press.

——— 1973. *America in Legend: Folklore from the Colonial Period to the Present*. New York: Pantheon Books.

Dundes, Alan. 1963. Structural Typology in North American Indian Folktales. *Southwestern Journal of Anthropology* 19:121–30 [reprinted in Dundes 1965:206–15].

———, ed. 1965. *The Study of Folklore*. Englewood Cliffs, NJ: Prentice Hall.

——— 1976. Structuralism and Folklore. *Studia Fennica* 20:75–93.

——— 1980. *Interpreting Folklore*. Bloomington: Indiana University Press.

———, ed. 1984. *Sacred Narrative: Readings in the Theory of Myth*. Berkeley: University of California Press.

——— 1987. *Parsing Through Customs: Essays by a Freudian Folklorist*. Madison: University of Wisconsin Press.

———, and Carl R. Pagter. 1975. *Work Hard and You Shall Be Rewarded: Urban Folklore from the Paperwork Empire*. Bloomington: Indiana University Press.

Edmonson, Munro S. 1971. *Lore: An Introduction to the Science of Folklore and Literature*. New York: Holt, Rinehart and Winston.

Erdész, Sándor. 1961. The World Conception of Lajos Ami, Storyteller. *Acta Ethnographica* 10:327–44 [reprinted in Dundes 1984:315–35].

——— 1963. The Cosmogonical Conceptions of Lajos Ami, Storyteller. *Acta Ethnographica* 12:57–64.

Eschholz, Paul A., and Alfred F. Rosa. 1970. Course Names: Another Aspect of College Slang. *American Speech* 45:85–90.

Evans, David. 1974. Techniques of Blues Composition among Black Folksingers. *Journal of American Folklore* 87:240–49.

# References Cited

_____ 1982. *Big Road Blues: Tradition and Creativity in the Folk Blues*. Berkeley: University of California Press.

Feintuch, Burt. 1987. The Joke, Folk Culture, and Milan Kundera's *The Joke*. *Western Folklore* 46:21–35.

Fife, Austin E. 1953. A Ballad of the Mountain Meadows Massacre. *Western Folklore* 12:229–41.

Firth, Raymond. 1960. The Plasticity of Myth: Cases from Tikopia. *Ethnologica* 2:181–88 [reprinted in Dundes 1984].

_____ 1973. *Symbols: Public and Private*. Ithaca: Cornell University Press.

Foley, John Miles. 1988. *The Theory of Oral Composition: History and Methodology*. Bloomington: Indiana University Press.

Foster, George M. 1964. Treasure Tales and the Image of a Static Economy in a Mexican Peasant Community. *Journal of American Folklore* 77:39–44.

Frazer, Sir James George. 1963 [1922]. *The Golden Bough: A Study in Magic and Religion*. One volume abridged edition. New York: The MacMillan Company.

Freud, Sigmund. 1953–1974 [1886–1939]. *The Standard Edition of the Complete Psychological Works of Sigmund Freud*. 24 vols. Trans. under the general editorship of James Strachey in collaboration with Anna Freud. London: Hogarth Press and the Institute of Psychoanalysis.

Gardner, Emelyn E. 1918. Some Counting-Out Rhymes in Michigan. *Journal of American Folklore* 31:531–36.

Georges, Robert A. 1970. Structure in Folktales: A Generative-Transformational Approach. *The Conch* 2:4–17.

_____ 1981. Proverbial Speech in the Air. *Midwestern Journal of Language and Folklore* 7:39–48.

Gerould, Gordon Hall. 1957 [1932]. *The Ballad of Tradition*. New York: Oxford University Press Galaxy Books.

Giuliano, Bruce S. 1976. *Sacro o Profano? A Consideration of Four Italian-Canadian Religious Festivals*. Canadian Centre for Folk Culture Studies, Paper No. 17. Ottawa: National Museums of Man.

Glassie, Henry. 1968. *Pattern in the Material Folk Culture of the Eastern United States*. Philadelphia: University of Pennsylvania Press.

_____ 1975. *Folk Housing in Middle Virginia: A Structural Analysis of Historic Artifacts*. Knoxville: University of Tennessee Press.

_____, Edward D. Ives, and John F. Szwed. 1970. *Folksongs and Their Makers*. Bowling Green, OH: Bowling Green University Popular Press.

Gmelch, George. 1971. Baseball Magic. *Transaction* 8:39–41, 54 [reprinted in Lehmann and Myers 1985:231–35].

Goffman, Erving. 1959. *The Presentation of Self in Everyday Life*. New York: Anchor Books.

Goldberg, Christine. 1984. The Historic-Geographic Method: Past and Future. *Journal of Folklore Research* 21:1–18.

Goldstein, Kenneth S., ed. 1960. *The Unfortunate Rake*. Folkways Record FA 2305.

Graburn, Nelson, H. H., ed. 1976. *Ethnic and Tourist Arts: Cultural Expressions from the Fourth World*. Berkeley: University of California Press.

Graham, Joe. 1981. The *Caso: An Emic Genre of Folk Narrative.* In *"And Other Neighborly Names"*, ed. Richard Bauman and Roger D. Abrahams, pp. 11–43. Austin: University of Texas Press.

Gregor, W. 1972 [1891]. *Counting-Out Rhymes of Children.* Norwood, PA: Norwood Editions.

Greenhill, Pauline. 1987. Folk Dynamics in Popular Poetry: "Somebody's Mother" and What Happened to Her in Ontario. *Western Folklore* 46:77–95.

Grider, Sylvia, ed. 1980. *Children's Folklore. Western Folklore* 34:159–265.

Gump, P. V., and Brian Sutton-Smith. 1955. The *It* Role in Children's Games. *The Group* 17:3–8 [reprinted in Dundes 1965:329–36].

Hendricks, William O. 1970. Folklore and the Structural Analysis of Literary Texts. *Language and Style* 3:83–121.

Hoffmann, Daniel G. 1952. Historic Truth and Ballad Truth: Two Versions of the Capture of New Orleans. *Journal of American Folklore* 65:295–303.

Hornbein, George, Marie Hornbein, Tom Keiter, and Kenneth Thigpen. 1982. *Salamanders: A Night at the Phi Delt House.* 14 minutes, color. State College, PA: Documentary Resource Center.

Howells, William. 1962 [1948]. *The Heathens: Primitive Man and His Religions.* Garden City, NY: Anchor Books and the American Museum of Natural History.

Hymes, Dell. 1981. *"In Vain I Tried to Tell You": Essays in Native American Ethnopoetics.* Philadelphia: University of Pennsylvania Press.

Inkeles, Alex, Eugenia Hanfmann, and Helen Beier. 1958. Modal Personality and Adjustment to the Soviet Political System. *Human Relations* 11:3–22.

Ives, Edward D. 1978. *Joe Scott: The Woodsman-Songmaker.* Urbana: University of Illinois Press.

Ivey, William. 1970. "The 1913 Disaster": Michigan Local Legend. *Folklore Forum* 3:100–14.

Jacobs, Melville. 1959. *The Content and Style of an Oral Literature.* Chicago: University of Chicago Press.

——— 1960. *The People are Coming Soon: Analyses of Clackamas Chinook Myths and Tales.* Seattle: University of Washington Press.

Johnson, Robbie Davis. 1973. Folklore and Women: A Social Interactional Analysis of the Folklore of a Texas Madam. *Journal of American Folklore* 86:211–24.

Jones, Ernest. 1930. Psychoanalysis and Folklore. In *Jubilee Congress of the Folklore Society: Papers and Transactions.* London: Folklore Society, 220–37 [reprinted in Dundes 1965:88–102].

Jones, Michael Owen. 1975. *The Hand Made Object and Its Maker.* Berkeley: University of California Press.

——— 1987. *Exploring Folk Art: Twenty Years of Thought on Craft, Work, and Aesthetics.* Ann Arbor, MI: UMI Research Press.

———, Bruce Giuliano, and Roberta Krell, eds. 1983. *Foodways and Eating Habits: Directions for Research.* Los Angeles: California Folklore Society [*Western Folklore* 40(1981): vii–137].

Jordan, Rosan A. 1975. Ethnic Identity and the Lore of the Supernatural. *Journal of American Folklore* 88:370–82.

# References Cited

_____ 1982. Five Proverbs in Context. *Midwestern Journal of Language and Folklore* 8:109–15.

Kalčik, Susan. 1975. "... like Ann's Gynecologist or the Time I was Almost Raped": Personal Narratives in Women's Rap Groups. *Journal of American Folklore* 88:3–11.

Kamenetsky, Christa. 1972. Folklore as a Political Tool in Nazi Germany. *Journal of American Folklore* 85:221–35.

_____ 1977. Folktale and Ideology in the Third Reich. *Journal of American Folklore* 90:168–78.

Kane, Steven M. 1974. Ritual Possession in a Southern Appalachian Religious Sect. *Journal of American Folklore* 87:292–302.

Kearney, Michael. 1984. *World View.* Novato, CA: Chandler & Sharp Publishers.

Kirshenblatt-Gimblett, Barbara, ed. 1976. *Speech Play: Research and Resources for the Study of Linguistic Creativity.* Philadelphia: University of Pennsylvania Press.

_____ 1978. Culture Shock and Narrative Creativity. In *Folklore in the Modern World,* ed. Richard M. Dorson, 109–22. The Hague: Mouton Publishers.

_____ 1983. Studying Immigrant and Ethnic Folklore. In *Handbook of American Folklore,* ed. Richard M. Dorson, pp. 39–47. Bloomington: Indiana University Press.

Klymasz, Robert B[ogdan]. 1973. From Immigrant to Ethnic Folklore: A Canadian View of Process and Tradition. *Journal of the Folklore Institute* 10:131–39.

_____ 1980. *Ukrainian Folklore in Canada.* New York: Arno Press.

Knapp, Mary, and Herbert Knapp. 1976. *One Potato, Two Potato: The Secret Education of American Children.* New York: W. W. Norton.

Kochman, Thomas. 1972. *Rappin' and Stylin' Out: Communication in Urban Black America.* Urbana: University of Illinois Press.

Kroeber, Karl, ed. 1981. *Traditional Literatures of the American Indians: Texts and Interpretations.* Lincoln: University of Nebraska Press.

Lawless, Elaine J. 1980. Making a Joyful Noise: An Ethnography of Communication in the Pentecostal Religious Service. *Southern Folklore Quarterly* 44:1–21.

_____ 1983. Shouting for the Lord: The Power of Women's Speech in the Pentecostal Religious Service. *Journal of American Folklore* 96:434–59.

Leach, Edmund. 1976. *Culture and Communication: The Logic by which Symbols are Connected.* Cambridge: Cambridge University Press.

Leary, James P. 1978. The Notre Dame Man: Christian Athlete or Dirtball? *Journal of the Folklore Institute* 15:133–45.

Lehmann, Arthur C., and James E. Myers. 1985. *Magic, Witchcraft, and Religion: An Anthropological Study of the Supernatural.* Palo Alto, CA: Mayfield Publishing Company.

Lessa, William A., and Evon Z. Vogt. 1965. 2d edition [1972, 3d edition]. *Reader in Comparative Religion: An Anthropological Approach.* New York: Harper and Row, Publishers.

Lévi-Strauss, Claude. 1963a [1962]. *Totemism.* Trans. Rodney Needham. Boston: Beacon Press.

_____ 1963b [1958]. *Structural Anthropology.* Trans. C. Jacobson and B. G. Schoepf. New York: Basic Books.

_____ 1967. The Story of Asdiwal. In *The Structural Study of Myth and Totemism,* ed. Edmund Leach, pp. 1–47. London: Tavistock.

Limón, José E. 1983. Legendry, Metafolklore, and Performance: A Mexican-American Example. *Western Folklore* 42:191–208.

Long, Eleanor. 1971. *"The Maid" and "The Hangman": Myth and Tradition in a Popular Ballad.* University of California Folklore Studies No. 21. Berkeley: University of California Press.

Lord, Albert B. 1960. *The Singer of Tales.* Cambridge: Harvard University Press.

Lowie, Robert H. 1917. Oral Tradition and History. *Journal of American Folklore* 30:161–67.

Malinowski, Bronislaw. 1954 [1925]. Myth in Primitive Psychology. In *Magic, Science and Religion and Other Essays* by Bronislaw Malinowski, pp. 93–148. Garden City, NY: Doubleday Anchor Books.

Martinez, Cervando, and Harry W. Martin. 1966. Folk Diseases among Urban Mexican-Americans: Etiology, Symptoms, and Treatment. *Journal of the American Medical Association* 196:147–50.

McAllester, David P. 1974. Riddles and Other Verbal Play among the Commanches. *Journal of American Folklore* 77:251–57.

McGeachy III, John A. 1978. Student Nicknames for College Faculty. *Western Folklore* 37:281–96.

Mieder, Wolfgang. 1981. The Proverbial Three Wise Monkeys. *Midwestern Journal of Language and Folklore* 7:5–38.

_____ 1982. Proverbs in Nazi Germany: The Promulgation of Anti-Semitism and Stereotypes through Folklore. *Journal of American Folklore* 95:435–64.

Mitchell, Carol. 1981. "Talking-Story" in *The Woman Warrior. Kentucky Folklore Record* 27:5–12.

Montell, William Lynwood. 1970. *The Saga of Coe Ridge: A Study in Oral History.* Knoxville: University of Tennessee Press.

Moore, Omar Khayyam. 1957. Divination—A New Perspective. *American Anthropologist* 59:69–74 [reprinted in Lessa and Vogt 1965:377–81].

Moore, Sally Falk, and Barbara G. Meyerhoff. 1977. *Secular Ritual.* Amsterdam: Van Gorcum.

Moorehead, Michael. 1981. The Use of Folklore in the Early Works of George Washington Cable. *Kentucky Folklore Record* 27:13–19.

Mullen, Patrick B. 1988 [1978]. *I Heard the Old Fishermen Say: Folklore of the Texas Gulf Coast.* Logan: Utah State University Press.

Oliver, Paul. 1963. *The Meaning of the Blues.* New York: Collier Books.

Olrik, Axel. 1909. Epische Gesetze der Volksdictung. *Zetschrift für Deutsches Altertum* 51:1–12 [translated and reprinted in Dundes 1965:131–41].

Opie, Iona, and Peter Opie. 1969. *Children's Games in Street and Playground.* Oxford: Clarendon Press.

_____ 1973. *The Oxford Book of Children's Verse.* Oxford: Clarendon Press.

_____ 1985. *The Singing Game.* Oxford: Clarendon Press.

Oring, Elliott. 1976. Three Functions of Folklore: Traditional Functionalism as Explanation in Folkloristics. *Journal of American Folklore* 89:67–80.

_____ 1978. Transmission and Degeneration. *Fabula* 19:193–210.

_____ 1981. *Israeli Humor: The Content and Structure of the Chizbat of the Palmah.* Albany: State University of New York Press.

# References Cited

_____ 1984. *The Jokes of Sigmund Freud: A Study in Humor and Jewish Identity*. Philadelphia: University of Pennsylvania Press.

Oster, Harry. 1969. *Living Country Blues*. Detroit: Folklore Associates.

Parsons, Elsie Clews. 1936. Riddles and Metaphors among Indian Peoples. *Journal of American Folklore* 46:172–74.

Passin, Herbert, and John W. Bennett. 1943. Changing Agricultural Magic in Southern Illinois: A Systematic Analysis of Folk-Urban Transition. *Social Forces* 22(1943):98–106 [reprinted in Dundes 1965:314–28].

Petersen, Albert J. 1976. The German-Russian House in Kansas. *Pioneer America* 8:19-27 [reprinted in Brunvand 1979:373–86].

Peterson, Sally. 1988. Translating Experience and the Reading of a Story Cloth. *Journal of American Folklore* 101:6–22.

Propp, V. 1968 [1928]. *Morphology of the Folktale*. Trans. Laurence Scott. Revised edition. Austin: University of Texas Press for The American Folklore Society and Indiana Research Center for the Language Sciences.

Radcliffe-Brown, A. R. 1939. *Taboo*. Cambridge: Cambridge University Press [reprinted in Lessa and Vogt 1965:112–23].

Raglan, Lord [Fitzroy Richard Somerset 4th Baron Raglan]. 1956 [1936]. *The Hero: A Study in Tradition, Myth, and Drama*. New York: Vintage Books.

Ramsey, Jarold W. 1977. *Coyote was Going There: Indian Literature of the Oregon Country*. Seattle: University of Washington Press.

_____ 1983. *Reading the Fire: Essays in the Traditional Indian Literature of the Far West*. Lincoln: University of Nebraska Press.

Renwick, Roger deV. 1980. *English Folk Poetry: Structure and Meaning*. Philadelphia: University of Pennsylvania Press.

Rosenberg, Bruce A. 1970. *The Art of the American Folk Preacher*. New York: Oxford University Press.

Rubel, Arthur J. 1960. Concepts of Disease in Mexican-American Culture. *American Anthropologist* 62:795–814.

Sacks, Harvey. 1974. An Analysis of the Course of a Joke's Telling in Conversation. In *Explorations in the Ethnography of Speaking*, ed. Richard Bauman and Joel Sherzer, 337–53. Cambridge: Cambridge University Press.

Samuelson, Sue. 1982. Folklore and the Legal System: The Expert Witness. *Western Folklore* 41:139–44.

Scott, Charles T. 1973. New Evidence of American Indian Riddles. *Journal of American Folklore* 76:236–41.

Shokeid, Moshe, and Shlomo Deshen. 1974. *The Predicament of Homecoming: Cultural and Social Life of North African Immigrants in Israel*. Ithaca: Cornell University Press.

Singer, Eliot A. 1984. The Whodunit as Riddle: Block Elements in Agatha Christie. *Western Folklore* 43:157–71.

Spicer, Edward S. 1977. *Ethnic Medicine in the Southwest*. Tucson: University of Arizona Press.

Stahl, Sandra K. D. 1977a. The Personal Narrative as Folklore. *Journal of the Folklore Institute* 14:9–30.

_____ 1977b. The Oral Personal Narrative in Its Generic Context. *Fabula* 18:18–39.

Stanley, David H. 1979. The Personal Narrative and the Personal Novel: Folklore as Frame and Structure for Literature. *Southern Folklore Quarterly* 43:107–20.

Stone, Kay. 1981. *Märchen* to Fairy Tales: An Unmagical Transformation. *Western Folklore* 40:232–44.

Swann, Brian, ed. 1983. *Smoothing the Ground: Essays on Native American Oral Literature.* Berkeley: University of California Press.

Taft, Michael. 1983. *Blues Lyric Poetry: An Anthology.* New York: Garland Press.

Taylor, Archer. 1966. "Neither Fish Nor Flesh" and Its Variations. *Journal of the Folklore Institute* 3:3–9.

Tedlock, Dennis. 1972. *Finding the Center: Narrative Poetry of the Zuni Indians.* New York: Dial Press.

Thompson, Stith. 1953. The Star Husband Tale. *Studia Septentrionalia* 4:93–163 [reprinted in Dundes 1965:416–74].

Titon, Jeff Todd. 1977. *Early Downhome Blues.* Urbana: University of Illinois Press.

Toelken, Barre. 1969. The "Pretty Languages" of Yellowman: Genre, Mode, and Texture in Navajo Coyote Narratives. *Genre* 2:211–35 [reprinted in Ben-Amos 1976].

_____ 1986. [1968]. The Folklore of Academe. In *The Study of American Folklore*, 3d ed., Jan Harold Brunvand, 502–28. New York: W. W. Norton.

Tuso, Joseph F. ed. 1971. Folksongs of the American Fighter Pilot in Southeast Asia, 1967–68. *Folklore Forum.* Bibliographic and Special Series No. 7:1–39.

_____ 1972. A Folk Drama—"What the Captain Means Is...", or that Interview You Never Saw on TV. *Folklore Forum* 5:25–27.

Vansina, Jan. 1965 [1961]. *Oral Tradition.* Trans. by H. M. Wright. London: Routledge & Kegan Paul.

Vogt, Evon Z. 1952. Water Witching: An Interpretation of a Ritual Pattern in a Rural American Community. *Scientific Monthly* 75:175–86 [reprinted in Lessa and Vogt 1965:364–77].

Wachs, Eleanor. 1978. "If Danger E'er Annoy": Folk, Popular, and Iconographic Sources for the Legend of the Battle of New Orleans. *Kentucky Folklore Record* 24:31–41.

_____ 1982. The Crime-Victim Narrative as a Folklore Genre. *Journal of the Folklore Institute.* 19:17–30.

Waugh, Butler. 1966. Structural Analysis in Literature and Folklore. *Western Folklore* 25:153–64.

Welsch, Roger L. 1968. *Sod Walls: The Story of the Nebraska Sod House.* Broken Bow, NE: Purcells.

_____ 1970. Sandhill Bailed-Hay Construction. *Keystone Folklore Quarterly* 15:16–34.

_____ 1976. Railroad-Tie Construction on the Pioneer Plains. *Western Folklore* 35:149–56.

_____ 1976–77. The Meaning of Folk Architecture: The Sod House Example. *Keystone Folklore* 21:34–49.

Wilgus, D. K. 1959. *Anglo-American Folksong Scholarship Since 1898.* Brunswick, NJ: Rutgers University Press.

# References Cited

Wilson, William A. 1973. Folklore and History: Fact Amid the Legend. *Utah Historical Quarterly* 41:40–58 [reprinted in Brunvand 1979:449–66].

———. 1976. *Folklore and Nationalism in Modern Finland.* Bloomington: Indiana University Press.

Wise, James. 1977. Tugging on Superman's Cape: The Making of a College Legend. *Western Folklore* 36:227–38.

Yankah, Kwesi. 1986. Proverb Rhetoric and African Judicial Processes: The Untold Story. *Journal of American Folklore* 99:280–303.

Yocom, Margaret R. 1982. Family Folklore and Oral History Interviews: Strategies for Introducing a Project to One's Own Relatives. *Western Folklore* 41:251–74.

Zeitlin, Steven J. 1980. "An Alchemy of Mind": The Family Courtship Story. *Western Folklore* 39:17–33.

———, Amy J. Kotkin, and Holly Cutting Baker. 1982. *A Celebration of American Family Folklore: Tales and Traditions from the Smithsonian Collection.* New York: Pantheon Books.

Zumwalt, Rosemary Lévy. 1988. *American Folklore Scholarship: A Dialogue of Dissent.* Bloomington: Indiana University Press.